A POLITICAL AND ECONOMIC DICTIONARY OF SOUTH ASIA

A POLITICAL AND ECONOMIC DICTIONARY OF SOUTH ASIA

Subrata K. Mitra
Siegfried O. Wolf
Jivanta Schöttli

FIRST EDITION

Routledge
Taylor & Francis Group
LONDON AND NEW YORK

First Edition 2006
Routledge
Haines House, 21 John Street, London WC1N 2BP, United Kingdom
(A member of the Taylor & Francis Group)

ISBN-13 978 1 85743 210 7

ISBN-10 1 85743 210 X

Development Editor: Cathy Hartley
Copy Editor and Proof-reader: Simon Chapman

Typeset in Times New Roman 10/12

Typeset by AJS Solutions, Huddersfield and Dundee
Printed and bound by MPG Books, Ltd, Bodmin, Cornwall

FOREWORD

The need for an easily accessible guide to the politics and economy of South Asia has gained in salience over the past decade. Comprising the states of Bangladesh, Bhutan, India, Nepal, Pakistan, Sri Lanka and the Maldives, and home to one-fifth of the world's population, the region has recently witnessed the opening up of its economies. In addition, the region has experienced regime changes, terrorist attacks, natural catastrophes and nuclear tests, as well as the meteoric growth of its service sectors—thanks to the alacrity with which its component states have taken to the internet and business outsourcing. These developments have rendered the region interesting to a motley crowd of international organizations, tourists, journalists and the ubiquitous business travellers. South Asia today bears the double distinction of being the site of vast, untapped potential for business opportunities *and* a potential threat to international order.

The twin legacies of colonial rule—a well-knit infrastructure of roads and railway links and widespread use of the English language in élite and governmental circles—have endowed South Asia with a potential advantage when compared to Central or South-East and East Asia, or, for that matter, Africa and Latin America. But an entrée to the economy and politics of the region has not been easy. The initial, post-independence emphasis on autarchic models of development did not encourage foreign direct investment. The dominant idioms of the national political economies, with a nostalgic carry-over from the days of the anti-colonial movements, expressed themselves more in terms of national self-assertion than in international or inter-state linkages.

The situation has changed vastly. Still, it is important for the outsider to note that the economy and politics of South Asia are an integral part of a deeper project of nation-building and national identity. The countries' economic and political institutions are anchored in indigenous categories and local contexts. For the western students of economics and politics, whose own experiences of these phenomena form part of a different historical trajectory, the *real* nature and purpose of many of these institutions and processes, as compared to their formal and putative roles, might come across as puzzling.

This *Political and Economic Dictionary of South Asia* intends to locate the reader in the midst of this fast changing and complex process which juxtaposes indigenous values and institutions of foreign provenance. This *interwoven* character of tradition and modernity is crucial to the South Asian reality—a point that the dictionary makes by putting in bold the institutional arrangements and conceptual innovations. Each state has two main sections on its economy and politics which contain the core facts in both domains. A keyword index to region-specific concepts helps locate them within these broad, generic categories. Finally, while each state has its own political, social and economic problems which are specific to its culture and history, the dictionary also draws attention to the common patterns of South Asia, which betray the shared origin of the institutions founded by the colonial rulers and the attempts of post-independence politics to come to terms with them.

The main political and economic organizations of South Asia, key concepts and their links to others of their ilk are the main features of this dictionary. However, like others of its genre, the dictionary has inevitably stretched from mere description towards the definition of concepts in terms of their philosophical depth and empirical context of the region. The dictionary has sought to focus on this crucial issue of the embedded-ness of South Asia's institutions by tracing their links to pre-modern culture and history. Comparing the fate of institutions across the states, one notices how the interaction of modern institutions and traditional societies has sometimes produced new mutations, historical evolutions, differentiations, and occasionally, political discontinuities. Independence has quickened the pace of politicization, causing some past anxieties to surface, sweeping aside the thin coating of acquired western modernity in some cases and tamed by the power of tradition in others. The material covered here has attempted to strike a balance between these competing polarities.

Whether it concerns state–economy relations or the interaction of traditional society and modern institutions, there is of course no standard South Asian 'model'. At one extreme lies Bhutan, where the indigenous idiom has become the legitimating instrument for a modernizing royalty. The same attempt, in Nepal, has been less successful, producing instead a violent mass upsurge. In India, the countervailing forces of politics have sustained the democratic process, causing modern political and economic institutions to acquire indigenous roots. This has not been as successful in Pakistan or Bangladesh, nor indeed in Sri Lanka, which had an early start in democratization compared to the other states of South Asia. The politics and economy of the island state of the Maldives have their own peculiarity in terms of the politics of the atolls, but as recent trends reveal, the slow stirring of multi-party democracy in South Asia has caught up with the secluded political life of this state of many islands.

A political and economy dictionary that aims at both breadth and depth would not have been possible without the diligent efforts of a band of dedicated researchers. We would like to thank Peter Braun, Lionel Koenig, K. Mahiuddin, Christoph Rehm, Kate Sullivan and Muhammad Tahir Noor who have sifted through enormous quantities of material in record time. We are grateful to them for their patience at coping with tight deadlines, meticulous efforts in tracking down obscure concepts and facts, and, above all, for their resourcefulness and good humour which have sustained the project through some trying times.

While we have tried to stay close to the descriptive role of the dictionary, the discerning reader will surely recognize the liberal, neo-institutional bias that underpins our approach to South Asia's economy and politics. As such, we are particularly grateful for the comments of Christine Bigdon, Alexander Fischer, Karl-Heinz Kraemer, Mobasser Monem, Malte Pehl, Dietmar Rothermund, Jyotirmaya Sharma and Peter Zingel, whose thoughtful comments have added a necessary sense of nuanced moderation. We would also like to take this opportunity to thank Cathy Hartley for her gentle and firm management of the project, and Simon Chapman for editorial guidance.

The dictionary attempts to make South Asia accessible to readers native to South Asia as well as to those from outside, approaching the vast region for the first time. The inter-disciplinary environment of the South Asia Institute of the University of Heidelberg, and its renowned library, recognized as a national resource centre by the German Research Council (DFG), have been among the most important sources of data. In addition, we would like to thank the Centre de Sciences Humaines, and the Centre for the Study of Developing Societies, both of New Delhi, and the University Library of Heidelberg. But most of all, the challenge and inspiration for the dictionary have come from the curiosity and motivation of our students. In dedicating this source book to them, it is our hope that they will look beyond the facts reported here in order to search for the logic that binds them together.

Subrata K. Mitra
Jivanta Schöttli
Siegfried O. Wolf

Department of Political Science
South Asia Institute
Heidelberg, June 2006

THE CONTRIBUTORS

Subrata K. Mitra is Professor and Head, Department of Political Science at the South Asia Institute, University of Heidelberg, and a Visiting Fellow at the Centre for the Study of Developing Societies, New Delhi. He was Executive Director of the South Asia Institute, Heidelberg (2002–04), and President of the Research Committee on Political Sociology of the International Political Science Association and the International Sociological Association (2002–06). Professor Mitra has been a consultant to several national and international organizations, including UNESCO, the French Institute for Public Opinion (Paris) and the European Union. His previous publications include *The Puzzle of India's Governance* (Routledge, 2006), *Democracy and Social Change* and *Culture and Rationality* (both Sage, 1999) and *Power, Protest and Participation* (Routledge, 1992)

Jivanta Schöttli is Lecturer in International and Comparative Politics in the Department of Political Science at the South Asia Institute, University of Heidelberg. A graduate of the London School of Economics and Political Science, she holds degrees in international relations and history, and economic history. Having lived and worked in Asian capital cities and studied links between India and Japan and India and China, her research currently focuses on the institutionalization of politics in India since independence in 1947.

Siegfried O. Wolf specializes in Comparative Politics and Political Theory. He is a Lecturer in Political Science at the South Asia Institute, University of Heidelberg. Before starting his academic career, Siegfried Wolf had a two-year apprenticeship at one of Germany's most established financial groups and has since worked for various consultancies specializing in political communication world-wide. He has conducted fieldwork in South Asia for his research in affiliation with the Centre de Sciences Humaines located in New Delhi. In addition, he is Deputy Editor and Managing Editor of the *Heidelberg Papers in South Asian Comparative Politics*.

CONTENTS

ABBREVIATIONS

ADB	Asian Development Bank
AIDS	Acquired Immune Deficiency Syndrome
AL	Bangladesh Awami League
BJP	Bharatiya Janata Party
BNP	Bangladesh Nationalist Party
BSP	Bahujan Samaj Party
c.	circa
CBMs	Confidence-Building Measures
CHT	Chittagong Hill Tracts
CPB	Communist Party of Bangladesh
CPI	Communist Party of India
CPI—M	Communist Party of India—Marxist
CPN	Communist Party of Nepal
CPN—M	Communist Party of Nepal—Maoist
CPN—UML	Communist Party of Nepal—Unified Marxist-Leninist
CTBT	Comprehensive Test Ban Treaty
DMK	Dravida Munnetra Kazhagam
DPA	Democratic Progressive Alliance
DRP	Dhivehi Raiyyithunge Party
EEZ	Exclusive Economic Zone
EPB	Export Promotion Bureau
EPZ	Export Processing Zones
EU	European Union
f.o.b.	free on board
FANA	Federally Administered Northern Areas
FATA	Federally Administered Tribal Area
FDI	Foreign Direct Investment
FYP	five-year plan
GDP	gross domestic product
GNH	Gross National Happiness
GNI	gross national income
GNP	gross national product
HIV	human immunodeficiency virus

HM	His/Her Majesty
IAS	Indian Administrative Service
ILO	International Labour Organization
IMF	International Monetary Fund
INC	Indian National Congress
IPKF	Indian Peace Keeping Force
ISI	Inter-Services Intelligence
LOC	Line of Control
LTTE	Liberation Tigers of Tamil Eelam
m.	million
MOU	Memorandum of Understanding
MP	member of parliament
MQM	Muttahida Qaumi Movement
MW	megawatt
NAP	National Awami Party
NAP—B	National Awami Party—Bhasani
NDA	National Democratic Alliance
NEFA	North East Frontiers Agency
NGO/s	Non-Governmental Organization/s
NPT	Nuclear Non-Proliferation Treaty
NWFP	North-West Frontier Province
OBC	Other Backward Classes
OECD	Organisation for Economic Co-operation and Development
PML	Pakistan Muslim League
PPP	Pakistan People's Party
PPP	purchasing power parity
RSS	Rashtriya Swayamsevak Sangh
SAARC	South Asian Association for Regional Co-operation
SAFTA	South Asian Free Trade Area
SAPTA	South Asian Preferential Trade Agreement
SCs	Scheduled Castes
SLFP	Sri Lanka Freedom Party
SMEs	small and medium-sized enterprises
STD	sexually-transmitted disease
STs	Scheduled Tribes
TULF	Tamil United Liberation Front
ULF	United Left Front
UN	United Nations
UNDP	United Nations Development Programme
UNFPA	United Nations Population Fund
UNHCR	United Nations High Commissioner for Refugees
UNICEF	United Nations Children's Fund
UNP	United National Party

UPA	United Progressive Alliance
UPFA	United People's Freedom Alliance
VHP	Vishwa Hindu Parishad
WHO	World Health Organization
WTO	World Trade Organization

NOTES ON THE ENTRIES

Within the country entries, the various sections have been organized thematically in (generally) the following order:

Political Development: Constitution; Executive; Legislature; Elections/Electoral System; Political Parties; Social Movements; Foreign Policy; Foreign Relations; Judiciary; Defence (Security); Military; Police; Riots; Terrorism; Miscellaneous (including Bureaucracy, Citizenship, etc.)

Economic Development: Economic Policy/Reforms; Private Sector; Public Sector; Population; Family Planning; Migration; Urbanization; Minority Groups; Agriculture; Land Reform; Food and Famine Prevention; Industry; Foreign Trade; Banking System; Foreign Direct Investment; Foreign Aid; Labour; Informal Economy; Child Labour; Power; Environment; Floods and Natural Disasters; Health; Education; Social Security; Poverty; Welfare; Gender Relations; Miscellaneous.

APPENDIX: COUNTRY-BY-COUNTRY LIST OF ENTRIES

The Appendix groups together entries by country. It aims to provide the reader with an overview of all the entries in the dictionary pertaining to a particular country, including those subheadings that can be found in the Political Development and Economic Development entries for each of the seven states of South Asia, as well as those which fall into the more general South Asia category.

A

Adhaalath Party

In August 2005 the Adhaalath Party, or Justice Party, became the third political party to officially register in the Maldives. The party was founded by Sheikh Hussein Rasheed Ahmed and is currently led by Dr Abdul Majeed Abdul Bari, with a major aim being the conservation of Islam in the Maldives. Following conflicting reports, it is unclear whether the political standpoint of the Adhaalath Party is closer to that of the **Dhivehi Raiyyithunge Party (DRP)**, which supports the government, or to the **Maldivian Democratic Party (MDP)**, which has tended to take a more opposing stance.

Adhikari, Man Mohan

Man Mohan Adhikari (1920–99), Prime Minister of Nepal from 1994 until 1995, was a politician who dedicated much of his life to the fight against authoritarian rule and the Nepalese monarchy. As leader of the **Communist Party of Nepal—Unified Marxist-Leninist (CPN—UML)**, Adhikari served as the first communist Prime Minister in Nepal, one of the few, and possibly the first, democratically-elected communists in the world to hold national office. During his time in office he initiated a number of reforms, including the Build-Your-Own-Village programme, to direct money to poor villages. Following his involvement in the struggle for Indian independence from the British, Adhikari returned to Nepal in 1946, and in the same year established the All-Nepal Trade Union Congress which led to Nepal's first, historical trade union movement on 4 March 1947. He later took a stand against the autocratic, party-less ***Panchayat* system**, and helped bring the communists into mainstream politics after the transition to democracy in 1990 ended King **Birendra**'s almost 20 years of absolute rule. In recognition of his service, Adhikari received a royal honour at his funeral procession, the only Prime Minister in Nepal ever to have received this level of recognition.

Aditya Birla Group

Having been founded as a cotton trading business in the mid-19th century, Shiv Narayan Birla's initial enterprise grew into India's second largest business group, with constituent flagship companies in heavy industries, telecommunications and finance. Under the leadership of former chairman Aditya Birla, the Birla Group is the world's largest producer of viscose staple fibre, the largest refiner of palm oil and, at home, the largest producer of aluminium in the private sector. A US $7,590m. conglomerate, more than 30% of its revenues flow from its operations across the world.

Advani, Lal Krishna

Lal Krishna Advani has been a prominent Indian politician and leader of the **Bharatiya Janata Party (BJP)** in the **Lok Sabha**. He is a close associate of **Atal Behari Vajpayee**. During his early career, he was known for his advocacy of a strong 'Hindu revivalist policy' which included a redefinition of Indian nationalism and a hard line against Pakistan. Accused of raising the emotions on the issue of **Ayodhya**, he created in 1990 and 1992 a major controversy by leading a '*Rath Yatra*' (chariot journey) across India to the city of Ayodhya. The second procession in 1992 culminated in the destruction of the '*Babri Mosque*'. Advani was arrested and accused of encouraging *communal* conflicts, detrimental to the secular basis of India. However, after the formation of the BJP-led **National Democratic Alliance (NDA)** government in 1999, Advani, like many other senior politicians, came to realize that without broad-based electoral support the BJP could never maintain a strong position of power. In this context his contribution to the party has been remarkable. He pursued the cause of Hindu revivalism with a clever electoral strategy and established a distinct but also flexible political and ideological identity. In addition, Advani provides his party with successful mass-mobilization techniques and a broad social base in the northern Hindi-speaking states ('Hindi Belt'). Born in 1929 in Karachi, Advani started his political career as a journalist, joined the **Rashtriya Swayamsevak Sangh (RSS)** in 1942 and rose from within its ranks to hold key positions in the Bharatiya Jana Sangh and its successor BJP. He was president in 1970–72 (BJS), 1973–77 (BJS), 1986–91 (BJP) and 1993–98 (BJP); and general-secretary and leader of the BJP in the **Rajya Sabha** in 1980–86, before joining the Janata Party, holding a cabinet position (Union Cabinet Minister, Ministry of Information and Broadcasting—1977–79) in the Janata Government of 1977. Between 1970 and 1989 Advani was a member of the Rajya Sabha (four terms) and, from 1979 until 1981, leader of the opposition in the Rajya Sabha; and he was elected to the ninth, 10th, 12th and 13th Lok Sabha. He held in the 13th Lok Sabha (1999–2004) the offices of Union Cabinet Minister, Home Affairs (1998–99, 13 October 1999–) and Deputy Prime Minister (since 1 July 2002) in the BJP-led coalition government. During a trip to Pakistan in June 2005 Advani became one of the few major Indian political leaders to visit **Jinnah**'s mausoleum. However, his positive comments on Jinnah created uproar within his own party as well as the ruling **Congress** party. After months of controversy Advani decided to step down as party president by the end of 2005.

Affirmative Action

Affirmative Action or positive discrimination gives specific preference to groups considered to be disadvantaged by the Hindu social structure (**caste system**) in India. The main target groups are **Scheduled Castes (SCs)**, **Scheduled Tribes (STs)** and, more recently, **Other Backward Classes (OBCs)**. To compensate for their social, economic and political inequality a quota of 22.5% of all government jobs, seats in educational institutions that have complete or partial government funding and electoral constituencies at all levels of government is reserved for SCs and STs. Enshrined in the Constitution under Article 15 (4) and Article 16 (4), the quota is roughly proportionate to their share in the population, a provision largely due to Dr B. R. **Ambedkar**. The issue of quotas for OBCs was less clear-cut and following those of various other commissions, the **Mandal Commission**'s report of 1980/81 recommended extending reservations to the OBCs with a quota of 27%. Implementation of this recommendation began in 1991 and caused extensive public protests. Although it is debatable whether affirmative action has brought about material and social betterment for 'backward' and 'discriminated' groups, it has been argued that a noticeable change has been achieved in the electoral sphere where members of SCs and STs have been brought into central roles that were unimaginable for them a few decades ago.

Agartala Conspiracy Case

Framed by the Pakistani government in January 1968 during the Ayub **Khan** regime, the Agartala conspiracy case implicated **Awami League** chief Sheikh Mujibur **Rahman**, together with 35 serving and former members of the armed forces and high government officials. They were accused of conspiring to bring about the secession of the east wing from Pakistan through armed revolt, with the help of the Indian government. The Pakistani government alleged that the accused had plotted against the country's national interest in a conspiracy initiated in the city of Agartala, India. In a separate declaration, the Home Department implicated Sheikh Mujibur Rahman in the conspiracy. He, together with many others, was detained in February 1969 and named as the prime conspirator. Initially, the government had planned a court martial, but it later opted to bring charges under civil law. The case began to be heard on 19 June 1968 before a special tribunal. However, confronted by a mass movement in East Pakistan, the Pakistani government decided to withdraw the case on 22 February 1969, thereafter releasing unconditionally all of the accused, including Sheikh Mujibur Rahman. (*See* **Bangla Movement**; **Bangladesh Liberation War**.)

Agrani Bank

Agrani Bank, one of three government-owned commercial banks in Bangladesh, has 891 branches, including 10 corporate and 30 authorized dealer branches which are responsible for foreign exchange. It commenced operations on 26 March 1972 with the assets and liabilities of the erstwhile Habib Bank Ltd and Commerce Bank Ltd, under the promulgation of Presidential Order No. 26 of 1972. In addition to traditional banking services, the Agrani Bank is involved in various income-generating and economic development projects.

Agricultural Development Bank Nepal (ADBN)

The Agricultural Development Bank Nepal (ADBN), previously the Co-operative Bank, was established in 1968 under the ADBN Act of 1967. Principally involved in development finances, ADBN mainly provides short-, medium- and long-term agricultural credit to individual farmers, groups of farmers, corporate bodies and village committees to enhance agricultural productivity. ADBN is an autonomous organization, supervised by the Ministry of Finance. Since 1984 it has also undertaken commercial banking operations in an attempt to mobilize urban resources for rural development.

Ahimsa

The term *ahimsa* refers to a concept of non-violence which advocates respect towards all kind of life. It has its origin in Sanskrit and is derived from the word *ahims*: *a-*, meaning 'not' and *hims* meaning 'injury'. As a religious doctrine it is primarily in practice in Hinduism, Buddhism and, particularly, Jainism. At the political level Mohandas Karamchand **Gandhi** utilized *ahimsa* as a key concept for mass mobilization in the independence movement. Based on *ahimsa* to challenge the British colonial ruler, he introduced the concept of ***satyagraha*** as a peaceful protest, in which it is aimed not to offend anybody or perceive anybody as an enemy. Five decades after Gandhi's assassination by a Hindu fanatic *ahimsa* continues to be a part of political culture and rhetoric in India.

Ahmadiyya/Ahmadis

An Islamic sect founded in the mid-19th century by Mirza Ghulam Ahmad. Today the Ahmadiyya community comprises roughly 4m. adherents in Pakistan. The fundamental difference between Ahmadis and the Sunni Muslim majority concerns the identity of the Promised Messiah, the reformer who the Prophet Muhammad foretold would appear after him. In 1973, during Zulfikar Ali **Bhutto**'s rule, a constitutional amendment effectively defined the Ahmadis as 'non-Muslim' and under **Zia** ul-Haq in 1978 a separate electorate system for non-Muslims, including Ahmadis, was installed. Persecution of and violence against the Ahmadis in Pakistan and partly in Bangladesh continues to be an issue. (*See* **All-Pakistan Muslim Parties Convention**; **Anti-Ahmadiyya Movement**.)

Ahmed, Tajuddin

Ahmed (1925–75) was Prime Minister of Bangladesh in exile. At the onset of the military crackdown, he left Dhaka on 25 March 1971 and organized the **Bangladesh Liberation War** from Indian territory. He is credited with having convinced Indira **Gandhi**, Prime Minister of India, to aid the liberation movement and to recognize Bangladesh even before Indian troops marched into East Pakistan's territory in December 1971. Once Bangladesh gained independence he returned to become Prime Minister, and subsequently held various ministerial posts after Sheikh Mujibur **Rahman** returned from Pakistan to become Prime Minister. Furthermore, he played a significant role in the constitutional process of the country. Ahmed was a close associate of Mujibur Rahman but had to step down from the Cabinet on 26 October 1974 owing to internal politics. After the assassination of Mujibur Rahman on 15 August 1975 (August Coup), he was arrested on 23 August and murdered within Dhaka Central Jail on 3 November, following the counter coup of Khalid Musharif, together with three other national leaders, Syed Nazrul Islam, A. H. M. Qamaruzzaman and M. Mansur Ali.

Aid-to-Bangladesh Consortium

Bangladesh remains heavily dependent on foreign aid for its development programmes. Japan, the USA, Middle Eastern and European countries are major aid donors to the country. The World Bank organized in October 1974 a consortium known as the Bangladesh Aid Group, comprising 26 international financial institutions and foreign governments interested in supporting the country's development activities. During the annual Bangladesh Aid meeting donors announce their annual commitment to Bangladesh, based on an assessment of the country's economy and an evaluation of the annual development programme. Dissatisfaction with the country's socio-economic development and the unstable law and order situation led to a recent decision to base future aid commitments on the government's success in improving stability and security.

Aid-to-India Consortium

The Aid-to-India Consortium was formed in 1958 by the World Bank Group and 13 countries, including Austria, Britain, Canada, Denmark, the Federal Republic of Germany, France, Italy, Japan, the Netherlands, Norway, Sweden and the USA, to co-ordinate foreign assistance to India. Aid was bilateral and mostly for specific development projects. In 1993 it was replaced by the India Development Forum. Backed by the World Bank, it has held annual meetings world-wide gathering Indian government officials and donor representatives together.

Aid-to-Pakistan Consortium

In 1960 the World Bank established the Aid-to-Pakistan Consortium because of Pakistan's dependence on foreign assistance. The consortium held 92% of Pakistan's outstanding disbursed debt in June 1991. Member states included the USA, Canada, Japan, the United Kingdom, Germany, France, and international organizations such as the World Bank and the ADB.

Akali Dal

Akali Dal (Eternal Party), also known as Shiromani Akali Dal, is a regional political party claiming to represent India's Sikhs. It describes itself as a moderate Sikh party and is controlled by the dominant Jat Sikh farming community of **Punjab**. Founded in 1920 as a political-religious movement, the Akali Dal sought to promote the political voice of Sikhs in issues pertaining to their interests, in particular to return the control of *gurdwaras* (Sikh temples) to the orthodox Sikh religious community, and to promote a return to the roots of the Sikh religion.

Following **Partition** and the reorganization of the states after independence, the charismatic Akali Dal leader, Master Tara Singh, launched the 'Punjabi Suba agitation' to form a state in which Sikhs would be a majority. In 1966 Prime Minister Indira **Gandhi** granted the demand and out of the state of Punjab was formed a Sikh-majority Punjab, with the Hindu-majority areas divided between **Haryana** and **Himachal Pradesh**. In 1967 Akali nominee Gurnam Singh took over as chief minister of Punjab. Over the next decade the political development of the Akali Dal was severely hampered by intervention from the ruling **Congress** party which, on various occasions, dismissed Akali state governments, as well as factionalism within the party. In the 1980s militancy and the demand for **Khalistan**, an independent Sikh state (a movement led by Sant Jarnail Singh **Bhindranwale**) added to the Akali Dal's troubles. The party continues to play a major role in state politics and has its headquarters in Amritsar. (*See* **Operation Blue Star**.)

Akhil Bharatiya Vidyarthi Parishad (ABVP)

The Akhil Bharatiya Vidyarthi Parishad (ABVP—All India Students Council) was founded soon after India's independence and formally registered on 9 July 1949. One of the fastest growing student organizations, it is affiliated with the **Sangh Parivar** and is one of the major political bodies at Indian universities. Its political activities on the campus encompass issues such as terrorism in Kashmir, migration into the border states from abroad, reservation and Mandal recommendations, unemployment and the economic reconstruction of India. The ABVP contests elections for student unions and has attempted to enter various university administration forums. (*See* **Jammu and Kashmir**; **Kashmir Dispute**.)

Aksai Chin

Located in the north-eastern section of Ladakh district in the Indian state of **Jammu and Kashmir**, about 38,000 sq km of the area known as Aksai Chin is a contested part of the border between India and China. A legacy of the British times, the border had remained informally delimited and was thus open to interpretation. There was heavy fighting in this area and in the **North East Frontiers Agency** during the 1962 border war between India and China and Aksai Chin has been under Chinese administration since. An icy and remote land, China's strategic interest lies in the fact that National Highway 219, a major connection linking Tibet and China's Xinjiang province, runs through it. India continues to claim Aksai Chin while China disputes India's control over the north-eastern state of Arunachal Pradesh. After 1962 the two countries agreed to respect the **Line of Actual Control**. (*See* **McMahon Line**.)

All-Assam Gana Sangram Parishad (AAGSP)

The All-Assam Gana Sangram Parishad (AAGSP—Assam Popular Struggle Association) was an alliance of small regional political parties and other non-political associations. Together with the **All-Assam Students' Union (AASU)** the AAGSP led a six-year-long agitation to expel foreign nationals illegally staying in Assam. In 1985 the AAGSP and the AASU signed the Assam Accord with the Indian government, bringing the movement to an end. The **Asom Gana Parishad (AGP)** was formed as a political party, successfully contesting elections to the state assembly. (*See* **North East India**.)

All-Assam Students' Union (AASU)

A powerful students' group that launched a bloody campaign to oust Bangladeshi immigrants between 1979 and 1985 and, again, from 1990. Increasingly, however, the All-Assam Students' Union (AASU) has appealed to the banned military **United Liberation Front of Assam (ULFA)** for an end to violence and has called for peaceful measures, such as tighter control over migrants to Assam and more industrial processing of Assam's natural resources, to stimulate the local economy. (*See* **North East India**.)

All-Ceylon Buddhist Congress

Formed on 18 October 1918 by Buddhist activists and headed by Dr. C. A. Hewavtharana, the original goal of the All-Ceylon Buddhist Congress was to aid the socio-economic development of Buddhists through charitable and developmental work. Today the organization is involved in reviving Buddhist education and festivals as well as environmental and relief work. (*See* **Buddhist Movement**.)

All-Ceylon Tamil Congress (ACTC)

Founded by G. G. **Ponnambalam** in 1944 and also known as the Tamil Congress, the All-Ceylon Tamil Congress (ACTC) was Sri Lanka's oldest Tamil party. In 1948 a faction broke away to form the Tamil **Federal Party (FP)** but the two streams came together in 1972 as the Tamil United Front which in 1976 came to be known as the **Tamil United Liberation Front (TULF)**. The TULF in 2001 joined the **Tamil National Alliance**.

All-India Anna Dravida Munnetra Kazhagam (AIADMK)

The All-India Anna Dravida Munnetra Kazhagam (AIADMK) is a regional political party in **Tamil Nadu** in India and has its roots in the **Dravidian** movement promoting Tamil identity. It was founded by M. G. Ramachandran (a popular cinema actor in South India, known as MGR) on 17 October 1972 as an offshoot from the **Dravida Munnetra Kazhagam (DMK)**, now the AIADMK's principal regional rival. Its headquarters are in Chennai (Madras). Under Ramachandran the AIADMK dominated politics in Tamil Nadu from 1977 until 1989. Following his death, personal rivalry split the party into two factions. The defeat of both factions and the DMK's 'political comeback' reunited the AIADMK under the leadership of Ms Jayalalitha Jayaram. The party has increasingly played a crucial part in coalition politics at the centre. Part of the **Bharatiya Janata Party**-led ruling coalition government in 1998, it withdrew in 1999 causing the government to fall and hold snap elections.

All-India Forward Bloc

The All-India Forward Bloc is a regional political party in **West Bengal**. It was founded by Subhas Chandra Bose on 3 May 1939. The ideology of the party promotes socialism, including nationalization of key sectors of the economy, land reform and redistribution. The party is an ally of the **Communist Party of India—Marxist** in West Bengal and forms part of the ruling **Left Front** government.

All-India Hindu Mahasabha (HMS)

The All-India Hindu Mahasabha (HMS) was originally founded as a social, cultural and religious organization, not as a political party. After the formation of the first Hindu *Sabha* (Assembly) in **Punjab** in 1907, this organization launched an 'All-India body' in 1915. The main targets were to safeguard the interests of Hindus, the social reform of Hinduism and the construction of a national Hindu community. This included a Hindu revivalist attitude, hostility towards 'Western influence' and, in particular, the prevention of the formation of Pakistan and the **Partition** of India. The foundation was conceived as an articulation of Hindu assertiveness as well as a reaction to Muslim organization and the implementation of separate Muslim constituencies. The HMS was mainly a provincial organization in northern India in its early years and initially functioned as one of several interest groups inside the **Congress** movement. Despite drawing support from other cultural organizations, such as Arya Samaj, the HMS could not secure any important position in the political life of post-colonial India.

All-India Majlis-e-Ittehadul Muslimen (AIMIM)

The All-India Majlis-e-Ittehadul Muslimen (AIMIM), also known as the All India Council of the Union of Muslims, is a regional political party in the Indian state of **Andhra Pradesh**. It was founded in 1927 by Bahadur Yar Jung 'for educational and social uplift of Muslims'. During its history, the AIMIM was involved in aggressive and violent politics, for example during the communal riots of the mid-1940s and in 1979. As a pro-Nizam party its central goal was the independence of an Islamic Hyderabad state. The party was banned in 1948 but reorganized itself in 1957, over the years developing into one of the leading representatives of urban Muslims. It is currently led by Asaduddin Owaisi and won one seat in the 14th **Lok Sabha** elections as part of the **United Progressive Alliance (UPA)** coalition.

All-India Radio (AIR)

All-India Radio (AIR) was formally set up in 1936 and is the main radio broadcaster in India. As a national service, it was planned, developed and operated by the Ministry of Information and Broadcasting until 1997 as an independent media unit. The first transmitters for sound broadcasting were privately owned and commenced operations in 1927 in Mumbai until the government nationalized them, bringing them under the Indian Broadcasting Service (IBR). In 1936 the IBR was renamed as the AIR, whose 215 broadcasting centres reach *c.* 90% of the total area and 97.3% of the population of India. Together with **Doordarshan** it is a division of **Prasar Bharati**, the Broadcasting Corporation of India.

All-India Railwaymen's Federation (AIRF)

The All-India Railwaymen's Federation (AIRF) was founded on 7 June 1925 in Mumbai and is today one of the largest labour organizations in India, with a membership of more than 1m. railway workers. This organization claims to be politically independent and democratic, free from interference by any political party or the government.

All-India Sikh Student Federation (AISSF)

The All-India Sikh Student Federation (AISSF) was formed by Sardar Swarup Singh in 1944, originally as the student wing of the **Akali Dal**. In the 1970s it broke off from the Akali Dal and drifted into the secessionist movement aimed at creating an independent **Khalistan**. While the AISSF made common cause with the movement for a Sikh homeland, it did not fight for it until militancy erupted under Sant

Jarnail Singh **Bhindranwale** in 1981 and a number of AISSF members joined ranks with the militants. The organization was banned between 19 March 1984 and 11 April 1985.

All-India Trade Union Congress (AITUC)

The All-India Trade Union Congress (AITUC) is the oldest trade union of India, established in 1920 and today one of the largest central trade union organizations. It was founded by the **Indian National Congress (INC)** as the mainstream labour organization of the independence movement, in which the AITUC played a significant role. Since independence it has been affiliated with the **Communist Party of India (CPI)**.

All-India Trinamool Congress/Nationalist Trinamool Congress (AITC)

The All-India Trinamool Congress/Nationalist Trinamool Congress (AITC) is a regional political party in India with its main support base in **West Bengal**. It was founded just before the 1998 general elections as an offshoot of the **Indian National Congress (INC)** by Mamata Banerjee. Initially the West Bengal Trinamool Congress (WBTC), it was soon renamed as the AITC. Prior to its electoral collapse in the 14th **Lok Sabha** elections of 2004, in which it won only two seats (in 1999 it had nine seats), the party had been the main opposition to the **Left Front** coalition of communist parties in West Bengal. After merging with a break-away faction of the **Nationalist Congress Party** the party now operates as the Nationalist Trinamool Congress.

All-Pakistan Muhajir Students Organization (APMSO)

Originally a breakaway faction of the *Jamaat-e-Islam* student wing, the All-Pakistan Muhajir Students Organization (APMSO) was founded by Atlaf Hussain in 1984. Later it came to be known as the **Muhajir Qaumi Movement (MQM)**. MQM has emerged as the main advocate of muhajir demands and in that capacity plays a major role in Pakistani politics.

All-Pakistan Muslim Parties Convention

The All-Pakistan Muslim Parties Convention was organized on 2 June 1953 in Karachi due to the pressures from an anti-Ahmadi movement called Thaffuz-ikhatm-i-nubuwwat. The convention declared Ahmadis to be a non-Muslim minority, called for Chaudhri Zafrullah Khan (an Ahmadi) to resign from the office of Foreign Minister and demanded that Ahmadis be removed from all key posts of the state. (*See* **Ahmadiyya/Ahmadis**.)

All-Pakistan Women's Association (APWA)

The All-Pakistan Women's Association (APWA) is a non-governmental organization operating to raise the socio-economic status and constitutional rights of women in Pakistan. It was founded in 1949 by Ra'ana Liaquat Ali **Khan**, wife of Pakistan's first Prime Minister. APWA has campaigned for the principles of equality, development, gender equality and social peace.

All-Party Hurriyat Conference (APHC)

The All-Party Hurriyat ('Freedom') Conference (APHC) was formed in September 1993 as an umbrella organization of more than 23 political, social and religious groups committed to the independence of Kashmir. Claiming to represent all people of the state **Jammu and Kashmir**, the APHC has refused to contest elections, its proclaimed goal being the independence of Kashmir for which, it is believed, it received substantial support from Pakistan. Over the years the Hurriyat had insisted that any talks on Kashmir be tripartite, with Pakistan, India and the Hurriyat as the participants. However, in September 2003 the APHC split into a hard-line faction (led by Syed Ali Ahah Geelani), and a moderate faction (led by Mirwaiz Umar Farooq) that claims to eschew violence, and in early 2004 the Deputy Prime Minister, L. K. **Advani**, of the **National Democratic Alliance (NDA)** government held two rounds of talks with the Hurriyat leadership, the first such interaction between the APHC and the highest levels of government. More recently, following a visit to Pakistan-administered Kashmir and to Pakistan by the moderate wing in June 2005, Prime Minister Manmohan **Singh** met with Mirwaiz Umar Farooq, suggesting that the hard-line faction is finding itself increasingly sidelined. (*See* **Kashmir Dispute**.)

All-Tripura Tiger Force (ATTF)

The All-Tripura Tiger Force (ATTF) was initially established as the All-Tripura Tribal Force on 11 July 1990 by a group of former Tripura National Volunteers. Operating in the north-eastern Indian state of Tripura as an active militant group, its main objectives are the expulsion of all Bengali-speaking settlers who entered Tripura after 1956; the restoration of land to tribals under the 'Tribal Land Revenue and Land Reforms Act' (1960); and the removal of names of migrants who entered Tripura after 1956 from the electoral roll. The ATTF's headquarters are located in Bangladesh and it has collaborated with the **United National Liberation Front (UNLF)** and the **National Socialist Council of Nagaland (NSCN)**. (*See* **North East India**.)

Alliance of Small Island States (AOSIS)

The Alliance of Small Island States (AOSIS), founded in 1990, is a coalition of small islands and low-lying coastal states that share similar environmental and development challenges and fears arising from their vulnerability to the adverse effects of global warming and rising sea levels. It operates as an international regime without formal organizational structures, to lobby and negotiate in the interest of Small Island Developing States (SIDS) within the United Nations system. The Maldives is a main driving force.

Al-Zulfikar Organization

A terrorist organization allegedly founded in 1981 by Murtaza Bhutto, the son of Zulfikar Ali **Bhutto**, to avenge his father's execution under the martial law regime of Gen. **Zia** ul-Haq. Operating from Kabul (Afghanistan), Damascus (Syria) and Delhi (India), it was involved in various subversive activities in Pakistan. The organization hijacked a Pakistani plane and killed a passenger in March 1981, demanding the release of political prisoners.

Ambani, Dhirubhai

Born in 1932 to a modest family in **Gujarat**, Dhirubhai Ambani went on to found first a textiles giant and, later, India's leading petrochemicals company, the Reliance Group. India's largest enterprise in the private sector, it became the first to challenge the government-run monopoly in the Indian petrochemicals industry in the mid-1980s. Revered at home as a national icon, Ambani's death in 2002 drew nation-wide and international tributes. The Reliance Group today has multinational ambitions in the areas of oil exploration, plastics and telecommunications, and is the only Indian private company to be included in the Fortune 500 list.

Ambedkar, Dr Bhimrao Ramji

Well known in India as the 'Father of the Constitution', Bhimrao Ramji Ambedkar was born in 1891. Unable to attend school during his childhood because of poverty, he was among the very few '**untouchables**' in British India to study abroad thanks to the patronage of Maharaja Sayaji Rao of Baroda. Following his return to India, after studying law in England and economics in the USA, he became the leader of the depressed classes movement, lobbying for special rights and representation. This social movement, with the slogan of 'Educate-Agitate-Organize', aimed at eliminating the **caste system** and bringing about the reconstruction of Indian society on the basis of the equality of all human beings. Ambedkar's demand for separate electorates for 'depressed classes' brought him into direct conflict with the **Congress** party and *Mahatma* **Gandhi**, who considered this as an opportunty for the British to divide Hindus on the basis of caste. When the Communal Award of 1932 granted separate electorates, Gandhi commenced a 'fast unto death', ultimately compelling Ambedkar to give in and replace separate electorates with reserved seats.

After independence, Ambedkar joined the Cabinet of Jawaharlal **Nehru** as Minister of Justice. He eventually became one of the main authors of the Indian Constitution of 1950 and a main advocate of the constitutional directive on **affirmative action**. Shortly before his death in 1956, he and thousands of his 'untouchable' followers converted to Buddhism in protest against the stringent Hindu caste system. There were many more conversions in the ensuing years. By the time of his death Ambedkar had established his third political party. He was honoured posthumously with the highest national honour, '***Bharat Ratna***', in 1990.

Andaman and Nicobar

Located in the **Indian Ocean**, in the Bay of Bengal, Andaman and Nicobar are island territories that became Indian territory at independence in 1947. The islands are far from India, the closest point being Chennai (Madras), 1,190 km distant by sea. The islands became a **Union Territory** in 1956, with its capital located at Port Blair. In 2001 the total population of the islands was reported to be 356,152, comprising a mix of Indian, Burmese and Malay descent. Most of the population are Hindu (67.5% in 1991) but there is also a fairly large Christian minority (24%) as well as Muslims inhabitants (7.6%). Five tribal groups, accounting for about 15% of the total population, live in government-protected tribal reserves. The Union Territory is represented by one seat in the **Lok Sabha**. Forestry, fishing and tourism are the main sectors of the economy. The islands, which have great potential for development, have gained strategic importance as the People's Republic of China has increased its presence in the Indian Ocean region (by leasing land from Myanmar). In 1998 the Indian government established the Far East Naval Command at Port Blair and in 2001 this was upgraded into a 'Joint-Services Command'.

Andhra Pradesh

Located in the south of India, Andhra Pradesh was the first linguistically-organized state in independent India. Formally established in 1953, the state of Andhra initially comprised the Telugu-speaking region of the Madras Presidency. In 1956, however, following the recommendations of the States Reorganization Commission, the Telugu area of 'Telangana' from the former Nizam state of Hyderabad was added to it to create Andhra Pradesh. The city of Hyderabad is the state's capital. Andhra Pradesh is India's fifth largest state in terms of area and population. According to the 2001 census of India, the state's population stood at 75.73m., accounting for 7.4% of India's total population. Nearly 80% of Andhra's workforce makes a living from agriculture and the state is known as the rice bowl of India. Hindus, including **Scheduled Castes (SCs)** and **Scheduled Tribes (STs)**, account for about 89% of the total population and Muslims, the largest minority, constituting about 9%, live largely in Hyderabad. Andhra Pradesh has one of the largest concentrations of SCs in the country, with about 59 of them represented in the state. The state assembly has 294 seats and 60 members in the national parliament (18 in the **Rajya Sabha** and 42 in the **Lok Sabha**). Andhra Pradesh comprises three main sub-regions: coastal Andhra, Rayalaseema and Telangana. Of the three, Andhra is the most developed and Telangana the least, a disparity that has been and continues to be a cause of contention and conflict in state politics. Politics in Andhra Pradesh captures the hurdles and opportunities that India's federal system has to offer. As a regional party, the **Telugu Desam Party (TDP)**, under the leadership of N. T. Rama Rao, managed to dislodge the **Congress** party, after more than two decades of Congress dominance, and to usher in a new period of party politics in the early 1980s. Later, in 1996, under N. Chandrababu Naidu (Rama Rao's son-in-law), the TDP acquired national significance, with influence that was out of proportion to its relatively small share of seats. At the same time, two powerful movements have come close to threatening the survival of the state: the violent struggle waged by the Naxalites during the 1960s and 1970s and the campaign for a separate Telangana state. Both movements, despite having lost some of their earlier momentum, continue to underlie contemporary Andhra Pradesh politics. Chief minister Chandrababu Naidu styled himself as a reformer and modernizer, referring to himself as 'CEO' of the state. To fulfil his priority of attracting foreign direct investment to the state, Naidu travelled widely, developing for the first time the image of a dynamic state connected to the world economy and internally through modern communications technology, pursuing its own 'foreign economic policy'. Nevertheless, in the 2004 national and state elections Naidu's party suffered under the double impact of an effective alliance strategy by the Congress party and the anti-incumbency factor expressed against Naidu's nine-year rule. Allied with both the Left parties and the newly-formed **Telangana Rashtriya Samithi (TRS)**, Congress made substantial gains in all three regions of the state.

Ansars and Village Defence Party (VDP)

The Ansar organization and the Village Defence Party (VDP) together constitute the largest paramilitary force in Bangladesh. Their main objectives are to assist the country's police forces in maintaining law and order, to take part in development programmes and social services and to help the army protect the country's territorial integrity and sovereignty. The Ansar organization was initially formed as an irregular auxiliary force to defend key governmental and public institutions, while the VDP was constituted in 1976 by Ziaur **Rahman** to carry out routine security duties in the villages. (*See* **Bangladesh Rifles**.)

Anti-Ahmadiyya Movement

The Anti-Ahmadiyya Movement does not accept the basic principles and the membership of the **Ahmadiyya** sect as part of the Islamic community of Pakistan. In 1992 the Movement issued a ***fatwa***, calling for an open ***jihad*** against Ahmadis. In 2003 radical Islamic groups in Bangladesh declared the Ahmadiyya community to be an 'un-Islamic sect'. (*See* **All-Pakistan Muslim Parties Convention**.)

Anti-Blasphemy Law

Incorporated in 1986, section 295/C of the Pakistan Penal Code (commonly known as the Blasphemy Act) imposes the death penalty on anyone who 'by words or visible representation or by an imputation or insinuation, directly or indirectly, defiled the name of Prophet Muhammad of Islam'. Furthermore, anyone found guilty of desecrating the Koran could be sentenced to life imprisonment under this law. Often abused and manipulated by religious fanatics to settle personal vendettas, this law has contributed to Pakistan's notoriety as an intolerant and fanatic society. Under pressure from many human rights organizations, the blasphemy law was revised in 2004, but only at a technical and procedural level.

Aphno Manchhe

A Nepali social mechanism, *aphno manchhe*, literally 'one's inner circle of associates', has become institutionalized in administrative and economic transactions. Decisions, instead of following formal rules, have tended to be influenced by informal sources, such as political influence, bribery and personal connections (*aphno manchhe*). (*See* **Chakari**.)

Arthasastra

The *Arthasastra* ('Science of Material Gain') is one of the earliest texts on statecraft in India, thought to have been written in the 4th century BC by Chanakya (also known as Kautilya). It advises that a number of key economic sectors should fall under the exclusive authority of the king to ensure a secure and prosperous economy.

Ashraf

A general term used in the international Muslim community, which gained importance in the process of Bangladesh's state formation. Traditional Muslims were divided by social origins into categories. Aristocrats known as *ashraf* (élite), were mostly Urdu speakers and maintained a distance from Muslim *jotedars* and peasants (*atraf* or *ajlaf*—ignoble) who identified themselves with the local culture and language. Initially, the leadership of the Muslim community in Bengal belonged to the *ashraf*. Cleavages within the *ashraf* community also exist, such as the **Shi'a–Sunni conflict**. In addition, the internal contradictions of Muslim society in Bengal were mirrored in their social and political life. While vernacular Muslim élites in favour of their local culture, especially the Bengali language, demanded a Muslim-dominated, independent and sovereign Bengal, in contrast, the *ashraf*, perceiving themselves as a high-born and ruling élite, were generally in favour of a single Islamic state in South Asia, by merging geographically dispersed Muslim majority areas. However, the creation of a territorially divided Pakistan in 1947 as the 'homeland' for all Muslims in the region, combined with the suppression of non-Urdu speakers by the *ashraf* in West Pakistan, led to a growing identity crisis among the majority people in Bengali-speaking East Pakistan, resolving the dichotomy between *ashraf* and *atraf*.

Asom Gana Parishad (AGP)

Asom Gana Parishad (AGP) is a regional political party in Assam (India), where it was founded and gained power in October 1985. It draws support from the **All-Assam Gana Sangram Parishad (AAGSP)** and the **All-Assam Students' Union (AASU)**. The party claims that Bangladeshi immigrants were an economic, religious, and cultural threat to the indigenous Hindu Assamese identity. The AGP held seven seats from 1985 until 1989 in the **Lok Sabha** and returned in 1996 with five seats as a part of the **National Democratic Alliance (NDA)** coalition (1996–99). It failed to gain any seats in the 13th Lok Sabha (1999–2004).

Associated Press of Pakistan (APP)

Created as a trust in 1947, Associated Press of Pakistan (APP) was taken over by the military government in 1961 due to financial crisis in the agency. It was made into a corporation, and merged with the Ministry of Information through an ordinance in 2002. The premier news agency of the country, APP reports, gathers, and distributes domestic and foreign news.

Association of Development Agencies in Bangladesh (ADAB)

The Association of Development Agencies in Bangladesh is an apex body and functions at the national level, co-ordinating and representing organizations of local, national and international NGOs working in Bangladesh. Founded in January 1974 as a loose coalition of foreign-aided NGOs involved in relief and rehabilitation activities, it has over the last two decades emerged as a co-ordinating body, with the aim of establishing NGO solidarity, promoting government-NGO relations, encouraging mutual co-operation, facilitating expertise and avoiding the duplication of programmes.

Atoll

Confusingly, in the context of the Maldives, the term Atoll serves a dual purpose, referring to the 26 natural Atolls comprising the republic, and to the 20 Atolls that function as administrative units.

Awami League – *see* Bangladesh Awami League

Awami National Party (ANP)

The Awami National Party (ANP) emerged in Pakistan in 1986, when four left-wing regional parties unified under the leadership of Wali Khan. It is only really represented in the **North-West Frontier Province (NWFP)**, and has co-operated in coalitions with both the **Pakistan People's Party (PPP)** and the **Pakistan Muslim League (PML)**.

Ayodhya Conflict

Ayodhya, a town in the north Indian state of **Uttar Pradesh**, gained international attention after the demolition of Babri Masjid on 6 December 1992 sparked communal violence across the country. The Babri Masjid (mosque), built in 1528 by a general of Babar, founder of the Mughal dynasty, has been a site of religious confrontation because some Hindus claim that the mosque was erected in order to replace an ancient Hindu temple built in the 11th century AD to mark the birthplace of Lord Ram, one of Hinduism's most revered deities. British rulers, when they annexed the kingdom of Avadh in 1856, put a railing around the mosque to separate places of worship, allowing the inner court to be used by the Muslims and a raised outer platform by Hindus.

Following India's **Partition** and the *communalized* atmosphere, the newly independent Indian government closed the site, placing it under guard. However, on the night of 22 December 1949 an idol of Ram was planted in the mosque, provoking riots that were quashed by the army and civil lawsuits filed by Hindu and Muslim leaders over the site's ownership. Declared a disputed site, the government locked the gates until the mid-1980s when the **Vishwa Hindu Parishad (VHP)** began an agitation to unlock the gates and build a temple for Ram. In 1986 a district and sessions judge of the Faizabad court ruled that the disputed site should be opened to the public for worship, triggering *communal* violence and protests. Both the **Bharatiya Janata Party (BJP)** and the **Indian National Congress (INC)** have used the issue in their quest for political power. In 1989, despite a Supreme Court ruling that no parties or groups could disturb the *status quo* of the Babri Masjid, Congress entered into an agreement with the VHP, allowing them to proceed with a foundation-laying ceremony for the Ram temple, and in 1992, with the BJP in power in Uttar Pradesh, VHP supporters tore down the mosque, prompting nationwide riots between Hindus and Muslims. In 2001 the VHP once again raised the '*Ram Jamnabhoomi*' (Ram's birthplace) issue, pledging to build a Hindu temple on the site, but this time the BJP-led **National Democratic Alliance (NDA)** government refused to condone the construction. Nevertheless, hundreds of 'volunteers' converged on the site and in 2002 at least 58 people were killed in an attack on a train in Godhra in **Gujarat** carrying Hindu activists returning from Ayodhya, sparking one of the country's worst riots. In April 2002 High Court judges started hearings to determine ownership of the site and in early 2003 archaeologists began a court-ordered survey to explore whether a Ram temple predated the mosque. The findings, however, remain disputed and criminal proceedings against the involvement of Hindu leaders in the 1992 destruction have been initiated.

Azad Kashmir

Azad Kashmir (Free Kashmir), together with the **Northern Areas**, constitutes almost one-third of the former princely state of **Jammu and Kashmir**, under Pakistani administration since the Indo–Pakistan war of 1947. Pakistan has divided these areas into two parts: 13,300 sq km as a nominally autonomous state of Azad Kashmir, and 72,496 sq km incorporated into Pakistan as the Northern Areas and administered as a *de facto* dependency. Azad Kashmir, with Muzafarabad as its capital, has a mountainous terrain and a population of more than 3m., many of whom are, however, settled in Europe, especially in the United Kingdom (almost two-thirds of British Pakistanis are of Azad Kashmiri origin). Foreign remittances from these expatriates have not only ameliorated the socio-economic conditions in regions such as Mirpur, but have also made a sizeable contribution to the total foreign exchange earnings of Pakistan. The politics of Azad Kashmir have mostly been influenced and dominated by prevalent trends in the political and military echelons of Pakistan. During its first 50 years Azad Kashmir has, almost uninterruptedly, been ruled by the Muslim Conference, a pro-establishment party, led by Sardar Qayyaum. Economically, the area is relatively underdeveloped and a long-running source of dissatisfaction has been Azad Kashmir's claim of a share in the royalties of the Mangala Dam (the second biggest dam of Pakistan after Tarbela).

B

Bahajan Samaj Party (BSP)

The Bahajan Samaj Party (BSP—Party of Society's Majority/Majority People's Party) is a political party in India, founded by Kanshi Ram on 13 April 1984 (the birthday of **Ambedkar**). The BSP frames its philosophy in terms of 'caste conflict' and seeks to build support among **Other Backward Classes (OBCs)**, **Scheduled Tribes (STs)**, and Muslims. Its main goal is to represent the **Dalits**. The party emerged from Kanshi Ram's earlier efforts to promote the interests of Scheduled Caste government employees and is linked with the aims of the 'apolitical' Backward and Minorities Employees Federation (BAMCEF). The BSP first came to political power in the northern Indian state of **Uttar Pradesh**, in alliance with the **Bharatiya Janata Party (BJP)**. The party produced the first Dalit ever to be a chief minister of Uttar Pradesh, Kumari Mayawati. However, outside the state of Uttar Pradesh the party has not been able to displace the Republican Party of India (RPI) as the leading party of the **Scheduled Castes** in **Maharashtra**. The BSP was implicated in several controversies, including, most notoriously, the so-called 'Taj Scam' (unauthorized commercial development at the World Heritage Site of the Taj Mahal) and also land deals, the formation of new districts and regularization of Dalit houses, etc.

Bahun

Nepali term for the hill caste of Brahmins who constitute 12.7% of the total population of Nepal. Together with the Thakuris and **Chhetris**, they dominate positions of power and leadership, including the political parties, media, judiciary, police force, the civil service and the army.

Bajrang Dal (BD)

Bajrang Dal (BD—'bajrang' is linked with Hanuman, the monkey god) is the youth wing of **Vishwa Hindu Parishad (VHP)**. It was established on 1 October 1984 in the Indian state of **Uttar Pradesh** with the aim of spreading political awareness among Hindus and resistance to anti-Hindu and anti-social elements. It claims a membership of 500,000 active workers and to be involved in various welfare measures. The BD is not as highly disciplined as the **Rashtriya Swayamsevak Sangh (RSS)**. Its motto is 'Seva, Suraksha, Sanskar' ('Service, Security, and Culture'), and its symbol is the *trishul*, the god Shiva's trident. In this context it is involved in various public campaigns, such as the Cow Protection Agitation and the Amar Nath Pilgrimage, and in social work among the underprivileged sections of the population. The BD has been closely associated with the VHP in the movement to 'liberate' Hindu holy shrines at Ayodhya and other sites where mosques now stand. It was banned for two years in 1992 by the Indian government for its role in the demolition of Babri mosque. (*See* **Ayodhya Conflict**; **Sangh Parivar**.)

BAKSAL – *see* Bangladesh Krishak Sramik Awami League

Balochistan

The largest of Pakistan's provinces, Balochistan covers 347,190 sq km (42% of Pakistan's total area) but has a population of only 7m., 7% of the country's total population. An extreme, arid terrain and scarcity of water in the region contributes to the harsh living conditions there. Basic development indicators in Balochistan are among the lowest in Pakistan, with female literacy rates reportedly below 15%. More than 80% of the province is designated as tribal area and governed through special laws. Three main tribes, the Baloch, Pashtun and Brahui, are predominant.

Balochistan became part of Pakistan in 1948. Armed uprisings by separatist forces have been a continuous phenomenon in this region, in 1948 itself and again in 1968 and 1973–77, but they have repeatedly been suppressed by the Pakistan military. The equitable distribution of resources is a continuous source of contention between the province and the centre, Balochistan alleging that its mineral resources, particularly natural gas, of which it has the largest reserves, benefit other provinces due to its own lack of industry.

Sharing a 960-km border with Afghanistan, the province has been badly affected by continuous instability in the neighbouring country which has led to an influx of arms, refugees and foreign militants into Balochistan. Since 2002 the government, with Chinese help, has been building a deep-sea port in the coastal town of Gawadar. Making use of its geo-strategic location, the hope is to project Gawadar as the world's gateway to Central Asia, bringing development and increased stability to the area.

Bandaranaike Family

One of the two foremost political families of Sri Lanka. S. W. R. D. Bandaranaike (1899–1959) established the **Sri Lanka Freedom Party (SLFP)** in 1951 and in 1956 led the party to eject the **United National Party (UNP)** from office. He personified a brand of nationalism that was unabashedly Sinhalese and Buddhist.

Following his assassination in 1959 his widow, Sirimavo Bandaranaike (1916–2000) took over, becoming the world's first female premier. She won elections in 1970. Their daughter, Chandrika Bandaranaike Kumaratunga (1945–), became leader of an opposition alliance in 1988 and was appointed Prime Minister in 1994. After winning presidential elections the same year her mother was installed as Prime Minister (she resigned in 2000) while Kumaratunga took over the presidency. She was re-elected as President in 1999, her term coming to an end in late 2005.

Bandh

The term *bandh* is derived from Hindi and used across South Asia. It means a general or state-wide strike, which is frequently associated with leftist pressure groups but, in practice, is not exclusive to them. (*See **Hartal**.*)

Bangalore

The South Indian city of Bangalore, with a population of 6,062,577, is the capital and the largest city of the Indian state of **Karnataka**. After India's independence in 1947 a deliberate attempt was made to develop Bangalore into a centre for science and research. Attracted to Bangalore because of its mild climate and strategic position far away from the country's sensitive borders, a number of key industries, such as Bharat Electronics Ltd (BEL) and Hindustan Aeronautics Ltd (HAL), were established by the government in Bangalore, together with national defence research laboratories and the Indian Institute of Science.

More recently Bangalore has become known as the 'Silicon Valley of India', famous for the concentration of high technology firms which spearheaded the boom in information technology (IT) in the late 1990s. Numerous industrial parks skirt Bangalore's suburbs where both Indian and multinational giants have operations, including the renowned **Infosys Technologies**. Despite the wealth and technology generated in Bangalore, the city's infrastructure remains neglected and under-developed. In mid-2005 a forum of Indian and international firms threatened to boycott flagship IT events unless the city government acted to improve conditions such as infrastructure in what is today one of Asia's fastest growing cities.

Bangla Movement

Language was a source of conflict between the two wings of Pakistan from the outset. Although the majority in East Pakistan spoke Bangla (constituting roughly 55% of Pakistanis at the time), Urdu was made the sole state language in 1948 under the newly formed government of Pakistan, established by Muhammad Ali **Jinnah**. Bengali students, politicians and the intelligentsia demanded that Bangla be made a second official language, alongside Urdu, as well as the state language of East Pakistan. Both Jinnah and his successor, Najimuddin, were vehemently opposed to this and, as a result, a language movement, the *bhasha andolon*, arose in 1948, gaining momentum over the years and reaching its climax on 21 February 1952. On this day, commemorated as martyrs' day, police forces opened fire on protesters, killing six Bengali youths and wounding many others in the aftermath. Bangla was finally recognized as one of the state languages in 1954, this recognition representing one of the first steps towards independence for Bangladesh. In 1999 UNESCO adopted a resolution to establish 21 February as International Mother Language Day in honour of those who sacrificed their lives in 1952. (*See* **Bangladesh Liberation War**; **Bangladesh Awami League (AL)**.)

Bangladesh, People's Republic of

The People's Republic of Bangladesh is located in the eastern part of South Asia, surrounded on three sides by India with which it shares 4,053 km of common border. To the south east is Myanmar, with which Bangladesh shares a 193-km common border, and in the south a coastline of 580 km forms part of the Bay of Bengal. Bangladesh is divided into six administrative units: Barisal, Chittagong, Dhaka, Khulna, Rajshahi and Sylhet.

Area: 144,000 sq km; capital: Dhaka; population: 146.7m. (UN, 2003), comprising ethnic Bengalis (*c.* 98%), tribal groups and non-Bengali Muslims; official language: Bangla (also known as Bengali); religion (1998 estimates): Muslims *c.* 88.3%, Hindus *c.* 10.5%, others *c.* 1.2%.

The supreme organ of government is the unicameral national parliament (Jatiya Sangsad) comprising 330 members, elected for a five-year term by popular votes from single territorial constituencies. The assembly elects the President as chief of state for a five-year term (renewable once) and also approves the Prime Minister, who is designated by the President.

History: Pakistan, which was formed in 1947 after the merger of East and West Pakistan into a single state, faced political unrest arising from differences in language, culture, levels of economic development and the geostrategic location of its two wings, which were separated by 1,600 km of Indian territory. East Pakistan was primarily populated by Bengalis, proud of the literary tradition of their language, Bangla, while the western part of Pakistan used Urdu as the main language—declared the official language of Pakistan in 1948 by Muhammad Ali **Jinnah**.

Denied a voice commensurate with the size of their population (in 1970 about 54% of the total population) in the administration of Pakistan, economic and political grievances gave rise to a growing sense of alienation. When, in the general election of December 1970, the **Awami League (AL)** of Sheikh Mujibur **Rahman** won a majority in the national legislature, he proposed framing a new constitution on the basis of his 'Six Points'. The negative response of West Pakistan to suppress calls for greater autonomy by the Eastern wing led to a declaration of independence on 27 March, which was followed by civil war. The Liberation War continued until 16 December 1971, when Bangladesh, with the help of intervention from India, became an independent, sovereign nation. The United Nations admitted Bangladesh in 1974.

Bangladesh has undergone a variety of regime changes since independence. The four pillars of democracy, nationalism, secularism, and socialism were supposed to sustain the nation, led by the father of the nation, first Prime Minister, and later President, Sheikh Mujibur Rahman. In 1975 the government of Bangladesh underwent its first change, moving from the original parliamentary system to a presidential one (that lasted until 1991). Gradually, Mujibur Rahman's socialist, democratic regime turned into an authoritarian, one-party, single-leader government that was quite different from what he had envisioned during the struggle for independence.

Sheikh Rahman was assassinated on 10 August 1975, the first of a number of political killings which have tarnished Bangladesh's politics since, and, after a short period of weak government, a military regime under Maj.-Gen. Ziaur **Rahman** and his **Bangladesh Nationalist Party (BNP)** ensued. Ziaur Rahman gradually liberalized the political system, removing restrictions on the press and on political parties which had been banned under Mujibur Rahman.

Ziaur Rahman was himself assassinated on 30 May 1981 and again, after a short interim government, military rule followed, with Lt-Gen. Hossain Mohammad **Ershad** at the helm. Ershad ruled the country with his **Jatiya Party (JP)** until his resignation in December 1991. Under his rule, Islam was introduced into the Constitution of Bangladesh, completing a trend that had started under Ziaur Rahman, who changed secular sections of the Constitution and replaced them with 'absolute trust and faith in Almighty Allah'. This shift towards Islam also had an impact on the foreign relations of Bangladesh.

When the government collapsed in 1990 as a result of increasing public pressure and a pro-democratic movement, relatively free and fair elections followed, together with a return to a parliamentary system in 1991. Ziaur Rahman's party, the BNP, won the country's first democratic elections and his widow, Begum Khaleda **Zia**, took over as Prime Minister. In 1996 Mujibur Rahman's daughter, Sheikh **Hasina** Wajed, and her AL took power through elections conducted under the observance of a neutral, **caretaker government**, which had been introduced some weeks before. Until the 2001 elections, when it was replaced by Khaleda Zia and the BNP, this party ruled without interruption.

Latest Elections: Legislative elections held on 1 October 2001 were won by the **Four-Party Alliance** led by Khaleda Zia and the BNP. The BNP and its alliance partners secured 46% of parliamentary seats, the party of Hasina Wajed, the AL, winning 42%, which translated into 195 seats for the BNP and 62 for the AL. Coalition partners of the BNP such as **Jamaat-e-Islami (Jammat)**, **Islamic Oikya Jote** and the **Manjur faction** of the JP won, respectively 18, two and four seats.

Recent Developments: Since the elections of 2001 the old disputes with India over the exchange of enclaves and the sharing of water have continued. Migration from Bangladesh to India has intensified problems between these two neighbours. Increasing cases of assaults on the Hindu minority and a strengthening of Islamic forces within the country are important concerns. The current political debate is dominated by the attempt to introduce a further tier of local governance by reviving an institution located at the village/ward level, called Gram Parishad or **Gram Sarkar**.

Bangladesh, Political Development

After independence Bangladesh introduced a legislature based on the Westminster system and formed a new government, with Justice Abu Sayeed Choudhury as President, and Sheikh Mujibur **Rahman** as Prime Minister after his release from a Pakistani prison in early 1972. The new government formed a constitutional committee to frame a constitution with four basic principles at its core: nationalism, secularism, socialism, and democracy. Promulgated on 16 December 1972, the Constitution provided for a Cabinet, collectively responsible to parliament, the *Jatiya Sangsad*. In the country's first parliamentary election, held in March 1973, the **Bangladesh Awami League (AL)** won 293 of the total 300 seats. The first parliamentary session was held on 7 April 1973. Two years later, however, a one-party presidential system was introduced, with a party system named the **Bangladesh Krishak Sramik Awami League (BAKSAL)**, under the fourth constitutional amendment. Under this new arrangement Sheikh Mujibur Rahman became President, with strong executive powers. With the assassination of Sheikh Mujibur Rahman in August 1975, state power was seized by coup leaders who were middle-ranking army officers. In a counter coup, Gen. Ziaur **Rahman** came to power in 1976 and continued until his own death by assassination in 1981. Rahman gradually consolidated his position, first by assuming the powers of Chief Martial Law Administrator and then, in April 1977, the presidency. In May a national referendum confirmed his position and policies. Having formed his own political party, the **Bangladesh Nationalist Party (BNP)**, in September 1977, he contested and won a presidential election in June 1978, defeating the AL candidate and further entrenching his position. In the second parliamentary election, held in February 1979, the BNP won 207 of the 300 seats and the AL emerged as the major opposition party, having won 39 seats.

As President, Ziaur Rahman replaced secularism as one of the major principles of the Constitution, adding instead references to the 'absolute trust and faith in Almighty Allah' and inserting Bismillah-ar-Rahman-ar-Rahim ('in the name of Allah, the Beneficent, the Merciful'). The principle of socialism was also modified, paving the way for a stronger role for the market.

After the assassination of Ziaur Rahman, Abdus Sattar, the Vice-President, become acting President for an interim period and was nominated as a BNP candidate in the presidential election of November 1981. He won the election but soon after, in March 1982, was forced to hand over power to the then military chief, Gen. H. M. **Ershad**, who remained in power until 1990. Under Ershad a third and fourth parliament were elected, but they are usually referred to as 'rubber stamp' parliaments. Following in the footsteps of his predecessor, Ershad also advocated religion as the basis of politics, declaring Islam as the state religion in the eighth constitutional amendment. Parliamentary democracy was revived with the fifth parliamentary election, held under a **caretaker government**, on 27 February 1991. The legislators returned to the parliamentary system, passing the 12th constitutional amendment without controversy. Begum Khaleda **Zia**, leader of the BNP (which won 140 of the 300 seats) became Prime Minister, in coalition with the **Jamaat-e-Islami**. However, the opposition party, the AL, organized demonstrations and strikes to force the BNP government to resign and to announce a new parliamentary election. Despite a boycott by the main opposition party, the fifth parliament fulfilled its tenure. In the sixth parliamentary elections of February 1996, Khaleda Zia was re-elected. The major opposition party boycotted the elections as fraudulent, demanding the dissolution of parliament and new elections. Finally, the sixth parliament adopted a neutral caretaker government system under the 13th constitutional amendment, to conduct parliamentary elections, which were held in June 1996. Under the leadership of Sheikh **Hasina**, the AL formed the government, completing its tenure despite a number of strikes, agitation, and walk-outs from parliament as well as a boycott, staged by the opposition party, the BNP. Sheikh Hasina handed power to the caretaker government for the eighth national parliamentary elections, held in 2001, in which the BNP emerged as the winner. Begum Khaleda Zia, chairperson of the BNP, formed a new government, in coalition with the Jamaat-e-Islami again. Although the AL also denounced this election as unfair and fraudulent, it has continued to attend parliament.

Constitution: The Constitution of Bangladesh was adopted on 4 November 1972. It provided for the separation of powers between an independent legislature, the executive, and judicial branches of the government. The original Constitution was formed on the basis of Mujibur Rahman's **Six-Point Programme** and the state was founded on the pillars of secularism, socialism and democracy. During the military rule of Gen. Ziaur Rahman Islamic references were inserted into the Constitution. The Constitution was changed and also suspended after the coup of 24 March 1982. Several amendments have been made to almost every section. The Eighth Amendment to the Constitution was added in 1988, recognizing Islam as the state religion and the 13th Amendment in 1996 provided for the system of a neutral, caretaker government. Amendments have also changed the political system several times, with a presidential system replacing the original parliamentary system envisaged in 1975. The separation of powers was then reintroduced after the last period of authoritarian rule, under Gen. Ershad, in 1991. In terms of the fundamental rights of citizens, all men and women are equal before the law, freedom of speech is guaranteed and a free press is ensured. However, in times of civil disorder and public protest the government has the authority under the Constitution to suspend these fundamental rights and to jail opponents without trial.

Executive: The Constitution of 1972 has been amended several times, creating changes in the nature of the executive. The form of government was changed from the original parliamentary system to a presidential system in 1975, included various military administrations and a return to a parliamentary system in 1991. Strengthening the President's position was the main motive behind the changes brought about by Mujibur Rahman and, later, by Maj.-Gen. Ziaur Rahman and Lt-Gen. Hossain Mohammad Ershad. Under the current constitutional arrangement, executive power is exercised by the Prime Minister, who is the head of government, directly or through officers subordinate to him. He or she is appointed by the President, and must be a member of the parliament (Jatiya Sangsad). In practice, the leader of the majority party is appointed as Prime Minister and if no party has a majority the leader of the coalition which has a majority in the parliament assumes this office. Furthermore, the Prime Minister heads the Council of Ministers (Cabinet). The members of the Cabinet are chosen by the Prime Minister and with him are collectively responsible to the parliament. Up to 50% of the ministers may be chosen from outside of parliament. The Prime Minister is required to consult the Council of Ministers before advising the President on important matters such as the dissolution of parliament or a declaration of emergency. However, the Prime Minister usually decides on major policies with little or no involvement by the President or parliament. The President, as the constitutional head of the state, is elected by the parliament for a term of five years and has limited executive powers compared to his predecessors, holding a largely ceremonial post. The supreme command of the military forces is vested in him and he is responsible for the formal appointment of the Prime Minister as well as the Chief Justice and other judges. However, the broad constitutional powers asssumed by the Prime Minister have been a focal point of criticism by each opposition, leading to the boycott of most parliamentary sessions at the Jatiya Sangsad. The separation of power remains a controversial issue, particularly due to interference by the executive in the lower tiers of the judicial system.

Legislature: Bangladesh has a unicameral parliament, the Jatiya Sangsad (JS), consisting of 300 members directly elected from an equal number of territorial constituencies on the basis of adult suffrage. In addition to the 300 seats, the Constitution provides for the reservation of a certain number of seats for women, who are elected by the directly elected members. Women may also be candidates in the general election. During the first parliament, 15 seats were reserved for women. The number was subsequently raised to 30, and then to 60 in the current, eighth JS. The legislature has a maximum term of five years from the date of the first sitting unless dissolved earlier by the President or extended under extraordinary circumstances, such as the country being engaged in war. Apart from the seventh JS, no legislature has yet been able to fulfil its five-year term owing to coups and counter coups, and to a lack of consensus between governing parties and the opposition.

The JS vests its authority in the presiding officer, who is designated as speaker, following the Westminster (United Kingdom) model. The speaker is assisted by several deputy speakers to conduct all parliamentary business. According to Article 74 (1) of the Constitution, they shall be elected from among members of the JS at the first sitting, which is presided over by the outgoing speaker. The Prime Minister is the leader of the house and is assisted by a deputy leader who he/she nominates. The President of the country is authorized to summon the JS on the written advice of the Prime Minister. The JS has its own independent secretariat to assist and provide necessary services to the speaker as well as to its members.

Elections/Electoral System: When Bangladesh became independent in 1971 it opted for a parliamentary system of government. This was replaced by a presidential system in 1975, but the country returned to the parliamentary system again in 1991. The Representation of the People Order 1972, the Conduct of Election Rules 1972, and the Code of Conduct 1996 laid the foundations for the procedures guiding elections. Article 122 of the Constitution provides several requirements for the enrolment of electors, who must be citizens of Bangladesh and not less than 18 years of age, must not have been declared by a competent court to be of unsound mind and are deemed by law to be residents of the constituency. Of the 300 parliamentary seats, 30 are reserved exclusively for women, who are elected from single-member territorial constituencies. They must also be citizens of Bangladesh and must have attained the age of 25 years. After the dissolution of parliament, whose tenure can be up to five years unless dissolved sooner, the next general election of members must be held within 90 days and is directed by the Election Commission and enabled by the neutral caretaker government (introduced under the 13th Amendment Act of 28 March 1996). This non-party caretaker government is expected to hold general parliamentary elections in a fair and free manner, keeping the process free from any partisan influence on the government machinery.

After the repressive Ayub **Khan** regime (1958–69) and the liberation war of 1971, Bangladesh held its first parliamentary election in 1973 in which the Bangladesh Awami League (AL), led by Sheikh Mujibur Rahman, won 291 of the 300 seats and 73.18% of the popular vote. Since then several modifications have been made, with subsequent elections becoming more and more an instrument for the legitimization and formalization of a regime instead of supporting the institutionalization of democracy. In the presidential election of 1978, Maj.-Gen. Ziaur Rahman emerged as the winner, with 76.63% of the popular vote. This success was followed by a major victory in the parliamentary election of 1979, in which his party, the Bangladesh Nationalist Party (BNP), won 207 of the 300 seats. Under the Ershad regime (1982–90) two parliamentary elections (in 1986 and 1988) were held, but both were tarnished by ballot-rigging and the latter was boycotted by the BNP as well as the AL. When the government collapsed in 1990 following a mass upsurge, a return to a parliamentary system took place and free and fair elections followed on 27 February 1991, in which the BNP won 140 out of 300 seats and Begum Khaleda Zia was installed as Prime Minister. The BNP also won 28 of the 30 reserved women's seats and entered into a coalition with the Jamaat-e-Islami, thus gaining 168 of 330 seats.

In the parliamentary elections of 1996 Khaleda Zia was defeated by Mujibur Rahman's daughter, Sheikh Hasina Wajed of the AL and the party won 146 seats in an election held under the newly introduced caretaker government. The most recent legislative elections were held on 1 October 2001 and the BNP and its alliance partners came ahead of their competitors, with 46% of the vote and 225 seats, whereas the AL captured only 42% of the vote and 62 seats. Elections since the 1990s can be broadly characterized as having been free and fair, although political violence and unrest usually occur at election time. (*See* Federalism.)

Political Parties Regulation (PPR): The Political Parties Regulation (PPR) was promulgated on 28 July 1976 by Gen. Ziaur Rahman in order to legitimize his regime and to reduce some of the restrictions on politics by allowing some political activities. Under this regulation, political parties were called on to apply for state approval and recognition of their organizations. As many as 60 political parties applied on the basis of their constitutions, programmes and manifestos to obtain the necessary permission to function legally. According to the PPR, 21 political parties were recognized by the state at that time. It is argued that the regulation had the effect of reintroducing fundamentalist political parties, like the Islamic Democratic League (IDL), building a new political platform for activists of the then banned Jamaat-e-Islami, as well as encouraging factional politics. With the promulgation of the PPR, Ziaur Rahman installed himself as President through a referendum and consolidated his power through the BNP.

Social Movements: Social movements played an important role in the independence movement in Bangladesh. The language movement (**Bangla Movement**) of the 1950s culminated in the **Bangladesh Liberation War** and the formation of Bangladesh. Since the struggle for independence, social movements have been prominent in organizing broad sections of society in an effort to overthrow undemocratic elements. For example, in 1990 a 15-party alliance, together with a student movement, succeeded in forcing Gen. Ershad to transfer political power to a neutral caretaker government, paving the way for elections and parliamentary democracy. Civil society organizations, including NGOs and community-based organizations, have gained significance in supporting peaceful alternatives to the country's socio-economic and political development. Due to Bangladesh's comparatively homogeneous society, sub-nationalist movements based on ethnic and religious lines have not emerged. The most significant separatist movement of ethnic groups has been that of the Chittagong Hill Tracts which signed a peace accord. (*See* **Chittagong Hill Tracts Conflict**.)

Foreign Policy: Despite significant changes in Bangladesh's foreign relations since 1971, two major pivots may be identified: concern about India's intentions as the regional hegemon and Bangladesh's neighbour; and the country's strong dependence on foreign development assistance. The need to secure economic aid from all possible sources has been one of the main concerns of the country's foreign policy and led in recent years to the adoption of economic diplomacy aimed at attracting foreign direct investment as well as the development of trade opportunities. A major achievement was the normalization of relations with Pakistan (diplomatic relations were established in 1976). A number of bilateral agreements were signed on cultural as well as economic, commercial and technical issues. Bangladesh remained unaligned during the Cold War, maintaining good relations with both the USA as well as the former Soviet Union. Additionally, an important goal of foreign policy was the establishment of closer ties with the Islamic world. In 1977, under Ziaur Rahman, mention of secularism in the Constitution was deleted and replaced with references to Islam. Bangladesh's relations with Islamic countries such as Saudi Arabia and the Gulf States were strengthened and included the opening of their markets to Bangladeshi labour and increased aid inflows. Because of close connections to India and the Soviet Union, relations with China (also a supporter of Pakistan) were problematic. China exercised its veto against Bangladesh's admission to the United Nations and closed its mission in Dhaka in 1972. Relations improved in the mid-1970s following the reconciliation with Pakistan and as India-Bangladesh relations deteriorated. Trade and cultural agreements, construction projects and military transfers were signed with China. Bangladesh also maintains good political relations with Japan as well as the Republic of Korea (South Korea) and bilateral trade and economic co-operation increased in the late 1980s when Japan became the largest aid donor to Bangladesh. Relations with its south-eastern neighbour Myanmar have been generally trouble-free apart from the **Rohingya issue**, an international refugee concern which remains a problem between the two countries. Apart from bilateral relations, Bangladesh plays an active role in reinforcing regional co-operation, President Ziaur Rahman having proposed and promoted the **South Asian Association for Regional Co-operation (SAARC)**. In addition, Bangladesh was a founding member of the **Bay of Bengal Initiative for Multi-Sectoral Technical and Economic Co-operation (BIMSTEC)**, and in 2001 joined the Indian Ocean Rim–Association for Regional Co-operation (IOR–ARC).

Bangladesh-India Relations: Bangladesh's relations with neighbouring India have often been difficult. Despite the fact that India supported Bangladesh during its liberation war in 1971, an inbuilt distrust is found in the foreign policy towards India, partly due to a perceived threat of Indian hegemonic ambitions to turn Bangladesh into a client state. Furthermore, India and Bangladesh share a 4,000 km border and there has been friction between the two countries, especially in the sensitive north east of India where the movement of people across the frontiers has been difficult to monitor, especially in the case of refugees, smugglers and militant elements flowing into India. The Ganges water-sharing dispute (**Farakka Issue**) is another long-standing source of tension between the two countries. In 1972 the Indo-Bangladeshi Treaty of Co-operation, Friendship, and Peace was signed, committing the parties to hold reciprocal consultations in the event of hostilities. Mujibur Rahman and the Bangladesh Awami League (AL) were criticized by opposition forces, in particular by leaders of the Bangladesh Nationalist Party, for agreeing to what was regarded as too pro-Indian a commitment. A number of other treaties were later signed by India and Bangladesh, targeting common problems such as water distribution, border disputes and migration problems. Remaining problems that resurface intermittently include ownership of the South Talpatti Island located in the Bay of Bengal, which leaves maritime boundaries undelimited and provides India with a trade advantage. A specific matter of concern has been the reported increase in activities of Islamic fundamentalist forces within Bangladesh and the danger that its territories and the porous Bangladesh–India border are being used by internationally active Islamic groups to carry out terrorist activities and destabilize sensitive areas in India.

Judiciary: The judiciary in Bangladesh consists of two main levels—the higher judiciary, constituted by the Supreme Court, and the subordinate judiciary at the local level. Within the Supreme Court is the High Court division and appellate division. Enforcement of fundamental rights and guarding the Constitution are its main objectives. The chief justice and other judges are appointed by the President in accordance with the advice of the Prime Minister. Subordinate courts are found at the district and *thana* level, but there are also, since 1999, metropolitan magistrates in the major cities (Dhaka and Chittagong) and a number of village courts, where most village cases end. There are also special courts, such as the loan court and the bankruptcy court following the Bankruptcy Act of 1997. Tribunal courts, such as the administrative tribunal and the labour tribunal, are found at the subordinate level. As far as religion is concerned, civil courts apply Muslim law in cases where the parties are Muslim, and if the law has not been abolished by an enactment of the legislature. Similarly, Hindu law is applied where the parties are Hindu. Although the Constitution provides for an independent judiciary, critics claim that there have been periods when the executive eclipsed judicial authority, as under Gen. Ershad's martial law, enacted in 1982, which forced the courts to serve the interests of the ruling regime. Judicial independence in contemporary Bangladesh is sometimes compromised, particularly at the local level, suffering from an archaic legal framework with cumbersome judicial procedure and corruption.

Defence (Security): Defence services are divided into the army, the navy and the air force. The President is the commander-in-chief of the three armed forces and the three service chiefs are equals in the national command structure. However, in practice, the army dominates the defence establishment. Each service maintains separate headquarters and is solely responsible for its own training and recruitment programmes. There is no joint command service element to promote inter-service co-operation and combined arms operations. The Ministry of Defence is technically responsible for overseeing the military and since 1991 the Prime Minister has reserved the defence cabinet portfolio. The primary mission of the regular armed forces is to defend the nation's territorial integrity against external attack. All three services have their own intelligence directorates, which collect tactical intelligence to support military operations. The directorate-general of national security intelligence is a separate civilian organization responsible for collecting foreign intelligence and monitoring internal political affairs. Apart from the three defence services, the **Bangladesh Rifles (BDR)** are responsible for border security. Although no serious military confrontation has occurred with India, the Bangladeshi defence planners have long regarded India as a regional bully. They believe that India has the capacity to destabilize the country by extending covert assistance to tribal insurgents or to the regime's domestic political opponents. The defence budget is the largest national budget item. Over the years defence spending has increased more than twentyfold. The army has received more than 50% of defence outlays. Navy and air force expansion has been less spectacular, although capital outlays for such high-cost items as ships and aircraft represent a substantial economic burden.

Military: Since independence the military has played a major role in Bangladesh's politics, which it has dominated for almost 14 years (Ziaur Rahman's regime from August 1975 to May 1981 and Ershad's rule from March 1982 until December 1990). The major force during the Bangladesh Liberation War in 1971 was the **Mukti Bahini** (the liberation army), elements of which were later inducted into the Bangladeshi military. The incorporation of the fighting elements from the independence struggle added to a basic cleavage between the traditional army establishment, perceived as freedom fighters, and post-independence formations such as the **Rakkhi Bahini** as well as new personnel recruitments. As a result, the armed forces of the country were not able to establish themselves as a monolithic political force, leading, among other reasons, to the various *coup d'états* and counter coups in the country. The army of Bangladesh, with its seven division strength, is one of the largest contributing forces to the United Nations for peace-maintaining operations across the globe. By 2002 the Bangladesh army had participated in as many as 26 UN peace-keeping operations, such as UNIIMOG (Iraq), UNPROFOR (Yugoslavia) and UNMEE (Ethiopia/Eritrea). Other major branches are the air force, formed in 1973, and the navy, constituted in 1971. Additionally, besides the coast guard, there are several paramilitary forces, such as the BDR, which patrols the border, the **Ansars and Village Defence Party (VDP)**, which is similar to a national guard, armed police battalions and national cadet corps. In addition to guarding the country from external attacks, the military provides 'assistance to the civil', which means aiding the implementation of law and order as well as providing logistical and manpower support during natural disasters. Military service is voluntary. The available military manpower (males aged 15–49) was recorded at 35,170,019 and the number of those 'fit for military service' at 26,841,255 in 2005. In 2004 military expenditure was estimated at 1.8% of the gross domestic product, amounting to US $995.3m.

Police: The Bangladesh police service originated from the colonial British-Irish constable system used on the subcontinent. The chief of the police service is the Inspector-General of Police (IGP), who controls all 10 branches of the police service under the indirect supervision of the home ministry. Police administration is divided into six civil ranges and one railway range. Each range is controlled by a Deputy IGP. In addition, three police commissioners are responsible for three divisional cities and 'Police Super' (SP) is the chief of the police administration at the district level, assisted by an Additional Police Super (ASP) and a number of Assistant Police Supers. Field-level police administration is organized into circles and police stations. Each circle is headed by an ASP and each police station is headed by an officer-in-charge (OC), assisted by sub-inspectors and assistant sub-inspectors. Police officers are categorized as gazetted and subordinate officers. Ordinary police constables constitute the base of the pyramid. However, it has been reported that the highest number of corruption cases were filed against the police administration. In a survey of 2,500 households, 96.3% claimed that it was almost impossible to get help from the police without money or influence.

Riots: Violent conflicts in Bangladesh have only in part been of ethnic origin. Riots are mainly carried out by various kinds of socio-political groups, including militant elements of student movements (*see* **Bangladesh Student Politics**), ***hartals*** of trade unions, the storm-troopers and ***mastans*** and their linked political parties. Today, a serious matter of concern is the gradual resurgence of the **Chittagong Hill Tracts (CHT) Conflict** which harbours 13 different tribes which, in the past, have maintained a special guerrilla force, the **Shanti Bahini**, which has fought since the mid-1970s for political independence, leading regularly to communal riots in the CHT region.

Terrorism: Until recently Bangladeshi officials denied the existence of terrorist structures in the country. However, in 2005 the government banned Islamic organizations such as the Jamiat-ul-Mujahideen (JMB) and Jagrata Muslim Janata Bangladesh (JMJB), a move interpreted by observers as a sign of increasing concern that Bangladesh might become a base from which both South and South-East Asian terrorists could operate. India, in particular, claims that militant elements from Bangladesh have been trying to destabilize its north-eastern region (*see* **North East India**). Since the attacks on the USA on 11 September 2001 it has been reported that Islamic terrorist groups may be operating from Bangladesh. Terror attacks within Bangladesh are also a real concern, particularly due to the political polarization of the country, which is split between the BNP and the AL. Since 2000 more than 100 people have been killed in bomb blasts. Highly co-ordinated attacks using more than 350 small bombs within about an hour of each other in 63 out of Bangladesh's 64 districts in 2005 were seen as warning signal of terrorist networks and infrastructure within Bangladesh.

Bureaucracy: The new republic of Bangladesh inherited a bureaucracy which had its origins in the Indian and, subsequently, the Pakistani civil service. Retaining the colonial civil service structure preserved a basic dichotomy between policy making, as formulated by the central bureaucratic institutions, such as ministries and their divisions, and policy implementation, by subordinated bodies, such as departments, agencies and governmental corporations. Various administrative reforms have been attempted, for example the introduction of the multi-purpose Bangladesh Civil Service (BCS) which is composed of about 30 separate services, each undertaking a specialized function and of which the Administrative Service is often referred to as the dominating or élite service. Members of all services are recruited through open competitive examinations conducted by the Bangladesh Public Service Commission, which follows a quota system. Critics claim that the BCS is highly politicized and corrupt, instrumentalized during the period of military rule in 1975–90, and fragmented due to attachments to political parties.

Citizenship: Article 6 of the Constitution determines and regulates citizenship. Before the promulgation of the Constitution, the government announced the Bangladesh Citizenship (Temporary Provisions) Order 1972 (President's Order No. 149 of 1972) to regulate citizenship, with effect from 26 March 1971. According to the second article of this order, citizenship is granted to every person who him/herself or whose father or grandfather were born in the territory of Bangladesh and who was a permanent resident of such territories on 25 March 1971, and continues to be a resident. Also, anyone who was a permanent resident of the territories now constituting Bangladesh on 25 March 1971, and who continues to be a resident, is deemed to be a citizen of the country. The article also stipulates that if a person owed, affirmed or acknowledged expressly or in conduct allegiance to a foreign state, he would not qualify to be a citizen of Bangladesh. Double citizenship has been allowed in the case of commonwealth countries. A gazette notification lists the countries in which a Bangladeshi national by birth can acquire foreign citizenship, without losing Bangladeshi citizenship. However, a person who acquires double citizenship, according to Articles 58 C and 66 of the Constitution, cannot become a member of parliament or an adviser of the caretaker government.

Corruption: The international anti-corruption watchdog Transparency International places Bangladesh at the bottom of 102 nations in its 2002 report. It reported that the protection of life and property and the dispensation of justice were largely absent. In the same year, a survey revealed that 96.3% of total households agreed that, without money or influence, it was almost impossible to get help from the police. Sixty-three per cent of households involved in court cases reported that without bribery of court officials proceedings would go no further. Seventy per cent confirmed that they had experienced unethical practices in admission procedures to hospitals as well as to institutions of education, where cash or influence was found necessary to gain admittance. The media was also heavily criticized, with a substantial number of households viewing newspapers as professionally unethical and partisan.

Decentralization: The challenges of decentralization in Bangladesh are long-running, dating from pre-independence times. At the heart of decentralization initiatives in the country is the reform of the local government structure. Each regime since the end of British colonial rule made various attempts to reform the local government structure, for socio-economic development as well as for political purposes. In this context, concepts of decentralization comprise four dimensions: political, administrative, financial and economic, aimed at transferring authority in planning and decision making from the central government to subordinate and local-level institutions. Currently, Bangladesh is divided into six administrative units, each placed under a divisional commissioner. Each division is subdivided into several *zila* (districts). The total number of *zilas* is 64, each headed by a deputy commissioner. The *zila* is further divided into rural and urban sub-districts, of which there are 463 rural sub-districts, called *upazilas* (formerly *thana*) and 260 urban sub-districts, comprising six city corporations and 254 municipalities. Below this third tier, in rural areas, is the union level, each *upazila/thana* consisting of several unions. Further, each union (of which there are 4,470) comprises several wards, a cluster of villages (gram level). Although the local tiers have to perform some administrative functions, institutions on the local tiers are only partly integrated into the administrative and political structure. However, decentralization strategies undertaken since independence remain transient and highly politicized, dependent on the electoral fortunes of governing parties at the centre. As a result, the *status quo* has been maintained, given that local institutions are completely dependent on the national government. Besides the union level, comprising elected councils, local institutions are largely unrepresentative.

Federalism: After 1971 the government of Bangladesh established a centralized political system. Federal elements are rudimentary and are implemented through the transfer of political decision-making authority to subordinate and local administrative levels, both in rural as well as urban spheres. Urban local governments are composed of six city corporations and 254 municipalities, also known as *pourashavas*, all of them provided with an elected council. Rural local governments have three tiers and a fourth has been suggested by the current government led by the BNP. The first rural tier of local governance is the *zila parishad*, a council at the district level. Despite the fact that elected councils have been proposed, *zilas* are still operated by the government-appointed executive secretariat, with no elected members. The sub-district level was originally represented by the *upazila parishad* (sub-district council), introduced in 1992. However, as with the *zila parishad*, the electoral constituents of the *upazila parishad* have remained suspended since 1992, but the BNP government has committed itself to reintroducing an elected *upazila* system. This institution has become the focal point of local planning and co-ordination of the government, operationalized through local administrative facilities such as the Thana Development Co-ordination Committee. The third tier consists of the union *parishad*, one of the oldest and currently, also, the only local government institution which is an elected body, exercising some degree of regional autonomy. The last (seventh) union *parishad* elections were held in 2003. Each union is subdivided into wards and each ward is composed of 1–2 villages (*gram*), provided with a ***gram sarkar*** (village council or government, formerly known as *gram parishad*). Despite the fact that a ward might comprise various villages, in this scheme one ward is considered as one village and, as a result, the *gram sarkar* complements and is partly integrated into the union *parishad*. The *gram sarkar* has been declared an elective institution, but so far elections have not been held and the government continues to favour nomination of members of this institution. In general, the introduction of distinct tiers of local governance, which could lay down the foundation for a truly federal structure in the country, remains a highly controversial and political issue at the crux of which is the attempt to embed local government institutions within the existing administrative structure and to gain control over them through appointments to them. However, non-elected local government institutions are not legally recognized by the Constitution.

Human Rights: To stabilize the rapid deterioration in law and order, governments in recent years have introduced and applied a strict anti-crime policy, as a result of which numerous cases of human rights violations have been reported, e.g. arrests without warrant, the use of torture, extrajudicial or so-called encounter killings by the police. Criticism has been particularly directed at the recently-formed **Rapid Action Battalion (RAB)**. In a nation-wide anti-crime and anti-terrorist campaign, codenamed 'Operation Clean Heart', in which some 40,000 troops took part, more than 200 people died and 10,000 were arrested. Politically-motivated detentions of journalists, politicians and others, as instruments of political repression, are reported and, despite the constitutional guarantee of fundamental and civil rights, including freedom of religion, there have been increasing attacks against religious and ethnic minorities or disadvantaged groups. Reported attacks against the **Ahmadiyya** community, declared as non-Muslims, and also on Buddhists, Christians and Hindus, have been an issue of concern and a source of tension with India, which accuses the Bangladesh government of turning a blind eye to attacks on the Hindu population. Violent clashes also continue between members of tribal groups in the Chittagong Hill Tracts, who concluded a peace agreement with the government in December 1997, and radical groups who oppose the peace accord, resulting in abuses on both sides. (*See* **Chittagong Hill Tracts (CHT) Conflict**.)

Inequality: Although Bangladesh has achieved some noticeable improvements in human development, according to various indicators the country is the only one in South Asia where social, economic and political inequality is increasing. Periods marked by a lack of democratic governance and sometimes open autocratic rule and the misuse of public goods contributed to the inequalities in distribution. Access to material, natural and financial resources as well as services of the state is monopolized by a minority comprising the established military, urban and rural political patrons and politicians and their parties. Unequal access to education has become an increasingly important problem, contributing to increasing income disparities between urban and rural areas as well as gender biases. The shift in economic policy towards industrialization has added to the impoverishment of the countryside. However, despite the high degree of inequality due to the country's social stratification, the disparities in access to health, land, employment opportunities and basic services, there has been no evidence of a major social or class conflict.

Nationalism: Concepts of nationalism in Bangladesh are marked by competition and conflict between secular and Islamic elements. Basically, there are two main streams: Bengali and Bangladeshi nationalism. Bengali nationalism underpinned the emergence of Bangladesh as an independent nation state, and has, as such, a regional connotation. Additionally, the idea of Bengali nationalism emerged from the spirit of a language movement with a decidedly secular alignment, which gathered momentum in the early 1950s as a counter ideology to West Pakistan nationalism and culminated in the Bangladesh Liberation War. Soon after independence in 1971,

Bengali nationalism promoted by the Mujibur Rahman government and the AL became a state ideology and was enshrined in the Constitution of Bangladesh. However, the principles of Bengali nationalism came under pressure in the late 1970s when the new military government veered towards a Bangladeshi nationalism, promoted by Ziaur Rahman and the BNP as the core of the Constitution through the fifth constitutional amendment. The argument used was that Bengali nationalism was foreign-biased, for, while it excluded non-Bengali groups within the country, it extended, linguistically, to include Bengali-speakers in the Indian state of **West Bengal**. In contrast, the opponents of Bangladeshi nationalism stress that it tends towards an Islamic bias, directed at the Muslims who make up almost 90% of the country's citizens, and which, following the assassination of Mujibur Rahman, was given primacy as the core of Bangladesh's nationhood. The debate over national identity is still a core issue in the country's politics.

Participation/Public Action: The Constitution grants the people of Bangladesh freedom of assembly and freedom of association, including permission to assemble and to participate in public gatherings and processions. In the last three decades the country has experimented with various forms of governance—democratic and military forms, and others which constituted a blend of both. Each has had an impact on participation and on the kind of public action taken, of which *hartals* have been the most significant. The criticism is often made that, through *hartals*, opposition forces took their political rivalries onto the streets, paralysing not only political institutions, but also hindering the pace of political and economic development of the country. The political culture and the behaviour of the two main parties, the AL and the BNP, have been held responsible for polarizing society around their distinguished leaders, a fact which has not helped promote the acceptance of parliamentary democracy among the people.

An immense number of new political parties, increasing from 14 in 1973 to 54 in 2001, which take part in the parliamentary elections, and voter turn-out which rose from 55.61% (1973) to 75.59% (2001) seem to be evidence of active political participation. However, remote and underdeveloped rural areas are only gradually gaining an awareness of their economic and political rights, primarily through the activities of civil society organizations which have emerged since the mid-1980s.

Bangladesh, Economic Development

The economy of Bangladesh, one of the poorest countries in the world, suffers the effects of overpopulation combined with environmental crises. In 2003 the annual rate of growth of the gross domestic product (GDP) was estimated at 5.8%, while GDP per capita was estimated at US $389. Exports generated total revenue of $6,200m. while imports cost $8,500m.

The first economic system introduced after independence, based on Mujibur **Rahman**'s socialism, was far from successful, failing to produce the rapid industrial growth necessary to tackle mass poverty and heavy dependence on foreign aid. During Ziaur **Rahman**'s rule the country initiated a piecemeal economic liberalization process. Between 1980 and 1990 Gen. **Ershad** denationalized many areas of the economy, as a result of which industrial production grew at an annual rate of 4.9%. During the 1990s the industrial sector shifted its emphasis to the garment industry and by 1995 industrial production had risen to 7.3%. By the late 1990s the government had reduced the pace of economic reforms, especially with regard to privatization, resulting in the loss of previous gains. This was highlighted by a precipitous drop in foreign direct investment in 2000 and 2001.

In June 2003 the **International Monetary Fund (IMF)** approved a three-year, $490m. plan as part of the Poverty Reduction and Growth Facility (PRGF) for Bangladesh. Seventy million dollars were made available immediately. In the same vein, the World Bank approved $536m. in interest-free loans. Inefficient state-owned enterprises and slow implementation of economic reforms, stalled in many instances by political infighting and corruption, frequent cyclones and floods, insufficient power supply and a rapidly growing labour force that has not been absorbed by the agricultural sector (in 2002 the rate of unemployment reached 40%) are major impediments to economic growth. Two further factors have weakened Bangladesh's economy. After 11 September 2001 the main export industry, ready-made garments, suffered in the global economic downturn and the annual growth rate in general exports declined from 18% to 8%. Second, the politics of confrontation, corruption, and slow reforms have, over the years, discouraged foreign investors. Nevertheless, with its huge supply of human resources, Bangladesh has the potential to become an attractive destination for foreign investment.

Economic Policy/Reforms: The pace of reform picked up momentum for the first time with the fall of Gen. Ershad in 1991 and the reintroduction of democratic governance in Bangladesh. Despite various changes of governance, the history of economic reform is characterized by two major landmarks: import liberalization and export-led growth leading to greater market-orientation and increased integration into the world economy. After periods of crisis-driven policies due to the burden of reconstruction and the recovery of a war-affected economy, accompanied by serious political instability, the guiding principle of economic policy was the achievement of macroeconomic stabilization. Adopting pro-poor strategies of human resource development and social protection, Bangladesh achieved an improvement of living standards for the average citizen, a noticeable reduction in population growth and an increase in life expectancy. The contemporary economic development programme by the government emphasizes the private sector, based on the enforcement of small export-orientated industries as the engine of future growth. The fundamentals for this strategy were laid down by the early creation of so-called 'export processing zones'. However, to operationalize this economic policy framework, major challenges have had to be tackled, such as corruption and, in particular, the rise of 'crony capitalism'. Nevertheless, in recent years the country's leading political parties, despite their entrenched rivalry, have developed a minimum consensus on economic policy matters, particularly towards strengthening market-oriented development within a democratic framework.

Private Sector: In the late 1970s the government initiated the process of privatization and introduced the new industrial policy in June 1982. This reversed the trend set soon after independence, when the government nationalized major industries such as jute, textiles, chemicals and other basic industries, banks and insurance. The government began to reverse its policy of nationalization because public-sector enterprises could not run profitably and efficiently, with many of them running into severe financial difficulties and management problems. A second factor for starting the process of privatization was the increasing pressure of aid-giving agencies. In 1976–92 about 500 state-owned enterprises were sold or returned to their former owners. The government created the Privatization Commission (later the Privatization Board) as the special agency to gradually transfer government-owned enterprises to the private sector. Furthermore, it has recently opened up new sectors, such as power generation, telecommunications, gas and oil exploration, transportation, ports and container facilities, banks and other financial sectors for private investment. Private investment (local and foreign) is forbidden in only five sectors that are linked to national-security (arms, ammunition and other defence equipment; production of nuclear energy; forest plantation and mechanized extraction within the bounds of reserved forests; security printing of currency notes and minting; and air transportation and railways). In other sectors the current government policy allows private investment without any ceiling, and registration is automatic. Private investment, both local and foreign as well as joint ventures, in the public sector are also permitted.

Public Sector: After independence Bangladesh's economy suffered from the aftermath of the liberation war as well as from the exodus of most non-Bengali entrepreneurs. The government, committed to a socialist model of development, enforced growth through state-owned enterprises (SOEs) to stabilize the economy of the country. Despite various initiatives of privatization, the public sector remains dominated by enterprises that are wholly or partly owned and controlled by the government. The majority of equity in the public sector is owned by the government either directly or indirectly, through governmental institutions. Three forms of public-sector enterprises operate in Bangladesh, including departmental undertakings, statutory corporations and joint-stock companies. The first type of enterprise is set up by executive actions of government bodies to provide public utilities and services at fair prices in the larger public interest. Examples include the Bangladesh Railway, Postal Department, Telephone and Telegraph Board, the Power Development Board, the Water Development Board, the Customs Department and the National Board of Revenue. **Bangladesh Bank (BB)** and Biman (Bangladesh Airlines) are examples of statutory corporations set up by an act of parliament. Their rules, objectives, functions and duties are defined and specified in the act itself. The SOEs together represent a heavy financial burden on the economy, leading to greater recognition by the government of the private sector's role in the country's economic development.

Population: One of the major problems of Bangladesh is its enormous over-population and steadily increasing population rate. With 146.7m. inhabitants (2003) and a growth rate of 2.06% (2003 estimate), the population has been forecast to almost double by 2050. With 994.3 persons per sq km (mid-2003 estimate) Bangladesh is, with the exception of very small countries such as Singapore and Bahrain, the most densely populated country in the world. Before the industrial development that took place in the 1980s, Bangladesh was the most rural nation in South Asia, with an urban population of 8.8% in 1974. By 2000 the urban population accounted for 24.5% of the total. In Dhaka alone the population grew from 335,928 in 1951 to 9.1m. Bangladesh has an ethnically homogeneous population, of which Bengalis account for 98%. Only around 1% belong to the tribal population, which lives primarily in the Chittagong Hills and comprises mainly the Chakmas, the Marmas (or Maghs), the Tipperas (or Tipras), and the Mros (or Moorangs), who have their own distinct cultural life. With regard to language and religion, the distribution is also very homogeneous, with Muslims accounting for 88.3% of the total population, Hindus for 10.5% and 1.1% belonging to other religions.

Family-Planning Policy: The fact that Bangladesh is the eighth most populous nation in the world has led the government to focus closely on family planning as a method of limiting population growth. A directorate within the Ministry of Health and Family Welfare was established in 1975 to provide family-planning services. In addition, health and family-planning clinics were established, especially in the rural areas, to provide clinical contraceptive services. Over the years the government has taken a series of policy and organizational decisions to promote family-planning programmes, including the integration of family-planning services into the health system and the involvement of NGOs in family-planning service delivery as well. As a result, the country has achieved significant improvements in demographic planning through substantially reduced population growth, fertility decline, gender equality and one of the fastest decreases in infant mortality in the developing world.

Migration: The history of migration in Bangladesh is characterized by three different phenomena. The exodus of people during the **Bangladesh Liberation War** of 1971 was the peak period of migration, when about 10m. refugees crossed the border into the Indian state of **West Bengal**. Most returned to the newly created Bangladesh after the war but an uncertain number remained in India. The second phenomenon emerged with the trend of emigration, which continued from the 1970s, when a significant imbalance in the human resources market, combined with political uncertainties, forced people to search for employment and better earnings abroad, particularly in the oil-rich countries of the Middle East. Between 1976 and 1997 more than 2m. people went abroad in search of employment and annual emigration between 1991 and 1996 was 200,000. The net migration rate in 2003 was 0.72 migrants/1,000 population. The basic migration law is the Immigration Ordinance of 1982, which specifies rules and regulations for migrant workers. The third and most concerning phenomenon is rural-to-urban migration, a major factor in internal migration resulting in a significantly increased rate of urbanization after independence. Apart from the last two major phenomena, which are classic examples of economic migration, there have been cases of people seeking asylum for religious and political reasons, such as the Hindus who have felt threatened by the emergence of radical Islamic elements in Bangladeshi society and politics.

Urbanization: Bangladesh's urban population, which was recorded at 702,000 in 1901, has increased more than fortyfold since, reaching 29m. in 2005. After independence the urbanization rate increased sharply because of growth in social and economic opportunities in the larger cities, poverty, natural disasters and adverse land-man ratios in the rural areas. With an annual average urban population growth rate of 3.4% between 1875 and 1995, Bangladesh is Asia's most densely populated country. Bangladesh's four metropolitan cities (Dhaka, Chittagong, Khulna and Rajshahi) account for nearly 50% of the national urban population, which already represents 25.5% of the total population of 135m. Dhaka, the major urban centre and capital, is already one of the largest cities in the world and its population is expected to increase from about 12m. in 2005 to as high as 22.8m. within the next 10 years.

Minority Groups/Communities: Bangladesh is a relatively homogeneous country. Of its 146.7m. (2003) residents, 98% are ethnic Bengalis, 1% belong to tribal groups and the remainder are non-Bengali Muslims. According to the 1991 census, 88.3% are Muslims, although Hindus form a sizeable minority of 10.5%. Some 1.2% are Buddhists, Christians, and animists. Tribal groups are largely found in the Chittagong Hill Tracts, which accommodate 13 different tribes, of which the Chakmas and the Marmas are the largest. The Constitution states that Islam is the official religion, but provides for the right to practise the religion of one's choice. Violence against religious minorities has reportedly been on the increase and is further complicated by the fact that the majority of Hindus traditionally vote for the opposition **Bangladesh Awami League (AL)**. Given the acute animosity between the AL and the ruling **Bangladesh Nationalist Party (BNP)**, violence is often politically motivated. Affirmative action is not provided for in Bangladesh's Constitution and so minority groups do not hold reserved seats in the legislature or in educational institutions. In 2004, of the 300 parliamentary seats, only seven were held by religious minorities. Land has been a highly contested issue for Hindu and tribal communities. The 2001 Vested Property Return Act has yet to resolve the claims of Hindus whose landholdings were expropriated by the government (then Pakistan) at the time of **Partition** in 1947. Autonomy and control over indigenous land also continues to be a problem with the Chittagong hill tribes, despite the peace accord of 1997. (*See* **Chittagong Hill Tracts (CHT) Conflict**.)

Tribes: Bangladesh has more than 30 tribes, of which the Chakmas, Marmas (or Maghs), Tipperas (or Tipras), and Mros (or Moorangs) are the largest groups According to the latest census, in 1991, the total tribal population numbered 1.2m., just 1.13% of the country's total population. Tribal groups are mainly located in the Chittagong Hills Tracts and in the regions of Mymensingh, Sylhet and

Rajshahi. They can be distinguished from one another by differences in dialect, dress, religion and customs. The majority of tribal peoples are Buddhists and a small number are Hindus, Christians and Animists. The government established the Tribal Cultural Institute at Rangamati town in 1978, and in order to encourage the participation of tribal peoples it reserved 5% of posts in both cadre and non-cadre services for them. A number of NGOs, including the Co-operative for Assistance and Relief Everywhere and the **Bangladesh Rural Advancement Committee (BRAC)**, have launched various programmes for tribal peoples, especially after the 1997 peace agreement between the government of Bangladesh and the Jana Sanghati Parishad (JSS).

Agriculture: Agriculture is the single largest sector in Bangladesh's economy. Despite progress towards greater industrialization in the late 1980s, agriculture is still essential to the economy of the country. In 2004 agriculture contributed 23.1% of the gross domestic product (GDP) and provided about 60% of national employment. Crops, forestry, fisheries and livestock are the main sub-sectors and contribute around 71%, 10%, 10% and 9%, respectively, to agricultural GDP. Rice is the principal crop and its production is given special importance as it is the country's staple food. The introduction of co-operative framing, a high-yielding variety of rice, improved irrigation and modern machinery have helped increase rice production. Jute, tea, sugar cane, potatoes, wheat and pulses are other important crops. Jute production, which has traditionally played an important role in Bangladesh's economy, is likely to decrease due to a declining share in the international market, while the tea sector, introduced in 1857, is gaining ground. Today tea is the fourth largest export earner of Bangladesh, the world's fifth largest tea exporter—the country produces 3% of the world tea crop from its 158 tea gardens.

Legal ceilings on land ownership, introduced to distribute extra land to the poor, have created small landholdings because of legal and illegal transfers within extended families. As a result, most of those engaged in agriculture are poor peasants, sharecroppers or agricultural labourers. The Land Reforms Ordinance of 1984 established crop shares: one-third of the produce for the owner, one-third for the sharecropper, and one-third to be split according to the costs of cultivation. Also in 1984 the Agricultural Labour Ordinance set minimum daily wages for agricultural labour at 3.28 kg of rice or its cash equivalent. Government policy with regard to agriculture has been guided by the dual objective of poverty reduction and sustainable development.

Land Reform (Ownership): Bangladesh is a land-scarce country. It was estimated in 1992 that 83% of Bangladesh's (113m.) people lived in rural areas and about 50% of them were effectively landless. Altogether, in rural and urban areas about 75% of people are landless while 10% of the population owns 50% of available land. Landless people usually migrate from village to city, particularly to the capital, Dhaka, to settle in slums. Increasing landlessness in rural areas is thus causing the rapid growth of cities in Bangladesh. Although each government since independence has introduced some form of land reform programme, these have usually met with limited success, primarily because of corruption and the local dominance of large landowners. In order to change land ownership and production relationships, a number of laws were framed in the direction of land reform, dating back to the formation of the Bengal Land Reforms Commission in 1940. An Acquisition and Tenancy Act (1950) fixed the ceiling for individual landholding at 100 *bighas* (one *bigha* refers in Bangladesh to 1,600 sq m, often interpreted as one-third of an acre). The ceiling was then increased to 375 *bighas* in 1961, but in 1973 it was reduced to 100 *bighas*, and, again, in 1984, to 60 *bighas*. The Land Reform Ordinance (1984) also gives some rights to sharecroppers. The ordinance established the rule of three shares: one-third of the produce for the owner, one-third for the sharecropper, and one-third split according to the costs of cultivation. The Ministry of Land is responsible for policy-making and for the supervision and monitoring of land reforms. For effective supervision of field offices, and the quick disposal of quasi-judicial cases, the Board of Land Administration was abolished and two new bodies, the Land Appeal Board and the Land Reforms Board, were established in 1989 under the Land Reforms Board Act and the Land Appeal Board Act. The main responsibility of the Land Reforms Board is to supervise the functioning of the field offices and the implementation of land reform measures, while the Land Appeal Board is empowered to consider appeals against the orders of the divisional commissioners under different laws relating to land administration and land management. In recent years a number of NGOs, including the Bangladesh Landless Association (BLA), have been involved in the movement for land reform.

Food and Famine Prevention: Food security in Bangladesh is closely related to total food production, food aid and internal food procurement. It is affected not only by floods and natural disasters but also by the immense growth of population, which reinforces pressure on the relatively narrow resource base of the country. There is still a gap between food demands and supply although the volume of production has steadily increased over the years. The shortage of food is usually met by international food aid as well as through imports from the international market. After independence, a great famine occurred in 1973–74, in which various factors played a part, including poor management of the food distribution system, natural disasters, material damage caused by the Bangladesh Liberation War (which amounted to about US $1,200m.) as well as inequalities in socio-economic relations. Between July 1974 and January 1975 more than 1m. people died, although the government's estimates are much lower. The Ministry of Food is responsible for the implementation and monitoring of food policy. In 1997 the Ministry of Health and Family Welfare formulated an additional 'Food and Nutrition Policy of Bangladesh', the main purpose of which was to improve the nutritional status of the population. Despite substantial improvement over the last 15 years, the country still suffers from one of the highest malnutrition levels in the world and widespread regional disparities. In particular, the rural population is affected by maternal and child undernourishment due to (chronic) protein-energy deficiency.

Industry: Bangladesh has a number of large, medium and small-sized industries in both the public and private sectors (e.g. jute, cotton, textiles, fertilizers, engineering, shipbuilding, steel, oil-refining, paper, newsprint, sugar, chemicals, cement and leather). The country was once one of the major exporters of jute, but in recent times the ready-made garments industry has replaced jute as the principal export-earner. Leather, ceramics, shrimps, fish, pharmaceuticals and frozen food are also major export sectors. The government has announced supportive policies for trade and introduced export processing zones (EPZ) to attract local and foreign investors through special facilities and incentives, including tax holidays for export-oriented industries, scope for 100% foreign investments and repatriation of profits. The annual rate of industrial growth fluctuated between 1996 and 2001, ranging from 4.92% to 8.32%.

Foreign Trade: Bangladesh's major exports include ready-made garments, jute, jute products, shrimps, leather and leather manufactures, and fish. Tea is the fourth largest export earner of the country—the world's fifth largest tea exporter. The USA is the most important market for Bangladeshi products, purchasing about 22.4% of exports in 2004. Other important destinations include Germany (14.5%), the United Kingdom (11.2%), France (6.9%) and Italy (4%). The main shortcoming of Bangladesh's export industry is its dependence on a large proportion of imported commodities. This led to a serious trade deficit in July–April of the 2005 financial year, when an increase of 65.9%, to US $2,882m., occurred, compared with $1,737m. in the 2004 financial year. In 2004 the major importers of products from Bangladesh were India (15.1%), China (12.5%), Singapore (7.5%), Kuwait (5.5%), Japan (5.3%) and Hong Kong (4.5%). In view of the sharply increasing trade deficit, the government in recent years has attempted to increase Bangladesh's export capacity. As a result, the European Union and Norway have already granted duty-free and quota-free market access for Bangladeshi goods. Canada is likely to provide Bangladesh the facility of duty-free and quota-free market access from January 2006 and efforts are under way to gain similar access to the USA, China, South Korea, Thailand, Russia and other countries. To promote export trade Bangladesh's government has offered a number of facilities, including cash incentives on various exportable products and reduced rates of interests on bank loans for exporters. An IDA-funded 'Bangladesh Export Diversification Project' has been undertaken to diversify export products and also explore newer markets for Bangladeshi commodities. To reduce dependence on imports, the government has incorporated changes to protect domestic industries as well as foreign exchange reserves. Due to the fact that Bangladesh's international trade is essentially seaborne, one of the major tasks is the extension and modernization of port facilities at Chittagong and Mongla.

Export Processing Zones (EPZ): Bangladesh has established export processing zones (EPZ) to attract potential investors in the country. Two EPZs, at Chittagong and Dhaka, became operational in 1983 and 1993 respectively, while EPZs in Comilla, Ishwardi, Mongla and Chittagong across the river will be operational within a few years. Altogether, 88,238 workers are employed in 253 units of the Chittagong and Dhaka EPZs, of which 132 were owned by foreign nationals, 60 were joint ventures and 61 were owned by Bangladeshi investors. The government established a Bangladesh Export Processing Zones Authority (BEPZA) in 1981 to promote, facilitate and co-ordinate foreign investment in the EPZs. Although largely state-driven, the private sector has also been permitted to build and operate EPZs.

Banking System: At the core of the banking system is the Bangladesh Bank, the country's central bank. Additionally, there are four nationalized commercial banks, five government-owned specialized banks, 30 domestic private banks and 10 foreign banks. The financial sector of the country is dominated by commercial banking services. From the late 1970s until the early 1980s the government attempted to promote the agricultural sector and private industry, resulting in changes to the financial sector. Two specialized banks, including Bangladesh Krishi Bank and Rajshahi Krishi Unnayan Bank, were created to meet the credit needs of the agricultural sector; and the Bangladesh Shilpa Bank (BSB) and the **Bangladesh Shilpa Rin Sangstha (BSRS)** were established to support the emerging private manufacturing sector. In this context, the Grameen Bank and local savings societies play an important role in rural areas and often offer better loan repayment rates than state-run banks. Until then, banks had been largely under tight state control. To enforce a market-oriented policy, in order to reduce distortions in the banking system, the Financial Sector Reform Programme (FSRP) was launched in the 1990s. Nevertheless, the banking system remains fragile, hampered by corruption, non-performing loans, overstaffing and political interference. To counter these distortions, the Bankruptcy Law 1997, the Bangladesh Amendment Act 2003, the Bangladesh Bank National Amendment Act 2003 and the Bank Company Amendment Act 2003 were passed.

Foreign Aid: As an underdeveloped country, Bangladesh depends heavily on foreign aid. Between 1979 and 2004 a total of US $22,500m. was disbursed by international donors. These huge flows of assistance were crucial for various achievements in the country's development, such as farming and attaining self-sufficiency in grain production. However, Bangladesh will continue to require substantial external assistance in its development and four trends have been identified. There is a basic tendency towards an increasing share of loans (63.17% in 2001) in total foreign aid, exceeding the proportion of grants (36.83% in 2001), which means there is a switch from donated foreign aid towards aid which has to be repaid after a certain period of time. Second, bilateral aid is declining while, in contrast, multilateral aid increased from 26.1% in 1971 to 57.4% in 1999. Third, there is also a transformation in the economic purposes of aid, visible in a new composition of the aid portfolio, consisting, in the case of Bangladesh, of food aid, commodity aid and project aid. The shares of commodity aid (13.42% in 2001) and food aid (3.71% in 2001) are significantly declining in favour of an increasing share of project aid (82.87% in 2001) that includes technical assistance. Fourth, foreign aid donors are increasingly imposing requirements, such as the democratization of local government, improvement of the law and order situation, introduction of economic and administrative reforms and enforced measures to curb corruption. As a result, the rate of disbursement is much lower than the rate of commitment of assistance. Today the donors of foreign aid to Bangladesh, which formed the **Aid-to-Bangladesh Consortium**, include bilateral donors, such as Japan, Canada, the USA and Germany, and multinational financial institutions (e.g. the Asian Development Bank and World Bank), as well as international agencies (e.g. the Swedish International Development Agency) and international organizations (such as the WHO and the UN).

Foreign Direct Investment (FDI): Bangladesh has a liberal policy towards foreign investment with regard to export-oriented industries and industries in the export processing zones (EPZs) and the high technology products sector. Foreign investment can be made either independently or through ventures on mutually beneficial terms and conditions. The government promulgated the Foreign Investment (Promotion and Protection) Act in 1980 to protect foreign investments, either directly or in co-operation with a domestic entrepreneur, especially in the EPZs. This act allows 100% foreign investment in any undertaking and does not impose any restriction on the repatriation of profits and income by foreign companies. Multiple visas and work permits for foreign investors and their expert professionals have been streamlined. All governments since 1991 have sought to promote foreign investments in all of the sectors except four, namely, arms/ammunition and other defence equipment and machinery; forestry; nuclear energy; and security printing. Among the FDI initiatives in the country, the leading sectors are banks, insurance companies, power-generation, pharmaceuticals, tobacco, the shoe industry, telecommunications, tea and cement. In 2004/05 FDI increased by 6.5%, reaching US $410m.

Foreign Investors' Chamber of Commerce and Industry (FICCI): The Foreign Investors' Chamber of Commerce and Industry (FICCI) was first established in 1963. After independence FICCI transferred its head office from Chittagong to Dhaka. FICCI provides the necessary support to multinationals and major joint venture companies operating in the country. Currently, FICCI has 129 ordinary members who have a minimum 50% foreign shareholding in their equity, and six associate members who have a foreign share of less than 50%. FCCI operates through a nine-member committee elected every two years by general members. The committee elects a president and a vice-president.

Labour: The labour force of Bangladesh in 2001 numbered 64.1m., of which it is estimated that 35% were engaged in the agricultural sector, 19% in industry and 46% in the services sector. Despite having a labour-intensive economy, socio-economic as well as domestic necessities have encouraged Bangladeshi labourers to migrate to other countries since the mid-1970s, when Middle Eastern states opened their job markets to Bangladeshis, attracting more than 70,000 workers. Malaysia and Singapore followed, leading to a further increase and in 1999 it was reported that 268,182 Bangladeshis were employees in foreign countries, sending remittances estimated at US $3,800m. in 2004/05. Most of these workers are unskilled and professionals form only the smallest part. The industrialization of Bengal, the area which was partitioned in 1947 to form East Pakistan and later Bangladesh, began in the 19th century during colonial times and in the early 1900s the first labour organizations were formed. Because of their close relationship to politicians, labour issues became a hot topic in national politics, which is still the case today. Privatization initiatives of the government have provoked strong responses, including a general strike in September 2003 which paralysed public life and was supported by the opposition. Unemployment (affecting some 1.7m. in 2000) and underemployment are major problems facing the country and labour laws as well as union rights continue to be ignored by many employers. In 2005 it was planned to privatize more than 100 enterprises, at the potential cost of some 150,000 jobs.

Informal Economy: Bangladesh is a typical example of an economy where the informal sector has always played an essential role. The informal sector contributed an estimated 35.6% to the economy in 2002 and employed more than two-thirds of the non-agricultural workforce. However, around 75% of informal employment is in trade and services. Street traders and vendors and itinerant, seasonal or temporary labour working on building sites or road work are typical examples of informal economic sources. Apart from this, drugs-trafficking, smuggling and corruption or bribery have also been lucrative forms of economic activity. The trafficking of weapons, especially small arms, is a particular concern.

Child Labour: Child labour in Bangladesh has to be addressed in the context of population growth, adult unemployment, lack of minimum wages, and the low quality of education. In 1999 an estimated 4.9m. children in the 5–14 years age group were employed as workers in Bangladesh, and within the 5–17 years age group around 7.9m. Of the second group, 6.4m. were working in rural and 1.5m. in urban areas. Generally employed in garment factories and engineering workshops, in the construction, domestic services and transport sectors, working conditions are often hazardous as little regard is paid to health and safety. The government has taken steps to implement various programmes to protect children's rights, especially in respect of labour. It passed the Primary Education Act and joined the Food-for-Education programme in 1993 as well as signing various conventions of the International Labour Organization (ILO) and the UN. In addition to these governmental efforts, the Bangladeshi Garment Manufacturers and Exporters Association, the ILO and UNICEF signed an agreement in 1995 to 'remove all child labourers from the garment sector'. A number of international and local NGOs undertake various projects that aim to eliminate child labour.

Trade Unions: The structure of the trade union movement in Bangladesh is more than 100 years old, rooted in the struggle for liberation from economic exploitation under the British colonial regime. The links with the independence movement, revolving around personalities, resulted in a close relationship between trade unions and the political parties in Bangladesh. In consequence, the trade union sector is often found to be highly fragmented, along the political and ideological lines of national politics, reflecting the personal rivalries of politicians and marked by violent behaviour. However, after independence in 1971 the nationalization of major industries resulted in a limited role for trade unions. After trade union activities were banned in the early 1980s, the **Sramik Karmachari Oikyo Parishad (SKOP)** emerged as the first national federation of trade unions in April 1983 and remains comparatively powerful. In recent years trade union activities have been particularly hampered by the establishment of Bangladesh's export processing zones, where their activities are banned. Today there are some 6,300 registered trade unions in Bangladesh, with some 1.9m. members.

Environmental Protection: Well known for its tremendous floods, resulting from the Padma and Brahmaputra river systems, Bangladesh is also located in a great cyclone hazard zone. A major threat to the natural environment, however, has arisen from ongoing industrialization, construction and the general overuse of natural resources for subsistence livelihood. Following the UN Stockholm Conference in 1972, the Environmental Pollution Control Ordinance of 31 March 1977 was the first official regulatory framework accepted by the government to control, prevent and abate environmental pollution in Bangladesh. Over the following decades several ministries were established, such as the Ministry of Environment and Forestry, which drafted and enforced rules, regulations, guide-lines and standards for pollution control and environmental protection. In the last decade environmental protection has become one of the priorities on the government's agenda, indicating growing concern about the rapid degradation of urban as well as rural environments. Important legislation includes the National Environment Policy of 1992, the National Environmental Action Plan of 1992, the Forest Policy of 1994, the Forestry Matter Plan (1993–2012) and the Environment Conservation Act of 1995.

Floods and Natural Disasters: Bangladesh is a natural disaster-prone country, situated in the world's hazard belts and subject to floods, droughts, tropical cyclones, tidal waves, windstorms and river bank erosion. The major natural disasters that occur periodically in this region are largely due to climatic and seismic factors and have had serious socio-economic implications through the loss of human and animal lives, destruction to infrastructure and other socio-economic assets. Severe floods are one of the major devastating and recurring phenomena in Bangladesh, having occurred in 1922, 1954, 1955, 1974, 1984 and 1987. Between 1987 and 2003 a total of 4,211 people died and as many as 80m. people are vulnerable to flooding each year. The government is trying to control settlement of the coastal regions in an effort to improve protection in those areas. Another common natural disaster is cyclones. The severe cyclones of November 1970 and April 1991 killed some 300,000 and 140,000 people, respectively, as well as causing property damage of more than US $3,000m. Tornadoes, which occur most frequently during the pre-monsoon period, are also major causes of damage to lives and property. Insufficient water supply and inefficient water usage has caused parts of the country to suffer from drought. In 1979 a severe drought devastated the country, causing widespread crop failure. Bangladesh is a part of the Bengal basin, which is also vulnerable to earthquakes, with major cities, including Dhaka and Chittagong, lying in one of the most seismically active zones in the world.

Health System/Policy: Bangladesh's government has been working towards the provision of health care to all citizens, through implementing a Health and Population Sector Programme (HPSP, 2003–08). Its main objective is to enforce sustainable improvement of the health, nutrition and family welfare status of the population. Health care in Bangladesh is offered at different levels of the system. Family-planning services operate at the grassroots level through 'Union Health Centres'. Health and family-planning workers work closely together with families, providing reproductive health care, child health care and communicable disease control. More than 400 *thana* Health Centres were established some 20 years ago to provide primary care. After the *thana* level, hospital services at the district level include general and specialized hospitals. Government hospitals, however, no longer inspire public confidence due to limited facilities and reports of corruption. As a result, the private sector has been performing better and foreign direct investment has also been allowed into the health sector. Even NGOs have been inducted into the health programme, e.g. the Bangladesh Rural Advancement Committee (BRAC). Nevertheless, health services are scarce. Most medical facilities are located in the municipal areas, while health service provision in the rural areas is still insufficient. It is estimated that less than 40% of the population has access to basic health care.

Education/Education Policy: Bangladesh has a low literacy rate of 43.1% (2003 estimate) and there is a disparity between female (31.8%) and male (53.9%) literacy rates which suggests that the education policies followed by successive governments have not been properly structured or have failed to achieve their target. The education system, with its beginnings in the colonial period, is divided into three different branches: the English Medium, the Bengali Medium and the Religious Branch, such as ***madrasas***. The education system is further divided into four levels—Primary, Secondary, Higher Secondary and Tertiary. There are 16 government universities and approximately 40 private universities. However, only about 60% of children attend school and only 40% of those who enter primary school actually complete it. Since the 1990s there has been a noticeable increase in the allocation of funds for education from the national budgets. According to UNDP reports, public expenditure on education between 1998 and 2000 was 15.7% of total government expenditure compared to 10.3% in 1990.

Non-Formal Primary Education (NFPE): Non-Formal Primary Education (NFPE) is an alternative method of teaching to provide minimum literacy for children from landless and destitute families. The Bangladesh Rural Advancement Committee (BRAC) pioneered the NFPE programme in 1985 and it has since extended over all the country. Currently 12,000 BRAC centres serve some 360,000 poor rural children and most NGOs working in the field have adopted this method of primary teaching. NFPE offers a three-year course in which students receive a functional education to prepare them for everyday life using an easy and flexible curriculum. Following its resolution at the World Summit for Children held in 1990, to bring 80% of its children under a literacy programme by 2000, the government actively supported the NFPE programme and helped spread the method of teaching through NGOs across the country.

Social Security/Policy: Bangladesh has no universal social security system and existing schemes are mainly restricted to employees in the formal and public sector, comprising civil servants, the army, police, and larger enterprises. However, the government does provide entitlements to people through its Annual Development Programme (in 2003 around 6.5% of the gross domestic product) which comprises entitlements for various social programmes. Such projects function generally in close co-operation with civil society organizations. For the aged population (57 or older) a monthly pension of around US $1.7 (July 2002), equal to 10% of average income and allowances for widows, distressed and deserted women, homes for the abandoned, dispossessed and disabled are provided by government agencies. Particularly vulnerable groups include the unemployed and those working in the informal sector.

Poverty: Despite receiving huge amounts of foreign aid (US $30,000m. since 1971), Bangladesh ranks amongst the five poorest countries in the world and approximately 45% of its population lives below the poverty line, defined in terms of people who do not have sufficient income and household production for a daily intake of 2,112 calories (WHO's poverty line). Thirty-six per cent of the population (1990–2001) live on less than US $1 per day and 82.8% (1990–2001) on less than $2 per day. This is mainly due to the fact that 80% of the population are dependent on agriculture for their livelihoods and encounter frequent natural disasters in the form of extreme floods, drought, cyclones, etc. In the 1990s some steps were taken towards reducing extreme poverty through economic and social reforms, such as the reduction of the population growth rate, which was brought down to an annual average of 1.5%, and government investment in health, education, the provision of social safety nets and support for microcredit programmes, which provided poor people with loans to start small businesses. Also, the deployment of NGOs is very high in Bangladesh. However, despite the government's initiatives to engage in poverty alleviation, as long as there is macroeconomic instability, poor infrastructure and bureaucratic harassment, the ability of people to accumulate private assets will be severely hampered.

Welfare: Although the Constitution of Bangladesh recognizes citizens' right to social security and support from governmental institutions during periods of need or indigence, an effective large-scale welfare system is non-existent. For the most part, the provision of support in the case of unemployment, illness, disability, widowhood, old age and other circumstances beyond control takes place within the traditional family and community networks. However, the processes of socio-economic transformation, accompanied by increased social mobility, migration, and urbanization, threaten to erode such informal social networks. Attempts to tackle this issue have been undertaken through various public works programmes, introduced to provide temporary, off-season employment to the extremely poor. Examples include the Food-for-Education programme, providing a small cash subsidy to destitute households whose children attend school, and the enforcement of community-based micro-insurance schemes to provide social protection and strengthen traditional informal safety nets.

Gender Relations/Empowerment: Despite traditional systems of gender relations in Bangladesh, the state recognizes and encourages equal participation of men and women in all walks of life. Women have steadily entered the jobs market, although primarily in the low-paid, underskilled ready-made garment sector, where female workers constitute 80% of the total workforce. Extra places are earmarked for women in the civil service. According to a UNDP report of 2001, adult female literacy (age 15 and above) was 30.8%, while the corresponding figure for males was 49.9%. This imbalance is also reflected in the overall composition of employment in Bangladesh, where 78% of the female labour force (1995–2001) was employed in agriculture and only 8% in industry. However, this scenario is bound to change over time as the country follows an equal opportunity policy with regard to employment in all sectors. Although both major political forces are headed by women and 30 additional seats are reserved for women in parliament, the parties tend not to nominate female candidates for general parliamentary seats, resulting in the fact that only 2% of seats were held by women in 2003.

Bangladesh Academy for Rural Development (BARD)

The Bangladesh Academy for Rural Development (BARD), formerly known as the Pakistan Academy for Rural Development (PARD), was founded in Comilla in 1959. It inaugurated a new system, known as the 'Comilla Model', comprising four project areas: the introduction of a rural two-tier co-operative system by organizing small farmers; the improvement of rural administration; the reconstruction and expansion of rural infrastructure; and the implementation of a model to utilize surface and ground water irrigation. The success of the project led to its nation-wide replication in 1962–63. The Comilla model also gained international attention and is applied in various rural development programmes world-wide.

Bangladesh Awami League (AL)

The Bangladesh Awami League (AL) is the older of the two major political parties of Bangladesh today. It was founded on 23 June 1949 as the 'East Pakistan Awami Muslim League' with Maulana Abdul Hamid Khan **Bhasani** as its chairman, Shamsul Haq of Tangail as its secretary, Sheikh Mujibur **Rahman** as its joint secretary and Yar Mohammad as its treasurer. The idea of a political alternative was raised by Hussain Shaheed Suhrawardy. It was rooted in an ideological and political conflict between him and the conservative faction of the **Muslim League (ML)**, contributing to the formation of a separate party with a secular spirit, representing

Bengali interests as a whole and pushed forward by the progressive faction of the East Pakistan wing of the ML. As a result, the AL (the term Muslim was soon dropped from the party's name) became a vanguard of the majority of Bengali people, expressing demands for provincial autonomy, the recognition of Bangla as one of the state languages and the improvement of socio-economic conditions in the Eastern wing of the country. It emerged as the first opposition party in Pakistan, successfully defeating the ML (winning 223 of 309 seats) in the 1954 election, as a major constituent of the United Front, a coalition of East Pakistan opposition parties. However, West Pakistan's élites refused to accept the democratic change of governance favouring East Pakistan interests, and instead dissolved the United Front ministry and imposed governor's rule. Subsequently, as a 'quasi oppositional party', the AL faced serious internal ideological cleavages on the questions of the foreign policy and autonomy of East Pakistan, finally leading to a split in 1957. A left-leaning, rural-based, pro-China faction, marked by a revolutionary approach, under the leadership of Bhasani formed a new political party, the **National Awami Party (NAP)**. A second faction, pro-western especially with regard to the USA and middle class-oriented, remained as the AL, building it up under the guidance of Rahman and Suhrawardy.

During the military rule of Ayub **Khan** (1958–69), political parties were banned. Rahman rejected the 1962 autocratic Constitution and organized political agitation, demanding that a new democratic constitution be framed. After the 1965 war between India and Pakistan, which revealed East Pakistan's vulnerability, he presented a **Six-Point Programme**. Rahman's formula was rejected by Ayub Khan and, along with other AL leaders, he was arrested for his alleged part in the **Agartala conspiracy case** in 1966. However, the AL's popularity grew and, supported by a student movement based on an extended 11-point programme, a mass uprising occurred in East Pakistan, culminating in the party's resounding victory in the 1970 elections. When Yahya Khan, then military ruler of Pakistan, refused to call on the AL to form a government at the centre, Rahman called, on 7 March 1970, for massive non-co-operation in East Pakistan, thus launching the struggle for independence. On the night of 25 March 1971 he was rearrested and the Pakistani Army began its armed crackdown. Thereafter, a government-in-exile was formed, with Syed Nazrul Islam as Vice-President (acting as President in the absence of Sheikh Mujibur Rahman, who declared the independence of East Pakistan before he was arrested) and Tajuddin **Ahmed** as Prime Minister. From India they led the war which ended on 16 December 1971 with the surrender of the Pakistani Army, following India's intervention.

After the liberation of Bangladesh, the AL was in power until 1975. During this period the AL framed a constitution providing for a parliamentary form of government and won world-wide recognition for the new nation. It arranged for the departure of Indian forces within three months of liberation and undertook a massive programme to rehabilitate people and reorganize government agencies. However, in the face of a grave economic crisis and an unprecedented flood in 1974, AL failed to ensure law and order in the country, resulting in the declaration of a state of emergency. The **Bangladesh Krishak Sramik Awami League (BAKSAL)** was formed and replaced multi-party, parliamentary democracy with a one-party presidential system. In late 1975 Rahman was assassinated together with all of the members of his family (apart from two daughters who were living abroad at this time) by mid-ranking military officers. Thereafter the military took power. In the early 1980s, under Gen. **Ershad**'s regime, the AL was reorganized, with its student, labour, youth and women's fronts consolidated under the leadership of Sheikh **Hasina**, daughter of Sheikh Mujib. The AL secured 39 seats and 76 seats, respectively, in the general elections held in 1979 and 1986, and, after the fall of the military regime, emerged as the main opposition party, winning 88 seats in 1991, at which point it began its campaign of boycotting parliament. Under the non-party **caretaker government** system, introduced by the 12th amendment, the AL won 146 seats in the seventh parliamentary elections and formed the government in 1996, completing a full five-year term. However, in 2001 the AL conceded defeat to the **Bangladesh Nationalist Party (BNP)** in the eighth parliamentary elections and returned to being the largest opposition party in parliament, which it subsequently boycotted. Sheikh Hasina is the elected president of the party and leader of the parliamentary group.

Bangladesh Bank (BB)

The Bangladesh Bank (BB) is the central bank of Bangladesh, established as a corporate body under the Bangladesh Bank Order 1972. It is responsible for managing the monetary and credit system, monitoring foreign exchange regulations as well as issuing currency and maintaining its value. It acts as the controlling, guiding and supervising organ of the country's banking system. Its head office is located in Dhaka.

Bangladesh Chemical Industries Corporation (BCIC)

The Bangladesh Chemical Industries Corporation (BCIC) is a public-sector corporation in Bangladesh, created in 1972 under the Ministry of Industries. Twenty-two chemical plants and product lines, producing fertilizers, paper pulp, basic chemicals, cement, sanitary wares, insulators, glass sheets, rayon/viscose yarn, rayon staple fibre, cellophane, soap and cosmetics, are under its control. The BCIC is seen as a leading example of corporate entrepreneurship, employing about 4,200 managerial and technical staff and about 27,200 workers.

Bangladesh Institute of Development Studies (BIDS)

The Bangladesh Institute of Development Studies (BIDS—Bangladesh Unnayan Gabeshona Protishthan) is a multi-disciplinary policy-oriented research organization which was established as the Pakistan Institute of Development Economics (PIDE) in June 1957. After the independence of Bangladesh in 1971, it was renamed the

Bangladesh Institute of Development Economics (BIDE) and, subsequently, in 1974, it was renamed BIDS. It is governed by a board of trustees and chaired by the Minister for Planning. It conducts basic research, focusing primarily on the socio-economic problems of Bangladesh, for purposes of planning and policy formulation.

Bangladesh Krishak Sramik Awami League (BAKSAL)

In the aftermath of the **Bangladesh Liberation War** and the subsequent gaining of independence, the country had to face severe economic challenges, a disastrous flood, and a deterioration in the law and order situation. Under then Prime Minister **Rahman** declared a state of emergency and instituted a one-party system, through the fourth constitutional amendment. As a result, in 1975 all political organizations were dissolved and Rahman refashioned his own party, the Bangladesh Krishak Sramik Awami League (BAKSAL), out of the **Bangladesh Awami League (AL)** and the Krishak Sramik Party. Rahman became chairman of the party, appointed a 15-member executive committee (that acted as a quasi-Cabinet), a 115-member central committee and five associated organizations. BAKSAL claimed to be tackling the social, political and economic issues of the country and various improvements, such as the reform of the bureaucratic sector, were achieved. However, critics see the system as a retrogression to authoritarian rule and as having created a lack of legitimacy in governmental institutions. Following the assassination of Rahman on 15 August 1975 the significance of BAKSAL gradually declined.

Bangladesh Liberation War

After the formation of Pakistan, in 1947, a cultural, political, economic and administrative gulf existed between its two wings, East Pakistan and West Pakistan, which were separated by about 2,000 km of Indian territory. A major difference was language, with Urdu the main and state-supported language in West Pakistan, and Bengali the suppressed language of the eastern part. This inequality resulted in an ethno-linguistic movement demanding that Bengali be made a state language. The movement, which met with violent repression, was transformed into a struggle for independence that began on 26 March 1971 and ended with the liberation of Bangladesh on 16 December 1971. Apart from the language grievance, Bengalis from East Pakistan, who constituted the majority of the country's population, had less representation in the civil service and military, and little influence over the country's economic policy. Most exports, the main commodity being jute, were produced in the east, but the allocation of earnings bore no relation to the contribution of that part of the country. Furthermore, most foreign aid was directed to West Pakistan, especially to the Indus River basin project, whereas in East Pakistan no such project was developed. While governmental and military infrastructure in the western wing were supported with high expenditures, no such investment was made in the eastern part. The Bengalis of Pakistan felt increasingly dominated and exploited by their western counterpart, this domination and exploitation being perceived as the equivalent of internal colonialism. The trigger for open conflict between East and West Pakistan was the 1970 general election results. Held on 12 December 1970, the election was contested by the major parties of each wing, the **Bangladesh Awami League (AL)** of Mujibur **Rahman**, dominant in the East, and the **Pakistan People's Party** of Zulfikar Ali **Bhutto**, dominant in the West. The former, having taken 162 of the 313 seats in the Pakistan parliament, was the winner. Consequently, it was expected that the AL, whose leader was advocating a new constitution on the basis of his **Six-Point Programme**, would form the government. However, this was blocked by the ruling military junta of Gen. Agha Muhammad Yahya Khan, who feared the loss of his own power and the loss of East Pakistan if he conceded Mujibur's demands. While the people of the eastern wing launched a civil disobedience movement in response to a call by Mujibur Rahman, attempts were made to negotiate a constitutional settlement with Yahya Khan until the events of 25 March 1971, when a military crackdown on East Pakistan was ordered and Mujibur Rahman was arrested and removed to West Pakistan. A war of independence was declared and clashes between the Pakistan army and AL supporters escalated. Ziaur **Rahman**, one of the most active and famous advocates of independence and, later, President of independent Bangladesh, declared the independent state at Chittagong on the night of 26/27 March. A *Mujibnagar* government, or government of the People's Republic of Bangladesh in exile, was formed in April by Tajuddin **Ahmed** and the Bangladesh movement, initiated as a movement for provincial autonomy, was transformed into a fully-fledged national liberation struggle. During the liberation war, which was waged over nine months and caused huge displacement of people and innumerable deaths, Bangladesh's **Mukti Bahini** (liberation army) received immense moral, diplomatic and material support from neighbouring India. Freedom fighters for this army were trained on Indian soil and a massive exodus of refugees across the border into the Indian state of **West Bengal** was allowed. In December 1971 the Indian army formally intervened in the war against Pakistan, bringing about the surrender of Pakistan's armed forces on 16 December 1971.

Bangladesh Nationalist Party (BNP)

The Bangladesh Nationalist Party (BNP) is one of the two major political parties in Bangladesh today. It was formed in 1978 as an amalgamation of splinter groups of different parties, including the **Muslim League**, the **Bangladesh Awami League (AL)**, the **National Awami Party (NAP—B)**, and almost all of the JAGODAL (Jatiyatabadi Ganotantrik Dal—Nationalist Democratic Party) and the Jatiyatabadi Front. Founded by Gen. (later President) Ziaur **Rahman** and state-sponsored, it is the only political party in South Asia to have been established by a military ruler. The major aims of the party were to legitimize his regime, to support the 19-point programme for the reconstruction and development of Bangladesh and to play an active role in the transition to a democratic political system. After Rahman's assassination in 1981, Abdus Sattar formally headed the party. However, the long-term question of leadership remained unresolved and the party faced a crisis in 1983, when it split into three factions: the BNP (Sattar), the BNP (Huda) and the BNP (Dudu-Nilu). A consolidation was achieved under the guidance of Rahman's widow, Begum Khaleda **Zia**, and drew strength from the anti-**Ershad** movement in the late 1980s. The BNP espouses Bangladeshi nationalism with an anti-Indian, anti-secular and pro-Islamic nuance, and supports a free-market economy and the conduct of subcontinental politics through **SAARC**. In the general elections of 1991 the BNP won 140 seats while its rival, the AL, won 88. In 1996 the party secured 116 seats and the AL 146. Led by Khaleda Zia, the BNP won the parliamentary elections held in 2001 at the head of a **Four-Party Alliance**, taking power for a fifth time.

Bangladesh Rifles (BDR)

The Bangladesh Rifles (BDR) is a paramilitary security force responsible for securing the country's borders and for controlling smuggling. When necessary it can support the regular armed forces for internal security as well as assist the police in maintaining law and order. It is a successor to the East Pakistan Rifles (EPR) which was reconstituted after the independence of Bangladesh. Currently it consists of 30,000 border guards, organized into 41 battalions, and operates under the authority of the home ministry. (*See* **Rakkhi Bahini**.)

Bangladesh Rural Advancement Committee (BRAC)

The Bangladesh Rural Advancement Committee (BRAC) was established as a relief and rehabilitation organization in 1972 by Fazle Hasan Abed after the independence of Bangladesh. The BRAC works with a specific target group, covering 70m. people who face extreme poverty, illiteracy, disease and physical and mental handicaps. BRAC is committed to assist the poor, especially women, to increase their access to economic and social resources in terms of poverty reduction and social development. The BRAC promotes income generation for the poor, mostly landless, rural population of Bangladesh, through micro-credit, health, education and training programmes, with over 26,000 regular staff and 34,000 part-time teachers in more than 60,000 villages across the 64 districts of Bangladesh. The BRAC currently includes a bank, a technological institute and a university.

Bangladesh Shilpa Rin Sangstha (BSRS)

The Bangladesh Shilpa Rin Sangstha (BSRS), or Industrial Loan Agency, is one of the country's specialized banks, established in 1972 with the objective of providing credit facilities and other assistance to industrial concerns and to encourage and broaden the country's base of investment. It provides medium- and long-term credit facilities for private-sector industrial projects, besides providing other necessary support for financing arrangements with foreign lending agencies, local banks and financial institutions for industrial concerns.

Bangladesh Student Politics

Student politics have been vibrant in Bangladesh since the first quarter of the 20th century. During the colonial period student movements were organized usually with the objective of spreading nationalist sentiment among the population. In later years student politics became enmeshed with party politics as parties began building their student wings. During the Pakistani period student organizations played a vital role in various movements (in 1952, 1966, 1969 and 1971), leading to the **Bangladesh Liberation War**. In the early 1990s student movements such as the All-Party Student Unions were instrumental in unifying the various political organizations, and forced the military government to restore democracy. Today, most political parties have their own student wings, using them to further patron-client relationships or factional interests, to the extent that even non-students are inducted as leaders. The engagement of students in politics has been criticized due to an increasing number of violent elements among their organizations, resulting in demands to ban them.

Bank of Bhutan – *see* Bhutan, Economic Development—Banking System

Bank of Ceylon (BOC)

The Bank of Ceylon (BOC) is the largest bank in Sri Lanka and has set up an international network with branches in London, Malé, Chennai and Karachi, and one joint venture bank in Nepal. BOC is backed and fully owned by the state and deals with the fields of government business, corporate banking, treasury operations, foreign exchange market and retail services.

Bank of Maldives PLC (BML)

The Bank of Maldives (BML) was founded on 11 November 1982 as a joint venture between the government of Maldives (50%) and the International Finance Investment Company (IFIC) of Bangladesh (50%). In the course of restructuring the BML, the contract with IFIC was not renewed and their shares were sold to the state trading organization, the Maldives Transport and Contracting Company. On 1 January 1993 BML was transformed into a public company. Currently, the 75% state-owned and 25% privately owned bank is the only bank to maintain branches outside of the capital (17 in total) and provides retail banking and other banking services.

BASIC Bank

The Bank of Small Industries and Commerce Bangladesh Limited (BASIC Bank) commenced operations in 1989 as a joint venture enterprise of the BCC Foundation and the government of Bangladesh. Following the closure of the Bank of Credit and Commerce International and, subsequently, of the BCC Foundation, the government of Bangladesh assumed 100% ownership of the bank on 4 June 1992.

Basic Democracies (BD—Pakistan)

Basic Democracies (BD), a reformed version of the local government system, was introduced in Pakistan by Gen. Ayub **Khan** in 1960 under the Basic Democracies Order, 1959. Under this the local government system was organized into five tiers: (i) union councils (rural areas), town and union committees (urban areas); (ii) *thana* councils (East Pakistan), *tehsil* councils (West Pakistan); (iii) district councils; (iv) divisional councils; (v) provincial development advisory council. Out of these five tiers, the union council was truly representative insofar as its 15 members were directly elected by the inhabitants of the union on the basis of universal adult franchise. The chairmen of the councils were elected from among the members. The other four bodies consisted of public representatives, officials and non-official members. Only the union and district councils had some specific duties. Introducing this new system, Gen. Ayub formed the national electoral college, consisting of 80,000 'basic democrats' from the two wings of Pakistan to elect the President and members of the national and provincial assemblies. By establishing parity between East and West Pakistan (40,000 basic democrats each) the actual majority of East Pakistan was neutralized. The basic democrats used their voting rights in the presidential elections of 14 February 1960. The system was abolished in 1969 after the fall of the Ayub regime.

Basu, Jyoti

Former Chief Minister of **West Bengal**, born in 1914, retired in 2001 ending a 55-year career in electoral politics. Defeating **Congress**, Basu was elected to the West Bengal legislature in 1946, eventually becoming the first Marxist Chief Minister in 1977. His government is credited with successfully handling the **Naxalite** and Gurkhaland movements, land reforms and democratic decentralization through the successful implementation of ***panchayati raj*** (local self-administration) and reducing poverty.

Bay of Bengal Initiative for Multi-Sectoral Technical and Economic Co-operation (BIMSTEC)

The Bay of Bengal Initiative for Multi-Sectoral Technical and Economic Co-operation, or BIMSTEC, groups together Bangladesh, Bhutan, India, Myanmar, Nepal, Sri Lanka and Thailand in a forum that aims to establish a free-trade area by 2017. Regional co-operation began in June 1997 with a ministerial meeting in Bangkok, Thailand, attended by representatives from Bangladesh, India, Sri Lanka and Thailand. Myanmar was admitted in December 1997, followed by Bhutan and

Nepal in February 2004. The inter-regional grouping aims to increase trade among member countries by taking advantage of their geographical location in the region of the Bay of Bengal and the east coast of the **Indian Ocean**, acting as a bridge between the five **SAARC** and two ASEAN (Myanmar, Thailand) countries.

The first BIMSTEC summit, attended by the seven Heads of State or Government, was held in Bangkok on 31 July 2004 in order to assess the challenges and opportunities for economic co-operation in the region, focusing on specific areas, including trade and investment, transport and communications, tourism, energy, human resources development, agriculture, fisheries, science and technology and people-to-people contact. Member countries also agreed to explore the expansion of co-operation into further areas, including those of culture, education, public health, protection of biodiversity, environment, information and communications technology, weather and climate research, natural disaster mitigation and management, and prevention of international terrorism and transnational crime.

BIMSTEC aims to promote and facilitate both inter-governmental and private-sector co-operation. The BIMSTEC Economic Forum represents both public and private sectors, while the BIMSTEC Business Forum focuses on the promotion of private-sector co-operation within the BIMSTEC region. Both make recommendations to be taken up at ministerial meetings. Since 1997, ministerial meetings have been held at least once every two years, with participation graduating from Deputy Minister of Foreign Affairs level to full ministerial level in December 2002. Co-operative activities are further facilitated and regulated through senior officials' meetings, economic/trade ministers' meetings, senior trade and economic officers' meetings, and the BIMSTEC Chamber of Commerce and Industry. Chairmanship of BIMSTEC is held by an individual country on an annual rotation basis.

Bharat

The mythical name for India, *Bharat* is evocative of religious and other symbols of traditional society. In the Constitution of India, Article 1 states that 'India that is, Bharat, shall be a Union of States'.

Bharat Ratna

The *Bharat Ratna* (Gem or Jewels of India) is the top Indian civilian award for outstanding service to the nation in the fields of art, literature and science, established by the President of India on 2 January 1954. It is awarded in 'recognition of public service of the highest order'.

Bharatiya Janata Party (BJP)

The Bharatiya Janata Party (BJP—Indian People's Party), together with the **Indian National Congress (INC)**, is one of the two major national political parties in India.

The evolution of the party from a small pro-Hindu movement in the first half of the 20th century to a major political force in the Indian parliament at the national level is one of the most interesting political phenomena in contemporary India. From a low point of two seats in the **Lok Sabha** in 1984, the party gained 85 in 1989, 160 in the 1996 elections and 182 in 1998. The BJP was formed in 1980, under the leadership of Atal Behari **Vajpayee** and Lal Krishna **Advani**, as the political inheritor of the Bharatiya Jana Sangh (BJS), a party established in 1951 by Shyama Prasad Mookerjee and with close ties to the **Rashtriya Swayamsevak Sangh (RSS)**. At the outset and over the course of its rapid rise to power, the party has drawn on the desire of many Hindus to see a more prominent role for Hindu culture within the institutions of the secular Indian state and to bring to an end the special treatment of minorities, such as the special status granted to the Muslim majority state of **Jammu and Kashmir**.

In 1998 the BJP contested the elections as part of the **National Democratic Alliance (NDA)** that comprised a number of small regional parties, most significantly the **All-India Anna Dravida Munnetra Kazhagam (AIADMK)** in **Tamil Nadu**, which later withdrew, contributing to the government's fall in April 1999. Although in power for less than a year, the BJP-led government went ahead with nuclear tests in May 1998. Elections were held again in 1999 and this time the NDA won an outright majority of 299 Lok Sabha seats, with Vajpayee sworn in as Prime Minister. Despite the ***Hindutva*** platform of the BJP and the calls to build a Ram temple in the city of Ayodhya on the same spot where the Babri mosque stood, the NDA government focused its energies on the economy. Policies pursued included the privatization of big government corporations, the liberalization of trade rules, the easing of foreign investment and ownership restrictions and tax reforms. However, the 2002 **Gujarat** riots tarnished the NDA government's period of office and reflected especially badly on the BJP as the Chief Minister of Gujarat, Narendra Modi, was a party member and faced charges of not only failing to contain but also of abetting the violence.

The defeat of the NDA in 2004, while a surprise to many, was seen as both a rejection of the BJP's brand of Hindu nationalism as well as a challenge to the economic buoyancy that the NDA's 'India Shining' campaign had attempted to portray and capitalize on. Altogether down by 44 seats, the BJP suffered its heaviest losses in the state of **Uttar Pradesh** where it had won 52 of the 80 Lok Sabha seats in 1996.

Bharatiya Kisan Union (BKU)

The Bharatiya Kisan Union (BKU), also known as the Indian Peasant Union, has its main support base in the north Indian states and has been active in organizing *kisans*, the working peasants. The *kisans* are divided into two broad sections, namely, the small, self-sufficient landowners who cultivate land with family labour and do not employ outside help; and those whose holdings are usually above the subsistence level. The BKU has grown to be dominated by the landowning section of *kisans* and has a political wing, known as Bharatiya Kranti Dal (BKD).

Bharatiya Mazdoor Sangh (BMS)

Bharatiya Mazdoor Sangh (BMS) is one of the largest labour organizations of India. It was founded on 23 July 1955 by Dattopant Thengadi. BMS claims that it is a productivity-oriented, non-political trade union, but is part of the **Sangh Parivar**. It claims a membership of more than 6,500,000, and is present in almost all states, covered by 32 All-India Industrial Federations. Its programme questions the appropriateness of class struggle for Indian conditions and seeks to cultivate harmonious relations between employers and employees. Furthermore, it rejects the theory of class conflict and promotes ***swadeshi***. BMS is represented on most of the bipartite/tripartite labour and industrial committees/boards constituted by the central government.

Bhasani, Maulana Abdul Hamid Khan

Maulana Abdul Hamid Khan Bhasani (1880–1976), popularly known as Maulana Bhasani, had a long political career from the 1930s. He was a founding member and president of the East Pakistan Awami Muslim League (**Bangladesh Awami League—AL**) before heading the Assam unit of the **Muslim League (ML)**. Early in 1957 he left the AL, opposing the pro-American foreign policy of the Suhrawardy faction, himself favouring closer relations with China, and again formed a new party, the **National Awami Party (NAP)**, with himself as president. He took refuge in India during the **Bangladesh Liberation War**, but soon after independence Bhasani led several protest movements against Mujibur **Rahman** and the AL government, opposing in particular the Bangladesh-India Treaty of 1972. He also viewed the **Farakka Issue** (barrage) as detrimental to Bangladesh's interests. For the country's first parliamentary elections in 1973 he formed an alliance of seven political parties, the All-Parties Action Committee, which broke apart over negotiations for future seat sharing. In 1974 he formed the All-Party United Front, comprising six parties, which also crumbled not long after, due to internal disputes. When the military came to power in 1975 he withdrew from active politics and continued to work in the educational sector until his death.

Bhattarai, Baburam

A senior standing committee member in the politburo of the **Communist Party of Nepal—Maoist**, Dr Bhattarai became politically active during his student days in India. He was a prominent spokesman during the pro-democracy movement in 1990 and considered by many to be a brilliant intellectual who, despite his rebel activities, continues to publish books on the political and socio-economic situation in Nepal. In 1996 Bhattarai and **Comrade Prachanda** launched the Maoist **People's War** and in 2003 Bhattarai led the Maoist negotiating team during the short-lived cease-fire with the government between January and August. (*See* **Jana Andolan**.)

Bhattarai, Krishna Prasad

K. P. Bhattarai (1924–), a member and former president of the **Nepali Congress Party**, was a key leader of **Jana Andolan**, the People's Movement. He served as interim Prime Minister of Nepal from April 1990 to May 1991, and again from May 1999 to March 2000. Bhattarai is well known for his long-running intra-party rivalry with G. P. **Koirala**, the first democratically elected Prime Minister following promulgation of the 1990 Constitution.

Bhindranwale, Jarnail Singh

A Sikh priest, or *Sant*, Jarnail Singh Bhindranwale became a political leader and a charismatic militant, leading the pro-**Khalistan** movement of the 1980s. Initially courted by Prime Minister Indira **Gandhi**, the support for Bhindranwale was meant to cut into the sphere of influence of the **Akali Dal**, the main rival to **Congress** in the state of **Punjab**. Bhindranwale's iconic stature, combined with growing violence and terror in the state as well as speculation of a Pakistani hand, began to worry the central government, which decided to take action in 1984. In an attack codenamed **Operation Blue Star**, the Indian army stormed Amritsar's Golden Temple, in whose precincts Bhindranwale and his followers had taken sanctuary. During the operation Bhindranwale was killed.

Bhopal Industrial Accident

Union Carbide India Ltd (UCIL) was established in 1934 and produced pesticides for use in the Indian agricultural sector. On 3 December 1984 an industrial disaster of unprecedented magnitude took place in the UCIL plant located in Bhopal, **Madhya Pradesh**, when methyl isocyanate gas leaked from a tank and spread through surrounding streets. At least 15,000 people died in the wake of the accident.

Bhutan, Kingdom of

The land-locked, Himalayan kingdom of Bhutan (*Drukyul*—Land of the Thunder Dragon), approximately the size of Switzerland, is situated between India and China. It is bounded on the north and north west by Tibet, with north-east India bordering its remaining frontiers. For administrative purposes, Bhutan is divided into 20 districts (***dzongkhag***). Area: 47,000 sq km; capital: **Thimphu**; population: official estimates in 2005 vary greatly, ranging from as high as almost 2m. to possibly as low as 810,000. Although it is generally difficult to place the Bhutanese people into specific ethnic categories, it is possible to subsume them under three main groups, the **Ngalong** of Tibetan origin; the **Sharchop** of Indo-Mongoloid/Burmese origin and the **Lhotshampa** of Nepalese origin; official language: **Dzongkha**. Besides this language of the ruling Ngalong, English is used in schools and commerce and Nepali is widely spoken, particularly in the south of the country; religion: Lamaistic Buddhist *c.* 75%, Hinduism *c.* 25%.

Bhutan is a monarchy whose executive authority resides with the King and a Council of Ministers (Lhengye Zhungtshog). They are assisted by the Royal Advisory Council (Lodoi Tsokde). The King is head of state, with the annually rotating chairman of the Council of Ministers serving as head of government. Both are accountable to the National Assembly, the legislative body, which has 150 members and meets biannually. In June 1998 a major political reform instigated by the King, Jigme Singye **Wangchuck**, announced that instead of being appointed, ministers would stand for open election. Bhutan has no political parties and no individual right of vote. Of the 150 members of the National Assembly, 105 are elected once every three years by village communities in a secret ballot, with one vote allotted to each household.

History: Buddhism was introduced into the region around the seventh century AD. The **Drukpa** school of Buddhism, from which the native name of the country is derived, was brought from Tibet to Bhutan by *Phajo* Drukgom Shigpo in the 13th century and is closely connected with the Ngalong élite. However, various sources stress that the Sharchop, who are followers of Nyingmapa Buddhism, are the older population group compared to the Ngalong. The Sharchop thus claim to represent an older school than the Drukpa. Without centralized rule from the mid-seventh to the 19th century, Bhutan relied on systems of local rule centering around clans and religious dynasties. Unification came about in 1616, when *Shabdrung* Ngawang **Namgyal**, a Tibetan *lama*, established the Bhutanese state on the basis of religious-secular rule. To secure Bhutan's identity as a Drukpa state, five wars were fought with Tibet and the Mongols, the last ending in victory for Bhutan, allowing a *Shabdrung* reincarnation to become head of state in 1734. The ensuing system of religious authority proved unstable, characterized by inner conflict and power concentrated in local rulers. In 1774 a peace treaty was signed with the English East India Company and from the late 18th century onwards Bhutan was brought under the umbrella of British Indian control. Following a war in 1864 it ceded its Duar territories, an area bordering India and controlled by Bhutan since the 18th century, to the British in return for annual compensation under the Treaty of Sinchulu. Towards the end of the 19th century political power had become concentrated in the governors of Paro and Tongsa districts and regional rivalry prevailed. The pro-British Tongsa governor, Ugyen Wangchuck (1862–1926), was knighted by the British for his co-operation and in 1907 he signed a coronation agreement with the British, under which he became King. This marked the beginning of the hereditary monarchy of Bhutan, which has since remained under the continuous rule of the Wangchuck family, as well as the end of civil war, and conflict with British India. Ugyen Wangchuck was succeeded by his son Jigme Wangchuck, who reigned from 1926 until 1952. During the four decades of their rule, Bhutan was unified and brought fully under the direct control of the monarchy. In 1910 the Treaty of Punakha was signed with the British, granting Bhutan sovereignty in internal matters on the condition that foreign policy would follow British advice. This arrangement was affirmed by independent India in 1947, which recognized Bhutan as a sovereign country. Two years later the Indo-Bhutanese Treaty returned areas of Bhutan annexed by the British, formalized annual subsidies to be received by Bhutan, and defined India's responsibilities in defence and foreign policy. The Indian Prime Minister Jawaharlal **Nehru**, visiting Bhutan in 1958, strengthened Indo-Bhutanese relations by announcing non-interference in Bhutan's internal affairs and support for its development efforts (a position maintained up to the present). Following China's occupation of Tibet in 1959, Bhutan altered its strategy of total isolation, recognizing the need to attract both Indian and international support. Bhutan has since become a member of several international bodies, joining the Colombo Plan in 1962, the United Nations in 1972, **SAARC** (as a founding member) in 1983, the **International Monetary Fund** and the World Bank in 1981, as well as the Non-Aligned Movement. The UNDP and Danish, Dutch, Japanese and Swiss bodies are all sources of foreign aid. The monarchy has played a key role in the modernization of Bhutan, with the third king, Jigme Dorje Wangchuck (1928–72), promoting education and technical development, and undertaking institutional change through the establishment (in 1952) of a National Assembly and a Royal Advisory Council. Other changes under his rule included reform of the civil service, the introduction of modern schools, and the abolition (in 1958) of slavery. The fourth and current king, Jigme Singye Wangchuck, officially crowned in 1974, has continued his father's policy of controlled modernization, focusing on the preservation of both the environment and Bhutan's unique culture, as well as an economic policy of self-reliance, referred to informally as **Gross National Happiness**. To gain greater visibility for Bhutan on the world stage, the international press was allowed, exceptionally, to cover the coronation.

Since the late 1980s the most contentious political issue in Bhutan has been the 'southern problem', revolving around the Nepali-speaking population of the south. Following a law passed in 1986 that granted citizenship to those who had settled in southern Bhutan prior to 1958, many ethnic Nepalis were categorized as illegal immigrants in the government census of 1988. New measures were subsequently introduced to enforce the citizenship law as well as to place more emphasis on the Tibetan-based Bhutanese culture. Nepali ceased to be a language of instruction in schools in 1989, and in the early 1990s the suppression of Nepalese cultural expression led to unrest and a demand for greater Nepali rights. The illegal **Bhutan People's Party (BPP)** began a campaign of violence and although an outright rebellion was contained, anti-government protests led to the arrest of many of those implicated in the disturbances. Since 1990 thousands of ethnic Nepalis and rebel supporters have fled from Bhutan to Nepal, claiming state persecution and human rights abuses. According to the UNHCR, some 120,000 people have been housed in refugee camps in Nepal and India.

Recent developments: In 1998 the king dissolved the Council of Ministers, announcing that ministers formerly appointed by him would instead be approved by the National Assembly. The resultant Council of Ministers was given more control over state affairs, with the head of government rotated annually among the cabinet members and the king remaining the head of state. The first draft of a new constitution was presented in December 2002, envisaging a parliamentary democracy with a constitutional monarchy. A revised version proposed by the king has been under discussion since March 2005 and foresees fundamental changes to the political procedures and institutions, moving towards a democratic constitutional monarchy by 2008.

Bhutan, Political Development

Bhutan's ninth five-year plan (July 2002–June 2007) was launched in July 2002, with a central focus on decentralization. The plan aims at devolving substantial autonomy to local government bodies and equipping them with the authority to execute development plans, primarily in rural infrastructure, health and education facilities and private-sector development. Since 2001 numerous changes have taken place in Bhutanese political institutions. The Council of Ministers established a committee of secretaries to increase efficiency, transparency and reduce corruption. In July 2001 the National Assembly passed the Civil and Criminal Procedure Code of Bhutan, a major judicial reform. The drafting of Bhutan's written constitution, which will separate and strengthen the legislative, judicial, and executive arms of the government, began in November 2001, representing the culmination of reforms initiated by King Jigme Singye **Wangchuck** in 1981. In its 2002 report the Royal Audit Authority (RAA) emphasized the need to promote good governance and increase transparency.

The royal government of Bhutan prioritizes the need to strike a balance between economic growth and the preservation of Bhutan's ancient traditions and culture. Human development, referred to as **Gross National Happiness**, forms a core national development objective and emphasizes the need for human resources investment. Sustainability is another key consideration, achieved through meaningful community participation in development activities. Bhutan's literacy rates and per capita gross national product have risen, and financial allocations to health and education sectors have been significant. Despite the government's efforts, Bhutan faces constraints, being a land-locked country with an adverse topography, a harsh climate, limited skilled manpower across all sectors, and very much dependent on foreign aid to support development. (*See* **Nepalese Issue/Conflict**.)

Constitution: Bhutan possesses no formal written constitution or bill of rights, although written rules, subject to periodical amendment and pertaining to the duties and powers of the *Lhengye Zhungtshog* (Council of Ministers), the *Lodoi Tsokde* (Royal Advisory Council) and the *Tshogdu Chenmo* (National Assembly) and the electoral procedures for their members, do exist. Bhutan may thus be described as a constitutional monarchy, based on the rule of law. The King commissioned a special committee in late 2001 to prepare a draft written constitution (Tsa-Thrim), which was formally submitted to King Jigme Singye Wangchuck in December 2002. A further draft was presented in mid-2003 and further revisions were made after submission to the districts for opinions and review. The current draft, proposed on 26 March 2005, envisages Bhutan as a 'democratic constitutional monarchy', with the planned introduction of a parliament on the basis of multi-party competition. The first national elections have been scheduled for 2008, for a government under a system of parliamentary democracy.

Monarchical System/Monarchy: Bhutan is one of the last two monarchies in the Himalayan region. Hereditary kingship as the main feature of its monarchical system is not an indigenous Bhutanese institution. It was introduced in 1907, during the time of British colonial rule in South Asia, by Ugyen Wangchuck (1907–26), the first King of Bhutan to abolish the extant Chhoesi system. Major challenges then were how to compensate for the lack of religious legitimacy demanded by the traditional leading monastic institutions and how to maintain territorial integrity in view of India and China as well as internal competing forces. Thus, King Jigme Wangchuck (1926–52) and King (since 1963 called **Druk Gyalpo**) Jigme Dorji Wangchuck (1952–72) consolidated the monarchical dynastic sovereignty based on the support of their own **Ngalong** community. Established as an absolute monarch, the fourth and current King Jigme Singye Wangchuck (1972–) has continued a policy of gradual transformation towards a constitutional system. Major steps towards a more pluralistic form of governance were the introduction of the National Assembly, the Block and District Development Committees and especially the Royal Vote of Confidence. (*See* **Namgyal, Ngawang**; ***Dratshang***.)

Bhutan Royal Government: Bhutan has created its own unique political and administrative system. Despite various reforms, the country is still characterized by a highly centralized system of governance. This system is based on three essential pillars: (1) the central machinery of the executive, judicial and legislative branches at the capital (**Thimpu**); (2) the local administration at the villages, blocks and the districts (sub-districts); and (3) the armed forces. Within these institutional arrangements the King (Druk Gyalpo) is the head of state, the commander-in-chief of the armed forces and the highest court, in addition to possessing extensive influence in the religious sphere of the country. The monarchy was able to preserve a patrimonial system, ensuring that higher positions and responsibilities in the government were assigned to members of the royal family. In this context, the overall objective of the government is to sustain the hereditary monarchy. Today the government consists of 10 ministers with their related departments, and several autonomous bodies, such as the Royal Audit Authority, the Royal Monetary Authority and the National Environment Commission.

Executive: Bhutan's executive authority is vested in the King (*Druk Gyalpo*), who is the head of state, and a Council of Ministers (*Lhengye Zhungtshog*), assisted by the Royal Advisory Council (*Lodoi Tsokde*). The King and the Council of Ministers are responsible to the National Assembly (Tshogdu Chenmo), which convenes twice a year. The Council of Ministers was established in 1968 with the approval of the National Assembly and was initially presided over by the King, who served as both head of government and head of state. In 1998 the annually rotating chairman of the Council of Ministers was made head of government, following a major governmental reform instigated by the King. In addition to the chairman, the Council of Ministers comprises nine other ministers, collectively responsible for 10 ministries, and the cabinet secretary. The Royal Advisory Council, although featuring in the 1953 constitution of the National Assembly, was fully established in 1965. Consisting of representatives of the monastic bodies, who serve one-year terms, and representatives of the people, who serve three-year terms, its central purpose is to advise the chairman of the Council of Ministers in his capacity as head of government and to supervise the general administration of Bhutanese affairs. Members may be re-elected, but not for consecutive terms. In permanent session, the Royal Advisory Council also acts as the *de facto* standing committee of the national assembly. All members of the Royal Advisory Council are concurrently members of the Council of Ministers and six are also members of the National Assembly.

Council of Ministers: The Council of Ministers (Cabinet), or *Lhengye Zhungtshog*, was established in 1968 by the King. Following political and administrative reforms, the *Lhengye Zhungtshog* has become the highest executive body in the country. It is responsible for day-to-day governmental business. The chairman of the council serves as the Prime Minister (*Lonchen*), a yearly rotating position. A Lyonpo (Minister) is nominated by the King and approved (elected) by the National Assembly for a fixed five-year term. (*See* ***Lhengye Nyamdrel Tshogchung***.)

Royal Advisory Council: The Royal Advisory Council, or *Lodoi Tsokde*, was established in 1965 and tasked with advising and assisting the King and the ministers in matters of governance. The Council consists of nine councillors, six (secret ballot) representatives of the people, elected by the National Assembly for three-year terms, two elected from representatives of the monastic bodies for one-year terms, and one member serving as the chairman of the Council (*Kalyon*).

Legislature: The *Tshogdu Chenmo* (National Assembly) was established in 1953, has a three-year term and convenes once a year in Thimpu. The number of members, being partly based on the population of the districts, is subject to periodic revision. In 2003 the *Tshogdu Chenmo* comprised 152 members, of whom 99, known as *chimis*, were elected by popular consensus. *Chimis* are representatives of Bhutan's 20 *dzongkhas* (districts) and serve a three-year term. The remaining members consist of 10 representatives of the central and district monk bodies, six members of the *Lodoi Tsokde* (Royal Advisory Council), and 37 civil servants nominated by the King. Of the civil servant members, 20 are *dzongdas* (district officers or majors), one is a representative of the Royal Bhutan Army, and the others are ministers, senior departmental secretaries or other high-ranking officials. The *Tshogdu Chenmo* enacts, revises and amends legislation, advises on constitutional and political matters and debates other important issues. Generally, decisions are arrived at by consensus, although a secret ballot facility exists for the resolution of controversial issues. Bhutanese law is largely based on Indian law and English common law. The speaker of the *Tshogdu Chenmo* is elected by its members for a three-year (renewable) term.

National Assembly (Tshogdu Chenmo): The unicameral *Tshogdu Chenmo* comprises the legislative institution of the political system of Bhutan and is responsible for the enactment, revision and amendment of legislation, in addition to advising on constitutional and political matters. Its membership has varied from 140 to 200 members, its size being redetermined every five years in accordance with the Constitution. Approximately two-thirds of the members are elected by popular consensus and serve a three-year term of office. Other members include monastic representatives, members of the Royal Advisory Council (*Lodoi Tsokde*) and civil servants.

Elections/Electoral System: Elections or referendums under universal suffrage have not been held in Bhutan. Since official recognition as an independent state in 1949, Bhutan's head of state has consistently been a member of the Wangchuk dynasty. The current head of government is *Lyonpo* Jigme Thinley (since 30 August 2003), who also serves as chairman of the Council of Ministers. The National Assembly (*Tshogdu Chenmo*), the unicameral parliament, was established in 1953 and convenes at least once a year in **Thimpu**. In 2003 it comprised 152 members, of whom 99 were elected by popular consensus at the district level. These 99 members, known as *chimis*, are representatives of Bhutan's 20 districts (***dzongkhas***) and serve a three-year term. The remaining members of the National Assembly consist of 10 monastic representatives from the regional monk bodies, who also serve a three-year term, and civil servants nominated by the King. Among the latter there are 20 *dzongdas* (district officers or majors), as well as various ministers, governmental secretaries and high-ranking officials. It is significant that not all members are elected simultaneously. Only 10 out of the 20 districts elect their representatives at the same time, leading to an overlap in their tenure. The royal decree, dating from 1953, embodies the conventions, procedures, and code of conduct for the National Assembly and its members. It grants one vote to each family in elections organized at the village level. Candidates for parliament are nominated in their respective districts by village heads and representatives of each family (***gung***), and must be at least 25 years of age. Following nominations at the village and local government levels, the speaker of the National Assembly declares the nominated members to be *chimis*. Not all *chimis* are elected concurrently, so overlaps in tenure occur.

Political Organizations: In accordance with long-standing legislation, there are no legal political parties in Bhutan. Candidates for election to the National Assembly run as individuals on a non-party basis. Many illegal opposition groups have, however, been formed in recent years and are mostly based ouside Bhutan, in Kathmandu, Nepal. The **Bhutan People's Party (BPP)** counts among the most well known and influential of these. Other opposition groups include the Bhutan Gurkha

National Liberation Front (BGNLF), the Bhutan National Democratic Party (BNDP), the Druk National Congress (DNC), the Human Rights Organization of Bhutan (HUROB), and the United Liberation People's Front (ULPF), all founded in the early 1990s.

Social Movements: Since political parties in Bhutan are illegal, socio-political organizations have appeared in the form of social movements, as in the case of the ethnic Nepalese (**Lhotshampa**) in exile, located in Nepal or in India's North East and **West Bengal**, and the Nepalese issue/conflict. These protest movements are characterized by the demand for a broader democratic foundation of governance, specifically, the provision of citizenship rights and political representation for the Lhotshampa, the abolition of feudal structures, and closer ties to India. Various attempts have been made, since the 1950s, to set up organizational platforms to mobilize particular ethnic groups, including the Bhutan State Congress (BSC) in 1952, the People's Forum for Human Rights Bhutan (PFHRB) in 1989, the Bhutan People's Party (BPP) in 1990 and the Bhutan National Democratic Party (BNDP) in 1992. Some sections of the Sharchop are organized too (e.g. Druk National Congress in 1992) to struggle against Ngalong dominance and to demand more influence in the decision-making process.

Foreign Policy: Following centuries of close ties with Tibet, China's expansionist policies led Bhutan to reorientate its foreign policy towards the south. From 1865 until 1947 Britain guided the kingdom's international affairs, with India taking over this role through the Treaty of Friendship between the Government of India and the Government of Bhutan of 1949. The Indian Prime Minister, Jawaharlal **Nehru**, visited Bhutan in 1958, strengthening Bhutan-India relations by announcing a policy (still in effect) of non-interference in Bhutan's internal affairs and support for its development efforts. Following China's actions in Tibet in 1959, Bhutan moved away from its policy of total isolation towards one of engaging both Indian and international support. None the less, until the 1970s Bhutanese foreign policy remained largely Indo-centric and inward-looking. The Indian annexation of Sikkim in 1975 and the deployment of an **Indian Peace Keeping Force (IPKF)** in Sri Lanka led to a reassessment of Bhutan's threat from the south, prompting a gradual reorientation of its foreign policy. Having gained UN membership in 1971 and created a Ministry of Foreign Affairs in 1972, the royal government established formal diplomatic relations with several other nations, primarily in South Asia and Scandinavia. Bhutan is today a member of several international bodies, having joined the Colombo Plan in 1962, **SAARC** (as a founding member) in 1983, and the **International Monetary Fund** and the World Bank in 1981. It has also actively participated in the Non-Aligned Movement. In recent years formal diplomatic ties have been established with Australia and Singapore (in 2002), and with Canada (in 2003). Bhutan does not have formal diplomatic relations with China. (*See* Bhutan-India Relations; Bhutan-China Relations; Defence (Security).)

Bhutan-China Relations: The People's Republic of China is perceived as a revolutionary power containing a serious threat for Bhutanese sovereignty. China has tried to destabilize the kingdom in the past, attempting to influence Bhutan's domestic affairs by encouraging communism. Relations worsened in the 1950s following China's invasion of Tibet in 1951, the Tibetan uprising and the flight to India of the Dalai Lama in 1959. At present Bhutan has no diplomatic relations with China, despite the 470-km border they share. Differences have arisen over the delineation of their common border. Border talks were initiated in 1959 but Chinese maps showing alterations of traditional Sino-Bhutanese and other Himalayan borders in Beijing's favour compelled Bhutan to impose an embargo on cross-border trade and pursue closer links with India. In the context of improving India-China relations, Bhutan started border negotiations in 1984 with China. A cautious re-evaluation of their relationship found expression in Bhutan's vote supporting the restoration of China's seat at the United Nations in 1971, and the Agreement to Maintain Peace and Tranquillity on the Bhutan-China Border in 1998.

Bhutan-India Relations: Amity towards India is at the core of Bhutan's foreign policy, characterized by the evolution from an exclusive and dependent relationship to a more balanced and strategic partnership. Despite the asymmetry in size India, unlike China, was never perceived as a threat to Bhutan's security or sovereignty. A landmark agreement was the Treaty of Friendship and Co-operation, signed in 1949, which not only brought the kingdom under India's security umbrella, but also guaranteed non-interference in Bhutan's internal affairs, while allowing India to advise Bhutan on international issues. As an important buffer state against China, Bhutan's political stability is part of India's security interests. To support this, India has, since 1961, been a major investor in Bhutan's development. India's economic assistance in more recent times has focused on developing Bhutan's hydroelectric capabilities, which already provide a crucial source of energy for India's West Bengal, and the improvement of infrastructure, an important source of employment for Indian labour. Besides the fact that India is Bhutan's major donor and trading partner, as a land-locked country the kingdom relies on Indian ports. On the political front, India has actively supported Bhutan in its foreign relations, helping it join the UN in 1971. In return, Bhutan has stood by India on issues such as its refusal to ratify the nuclear non-proliferation and comprehensive test ban treaties and its nuclear test in 1998. In addition, Bhutan's China policy operates in accordance with India-China relations. India has tried to avoid involvement in the issue of ethnic Nepalese refugees, some 100,000 of whom are estimated to be living in camps in Nepal as well as many thousands in India, arguing that this is a bilateral issue between Nepal and Bhutan. Despite the close interaction between the two countries, Bhutan is not completely bound by India and exercises sovereignty in the attempt to diversify its foreign relations. (*See* **Indian Military Training Team (IMTRAT)**.)

Bhutan-Nepal Relations: Non-resident diplomatic relations were established between the two Himalayan kingdoms in 1983. Despite having shared an open border, trade remains minimal between the two countries and relations continue to be marked by tensions over the issue of refugees in Nepal. Recurited by Bhutanese authorities in the early 1900s to extract timber from forests in the southern foothills, Nepalese labourers were allowed to stay on as tenant famers in the areas that had been cleared. Under the Nationality Law of 1958 these groups were granted Bhutanese citizenship. However, as the number of Nepalese economic migrants across open borders increased during the 1960s it became a politicized issue in the 1980s, when citizenship laws introduced new restrictions and requirements. A governmental policy of strengthening national integration through the promotion of a national dress and language and the removal of Nepalese as a third language in schools added to a sense of discrimination and oppression amongst southern Bhutanese, namely the Lhotshampa. Instability and acts of violence increased during the late 1980s, launched by dissidents who also began to operate from India and Nepal. The large-scale expulsion of ethnic Nepalese in the 1990s, termed as 'illegal immigrants' or 'non-nationals' by the Bhutanese government, caused relations to deteriorate substantially and remains an unresolved issue and source of tension. It is estimated today that more than 100,000 'stateless' ethnic Nepalese are living as refugees in camps in Nepal. A joint Bhutan-Nepal verification team was set up in 2003 to categorize the refugees, but progress has been slow.

Judiciary: Bhutanese law is based on civil and criminal codes which stem from those laid down by the *Shabdrung* Ngwang Namgyal in the 17th century. An independent judicial authority was established in 1961, and the High Court in 1968. Each district posesses a *Dzongkhag Thrimkhang* (district court), presided over by a *Thrimpon (*Judge*)*, and where most cases are tried. Civil disputes of a less serious nature may be settled by a village headman. All district court appeals are settled by the *Thrimkhang Gongma* (High Court), which is presided over by the chief justice and seven other judges, who are appointed by the King. The supreme court of appeal is the King, who hears appeals arising from High Court adjudications. All citizens possess the right to petition the King through the office of the *gyalpoi zimpon* (court chamberlain).

Department of Legal Affairs (DLA): The Department of Legal Affairs (DLA) was formed in 2000 by the government as an autonomous body to deal with increasingly complex legal issues in Bhutan. After the establishment of the **Thrimkhang Gongma** (High Court), the DLA represented a major transformation in the structure of Bhutan's judiciary and an essential step towards restructuring and strengthening governmental institutions. The DLA offers legal services, including the drafting of laws, particularly in the international context, programmes and modules in judicial education and training. Besides a prosecution division with civil and criminal sections, to indict offenders on behalf of the government, it maintains a special unit for human rights issues. There are indications that the DLA will be upgraded into a Ministry of Law.

Defence (Security): Strategically positioned between India and China, Bhutan has so far faced no major security threat. Apart from the presence of 100,000 Bhutanese refugees on Nepalese soil, which has strained relations with that country, Bhutan is not involved in any international disputes. Nevertheless, the **Naxalite Movement** in

India's West Bengal and separatist movements in North East India have heightened Bhutan's security concerns.

Bhutan came under the Indian security umbrella in a 1949 Treaty of Friendship. While no concrete aid for defence was promised, in 1958 the Indian Prime Minister declared that an act of aggression against Bhutan would be regarded as an act of aggression against India. The Royal Bhutan Army (RBA) was established with Indian assistance in the 1950s and close co-operation continues, with the RBA receiving regular training from an Indian team. Officially numbering just over 6,000, the RBA is under the direct command of the King. The growing threat of Indian militants establishing military bases on southern Bhutanese territory led to a significant strenghtening of the RBA, the Royal Bhutan Guards and the Royal Bhutan Police (RBP). In early 2004 joint operations with India were carried out to flush out suspected rebels from the outlawed groups, the **United Liberation Front of Assam (ULFA)** and the **National Democratic Front of Bodoland (NDFB)** in Bhutan.

Military: The security forces comprise the Royal Bhutan Army (RBA), the Royal Bhutan Police (RBP), and the Royal Bodyguards. In July 2004, together, they employed 14,209 personnel, and military expenditure amounted to US $11.2m., or 1.9% of gross domestic product, in 2003. The Royal Bhutan Army was established as an organized military force in the 1950s with support from India, and in response to the Chinese occupation of Tibet. Consisting of around 6,000 personnel, it is under the direct command of the King, with day-to-day operations overseen by the chief of operations. Recruitment is on a voluntary basis and is supplemented by a form of conscription. Military training facilities are provided by an Indian Military Training Team (IMTRAT), with other training facilities and camps spread throughout the country. The army's primary duties have traditionally centred around border defence, but it has also assisted the RBP in the execution of internal security duties. Organizationally subordinate to the RBA, the RBP was established in 1965 and also operates under the command of the chief of operations of the army. The Royal Bodyguards are responsible for the security of the King and the members of the royal family.

Police: The RBP was established on 1 September 1965 with personnel reassigned from the RBA. Subordinate to the army and under the command of its chief of operations, the Royal Bhutan Police has headquarters in each district and sub-district. Recruits undergo basic training at the Police Training Centre in Jigmiling, Geylegphug District. Advanced training, in areas such as criminology, takes place in India, Singapore and other countries. Significantly, the RBP recruits women for active service. In addition to general police functions, police officers also perform border patrol duties.

Riots: Riots and insurgents are a comparatively recent phenomenon in Bhutan and have appeared as the result of, generally, three types of grievance: (1) inter-élite rivalries, which have culminated in political assassinations and attempts to overthrow the government, a well-known example being the assassination of the reformer *Lonchen* Jigmie Palden Dorji in 1964 and a subsequent *coup d'état*; (2) the refusal of Indian militant groups to dissolve their camps and to leave the country has led to various conflicts with the Bhutanese Armed Forces; and (3) there have been acts of violence linked with the Nepalese issue/conflict in southern Bhutan. The government regards the last two as threats to national security and the integrity of the country.

Terrorism: Various militant groups have made their base Bhutan, for example the **United Liberation Front of Assam (ULFA)**, the **National Democratic Front of Bodoland (NDFB)**, the **Bodo Liberation Tigers Force (BLTF)** and the Kamatapur Liberation Organization (KLO). While the first three have been largely engaged in operations in North East India, they are recognized as a serious threat to Bhutan's national security and political stability. Cross-border activities, intimidation and militarization of the population have hampered local economies and even threatened to undermine friendly Bhutan-India relations. In late 2003, following unsuccessful negotiations for a peaceful retreat of militants from Bhutan, the Bhutanese military took action to eradicate rebel bases in southern Bhutan. (*See* **Nepalese Issue/Conflict**.)

Block Development Committees: The Block Development Committees, or *Gewog Yargye Tshogchung* (GYTs), serve as an interface between elected representatives and the governmental bureaucracy, which has the status of an observer during the formulation of development strategies. The GYTs were also set up to re-establish control, ownership and responsibility for the maintenance of collective local resources. With similar functions and powers to the District Development Committees, the GYTs operate at the Block (*gewog*) level, representing groups of villages. Thus, the GYTs promote self-organization at the micro-level, deepening house-to-house direct political participation. Corresponding to the number of Blocks, there are currently 201 of these institutions.

Bureaucracy: While Bhutan did not benefit from experienced and functional colonial bureaucratic structures, it also did not import any, posing a significant challenge for development efforts. Since modernization started in 1961, there has been a steady growth of political, administrative and judicial institutions, with the aim of creating a lean and efficient civil service. Bhutan's bureaucracy is currently setting up ministries and various independent and semi-autonomous agencies, operating at three different levels. Apart from the national level, the bureaucracy is gradually extending to the district and sub-district levels, and in recent years there has been a steady growth of bureaucracy in the local units of blocks and villages. At the same time, the government has improved capacity to generate a well-trained, educated and qualified bureaucracy forming the core of the ruling élite and the dominant intelligentsia. Critics claim that the gap between state, society and the bureaucracy has produced a power vacuum, limiting the scope and efficiency of democratic structures at the local level.

Citizenship: Citizenship is a major issue in the politics of Bhutan and has been the cause of crises. To implement a restrictive migration policy the government passed various amendments modifying the provisions for obtaining Bhutanese citizenship: (1) the Nationality Law of Bhutan (Citizenship Act) enacted in 1958 granted citizenship to a foreigner who had been in Bhutan for at least 10 years and owned agricultural land; (2) the Bhutan Citizenship Act of 1977 modified the 1958 Act by changing the minimum period of residence (now 20 years for civil servants and 20 years for non-governmental employees) and introduced the requirement of knowledge about **Dzongkha** and the history of Bhutan. The attachment of citizenship to land property was dropped and the loyalty oath was specified in more detail, including reference to **Tsa-Wa-Sum**; (3) the Bhutan Citizenship Act of 1985 declared all people whose names were not registered in the census register maintained by the Ministry of Home Affairs on or before 31 December 1958, to be non-nationals. A cut-off year, 1958, was declared for granting citizenship, but without the need to prove a minimum period of domicile in Bhutan. Opponents of the Citizenship Act of 1985 argue that there is great room for interpretation, and that the provisions can be misused with regard to migration. Furthermore, since the Ministry of Home Affairs did not exist until 1968, the need to obtain proof of one's registration has turned the granting of citizenship into a non-transparent procedure. Those most affected by the amendments were the Lhotshampa in south Bhutan who, lacking the necessary documents, were unable to fulfil the necessary requirements to gain citizenship.

Bhutan Citizenship Act 1985: Bhutan's third act on nationality and citizenship was adopted by the National Assembly (*Tshogdu Chenmo*) in 1985. This retroactive act provided for citizenship by birth (where both parents were citizens of Bhutan), by registration (for census-registered persons permanently resident in Bhutan in or before 1958), or by naturalization (requiring recorded residence of 15 years for government servants or individuals with only one citizen parent and 20 years for all others, spoken and written competence in Dzongkha and written tests on the culture, customs and history of Bhutan). The 1985 Act was implemented through the 1988 census, which aimed at identifying foreigners and 'bona fide' Bhutanese nationals on the basis of the new act.

Corruption: Data or indices on corruption are only partially available in Bhutan, although the phenomenon is an emerging concern. Inefficiency, ineffectiveness, irregularities, negligence, and minor misfeasance, as well as nepotism and favouritism, are common and declared, by the government, to be symptomatic of a growing economy. Although hard evidence is difficult to come by, corruption is prevalent in both government and the private sector. Major areas prone to corruption include procurement, engineering and construction works, stores and equipment, revenue receipts, cash collections and handling, and commissions on sales. In addition, there are numerous cases of wrong payments, illegal contract arrangements, and bribery disguised as traditional gifts. To tackle the issue of corruption, Bhutan has undertaken various measures. It signed the UN Convention against Corruption in 2004, launched a 'Fraud Alert System' where citizens could post information on corrupt practices and established the Royal Audit Authority (RAA). A current draft of the constitution (as of 26 March 2005) provides for a new anti-corruption agency.

Decentralization: Apart from economic modernization and liberalization, the royal government has taken steps to decentralize administrative structures, including the devolution of various regulatory, political and financial powers. In 1979 the first step was taken through the transfer of powers to the districts (***Dzongkhag***). This was consolidated in 1981 with the establishment of a District Development Committee in each of the 20 districts, which are further divided into *gewogs*, or blocks. In 1990 the Block Development Committees were introduced. Such steps sought to promote decentralization by delegating authority and transferring manpower from central agencies to regional and local administrative structures as well as encouraging greater engagement in and efficiency of decision-making on developmental issues. (*See* Political Participation.)

District Development Committee: The District Development Committee, or Dzongkhag Yargye Tshogchung (DYT), is the interface between the elected representatives of the people and the bureaucracy of the Bhutanese government. These committees are empowered to formulate plans and propose agendas for debate in the National Assembly. Corresponding to the division of the country into 20 districts (*dzongkhags*), there are 20 DYTs. The size of DYT membership ranges from 20 to 60 depending on the district's size and population. The DYT provides the institutional framework to promote further administrative reforms and to foster socio-political awareness among the people, as well as encouraging their political participation.

Federalism: Bhutan is characterized by a centralized monarchical form of governance with a cautious approach towards incorporating federal elements into the political structure. So far, federalism in the country has been pursued through administrative decentralization of executive and judiciary functions. Federalism on a territorial basis is perceived by the ruling élite as more of a threat to the unity of the country than as an opportunity to integrate ethnic communities, especially the Lhotshampa. However, economic development and the consequent social mobility as well as rural-urban migration have reduced ethnic concentration as the essential constituent of a territorial federal structure.

Human Rights: While a draft constitution is under discussion, there is as yet no written constitutional framework providing for the protection of fundamental political and human rights. The King continues to exercise strong, active and direct power over the government and political parties as well as human rights organizations, and NGOs are prohibited. While the law provides for the freedom of religion, the government restricts this in practice. Buddhism is the state religion and the government subsidizes monasteries and shrines of the **Drukpa** school. Although the King declared major Hindu festivals as national holdiays, there are no Hindu temples in Thimphu, despite the migration of many ethnic Nepalese, a large proportion of whom are Hindus, to the city. According to reports, permission from the government to build a Hindu temple is required but rarely granted.

Freedom of movement is also restricted, particularly in the border areas. Ethnic Nepalese in the south of the country claim that they are frequently denied security clearances that are necessary for passport forms. Furthermore, under the 1985 citizenship law many ethnic Nepalese lost their citizenship, creating the highly contentious issue of almost 100,000 ethnic Nepalese refugees in camps across the border in Nepal since the early 1990s.

Bhutan has ratified only two of the major international human rights conventions, on the elimination of discrimination against women and the protection of children's rights.

Inequality: Bhutan is a comparatively egalitarian society where social and economic inequities have not emerged as serious concerns in recent years. Steps towards the equal treatment of all Bhutanese were the abolition of slavery and serfdom in 1958. Furthermore, the government established various programmes of land reform, especially the introduction of a royal land grant (**Kidu system**). Ethnic groups such as the major community of Lhotshampa accuse the government and ruling élite of limiting access to economic and political resources in favour of the Ngalong. A certain degree of inequality related to malnutrition or seasonal food insecurity in geographically remote and isolated communities is visible. In addition, through modernization, regional disparities in economic development and income inequalities have arisen. Other social issues, such as gender relations and poverty, are marginal compared to other South Asian countries. (*See* **Nepalese Issue/ Conflict**.)

Nationalism: As a result of the Nepalese Issue/Conflict, there was a surge of nationalist sentiment on the part of tradition-orientated Bhutanese. With the passing of restrictive citizenship acts and the adoption of the cultural policy, ***Driglam Namzha***, the Bhutanese government switched from a liberal attitude towards a policy of Bhutanization, seen by the Nepalese as an assimilative and exclusive, culturally-based nationalism of the Drukpa identity group. The result of these socio-political tensions was the expulsion and flight of large numbers of Nepalese immigrants, creating, in the process, a pan-Nepali identity among the refugees and those still resident in Bhutan. Drawing on this, the Bhutanese government occasionally voices concern about being marginalized in their own country and the emergence of a Nepali nationalism based on the imagined concept of a 'Greater Nepal'. While there is little concrete evidence either in Nepal, India or Bhutan of such an idea taking actual shape, the term is used to stoke an imagined threat to the country's identity, cultural heritage and political structure.

Participation/Public Action: A gradual decentralization of decision-making was implemented at the beginning of the fifth Five-Year Plan in 1981. The overall objective was to encourage grassroots participation and responsibilities by involving citizens in the process of planning and implementing development programmes. The royal government enlarged opportunities for political participation at the national level through the creation of a number of new institutions such as the National Assembly (*Tshogdu Chenmo*). The creation and strengthening of local institutions, such as the District Development Committees and the Block Development Committees within the process of political and administrative decentralization has had positive outcomes, such as increased active participation, transferred power to the community and greater political consciousness. However, it must be emphasized that people of Nepalese origin have generally been much more politically engaged than the **Drukpa** who have not as yet organized politically in any significant way. An obvious reason for this might be that political parties have been considered undesirable. However, the promulgated introduction of nation-wide parliamentary elections in 2008 and the establishment of a multi-party system on the basis of an envisaged democratic constitutional monarchy ought to change this in the near future.

Royal Civil Service Commission (RCSC): The Royal Civil Service Commission (RCSC) is an autonomous body established in 1973 as the Department of Man-power. Following various reconstitutions, it works as a co-ordinating agency to formulate and implement human resource policies and is responsible for the rational administration of the civil service. A major focus of the RCSC is to prevent the politicization of the bureaucracy.

Royal Pardon: The term royal pardon, as used in Bhutan, refers to the forgiveness of a crime and the penalty associated with it and is primarily associated with the law of Tsa-Wa-Sum. It is granted by the King, the head of state, on specific occasions, usually on 17 December, to mark the National Day.

Royal Vote of Confidence: The introduction of a vote of confidence is one of the major steps that has been taken towards introducing democratic elements into the monarchical system in Bhutan. It was proposed by King Jigme Dorji Wangchuck in 1969 and slightly modified in 1970 to ensure that the National Assembly could remove the Druk Gyalpo through a vote of no-confidence based on a two-thirds' majority. Established against the will of the the people's repre-sentatives, it is difficult to imagine this provision actually being applied in Bhutan. However, the King has none the less, in theory, lost his veto power in the National Assembly and should he forfeit the confidence of this institution, the Wangchuck family member who is next in line of succession would automatically be enthroned.

Bhutan, Economic Development

Gross domestic product (GDP) at purchasing power parity (PPP): US $673.2m.; GDP per capita at PPP: $2,060 (2003 official estimate); currency: *ngultrum* (BTN).

Bhutan's economy, one of the world's smallest and least developed by all measures, started the process of modernization in 1961, when the country emerged from a period of self-imposed seclusion. Through the formulation and implementa-tion of five-year plans (FYP), the government has followed a model of planned economic development. The first four FYPs (1961–81) focused on developing a basic infrastructure, especially a road network to reduce the country's physical isolation, to connect inner areas of Bhutan and to improve communications, necessary for further growth. The fifth and sixth FYPs (1981–92) were designed along World Bank, **International Monetary Fund (IMF)** and ADB guide-lines, turning attention to privatization of the public sector and promotion of export-orientated sectors, including industry, mining, trade, commerce and power-generation projects. The seventh FYP (1992–97) was characterized by the attempt to consolidate achievements of previous development projects, internal resource mobilization and human resource development. During the eighth FYP (1997–2002) the concept of sustainable development took root and decentralization measures were introduced. Political turbulence in Bhutan's southern districts (*see* **Nepalese Issue/Conflict**), where most of the country's industrial enterprises are located, has hampered economic development of the country. The present FYP (2002–07) will incorporate a *gewog*-based planning process and prioritizes infrastructure development to invigorate the private sector, improvement of social services and preservation and promotion of Bhutan's culture and environment. Today the overall performance of the economy indicates its fundamental macro-economic stability, while at the same time highlighting its vulnerability due to its dependence on other countries, especially India. Furthermore, the nation's economic structure is still based on subsistence agriculture. However, GDP is estimated to have grown by around 7.1% in the 2004/2005 financial year. Hydropower projects have been a major contributor to economic growth in the past and are likely to continue to be the main constituent of future development.

Economic Policy/Reforms: Bhutanese economic policy is characterized by the official development strategy known as **Gross National Happiness (GNH)**, which aims at balancing economic growth with social, political and cultural development. To implement the GNH, economic policies follow the guide-lines of five-year plans. Two main areas of future development have been identified: the production of hydropower and natural resource-based processing industries, and the development of small and micro (cottage) enterprises. Among these, off-farm employment, rural industrialization, horticulture, tourism (cultural, sports and eco-tourism) and specialization in niche markets using Bhutan's rich biodiversity will be enforced. The government has gradually introduced several economic liberalization policies to encourage private-sector development, especially in trade, mining, industry and financial sectors. At the same time Bhutan is attempting to minimize its dependence on foreign aid donors and has incorporated a threefold strategy of diversifiying financial backers, increasing domestic revenue, and restricting the pace of development.

Private Sector: The private sector in Bhutan emerged three decades ago. Still in its infancy, it is characterized by an unbalanced industrial diversification, and dominated by small and medium-sized enterprises (SMEs) operating in small-scale production and service industries, including commercial trading. By the end of 2000 the government had issued around 21,000 industrial and trading licences. The development of the private sector is hampered by several factors, including a lack of entrepreneurial culture; restrictive legal and regulatory frameworks especially for the financial sector, such as interest rates and the tax system; shortages of labour (both skilled and unskilled), technical expertise as well as technology and raw materials; small production capabilities; and a limited, fragmented domestic market with insufficient physical infrastructure, such as roads and electricity. To invigorate private-sector growth the government has adopted various strategies, introducing more conducive regulatory and legal provisions and the partial or full privatization of several state-owned enterprises (like tourism or surface transport).

Public Sector: The public sector plays a pervasive role in Bhutan's economy and was considered to be the main engine of Bhutan's development, dominating all major activities and initiatives. Apart from agriculture, the private sector was virtually non-existent until recently because its development was considered as contradictory to the core assumptions underlying the philosophy of Gross National Happiness. Today, the government recognizes that the role of the state and the dominance of the public sector constrain a flourishing private sector. However, the public sector is still the major employer in the country and public employment is coveted as a badge of honour and status, with many Bhutanese still reluctant to enter the private sector because of perceived job insecurities and uncertain career prospects.

Population: The population at July 2003 was estimated at 2,139,549, although other estimates cite figures as low as 810,000. The capital, **Thimpu**, is home to a population of between 50,000 and 65,000. In 2003 the proportion of the population under 15 years of age was estimated as being a high 39.6%, with 56.4% of the population falling between the ages of 15–64, and 4% over the age of 65. The male/female sex ratio is 1.07. Average life expectancy lies at 53.58 years, with the estimated birth rate at 34.82 births per 1,000 population and the death rate at 13.47 deaths per 1,000 population. The total fertility rate stands at 4.94 children per woman, with an infant mortality rate of 104.68 deaths per 1,000 live births. The prevalence of HIV/AIDS in adults was estimated in 2001 as being less than 0.1 %, with fewer than 100 people estimated in 1997 as living with HIV/AIDS.

Family-Planning Policy: Family planning in Bhutan was integrated into the health care delivery system in 1971, initially covering a limited geographic area and offering few contraceptive methods. In 1981 the National Institute of Family Health (NIFH) was created, expanding and modernizing family planning throughout the country. Numerous reproductive health campaigns were initiated from 1995 onwards in response to the findings of Bhutan's 1994 national health survey, which identified poor reproductive health indicators. Goals of the reproductive health programme, to be achieved by the end of the ninth five-year plan in 2007, include improving family-planning knowledge, increasing the contraceptive prevalence rate from 30.7% (2000 estimate) to 100%, reducing population growth to 2% or less and the total fertility rate to three or less.

Migration: Regarding migration, Bhutan has had to face two challenging issues. An increasing internal, rural-urban migration, has affected the two larger urban areas, Thimpu and **Phuntsholing**. Surveys reveal that 72% of the urban population are migrants from rural areas, that most migrants are aged 16–30 years and that 63%

have primary education or more. This migration results from the lack of opportunities in rural areas and the uneven geographical terrain that limits land use. The movement of people from the south of the country towards Nepal or **North East India** and **West Bengal** and North East is another source of migrants, although this phenomenon is classified under Bhutanese law as 'illegal immigration'. In this context, the royal government has been involved in an ongoing confrontation over the problem of migrants, an issue that has both economic and ethnic dimensions. (*See* **Nepalese Issue/Conflict**.)

Urbanization: The process and problems of urbanization are relatively new phenomena in Bhutan. Over the last four decades, with road construction and improved transport facilities that have increased accessibility, rural communities have come under the influence of larger settlements, which have then grown into towns. In addition, with the expanding population and the lack of employment opportunities in rural areas as well as the attractions of urban settlements, such as better health facilities and alternative employment, there has been a marked increase in rural-urban migration. Half of the urban population resides in the two largest urban centres—Thimphu, the capital, and Phuntsholing. The rest of the population is distributed in 26 urban centres and 26 satellite towns, declared as 'larger settlements' with individual populations ranging from 500 to 10,000. The current annual rate of population growth is around 10%, and it has been estimated that in 2006 the population of Thimpu will reach approximately 100,000, compared with 46,000 in 1999. Responsibility for town planning and the development of urban infrastructure for all urban centres lies with the National Urban Development Corporation.

Minority Groups/Communities: Bhutan's society is multi-ethnic, being composed of several distinct communities whose differences rest on ethnicity, profession, social structure, beliefs and values. The people of Bhutan consist of so-called indigenous groups as well as immigrants from neighbouring countries, namely Nepal, India, Myanmar (Burma) and Tibet (China). Based on the criteria of ethnic origin, the majority of Bhutanese can be separated into three groups: the **Ngalong** (of Tibetan origin); the Sharchop (of Indo-Mongoloid/Burmese origin); and the **Lhotshampa** (of Nepalese origin). These three broad categories do not constitute monolithic blocks and within them are minor communities of varied socio-economic, ethnic and cultural backgrounds. Furthermore, there are indigenous ethnic groups or tribes, for example the Brokpas, Mons, Khens, Birmis, Dayas, Lepchas, Bodos or Tephoos, to add to these categories. Besides this ethnic clustering there is also a religious categorization. According to official claims, the majority of Bhutanese are Buddhists, who follow the **Kagyupa School**, namely the **Drukpa** branch of it. The various religious minorities are Hindus, Christians, followers of the Nyingmapa School of the Mahayana Buddhism, animists and Muslims, also known as Kaches.

Tribes: Bhutanese society is a complex mix of indigenous and migrant communities. Together with the three major social groups, the Ngalong, Sharchop and

Lhotshampa, there are various minor ones, including the tribal populations of Bhutan. The origin and history of many tribes, especially those located in remote parts of the country, is little known. However, the country's most significant minor communities or tribes are: Brokpas (a nomadic community in central Bhutan, of Tibetan origin), Mons (or Monpas, living in the east and south east, considered to be the oldest inhabitants), Khens (located in central Bhutan, with Indo-Mongoloid features), Birmis (a nomadic group in the east), Lhops or Doyas (a tribe in the south west who claim to be aboriginal inhabitants), Lepchas (a very small community in the west, of Sikkimese or Indian-Nepali origin), Bodos (a community in the south) and Tephoos (a group in north Bhutan, of Indian origin). The majority of these groups are Buddhist, some Hindu and a few follow different religions, particularly animism. A main concern for these tribes has been the loss of their identity due to the government's cultural policy which has led in the past to various conflicts. (*See* ***Driglam Namzha***.)

Agriculture: Bhutan has an agrarian-based economy, with 94% of its citizens engaged in agriculture, livestock rearing and fishing. Agriculture contributed an estimated 35.9% of gross domestic product (GDP) in 2001. Around 9% of the land is used for crop cultivation or permanent pasture. Agriculture in Bhutan has traditionally been on a small-scale, subsistence level and, due to a shortage of cultivable and pasture land, limited technical knowledge and lack of skilled labour, agricultural development has been slow. In early 1988 the newly established Bhutan Development Finance Corporation (BDFC) took over from the Royal Monetary Authority (RMA) of Bhutan in its administration of rural credit schemes, providing loans for land improvement and livestock, seasonal requirements, and longer-term development plans. In the same year, the BDFC received a US $2.5m. loan from the ADB. Major irrigation schemes were carried out in southern and central Bhutan to improve the quality and quantity of water sources. The Ministry of Agriculture's objective of achieving food security, namely the balancing of import costs with the returns from cash crop exports, was officially achieved by 1999.

Land Reform (Ownership): Land ownership and reforms continue to be a central issue in Bhutan. Since the agriculture sector is still dominated by subsistence farming, rural socio-economic well-being depends on landholdings as the major indicator for wealth or poverty. The royal government has introduced some land reform measures as poverty alleviation instruments. The first Land Reforms of 1952, the ***Thrimshung Chenmo*** in 1959 and the Land Act of 1978 dealt with tenure rights over agricultural land. The introduction of registration or recording of land enhanced credibility and legitimacy in matters of inheritance and established tenure rights over property to the individual farmer for land that he had traditionally cultivated. These reforms had two components: first, an option was given to tenants and former slave or serf families to acquire land for their own cultivation under governmental observation; and, second, the ceiling on land ownership was fixed at about 10–12 ha depending on the type of land and the area in which it was situated. These measures sought to abolish remnants of the feudal system, to prevent the emergence of dubious moneylending practices and achieve progress towards the equal treatment of all citizens. The right to sell or transfer land or any immovable property to a person who is not a citizen of Bhutan, except in keeping with laws enacted by parliament, is forbidden. (*See* **Kidu System**.)

Food and Famine (Prevention): Widespread famines are not a common occurrence in Bhutan. However, due to a susceptible ecological environment parts of the country are vulnerable to transient food insecurity, seasonal hunger and malnutrition. Small landholdings, low productivity, the increase of population and natural disasters are common causes of food shortages. Close kinship and traditional social support systems are coping mechanisms for the Bhutanese. For some communities, forest foods are a major component of traditional diets, adding to the need to preserve forest endowments as a buffer against food insecurity. National policy aims at food security by increasing the production of cereals to achieve self-reliance and boosting agricultural production, including cash crop exports to finance additional food imports. (*See* Poverty; Floods and Natural Disasters.)

Industry: The industrial sector of Bhutan remains largely underdeveloped, accounting for just 18% of GDP and employing a very small proportion of the workforce. The majority of production is of the cottage industry type, in addition to cement, wood products, processed fruits, alcoholic beverages, and calcium carbide. The larger industries, established since Bhutan's economic modernization began in the 1960s, are modern and operate with labour-saving technology. Tourism has developed into an important industry in Bhutan since its introduction in 1974, becoming the largest earner of foreign exchange. The number of foreign visitors, though highly restricted except for Indian nationals, reached nearly 5,600 in 2002, with tourist receipts reaching US $7.4m.

Foreign Trade (Import/Export): Traditionally the majority of Bhutan's foreign trade was with Tibet, but by 1960, following the closure of the Bhutan-China border, formal trade was reorientated towards India, now Bhutan's most significant trading partner. Trade and transit arrangements between India and Bhutan were signed in 1972, 1983 and 1990. A trade agreement was also signed with Bangladesh in 1980, and renewed in 1990 and 2003. Exports reached US $154m. f.o.b. in 2000, primarily in the form of surplus hydroelectric power (to India), timber, wood products, spices, cement, fruit and handicrafts. In 2004 87.9% of exports went to India, 4.6% to Bangladesh, and 2% to the Philippines. Imports amounted to approximately $196m. c.i.f. in 2000, and consisted mainly of fuels, grains, machinery, vehicles, and fabrics. Of imported commodities in 2004, 71.3% came from India, 7.8% from Japan, and 3% from Austria. Since 1976, tourism, although a highly restricted actvity, has become Bhutan's largest source of foreign exchange earnings.

Banking System: The Royal Monetary Authority (RMA), established in 1982, is Bhutan's central bank with headquarters in Thimpu. It is responsible for issuing currency, implementing monetary policy, co-ordinating the activities of financial institutions, and holding the government's foreign exchange earnings. The Bank of Bhutan (BOB), the country's only commercial bank, was established in 1968 as a joint venture with the Chartered Bank of India. Its assets were taken over by the State Bank of India in 1970, which currently holds 25% of its shares. The remaining majority is held by the royal government of Bhutan. The BOB provides financial loans to traders, industrialists, civil servants and small businessmen. The Bhutan Development Finance Corporation (BDFC), established in 1988, took over from the RMA in the administration of financial assistance to small- and medium-scale industrial and agricultural producers and was privatized in 1991. Non-bank financial institutions include the Royal Insurance Corporation of Bhutan (RICB), established in 1975, and acting as a provider of both general and life insurance; the Government Employees Provident Fund (GEPF), established in 1986, managed on behalf of the government by the RICB and responsible for investments from civil servants; and the Unit Trust of Bhutan (UTB), established in 1975 to encourage investment by Bhutanese within the domestic economy. The GEPF, UTB and other non-bank institutions are small and constrained by the rudimentary use of money in the Bhutanese economy.

Foreign Direct Investment (FDI): The royal government's policy towards foreign capital has been a restrictive one. Among the reasons to keep investors out of Bhutan, the main ones have been the need to protect the country's underdeveloped private sector and to shield Bhutanese identity and culture from external influences. Due to growing financial demand for necessary development schemes, in particular to generate employment, and Bhutan's limited public as well as private funds, government policy towards foreign direct investment (FDI) has undergone cautious change. Non-nationals may hold 20% of equity in joint ventures. Among the first foreign investors were the State Bank of India in 1971 and the Marubeni Corporation (Japan) in 1990. The private sector has strongly emphasized the need for FDI to broaden employment and training opportunities, to promote the transfer of technology and to deepen the economic and revenue base. Nevertheless, the governmental approach to FDI is still seen as conservative by investors, and the need for greater simplification of provisions and the liberalization of licences as vital to encourage FDI.

Foreign Aid: The influx of capital into Bhutan is mostly in the form of foreign aid rather than foreign direct investment. Bhutan has, in the past, depended on India, which largely financed the first three development plans (1961–76). More recently, Bhutan has had an aid inflow from several bilateral donors, which are also development partners, providing capital investment in the form of technical co-operation, project assistance or foreign volunteer programmes. Bhutan has also been a donor in South Asia, for example in 1987, when it provided disaster relief aid to Maldives, Bangladesh and India.

Labour: Until recently Bhutan was categorized as a labour-deficient country, characterized by its significant dependence on India due to its basic need for semi-skilled and unskilled labour for major development projects. The shortage still exists because of a mismatch between the demand for and supply of human resources. As a result, the primary challenge is not the lack of employment opportunities but the insufficient quality of the labour force. In 2004 the presence of an expatriate workforce was estimated at more than 34,000.

According to the government, in 2004 the rate of unemployment increased to 2.5% from 1.8% in 2003. However, this comparatively small rate of unemployment is largely invisible because of the still existing social safety nets extended by the joint family system. In addition, through development efforts in the educational sector, the country will be able to gradually provide a more qualified labour force. In future, a cause for concern, however, will be an increasing income gap between the new developing sectors and traditional sectors, and rural-urban migration and its negative impact on farming and agricultural development.

Informal Economy: The informal economy in Bhutan mostly consists of trade in goods like yarn, rice, sugar and aluminium with India. Such economic activities are tolerated and overlooked by the government, condoned partly because of remote geographic conditions and linked disadvantages of Bhutan. It is, however, estimated that the informal trade balance is significantly in favour of India. An increasing concern is the movement of illegal drugs.

Child Labour: The improvement of children's social environment is at the centre of Bhutan's development strategy. Concerted efforts have been made to draw up a coherent legal framework to protect the interests of children and youth. Bhutan ratified the Convention on the Rights of the Child (1990), was part of the World Summit for Children (1990) and the World Declaration and Plan of Action for Children's Survival, Protection and Development (1991). The government implemented the National Plan of Action for Children and introduced a minimum working age of 18 years. However, the phenomenon of child labour is largely a seasonal one in the agricultural sector, or else takes place within the home, making it difficult to monitor. Records on the involvement of children in compulsory labour are not available.

Compulsory Labour: In the past a Bhutanese citizen was obliged to provide three categories of compulsory labour and free labour, irrespective of gender: (1) *Chunidom*, a nominally paid labour performance, had to be provided over a one-month period to implement development projects by the central government; (2) *Zhapto Lemi*, a non-paid labour performance, supported development schemes by governmental institutions at the district level; (3) *Googda Woola* supplemented the first two kinds of labour and involved seven–15 days per household, per year of nominally paid labour in the form of ***Dzong*** (district) maintenance. Hiring a replacement labourer or payment of cash in lieu of labour was possible. Today, this system has been modified by the government and appears as voluntary community service. (*See* Labour.)

Environmental Protection: Bhutan has given special attention to conserving biodiversity and the country's rich natural resources. Environmental protection is an integral consideration in all of the governmental development agendas, which are based on holistic Buddhist concepts as well as on principles of sustainability. The government has declared that it will maintain forest cover at 60% and has identified more than 26.23% of the country's total territory as established protected areas and an additional 9% as biological corridors. To prevent the over-exploitation of natural resources, Bhutan applies a restrictive policy, particularly in fields such as tourism (ecotourism), energy and mineral quarrying. However, Bhutan's conservationist ethos faces the challenge of rapid population growth, urbanization, industrialization and unsustainable agricultural methods. To minimize the negative impact, the government has established a **Bhutan Trust Fund for Environmental Conservation**. The National Environment Committee (NEC) was founded in 1989 to co-ordinate environmental protection activities and to monitor the environmental impact of economic development. A national environmental strategy, called 'the Middle Path', serves as a policy framework to guide current and future environmental conservation.

Green Belt Policy: A term that refers to the idea of establishing a 1 km-wide corridor along the Indo-Bhutan border, the official reason behind the Green Belt was to check erosion and prevent floods in India. The government has not been able to implement this idea in the face of immense opposition to the negative impact it would have on the population living in the southern districts of Bhutan. Approximately 20%–30% of residents would be displaced. Furthermore, this policy has been seen as part of an official effort to culturally assimilate the Nepali-speaking Lhotshampa by dissolving their geographical concentration. (*See* **Nepalese Issue/ Conflict**.)

Floods and Natural Disasters: As part of the geologically fragile Himalayan area, Bhutan has faced various disasters. Landslides, caused by heavy rain, have in the past cut off roads and other communications, and damaged bridges and irrigation channels in many regions of the country. Apart from landslides and river erosion, there is the hazard of floods caused by glacial lake outbursts. Melting water from receding glaciers, especially in northern parts of the country, are a problem since the remaining unconsolidated debris adds to the possibility of future landslides.

Health System/Policy: The health status of Bhutan's population has improved radically over the last two decades, with life expectancy increasing from 45.6 years in 1980–85 to 62 years by 2001. This increase can be attributed to improvements in living conditions, sanitation and water supply, nutrition, maternal and child health care, immunization and the control of communicable diseases. The health care system provides access to essential health care services for about 90% of the population. Modern medical facilities were introduced in 1962, as part of the first Five-Year Plan (1962–67). Prior to the practice of modern health care, Bhutan relied solely on traditional medicine, which continues in tandem with modern allopathic methods. The emphasis on primary health care initiated in 1978 has generated one of the best-organized primary health care systems in the region. Despite the high cost of health care service delivery due to a scattered population across difficult terrain, Bhutan has achieved a fairly uniform distribution of basic health units, district hospitals, and regional referral hospitals. Primary health care coverage expanded from 65% in 1990 to more than 90% in 2002. Human resources for the health sector have steadily increased, yet Bhutan still faces a shortage of medical personnel. There is no institute for the training of medical doctors, who must consequently receive their training abroad. In 2000 there were just 109 medical doctors in the country. The government's commitment to preventing the spread of HIV is very high. Bhutan's national STD/AIDS control programme was started in 1988, even before the first HIV infection was detected in 1993. In 2003 Bhutan reported just 42 cases of HIV/AIDs. Basic health care services and essential drugs are provided free and so far there has been no involvement from the private sector. In the past, donors, including the government of India, UNICEF, UNFPA, and WHO, have played a significant role in supporting the health sector. Total national health expenditure for 2000 was 12.2% of total government expenditure, with government spending on health care accounting for 52% of total health expenditure. External resources for health formed 27.5% of public expenditure on health in 2000.

Education/Education Policy: Education has traditionally been an important part of religious life in Bhutan, and monastic education continues today in several state-supported religious institutions. Modern state education was introduced by the reformist King, Jigme Dorji **Wangchuck**, during the 1960s. Although not compulsory, it is, apart from nominal fees, virtually free. Post-secondary education is also paid for by the state. Despite the expansion of formal education for children, adult illiteracy rates remain high. Primary education begins at six years of age and lasts for five years, with secondary education continuing for a total of five years and following a syllabus influenced by both British and Indian practices. The medium of instruction is English, and **Dzongkha**, the official national language, is a compulsory subject. Annual school enrolment has, on average, grown by about 8% annually and primary education enrolment rates climed from 73% in 1998 to 81% in 2003. At primary school level female enrolment rates are now virtually on a par with those for males. Post-secondary education is possible at one degree college, seven post-secondary education institutes, four technical institutes, one teacher training college and one institute of management. A number of Bhutanese students receive higher education at universities abroad. Despite growing enrolment rates, adult literacy, at 54% (2005 estimate), falls below the regional average and female literacy levels remain much lower than those for males (males: 56.3%; females: 28.2% in 1998).

Social Security/Policy: Bhutan's social security system is one primarily based on traditional institutions, such as family networks or the Kidu system. However, with increased economic mobility and the processes of rural-urban migration, the structure of Bhutanese society is gradually changing. The royal government has responded to this development through a long-term strategy of building up a formal social security system. Some social policy measures have been implemented, for example the National Pension and Provident Fund in 2000, and there have been various sustainable livelihood programmes, such as the Rural Credit Programme, in place since the 1980s. The budget allocation for social-sector expenditure in the ninth five-year plan (2002–07) constitutes about 11.5% of GDP on an annual basis.

Poverty: Poverty has been recently recognized as an issue in Bhutan. Despite the fact that it is one of the least developed countries it does not suffer from extreme poverty. According to official surveys, the percentage of Bhutanese below the national poverty line (people who live on less than US $200 per year) was 31.7% in 2003. The incidence of poverty has been limited to a significant extent by the public welfare system and a wide range of broad poverty measures by the government, as well as private, traditional safety nets. Nevertheless, forms of deprivation are faced by certain sections of society, in specific parts of the country and during different seasons in terms of access to food, education and basic health. In this context, poverty has been identified as a multi-dimensional phenomenon, not limited to income alone but including access to social services and market opportunities. The government has identified various indigenous causes and factors leading to poverty, including limited ownership or access to productive assets (especially the lack or inadequate size of landholdings); remote locations and a difficult terrain hindering access to social and economic resources; slow expansion of non-agricultural employment alternatives; large families and rapid population growth; shortage of labour in rural households due to migration; limited provision of higher education facilities; and natural disasters. However, with its moderate levels of urbanization and the comparatively small size of urban settlements, poverty in Bhutan is very much still a rural phenomenon, although poverty in urban settlements is emerging.

Welfare System: The absence of extreme poverty in Bhutan has been largely the result of a well-planned welfare system. Education and health services are provided free, and supported by traditional safety nets such as the Kidu system. The majority of households now have access to these social benefits. Influenced by Buddhist concepts, the government recognizes that the community must provide for both the spiritual and social-economic welfare of the individual. Therefore, economic growth, as well as conserving religious institutions and traditions, is seen as essential to supporting and nurturing the various needs of society. (*See* Social Security/Policy; ***Dratshang***.)

Gender Relations/Empowerment: Compared with its Buddhist neighbour, Nepal, gender relations in Bhutanese society are relatively balanced. Women benefit from a favourable socio-economic context (property rights, female ownership, matrilineal family system) and the current legal system covers issues of separation, adultery, divorce and child custody. More significant are the positive social indicators in education and health which are far more advanced than in neighbouring countries. However, certain gender issues, such as the under-representation of woman in the government, public offices and civil service, remain to be tackled. (*See* **National Women Association of Bhutan (NWAB)**.)

Marriage Act of 1980: The Marriage Act of 1980 corresponded with the Bhutan Citizenship Acts of 1958 and 1977 and was implemented to restrict and control the marriage of Bhutanese citizens with non-nationals, especially Nepalese. In accordance with the provision, a national who marries a non-national undergoes severe penalties. Access to various economic resources provided by the government have been denied, such as assistance in the form of land, seeds, loans, livestock, and health benefits as well as jobs in the public sector. (*See* **Nepalese Issue/Conflict**.)

Royal Audit Authority (RAA): The Royal Audit Authority (RAA) is Bhutan's supreme audit institution, responsible for auditing public-sector agencies and, since 1999, primarily responsible for enhancing accountability in the government. It is an independent body, detached from the bureaucracy, and is seen as one of several official measures to devolve authority and power and to improve the efficiency and transparency of governance.

Bhutan Broadcasting Service Corporation (BBS)

The Bhutan Broadcasting Service Corporation (BBS) is the national broadcasting company in Bhutan, providing radio and television services. Set up in 1973 by members of the National Youth Association of Bhutan (NYAB), the objectives of the company are twofold: (1) informing, educating and entertaining; and (2) promoting Bhutan's culture, heritage and national as well as regional languages. The radio service is nation-wide, while television services are still limited to the area (valley) around **Thimpu**.

Bhutan Chamber of Commerce and Industry (BCCI)

The Bhutan Chamber of Commerce and Industry (BCCI) is a non-profit-making NGO based in **Thimpu**, established in 1980 under government sanction. The apex forum for the business community, its primary objective is to facilitate trade and stimulate industries through promoting and developing Bhutan's private sector. It also actively liaises between the government and the business community on policy issues, interpreting policies and disseminating business information to members and relevant international agencies, and providing guidance and technical assistance in business planning. The BCCI has the right to nominate one member for the National Assembly.

Bhutan Development Finance Corporation (BDFC) – *see* Bhutan, Economic Development—Banking System

Bhutan People's Party (BPP)

The Bhutan People's Party (BPP) is illegal due to a national ban on political parties in Bhutan. Founded in 1990 in Bhutan as a successor to the People's Forum on Democratic Rights, itself established in 1989, it operates in exile from Khatmandu today. Mainly made up of Hindus of Nepalese origin, the BPP views itself as anti-corruption rather than anti-monarchy, advocating transformation of the hereditary monarchy into a constitutional monarchy. Other main objectives of the group include judicial reform; freedom of religion, language, speech and the press; equality of ethnic groups; and the unconditional release of all political prisoners. The BPP was involved in the staging of large demonstrations in southern Bhutan in September 1990, protesting against **Drukpa** domination and demanding political reform.

Bhutan Trust Fund for Environmental Conservation (BTF)

The Bhutan Trust Fund for Environmental Conservation (BTF), established in 1991 by the government, is the world's first environmental trust fund. Its main objective is to promote sustainable development. The BTF offers financial support for projects and activities that develop long-term environmental protection.

Bhutto, Benazir

The daughter of Zulfikar Ali **Bhutto**, Benazir Bhutto was born in Karachi, Pakistan, in 1953. Completing her early education in Pakistan, she later attended Radcliffe College and Oxford University, where she studied for a degree in Philosophy, Politics and Economics. In 1988 Benazir won the general elections as head of the **Pakistan People's Party (PPP)** with a small majority and was forced to form a coalition government with the **Muttahida Qaumi Movement** and independent members of the National Assembly. She was the first woman to head an Islamic country. The Bhutto government collapsed in 1990 when the MQM withdrew its support. Though the government did not enact any major legislation during its 20 months in office, it strengthened the democratic process in Pakistan by allowing greater freedom of the press and encouraging competition among political parties. Her government improved relations with the USA, the Commonwealth nations and also, to a certain extent, with India until the **Kashmir dispute** was revived in 1990. In the same year the PPP was replaced in government by its main rival party, the **Pakistan Muslim League (PML)**, which won more than two-thirds of the seats in the National Assembly. For the first time in Pakistan's history a democratically elected government was followed by a democratically elected successor and Benazir Bhutto was to return as Prime Minister in 1993. In November 1996 President Farooq Leghari, a former ally, dismissed Bhutto, accusing her of having sponsored police hit squads, condoned bribery and almost bankrupted the government. Since 1996 Benazir Bhutto has lived in exile in London and Dubai, thereby escaping imprisonment for corruption. She was excluded from Pakistan's parliamentary elections in 2002.

Bhutto, Zulfikar Ali

Born in 1928 and educated abroad, Zulfikar Ali Bhutto began his political career as Pakistan's Commerce Minister in 1958. In 1966, ready to launch his own political ideas, Bhutto formed the **Pakistan People's Party (PPP)** with an agenda that combined Islam with socialism. In the 1970 general elections the PPP won a large majority in West Pakistan but failed to reach an agreement with Sheikh

Mujibur **Rahman**, the majority winner of East Pakistan, leading to the 1971 war that resulted in the formation of Bangladesh. Bhutto was installed as martial law administrator and President and, through shrewd bargaining, is credited with having held his ground over the **Simla Agreement** of 1972, in which he refused to commit himself, in writing, to recognizing the **Line of Control (LoC)** as an international border.

Bhutto's programme of nationalization in 1972–77 and his attempts to concentrate power in the hands of the Prime Minister, following the new 1973 Constitution and his own installation as Prime Minister, gradually lost him allies. Announcing general and provincial elections in 1977, Bhutto and the PPP were ultimately accused by the opposing **Pakistan National Alliance (PNA)** of electoral fraud, triggering a mass protest movement and a military coup by Gen. **Zia** ul-Haq, who imposed martial law. Bhutto was subsequently arrested on charges of authorizing the murder of a political opponent. Following a two-year trial, Bhutto was found guilty and hanged on 4 April 1979.

Bihar

Located in northern India, Bihar shares an international border with Nepal. The state of Bihar was formed soon after India's independence in 1947 with Patna as the state capital. In 1956, in accordance with linguistic reorganization of the states, land was transferred to **West Bengal** along the south-eastern border, and in 2000 the mineral-rich state of **Jharkhand** was carved out of Bihar's southern forest regions. In 2001 Bihar's population was recorded at 82,998,509 making it the third most populous state in the Union. Bihar's population is overwhelmingly Hindi-speaking, Hindu by religion (83.2% of the total population, according to the 2001 census) and largely rural. Bihar is the poorest state in the Union, a result of maladministration, inter-caste and *communal* conflict (the state recorded the lowest literacy rate in the country in 2001). Agriculture is the mainstay of the population. Bihar has a bicameral legislature with a state assembly of 243 seats and the state returns 40 members to the **Lok Sabha**. In the 1989 Lok Sabha elections, the Janata Dal (JD), marking the rise of a powerful backward caste movement, displaced the **Congress** party from Bihar's state government. Its success was confirmed by a number of elections in the 1990s accompanied by the emergence of party supremo, Lalu Prasad Yadav. His break with the JD in 1997 to form his own **Rashtriya Janata Dal (RJD)** created a new force in state politics, targeting the disadvantaged sections of Bihar's population, principally Muslims and Yadavs (a backward Hindu caste). Under Yadav's leadership, the RJD established itself as the largest party in the 2000 assembly elections, winning 124 seats of the assembly's 324 seats in undivided Bihar, with the **Bharatiya Janata Party (BJP)** emerging as the largest opposition party. Since then the RJD has aligned itself with the Congress, projecting the alliance as a secular front against the BJP and **Janata Dal—United (JD—U)** alliance (which dates from the mid-1990s). Despite corruption charges, extensive investigation by the Central Bureau of Investigation (CBI), dismissal from office, prison sentences and a notable deterioration in law and order under his rule, Yadav's charisma and following amongst the poor have endured. In the 2004 general elections the RJD emerged as a key ally of the Congress, having won 22 Lok Sabha seats, earning Yadav the position of Minister of Railways. However, state elections in February 2005 produced a hung assembly and the imposition of President's Rule. Smaller forces, such as the fledgling **Lok Jan Shakti Party (LJSP)** with its **Dalit** platform (*see* '**Untouchables**'), were able to erode the electoral base of both the RJD and JD—U. In elections held in October 2005 the JDU, in alliance with the BJP, won 143 seats in the 243-member assembly.

Biju Janata Dal (BJD)

The Biju Janata Dal (BJD) is a regional party in the Indian state of **Orissa** led by Naveen Patnaik (party president and Chief Minister of Orissa). It is an offshoot of the Janata Dal, an ally of the **Bharatiya Janata Party (BJP)** and part of the opposition **National Democratic Alliance (NDA)**. It won 11 seats in the 14th **Lok Sabha** in 2004.

Bikalpa Dhara Bangladesh (BDB)

The Bikalpa Dhara Bangladesh (BDB) is a political party in Bangladesh, founded in 2004, and led by Prof. Badruddoza Chowdhury. Its main aims are to combat terrorism, corruption and poverty. It expressed its solidarity with the current **Fourteen-Party Opposition Movement** and is involved in various campaigns against the ruling **Four-Party Alliance**.

Biraderi System

Biraderi, literally meaning 'brotherhood', describes tribal networks or an extended clan based on allegiance and solidarity in Pakistan. Providing an extended social network for co-operation and assistance for the individual, it also includes personal commitment and constraints. Being an identity- and solidarity-forming schema, the *biraderi* system can partly be compared to the Hindu **caste system**.

Birendra, King

Birendra Bir Bikram Shah Dev (1945–2001), son of King **Mahendra** (1920–72), was crowned in February 1972 and ruled Nepal as king until his death in 2001. Educated at premier institutes in India, the United Kingdom, Japan, and the USA, King Birendra ruled absolutely for 18 years until the people's movement of 1990 challenged his regime. On 8 April 1990 he ended the (almost) 30-year ban on political parties and gradually, over the following months, a multi-party system emerged, the ***Panchayat* system** was dissolved, and the king's status was effectively reduced to that of a constitutional monarch. King Birendra suffered an unexpected and violent death when, according to official accounts, he and most of his family, including his wife Queen Aiswarya, were killed by his eldest son and heir, Prince Dipendra, in an apparent murder-suicide. (*See* **Jana Andolan**.)

Bodoland Movement

The Bodos, a plains tribe who were amongst the earliest settlers in the Indian state of Assam (*see* **North East India**), initiated a movement protesting against the dispossession of their land by Bengali and Assamese settlers. In the late 1980s their demands extended to a separate Bodoland and in 1988 the **National Democratic Front of Bodoland (NDFB)** was founded to initiate a guerrilla war. In February 1993 the Indian government managed to broker a 'Bodo Accord' and in 2003 negotiations led to the creation of an elected Bodoland territorial council, comprising areas of lower Assam. In May 2005 a cease-fire was signed between the government and the NDFB, a breakthrough agreement after two decades of insurgency.

Bofors Scandal

The Bofors Scandal erupted in India in 1987 when a Swedish radio channel claimed that a Swedish arms company, Bofors, had paid millions of dollars in bribes to secure a US $1,400m. sale of howitzer guns to the Indian army. Creating political uproar in India, the Bofors Scandal came to symbolize political corruption, tarnishing then Prime Minister Rajiv Gandhi's image and contributing to the defeat of his party in the 1989 general elections. Investigations into the Bofors case have been slow, with the Central Bureau of Investigation charging various high-profile politicians and international businessmen. Although Rajiv Gandhi himself was also suspected of having received bribes, his name was cleared in early 2004 when the Delhi High Court ruled that there was no evidence of his personal involvement.

Bombay Stock Exchange (BSE)

The Stock Exchange in **Mumbai**, known as the Bombay Stock Exchange (BSE) and listing more than 3,500 companies, is the largest of India's more than 20 stock exchanges. Established in 1875 as 'The Native Share and Stock Brokers Association', it is older than its counterpart in Tokyo and is also one of Asia's oldest stock exchanges. The average number of daily trades in the financial year 2004–05 was around 1m., giving it one of the highest hourly rates of trading in the world. The average daily turnover of the Exchange during the above period was around US $463m. The BSE 'Sensex' is the widely used market index for the BSE.

Border Security Force (BSF)

Established in 1965, India's Border Security Force (BSF) is responsible for protecting the country's 15,106.7 km of land border running through 92 districts in 17 states. The BSF is one of seven central police forces under the Union government.

Buddhist Movement (Sri Lanka)

Sri Lanka is the oldest continually Buddhist country, Theravada Buddhism being the major religion in the island since its official introduction in the second century BC. Nearly 70% of the country's population are followers of Buddhism while 15.5% are Hindus. The Constitution accords Buddhism the 'foremost place', but stops short of recognizing it as the state religion. There is a Ministry of Buddha Sasana and Religious Affairs. The Buddhist clergy is a powerful element in Sri Lankan politics and all mainstream Sinhalese-majority political groups have a band of Buddhist monks loyal to them. Even the Marxist **Janatha Vimukhti Peramuna (JVP)** or People's Liberation Front, has its Buddhist supporters. Two failed armed uprisings by the JVP in 1971 and 1987 had the backing of monks. Religion has tended not to play a significant role in the civil conflict, which is essentially rooted in linguistic, ethnic and political difference, but in September 1959 a Buddhist monk shot dead the then Prime Minister Solomon **Bandaranaike**, as he moved to offer concessions to the Tamils. In 2004 the world's first all-clergy party of Buddhist monks, the **Jathika Hela Urumaya (JHU)** or National Heritage Party, contested parliamentary elections, unexpectedly winning nine seats. A potential new source of instability for the coalition government, the JHU campaigned on the promise of establishing a *Dharmarajya* (the ideal Buddhist state) in Sri Lanka, drawing support from urban, middle-class voters disenchanted with mainstream Sinhala parties. (*See* **Patriotic National Movement (PNM)**.)

Bullock Capitalists

The concept of Bullock Capitalism (a term coined by the academics Rudolph and Rudolph) provides a dynamic link between the traditional and the modern sectors of the Indian economy. Bullock capitalists are small-scale, self-employed, substantial family farmers and possess considerable social and economic heterogeneity. Politically, the ubiquitous bullock capitalists present themselves as opponents of both industrial capital and the urban sector in the name of remunerative prices and better terms of trade between the countryside and the city. Their presence serves to articulate agrarian politics in sectoral rather than class terms and provides a dynamic link between the legitimacy of the state and expansion of the rural economy. The bullock capitalists became a dominant class in the Indian countryside in the 1960s following the success of the **Green Revolution**. The vast rank of bullock capitalists is a powerful indicator of both the vitality of the process of capital formation in the countryside and the effectiveness of social limits to the growth of predatory capitalism.

C

Caretaker Government (Bangladesh)

The term caretaker government refers, in the context of Bangladeshi politics, to a neutral, non-partisan and non-party interim government responsible for ensuring free, fair and impartial general elections after a parliament's mandate ends and to supervise during the election period. To provide the caretaker government with the necessary legitimacy, the 13th amendment to the Constitution was passed on 26 March 1996. According to this, such a government must take office within 15 days of the dissolution of parliament and it must organize general elections within 90 days of the dissolution as well as giving the Election Commission all the support necessary for holding free and fair parliamentary elections. The caretaker government consists of a Chief Adviser at its head and not more than 10 other advisers, all appointed by the President to whom it is also collectively responsible. The Chief Adviser is usually the most recent retired Chief Justice, who functions as Prime Minister. The temporary government exercises executive powers until a new Prime Minister has been appointed and his regular Cabinet formed. However, it is not empowered to make any policy decision that lies beyond the electoral remit or which may influence the election results, except to run the necessary day-to-day administration and ordinary routine procedures of governance. Under this constitutional framework two caretaker governments have so far been installed, one in 1996 and a second in 2001.

Caste System

India's local castes, or ***jatis***, are the basic social units that still govern marriages, social networks, food taboos and rituals in the country. There are more than 2,000 *jatis*, traditionally divided into four hierarchically ranked broad categories called *varnas*, namely, the Brahmins who performed the traditional function of priests, the Kshatriyas, who were the rulers and the warriors, the Vaisyas, who were the mercantile classes, and the Sudras, who were the service groups, agriculturalists and artisans. The '**untouchables**', so called because of the polluting functions, such as scavenging, which they traditionally performed, were an integrated part of Indian society but were considered to be impure and were not even part of the formal *varna* system.

Traditionally, the caste system presupposed the interdependent relationship of occupational groups, referred to as the ***Jajmani* system**, within which *jatis* were linked to one another through ties of reciprocal economic, social and political obligations. The relationship of the lower castes to the high-caste landowners, for example, was hereditary, but their dependent status entailed certain rights, such as a share of the harvest. The system was meant, however, to emphasize social hierarchy and inequalities of power, wealth and status. These oppressive aspects of the caste system have been increasingly contested through social movements, legislation as well as electoral mobilization, particularly in the case of the former 'untouchables', who by constitutional requirement are beneficiaries of reserved jobs in public services as well as educational institutions. Many Indians see the caste system as the cause of India's social fragmentation and economic backwardness, but for a vast number castes are the only basis of identity and social interaction. Interestingly, democracy and economic growth seem to have engendered a new 'political caste' that is regarded as an instrument for the promotion of collective interest by social groups that form caste associations and political linkages with competing parties for that purpose. By becoming an instrument of both the citizen and the politician, caste has taken on a new role of raising consciousness, in the process undermining the ideological basis of social hierarchy and the more odious aspects of caste domination. (*See* **Affirmative Action**.)

Centre of Indian Trade Unions (CITU)

Established in 1970 in Calcutta (today Kolkata), the Centre of Indian Trade Unions (CITU) is today one of the five largest central trade union organizations of India. Politically, it is affiliated with the **Communist Party of India—Marxist** and rooted in a militant strain of the trade union movement based on the concept of class struggle.

Chakari

Originally a concept in Hinduism meaning to wait upon, serve, appease or to seek a favour from a god, in Nepal the contemporary practice of *chakari* describes the offering of gifts and services. Like ***aphno manchhe***, *chakari* functions to facilitate decision-making and to counter the high transaction costs of Nepal's bureaucracy.

Chand, Lokendra Bahadur

Appointed by King **Gyanendra** as Prime Minister of Nepal on 11 October 2002 after the elected government under the **Nepali Congress** was dismissed. A palace loyalist, Lokendra Bahadur Chand accepted the position for the fourth time. In 1997 Chand was Prime Minister for two years as part of a coalition government, representing his party, the **Rashtriya Prajatantra Party (RPP)**. Chand was forced to resign in mid-2003, amid protests by opposition parties that his appointment had been unconstitutional and growing Maoist violence.

Chandigarh

Designed in the 1950s to be a model town for the newly independent state of India, Chandigarh was constituted as a **Union Territory** in 1966 to serve as capital city to both the states of **Haryana** and **Punjab**. The city was to be transferred to Punjab in 1986 but disagreement over the territories to be given to Haryana in return indefinitely delayed the process. As a Union Territory, Chandigarh has no legislature and is the responsibility of the Ministry of Home Affairs. It returns one member to the **Lok Sabha**, which has been held since 1991 by the **Indian National Congress (INC)**.

Chhattisgarh

Part of **Madhya Pradesh** until November 2000, the Indian state of Chhattisgarh is located in the central region, with its capital in Raipur. Hindi is the most widely spoken language and the main local language is Chhattisgarhi. In 2001 Chhattisgarh had a population of 20,833,803, one-third of it comprising tribes and a significant proportion coming from the **Scheduled Castes**. The state's main religion is Hinduism and there are also small communities of Muslims and Christians. Agriculture is the most important sector of the economy but the mining industry of the state produces an essential supply of minerals and ores for the rest of the country. The state assembly has 90 seats and Chhattisgarh returns 11 members to the **Lok Sabha**. Demands for a separate state based on regional distinctiveness date back to the mid-1920s. A separatist movement emerged in the 1970s, but it was only in the late 1990s that both the **Congress** and the **Bharatiya Janata Party (BJP)** recognized the claim. Initially a Congress-held state, organizational weakness in the party, together with the presence of the **Nationalist Congress Party (NCP)**, which split the votes, enabled the BJP to win 52 of the 90 state assembly seats in the 2003 state election. The BJP's ascendancy in the state was confirmed in the 2004 parliamentary elections in which it won 10 Lok Sabha seats. In addition to capitalizing on dissatisfaction with the performance of the Congress in the state's first government, the BJP has also managed to make inroads into tribal areas through extensive grassroots activism conducted by the **Rashtriya Swayamsevak Sangh** in the form of providing schooling and health services and reconversion programmes aimed at bringing back to Hinduism tribals who were converted to Christianity by missionaries.

Chhetris

Among Nepal's numerous castes and ethnic groups are the Chhetris in the hill areas who, after the Brahmins (**Bahun**) and together with the Thakuris, are upper castes.

Together these groups dominate positions of power and leadership including the police force, the civil service, the army, judiciary, education system and media, despite constituting only 30% of Nepal's population.

Chhoesi

The term *Chhoesi* is used in Bhutan to refer to a dual system of government that prevailed from 1650 to 1907, comprising a temporal head (*Druk Desi*) and a religious leader (***Je Khenpo***) as the leading institutions of the country's socio-political system. It was established by Ngawang **Namgyal** and is recognized as a significant landmark in the genesis of Bhutan's structure of governance. Various aspects of the *Chhoesi* still exist and continue to play a significant role in the country's development process. (*See* ***Dratshang***; **Council for Ecclesiastical Affairs (*Dratshang Lhentshog*)**.)

Chimi

A term used in Bhutan to refer to an elected member of the National Assembly. The *chimi* is elected through direct popular consensus at the district level. The number of seats from each district depends on the size of the population.

Chipko Movement

A social movement in northern India, the Chipko Movement fought for the protection of the Himalayan forests. Based on Gandhian principles, the movement used strategies of non-violent protest and attracted attention with its tactic of village women hugging trees to prevent them from being chopped down. The first protest action took place in April 1973 and the movement had its major success in 1980 when it secured a 15-year ban on 'green felling' in the Himalayan Forests of **Uttar Pradesh**. The movement, pioneered and publicized effectively by successful leaders such as Sundarlal Bahuguna, was the first of its kind to gain nation-wide attention and followers. It was also crucial in highlighting the need for an environmental policy that addressed people's needs as well as the protection of natural resources. (*See* **Gandhi**, Mohandas Karamchand.)

Chipon

The term *chipon* refers to an elected village co-ordinator, functionary, or representative in Bhutan. This institution, an essential constituent of the Block Development Committee, plays an important role in integrating the Bhutanese into the political as well as development process. The *chipon* has to fulfil various legal and administrative functions, making it an important interface not only between district and village but also between the state and society. (*See* ***Gup***.)

Chittagong Hill Tracts (CHT) Conflict

The Chittagong Hill Tracts (CHT) conflict is rooted in a confrontation between the Muslim majority and non-Muslim tribal minority, which has increasingly felt politically and economically marginalized within Bangladesh. This perceived marginalization resulted in a separate identity, a claim to regional autonomy and a militant movement. The CHT is an extensive hill area of some 13,000 sq km that constitutes around 10% of Bangladesh's territory. Located in the south east, the CHT borders Myanmar as well as the Indian states of Tripura and Mizoram (*see* **North East India**). In addition to its rich natural resources (especially of natural gas, coal and copper) and its geostrategic position, this socially, politically and economically underdeveloped area is of special concern to the national government due to the numerous tribes who live in it. With 13 different tribes (the Chakmas and the Marmas being the largest), various state economic policies have led to the displacement of these indigenous tribal populations and the disruption of their livelihoods by, for example, prohibiting access to forest areas, declared as reserve forests. The feeling of oppression was enforced by the increasing number of non-tribal people encouraged by the government to settle in the CHT, causing shortages of cultivable land. Demands for improved socio-economic conditions as well as for more political autonomy by these tribal groups can be traced back to pre-independence days. They have been fighting since the mid-1970s, with the help of the **Shanti Bahini**, against the resettlement of immigrants from the plains in the CHT. Three issues are at the core of the conflict: the autonomy of the CHT, the withdrawal of settlers from outside, and the demilitarization of the area. Since the 'CHT Treaty' of 1997 between the Jana Sanghati Parishad and the government of Bangladesh, there has been a cease-fire and an ongoing peace process. Nevertheless, sporadic violent incidents continue to be reported.

Choudhury, Badruddoza

Dr Badruddoza Choudhury (1932–), President of Bangladesh from 2001 until 2002, resigned at the request of the ruling **Bangladesh Nationalist Party (BNP)** owing to his failure to pay respects to the party's founder, Ziaur **Rahman**, on the anniversary of his death. Having entered politics in 1979, for decades Choudhury had been an influential figure in the BNP, having been its founding secretary-general, an education minister and foreign minister. Following his resignation Choudhury became one of BNP's harshest critics, launching a new political party, named **Bikalpa Dhara Bangladesh**, in 2004.

Comilla Model – *see* Bangladesh Academy for Rural Development (BARD)

Communist Party of Bangladesh (CPB)

The Communist Party of Bangladesh (CPB) was founded in 1968 by Moni **Singh** as an independent party, the East Pakistan wing of the Communist Party of Pakistan. It originated as a regional branch committee of the Communist Party of undivided India, which was established in 1920, at Tashkent. The current president and general secretary of the CPB are, respectively, Monjurul Ahasan Khan and Mujahid ul-Islam Selim. The party is part of the opposition **Eleven-Party Alliance**. The youth organization of the CPB is the Bangladesh Youth Union, and the students' organization is the Bangladesh Students Union.

Communist Party of India (CPI)

The Communist Party of India (CPI) is a national political party with strongholds in the Indian states of **West Bengal** and **Kerala**. The party was founded on 26 December 1925 with the main objective of creating an alternative mass organization to the independence movement led by the **Indian National Congress (INC)** and headed by Mohandas Karamchand **Gandhi**. The party split in 1964 when a faction broke away under the name of the **Communist Party of India—Marxist (CPI—M)**.

In recent years the party has shifted from an anti- to a pro-Congress position. Today the CPI as a national party is part of various regional alliances: in Kerala it is part of the **Left Democratic Front (LDF)** and in **Tamil Nadu**, part of the Progressive Democratic Alliance (PDA). As a part of the **Left Front** in Tripura and **West Bengal** it is supporting the ruling **United Progressive Alliance (UPA)** with the INC as its main constituent, but without forming part of the government. Currently the party is led by A. B. Bardhan. It won 10 seats in the 14th **Lok Sabha** elections in 2004.

Communist Party of India—Marxist (CPI—M)

The Communist Party of India—Marxist (CPI—M) has its main support in the states of **West Bengal**, Tripura (*see* **North East India**) and **Kerala**. The party emerged out of a split in the **Communist Party of India (CPI)** in 1964, when the left faction organized itself as a party and Jyoti **Basu** became a prominent leader of the CPI—M. Despite the fall of communism and the demise of many communist parties around the globe, the CPI—M still plays an important role in the electoral and political landscape of Indian democracy. As a vocal and influential component of the opposition in the parliament, the CPI—M, with some of its allied trade unions, articulated a vital part of the spectrum of political opinion throughout the 1990s. Moreover, in some of India's federal states, the CPI—M has been the governing party for long periods post-independence, the most notable case being the large state of West Bengal where it famously represents the world's longest serving democratically elected communist government. Party ideologists have had to come to terms with multiculturalism, democracy and liberalization of the economy in India. While the CPI—M has shown great flexibility in dealing with the contradictions between communist ideology and the forces of *realpolitik*, documentary evidence shows that these issues are rigorously debated within the party. In order to sustain its parliamentary communism, the party has made deliberate efforts to broaden the social base of its membership. Following the 2004 general elections in which the CPI—M won 43 seats and emerged as the third largest party in the parliament, it declined an invitation to join the government at the centre, choosing instead to support the ruling **United Progressive Alliance (UPA)** from outside.

Communist Party of Nepal (CPN)

Formed in 1949 by exiled leaders in India as the Nepal Communist Party (NCP), by which name it is also still known. Numerous communist factions and splinter groups have emerged since, a result of personal differences amongst party leaders as well as disputes within the international communist movement. Even during the party-less ***Panchayat* system** between 1960 and 1990, communist activists maintained their base of support amongst peasants, workers and the poor. Influenced by the **Naxalite Movement** led by Charu Majumdar and Kanu Sanyal in the neighbouring Darjeeling district of India and inspired by Mao's Cultural Revolution, radical ideas entered south-east Nepal in the late 1960s, leading to the formation of a number of Maoist splinter groups of the NCP.

The United Left Front, a loose union of seven communist groups, organized the **Jana Andolan** for the restoration of multi-party democracy together with the **Nepali Congress** in early 1990. The two leading constituents of the United Left Front, the Communist Party of Nepal (Marxist-Leninist) and the Nepal Communist Party (Marxist) joined in early 1991 under the name **Communist Party of Nepal—Unified Marxist-Leninist (CPN—UPL)** to make significant gains in the 1991 parliamentary elections and emerge as the second largest political party in Nepal under the leadership of its president, Man Mohan **Adhikari**. More radical communist groups with Maoist orientations formed an election platform as the United People's Front Nepal (UPFN) and became the third strongest party in the 1991 elections. The split of this radical front in 1993 and rejection of the remaining UPFN group around Dr Baburam **Bhattarai** as a contestant party for the 1994 elections, led to the formation of the **Communist Party of Nepal—Maoist** that started a militant insurgency against the Nepali state in early 1996. The share of votes for the CPN—UPL grew steadily during the 1990s. The party won the local elections of 1997 with an absolute majority. Only a prior split of the party prevented it from becoming the leading political party in the 1999 parliamentary elections, with an absolute majority of seats and a relative majority of votes. Both factions of the party rejoined in 2002. (*See* **People's War**.)

Communist Party of Nepal—Maoist (CPN—M)

One of several splinter groups from the **Communist Party of Nepal (CPN)**, the Communist Party of Nepal—Maoist (CPN—M) was formed in mid-1994 under the leadership of Pushpa Kamal Dahal, referred to as **Comrade Prachanda**. The party claims allegiance to the ideals of the Chinese Cultural Revolution. After the downfall of the **Adhikari** government in 1995 and government action against Maoist forces in western Nepal, the CPN—M launched on 12 February 1996 a **People's War** aimed at overthrowing the monarchy and replacing it with a new people's republic. Dr Baburam **Bhattarai** emerged as a spokesman of the party, leading it in the failed cease-fire negotiations with the government in 2003. In 2003 the US Department of State placed the CPN—M on its list of terrorist organizations.

Communist Party of Nepal—Unified Marxist-Leninist (CPN—UML)

Also known simply as Unified Marxist-Leninist (UML) and Nepal Communist Party. Emerging in the aftermath of the **Jana Andolan**, the CPN—UML was the result of a merger between two principal communist groups, the Communist Party of Nepal—Marxist and the CPN—Marxist-Leninist, just four months ahead of the May 1991 elections. Like Nepal's other communist groups, both parties claimed to be the true heirs to the original **Communist Party of Nepal** founded in Calcutta in 1949 by a former **Nepali Congress** secretary.

Under the leadership of Man Mohan **Adhikari** the party emerged from the 1991 elections as the main opposition force in parliament with 69 seats, winning decisively in the eastern hill districts and the **Tarai** region. In the 1994 elections, the UML, with 88 of the 205 seats in the *Pratinidhi Sabha*, the house of representatives, emerged as the largest party. Opting to form a minority government under Prime Minister Adhikari, the UML was in power for just nine months, during which it committed itself to more moderate policies than its radical election pledges. Nevertheless, an ambitious 'Build Your Own Village' campaign was launched to increase decision-making power at the community level in development programmes and a commission was formed to investigate the land reform issue. In response, opposition parties accused the UML of using populist policies to garner more votes, culminating in a vote of 'no confidence' on 10 September 1995 in which the UML was defeated.

Divided internally between the ideological purists and the less radical, more pragmatic members of the party, the UML ultimately split in 1998 when about half of the party's parliamentary deputies formed a breakaway faction, the CPN—Marxist-Leninist. As a result the UML obtained 71 seats in the 1999 elections. Without the split the CPN—UML would have quite likely won an overwhelming absolute majority of seats and, also, a clear majority of votes.

Comprehensive Test Ban Treaty (CTBT)

Initially proposed during the 1950s, the 'big five' nuclear powers—the USA, Russia, China, the United Kingdom and France—backed talks leading to the creation of the Comprehensive Test Ban Treaty (CTBT) at the United Nations in September 1996. The treaty aims to ban all nuclear explosions but cannot be enforced until 44 individually-named states, known or believed to have nuclear reactors capable of making material required for a nuclear bomb, have ratified it in their own legislatures. To date, 33 of these states have complied. Among the significant nuclear states that have refrained from ratifying the CTBT are Pakistan and India. (*See* **Nuclearization**.)

Comrade Prachanda (Pushpa Kamal Dahal)

Commonly known as Chairman or Comrade Prachanda, Pushpa Kamal Dahal is the leader of the **Communist Party of Nepal—Maoist (CPN—M)**. Having spent his early years in western Nepal, Prachanda became politically active in the early 1970s when a communist uprising in the south-easternmost district of Nepal occurred under the influence of the **Naxalite Movement** in neighbouring India. By the mid-1980s Prachanda and Dr Baburam **Bhattarai** had emerged as the two key Maoist leaders. On 4 February 1996 the **Nepali Congress**-led coalition government was presented with a list of 40 demands related to 'nationalism, democracy and livelihood' and an ultimatum threatening civil war if these were not met. (*See* **People's War**.)

Confederation of Indian Industries (CII)

The Confederation of Indian Industries (CII), originally founded in the city of Calcutta (Kolkata) as the 'Engineering and Iron Trades Association' in 1895, is a prestigious corporate association in India. Since liberalization of the Indian economy, CII has been the most visible business association in India with more than 4,700 member companies, a vibrant network of 35 offices in India, 11 overseas and institutional partnerships with 216 organizations in 94 countries.

Confidence-building Measures (CBMs)

Confidence-building measures (CBMs) are the collective or unilateral action of states aimed at increasing the transparency and predictability of another state's behaviour in the area of concern. These measures can be military, diplomatic, economic and cultural. In the case of India–Pakistan rivalry, CBMs have been of paramount importance, especially after the overt declaration of nuclear capabilities in 1998 and the almost year-long standstill on the brink of war in 2001–02. Both countries have a long history of CBM creation but a poor record of implementation.

Recognizing their precarious positions, both have, since 2002, tried to enlarge the scope of existing CBMs in order to reduce the likelihood of an accidental nuclear conflict, and to present themselves as responsible nuclear powers in the international community. There is also a growing realization in both governments that no stable solution is possible without popular support in both countries. As a result, CBMs to ensure and improve people-to-people contact, such as the Srinagar–Muzaffarabad bus service for public travel and a truck service for trade, have been given high priority. Similar bus services for the Lahore–Amritsar, Nankana sahib–Amritsar and Poonch–Rawalakot routes and a railway link between the state of **Rajasthan** in India and the province of **Sind** in Pakistan are being explored. Another important measure under consideration is the establishment of meeting points across the **Line of Control (LoC)** for divided families of Kashmir. (*See* **Kashmir Dispute**.)

Among military CBMs, the more important include finalizing an agreement on the pre-notification of ballistic missile tests, a nuclear hotline between foreign secretaries of both countries, a hotline connection between the Director General Military Operations (DGMOs) to reduce chances of misunderstanding over each other's military movements, prior notification of military exercises at specified locations, especially those in the vicinity of the LOC, an agreement of no attack on each other's nuclear facilities, and a bilateral accord on prohibiting the development, production and use of chemical weapons. An initial agreement on a prospective gas pipeline running from Iran to India via Pakistan was hailed as a landmark in the politico-economic history of the hostile neighbours. Other CBMs under development are communication links between the Pakistan Maritime Security Agency and the Indian Coast Guards, a bilateral air services agreement and a shipping protocol.

Congress – *see* Indian National Congress

Congress System

'Congress System' refers to the main conceptual and analytical features of India's system of one-party dominance in 1947–67. In this period there was uninterrupted rule by the **Indian National Congress**, both in the central government as well as in the constituent states of the union, except for a brief interlude of communist rule in **Kerala** in 1957–59. Non-Congress parties of the Left and Right had full freedom to operate during this period but they functioned more as parties of pressure than as alternatives to the Congress as ruling parties. The period came to an end after the fourth general election of 1967, when broad-based, anti-Congress coalitions were formed which reduced the strength of the Congress in the centre and replaced it as the party in power in some states.

Council for Ecclesiastical Affairs (*Dratshang Lhentshog*)

Bhutan's ***Dratshang*** Lhentshog, which was founded in 1984 by the royal government to replace the Central Board for Monastic Studies, operates as a kind of apex organization for various centres, schools and religious bodies. In addition to enforcing the state's control over the religious sphere, the institution aims to conserve Buddhism as the state religion and to ensure its influence during the process of socio-economic and political transformation.

D

Dadra and Nagar Haveli

Located on the west coast of India, Dadra and Nagar Haveli are two enclaves which formerly belonged to Portugal. Acquired by India in 1954, they became a **Union Territory** in 1961 when other Portuguese domains were incorporated. The population in 2001 was recorded at 220,490 of which a large part were registered as tribals. A majority of the people are Hindu (93.5% in 2001), while there are also small Muslim and Christian communities. The territory remains largely underdeveloped, agriculture being the principal economic activity. Major water projects have aided irrigation but have also caused some villages to become submerged.

Dalit

Dalit may be translated from Hindi as 'crushed' or 'oppressed' and refers to a person who falls outside the four *varnas* of the Hindu **caste system** and is considered to be below them. Typical occupational groups that fell into this category included leather-workers, scavengers, poor farmers and labourers. Traditionally this meant, for example, that Dalits were forbidden to worship in temples or to draw water from the same wells as caste Hindus.

Other terms have been used to refer to Dalits, including ***Harijan***, which was coined by *Mahatma* **Gandhi**, and 'untouchable', the use of which is now banned under the Constitution of India. Dalits themselves are not a single identifiable race or caste and can be divided into various subcastes with their own hierarchical order. Following independence and as a result largely of **Ambedkar**'s efforts, a **reservation policy** was introduced to ensure that Dalits would obtain a proportionate political voice. A successful Dalit movement burgeoned in the 1990s when a Dalit identity served as a basis for political mobilization and parties, particularly in the states of **Bihar** and **Uttar Pradesh**.

Daman and Diu

Two enclaves on the north-western coast of India, Daman and Diu became a **Union Territory** in 1961. Following a military operation to 'liberate' the territories under Portuguese rule, Daman and Diu were at first administered together with **Goa**, which became a separate state in 1987. The population in 2001 was enumerated at 158,204, including Hindus (89.7%), Muslim (7.8%) and Christian (2.1%) minorities, and others. The language and culture of the enclaves are largely Gujarati and the territory is primarily dependent on fishing and tourism.

Delhi

Located in northern India, the National Capital Territory (NCT) of Delhi is almost entirely surrounded by the state of **Haryana**, except on the east where it borders **Uttar Pradesh**. Under the British, the administrative capital of India was shifted in 1911 from Calcutta (now Kolkata) to Delhi, where a new administrative capital—'New Delhi'—was constructed in 1931. The city's strategic importance, for the British and earlier rulers, was its location on the main route from the north west into the Gangetic heartland of North India. Delhi remained the capital of independent India, becoming a Union Territory in 1956. With the aim of preventing the national capital from becoming a political arena, Delhi was given the municipal corporation of Delhi as its only representative institution. In 1966 this was supplemented by a metropolitan council. Demands for statehood increased during the late 1980s, resulting in the compromise of semi-statehood, granted by the 69th Amendment Act of 1991. This created the national capital territory under which Delhi was given special status, and its own legislature. Under the new territorial arrangement, Delhi has a legislative assembly of 70 seats and returns seven members to the **Lok Sabha**.

Pre-**Partition** Delhi was a predominantly Muslim city. Following independence and Partition in 1947 there was a large-scale exchange of populations between India and Pakistan, one of the results of which was that Delhi became a largely Hindu city, full of refugees from the old **Punjab**. According to the 2001 census the main religious groups are Hindus (82.0%), Muslims (11.7%) and Sikhs (4.0%). The population of the NCT was recorded at 13,850,507 in 2001. Delhi is the most urbanized of states and territories in India, with 93.2% of its population (as enumerated in 2001) classified as urban. The city of Delhi, also the capital of the NCT, is the country's second largest and is a major commercial, financial and industrial hub, attracting migrant workers, particularly from neighbouring Haryana and Uttar Pradesh. Services are the largest component of the economy, contributing about 77% to net domestic product in 2001/02. Elections for Delhi as an NCT were held for the first time in 1993 and were won by the **Bharatiya Janata Party (BJP)**, which took 49 seats. However, in the 2003 assembly elections the **Indian National Congress** secured an absolute majority, winning 47 of the 70 seats. Bolstering this was the performance of the Congress in the 2004 general elections, in which it won all but one of Delhi's Lok Sabha seats, an overwhelming reversal of fortune for the BJP which had held all seven parliamentary seats after the 1999 general elections. The erosion of the BJP's position is partly attributed to factionalism within the party, dissatisfaction amongst migrant workers (a large constituency in Delhi's electorate), who had not benefited from the **National Democratic Alliance**'s **(NDA)** economic policies, as well as the BJP's decision to field candidates who were sitting MPs and vulnerable to an anti-incumbency vote. At the same time, the Congress government, led by Chief Minister Shiela Dixit since 1998, has proven highly popular, tackling a number of 'good governance' issues that have long plagued Delhi residents, including public transport, water and electricity supply, law and order, pollution and unauthorized dwellings.

Democracy Day

Celebrated around 18 February in Nepal (the exact date varies according to solar and lunar calendars), 'democracy day' commemorates the return of King **Tribhuvan** from exile to Nepal in 1950 and the Delhi compromise which brought about the end of the Rana system and ushered in an interim government. Tribhuvan promised to introduce a democratic system and to hold elections for a constituent assembly within two years, neither of which happened. Nevertheless the day has great symbolic value in Nepal.

Democratic Action Committee (DAC)

In January 1969, several opposition parties in Pakistan formed the Democratic Action Committee (DAC) and launched an agitation against the military regime of Ayub **Khan**. The alliance was headed by Nawabzada Nasrullah Khan and was directed towards restoring democracy in Pakistan.

Democratic Progressive Alliance (DPA)

The Democratic Progressive Alliance (DPA) is a multi-party alliance in the south Indian state of **Tamil Nadu** and was formed by the **Dravida Munnetra Kazhagam (DMK)**, under the leadership of its president, M. Karunanidhi, to contest the 2004 general elections, in which it won all 39 **Lok Sabha** seats. The DMK was a former constituent of the **National Democratic Alliance (NDA)**. After various disputes over the NDA's Common Minimum Programme, e.g. the anti-conversion Act of the Tamil Nadu government in 2002, the DMK and some other parties withdrew from the NDA to create the DPA which then became a constituent of the ruling **United Progressive Alliance (UPA)** at the national level. The DPA includes the **Congress**, the **Marumalarchi Dravida Munnetra Kazhagam (MDMK)**, the **Pattali Makkal Katchi (PMK)**, the **Communist Party of India—Marxist**, the **Communist Party of India (CPI)** and the Indian Union Muslim League (IUML).

Dhaka Stock Exchange Ltd (DSE)

The Dhaka Stock Exchange Ltd (DSE) came into operation on 28 April 1954 as the East Pakistan Stock Exchange Association Ltd. It was renamed in 1962 as the East Pakistan Stock Exchange Ltd, and again, in 1964, as the DSE Ltd. It formally commenced trading in 1956 with an authorized capital of Rs. 300,000 and divided into 150 shares. In February 2006 there were 267 listed issues (companies and debentures) and market capitalization was around US $1,671m. The DSE gained momentum under the government's policy of liberalization, and the attraction of foreign investment by permitting non-residents to invest freely in Bangladesh via this capital market. A second stock exchange in operation is the Chittagong Stock Exchange.

Dharma

The term *dharma* is one of the key concepts of religions such as Hinduism, Buddhism or Jainism which have their origins in India. Common translations render it as 'right way of living', 'divine law', 'path of righteousness', 'natural harmony', 'order', 'duty' or 'obligations', among others. However, *dharma* can have various meanings. In Hinduism, *dharma* (Sanskrit) is a universal and eternal law (*sanatan dharma*), both a religious and a moral one, under which each individual or group must play a particular role by performing certain, appropriate duties, that depend on one's class, status, and station in life. In Buddhism, on the other hand, *dharma* (or *dhamma* in Pali) means the universal truth common to all individuals as the body of teachings and practice expounded by the Buddha. In Jainism, *dharma* is commonly understood as moral virtue.

Dharna

The term *dharna*, derived from Hindi, is used across South Asia. It came to prominence as a mode of political protest during the turbulent 1960s through the barricading of public places as a form of sit-in.

Dhivehi Raiyyithunge Party (DRP)

The Dhivehi Raiyyithunge Party (DRP), or Maldivian People Party, is the second registered political party in the Maldives and is led by the current President, Maumoon Abdul **Gayoom**. The current political landscape is dominated by a confrontation between the opposition **Maldivian Democratic Party (MDP)** and the government-oriented DRP, consisting of top bureaucracy and business leaders. The party's primary goals include greater prosperity for the people, increasing public participation in governance, promoting Islamic principles, maintaining peace and harmony, and protecting national unity and identity. Following campaigns of recruitment and efforts to raise party awareness, the DRP comprises approximately 25,000 members (2005). However, observers claim that the party is dominated by Gayoom, hindering the development of internal democratic procedures and the transformation into a party of more general appeal.

Didi, Abdulla Afif

A leading politician of a local separatist movement in the southern Atolls of the Maldives that emerged in the pre-independence period. The movement culminated in 1959 in the promulgation of a short-lived state, the United Suvadive Republic, comprising around 20,000 citizens and four Atolls—North Huvadhu Atoll (GA), South Huvadhu Atoll (GDh), Fuvahmulah (Gn), Addu Atoll (S)—collectively known to the separatists as the Suvadiva Atolls. Didi served as the leader of this state until **Malé** forcefully took over in 1962. The separatist ideas of Didi and his movement today find expression in the pro-British attitude of the southern Atolls and their suspicion of the centre, in particular regarding procedures for distributing political and socio-economic resources.

Didi, Muhammad Amin

Muhammad Amin Didi, a modern and Western-orientated Maldivian statesman, served the country as Prime Minister (chairman, Council of Regency) under the sultanate in the 1940s and, following its suspension, as President of the First Republic. After seven months Amin Didi was overthrown and the sultanate reinstated in February 1954. Critical food shortages combined with unpopular measures, such as a total ban on tobacco, made it easier for Amin Didi's opponents to rally against him. Despite his short-lived presidency, he implemented various social and economic reforms in the education system and is recognized as a promoter of women's rights. Amin Didi is recognized as a reformer and father of nationalism in the Maldives.

Didi, Sultan Muhammad Farid (Fareed)

As an elected Sultan in 1954, Muhammad Farid Didi became the first head of state of the Maldives after independence in 1965. He remained in power until he was overthrown by a popular referendum, initiated by Ibrahim **Nasir**, which abolished the sultanate and introduced the second republic in the Maldives. He was forced into exile in Sri Lanka where he later died.

Donoughmore Commission

A Royal Commission in 1924 sent from Britain to propose constitutional changes to improve representative government in Ceylon, later Sri Lanka. The result was the Donoughmore Constitution, promulgated in 1931, which experimented with participatory democracy while keeping power firmly in British hands. It is criticized for having introduced universal adult suffrage without communal representation, enabling the Sinhalese to obtain an absolute majority over the combined strength of all other ethnic groups in the 1931 state council elections and triggering the emergence of parties along ethnic lines, such as the **All-Ceylon Tamil Congress**. For the Tamils, the Donoughmore Constitution was seen as a capitulation to Sinhala nationalism and political dominance. (*See* **Soulbury Commission**.)

Doordarshan

Doordarshan is a public broadcast terrestrial television channel in India operated by **Prasar Bharati**. It has the widest and largest viewership in India and the most extensive infrastructure of studios, making it one of the largest broadcasting organizations in the world. Its network of 1,314 terrestrial transmitters covers more than 89.6% of the population.

Dr Reddy's Laboratories Ltd

Founded in 1984, Dr Reddy's is one of the leading pharmaceutical companies in India and also has operations in more than a dozen countries. Dr Reddy's manufactures generic versions of existing pharmaceutical drugs which are sold in India and other developing countries where there are no pharmaceutical patent laws. Once the original patent expires Dr Reddy's also exports to the USA and other industrialized countries. Dr Anji Reddy, the founder, is a national icon for his efforts to bring affordable medicines to the masses. Dr Reddy's Foundation for Human and Social Development and the Naandi Foundation work on sustainable development initiatives.

Dragpo tewa

A political and philosophical concept drawn from Buddhism, literally translated as the 'centre of violence'. It is used in Bhutan to describe a strategy of governance including violent and forceful elements that are commonly recognized as contrary to the idea of peaceful conflict management. (*See* ***Zhiwey Zhung yog***.)

Dratshang

The term *Dratshang* is used in Bhutan and refers to a monastic body. The central monastic body (*Dratshang Lhentshog* or **Council for Ecclesiastical Affairs**) is headed by the ***Je Khenpo*** and represents, as chief abbot, the Buddhist clergy of the country. Despite the increasing control of the state over the religious sphere, it continues to play an important role not only in the spiritual and cultural life of the people but also in significant government institutions such as the National Assembly and the Royal Advisory Council. (*See* **Bhutan, Political Development**.)

Dravida Munnetra Kazhagam (DMK—Dravidian Progress Party)

The Dravida Munnetra Kazhagam (DMK—Dravidian Progess Party) is a regional political party in **Tamil Nadu**. It was founded by C. N. Annadurai (a popular film script writer) in 1949 as an offshoot from Dravida Kazhagam. The party's ideology originally had anti-north India, anti-Hindi and anti-Brahmin tendencies. The party proclaimed cultural, economic and political domination of the south by the north and opposed the retention of Hindi as an official language, seeking more autonomy for the states. The party is also described in the political arena as a Tamil nationalist party representing the interests of middle- and lower-caste Tamil speakers. The party gained representation in the **Lok Sabha** for the first time in 1957 and in 1972 lost some of its support to the splinter group **All-India Anna Dravida Munnetra Kazhagam (AIADMK)**. It contested the 1998 national elections in alliance with the **Bharatiya Janata Party (BJP)** and was part of the ruling **National Democratic Alliance (NDA)** until the general elections of 2004.

Dravidian

The Dravidian linguistic family is distinct from the Indo-Aryan, Munda and Tibeto-Burman families of languages found in India. Dravidian also refers to the people, region and culture of southern India. A Dravidian movement, launched in **Tamil Nadu** in the early 20th century, was founded upon a reformist, anti-Brahmin and rationalist philosophy. C. N. Annadurai, charismatic leader of the **Dravida Munnetra Kazhagam (DMK)**, transformed this socio-cultural movement into a political party.

Driglam Namzha (Culture Policy)

The royal decree of Driglam Namzha, understood abstractly as 'the principles of Bhutanese customs and traditions' and, more concretely, as 'national dress and language', was issued by King Jigme Singye in 1989, and enforced by the Bhutanese government in the same year. *Driglam Namzha*, alongside other measures, was intended to forge a distinctive Bhutanese national identity on the basis of the culture of the ruling **Ngalong**, deemed by the King to be the country's main resource. The *Driglam Namzha* includes the mandatory wearing of the national costume (*gho* for men and *kira* for women) on formal occasions. Reports suggest, however, that the dress code is often applied beyond the stipulations of the King's decree, extending even to everyday life. Failure to abide by the dress code of *Driglam Namzha* may result in short-term imprisonment or the imposition of a fine. The **Dzongkha** language, mother tongue of the Ngalong people of the west highland districts, was declared the national language of Bhutan by the King in 1961. In 1989 the Nepali language was taken off the curriculum of educational institutions and all materials in Nepali were removed from schools.

Druk Gyalpo (Dragon King)

The Druk Gyalpo (Dragon King) is head of state in the constitutional monarchy of Bhutan and the apex of the political system. Bhutan's hereditary monarchy has remained within the **Wangchuck family** since it was established in 1907. Succession to the throne depends on male primogeniture from amongst the legitimate descendants of the first Druk Gyalpo, Ugyen Wangchuck. King Jigme Singye Wangchuck is Bhutan's fourth and current King. (*See* **Bhutan, Political Development**—Monarchical System/Monarchy.)

Drukpa

Derived from '*druk yul'*, the indigenous phrase to describe inhabitants of Bhutan, Drukpa refers to the ruling faction in Bhutanese society. Furthermore, it refers to a major school (the **Kagyupa School**) of Tibetan Buddhism that only the **Ngalong** ethnic group adheres to. As a result the term is used to connote a 'Drukpa identity group', constituting a cultural pillar of the nation as distinguished from the **Lhotshampa**, who constitute a second category. In this context, there is the tendency among Ngalongs to subsume the **Sharchop** under their own identity group to broaden their socio-political base. However, the Sharchop belong to the Nyingmapa school of Buddhism, which has faced discrimination according to critics. Due to the absence of statistical data, however, it is not clear whether the majority of Bhutanese follow the Drukpa branch of the Kagyupa or the Nyingmapa school.

Drukyul

A term derived from **Dzongkha** and used in Bhutan as the name for the country. It means literally 'Land of the Dragon'.

Dzong

This term, used in Bhutan to mean fortress, castle, palace, as well as temple or monastery, refers to the structure of a building constructed to accommodate a political or religious institution. Usually it is the centre of all regular and administrative activities in a district and houses the head office of the *Drangpon* (literally 'law chief', formerly known as *Thrimpon* or *Dzongpon*), who perform the functions of a district magistrate in the civil administration. Through the process of decentralization various responsibilities are transferred from the *Dzongs* to the village level.

Dzongkha

Dzongkha refers to the mother tongue of the ruling **Ngalong** élite in Bhutan. Since 1961, when it was elevated to the national language, Dzongkha has been the official language as well as, alongside English, the language of administration. The word Dzongkha derives from ***Dzong***, meaning fortress, castle, palace, etc., and *Kha*, meaning language. Thus it literally means language of the palace. It is very similar to the Tibetan language and deeply influenced by the classical religious language

Choekey. As Dzongkha is the mother tongue of only 20%–30% of the population, minority groups such as the Nepali-speaking **Lhotshampa** have felt discriminated against. (*See* **Driglam Namzha**.)

Dzongkhag

The term *Dzongkhag* is used in Bhutan to refer to a district as a political and administrative unit, headed by a *Dzongda* (District Administrator). Sub-districts are described as *Dungkhag* and formed by various ***gewog*** (blocks) and headed by *Dungpa*. In recent years the *Dzonkhag* as well as the *Dungkhag* and *gewogs* have gained momentum in the process of decentralization.

E

Eelam

In its original form, 'ila-m', the Tamil term referred to the whole island. Later derivations include 'Eelam'. With the **Federal Party**'s **(FP)** emergence in Sri Lanka the 1950s the term began to be politicized but it was in the 1970s that militant Tamils used it to connote a separate state or 'traditional homeland', comprising the Northern and Eastern Provinces. (*See* **Liberation Tigers of Tamil Eelam—LTTE**; **Tamil Language**).

Eelam People's Democratic Party (EPDP)

Led by Douglas Devananda, who was cabinet minister in **Kumaratunga**'s government, the Eelam People's Democratic Party (EPDP) broke away from the **Eelam People's Revolutionary Liberation Front (EPRLF)** around 1988. Since 1990 it has fought alongside the Sri Lankan Army against the **Liberation Tigers of Tamil Eelam (LTTE)** and since 1994 has been the most significant force in electoral politics in **Jaffna**. Its members and property have come under frequent attacks by the LTTE, as a result of which the EPDP and other Tamil parties, such as the **People's Liberation Organization of Tamil Eelam (PLOTE**, also **PLOT)**, received government arms for self-defence, putting such parties in the awkward position of being categorized as 'Tamil paramilitary groups' under the 2002 ceasefire accord. (*See* **Tamil Language**.)

Eelam People's Revolutionary Liberation Front (EPRLF)

Having split from the Marxist Eelam Revolutionary Organization of Students in 1980, the Eelam People's Revolutionary Liberation Front (EPRLF) became the Indian government's ally and the leading party in the North East Provincial Council created under the 1987 **Indo-Lanka Accord**. In 2001 a faction of the EPRLF joined the **Tamil National Alliance (TNA)**.

Eleven-Party Alliance

The Eleven-Party Alliance is a grouping of 11 leftist groups and liberal democratic parties in Bangladesh, including the Communist Party, the **Gano Forum**, the Workers Party and the Workers Peasants Socialist Party. It is one of the major forces in opposition since the general elections held in 2001. The coalition claims to work towards the restoration and protection of a secular order and against fundamentalist tendencies in the country. Despite the original intention to build up a political alternative to the **Bangladesh National Party (BNP)** and the **Bangladesh Awami League (AL)**, the Eleven-Party Alliance takes part in the **Fourteen-Party Opposition Movement** led by the AL.

Emergency – *see* India, Political Development

Ershad, Gen. Hossain Mohammad

Gen. Hussain Muhammad Ershad, chief-of-staff of the army, seized control of the Bangladesh government in a military coup on 24 March 1982. He proclaimed martial law, appointed himself as Chief Martial Law Administrator, suspended the Constitution and assumed the presidency in December 1983. Controversial elections for parliament were held under his rule and then followed by a presidential election in 1986. The **Jatiya Party (JP)**, led by Ershad, won the majority of legislative seats and Ershad himself won the presidential elections. In 1990 civil protests organized by the **Bangladesh Awami League** (led by Sheikh **Hasina**) as well as the **Bangladesh Nationalist Party (BNP)**, spearheaded by Khaleda **Zia** and against his authoritarian rule, began and, unable to repress them, Ershad was forced to resign in December. In the following years Ershad was jailed several times due to his involvement in corruption during his tenure in office.

Export Promotion Bureau (EPB)

The Export Promotion Bureau (EPB) of Bangladesh is a government agency headed by a chairman under the Ministry of Commerce and entrusted with the responsibility for promoting exports. The main functions of this organization are to formulate policy and programmes for the active promotion of exports and to co-ordinate export development efforts. Exploring potential markets for Bangladeshi exports, organizing participation in international trade fairs, it also assists in the settlement of disputes related to export-related transactions. The EPB is responsible for gathering detailed business information about products from manufacturers and exporters to foreign markets.

F

Farakka Issue

The Farakka Issue refers to a controversial river management project that was taken up by the Indian government to serve the twin purpose of regulating the amount of Ganga water to flow out from the Indian territory into Bangladesh and to ensure that sufficient water is diverted to Hooghly River to enable the regular flushing of silt at Calcutta (Kolkata) port. The structure of Farakka barrage was completed as early as 1971. It was an issue that affected India-Pakistan relations prior to the emergence of Bangladesh and has continued subsequently. The negotiations on sharing of Ganges waters at Farakka started in 1960 when the **Indus Waters Treaty** was signed, but there was little progress. Since the emergence of Bangladesh the issue has changed in its political complexion. Several meetings have been held at ministerial level, but no mutually acceptable solution was reached until 1977, when an agreement was signed for five years, at the end of which it was replaced by an MOU. The MOU was valid until 1988. In 1989–96 no agreement/treaty existed between India and Bangladesh. On 12 December 1996 the Prime Ministers of both countries signed a treaty on the sharing of the Ganges waters for 30 years, renewable on mutual consent.

Fatwa

A *fatwa* is a legal pronouncement in Islam, issued by an expert in Islamic law on a specific issue. *Fatwas* are usually pronounced at the request of an individual or a judge to settle a question where *figh*, Islamic jurisprudence, is imprecise. A scholar issuing a *fatwa* is known as a *Mufti*. Because of the lack of a centralized Islamic priesthood, there is no generally accepted agreement as to who is qualified to issue a *fatwa*.

Federal Party (FP)

Founded by S. J. V. Chelvanayakam in 1949, the Federal Party (FP) became the main Tamil party in Ceylon in 1956. It was a founding partner of the Tamil United Front, later the **Tamil United Liberation Front (TULF)**, and was one of the first to suggest the idea of federalism as a solution to the ethno-political conflict. It was recently revived within the **Tamil National Alliance**, which contested the 2004 elections in Sri Lanka under the FP (also known as Illankai Tamil Arasu Kachchi) banner. (*See* **Eelam**; **Tamil Language**.)

Federally Administered Northern Areas (FANA)

The Federally Administered Northern Areas (FANA) of Pakistan, comprising mainly Baltistan, Gilgit and Hunza, are strategically a very important region—of 72,496 sq km with a population of almost 1.1m.—located in the extreme north of Pakistan and bordering with India, Afghanistan and China. The area has been under Pakistani administration since the first war between India and Pakistan in 1948. Though administered as a *de facto* union, accession of the area has not been formally accepted by Pakistan lest India interpret it as a validation of the *status quo* in the **Kashmir dispute**. The resultant ambiguity and lack of political representation has been a continuous cause of frustration amongst the region's inhabitants. (*See* **Jammu and Kashmir**.)

Federally Administered Tribal Area (FATA)

Pakistan's Federally Administered Tribal Area (FATA), consisting of seven administrative agencies spread over about 27,000 sq km, is outside the legal, judicial and geographical jurisdiction of all of the four provinces of Pakistan. Bordering on Afghanistan, its population is mainly Pashtuns who are ruled according to a traditional ***jirga*** system, with the Pakistani government exercising only nominal control through a political agent. As a whole, the region is underdeveloped, with low literacy rates and little infrastructure. Its rugged mountainous terrain and special legal status has traditionally made it a favourite hideout for outlaws.

Federation of Indian Chambers of Commerce and Industry (FICCI)

The Federation of Indian Chambers of Commerce and Industry (FICCI) was founded in 1927 under the guidance of Mohandas Karamchand **Gandhi** to accumulate support and bring together various forces in India under a broader movement for India's independence. Together with the Associated Chambers of Commerce and Industry, FICCI functions as the apex chamber of commerce for trade associations and industry in India. A key actor in policy formulation and the socio-economic transformation of the country, it has gained a significant role in the making of government economic policy, advocating greater private-sector participation, free markets, exports and foreign direct investment.

Four-Party Alliance

Bangladesh's Four-Party Alliance, formed at the beginning of 1999 to contest the 2001 parliamentary elections and led by the **Bangladesh Nationalist Party (BNP)**, was voted into office with a two-thirds' majority in the country's eighth national parliamentary elections, held in October 2001. The alliance included two hardline Muslim parties, the **Jamaat-e-Islami** and the **Islamic Oikya Jote (IOJ)**, and one faction of the **Jatiya Party** (Naziur or Naziur Firoz), led by Naziur Rahman Manzur (**Manjur Faction**). Among the four alliance partners, the BNP alone won 195 seats, the Jamaat-e-Islami, one of its major partners, 18, IOJ two and the Jatiya Party (Naziur) four. The alliance government is often blamed for providing support to Islamic fundamentalist groups.

Fourteen-Party Opposition Movement

The Fourteen-Party Opposition Movement designates a grouping of parties in opposition since 2001 in Bangladesh and led by the **Bangladesh Awami League (AL)**. Other components are the **Eleven-Party Alliance**, **Jatiya Samajtantrik Dal (JSD)**, and the **National Awami Party (NAP)**, headed by Muzaffar Ahmed.

G

Gakid

A term used in Bhutan to refer to a spiritual concept derived from Buddhism and meaning happiness and peace, *Gakid* corresponds with the economic philosophy of ***Peljor Gongphel***, which emphasized the need to channel and balance the undesirable effects of indiscriminate modernization. (*See* **Gross National Happiness**.)

Gan

In 1956 an agreement between the British and Maldivian governments allowed the British air force to establish a base on the southern Gan Island (Addu **Atoll**). Another agreement in 1960 extended its use for a period of 30 years, in return for which the British were to pay the Maldivian government. Due to its economic impact on the inhabitants of the southern Maldivian islands, the Royal Air Force base was increasingly seen by the central government in **Malé** as a disturbing factor in domestic affairs, becoming a critical issue in UK-Maldives relations. The crisis culminated in a separatist movement aimed at the formation of a United Suvadive Republic (*see* **Didi**, Abdulla Afif). In 1975 the United Kingdom decided to close the air base. The strategic significance of Gan Island was reinforced in 1977 when the Soviet Union offered US $1m. to lease the base. The decision to refuse the Soviet offer was seen as being in keeping with the islands' policy of non-alignment.

Gandhi, Indira

Born in 1917 in Allahabad, Indira was the only child of Jawaharlal and Kamala **Nehru**. In 1942 she married, initially against Nehru's wishes, Feroze Gandhi, a Parsi (and no relation to Mohandas **Gandhi**), acquiring the charismatic surname that created the enduring Nehru-Gandhi political lineage. Indira Gandhi became her father's closest confidante, observing and learning first hand from his years as Prime Minister (1947–64). During his lifetime Indira Gandhi became Congress president (in 1959), but at his death it was still unclear whether she would pursue a career in politics and whether she would be able to sustain one. When Prime Minister Lal Bahadur Shastri died in office in 1966, Indira successfully contested to succeed him as party leader and subsequently became one of India's strongest Prime Ministers.

By using her powers of patronage and intrigue, she subverted the checks and balances that characterize the parliamentary form of government, centralizing her personal authority and causing the **Indian National Congress (INC)** to split in 1969 over support for her leadership. Winning a sweeping victory in 1971, through her famed *garibi hatao* ('remove poverty') campaign, Indira's popularity received a further boost when India went to war in 1971, successfully dismembering Pakistan to create Bangladesh. Drastic policies included her decision to nationalize banks, the 1971 20-year Treaty of Peace, Friendship and Co-operation signed with the Soviet Union that further aggravated relations with the USA, together with India's first nuclear test, the peaceful nuclear explosion of 1974 (*see* **Nuclearization**), and, most dramatically of all, the imposition of emergency rule in 1975, marking the only break in India's democracy since independence. In 1977, misjudging her own popularity, Indira Gandhi advised the President of India to dissolve the **Lok Sabha** and call for fresh elections. Indira Gandhi lost the elections, leading to the formation of the first non-Congress government at the centre under a Janata Party coalition. She returned victorious, leading the Congress (I) in the 1980 elections. Her third term in government was marked by growing conflict in **Punjab** and the rise of Sikh militancy and secessionism in **North East India**. When militants led by Jarnail Singh **Bhindranwale** occupied the Golden Temple in Amritsar, Indira Gandhi ordered the army to storm what was the holiest site for Sikhs in June 1984. The military assault, codenamed **Operation Blue Star**, and the general crackdown on Sikhs under Operation Woodrose, outraged Sikhs and on 31 October 1984 Indira was assassinated by her Sikh bodyguards. Both her sons, Sanjay and Rajiv, were involved in politics. Sanjay Gandhi, Indira's favourite, was being groomed as her successor when he died in a plane crash in 1980. Rajiv Gandhi, who became Prime Minister on his mother's death, was killed by a suicide bomber from the Sri Lanka-based Tamil militant group, the **Liberation Tigers of Tamil Eelam**, in May 1991. (*See* **India, Political Development**—Emergency.)

Gandhi, Mohandas Karamchand

Mohandas Karamchand Gandhi, also known as the *Mahatma* (Great Soul), was an iconic figure in the Indian independence struggle. Born on 2 October 1869 in **Gujarat**, Gandhi trained as a barrister in England, and developed a technique of resistance which he called ***satyagraha***, or non-violence, to fight injustice while in South Africa where he had been sent to settle a case between two Indian Muslim businessmen. The South African experience also taught Gandhi the importance of cross-community coalitions, a theme that translated itself into Hindu-Muslim unity, which became a salient feature of Gandhi's politics upon his return to India in 1915. Under his leadership, the **Indian National Congress (INC)** became increasingly conscious of the gap between the predominantly urban middle-class Congress and the Indian masses, shifting its attention to the Indian peasantry to create a mass movement. Consequently, the INC steadily broadened its reach both in terms of social class and geography. In 1918, while introducing *satyagraha* to India, Gandhi courted arrest in support of the indigo plantation workers of the British province, **Bihar**. There were similar movements in the provinces of **Punjab**, Gujarat and other parts of India. To expand the non-violence movement, Gandhi advocated the spinning of one's own cotton (*khadi*) as a means to include women, as well as the boycott of foreign-made goods. In choosing civil disobedience to resist the salt tax imposed by the British and much resented by Indians, he led the famous 1930 Dandi March of about 400 km which ended at the seaside and the illegal production of salt, capturing attention and mobilizing support across the country, demonstrating his brilliance as a strategist. When the British rulers responded with repressive measures, they only intensified the struggle, imprisoning Gandhi on many ocassions but often releasing him for fear of the repercussions if he died under British imprisonment.

Vehemently opposed to **Partition**, by the time of independence senior Congress leaders like Jawaharlal **Nehru** and Sardar Patel convinced him that it was the only way to avoid a civil war. After independence Gandhi focused on Hindu-Muslim relations, launching a fast-unto-death to end communal violence and to compel the government to transfer money that had been promised to Pakistan. In **Delhi**, to try to stem the communal violence arising from Partition, Gandhi was shot and killed on 30 January 1948 by a Hindu extremist who considered him too conciliatory towards Muslims.

While Gandhi's techniques of non-violent resistance and leadership during the freedom struggle are deeply revered, his ideas of non-party government, decentralization of power and authority, and focus on cottage industry were largely ignored during the framing of the Indian Constitution.

Gandhi, Sonia

Sonia Gandhi (widow of Rajiv Gandhi—*see* **Nehru-Gandhi Family**) took over chairmanship of the ruling **United Progressive Alliance (UPA)** following the 2004 elections and on 28 May 2005 was re-elected as president of the **Indian National Congress (INC)**. Born on 9 December 1946 into a traditional Roman Catholic household in Italy, Sonia married Rajiv Gandhi in 1968, moving into the house of her mother-in-law, the Prime Minister Indira **Gandhi**. Following her husband's assassination in 1991 there were calls for her to enter politics which she resisted until 1998, when she assumed leadership of the Congress. For the 2004 elections, Sonia Gandhi entered wholeheartedly into the campaign, revitalizing the Congress and unseating the **National Democratic Alliance (NDA)**. A storm of controversy arose over the possibility of a foreign-born and naturalized person becoming Prime Minister and prominent leaders of the **Bharatiya Janata Party (BJP)** threatened a nation-wide agitation. However, Sonia Gandhi surprised everyone by renouncing the post and suggesting Manmohan **Singh** for the post instead, a political move that demobilized opponents, generated adulation and allowed her to remain the steering force of the Congress in the UPA coalition. In the 2004 elections both of her children attracted public attention, her son Rahul contesting and winning from Amethi in **Uttar Pradesh**, and her daughter, Priyanka, energetically campaigning for her mother. Both are being groomed to possibly assume the Nehru-Gandhi mantle in the near future. Sonia represents the seat of Rae Bareilly, also in Uttar Pradesh.

Gano Forum (People's Forum)

The Gano Forum is a political party in Bangladesh founded in 1993 as an amalgamation of factions splintering from the **Bangladesh Awami League (AL)**, the **Communist Party of Bangladesh (CPB)**, led by Saifuddin Ahmed Manik, and the National Socialist Party, led by Shajahan Siraj. The party was formed under the leadership of Dr Kamal Hossain, who had been a member of Sheikh Mujibur **Rahman**'s Cabinet. The main slogan of this party is 'violence-free politics, economic progress at the grassroots and basic amenities for all'. The Gano Forum is part of the **Eleven-Party Alliance** in opposition since 2001.

Gawadar Project – *see* Balochistan

Gayoom, Maumoon Abdul

Born in 1937 in **Malé**, Maumoon Abdul Gayoom, after studying in Cairo, Egypt, and lecturing in Islamic studies, returned to serve in the Maldivian government in various ministerial posts, and as Maldivian representative to the UN. In 1978 he succeeded Ibrahim **Nasir** as President of the Maldives. In the elections of 1978, Gayoom obtained more than 90% of the vote, a feat which he repeated in the elections of 1983, 1988, 1993 and 1998. In November 2003 he was re-elected, enabling him to remain in power until November 2008 and making him the longest-serving active ruling political leader in Asia. Since his assumption of office, Gayoom has successfully ensured his power by occupying important positions in the bureaucracy and ministries with members of his family as well as, according to his critics, suppressing opposition movements. During more than 28 years in power he has faced three attempted *coups d'état*. Following national and international pressure, Gayoom introduced political reforms, notably the Political Parties' Regulation 2005, allowing parties officially to register. In the emerging context of organized political competition, he supports the **Dhivehi Raiyyithunge Party (DRP)**, which acts as his own political platform. Gayoom's political priorities have included managing security problems, environmental protection, socio-economic development of the remote Atolls and outer Islands, the preservation of Islamic culture as well as the prevention of fundamentalism.

Gewog

Gewog refers in Bhutan to a district as a political and administrative unit and comprises various villages (*zomdus*). (*See* ***Dzongkhag***.)

Gherao

Gherao is a term used in South Asia and generally meaning the encirclement of a person or picketing of office buildings to realize a demand. During the 1960s in East Pakistan it was introduced as a form of political protest widely applied by opposition parties to pressure the government with claims for greater autonomy. The most recognized *gherao* of this time was the mass upsurge of 1969, which included the surrounding of the governor's house. Following Bangladesh's independence, it became a popular form of protest there, frequently used by political parties, trade unions and student organizations. The Prime Minister's office and secretariat, and local administrators' offices and even universities' vice-chancellors' offices are often *gheraoed*, with protestors preventing people from leaving their offices.

Goa

India's smallest state in terms of size, Goa is also the richest in terms of per capita income. Located on the west coast, Goa was a Portuguese colony until 1961, when the Indian armed forces 'liberated' or 'annexed' Goa, depending on the perspective taken of Prime Minister **Nehru**'s decision to use force. The administrative capital of Goa is Panjim, the legislative capital Porvorim and the court of appeal is the High Court of **Maharashtra** in **Mumbai**. Konkani is the state's official language. The Goa assembly consists of 40 members; and the state has two seats in the **Lok Sabha**. Uniquely, Goa is the only state with a uniform civil code in practice, a Portuguese legacy that was retained. Goa is among the country's premier tourist destinations and has one of the highest road network densities in India. While Hindus constitute a majority, congregated largely in the north, there is a solid Roman Catholic minority which forms about 28% of the electorate and which has played a decisive role in both Lok Sabha constituencies. In 1999 the **Bharatiya Janata Party (BJP)**, riding a strong anti-**Congress** wave, managed to capture both seats, but in 2004 voting appeared split along religious lines, with the Hindu vote going to the BJP and the Catholic vote to the **Nationalist Congress Party**/Congress alliance. The imposition of President's Rule in March 2005, following a hung assembly, and the subsequent decision to hold early by-elections instead of dissolving the house and holding fresh assembly elections, raised questions about the impartiality of Goa's Governor and highlighted the delicate nature of state-centre relations.

Gono/Gana Adalat

Terms used to refer to a kind of people's court in Bangladesh, initiated by the political activist Jahanara **Imam** in Dhaka in 1992. Its overall objective was to try collaborators and war criminals of the **Bangladesh Liberation War** in 1971. As a public extraordinary judicial institution it was promoted and set up by the Ghatak Dalal Nirmul Committee, a 12-year public movement to eliminate traitors and collaborators. The Adalat was formed with 11 judges, chosen by this committee and held a number of open public hearings at Ramna Green in Dhaka, where charges were brought against leading members of the pro-Pakistani forces.

Gram Sarkar (*Gram Parishad*)

Formerly known as *swanirvar gram parishad*, a system of local governance in Bangladesh based on self-reliant (***swanirvar***) villages, *gram sarkar* was introduced by former President Ziaur **Rahman** in 1980 to strengthen the support base of the **Bangladesh Nationalist Party (BNP)** in rural areas. Each ward, comprising 1–2 villages, should have a *gram parishad*, headed by a *gram padhan* (village chief) and comprising elected members representing landless peasants, women, youth, landed peasants, shopkeepers, fishermen and artisans. Its main objective was to deal with local, day-to-day challenges, including family disputes, health and population control, food production and law and order. Having no revenues of their own, the *gram parishad* were not able to fulfil their responsibilities, but can be seen as an attempt to challenge the landed élite and to integrate disadvantaged groups into the political process. The Self-Sufficient Village Government Plan ended in 1980. However, in 2003 the *gram parishad* system was reshaped as a scheme of *gram sarkar*, and introduced for a second time by the government. The proposed 13-member *gram sarkar* comprises, besides its chairman, the *gram sarkar prodhan* (union *parishad* member elected from the ward), and other members, both men and women, elected in a general meeting of the voters of the ward under the supervision of a 'prescribed/directing authority'. However, given that the authority is reportedly in favour of nominated rather than elected members, local government continues to be a major political issue in the country. In August 2005 the High Court declared *gram sarkar* in its current non-elective form as illegal and unconstitutional, but this judgement was overturned by the Supreme Court and the issue remains undecided.

Grameen Bank Project

The Grameen Bank Project was first put into action in 1976 in the Chittagong Hill Tracts (*hathazari* subdistrict) of south-east Bangladesh by Professor Muhammad Yunus. It was launched as an action research project to create a credit delivery system, specifically for the landless and poor in both rural and urban slum areas by organizing them into groups for credit disbursement and other banking services. The project provides credit without collateral for a large range of micro-activities for income and employment generation and asset creation. Between 1976 and 1983 it expanded throughout the country and was transformed into a formal bank under a special law passed in 1983. Ninety-four per cent of total equity is owned by the poor borrowers and the remaining 6% is government-owned. As of July 2004 there were 3.7m. borrowers, 96% of whom were women. With 1,267 branches, Grameen Bank provides services in 46,000 villages, more than 68% of the total. Its positive impact on poor and formerly poor borrowers has been documented by many independent studies.

Gramodaya Mandalas

Drawn from the term *Gramasabhava* which described the traditional village council system in Sri Lanka, the *Gramodaya Mandala*, or Village Development Council, was introduced from 1981 onwards in a bid to increase people's participation in local government. Not particularly successful, the *Pradeshiya Sabha* system, an elected rural regional council, replaced the village councils in 1987.

Green Revolution

The term Green Revolution in general refers to an economic and agricultural development strategy introduced by Western aid organizations in poor countries in co-operation with local planners to achieve self-sufficiency in food grains. The various projects included the following components: (1) expansion of farming areas; (2) adoption of new technology to improve the technical aspect of agricultural production (use of heavy machinery for harvesting and irrigation methods); (3) the use of high-yielding cereal grains and genetically improved seeds; and (4) the use of chemical fertilizers, pesticides and herbicides. In the Indian context, the term Green Revolution is usually applied to the period from 1967 to 1978, in which the above-mentioned strategy was applied to make India self-sufficient in food grains. The programme was started with help from the US Rockefeller Foundation. Despite the fact that many analysts in India and abroad see it as a successful development strategy, critics have claimed that it was used by decision-makers for political purposes and that the Green Revolution in India created wide economic and inter-state disparities. Higher crop yields were attained primarily in northern and north-western India, in areas with assured supplies of water, large inputs of fertilizers and adequate credit systems, as was the case in states such as **Punjab**, **Haryana** and western **Uttar Pradesh**. Others, such as **Andhra Pradesh** and **Tamil Nadu**, lacking the requisite inputs, did not experience the same beneficial results.

Gross National Happiness (GNH)

The term Gross National Happiness or National Contentment was coined by the royal Bhutanese government as a benchmark and developmental goal. As the overarching philosophy of development, it expresses the conviction that all development strategies must contribute to both the material well-being as well as the spiritual, emotional and cultural needs of the Bhutanese people. Each modernization strategy must maintain a balance between the material and non-material needs of individuals and society. The four core principles of GNH are: (1) economic growth and development; (2) preservation and promotion of cultural heritage (in this case that of the ruling élite); (3) preservation and sustainable use of the environment; and (4) good governance. Underlying these four pillars is the belief that GNH is more important than gross national product.

Gujarat

Located in western India and bordering partly with Pakistan, Gujarat is one of India's most urbanized, industrialized and prosperous states and is also the birthplace of *Mahatma* **Gandhi**. The state was created in 1960 out of the predominantly Gujarati-speaking areas of the state of Bombay and a new capital city, named Gandhinagar, was built in 1970. Gujarat has a legislative assembly of 182 seats, of which 26 are reserved for **Scheduled Tribes**, reflecting the large proportion of tribes in the state (in 2001 they represented 14.8% of the population). The state returns 26 members to the **Lok Sabha**. While Hindus constitute a majority (89.1%), there is a significant Muslim community (9.1%) and Gujarat is one of the main centres for Jains. The **Congress** party dominated state politics until 1995, when the **Bharatiya Janata Party (BJP)** came to power, and the state became a BJP stronghold. Communal tensions came to a head in 2002 when a train carrying returning Hindu pilgrims and activists from Ayodhya was attacked at Godhra railway station. A Muslim mob was blamed, sparking riots across parts of Gujarat. State ministers and the police were criticized for not having done enough to protect the Muslim community and for even having abetted the violence, instigating an investigation by the National Human Rights Commission and later the Central Bureau of Investigation. However, in the assembly elections of 2002 the BJP secured two-thirds of the seats, although this victory was undermined by the results of the 2004 national elections in which the Congress made some inroads. Voting, it was observed, was not along obvious communal lines, the BJP's losses being attributed more to infighting and to gains made by Congress in rural constituencies.

Gung

A term used in Bhutan to refer to the smallest administrative unit, the household, which occupies a central position in development strategies as well as in the country's judicial and legislative systems.

Gup

A term used in Bhutan to refer to the elected head in the administrative and socio-political unit of the block, or *gewog*. The *gup* has been an essential feature of Bhutanese rural life since the 17th century and has traditionally acted as an intermediary between community and state. With decentralization, the responsibilities of the *gup* have increased rapidly to encompass a role in the expanding local administrations, including fostering good co-operation between the different levels of administrative units, official communication, planning and drafting agreements between different parties, evaluating government policies in the local context and suggesting remedies where needed. The *gup* may be assisted by the ***chipon*** (elected village co-ordinator) and the *mangi-ap* (village elders).

Gurkha (Gorkha)

Gurkha is the British (and Indian) Army term for recruits from any tribe of Nepal. They were and are renowned for their bravery and loyalty in service. The term derives its name from Gorkha, a west Nepal town which was the original seat of the present Shah dynasty.

Gyanendra, King

In June 2001 Prince Gyanendra became Nepal's King following a massacre of most of the royal family, ostensibly by the crowned prince, Gyanendra's nephew, Dipendra. For the first time in recent history, the monarch's coronation was greeted with hostility as riots and rumours of a conspiracy broke out. Less than two years later, on 4 October 2002, Gyanendra assumed executive powers and on 1 February 2005 a national emergency was declared and the government sacked, mirroring the events of 1960 when power was wrested by the palace. Reasons cited for the King's direct rule include the need to combat the ongoing Maoist insurgency, paralysis and infighting amongst political parties and corruption, although in reality there has been a suppression of fundamental rights as well as the rejection of peace proposals by the Maoists.

H

Harijan

A term coined by Mohandas Karamchand **Gandhi**, *Harijan* means *Children* or *People of God*. It was used by him as an alternative to '**untouchables**' and emerged in the early 1930s during the differences between him and **Ambedkar** on the issue of representation based on separate electorates. The use of the term *Harijan*, however, was seen by members of the community as being a way of making 'untouchability' more acceptable to caste Hindus, not of bringing about a change in their status. Later, in the 1960s, the term **Dalit**, deriving its significance from the material, social experience of its subjects, gained favour even over the state-constituted category of **Scheduled Castes (SCs)**.

Harkat ul-Ansar/Harkat ul-Mujahideen (HuM)

The Harkat ul-Ansar, now known as Harkat ul-Mujahideen (HuM), was founded in 1980 in Karachi, Pakistan, in order to fight in Afghanistan. It is a merger of two Islamic groups, Harkat ul-Jihad al-Islami and Harkat ul-Mujahedin. Based on a pan-Islamic ideology, it adopted an explicitly anti-Indian attitude, supporting the accession of Kashmir to Pakistan and becoming one of the most significant terrorist groups operating in Kashmir. (*See* **Jammu and Kashmir**; **Kashmir Dispute**.)

Hartal

Hartal or its synonym ***bandh*** are indigenous political terms used in India and meaning to mobilize mass support through the cessation of work (general strike).

Haryana

Situated in the north of India, Haryana, a constituent state of the Indian Union, was formed in 1966 from the Hindi-speaking parts of the **Punjab** region. Haryana continues to share its capital, **Chandigarh**, with the state of Punjab. Hindus constitute a majority, accounting for 88.2% of the population, followed by Muslims (5.8%) and Sikhs (5.5%). Amongst the most prosperous states of India, Haryana's economy is primarily agricultural and produces a large surplus of grain for external sale. Haryana has a legislative assembly of 90 seats and returns 10 members to the **Lok Sabha**. Within Haryana's agrarian population, the land-owning Jat community is the most powerful and has played a significant role in state politics (today comprising about 25% of the state's electorate). In 1977 the Haryana Lok Dal, a party strongly supported by the agricultural Jats, took power in the state on the strength of anti-**Congress** feeling after the 1975 emergency. Lending support first to the **Bharatiya Janata Party (BJP)** government (1977–80) and then to that of the National Front (1989–90), the Lok Dal was a player in national politics. In 1991 the Congress regained Haryana, taking advantage of a four-cornered contest with the Lok Dal, the Haryana Vikas Party and the BJP that split the vote. Similarly, for the 2004 general elections and the 2005 assembly elections no grand alliances were formed, ultimately benefiting the Congress which is the only party that manages in Haryana to appeal across major caste and community divisions. Congress won nine of the 10 Lok Sabha seats and, in a landslide victory, took 67 seats in the legislative assembly.

Hasina Wazed, Sheikh

Sheikh Hasina, the second woman to become Prime Minister of Bangladesh (1996–2001), was born in 1947. She began her political career during her student days—she was vice-president of her college students' union in 1966–67 and a member and secretary of the Rokeya Hall Unit of the Bangladesh Chhatra League (student wing of the Bangladesh Awami League—AL) at Dhaka University. She entered national politics in the late 1980s, five years after the assassination of her father, Sheikh Mujibur **Rahman**, was elected president of the AL in 1981, and has since been its leader. In 1983 Sheikh Hasina formed a 15-party alliance to launch a movement against Gen. **Ershad**. Her party (a leading constituent of an eight-party alliance), together with the **Bangladesh Nationalist Party (BNP)**, led by Khaleda **Zia** who was later to become Sheikh Hasina's arch rival, lent its support to the student movement, finally overthrowing the Ershad regime in 1990.

Following the 1991 national elections, Hasina's AL emerged as the largest opposition party. She led numerous movements to contest the BNP government and under her leadership the AL launched a campaign with other major parties to boycott the government's decision to hold elections in February 1996. Yielding to the pressure, a **caretaker government** was established to oversee elections in June 1996 and, together with the **Jatiya Party**, the AL formed the new government. Under her leadership a key water treaty was concluded with India in 1996, and an important peace accord with tribal groups in the Chittagong Hill Tracts was signed in 1997. Accused increasingly of corruption and of being pro-Indian, Sheikh Hasina was voted out of office in the parliamentary elections of October 2001. She returned to parliament as leader of the opposition.

Himachal Pradesh

Located in the north west of India along the foothills of the Himalayas, Himachal Pradesh shares an international border with China in the east. Himachal Pradesh was formed in 1948 as a union of 30 former princely states, with additional territory gained in 1954 and 1966, officially becoming the 18th state of the union in 1971, with Shimla as its capital. Although a predominantly Hindu state (Hindus made up 95.4% of the population in 2001), Buddhism has had a strong influence on the largely rural population and Dharamsala, home to the Dalai Lama (the exiled Tibetan leader), is located in Himachal Pradesh. Making use of the tremendous waterways in the region to produce hydroelectric power, the Bhakra-Nangal Dam, one of the highest in the world at 225 m, provides essential electricity for **Delhi**, **Haryana** and **Punjab** and irrigation water for **Rajasthan**. The legislative assembly of Himachal Pradesh comprises 68 seats and the state returns four members to the **Lok Sabha**. Since its creation in 1971, **Congress** has governed the state five times and the **Bharatiya Janata Party (BJP)** three times. The state elections held in 1991 and 1998 were closely contested, with the BJP just managing to displace the Congress government. In 2003, however, Congress won 43 assembly seats while the BJP retained only 16. In the 2004 parliamentary elections Congress won three of the state's four seats in the Lok Sabha.

Hindi-Chini bhai bhai

A term coined by the **Nehru** administration during the first euphoria following India's independence, literally meaning 'Indians and Chinese are brothers'. It expressed the hope invested in a new post-colonial Asia as an independent force in world politics. However, after the 1950s border conflicts and a war in 1962 between India and China, together with unresolved border issues such as **Aksai Chin** and the **McMahon Line**, the slogan began to lose its lustre.

Hindustan

The term Hindustan has its roots in the Persian language, meaning 'Land of the Hindus'. 'Hindu' refers to the inhabitants of the region, Hind. Geographically Hindustan is a historical name for northern India, comprising, imprecisely, the five **Punjab** rivers and the Gangetic plains. It is also a term that was used by the Mughals. In modern-day politics Hindustan is another name for India (**Bharat**).

Hindutva

Hindutva (literally 'hinduness', the quality of being Hindu) was a term originally coined by Vinayak Damodar **Savarkar** in his book *Hindutva: Who is a Hindu?* published in 1923. He regarded all inhabitants of the Indian subcontinent as Hindus, and specifically those who (1) regarded it as their fatherland (*Pitribhu*); (2) descended from Hindu parents; and (3) considered this a 'land where one can acquire religious merit' (*Punyabhumi*). According to Savarkar, these constituted the three 'essentials of Hindutva': a common nation (***rashtra***), a common race (*jati*) and a common civilization (*sanskriti*). Savarkar used the term *Hindutva* to emphasize its distinctiveness from the word *Hinduism*, which he associated with disunity and social as well as political grievances among the Hindu community. One of the main purposes behind the concept of *Hindutva* was to construct a collective identity to support the cause of 'Hindu-unity' (*Hindu Sanghatan*) and to avoid too narrow a definition of *Hinduism*, which had the consequence of excluding Buddhists, Sikhs and Jains from the Hindu community. Later, Hindu-nationalist ideologues transformed Savarkar's original *Hindutva* concept into a strategy to include non-Hindus, in order to widen their social base, and for political mobilization. Against this background *Hindutva* faces the challenge of determining the ambit of the intended Hindu nation, the Hindu *rashtra*, for which it will provide the ideological justification and legitimization. Today, *Hindutva*, as an ideology adopted by the **Sangh Parivar**, promotes a form of cultural nationalism and is used in this sense as the equivalent of Hindu nationalism. In this function the concept has emerged in recent years as a key instrument in electoral campaigning in India.

Hizbul Mujahideen (HM)

The Hizbul Mujahideen (HM) was founded in 1989 as a militant wing of the **Jamaat-e-Islami** and is one of the most active and largest terrorist groups operating in Kashmir. As a pro-Pakistani organization it stands for the integration of **Jammu and Kashmir** with Pakistan, as well as its Islamicization. It was reportedly originally formed as a counter to the **Jammu and Kashmir Liberation Front**, which advocated complete independence for the state. With its headquarters in **Azad Kashmir**, the government of Pakistan has been under international as well as Indian pressure to ban this militant outfit. In December 2005 the European Union added the HM to its list of banned terror groups. (*See* **Kashmir Dispute**.)

Hossain, Kamal

Dr Kamal Hossain, an eminent barrister and leader of the **Bangladesh Awami League (AL)**, was a government minister in 1972–75. He is recognized as one of the major contributors to drawing up the new Constitution for the country as chairman of the Constitution Drafting Committee, Constituent Assembly of Bangladesh, 1972. He finally left the AL and formed a new party in 1990, named **Gano Forum (People's Forum)**, of which he became chairman. He is associated with a number of national and international organizations and has held the chairmanship of Committees on Legal Aspects of Sustainable Development, International Law, Bangladesh Legal Aid and Services Trust.

Hundi System (Pakistan)

The term 'Hundi System' is used to describe an informal system of money-laundering and camouflage in Pakistan. This includes, for example, 'money changers' who handle the transfer of money from one place to another without using the formal channels of a banking system. The 'Hundi System' came under scrutiny following 11 September 2001, when it was revealed that the terrorist attacks that took place on that day had been partly financed through the 'Hundi System' network.

I

Imam, Jahanara

Jahanara Imam (1929–94), prolific writer and Fulbright scholar, was idolized in Bangladesh as 'Shaheed Janani' ('Mother of Martyrs'). Today she is well known as a socio-political activist who headed the struggle to oppose the rehabilitation of pro-Pakistani collaborators, e.g. the anti-liberation figure, Golam Azam, who was accused of being a war criminal and a mass murderer. Imam's husband was killed by the Pakistani army during interrogation and her son, Rumi, a recognized member of the **Mukhti Bahini**, went missing in action during the **Bangladesh Liberation War** of 1971. During the war she wrote a diary, *Ekattarer Dinguli* ('The days of '71', published in English as '*Of Blood and Fire*'), which gained attention as an evocative documentation of these times. She entered the political arena as the co-ordinator of the Ghatak-Dalal Nirmul Committee (Committee to Exterminate Traitors and Collaborators), under which she set up the **Gono/Gana Adalat** (people's court), asking for the people's verdict against the collaborators of 1971, and to maintain the spirit of the struggle for liberation among the people after independence.

India, Republic of

The Republic of India has an area of 3,287,590 sq km, a coastline of 7,000 km and shares land borders with Tibet and Nepal to the north, Bangladesh to the east, Bhutan and Myanmar to the north east and Pakistan to the north west. Capital: New Delhi; population: 1,029,991,145 (2001 estimate), comprising Indo-Aryan (72%), Dravidian (25%), Mongoloid and others (3%) (2000); religion: Hindu (80.5%), Muslim (13.4%), Christian (2.3%), Sikh (1.9%); others, including Buddhist, Jain, Parsi (1.8%); unspecified 0.1% (2001 census); official languages: Hindi is the national language and English is widely used, but there are 14 other officially recognized lanugages—Bengali, Telugu, Marathi, Tamil, Urdu, Gujarati, Malayalam, Kannada, Oriya, Punjabi, Assamese, Kashmiri, Sindhi and Sanskrit. Executive power is formally vested in the President who is elected by an electoral college consisting of elected members of both houses of parliament and the legislatures of the states. The Union of India consists of 28 states and seven **Union Territories**.

History: After two centuries of British colonial rule, India gained independence on 15 August 1947. **Partition** claimed the lives of thousands and led to the death of *Mahatma* **Gandhi** who had been trying to stem the communal violence that had been unleashed. The constituent assembly, which met from 1946 until 1950, adopted the model of British parliamentary democracy, separating power between the executive, the legislature and the judiciary. The Constitution of independent India was promulgated on 26 January 1950, today celebrated as Republic Day. Among the challenges facing the new country were the need to integrate the more than 500 princely states, the conflict over Kashmir (*See* **Kashmir Dispute**) which had erupted in 1947 and demands for reorganizing states along linguistic lines (*see* **Linguistic Regionalism**). The **Indian National Congress (INC)**, under the leadership of Jawaharlal **Nehru**, India's first Prime Minister (from 1947 until 1964), remained the largest and strongest party after independence. Nehru and the party exercised a great influence on Indian politics, with the INC holding substantial majorities at the centre and in virtually all states. During Nehru's 17 years in power, through three general elections (in 1952, 1957 and 1962), the foundations of an economic and foreign policy that were to shape post-colonial India's economic and political development were laid. Nehru died in 1964 and was succeeded as Prime Minister by Lal Bahadur Shastri who led the country during the 1965 war with Pakistan and the subsequent **Tashkent Agreement**. Following Lal Bahadur Shastri's sudden death in January 1966, the INC was headed by Nehru's daughter, Indira **Gandhi**, until her assassination in 1984. Winning an election in 1967 which ended the general pre-dominance of Congress in the states (*see* **Congress System**), Indira Gandhi was Prime Minister until 1977. Faced with opposition from within her party, which split in 1969, Indira Gandhi consolidated her position with a victory in the 1971 elections and the war with Pakistan in August 1971 that led to its dismemberment, the creation of Bangladesh and the **Simla Agreement**. Nevertheless, a popular campaign, led by J. P. **Narayan**, capitalizing on widespread economic and political discontent, threatened Indira Gandhi enough for her to declare a state of emergency in 1975. Elections were called in 1977 and Indira Gandhi was defeated and the INC replaced for the first time at the centre. The Janata government, a coalition of opposition parties, was formed under Prime Minister Morarji Desai, but, owing to rifts within the alliance, lasted only until 1979. A government formed at the invitation of the President also failed to gather enough support, resulting in elections being held in 1980 and Indira Gandhi's return to power with an overwhelming victory.

Indira Gandhi's second term of office was marked by violent regional and religious separatism in the states of **Punjab** and **North East India**, which concluded in 1984 when she was assassinated by Sikh members of her own personal guard. Swept into power on a wave of sympathy, Indira Gandhi's son, Rajiv Gandhi, came to power in an unprecedented triumph for the Congress. Adopting a less confrontational approach towards opposition members and leaders of various regional movements, Rajiv Gandhi appeared to be a modern, progressive Prime Minister. Nevertheless, demands for an independent **Khalistan** continued in Punjab. Faced with allegations of corruption due to the **Bofors Scandal**, events in Sri Lanka, where an **Indian Peace Keeping Force (IPKF)** was caught in a civil war, and the **Ayodhya Conflict**, the Congress suffered a massive decline in support in the 1989 elections. The **Bharatiya Janata Party (BJP)** emerged as a significant force, winning 88 seats in total and initially extending support to V. P. Singh's short-lived National Front government. In the 1991 elections the BJP established itself as the strongest opposition party, Congress returning to power under Narasimha **Rao** who, after Rajiv Gandhi's assassination in 1991, took over leadership of the party in an interim capacity. Facing a serious foreign exchange and fiscal crisis, the new government launched a programme of economic reforms. That both Congress and the BJP entered into pre-poll alliances for the 1996 elections demonstrated the growing importance of regional parties, such as the **All-India Anna Dravida Munnetra Kazhagam (AIADMK)**, and the **Shiv Sena**. The BJP won the largest number of seats but failed to achieve a majority, giving way after a 13-day period in government. A 13-party coalition emerged to form a government known as the United Front, under the former chief minister of Karnataka, H. D. Deve Gowda. His government lasted less than a year, the Congress Party withdrawing its support in March 1997. Inder Kumar Gujral replaced Deve Gowda as Prime Minister at the head of a 16-party United Front coalition which also collapsed when Congress withdrew its support, in November 1997. In the elections of 1998 the BJP emerged as the biggest party, increasing its tally of **Lok Sabha** seats from 160 to 182 and forming a coalition government under Prime Minister **Vajpayee**. A political stalemate caused by the withdrawal of the AIADMK in April 1999 caused the government to lose a vote of confidence by just one vote. Fresh elections were called and in 1999 a 24-member BJP-led alliance, the **National Democratic Alliance (NDA)**, won an outright majority.

Latest Elections: Deciding to hold early elections in April and May 2004, the BJP projected its achievements in terms of the economy while the Congress highlighted the growing wealth gap and the rural poor. Sonia **Gandhi** and her children, Priyanka and Rahul Gandhi (*see* **Nehru-Gandhi Family**), played leading roles in the campaign. Winning 145 seats, the Congress-led **United Progressive Alliance (UPA)** formed a coalition government, with the support of the left parties from the outside. While it was assumed that Sonia Gandhi, as leader of Congress, would become Prime Minister, she announced, shortly after the election results became known, her decision to support Manmohan **Singh** instead.

Recent Developments: In June 2004 L. K. **Advani** was elected as parliamentary leader of the BJP and leader of the opposition and in October 2004 also became BJP president. However, by the end of 2005 both leaders had stepped down, Vajpayee announcing his retirement from active politics and Advani resigning as party president.

India, Political Development

Since independence in 1947, India's political development has been marked by a transformation of the party system, the extension of participation and the federalization of the polity (*see* Federalism). The initial 'one-party dominant system' with the **Indian National Congress (INC)** at the centre was commonly referred to as the '**Congress system**'. From 1977 the system moved towards a competitive multi-party system, with parties forming along the whole left-right spectrum of politics. During the anti-colonial movement the INC had acted as a meeting point for people of all social backgrounds. Led by members of the **Nehru-Gandhi Family**, it dominated post-independence politics both at the national level and in the states for much of modern Indian history. In the 1980s, and, more dramatically, in the 1990s, it lost its dominant position as a quasi-two-party system evolved with the rise of the **Bharatiya Janata Party (BJP)**. It should be noted that the plurality voting system is partly responsible for the INC's hegemonic position, since no party has ever been able to muster an absolute majority of votes in a national election.

Over time, smaller regional parties have also gained greater significance. Since the second half of the 1990s, for example, regional parties such as the **Telugu Desam Party (TDP)** from **Andhra Pradesh**, or the **Biju Janata Dal (BJD)** from **Orissa**, have played a decisive role not just as governmental parties in their respective states, but also as key partners in alliances with national parties at the centre. As a result the two major national parties—the INC and the BJP—have been dragged into pre-poll alliances aiming to achieve the most convenient seat-sharing arrangement in terms of the seat/votes ratio. This growing need for coalition-building strategies has become a major feature of party politics in the last two decades, as demonstrated by the BJP-led **National Democratic Alliance (NDA)** and the INC-led **United Progressive Alliance (UPA)**. While most national governments managed to serve their respective terms on the basis of clear majorities, in the 1990s there was a series of minority or unstable coalition governments. Violent ethnic and religious conflicts have aggravated the sense of political instability. Among others, these have included **Operation Blue Star**, military action against Sikh terrorists in Amritsar in 1984, and, shortly afterwards, Prime Minister Indira **Gandhi**'s assassination and the destruction of the Babri Mosque, in the context of the **Ayodhya Conflict** in 1992.

Nevertheless, national policies, with regard to broad economic development, foreign affairs, and the secular character of the state, have remained stable despite several changes of government. All in all, India, after more than five decades of independence, can be regarded as a successful multicultural, post-colonial state with democratic institutions that may not have always been able to preclude political violence or temporary challenges to law and order, but which have over time managed to incorporate dissidence and opposition into the political process.

Constitution: The Constitution of the Republic of India came into force on 26 January 1950, which is celebrated each year as Republic Day. The Constitution was adopted by a constituent assembly that was formed before independence in 1946 and which, after 1950, became the provisional parliament of India until elections in 1952. Following **Partition** in 1947, the assembly comprised 299 members, mostly indirectly elected by members of the provincial legislative assemblies and members representing the Indian princely states. Key figures included Dr B. R. **Ambedkar**, regarded as the father of the Constitution, Jawaharlal **Nehru** and *Mahatma* **Gandhi**.

The longest written constitution of any independent nation, the Indian Constitution contains 395 articles and 12 schedules. Laying down the basic structure of government, the Constitution also establishes democracy, socialism, secularism and national integration as national goals. The Constitution of India draws extensively on Western legal traditions, but distinguishes itself in terms of its aspirations to end socio-economic inequities. The result was the separation of powers among the executive, legislature and the judiciary at the national level, represented by the President and the Council of Ministers, the parliament and the Supreme Court respectively. Furthermore, a division of powers is provided for in a federal system.

Fundamental Rights (Articles 12–35) embodied in the Constitution are guaranteed to all citizens and include individual rights such as equality before the law, freedom of speech and expression, freedom of association and peaceful assembly, freedom of religion and the right to constitutional remedies for the protection of civil rights, such as habeas corpus. In addition, the fundamental rights aim at rectifying past inequalities, abolishing '**untouchability**', prohibiting discrimination on the grounds of religion, caste and gender, and forbidding forced labour. Furthermore, minority rights are ensured through the right to preserve a distinctive language and to organize educational institutions.

An important feature is the Directive Principles of State Policy (Articles 36–51). Though not legally enforceable, these act like guide-lines, identifying goals such as a uniform civil code and the organization of village *panchayats* (*see* ***Panchayati Raj***) as units of self-government, which was adopted under the 73rd and 74th amendments of 1992.

Drawing from the 1935 Government of India Act, the Indian Constitution in fact contains many emergency clauses dating from colonial times as well as a tendency to concentrate power in the hands of the central government, particularly in the office of the Prime Minister. A system of checks and balances has, however, emerged, particularly with the assertiveness of the Supreme Court and election commission and the growing power of regional parties, resulting in coalition governments at the centre.

Schedules can be added to the Constitution by amendment. Among others, the 12 existing schedules cover the designations of the states and **Union Territories**, allocation of seats in the **Rajya Sabha** and **Lok Sabha**, provisions for the **Scheduled Castes (SCs)** and **Scheduled Tribes (STs)**, state, union and concurrent lists of responsibilities. Amendments normally require the support of at least two-thirds of the two houses to be passed. Despite this, the Indian Constitution is one of the most frequently amended in the world, with the first amendment passed only one year after the Constitution had been promulgated. In 1973 the landmark case of *Kesavananda Bharati vs. The State of Kerala* produced a ruling which posited that, under Article 368, parliament is not able to alter the basic structure or framework of the Constitution. Under Indira Gandhi, the 42nd amendment of 1976, which also inserted the words 'socialist' and 'secular' into the preamble, sought to prevent any court from reviewing constitutional amendments, with the exception of procedural issues concerning ratification. However, in *Minerva Mills vs. Union of India* 1980, clauses (4) and (5) of Article 368 inserted by the 42nd amendment were struck out by the Supreme Court as violating the basic structure of the Constitution, thereby reaffirming its power of judicial review.

Executive: The President combines the ceremonial roles of the head of state with some substantive powers as well. Under the Constitution, executive power is formally vested in the President. The Constitution provides the President with the authority to suspend fundamental rights and declare a state of emergency under Article 352, to impose President's Rule in a region under Article 356 (the state is then ruled directly by the union executive), and a provision for financial emergency under Article 360 which has not so far been used. However, the President is expected to exercise these powers on the advice of the Council of Ministers, which has as its head the Prime Minister. Advice given to the President by the Prime Minister, as stipulated by the Constitution, cannot be enquired into by a court of law. Furthermore, the Constitution requires that important presidential proclamations be laid before parliament for approval within two months of their announcement, failing which they will lapse. The President also appoints the Prime Minister and has the authority to dismiss him, although this has not yet happened. Elected for a five-year term through a procedure that involves the political representation and active participation of all the country's regions as well as the national parties, the President is eligible for re-election and may be impeached for violation of the Constitution. Election occurs through proportional representation by a simple transferable vote, a complicated voting procedure designed to ensure uniformity among the states as well as parity between the regions as a whole and the nation. The fact that both offices were occupied by leaders from or supported by Congress party facilitated co-operation during the early years of the republic (Prime Minister Jawaharlal Nehru and President Rajendra Prasad). In contrast to many developing countries, the appointment of the highest elected executive of India has been conducted through a regular and democratic process. However, India's democratic government was seriously compromised in 1975 through the imposition of a national emergency. Furthermore, the dismissal of elected governments at the regional level has been and continues to be an instrument used for political purposes. K. R. Narayanan, a former President (1997–2002) who was born into a family of former '**untouchables**', set an important precedent by twice declining the advice of the Council of Ministers to impose President's rule, first in **Uttar Pradesh** in 1997 and then in **Bihar** in 1998. On both occasions the states were ruled at the time by a party opposed to the one in power at the centre. Others, like Presidents Sanjova Reddy (1977–82), Zail Singh (1982–87), Dayal Sharma (1992–97) and Abdul Kalam (2002–) have also exercised their presidential prerogative.

As the connecting link between the ministry and the President, as well as between the ministry and parliament, the office of Prime Minister continues to be, as Nehru once described it, 'the lynchpin of Government'. Nevertheless, the coalitional nature of contemporary Indian politics requires much more consultation with other parties, leading sometimes to the open articulation of defiance against the authority of the Prime Minister, which would have been unthinkable during the days of Nehru. The extensive powers vested in the President are in fact exercised by the Prime Minister who, together with the ministers, controls and co-ordinates the departments of government and determines policy through the submission of a programme for parliamentary action. When the Prime Minister commands the majority in the Lok Sabha, his government is secure, but if defeated on any major issue, or if a no-confidence motion is passed, he must, by the conventions of cabinet government, resign but may officiate as Prime Minister until the next elections. After his government lost a vote of confidence in April 1999, Atal Bihari **Vajpayee** continued to lead an interim administration until elections were held in October. Since 1977, when the first non-Congress government came into power (under a BJP-led coalition), governments have been less stable and a number of Prime Ministers have had to resign as a result of party splits or no-confidence votes before completing their full term. Other practices of cabinet government have become institutionalized in India as well. The Cabinet provides the necessary backing to the Prime Minister. It also provides a balance to his authority through its collective weight. This model was sorely tested during the tenure of Indira Gandhi, whose authoritarian tendencies and distrust of colleagues undermined the Cabinet's role in providing policy and administrative leadership. However, subsequent developments have restored the conventions of parliamentary government and the principle of collective responsibility. Under collective responsibility, each minister accepts and shares responsibility for all decisions of the Cabinet. A dissenting member is morally bound to resign and may not vote against government policy in parliament. In addition, the principles of consensus and accommodation as core values of the political system are so deeply entrenched that even after the end of Congress dominance and the coming of non-Congress governments, there has been no radical discontinuity in civil servants, policy mechanisms or even policy orientations. Following the victory of the Congress-led UPA in the 2004 parliamentary elections it was expected that Congress president Sonia **Gandhi** would, according to convention, become the Prime Minister. Instead, she proposed Congress member Manmohan **Singh**. Soon after, Sonia Gandhi was appointed chairperson of the newly created National Advisory Council (July 2004), ostensibly to monitor the implementation of the UPA's Common Minimum Programme.

President's Rule: A legacy of vice-regal emergency powers dating from colonial times, Article 356 of the Indian Constitution provides for President's rule, allowing the national Cabinet to disband a state legislature under certain conditions. During the first two decades of independence, under Prime Minister Jawaharlal Nehru, Article 356 was invoked twice, famously in the case of **Kerala** where the elected communist government was dismissed in 1959. President's rule has been frequently invoked when the ruling state government has been unable to obtain the required parliamentary majority in the state legislature. Resorting to Article 356 has also occurred when the state government has been unable to cope with a crisis, irrespective of whether a parliamentary majority is retained, as in the cases of Nagaland, **Punjab** and Kashmir, where instability caused by separatist movements provided the justification to suspend the democratic process.

In the 1990s the provision for direct rule was challenged and in 1994 the Supreme Court ruled against the misuse of Article 356 and, furthermore, held that any proclamation under Article 356 would be subject to judicial review. While this has introduced some checks to potential misuse of the article and President K. R. Narayanan in October 1997 refused the union Cabinet's recommendation to impose President's rule in Uttar Pradesh and, again, in 1998 for Bihar, the Article has been invoked more than 100 times since 1950.

Legislature: At independence in 1947 the constituent assembly was drawing up the Constitution of India. Between January 1950, when the Constitution was adopted, and 1952, when the first general elections were held, the constituent assembly also acted as an interim legislative body. In May 2004 the 14th Lok Sabha was formed. The Lok Sabha, or lower house, is closely modelled on the British House of Commons. However, unlike Britain, India is a federation and has borrowed features of the American system, such as the Rajya Sabha, the upper house, which resembles the US senate. Reflecting the philosophy of social justice that underpinned the Freedom Movement, some special features characterize the Indian legislature, e.g. the quota system of 'reserved' seats for former 'untouchables' and tribals. The Lok Sabha may comprise a maximum of 545 seats, of which 543 are directly elected on the basis of adult suffrage from single-member constituencies, a simple majority deciding the winner. Two members of the Anglo-Indian Community may be nominated by the President if, in his opinion, the community is inadequately represented in the house. The term of the Lok Sabha is five years unless extended under emergency conditions, which has happened only once, during the emergency of 1975–77. The Constitution specifies that the Lok Sabha must meet at least twice a year, with no more than six months between sessions. The business of parliament is transacted primarily in English or Hindi, but provisions are made for the use of other Indian languages. A number of parliamentary committees function as watchdogs over the executive or as information providers. The first hour of the parliamentary day (known as zero hour) is devoted to questions that bring ministers under public scrutiny, but the Lok Sabha's ultimate control over the executive lies in the motion of no-confidence that can bring down the government.

The Rajya Sabha consists of a maximum of 250 members, of whom 12 are nominated by the President for any outstanding expertise of knowledge they may have in a specific area. Reflecting the federal principle, the allocation of the remaining seats among the regions corresponds to population, with the members being elected by the state legislative assembly for a term of six years. The terms are staggered, as in the US senate, so that one-third of the members stand for election every two years. The parliament is the supreme law-making body of the federal government and can make laws on a wide variety of subjects mentioned in the seventh schedule of the Constitution under 'Union List'. The parliament can also make laws in subjects mentioned in the 'Concurrent List', which covers areas that the states can also pass legislation on. In the case of conflict, union laws prevail. In addition, parliament can make laws in areas not mentioned in the Constitution at all. The legislative process follows British practice, with laws initiated in the form of government or private members' bills. All bills, except money bills with implications for spending, revenue, borrowing or India's financial reserves, which fall only under the Lok Sabha's authority, can be introduced in either house. Ordinary bills go through three readings in each house and at the second stage the bill may be referred to a select or joint committee of both houses. Once a bill has been passed by both houses, it requires the assent of the President in order to become a law, at which point the President can ask for technical and expert advice before making a decision. Other constitutional powers of the Lok Sabha include the ability to approve and remove members of the Council of Ministers, approval of central government finances, delimitation of state and Union Territory boundaries and amendment of the Constitution. There have been clashes with the Supreme Court over the extent to which parliament may amend the Constitution. The legislature of most states consists of only one house (the legislative assembly), whose members are directly elected by state residents for a period of five years. The choice of unicameralism or bicameralism was left to the states, depending on their assessment of costs and needs in running a second chamber. Any legislative assembly may create or abolish a legislative council (second chamber) through a majority of two-thirds, followed by an act of parliament.

Elections/Electoral System: Under the British Raj the elective principle was introduced into local bodies in India in 1884 and into provincial councils in 1892 and was progressively expanded through phases of reform. In 1909 the Morley-Minto reforms extended elections to the state legislative councils, expanding suffrage and introducing communal electorates (separate electorates for the Muslims). The Montagu-Chelmsford reforms of 1919 divided authority between the central and state governments and enfranchised 5m. Indians. The Government of India Act of 1935 increased the electorate to 30m. Following independence in 1947 the Constitution of India (adopted in 1950) made suffrage universal for all men and women at the age of 21 (in 1989 this was changed to 18) and the system of communal electorates was abolished. The country's first general elections were held in 1951/52. In 1951 more than 173.2m. registered to vote and in the 14th general elections, held in May 2004, more than 670m. people were eligible to vote, making India the largest democracy in the world. Under India's parliamentary system of government a core commitment is the holding of regular, free and fair elections. These elections determine the composition of the government, membership of the two houses of parliament, the state and Union Territory legislative assemblies, and the presidency (elected indirectly through an electoral college). The country is divided into 543 parliamentary constituencies, each of which returns one member to the Lok Sabha, the lower house, on the basis of a first-past-the-post system. The size and shape of the parliamentary constituencies are determined by a Delimitation Commission which has tried to create constituencies with roughly the same population. As a result, the boundaries of the constituencies are meant to be examined after each 10-yearly census in the light of changes in the population. Adjustments of this kind, however, have been suspended since the 1970s due to the stark difference in birth rates between northern and southern states. Elections to the Lok Sabha and to every state legislative assembly have to take place every five years unless called earlier. If a government can no longer command the confidence of the Lok Sabha, the President can dissolve parliament and call a general election. The Constitution states that elections must be held within six months of the last session of the dissolved Lok Sabha. The Election Commission, set up in January 1950, decides the schedule for elections and has to take into account weather, the agricultural cycle and security considerations. Elections are usually staggered over a period of one month to allow security forces to move from one part of the country to another. Any Indian citizen registered as a voter and aged 25 years or more can contest elections, either sponsored by a registered party or as an independent. In the reserved seats—79 for Scheduled Castes (SCs) and 41 for Scheduled Sribes (STs)—in the Lok Sabha, candidates can only come from the respective group although all registered voters are eligible to vote. A constitutional amendment to introduce reservations for women is under discussion. Voting is by secret ballot and in the 2004 Lok Sabha elections 800,000 polling booths were set up across the country. For the 2004 elections electronic voting machines were used for the first time instead of ballot boxes. Political parties must be registered with the Electoral Commission and registration is dependent on whether the party is deemed to be committed to the principles of democracy and secularism, holds organizational elections and has a written constitution. Party symbols must be allocated as they enable illiterate voters to identify candidates. Elections in the past have been extravagant events and, in order to introduce greater accountability and equality, tight limits on the amount of money a candidate can spend during the campaign have been imposed. The official campaign period lasts for two weeks from the drawing up of nominated candidates and officially ends 48 hours before polling closes. Voter turn-out has steadily increased over the years, particularly amongst women and members of the Scheduled Castes and Scheduled Tribes, where it has almost reached the national average. In 1951 overall electoral participation was recorded at 45.7%, reaching a peak of 64.1% in the 1984 elections. In 2004 voter turn-out was 57.9%. In addition, the number of candidates contesting each election has grown from an average in 1952 of 3.6 per constituency to 25.6 in 1996. In 1996 certain remedial measures were taken to make it more difficult to stand as a candidate, such as increasing the size of the deposit and requiring a larger number of supporters for a nomination. As a result, in the 1999 Lok Sabha elections the proportion fell to 8.6 per constituency. The resilience and value attached to the electoral system was made evident in the 1977 elections, which followed a period of authoritarian rule (1975–77) under the emergency declared by Prime Minister Indira Gandhi. Calling elections in the belief that she would be re-elected, the electorate instead punished her by throwing the Congress party out of office. The 1977 elections also marked a watershed in India's party politics, bringing to power for the first time a non-Congress government at the centre under the Janata Dal, a fusion of the four main opposition parties. Until then, the first-past-the-post system had enabled Congress to win majorities in the legislature and, together with a fragmented opposition, had resulted in a one-dominant party system. Since 1977, with the emergence of coalition politics and a multi-party system, Congress majorities have disappeared and small changes in vote share can now have a dramatic impact upon the resulting parliament. In 1996 yet another unprecedented situation emerged when a coalition government was established by the United Front, a combination of 13 parties with opposed ideologies, as an alternative to both the largest party, in terms of seats, the BJP, and the second largest, Congress.

The electoral process is widely regarded as free and fair, and the Electoral Commission is highly respected, independent and rigorously enforces the 'model code of conduct' which sets out what political parties and candidates can and cannot do in the run-up to elections. Electronic voting machines have helped to counter problems of ballot rigging. However, a serious problem is the appeal to sectarian forces during election time that can and has fuelled violence. Transitions from one government to the next have nevertheless generally been smooth. Elections to the state assemblies (the *Vidhan Sabhas*) are carried out in the same manner as the Lok Sabha elections, with states and Union Territories divided into single-member constituencies and implementing a first-past-the-post system. The assemblies range in size according to population, the largest being that of Uttar Pradesh, with 403 elected members, and the smallest that of **Pondicherry** (a Union Territory), with 30.

Social Movements: Social movements have played an important role in India's political development. Operating through extensive grassroots networks, they have focused on numerous issues, employing various methods. In the early years after independence Ambedkar symbolized the struggle to reform the **caste system** and improve the conditions of the SCs, giving rise to the **Republican Party of India** that represented not only former 'untouchables' but also the labouring class. Most of the major political parties, such as the Congress, the BJP and the communist parties, have institutionalized links with student, labour and women's movements, but since the 1970s the NGO sector has been growing in size and importance. Amongst agricultural labourers, constituting a large percentage of the country's labour force and heavily under-unionized, Gandhian volunteer organizations have campaigned against bonded labour, for the improvement of educational facilities and for the implementation of the Minimum Wages Act. Movements have also turned into armed struggles. The Telangana insurrection in Andhra Pradesh began in 1946 as a peasant movement against low wages, forced labour and the misappropriation of land. The movement came under the leadership of the **Communist Party of India (CPI)** by mid-1948, which advocated guerrilla warfare to destroy the existing power structure, inspiring others, such as the land-grab movement of the mid-1950s and the **Naxalite Movement**. Environmental concerns emerged in the 1970s, with forest-dwellers and tribals initiating movements to protest against encroachments or restrictions on their rights. Among the most famous were the **Chipko Movement** and, later in the 1980s, the **Narmada Dam** movement. In response, the state has used methods of repression and co-option. Reservations have been introduced in jobs and educational institutions for backward castes and tribes, and programmes and agencies have been established to uplift the poor, such as the **Integrated Rural Development Programme (IRDP)**. At the same time, power-holders have been able to suppress the demands of the poor and disadvantaged with the collusion of the police and local government. (*See* '**Untouchability**'; **Scheduled Tribes**.)

Emergency: The Indian Constitution identifies three types of emergencies that may justify the suspension of fundamental rights, each of which must be approved by parliament. The first is a 'National Securities Emergency' (Article 352), under which the President, acting on the Prime Minister's advice, may proclaim a state of emergency if the 'security of India, or any part of its territory is threatened by war, external aggression or armed rebellion'. When Article 352 is invoked, Articles 353 and 354 enter into operation, allowing the central government to suspend federal provisions and assume direct control over the states and revenue. A 'Constitutional Emergency in the States' (Article 356) occurs when the President, acting on the advice of the governor of a state and the Prime Minister, proclaims a state of emergency in that state because the normal process of government cannot be carried out in accordance with the Constitution. The third type, a 'Financial Emergency' (Article 360), may be declared by the President, acting on the Prime Minister's advice, if the country's financial or monetary stability is threatened. Article 352 was invoked by the Congress government of Indira Gandhi during the war with Pakistan in 1971, leading to the creation of Bangladesh. The same article was invoked by Indira Gandhi in the name of maintaining internal security when a 'National Emergency' was declared between June 1975 and March 1977. Faced with growing allegations of electoral fraud for the 1971 elections, a conviction by Allahabad High Court on 21 June 1975 proved to be the final trigger. Finding the Prime Minister guilty of using government machinery for election purposes, the court ordered her to be removed from her parliamentary seat and banned from contesting the next election. In support of the verdict, labour and student union strikes swept across the country and protests in the captial were led by J. P. **Narayan** and Morarji Desai. Assuming extraordinary powers under Article 352, the government suspended fundamental rights, postponed general elections and incarcerated more than 150,000 people, including several members of parliament who stood up against it as well as leaders such as J. P. Narayan. This was the first major trial for India's democracy and one of the most controversial periods in the country's political development. During this period Indira Gandhi introduced a 20-point economic programme to increase agricultural and industrial production, improve public services and fight poverty and illiteracy. In addition, amendments to the Constitution were passed exonerating her from the charges of electoral fraud. Furthermore, President's Rule was declared in **Gujarat** and **Tamil Nadu** where anti-Indira Gandhi parties ruled. On 23 January 1977 fresh elections were scheduled for March and all political prisoners were released. The national emergency officially ended on 23 March 1977 and in the subsequent elections Congress suffered its first defeat in parliament, with the Janata Party alliance of opposition parties taking power and Indira Gandhi losing her own constituency seat.

After the Congress party's defeat, the conditions for declaring an emergency were made more stringent, although instability in the 1980s due to separatist movements and terrorism led to amendments and to legislation granting special powers.

Anti-defection Law: In 1985 the government of India under Prime Minister Rajiv Gandhi introduced anti-defection legislation in the form of the Tenth Schedule by the 52nd Amendment of the Constitution. This legislation stipulated that a member (whether elected as a candidate of a political party, as an independent or as a nominated member) of either house of parliament or any legislative assembly in the states or Union Territories would be disqualified if he/she gave up voluntarily membership of the political party he/she belonged to at the time of election, or if he/she voted or abstained from voting contrary to the directions of his/her party or of a person authorized by that party to give such directions without obtaining prior or subsequent permission from that party. To further curb the problem of defections the NDA government amended the Tenth Schedule in 2004 by deleting Section 3 which had legitimized splits or mergers involving a group constituting one-third of members of a party in the legislature. New restrictions introduced through the 91st Constitutional Amendment Act bar defections both individually or as a group. Those opposed to stringent anti-defection laws claim that they threaten the very idea of democracy by discouraging individual political dissent.

Horse Trading: Political term for the process of bargaining within the parliamentary sphere when political parties resort to unscrupulous means to lure members from another party to put together the majority required to form a government. Sometimes the defectors are rewarded with ministerial berths and often with monetary gain. In India it is recognized as a form of corruption at the highest political level. To reduce the chaos caused by the numerous splits and mergers that result from horse trading, the anti-defection law was passed in 1985.

Foreign Policy: Prime Minister Jawaharlal Nehru dominated Indian foreign policy-making for the first 17 years after India's independence, establishing the pillars of non-alignment and ***Panchasheela***. During the 1950s and 1960s India gained an unnaturally high international profile partly on the basis of Gandhi's legacy and Nehru's engagement in foreign affairs. A founder member of the UN, India has always been a major contributor to UN peace-keeping missions. Initiatives of Nehru include the Non-Aligned Movement (launched in collaboration with Tito and Nasser in 1956) and an Afro-Asian solidarity movement initiated in 1955. However, by the mid-1960s India had experienced a humiliating defeat by the Chinese in 1962 and a war with Pakistan, prompting a rethink of foreign policy (*see* Military). Under Prime Minister Indira Gandhi India began to more actively assert its power, tilting towards the Soviet Union with the treaty of 1970 and the war with Pakistan in 1971 that led to its dismemberment and the creation of Bangladesh. This trend was continued under Prime Minister Rajiv Gandhi who sent an **Indian Peace Keeping Force (IPKF)** to Sri Lanka in 1987 and made a landmark visit to China in 1988.

With the end of the Cold War and the loss of the Soviet Union as a veto-wielding ally in the UN Security Council, India was forced to revise its foreign policy thinking. Under Prime Minister Narasimha **Rao**'s government a 'Look East' policy was developed, reviving India's links with the ASEAN region. First a sectoral dialogue partner of the ASEAN in 1992, India became a fully-fledged dialogue partner in 1997 and a summit partner in 2001. Also initiated under the Rao administration, and continued by subsequent governments, was the greater emphasis given to trade and co-operation, a central feature of agreements concluded with the European Union, Russia, the USA and China in the 1990s as well as with South Asian countries, in an attempt to improve India's relations with its neighbours. The establishment of diplomatic relations with Israel in 1992, the nuclear tests of 1998 (*see* **Nuclearization**), the lobbying for a permanent seat on the UN Security Council, the 'Next Steps in Strategic Partnership' with the USA in July 2005, each groundbreaking, represent a new pragmatism in Indian foreign policy. Along with the economic reforms of the 1990s launched by the Congress government under Narasimha Rao and continued by Prime Minister Vajpayee under the NDA, a more active economic diplomacy has been pursued to attract foreign investment as well as increase India's bargaining power on the international stage through institutions such as the World Trade Organization.

Non-Alignment: The policy of avoiding ideological affiliations with either of the major power blocs during the Cold War, non-alignment came to officially characterize Indian foreign policy. Not meant to be a position of neutrality, non-alignment was rather an instrument of foreign policy to enhance India's manoeuvrability, particularly in the securing of foreign aid.

India-China Relations: As the two largest countries in Asia, sharing a 2,000-km contested border and, additionally, as emerging economic powers in the international system, the relations between India and the People's Republic of China (PRC) are of critical importance. This was appreciated by Prime Minister Jawaharlal Nehru and efforts were made to engage in peaceful relations with the newly communist

PRC, India being one of the first countries to establish diplomatic relations with it, in 1950. A high-point of the so-called '**Hindi-Chini Bhai Bhai**' spirit was the 1954 *Panchasheela* agreement which committed the two countries to 'peaceful coexistence'. India recognized China's suzerainty over Tibet, voluntarily giving up its military, communications and other rights which India had inherited from the British. This area, traditionally a buffer zone between the two neighbours, gained particular significance following the discovery of a completed Chinese road running through the **Aksai Chin** region of the Ladakh District of **Jammu and Kashmir**. Disputes over maps showing the **McMahon Line**, together with the flight of the Dalai Lama to India in 1959, raised tensions between the two countries. Following border clashes, on 10 October 1962 Chinese forces attacked India, easily defeating the unprepared and ill-equipped Indian forces and occupying strategic points in Ladakh and the **North East Frontiers Agency (NEFA)**. China declared a unilateral cease-fire on 21 November and withdrew 20 km behind a **Line of Actual Control (LAC)**. Relations with China worsened during the 1960s as China-Pakistan relations improved and, taking advantage of the Sino-Soviet split, India in the 1970s drew closer to the Soviet Union. In 1976 ambassadorial links were restored but border discussions remained stalled until the late 1980s. Rajiv Gandhi travelled to China in 1988, the first visit by an Indian Prime Minister since that of Nehru in 1954, and opened new avenues for cultural and economic ties and co-operation as well as establishing a joint working group on the boundary question.

A series of high-profile visits between the two nations helped to further improve relations and boost economic interaction, with Prime Minister Narasimha Rao visiting China in 1993 and signing the Agreement on the Maintenance of Peace and Tranquillity along the Line of Actual Control. In 1996, during a state visit to India by Chinese President Jiang Zemin, the two countries agreed to confidence-building measures along the disputed border. Although relations suffered a set-back when, following the 1998 nuclear tests, the Indian defence minister cited China as India's 'potential threat number one', Indian officials quickly confirmed their committment to friendly relations with China. Prime Minister Atal Bihari Vajpayee's visit to China in 2003 shifted the emphasis to trade, economic co-operation and investment, reflecting the rapid growth in bilateral trade that had occurred, from US $338m. in 1992 to US $7,600m. in 2003 and US $13,600m. in 2004.

Despite improved relations and a deeper economic relationship, the border remains a potential source of friction, with India claiming Aksai Chin, and China disputing territory in India's north-eastern state of Arunachal Pradesh (*see* **North East India**). Pakistan-China relations, as well as China's support for regimes in India's near neighbourhood, have also been a concern to India.

India-Pakistan Relations: Gaining independence one day apart from each other in August 1947, India and Pakistan were carved out of British India, their freedom struggles led by the Congress and the All-India Muslim League respectively. Sharing deep cultural similarities, particularly North India and Pakistan, Partition divided families, separated religious communities from their holy sites, for example the Sikhs in India from the birthplace of Guru Nanak Dev, close to Lahore, as well as creating a bitter feud that has lasted more than 50 years. India and Pakistan's borders include the disputed **Line of Control (LoC)** in Kashmir and an international border running along the Indian states of Punjab, **Rajasthan** and Gujarat and the Pakistani provinces of Punjab and **Sind**.

Out of the three full-scale wars fought, two have been directly related to the **Kashmir Dispute**. In 1947–48 the first war resulted in a cease-fire that was to become the *de facto* border in the north. In an attempt to change the *status quo*, Pakistan initiated a second war in 1965 that resulted in the **Tashkent Agreement** which maintained the cease-fire line. The third war in 1971 led to the creation of Bangladesh and ended with the **Simla Agreement** of 1972 that established the LOC in Kashmir. The border in this region has remained contested, with fighting taken to the extreme heights of the **Siachen Glacier** ever since 1984. Attempts at negotiations and dialogue between the two nations have failed on every occasion, one of the few treaties to function being the **Indus Water Treaty** concluded in 1960. Apart from indigenous causes to the long-running rivalry, such as the rise of Pakistan's powerful military élite, the emergence of Islamic fundamentalism and India's allegations that Pakistan aided Sikh terrorists in Punjab in the 1980s and Kashmiri militants in the 1990s, there have been external intervening factors, such as the Cold War and extra-regional players. During the Cold War, India and Pakistan found themselves on opposite 'sides', Pakistan a strategic ally of the USA and India officially maintaining a policy of non-alignment but tilting towards the Soviet Union. Pakistan's close relations with China added to India's security concerns, particularly after the 1965 war when the threat of a two-front war, with Pakistan to the west and China to the east, became a real one.

Despite the end of the Cold War and a series of civilian governments in Pakistan under Benazir **Bhutto** and Nawaz **Sharif** in the 1990s, relations between the two countries seemed to worsen. Discussions, begun in 1990, over **confidence-building measures (CBMs)** were cancelled in June 1992 following mutual expulsions of diplomats for alleged espionage activities. With the emergence of an armed ethno-nationalist movement within Indian-administered Kashmir, the state of Jammu and Kashmir, discussions on the Kashmir issue were frozen. In June 1994 the Indian Army began to deploy a new missile, *Prithvi*, which had the capacity to reach most parts of Pakistan and in April 1998 Pakistan tested its new intermediate-range missile, capable of reaching deep into Indian territory. Both countries went nuclear in May 1998, raising fears that an arms race had been initiated (*see* **Nuclearization**). Talks were resumed, with Prime Minister Vajpayee crossing the land border to inaugurate the first passenger bus service between the two countries. The Lahore Declaration was signed in February 1999, pledging peace and stability. Tensions, however, soon returned to the fore, culminating in the **Kargil** crisis in mid-1999.

After the military coup of 1999 by President **Musharraf**, the two states came close to yet another war in 2002 when, following an attack on its parliament in

December 2001 that India blamed on Pakistan-sponsored terrorists, India mobilized troops along the border. Pakistan responded and the possibility of nuclear war between two neighbours once again arose. Brought back from the brink through international pressure and diplomacy, a peace process was finally initiated in April 2003 by Prime Minister Vajpayee. A cease-fire was implemented along the LoC and in January 2004, at the Islamabad **SAARC** summit, the countries agreed to resume a 'composite dialogue' on all major issues. Despite a change of government in India in May 2004, the dialogue continued with the high-profile visit of President Musharraf to India in April 2005. Issues to be covered by the composite dialogue included Kashmir and CBMs as well as several other long-running conflicts, such as the Siachen Glacier and Sir Creek, a maritime dispute over an estuary, believed to hold oil and gas desposits, separating Gujarat and Sind. Water-sharing disagreements also relate to Kashmir where India wants to build a barrage across the mouth of Wullar Lake which Pakistan argues will be used to deprive its farmers of irrigation water.

Positive developments have been largely in terms of 'people-to-people' contact, such as the resumption of air, train and bus services, cricket matches, cultural exchanges and the provision of medical facilities. Following the earthquake of October 2005 the two countries collaborated to open crossing points along the LoC to enable families to visit relatives across the border and to facilitate the transport of aid to isolated areas. While there is no formal trade agreement between the two countries, it is estimated that the annual value of illicit trade is more than US $1,000m., demonstrating the substantial potential for closer commercial links. Nevertheless, critical hurdles in the India-Pakistan relationship remain. Both countries continue to invest heavily in defence, contributing to spiralling costs and mutual insecurity. The role of the USA, particularly since President Clinton's landmark visit to India in 2000 and the 2001 terrorist attacks in America which revived Pakistan's strategic importance, could be either a stabilizing or a destabilizing force as it engages more extensively with India.

India-Russia Relations: From the early 1950s and throughout the Cold War India and the Soviet Union maintained close co-operative ties. India's policy of non-alignment enabled it to accept Soviet aid in the sectors of industrial development, defence production and arms purchases, without falling exclusively into the Soviet sphere of influence, balancing this with copious foreign aid from the USA, particularly for food under the PL480. By 1965 the USSR was the second largest national contributor to India's development and one of India's few supporters in the international arena on issues such as Kashmir and, in 1971, Bangladesh. Under Prime Minister Indira Gandhi relations peaked with a 20-year Treaty of Peace, Friendship and Co-operation concluded in 1971, which, while not a mutual security treaty, helped counterbalance the emerging Pakistan-USA-China triangle. During the 1980s numerous high-level visits took place, in the course of which Prime Minister Rajiv Gandhi made four official trips to the USSR. Following the disintegration of the USSR and the demise of the bipolar international system, India lost an important ally in the international system and particularly in the UN Security Council. A new Treaty of Friendship and Co-operation that was signed in 1993 discarded the old security clauses that were directed specifically against the USA and China. Defence-related trade continues to form the bedrock of Russia-India relations. The purchase by India of a Russian aircraft carrier was finalized in January 2004, but the previous patron-client relationship has gradually shifted towards one of joint research and production, particularly in the case of scientific co-operation in the field of space and rocket technology. A new area of common strategic interest is linked to the energy sector, with India seeking to increase energy imports from Russia and the Central Asian republics. Significantly, Russia-India ties survived the transition to a post-Cold War world, with both sides recognizing and building upon the foundations of a time-tested relationship.

India-USA Relations: With the end of the Cold War and India's more outward-looking economic policy, relations between the USA and India have strengthened and deepened. Today, the USA is India's most important trading partner (with the value of bilateral trade in 2004 recorded at US $21,700m.), largest investor (with a 17% share) and military ties have also been intensified. In retrospect, the US-led sanctions imposed on India in the wake of the 1998 nuclear tests appear to have been a short-term disturbance to a long-term trend towards closer economic and security relations. In March 2000 US President Bill Clinton visited India, the first such visit by an American President in 22 years, and in September of that year Indian Prime Minister A. B. Vajpayee reciprocated, initiating a string of high-level exchange visits between the two countries. Prime Minister Manmohan Singh's visit to Washington, DC, in July 2005 successfully concluded the 'Next Steps in Strategic Partnership' to expand co-operation in space, civil nuclear energy and high technology.

The recent moves towards greater co-operation and trust between the two countries represent a considerable reversal from earlier times when different strategic and ideological factors strained relations. During the 1970s India-USA relations reached a nadir. In 1971, while the USA initiated a new relationship with China, India signed a friendship treaty with the Soviet Union. As the situation in East Pakistan deteriorated, the USA continued to supply arms to Pakistan and Prime Minister Indira Gandhi's November 1971 visit to Washington is remembered for the sour personal relations between her and US President Nixon. When war broke out in December 1971 and India intervened in East Pakistan, the USA's subsequent deployment of a nuclear-powered aircraft carrier to the Bay of Bengal left many in India convinced that the USA was a major security threat to India. After Nixon terminated a substantial amount of economic assistance, India began to clamp down on the flow of American scholars and intensified criticism of American policies in Cambodia and Viet Nam on the international stage. Relations improved throughout the 1980s despite divergent views on issues such as the Soviet intervention in Afghanistan, America's policies towards the Middle East and, particularly, Pakistan. In the early 1990s economic reforms stimulated an influx of American investment and technology and the end of the Cold War allowed for greater 'normalcy' in relations, in particular a more even-handed US approach to the Kashmir problem. India's 1998 nuclear tests automatically triggered US-imposed sanctions, but the arguments for good relations proved strong when, in 2001, these were lifted and a new convergence of interests emerged in the form of combating international terrorism and religious extremism. Closer defence relations have included joint naval exercises, the June 2005 landmark 10-year 'defence framework' and strategic partnership to help facilitate joint weapons production, co-operation on missile defence and the transfer of technology. Negotiations are under way to enable India to buy nuclear fuel and parts for civilian reactors provided these sites are open to inspection. The US-India economic dialogue was revitalized in 2005 as a channel to resolve commercial disputes and to boost bilateral trade and investment.

Judiciary: Article 214 of the Indian Constitution states that there shall be a High Court with full legal powers responsible for each state. There are 18 High Courts, each comprising a chief justice and seven other judges whom the President appoints. At the lowest rung of the judiciary are the district and session courts, the former presiding over civil cases and the latter over criminal cases. The Supreme Court, the apex body of India's judicial structure, has original, appellate and advisory jurisdiction and its exclusive original jurisdiction extends to disputes between the union government and one or more states and in disputes involving two or more states. It has appellate jurisdiction in any case, civil or criminal, that involves, by its own certification, a substantive question of law in the meaning and intent of the Constitution. The Supreme Court is the interpreter and guardian of the Constitution. Unlike the British system, where no court may hold an act of parliament invalid, all legislation passed in India by the union government or the states must be in conformity with the Constitution, and the constitutionality of any enactment is determined under the power of judicial review by the Supreme Court. The Supreme Court has gone as far as to state, in the landmark *Kesavananda Bharati* case (1973), that parliament, born of the Constitution, lacked the authority to amend the 'basic structure' of the Constitution. Judges appointed by the President shall serve as long as the President wishes them to serve ('during the pleasure of the President').

The Supreme Court of India has been vested with the power to give advisory opinions on any question of fact or law referred to it by the President (Article 143). The advisory opinion, however, is not binding on the government nor is it executable by law. The Supreme Court has been involved in such contentious issues as the **Ayodhya Conflict**, which has helped bring the dispute into the institutional structure rather than let it slip out of the political process of adjudication altogether.

Since the core judicial doctrine of the Constitution of India puts the 'procedure established by law' as superior to the American doctrine of 'natural justice', the Supreme Court was initially accorded a status below the parliament but above the national executive in terms of authoritative interpretation of the law. Gradually, however, the Supreme Court has asserted its supremacy in such matters and the evolution has been facilitated by the steady erosion of the massive legislative majorities at the disposition of the executive during the early decades after independence, the growing influence of the media and the mobilization of interest groups at the national level. The emergency rule of Indira Gandhi (1975–77) dented its authority and autonomy, but since then the court has re-established itself. Perhaps the most serious shortcoming of the Indian judiciary has been the slowness of procedure and the immense backlog of cases. It is estimated that there are about 3m. cases pending in the courts of India. While corruption, especially at the lower levels, is certainly one of the causes for delay, the sheer volume of cases filed is proof of the high esteem and trust that the Supreme Court has managed to retain in the eyes of the public, unlike other state institutions. In recent times judicial activism has extended to public interest litigation, a new doctrine under which the court has appointed itself as the guardian of vulnerable social groups and neglected areas of public life, such as the environment.

Uniform Civil Code: Article 44 of the Indian Constitution envisages a Uniform Civil Code for a population of more than 1,000m. of numerous different religious backgrounds and personal laws. The Constitution at the same time allows members of different faiths to follow their own religious laws. Under Prime Minister Jawaharlal Nehru the process of restructuring Hindu law was initiated through four controversial enactments in the 1950s. However, codification was left incomplete and the resulting ambiguities came to be challenged in courtrooms and academic analyses. Revived by the BJP, which called for similar reform of Muslim personal law as the next step towards a Uniform Civil Code, this became a hotly contested issue. (*See* **Shah Bano Case**.)

Defence (Security): For British India a crucial pillar of defence policy was the creation of buffer zones along the border areas. Following independence this strategy crumbled as both Pakistan and China emerged determined to assert their newly acquired sovereignty. On both flanks India's borders were contested, the first Kashmir conflict of 1947/48 and the Sino-India war of 1962 leaving in their wake the unresolved disputes over territory that remain a hindrance to regional stability. India's defence challenges reflect the dilemmas of a country that is by far the largest in the regional neighbourhood (*See* **Kashmir Dispute**.). Whilst the smaller states of Nepal and Bhutan depend on Indian military protection, trade and economic support, they have also perceived India to be a regional hegemon and bully. Thus, despite India's efforts to engage its neighbours through bilateral agreements, such as the 1950 Nehru-Liaquat Pact, the India-Nepal Treaty of Peace and Friendship, also of 1950, and the 1987 **Indo-Lanka Accord**, these have not earned their trust and loyalty. Whether India will decide to invest more in SAARC's potential to act as a multilateral security arrangement remains to be seen. Internal security challenges include low intensity conflicts (ethnic, tribal, communal, and also involving left-wing movements) and the increasing frequency and audacity of terrorist attacks directed at soft targets calculated to inflame communal sentiments, to disrupt the economy, as in the 1993 **Mumbai** blasts, or even to undermine the political system, as with the strike on parliament in 2001. Cross-border infiltration and terrorism have demonstrated that border issues and relations with neighbouring countries remain the main challenge for India's defence forces. The 1998 nuclear tests (the first were carried out in 1974), conducted under the BJP-led government, spurred fears of a resurgent India with military ambitions. However, while defence expenditure has increased over the last decade, it still represents only a modest proportion of gross domestic product (2.5% in the 2004 budget) compared with Pakistan or China.

Military: After independence, under Prime Minister Jawaharlal Nehru's leadership, the Indian military was accorded low priority and defence expenditure was kept at less than 1% of the GDP. Funds were limited and at the time it was thought that, other than Pakistan, graded a 'second class military power', there was no threat requiring military preparedness. Low defence spending was part of a larger strategy of non-alignment and keeping the military under civilian control. Since then India has fought four major conventional border wars (in 1947/48, 1962, 1965 and 1971) and the battle at **Kargil** (1999). As a result, military expenditure has risen sharply, reaching US $16,970m. in 2004.

The responsibility for national defence rests with the Cabinet and instructions are discharged through the Ministry of Defence. There are three Service Chiefs (for the Army, Navy and Air Force) with the Supreme Command of the Armed Forces vested in the President. Following the humiliating defeat by China in 1962, the Indian forces underwent massive expansion, with the intention of building up the capability to fight a two-front war, engaging both China and Pakistan. As a result, India has the third largest standing, volunteer army, with around 1m. men in the defence forces. However, India's military expenditure as a percentage of GDP (2.5%) is below the world average of 3%. In the 2004 budget the UPA surprised many by announcing an increase in the defence budget of more than 27% for the 2004–05 fiscal year. This reflected plans for increased arms procurements and modernization of all three services. India has long been an active participant in UN peace-keeping missions. India is currently the third largest contributor of troops to the UN.

Police: The **Indian Police Service (IPS)** is the premier police service in India and a branch of the Ministry of Home Affairs. A successor to the colonial Indian Police, the IPS is still substantially governed by the Police Act of 1861. The IPS was established in 1949 and is, together with the **Indian Administrative Service (IAS)** and the Indian Forest Service, an all-India service. Recruitment for the IPS is made by the union government and selections are based on a competitive civil service examination. Apart from the IPS, each state has its state police services. In addition to the regular police force, there are paramilitary forces such as the **Border Security Force**, the Central Reserve Police Force, the Indo-Tibetan Border Police and the Central Industrial Security Force.

Police reform has been a key topic both at the state and central level, with numerous commissions initiated to examine the problems and suggest improvements. In 1977 the government of India instituted the National Police Commission (NPC) to comprehensively review the police system. Producing eight reports between 1979 and 1981, the Commission advocated the need for effective and credible police accountability mechanisms, improved morale through better working, living and service conditions of the police, and replacement of the 1861 Police Act. Other problems noted were the illegitimate interference of politicians in the police organization and the negative public perception of the police. Although the NPC was disbanded, its recommendations remain valid today.

Central Reserve Police Force (CRPF): The Central Reserve Police Force (CRPF) is one of the most important armed police forces in India. It was founded in 1949 and evolved from the Crown Representative's Force (formed in 1939). Its primary role is to aid and assist the states and Union Territories in internal security management and to maintain law and order in the country. The CRPF had to undertake various counterinsurgency duties and is part of UN peace-keeping forces. Today it plays a significant role in the general elections as well as in the state assembly elections with regard to security arrangements. Currently the force is composed of around 170,000 personnel.

Central Industrial Security Force (CISF): The Central Industrial Security Force (CISF) was set up under the Central Industrial Security Force Act of 1968 on 10 March 1969 and transformed into an armed force on 15 June 1983. Today it is, with a strength of around 100,000, one of the largest paramilitary forces of the Indian Union, operating under the direction of the Home Ministry. It is responsible for the security of public areas, such as atomic power plants, space installations, defence production units, mints, oil fields and refineries, major ports, and air ports, among other facilities.

Central Bureau of Investigation (CBI): The Central Bureau of Investigation (CBI) is India's premier investigating agency. It is run by the federal government and was established in April 1963, evolving from the Special Police Establishment (SPE). The overall objective of the CBI is the preservation of values in public life and ensuring the health of the national economy. It deals with anti-corruption matters as well as major conventional and economic crime. The CBI must receive a state government's permission before investigating a crime in that state. To counter allegations of politicization, proposals have been made to increase autonomy and transparency, for instance in the selection of officials for top posts.

Research and Analysis Wing (RAW): India's premier external intelligence body, the Research and Analysis Wing (RAW) was created in 1968 out of the Intelligence Bureau which then handled both internal and external intelligence and which, since, has been responsible for activities at home. RAW reports directly to the Prime Minister's office and its operations and structure are highly secretive. Pakistan and other neighbouring countries are the primary focus of RAW.

Riots: Between 1946 and 1948 communal riots rocked the subcontinent, causing more than 1m. deaths, especially during the massive exchange of population in 1947 when Partition led to the establishment of Pakistan and an independent India. Since then riots have largely been the result of inter-community tensions and have erupted intermittently across India. Research on the incidence of lethal ethnic riots between 1950 and 1995 reveals that four out of the 28 states have been worst affected and a disproportionate share of deaths caused by Hindu–Muslim violence has occurred in cities, although a vast majority of the population lives in rural areas. Eight cities feature most prominently, including Mumbai, Ahmedabad, Aligarh, Hyderabad, Meerut, Baroda, New Delhi and Kolkata, which together accounted for 46% of all riot deaths between 1950 and 1995. In 2002 the riots of Gujarat, instigated by the incineration at Godhra station of a train carrying Hindu pilgrims returning from Ayodhya, were amongst the country's worst. More than 1,000 were killed, of whom most were Muslims, in the riots that followed. The state government of Gujarat was blamed for not providing effective protection to Muslim communities and for not taking sufficient preventive action to stem the violence and retaliation. Accusations went so far as to claim that the police had deliberately failed to quell anti-Muslim violence. Galvanized into action by the Gujarat atrocities, government institutions such as the National Human Rights Commission (which launched an investigation) and the National Commission for Minorities, as well as the judiciary, issued strong rebukes against the state government.

The anti-Sikh riots of 1984, following Prime Minister Indira Gandhi's assassination by her Sikh bodyguards, when more than 3,000 Sikhs were killed in **Delhi** and thousands across the country, was another case of extreme communal violence. Released in the summer of 2005, the Nanavati Commission report, the result of an official investigation, was the 11th in a series of official reports examining the anti-Sikh riots.

Terrorism: Since independence in 1947, India has faced a variety of violent movements, ranging from left-wing guerrillas and fundamentalist Islamic terrorists to internal ethnic insurgencies. The insurgencies in Punjab and Jammu and Kashmir have caused the bulk of casualties. In the 1970s and 1980s the separatist, pro-**Khalistan** movement led to the assassination of Prime Minister Indira Gandhi in 1984 and a crackdown by the state's security forces. Since the early 1990s terrorism has taken a heavy toll on civilians in Jammu and Kashmir. International networks of finance, arms smuggling, instability in neighbouring countries and the influx of foreign militants are challenges for intelligence-gathering organizations such as the Central Intelligence Bureau and the Research and Analysis Wing (RAW).

Attacks have also been targeted outside disturbed areas, seeking to cause instability to the whole country. For example, acts of violence against religious communities are designed to stir up communal riots, while the Mumbai blasts of 1993, partly at the **Bombay Stock Exchange (BSE)**, were meant to undermine investor confidence.

Over the last 30 years various laws have been passed to deal with civil unrest, insurgency and terrorism. Two were specifically directed at terrorism: the Terrorism and Disruptive Activities (Prevention) Act (TADA) of 1985 and the Prevention of Terrorism Act (POTA) in 2002. Both sought to distinguish terrorism from other criminal activities but faced problems in defining terrorism and the danger that such laws can be abused by civil authorities, used to suppress political forms of dissent and protest. Like its predecessor, POTA faced much criticism and, under the newly-elected UPA, was repealed in late 2004 and substituted by an existing Unlawful Activities (Prevention) Act (UAPA).

In general, India's strategy towards terrorism has been to take forcible police action to blunt terrorist groups and then employ maximum efforts to restore democratic processes, even if in the process former militants have been elected (*see* **Mizo National Front**).

Since the 11 September 2001 attacks on the USA, India's concerns about state-sponsored or 'cross-border terrorism' from Pakistan has received greater attention, with **Lashkar-e-Toiba (LET)** designated as a foreign terrorist group by the USA in 2001 and **Hizbul Mujahideen (HM)** by the EU in 2005.

Bureaucracy: One of the main achievements of the Indian political system has been to set up a bureaucratic apparatus that is both professionally organized and politically accountable. Once again, India has added practices gleaned from other political systems to the indigenous tradition. The Indian bureaucracy is an enormously complex system that combines national or all-India services with regional and local services, technical and managerial staff running public-sector undertakings. Public recruitment by merit with stiff competitive examinations for the upper echelon is the general rule, with political appointments such as occur in the USA being rare. The main services, such as the Indian Administrative Service (IAS) and the Indian Police Service (IPS), retain some of the features of their pre-independence structures, but, like the rest of the leading services of India, have been reorganized in a manner to create a federal balance in recruitment, with special attention being paid to the representation of the former 'untouchables', tribals, and women. Recruitment is supervised by the Union Public Service Commission (UPSC), an independent advisory body appointed by the President of India, and extensive new facilities have been created for training new recruits. Although candidates are recruited centrally, the IAS is composed of separate cadres for each region, to which they are permanently allotted. However, regional loyalties are balanced by the provision that at least half of the members of the IAS cadre come from outside the region with the mandatory provision of having to learn and pass exams in the regional language. Pressure for local control over the IAS has been mounting in recent years. Some would argue, citing the cases of corruption and political collusion with local parties and interest groups, that the IAS is no longer the 'steel frame' that it used to be. But such cases are still exceptional. Most of the time regional and district administrations seek to combine rule of law, efficient management and co-ordination, and, increasingly, local democracy. These values are often hard to reconcile in practice: the extent to which a regional government succeeds in achieving this ideal acts as a crucial parameter of how successful it is in achieving the goal of democratic governance.

Cattle Preservation Bill: The 'Indian Cattle Preservation Bill' was placed on the floor of the parliament as a private member's bill by Seth Govind Das, a Congress member of parliament, in 1955. The bill sought a ban on the slaughter of cows and provided another example of the potential for political controversy in India of the role of religion in the public sphere and the political dilemma to which it led. The principal arguments of the bill's advocates were quite wide-ranging in character. Cattle preservation was, they argued, a national commitment, a solemn pledge made in Article 48 of the Constitution to prohibit the slaughter of cows and calves and other milk and draught animals and a measure that reflected a deeply rooted component of national culture.

Citizenship: The Constitution of India provides for a single citizenship for the entire country. The provisions relating to citizenship are contained in Articles 5–11 in Part 2 of the Constitution. The Citizenship Act adopted by Parliament in 1955 provides for acquisition and the determination of citizenship through birth, descent and registration. In an attempt to engage the widely-spread Indian diaspora, the Citizenship (Amendment) Ordinance 2005 made provisions for a new form of Indian nationality, that of the overseas citizens of India. While the Constitution initially did not permit dual nationality, new legislation allows overseas Indians, termed 'Person of Indian Origin' (PIO), who migrated from the country after 26 January 1950 to apply for a form of dual citizenship. An overseas citizen of India cannot enjoy full citizenship rights and, even if resident in India, cannot vote or take up public employment. The new legislation primarily provides travel and residency privileges similar to the 'PIO card' scheme which provides the holder various benefits, such as visa-free entry into India for 20 years.

Corruption: Corruption in India's public services is widespread. A report by Transparency International in 2002 placed India amongst the 30 most corrupt countries in the world. A separate study found that nearly one-half of the people who had had to use public services had needed on occasion to pay a bribe. The police is generally considered one of the most corrupt institutions. The Central Bureau of Investigation (CBI) registers hundreds of cases under the Prevention of Corruption Act each year, but the backlog of cases results in long delays before any verdict can be delivered. While a number of states have appointed ombudsmen to tackle the prevalence of corruption, the problem continues. Transparency International ranked Kerala as the least corrupt Indian state in 2005. A lack of transparency and accountability in government services has emerged as one of the prime complaints from citizens. New initiatives include e-governance which, through computerization, aims to reduce the scope for corruption by introducing streamlined and anonymous procedures in areas such as tax collection. Since independence in 1947 a number of corruption scandals have rocked the country, one of the most notorious being the **Bofors Scandal** in the 1980s.

Decentralization: The Republic of India is a federal union composed of 28 states, each with its own state legislature and numerous local government bodies within its territory. Besides these, there are also six Union Territories governed directly by the union government which may have one or more local government bodies within their territory. Local government is divided between the rural authorities (*see* ***Panchayati Raj***) and urban authorities (municipalities). Each sector is further subdivided into a number of categories based on population. The 74th Constitutional Amendment Act of 1992 aimed at granting more power and authority to urban local bodies, dividing them into *nagar panchayats* (for emerging urban areas), municipal councils (for smaller urban areas) and municipal corporations (for larger urban areas). In the rural sector there are *gram panchayats* (villages with an average population of *c*. 1,000), the *panchayat samitis* (*c*. 100 villages) and the *zilla panchayats* (*c*. 1,000 villages or 1m. people). All councillors are directly elected by the first-past-the-post system and one-third of all seats are reserved for women. Reservations for Scheduled Castes and Scheduled Tribes depend on the proportion of the local population they make up. Local government is responsible for a limited number of services, such as water supply, sanitation, waste disposal, burials, street lighting, primary education and roads. More recently it has been granted a greater role in economic development, particularly in poverty alleviation. Revenue can be raised through taxes but is largely drawn from transfer payments and loans obtained from the state government.

Directive Principles of State Policy (DPSP): The Directive Principles of State Policy (DPSP) are a part of the Indian Constitution (Part 4) which provides guidelines for the creation of a social order based on social, economic and political justice. The aim of these principles is to ameliorate social and material disparities and to provide the conditions for the creation of a civil society in India. In contrast to the Fundamental Rights the DPSP are non-justiciable.

Federalism: The preference for a federal division of powers was encapsulated in the decision of the INC during the 1920s to organize its provincial committees on the basis of linguistically contiguous areas. The Government of India Act 1935, provided for a federal structure and, while not implemented under the British, became the basis for India's Constitution.

Nevertheless, numerous special features of the Indian Constitution give it its highly centralized form. The constituent states, for example, do not have their own separate constitutions. Under Article 370 an exception was made in the case of Jammu and Kashmir, which acceded to the union on the condition that the central government would not interfere with the internal affairs of the state. The Constitution, in the tradition of written agreements between the centre and the states, defines the division of powers between both sides in the seventh schedule. The Union List, spanning 97 items, gives the centre exclusive authority to act in matters of national importance while the State List, covering 66 items, includes issues of local and regional importance, such as public order and police, welfare, health, education and land revenue. Finally, the Concurrent List contains 47 items over which both centre and the state share legislative competence, including, most importantly, civil and criminal law, social and economic planning. The residual power lies with the Union, and unlike the classic model of federalism, in India the central government, acting though parliament, can create new states, alter the boundaries of existing ones and even abolish a state without recourse to constitutional amendment. The central government is vested with a variety of powers that enable it, under certain circumstances, to extend its authority to the executive and legislative domains of the states. These special powers take three forms: (1) the emergency powers under Articles 352, 356 and 360; (2) the use of Union Executive powers under Articles 256, 257 and 360; and (3) special legislative powers granted under Article 249. The emergency powers enable the Union Executive to transform the federation into a unitary state, with the President's assent. However, even under non-emergency conditions, if the national interest so requires, the central government may assume executive powers over regional governments. In addition the central government has vast powers over the collection and distribution of revenue, which makes the states heavily dependent on the central government for financial support. Most of the lucrative taxes, such as income tax, corporate tax and customs duties, are collected by the central government and shared with the states under a formula designed by the independent Finance Commission, appointed by the President. The Finance Commission distributes funds every five years (as enshrined in the Constitution) and the Planning Commission (based on a cabinet resolution only) allocates the funds to the states.

Despite these centralizing tendencies, the Indian political system has developed a pattern of co-operation between the centre and states, aided by economic growth and liberalization in some cases, the assertion of cultural identity and the demands for autonomy in others. With the change towards multi-party democracy and coalition government, India's regional governments have come into their own, as countervailing forces to the central government. The adoption of regional languages as administrative languages has also brought government closer to the people, further legitimating the state rather than acting as a fragmentary force. (*See* **Linguistic Regionalism**.)

Human Rights: India has accepted and ratified five international human rights treaties, namely, the International Covenant on Civil and Political Rights (CCPR), the Convention on the Elimination of All Forms of Discrimination against Women (CEDAW), the Convention on the Elimination of All Forms of Racial Discrimination (CERD), the Covenant on Economic, Social and Cultural Rights and the Convention on the Rights of the Child (CRC). The Convention Against Torture and Other Cruel Inhuman or Degrading Treatment or Punishment and the CRC-Optional Protocols OP-AC and OP-SC have been signed by the Indian government but not yet ratified by the parliament. In 1993 the Indian government adopted the Protection of Human Rights Act and installed the National Human Rights Commission, whose remit is to observe adherence to human rights. The Prevention of Terrorism Act, which was often criticized by human rights activists, was also repealed under the Congress-led government in 2004. Counterinsurgency operations in Jammu and Kashmir continue to claim a high toll on the civilian population. In 2003 Amnesty International alleged that more than 340 civilians were killed. The Armed Forces Special Powers Act, in effect in Jammu and Kashmir and parts of **North East India**, grants the police extraordinary powers of arrest and detention and human rights groups allege that security forces operate with virtual impunity in areas under this Act. While minority rights and religious freedom are protected under the Constitution, concerns have been voiced about the failure of the Gujarat government to arrest and convict those responsible for the communal violence of 2002.

Inequality: By nature of its size, India is inevitably a country of multiple differences and persistent disparities, the many potential axes of inequalities including religion, caste, income, gender, age, tribe and region. The impact of India's economic reforms in the 1990s on indicators of inequality is much debated. Some point to an improved Gini coefficient (a measure of income disparity and uneven distribution), whilst others hold that the 'trickle down' of wealth has not been apparent amongst India's burgeoning poor and that inter-state and urban-rural divides have widened. Regional differences are attributed to various factors, including geography, richness of natural resources and the quality of state government as well as the levels of existing human capital. Traditionally one of the most deprived sections of society, the Scheduled Castes (SCs) and former 'untouchables' or **Dalits** were denied equal opportunities and mobility across social boundaries and occupation groups under the rigidities of the caste system. Through **affirmative action** the state has actively intervened to uplift SCs, together with the Scheduled Tribes (STs). However, literacy rates are still much lower amongst SCs and STs compared to all-India levels and most of them, dependent on wage labour in agriculture, suffer from unequal access to land and capital markets. The gender divide is another critical fault line in Indian society and economy, and although progress has been made, high male/female differences persist on almost all human development indicators. Despite wide socio-economic disparities across the country and within states, political participation amongst disadvantaged groups has grown over the years. Political parties have been formed to promote interests specific to their groups (*see*, for example, **Bahajan Samaj Party**), and their leaders have emerged as powerful players in Indian politics.

Nationalism: The emergence of Indian nationalism prior to independence is traced by some to the mutiny of 1857, also referred to as the first war of independence. With the formation of the INC in 1885 and, later, under the leadership of *Mahatma* Gandhi, the movement gathered momentum as a nation-wide freedom struggle. Parallel nationalist ideologies did emerge in the form of social reform and religious revival movements like the Arya Samaj and Brahmo Samaj, the campaigns of Sir Syed Ahmed Khan resulting in the formation of Aligarh Muslim University. Key individuals who directly and indirectly led to streams of nationalist thinking drawn from Hinduism include Sri Aurobindo, Swami Vivekananda and **Savarkar**. With independence, the aftermath of Partition, the assassination of Gandhi by a

Hindu fanatic, the Kashmir Dispute and the rise of an Islamic Pakistan, religion-based nationalism in India was seen as irrational and dangerous. Instead, under the Congress governments and the leadership of Prime Minister Jawaharlal Nehru secularism and economic self-reliance were promoted as the basis for an Indian national identity. Nevertheless, various forms of cultural nationalism have threatened the unity of the Indian state, including the rise of sub-national, secessionist movements based on language (Tamil), on religion (Khalistan) and on ethnic differences (North East India).

More recently, the rise of Hindu Nationalism has been observed, together with the emergence of the BJP as a national player in electoral politics. On the one hand recognized as the maturing of politics, with the evolution of an alternative to the INC, the BJP's links with the **Sangh Parivar**, especially the **Rashtriya Swayamsevak Sangh (RSS)**, the potency of issues such as Ayodhya and the outbreak of communal clashes, are reminders of the dangers that a religious nationalism poses to a multinational state like India. At the same time, the limits to Hindu Nationalism might be found in the checks and balances created by powerful regional parties that have become important players in coalition politics at the centre. Examples include the **All-India Anna Dravida Munnetra Kazhagam (AIDMK)** and the **Dravida Munnetra Kazhagam** from Tamil Nadu.

The nuclear tests of 1998 and record levels of economic growth are seen as potential grounds for stronger nationalism, reflected in a more aggressive economic diplomacy and jingoist foreign policy.

Participation/Public Action: Indicators of political participation in India have on the whole been consistently positive, despite the country's deep income disparities, low literacy levels and gender inequity. In 1952, for example, when the country held its first elections after independence in 1947, voter turn-out was recorded at 44.87%, and levels since have been maintained between 55% and 61%. Furthermore, electoral participation has not been markedly differentiated along gender, caste or community lines. In formulating the 1950 Constitution various decisions were taken to stimulate and increase the participation of the masses. Universal adult franchise and direct elections to a central parliament and state legislatures, it was hoped, would encourage mass involvement in the political process and give rise to issues relating to broad economic and social problems rather than narrow parochial interests based on caste, language or religion. Affirmative action through the reservation of seats in national and state legislatures was introduced to ensure that Scheduled Tribes and castes would have a voice in decision-making. Furthermore, the community development programme of the 1950s and the institutionalization of ***Panchayati Raj***, a decentralized form of government at the village level, aimed at encouraging rural participation. In 1992 the 72nd constitutional amendment introduced reservations for women in local elected bodies. Contrary to fears of caste being a source of divisive loyalties, horizontal mobilization along caste lines has led to the emergence of caste movements, even caste-based political parties, furthering participation in civil society as well as politics. Examples include the Bahajan

Samaj Party and the **Samajwadi Party**. In the 1970s there was a surge in NGOs, spearheading social movements in environmental and women's issues. Protests and popular agitation are often able to mobilize huge numbers and to catch widespread media attention, as in the case of the Narmada Dam movement in the late 1980s. In addition, trade unions, farmer organizations and student unions have played an active role in Indian politics.

Third Front: The idea of a 'third front' in Indian politics emerges periodically. Attempts to convert anti-Congressism in the 1960s into a third front alternative to the Congress party succeeded only in 1977 when, united under the banner of the Janata Party, opposition parties came to power briefly. In 1989 the left parties and the BJP propped up a national front and for the 1996 Lok Sabha elections, in a bid to keep both Congress and the BJP out of power, a united front was formed. In each case regional parties were crucial, at times undermining coherence and stability at the centre.

India, Economic Development

Gross domestic product (GDP) at purchasing power parity—PPP): US $3,319,000m. (2004 estimate); GDP per capita at PPP: $3,100 (2004 estimate) *agriculture:* 21.4%; *industry:* 27.0%; *services:* 51.5% (2004 estimates); *exports*: $69,180m. f.o.b. (2004 estimate); *imports*: $89,330m. f.o.b. (2004 estimate); currency: Indian rupee (INR). India's economic development since independence in 1947 can be broadly divided into three distinct periods: 1947–64, the **Nehru** years and the emergence of a closed economic system with some economic growth; the mid-1960s to 1980, which produced a closed, socialist and stagnant economy; and, since the mid-1980s, a process of reform, gradual liberalization and accelerating growth rates. Heavily influenced by the philosophy of self-reliance (*see* **Swadeshi**), advocated by the **Indian National Congress (INC)** during the freedom struggle, and the socialist ideals of the time, policy-makers in independent India sought to combine an activist state with the requirements of a democratic system and the legacy of capitalist and proto-capitalist institutions of the past. Opting for a mixed economy model, the Planning Commission was established in 1950, but was to function more as an appendage to the Prime Minister's Office. Its mandate was to direct and co-ordinate the economy through five-year plans.

India's leaders at independence faced a number of tremendous economic challenges. Agriculture, by far the dominant sector of the economy, was characterized by low productivity, insufficient production and distribution, poor irrigation and, as a result, high vulnerability to drought, as well as by a feudal land tenure system that deprived tillers of the right of land ownership. In addition, acute poverty and underemployment were widespread across the country. Nevertheless, at independence India was better off than most post-colonial states in terms of the possession of credit reserves, the diversification of its industrial base and the extent of the indigenous network of stock exchanges. To cope with the need for rapid and balanced economic growth, the first two five-year plans (1951–55 and 1956–60) adopted strategies that endorsed export pessimism (which discounted the role Indian exports could play in stimulating economic growth) and savings pessimism (which discounted the belief that private savings would be able to finance capital accumulation), and displayed a general distrust of multinationals, of large private industrialists and, gradually, of the market itself. However, it must be noted that during the 1950s and early 1960s this approach reflected the general line of thinking amongst economists within and outside India. During this period the basic structure of a mixed economy was installed, including a clear demarcation of areas falling under the private and public sectors and the beginnings of a regulatory economy to curtail the freedom of private business. The same regulatory agencies which during the Second World War had controlled the use of foreign exchange, the distribution of supplies and allocation of resources were expected to play a developmental role. The focus was to be heavy industry, in the belief that infrastructure and basic industries would spur growth and enable the transition from a traditional, agrarian society to a modern, industrialized economy. Viewed as the golden years of planning, the period 1956–65 registered a growth rate of 7% in manufacturing output, mostly the result of expansion in the public sector, and overall GDP growth of 4%. The import substitution strategy and protectionism granted to domestic industry also enabled private business to record high profits. Grand irrigation and power-generation projects such as the Bhakra-Nangal Dam, completed in 1954, helped raise agricultural growth from a pre-independence annual average of less than 1%–2%. The phase of slow growth and industrial stagnation that was to settle in after the death of Nehru in 1964 was partly the result of prioritizing heavy industry at the expense of agriculture, the further restrictions introduced by Prime Minister Indira **Gandhi** in the 1970s as well as the population explosion of the 1950s and 1960s. At an annual average rate of 2.1%, population growth absorbed all economic surpluses. The restrictions on private trade and dependence on cheap subsidized imports under the PL 480 programme combined to reduce incentives to increase yield and marketed surplus. Maintaining a low GDP growth rate of 3.5% in 1966–80, India seemed unable to surpass what was derided as the 'Hindu rate of growth'. During the early 1970s bureaucratic controls through licensing were extended, alongside the general trend towards centralized decision-making under Indira Gandhi. Nationalization took place in banking, insurance and mining. Large segments of trade in bulk goods were brought under government control, and as a result of centralization consumer goods production fell dramatically. To give the country's policies constitutional backing, the 42nd Amendment of 1976 inserted the words 'Socialist and Secular' before 'Democratic Republic of India' in the preamble to the Indian Constitution. In 1981–82, during her second term of office, Indira Gandhi initiated modest reforms in response to continuous balance of payments crises. The control regime was relaxed to encourage production in designated 'core' sectors, with export potential and restrictions generally eased to facilitate economic transactions and investment, a process that was continued under

Rajiv Gandhi. Real structural reforms, however, only followed in the 1990s, when India engaged in what might be called full-blown liberalization under the stewardship of Prime Minister Narasimha **Rao** (1991–96) and finance minister Manmohan **Singh**. A result of this has been that in 2004 India attained a GDP growth rate of 8.2%, making it one of the fastest growing economies in the world. Nevertheless, regional and state disparities in economic growth, human development and poverty levels are an enduring problem.

Economic Policy/Reforms: Following independence, the government of India passed an industrial policy resolution which provided for a mixed economy. In practice, this socialist-inspired policy aimed at self-reliance and sought to achieve this through a large public sector coexisting with private enterprise, along with extensive controls on the private sector. This policy led to what was generally called the 'Hindu rate of growth', a low but steady annual economic growth rate of about 3.5%, but also a growing fiscal deficit, which reached 8.3% of India's GDP during the Gulf War in 1991. Although 1991 is conventionally given as the year when structural reforms of the economy were initiated, the economic reform process in India has its roots in the 1980s, when the limitations of the earlier strategy based upon import substitution, public-sector dominance and extensive government controls over the private sector had become evident. However, the 'half-hearted' liberalization first introduced by Prime Minister Indira Gandhi and later continued by her son, Rajiv Gandhi, was limited to liberalizing particular aspects of the control system. The fiscal crisis of 1991 led to both a broad stabilization package, proposed by the **International Monetary Fund**, to handle the short-term external balance of payments problem (which resulted in the near-exhaustion of India's foreign-exchange reserves), as well as to a longer-term reform agenda aimed at dismantling the '**Licence Permit Raj**' system (a bureaucratic control regime) and allowing market forces a bigger role in the economy. These reforms, initiated by Prime Minister Narasimha Rao and then finance minister Manmohan Singh, included a liberalized foreign investment and foreign exchange regime, significant reductions in tariffs and other trade barriers, reform and modernization of the financial and banking sectors and significant adjustments in government monetary and fiscal policies.

Since the beginning of the reform process India's GDP has grown at a consistent annual rate of about 7% (excluding 1992–93, when the economy was still experiencing the shock of radical reforms). Foreign direct investment has increased nearly tenfold since 1991 and the current account deficit has turned into a surplus over the last years. The reason why GDP growth has remained strong since 1991 is primarily due to the contribution of non-agricultural sectors, in particular services, which in 2004 were the main component of the Indian economy, contributing about 51.5% of GDP. This has enabled the economy to withstand a steep decline in the agricultural sector. Nevertheless, the speed of the reform process has slowed as the external finances pressure decreased. Supporters of the reform process see this as the main reason why poverty levels have not been brought down and advocate what are known as 'second generation' reforms, including fiscal consolidation, downsizing of the government, a continuation of tax reforms, reforms in the power, road and ports sectors as well as completion of reform in the telecommunications industry.

Following the **Lok Sabha** elections of 2004, there were apprehensions among supporters of the liberalization process that a communist-backed government led by the Congress party would reverse the reform process. These fears, however, seemed groundless as, since 1991, none of the four successive governments has undermined or discounted the need for economic reforms, despite anti-reform statements made during electoral campaigns. Nevertheless, the government has publicly admitted that the challenge remains one of harnessing the growth stimulated by economic reforms to benefit the poor and rural sectors in general.

Mixed Economy: Soon after India's independence in 1947, the Industrial Policy Resolution of 1948 demarcated the scope for development of industries in the private sector and provided for the reservation of certain areas for exclusive development under the public sector, initiating a mixed economy approach to industrial development. Just emerging from a war economy and the controls imposed during the Second World War, the representatives of India's private enterprise were not averse to a mixed economy model in which the state would invest in heavy industry, leaving light, consumer industry to private initiative. The views of prominent industrialists were expressed in the 1944 Bombay Plan.

Private Sector: At independence in 1947 India had a small but relatively well-established private sector, with important business families, such as the Tatas (*see* **Tata Group**) and the Birlas, whose cotton mills and manufacturing factories provided the basis for India's industrial development. Private entrepreneurship was, however, severely restricted over the next three decades, limited to certain sectors under the country's mixed economy and controlled through the 'License Permit Raj'. Competition was curtailed and a few favoured private companies had a monopoly, particularly in the production of consumer goods, which were generally of poor quality.

With the reforms of the early 1990s initiated by the Narasimha Rao government, the economy was gradually liberalized and opened up to external competition. India's entrepreneurs responded to the new opportunities, particularly in the information and technology sector which boomed in the 1980s with companies like **Infosys Technologies** and **Wipro Infotech** excelling on the world market. Pharmaceuticals followed in the area of generic medicines, **Dr Reddy's Laboratories** and **Ranbaxy Laboratories** leading the way. Conglomerates such as the Tata Group, **Aditya Birla Group** and **Reliance** are India's largest private firms.

The success of India's home-grown and internationally competititve companies is attributed to the existence of strong capital markets, an advanced legal system and a democratic political system that supports reforming state-owned enterprises and privatization.

Public Sector: India's public sector includes the government bureaucracy at central, state and local levels, enterprises that are run directly by the government, such as the postal services, railways and parts of the telecommunications sector, and enterprises that are incorporated as independent companies both in the industrial and services sectors. At independence in 1947 leaders such as Prime Minister Jawaharlal Nehru envisioned the public sector as running the 'commanding heights of the economy', propelling industrialization through heavy industry and preserving the country's autonomy, as well as providing for the social welfare needs of its employees. By the late 1970s industrial stagnation had prompted a rethink about the role of state-owned enterprises (SOEs), many of which had become a drain on state resources. As part of the economic reforms launched in 1991 by Prime Minister Narasimha Rao and then finance minister Manmohan Singh, a disinvestment policy was launched, with the number of industrial sectors reserved for the public sector cut from 17 to eight and then to four 'strategic' enterprises of defence, atomic energy, specified minerals and railway transport. Dismantling the 'Licence Permit Raj' exposed the public sector to greater competition while 'sick' SOEs were to be restructured or a small percentage of government equity sold off. While each of the five governments of the 1990s maintained a commitment to disinvesment, the extent and method has been a sensitive issue, particularly how a government selects which SOEs should be supported. SOEs which have the potential to do well are referred to as the *Navratna* (nine jewels). In the budget of 1999–2000 of the **National Democratic Alliance (NDA)**, privatization was mentioned for the first time and 'strategic sales', the transfer of a controlling stake to a private party in one go, became more common. Industrial sector privatization can be authorized either through an executive order, and if acquired through a parliamentary act requires parliamentary approval. Financial sector liberalization is overseen by the **Reserve Bank of India (RBI)**.

Population: In the 2001 national census India's population was enumerated at 1,027,015,247, the second after that of China to cross the 1,000m. mark. Although in absolute terms there has been an increase of 181m. since 1991, growth per decade declined from 23.86% in 1981–91 to 21.34% during 1991–2001, the sharpest fall since independence in 1947, reflecting a decrease in fertility rates. Between 1951 and 1991 India's population more than doubled, rising from 361m. to 845m., an instance of rapid growth similar to that of most developing countries. While birth rates declined due to better family planning and education, improved life expectancy and better health conditions meant that population growth was not checked. Given the age structure of India's population, the rate of population growth is not expected to dramatically change in the near future and it is estimated that India will overtake China as the world's most populous country by 2050. Studies, for example, reveal that every second Indian is under 18 years of age, heralding new challenges for the government in terms of education facilities, job opportunities and care of the aged. Compounding this challenge is the still immense proportion of illiterate people (296m. of those aged seven years and over in 2001), with striking differences reported across states and the rural-urban divide. While overall the sex ratio has improved compared to previous years, reaching 933 females per

1,000 males, many of the states, particularly in the age group of 0-6, report low female numbers. Population growth has also led to a rapid increase in the average density of population (from 117 per sq km in 1951 to 324 per sq km. in 2001) and although India is still regarded as a 'land of villages', urban agglomeration has been high, a result of city population growth as well as the rural exodus to cities. Among the major states, **West Bengal** is the most thickly populated and the **North East India** region the least.

Family-Planning Policy: In 1952, just five years after independence, India's leaders implemented one of the developing world's first national government-sponsored family-planning efforts. Ever since, population stabilization has been a central concern in India's five-year plans. The National Planning Policy adopted in 1976 represented a reorientation in strategy, with family size thought to be a function of poverty. An integrated development programme aimed at improving general welfare was formulated. While education about the population problem became more widespread, government-enforced sterilization, spearheaded by Sanjay Gandhi, then-Prime Minister Indira Gandhi's son, during the emergency period of 1975–77, called into question the propriety of state-sponsored birth control. Subsequently, population control became a politically taboo subject, with more emphasis being given to health education and awareness-raising initiatives. During the 1980s, family-planning programmes were implemented through the state governments with central government financial assistance. In rural areas, a pre-independence network of primary health centres had to be extended and by 1991 India had more than 150,000 public health facilities offering family-planning programmes. Despite such efforts, the 1991 census revealed one of the most rapidly growing populations in the world. Over-centralization of policy formulation had resulted in population control programmes that did not cater to regional differences and local attitudes toward birth control. Furthermore, the strong cultural preference for sons continued to encourage parents to have children until a son was born. In 2000 a new national population policy was adopted. Through awards and incentives the hope is to encourage the country's poorest couples to have just two children and to generally discourage marriage before the age of 21.

Migration: According to the 2001 census, some 307m. people, or 30% of the Indian population, were migrants by place of birth (those enumerated at a village or town other than their place of birth). Seen historically, there has been a steady inrease in the number of migrants, who were enumerated at 144m. in 1961. According to the 2001 census, **Maharashtra** received the largest number of migrants (7.9m.) by place of birth from other states and other countries. Among males, the most important reason for migration cited was to seek work and employment. The census also noted that intra-state migration tended to be mainly from one rural area to another, while inter-state migration was largely from rural to urban locations. Migration from neighbouring countries was predominantly from Bangladesh, the majority probably having come during the Bangladesh War of 1971.

The Indian community abroad is substantial, a first wave having migrated in the 19th century, driven by the economic compulsions generated by colonialism and spreading across the British empire to countries in Africa, South-East Asia, Fiji and the Caribbean. A second wave occurred in the second half of the 20th century, when India's 'brain drain' occurred as skilled professionals opted for the West over India's sluggish and controlled economy. In the 1970s semi-skilled labour migrated in large numbers to the Gulf, in response to the oil boom. Today it is estimated that the Indian diaspora numbers more than 20m. A booming economy is expected to generate the return of many overseas Indians. To encourage this trend and attract investment, the government of India has recently made amendments to its citizenship laws.

Urbanization: The 1951 census after India's independence reported a high (3.5%) annual rate of urban growth in the 1940s, partly reflecting the massive immigration caused by **Partition** and the rehabilitation of refugees around a few urban centres. An even higher annual rate of 3.8% was recorded in the 1970s as numerous new towns emerged across the country. While India's level of urbanization continues to be low (about 28% in 2001), the absolute numbers are very large. The 2001 census reported an urban population of 285m., having grown since 1991 at an annual rate of 3.1%. Six of the world's 20 largest metropolises were in India and, according to the 2001 census, there were 35 Indian cities with a population of more than 1m., with Greater **Mumbai** having the highest—16.4m. However, the 2001 urban population levels have turned out to be lower than most predictions and, contrary to expectations, a deceleration in urban growth has taken place over the last 30 years despite the economic expansion in non-agricultural sectors, which ought to have caused a boom in urban living. This is partly because, while larger towns have grown, there has not been a general increase of urban centres in the lower categories.

State and city governments are trying to create urban centres that will attract local and international investment by favouring 'high value', commercial and industrial activities and the relocation of low-income and slum colonies to city peripheries. However, land scarcity and infrastructure deficiency continue to challenge urban developers as well as the growing urban poverty in Indian cities.

Despite the 74th Constitutional Amendment of 1992, which gave greater powers and responsibilities to urban local bodies, the financing and planning of infrastructure projects remains primarily centralized. State authorities continue to dominate decision-making in areas such as urban land development, the provision of public transport and housing, but lack the requisite resources and flexibility to respond to a growing city's demands.

Minority Groups: A fundamental challenge for India has been safeguarding the interests of minorities while at the same time preserving the degree of cohesion and uniformity necessary for a tolerant, plural society. As a result, the framers of the Constitution did away with the system of separate electorates for minorities introduced by the British and considered to be divisive, opting instead for 'protective discrimination'. While **Scheduled Castes (SCs)** and **Scheduled Tribes (STs)** have been granted reservations in the Lok Sabha and assembly seats, in public-sector employment, religious and linguistic minorities are granted the special rights to conserve their language (Article 29) and to establish and administer educational institutions (Article 30). Articles 25–28 accord all communities the right to freedom of religion.

Nowhere in the Constitution is the term 'minority' defined, but at the time of its framing the politically recognized minorities included Muslims, Sikhs, Christians, Parsis and Anglo-Indians. The problem, however, has been how to specify the geographical unit with reference to which a minority is identifed. Furthermore, large sections of the recognized minorities are in fact majorities in certain states, as is the case with Muslims in **Jammu and Kashmir**, Sikhs in **Punjab** and Christians in Nagaland. The 2001 census recorded Muslims as the largest minority group, constituting 13.4% of the country's population, while Christians made up 2.3% of the total and the Sikhs 1.9%. The dwindling Parsi population was estimated at about 69,000. Even the majority community of Hindus (80.5%) are often described as comprising a vast number of sub-caste minorities. Majority-minority relations occasionally clash in the form of communal riots. Other grievances include the tendency of Hinduism to subsume members of other religions, such as Jains, Buddhists and Sikhs, and the fact that while state boundaries were redrawn on a linguistic basis (*see* **Linguistic Regionalism**) most states have significant linguistic minorities.

Backward Castes/Classes (Commission): Next to the Scheduled Castes and Scheduled Tribes, India's Constitution recognizes those lower castes which face social exclusion as 'Socially and Educationally Backward Classes' (and also the Other Backward Classes—OBCs). Backward Classes usually belong to the Sudras, the lowest of the four *varnas* (broader caste groups), and constitute about one-half of India's total population. The decision to include castes on the list of Backward Classes is made by the National Commission for Backward Classes (NCBC). This list currently includes 2,268 castes. In addition to financial assistance and educational programmes, the Indian government has introduced a 27% job reservation quota for OBCs in government employment.

Agriculture: While the share of agriculture in India's economy fell from more than one-half of the GDP in 1950 to less than one-quarter in 2004, the share of the population dependent on agricultural income declined less steeply, from 77% to 62%. Out of the 55% of India's total land space available for cultivation, only about 33% is under assured irrigation, the rest being highly dependent on monsoon rains. India none the less managed to increase production of staple cereals more than fourfold between 1950 and 2000, attaining self-sufficiency in food and changing from a food importer to a food exporter. In 2001 agricultural products contributed 14.2% of total exports. The Gangetic Plain, extending from Punjab to Assam, is the most intensively farmed part of the country. At independence in 1947, faced with a growing and mainly rural population, one of the primary goals of India's first generation of planners was to attain self-sufficiency in food production. The first two five-year plans focused on removing basic socio-economic constraints through land reform, changes in the village power structure and by encouraging citizen participation in the hope of stimulating agricultural output. The continuing shortages of the 1960s prompted a concerted drive to improve irrigation and distribute better seeds and fertilizer, a phase that became known as the **Green Revolution**. To encourage the use of higher-yielding seeds, the government set up a system of procurement and minimum support prices to offset the lowering of market prices that would follow increased output. Under this scheme the government would procure grain from producers in difficult years, when crops fell short of needs, at lower-than-market prices, promising to buy at higher-than-market prices in good years, to cover costs of production and ensure reasonable profits. Ultimately, the strategy was largely to the benefit of the large-scale holdings, creating a powerful political lobby among the 10% who controlled almost 65% of total arable land. Despite the reforms of the 1990s that opened up the economy to foreign investment and goods, private investment in the agricultural sector remains small. Extensive market regulation, limited processing plants, the dominance of small-scale enterprises and intermediaries and poor rural road and transport facilities account for the relatively small number of organized chain stores across India. Furthermore, through what is known as the 'food subsidy', the Indian government covers the cost of price support, distribution and storage of wheat and rice, amounting to about 5% of all government expenditure in 2002, as well as subsidizing farm inputs such as fertilizer and power. Since independence, when five-year planning was introduced, plan priorities, policies and resource allocations have been centrally decided. Food and price policy are also decided by the central government despite the fact that agriculture is identified as a state responsibility in the Constitution. Achieving political consensus for further reform in the agricultural sector is difficult given the numbers involved and the importance of the farmers' vote. Meanwhile, the government, under pressure from the farmers' lobby, provides subsidized inputs and purchases grain at higher-than-market prices, which, in combination with mounting distribution and storage costs, results in a situation in which stockpiled food is simply beyond the means of poor consumers. However, as India's economy integrates further with the international economy, so different players emerge with new demands and challenges. For example, in order to meet global requirements of reliable production and consistent quality, agribusinesses increasingly rely on contract farming, an arrangement for which the legal framework has yet to be fully defined. (*See* **Bullock Capitalists**.)

Land Reform (Ownership): Under the Constitution, responsibility for land reforms lies with India's state governments. Since independence state governments have implemented a large number of land reforms, including legislation setting a ceiling on land ownership by individuals, and legislation regulating land tenancy. Overall, these land reforms were successful in fundamentally changing the traditional feudal land ownership system still present under the British Raj into a system where land is more equally distributed among peasants, and most of the large landholdings have disappeared. Most reforms were aimed at removing intermediaries from land relations, the most pervasive form being the *Zamindari* system. *Zamindar* denotes a landowner who receives rent without cultivating the land himself. The initiatives and success in redistributing land vary among India's states. The attempts to reform land ownership were most rigorously implemented after 1978 by the communist state government of West Bengal, which was able to redistribute land to the landless cultivators on a large scale. The neighbouring states of **Uttar Pradesh** and **Bihar**, on the other hand, made the least progress in redistributing land ownership. Progress in the field has been stymied by court cases and severe violence between the landless and the militias of the rich landowners. Since the liberalization of India's economy in 1991, land reform legislation has come under increasing scrutiny. In particular, the restrictive laws on land ceilings are considered by many to be ineffective tools for rural development.

Co-operatives/Co-operative Movement and Farming: The co-operative, as a voluntary organization to pool resources, has a long history of development in India dating back to the late 19th century. After independence co-operatives assumed an important role in programmes of poverty alleviation and economic development. In the first Five-Year Plan it was specifically stated that the success of the Plan would be judged, among other things, by the extent to which it was implemented through co-operative organizations. Early co-operatives were primarily intended to provide credit to farmers and to rural agro-industrial ventures. The second Five-Year Plan encouraged the co-operative movement by adding marketing, warehousing, trading and other economic functions to its activities. Examples of highly successful co-operatives include the Indian Farmers' Fertilizer Co-operative, the National Federation of Co-operative Sugar Factories and co-operatives for the marketing and distribution of cotton. Dairy co-operatives operating under the National Dairy Development Board were behind the success of the 'White Revolution' which enabled India to become the largest producer of milk in the world, the result of a national marketing strategy in the 1970s that created a chain of dairy processing plants, collection stations and a national milk transportation grid. The National Co-operative Union of India is the apex organization promoting the co-operative movement.

Food and Famine Prevention: In the 1950s and 1960s India relied on US food aid, the PL480 programme providing rice imports, to meet the needs of its growing population. Through extensive irrigation projects, a public distribution system of providing food grains at affordable prices and the Green Revolution of the 1970s India managed to achieve self-sufficiency in all food items and has become one of the world's largest rice producers. Since independence in 1947 India has successfully prevented famines. In the last substantial famine, which occurred under British rule in 1943, about 3m. people died in Bengal. Post-independence there have been many occasions of substantial crop failures, often covering large regions, and sharp declines in national food availability, but threatening famines have been tackled by the government through public distribution systems based on fair price shops, before they could become major killers. Increasing efficiency at averting famine conditions is noticeable in the way the government reacted, without major external assistance, to threatening situations in Maharashtra in 1973, in West Bengal in 1979 and in **Gujarat** in 1987 (caused by one of the worst droughts of the century) compared to the case of near-famine in Bihar in 1967. Nevertheless, per capita food availability remains meagre and the FAO classifies India as a low-income, food-deficit country. According to international measurements, about 40% of India's population live in chronic poverty, consuming less than 80% of minimum energy requirements. Cereals remain the staple food in India, with the average Indian diet remaining largely deficient in green leafy vegetables, meat, fish, milk and milk products.

Public Distribution System (PDS): The Public Distribution System (PDS) is meant to ensure availability of foodgrains to the public at affordable prices and to enhance the food security of the poor. The allocated commodities include wheat, rice, sugar and kerosene oil. Its 400,000 Fair Price Shops (FPS) make the PDS probably the largest national food-distribution system in the world. In June 1997 the Indian government additionally installed the Targeted Public Distribution System (TPDS) with a specific focus on the poor.

Industry: At independence in 1947 India produced only a few industrial products, namely, cotton textiles, jute, some iron and steel and a few consumer goods. The growth of other industries had been stymied by lack of capital and a colonial policy based on the import of manufactured goods from Britain and the production of commercial export crops such as cotton and jute. In the 1950s and 1960s massive efforts to industrialize the country through a planned economy and state-owned industries in core areas, such as mining, steel production, railroads and armaments, were made. To attain self-sufficiency, India aimed at producing everything itself, covering an impressive array of goods, from toothpaste to cars. Imports were strictly curtailed by the government and an intricate web of licensing controlled the pattern of industrial development, which was biased towards heavy industry. By the mid-1960s modest economic growth had been achieved, together with a diversified industrial base and the establishment of successful indigenous industries, such as car manufacturing. However, the protectionism under such a regime failed to create internationally competitive companies and as a result manufacturing was not the same driving force of India's economy that it was in the newly industrialized, export-oriented South East Asian countries. In the mid-1980s efforts were made to stimulate the industrial sector and to promote exports by abolishing some of the licensing regulations. The New Industrial Policy of 1991 went dramatically further, with tariff reductions, currency devaluations, the easing of restrictions on foreign investment and imports, liberalized interest rates and tax reforms, all of which suddenly lowered the barriers to entry for foreign firms and products. Unable to match the competition, Indian industry registered a decline in production and capital formation in the manufacturing sector in 1999, the production growth rate falling from 6.6% in 1999/2000 to 2.8% in 2001/02. To combat this the government turned its attention to investing in research and development as well as in infrastructure to improve the operating environment of industry. In 2004 the industrial sector contributed just 27% of the gross domestic product, while services (trade, tourism, banking, transport, communications) contributed almost 51.5%. Poor infrastructure, cumbersome bureaucracy, reservation of key products for small-scale industry, labour market rigidities and the need to restructure public-sector enterprises (especially in power, rail and road transport) continue to hamper industry.

Foreign Trade: India's international trade, dominated by primary exports after independence, slowly began to change during the 1960s when the country commenced exports of manufactured goods on a modest scale. This process of transformation suffered a severe set-back during the oil crisis of the 1970s. Since then, India's trade balance has turned increasingly negative, making the liberalization of its over-regulated market urgent. Economic reforms started in 1991, when the government of Narasimha Rao lifted many of the strict import and export controls as well as the high tariffs, slowly converting India into a lucrative market for international companies and financial institutions. Since then, despite occasional criticism by the proponents of traditional ***swadeshi*** politics, India has been gradually integrated into the international market economy. Manmohan Singh, who initiated India's economic reforms as finance minister in 1991, became India's Prime Minister in 2004. Since 1991 the value of India's exports has increased from US $18,000m. in 1991–92 to $62,000m. in 2003–04, while the value of its imports rose from $19,000m. in 1991–92 to $75,000m. in 2003–04. India's major trading partners are the USA, China (including Hong Kong), the United Kingdom, Japan, and Germany. The main export commodities are textile goods, gems, engineering goods and chemicals. The main import commodities include crude oil and petroleum products, machinery and fertilizers.

Associated Chambers of Commerce and Industry (ASSOCHAM): Established in 1920 under the patronage of British and Indian industrialists, the formation of the Associated Chambers of Commerce and Industry (ASSOCHAM) of India represented the culmination of a historical process that brought together the three oldest regional chambers of Bengal (Calcutta, or today, Kolkata), Bombay (today, Mumbai) and Madras (today, Chennai). Soon after the **Federation of Indian Chambers of Commerce and Industry (FICCI)** was set up, representing the nationalist leanings amongst the business community. ASSOCHAM is today amongst the leading, nation-wide chambers of commerce. With more than 1m. corporate and individual members, ASSOCHAM also advises the government on policy issues and promotes bilateral economic issues.

Banking System: The Indian banking system is characterized by a large number of banks with mixed ownership. In 2004 the commercial banking segment comprised 27 public-sector banks in which the government had majority ownership; 40 private-sector banks; and 33 foreign banks. Total bank assets constituted about 70% of GDP in 2003–04, of which public-sector banks possessed 75% (compared with more than 90% in 1991) while private and foreign banks held about 25%. The central bank, the Reserve Bank of India (RBI), was established in 1935 and nationalized in 1948. Functioning as an adjunct to the Ministry of Finance, the RBI was compelled to invest in government securities and meeting the targets of directed lending for strategically important industries. All large private banks were nationalized first in 1969, and then in 1980 under Prime Minister Indira Gandhi. Drastic financial sector reforms were initiated in 1991 and 1992 in response to a fiscal crisis characterized by a public deficit equivalent to 10% of GDP, a current account deficit equivalent to 3% of GDP, an inflation rate of 10% and growing domestic and foreign debt. Among the reforms were liberalization of the interest rate regime, the lifting of entry restrictions on foreign banks, facilitating the setting up of new private banks, a diversified ownership of public-sector banks and greater transparency in the balance sheets to improve accountability and supervision in accordance with international standards. The RBI remains the sole issuer of currency and implements and monitors the government's monetary policy. Wide-scale privatization of public-sector banks has not taken place, the Indian government opting instead for a gradual process of restructuring through increased competition.

Foreign Direct Investment (FDI): Foreign direct investment (FDI) flows into India have risen since the 1990s but remain low in comparison with other emerging markets. In 2002 India received FDI inflows equivalent to less than 1% of GDP whilst those received by China were equivalent to 3.7% of GDP. In dollar terms this was 15 times the amount received by India. Reasons for the underperformance of FDI in India include labour market inflexibility, relatively high tariffs and the limited scale of export processing zones. Furthermore, different definitions of FDI account for some of the gap between China and India. For example, China includes as FDI, domestic money received via Macao, Taiwan and Hong Kong. Also, the resources of India's expatriate community have only just been mobilized unlike the overseas Chinese across East Asia who have been investing in China since the early 1980s. Prior to 1991, FDI proposals were considered case-by-case and strictly controlled by the government. Liberalization in the 1990s gradually altered this. Since 2000 FDI up to 100% investment is freely allowed in all sectors, except for arms and ammunition, atomic energy, railway transport, coal and lignite and mining, and is automatically approved, provided the Reserve Bank is notified within 30 days. In 2004 **Andhra Pradesh**, **Karnataka**, Maharashtra and **Tamil Nadu** which, because of India's federal structure, are allowed to design their own investment policies and incentives for FDI, together with national capital territory, **Delhi**, attracted the greatest percentage of FDI inflows into the country. Since the late 1990s, with the expansion of home-grown firms such as Tata Group, Wipro Infotech, Reliance (*see* **Ambani**, Dhirubhai, Dr. Reddy's Laboratories and **Infosys Technologies**), India's outflows of FDI have expanded. Between 1999–2005 the USA was the most important destination of Indian outward FDI, followed by Russia, with Indian investment targeting mainly the manufacturing sector. In

2003–04 FDI into India amounted to US $4,673m., with most proposals coming from the USA, followed by Mauritius and the United Kingdom.

Foreign Aid: In the first 30 years after independence in 1947 foreign aid played a significant role as a means of providing foreign exchange. Until the early 1980s almost all the foreign exchange requirements of the country's balance of payments on the capital account were met through foreign aid. Foreign aid was also invaluable in the form of food assistance, particularly through the PL-480 programme from the USA. The Green Revolution of the 1960s was financed greatly with foreign assistance as was the co-operative movement of the 1970s and 1980s, giving rise, for example, to the White Revolution.

With India's economic growth since the reforms of the early 1990s and expanding foreign reserves (recorded at US $141,500m. in March 2005), India announced that it would only receive government-to-government aid from a club of six donor countries. In an attempt to shed its image of aid recipient, India seeks to enhance its own role as an aid donor. India is already a significant donor to several sub-Saharan African countries and, since 2002, has extended US $500m. for reconstruction in Afghanistan. However, 60% of India's aid budget comes from multilateral lenders, such as the World Bank, which continues to provide crucial assistance for infrastructure and social sector projects.

Labour: Estimates in 2005 put unemployment at 9%, although, given India's huge informal economy, this figure is difficult to assess. More than half of India's workforce is engaged in the agricultural sector which, compared to industry, has remained relatively un-unionized. Trade unionism in India has gone through four broad phases, corresponding to structural changes in the economy. The first phase, from 1950 to the mid-1960s, saw the government pursuing a planned economy and an import substitution strategy which corresponded with the rise of public-sector unionism. The two main federations then were the **Indian National Trade Union Congress** and the communist **All-India Trade Union Congress (AITUC)**. The second phase, from the mid-1960s until the late 1970s, a period of relative economic stagnation and political instability, witnessed rising labour discontent, inter-union rivalries and industrial conflict. Organizations such as the Hind Mazdoor Sabha emerged as leading voices in the labour movement. Between 1980–91 a third phase of uneven economic development, decentralized bargaining and independent trade unionism gained ground and inter-state, inter-regional variations in the labour-management regimes grew wider, with unions strengthened in the more prosperous economic sectors. The fourth and as yet incomplete phase started with the economic reforms of the early 1990s and has been characterized by demands for greater labour-market flexibility, especially in employment and industrial dispute management, where the state has traditionally played an active role. Reforms are considered vital to stimulate India's manufacturing sector, but are resisted particularly by the left parties, which, since 2004, lend outside support to the ruling **United Progressive Alliance (UPA)** coalition. Other pressing challenges include the need to tackle the prevalence of child labour and bonded labour (work which is done in order to repay debt, and which is passed down the generations). In 1976 an act of parliament formerly abolished the bonded labour system but the practice persists, especially in states where highly feudal structures remain in place.

Informal Economy: It is estimated that the informal sector in India employs almost 90% of the labour force, producing some 60% of the country's GDP. It encompasses farming, fishing, forestry, cottage industries, petty vendors and small-scale, mechanized industry in rural and urban areas. Referred to as the 'unorganized sector' in India, official policy was initially one of neglect. With the gradual process of economic liberalization started in the mid-1980s, the size and significance of the informal economy received greater attention. A Second National Commission on Labour was set up in 1998 with the specific goal of formulating legislation to increase protection in the unorganized sector in light of the effects of liberalization and globalization. The report of the Commission highlighted the low wages, the high percentage of women workers, child labour and the existence of debt bondage that characterized the unorganized sector.

India's black economy, its size estimated sometimes at as much as half of the economy, continues to grow despite efforts by the finance ministry to amend tax laws, to lure black money through amnesty schemes and warnings. Significantly, it is reported that the growth of the underground economy is not in the primary (agricultural) or secondary (industrial) sectors, but in the tertiary services sector. Corruption is considered to be a major reason behind the black economy, with people at every level of society confronted with the need to pay bribes in order, for example, to overcome bureaucratic delays or facilitate procedures.

Child Labour: Although all forms of bonded or forced labour are prohibited in India by Article 23 of the Constitution, bonded child labour is still one of the most striking problems of Indian society. Data based on the Indian census reveal that there were nearly 13.6m. child labourers in 1981, of whom more than 90% were **Dalits** (*see* **'Untouchables'**). These data show that the majority of rural child workers are employed in cultivation and agricultural labour, whereas urban child labourers are distributed differently. Since 1981 no relevant data regarding the incidence of child labour has been collected by the Indian government. Extrapolations of the 1981 data by the Indian government place the current number of child labourers at 17m.–20m., whereas NGOs, such as Human Rights Watch, estimate the number to be as high as 60m.–115m. The reasons for the high incidence of child labour in India are to be found in structural features such as the high rate of poverty, the absence of social welfare schemes and easy access to loans and the **caste system**, as well as the simple fact that child labour is about 80% cheaper than adult labour.

Atomic Energy Commission (AEC): The Indian Atomic Energy Commission (AEC) is the principal policy-planning body for India's nuclear energy programme and has offices in New Delhi and Mumbai. It was first set up in 1948 as part of the government's Department of Scientific Research, which had been created a few months earlier. The first AEC had three members, under the chairmanship of Homi

J. Bhabha, known as the chief architect of India's nuclear programme. Initial activities included uranium exploration and mining. The AEC was made part of the Department of Atomic Energy (DAE) in 1958. Development of nuclear power and related activities are carried out in various units under the AEC/DAE. The actual growth of nuclear power has, however, been modest. In 2005 it was reported that total installed nuclear power generation capacity represented less than 3% of the country's total installed electricity generation capacity. The Bhabha Atomic Research Centre, also under the DAE, is India's premier nuclear research and development centre. (*See* **Nuclearization**.)

Environmental Protection: India suffers under the dual impact of poverty-induced environmental degradation as well as pollution caused by affluence (growing demand for vehicles and consumer goods) and an expanding industrial sector. While extensive environmental legislation exists, grassroots movements have traditionally played an active role, exerting pressure on the government's development plans as in the case of the **Narmada Dam**, or the **Chipko Movement**. Following the 1984 **Bhopal Indutrial Accident**, environmental awareness and activism in India increased significantly. The Environmental Protection Act of 1986 created the Ministry of Environment and Forests, responsible for administering and enforcing environmental laws and integrating environment policies as part of sustainable development. Despite the existence of a legal and regulatory regime, enforcement has been the challenge. To tackle air pollution in the capital, New Delhi, one of the worst affected cities, the government introduced strict emission standards for all vehicles and high punitive fines, a strategy which has proven highly successful. Since 2002 India has been a signatory to the Kyoto Protocol and has the potential to play an important role in carbon-emissions reduction. While India continues to rely mainly on coal for energy, a number of alternatives, including natural gas, solar and wind projects, are being explored under the auspices of the Ministry of Non-Conventional Energy Sources. In rural and agricultural areas, where more than 70% of the population live and are usually dependent on natural resources for their livelihood, the environment has undergone some of the worst degradation. Pressures of population, as well as the growing demands of the market, have led to soil degradation and deforestation through excessive farming and firewood collection. The availability of safe drinking water is considered to be one of India's most pressing future challenges, with shrinking groundwater tables and water supplies contaminated by bad waste management, both domestic and industrial. Agriculture consumes nearly 80% of the country's utilizable water which, furthermore, tends be subsidized by the state.

Floods and Natural Disasters: Given its continental dimensions and geographical position, India suffers from a host of natural disasters, including floods, droughts, cyclones, earthquakes and, in 2004, the **Indian Ocean** tsunami which left more than 10,000 dead, affecting particularly the **Andaman and Nicobar** Islands and the coastal habitations of Tamil Nadu. Densely populated areas, poor housing, faulty development planning and an infrastructural system that often cannot cope with the suddeness and magnitude of disasters, results in the extremely high death tolls of natural disasters in India. For example, the cyclone of 1999 killed more than 10,000 in **Orissa** and more than 16,000 died in the 2001 Kutch earthquake in Gujarat. Of the 35 states and territories, 22 are recognized as disaster-prone. It is estimated that 28% of the country's total cultivable area is drought-prone and 57% earthquake-prone. Furthermore, India is one of the worst cyclone-affected parts of the world, with severe tropical cyclones striking the east and west coasts every year. Under the Indian Constitution, disaster management falls under state responsibility. A National Crisis Management Committee exists to mobilize central resources and attempts are under way to improve disaster response, early warning systems and rehabilitation measures.

Health System/Policy: India's eighth Five-Year Plan (1992–97) identified 'human development' as its focus, with population control and health listed as two of its top priorities. Nevertheless, despite intensified efforts on the part of the government, enormous health problems continue to afflict the country's population. While overall health conditions have improved, with life expectancy rising (males: 60; females 63 in 2003) and infant mortality rates falling (males: 85 per 1,000; females 90 per 1,000 in 2003), India's living standards for the vast majority are still among the lowest in the world. Nearly half of all children under the age of five are malnourished and a high proportion of the population continues to suffer and die from preventable infections and from pregnancy and childbirth-related complications. New health threats include HIV/AIDS, which has affected an estimated 3.5m. Indians. Major constraints facing the health sector include limited resources, the lack of an integrated multi-sector strategy, poor disease surveillance and response systems and underinvestment in basic facilities, such as the provision of clean drinking water and sanitation. The health sector is characterized by a vast government sector, providing publicly financed health services free of cost, from the primary to tertiary level, accounting, in 2001, for about 17.9% of total expenditure on health; and by a fee-levying private sector that accounts for about 82% of overall health expenditure. Under such a financing system, inequities in the health service are exacerbated, with the poor forced to rely on sub-standard government facilities. Furthermore, under the Constitution, the provision of health care is primarily a state responsibility, resulting in wide inter-state differences in health indicators. States such as **Kerala**, Punjab and Tamil Nadu have twice the rate of per capita public health spending of Bihar and **Madhya Pradesh**.

Education/Education Policy: India's overall literacy rate (literacy being defined in India as the ability to sign one's name) in the 2001 census was calculated at 65.2%. In 1991–2001 the number of illiterates declined for the first time since the 1951 census, by almost 32m. in absolute terms. Large inter-state variations persist, the state of Kerala at one end with more than 90% and Bihar, at the other, registering less than 50% literacy. In rural areas the literacy rate increased from about 36% in 1981 to 59% in 2001 and in urban areas from 67% to 80%. The national policy on education states that elementary education is compulsory, although this is hard to implement and monitor.

Total expenditure on the education sector in 2001/02 was 4.02% of the GDP. The responsibility for educational development rests largely with the state governments while the central government sets general objectives and aids the more backward states. A number of states have successfully raised literacy rates by targeting drop-out rates instead of enrolment, at the primary and secondary school levels. The mid-day meal scheme, particularly effective in Tamil Nadu, successfully increased the retention rate of students, together with other measures, such as changing the curriculum to include vocational training and flexibility in school terms to suit seasonal demands for labour in rural areas. The gender gap in literacy levels, however, continues, with male literacy at 76% in 2001 (compared with 56% in 1981) and female literacy at 54% (compared with 30%). Government-sponsored initiatives focusing on the education and empowerment of women have been made at the village level. In 2004 there were more than 15,000 state-backed colleges across the country, reflecting a nation-wide expansion in higher education enrolment over the past two decades. As the government tends to focus on primary and secondary education, private participation in higher education has grown over the years, particularly in the form of engineering colleges and the prestigious Indian Institutes of Technology (IITs) and Indian Institutes of Management (IIMs).

Social Security/Policy: India's expenditure on social services has been very small, even in comparision with other developing countries. What existed in the past covered public servants and administrative staff, leaving the vast majority of the population to rely on informal arrangements such as the extended family, caste or tribal ties. In 1995 the government of India introduced for the first time an all-India protective type of social security scheme, the National Social Assistance Programme, which provided assistance to poor households in the event of old age, death of breadwinner and maternity. An important pillar of India's social protection policies has been the food programme, implemented in the late 1960s and part of a wider poverty-alleviation scheme.

Sections of society that are least protected include the informal sector (almost 90% of the total workforce), India's large aged population, which depends on the family as a support system, the disabled and the tribal populations.

A major initiative in the social sector launched under the current UPA government is the National Rural Employment Guarantee scheme, which promises wage employment to every rural household, in which adult members volunteer to do unskilled manual work, guaranteeing at least 100 days' employment.

Poverty: India's 2005 union budget announced increased spending on primary education, health and rural infrastructure. This three-pronged approach to combating poverty and improving the life of ordinary citizens, a bid to pursue economic development with 'a human face', represents a move towards an integrated poverty-eradication strategy. Traditionally, the Indian government has implemented an income-based measurement of the poverty line, defined by the Planning Commission as the per capita monthly expenditure of Rs 49 for rural areas and Rs 57 for urban areas in terms of 1973–74 prices, corresponding, respectively, to daily calorie intakes of 2,400 and 2,100. However, while per capita income levels have generally risen (more than doubling in 1951–96), this has not translated into a faster poverty reduction path. Official estimates record a fall in the incidence of income poverty from about 36% in the early 1990s to somewhere between 25% and 30% in the early 2000s, but exact figures are disputed due to survey data discrepencies. Stark regional difference have intensified with extreme poverty concentrated in rural areas of Bihar, Madhya Pradesh, Uttar Pradesh and West Bengal. Furthermore, child and infant mortality rates continue to be unacceptably high, with one in every 11 Indian children dying in the first five years of life for lack of low-technology and lost-cost interventions. Malnutrition, according to a 2005 UNDP report, has barely improved in the last decade and affects about half the country's children.

Explanations for India's slow battle against poverty have highlighted the country's poor human development indicators, in particular pervasive gender inequalities, combined with rural poverty, which has undermined the potentital to convert growth into development. Female mortality rates remain higher than male mortality rates up to the age of 30. Girl children are generally given less education and medical attention, affecting both mortality rates and the health of their offspring. The link between gender inequality and income poverty is supported by states such as Kerala, where girls are twice as likely to become literate and five times more likely to reach their fifth birthday than girls born in Uttar Pradesh.

Public expenditure has been vital in India's income poverty reduction and the government has introduced several poverty alleviation programmes over the years, the public distribution system of subsidized food being a well-known example. States have experimented with different models. Tamil Nadu, for example, achieved rapid progress in education through increased funds, together with improved accountability mechanisms of service providers and incentives such as free school meals and free textbooks aimed at poor households.

Welfare: While India has made progress in human development since independence in 1947, its overall performance compares unfavourably with other developing countries. Improvements in health indicators such as life expectancy and infant mortality rates have been much slower than expected and there is widespread undernutrition among women and children. The UNDP's *Human Development Report 2005* ranks India 127th out of 177 countries in terms of a composite Human Development Index. Progress has varied across the states, with Kerala having achieved high levels of human development and the so-called 'BIMARU' states of Bihar, Madhya Pradesh, **Rajasthan** and Uttar Pradesh having performed particularly badly.

Population control has long been the central focus of governmental welfare programmes in India, starting with a family-planning programme in 1952. The programme evolved gradually from awareness and information activities to clinical services, and under a target-oriented system the central government directed each state to achieve replacement fertility levels by a certain year. Criticized for being too centralized, the Indian family-planning programme began in the 1990s to do away with quantitative targets, encouraging states to develop their own system of performance planning and monitoring based on an assessment of community needs. At the same time, a shift towards reproductive and child health has been pursued to bring down high maternal and infant mortality rates, with greater emphasis being placed on rural areas through the National Rural Health Mission. (*See* Education, Health System/Policy.)

Gender Relations/Empowerment: Indicators of women's relative position in Indian society and the economy suggest that while there has been a great improvement over the last 50 years (life expectancy has increased, mortality rates have dropped), there are entrenched biases against females. The sex ratio for the 0–6 cohort has declined continuously, most likely because of greater neglect of girl children and the wider practice of female foeticide as a result of modern medical techniques to determine the sex of the foetus (*see* Population). India's maternal mortality rates have declined very slowly, reflecting a rural-urban divide, poor infrastructure and limited education about health. According to a WHO report in 2005, India has the third highest mortality rate in Asia.

The state has taken an active role, seeking to improve employment opportunities, encourage female participation in decentralized political institutions and processes as well as addressing persisting social and legal inequalities as in the case of succession and ownership rights. Providing or taking a dowry was made illegal in 1961, although the practice still occurs widely and women continue to suffer from societal violence. Under the 73rd Amendment of 1992, one-third of local ***Panchayati Raj*** seats are reserved for women, allowing them a greater voice in decision-making and the possibility of directing local governance to issues that have a direct impact on women and children. Extending reservations to legislative and state assemblies has also been much discussed but not implemented.

The fast-growing software and information technology sector, as well as back office work subcontracted by multinational companies, has increased employment for urban, educated women and on comparatively good salaries. Microcredit and self-help loan schemes launched by private individuals and NGOs have had some success in providing rural women with greater income and a greater say in the allocation of household finances.

National Development Council: The National Development Council (NDC) is the most important decision-making body in the development sector. It consists of the Prime Minister, the Cabinet and the Chief Ministers of all the states. Development plans are generally prepared by the Planning Commission and submitted to the NDC, which has the authority to adopt the plans with or without amendments.

India Trade Promotion Organization (ITPO)

The India Trade Promotion Organization (ITPO) was established on 1 January 1992 to implement policy reforms in the economy, trade and industry as an enterprise of the national Ministry of Commerce. As a premier trade promotion agency it promotes India's external export drive and provides a wide spectrum of services to trade and industry. To fulfil this aim, the ITPO has built up an extensive infrastructure as well as information facilities which are available to exporters both in India and abroad.

Indian Administrative Service (IAS)

The Indian Administrative Service (IAS) is a successor to the Indian Civil Services (ICS). It was formally constituted in 1947. Entrants to this service are recruited through competitive examinations conducted by the Union Public Service Commission (UPSC), appointed by the President of India. As the executive arm of the government, the IAS is engaged with the implemention of govermental decisions at the central and state levels. Its responsibilites include development functions, issues of law and order and general administration.

Indian Federal Democratic Party (IFDP)

The Indian Federal Democratic Party (IFDP) is a regional political party in south India, founded in 2002 in **Kerala** and led by P. C. Thomas, who crossed over from the Kerala Congress (M), from which he was elected to the 13th **Lok Sabha**. He joined the **National Democratic Alliance (NDA)** as an ally of the **Bharatiya Janata Party (BJP)** and became a Union Minister. The IFDP won one seat in the 14th Lok Sabha elections of 2004.

Indian Military Training Team (IMTRAT)

The Indian Military Training Team (IMTRAT) was set up as a result of a joint defence agreement between Bhutan and India, in 1965. Based in **Thimpu** and three district capitals, Haa, Tashigang and Wangdiphodrang, its role is confined to training the Royal Bhutanese Army. Additionally, IMTRAT relays India's security interests and serves as an outpost of the Indian army towards China.

Indian National Congress (INC)

One of the oldest parties in the world and the first all-India political association, the Congress party continues to be a major player in Indian politics, a position it occupied during the critical years of India's transition from colonial rule to independent democracy. Founded in 1885, the Congress was an annual gathering of the educated élite of British India in which Sir Alan Octavian Hume, a retired British civil servant, played a crucial role in bringing together Indian nationalists of different hues within one organization. Funtioning initially as a pressure group petitioning the government for political and administrative reforms, the Congress became a mass membership party under the leadership of *Mahatma* **Gandhi** from 1920 onwards. Devoting attention to the Indian peasantry and the need for radical social reform, the party extended its reach both socially and geographically.

Provincial elections held under the Government of India Act of 1935 endowed the Congress party with valuable experience in electoral campaigning and, subsequently, governance.

It was the chief political party in the constituent assembly that produced the Indian Constitution and, on winning the first general election in 1952, assumed office. Following independence, Prime Minister Jawaharlal **Nehru** and the Congress government articulated the core values of India's political culture in terms of Indian nationalism, social democracy, economic self-reliance through the Mixed Economy and secularism. The party held considerable majorities in the **Lok Sabha**, as well as continuous control over almost all regional governments in India from 1947 until 1967—known as the '**Congress System**'. Under the leadership of Nehru the INC won elections in 1952, 1957 and 1962, Nehru coming to symbolize Congress culture in many ways, playing an important role in the socio-economic transformation of India and building a national ethos based on the principles of socialism and democracy. After his death in 1964, the Congress came under the grip of a group known as 'the syndicate', a gathering of powerful state leaders with control over regional congress organizations. Their power was slowly dismantled under the leadership of Indira **Gandhi** (Prime Minister in 1966–77 and 1980–84), who systematically replaced Chief Ministers until the inner Congress caucus consisted almost exclusively of a few trusted advisers and relatives, which later came to include, prominently, her younger son, Sanjay. With Indira Gandhi at the helm from 1966, the INC went on to win the 1967 and 1971 elections, but following the emergency of 1975–77 Congress suffered its first parliamentary defeat in the 1977 elections, splitting for a second time in 1978. Congress first suffered a major split in 1969 as a result of opposition within the party to Indira Gandhi's socialist programme and leadership style. The Congress Party Organization, Congress (O), was formed with its own president, national committee, and parliamentary party, although less than one-quarter of the Congress members of parliament joined its ranks. In 1971 Congress (O) won 15 seats in the Lok Sabha, but later saw its support dwindle, changing its name in 1985 to Congress (Secular). In that year it won five seats, and just a single seat in the 1989 election. Indira Gandhi's party, regarded as the successor to the original Congress party, known as Congress—Requisitionist or Congress (R) because of a requisitioned party meeting summoned by Mrs Gandhi during the split, lost seats only temporarily, gaining votes and seats in the 1971 elections. The second split in 1978 saw forces loyal to Indira Gandhi breaking off to form Congress (Indira), or Congress (I), confirmed as the official Congress party in 1981. Despite being a faction, this party took control and continued Congress policies and agenda. Achieving an impressive victory in the 1980 elections, it proved Congress (I) to be more effective than the rival Congress party. In October 1984 Indira Gandhi was assassinated by Sikh extremists and was succeeded both as leader of Congress (I) and as Prime Minister by her son Rajiv Gandhi (Prime Minister in 1984–89), who led the party to a tremendous victory in the parliamentary elections of 1984–85. During the 1990s, however, the Congress party witnessed the rise of a new rival, the **Bharatiya Janata Party (BJP)**, coming to terms with its declining fortune when it formed a minority government in 1991 under Narasimha **Rao** which nevertheless lasted its full term.

Internal disputes, organizational decay, a growing number of political and powerful regional parties, an inability to keep pace with social changes in many districts or to maintain its old electoral coalition of high castes, **Scheduled Castes (SCs)** and Muslims, have all contributed to a weakening of support for the Congress party. In the general election of 1998 it finished well behind the BJP and in 1999 suffered its worst electoral defeat in more than 50 years, winning only 114 of 545 seats in parliament but still the largest percentage of votes, 28.30%. However, the victory of Congress, under the leadership of Sonia **Gandhi**, in the 2004 general elections, leading to the formation of a Congress-led **United Progressive Alliance (UPA)** government, has once again shown the resilience of the party.

Indian National Trade Union Congress (INTUC)

The Indian National Trade Union Congress (INTUC), established in 1947, is the largest central trade union organization in India and is affiliated with the **Indian National Congress (INC)**. It has an anti-communist bias and claims that its policies and programmes draw inspiration from Mohandas Karamchand **Gandhi**'s ideas on the economic and social development of the country, which ought to be based more on human considerations than on economic ones.

Indian Ocean

Covering an area of 68.556m. sq km, the Indian Ocean is the third largest of the world's five oceans. Located between the two bigger ones, the Atlantic and Pacific, it serves as a major sea route connecting the Middle East, Africa and East Asia with Europe and the Americas. Four critically important access waterways feed into the Indian Ocean: the Suez Canal (Egypt), the Strait of Hormuz (Iran-Oman), Bal el Mandeb (Djibouti-Yemen) and the Straits of Malacca (Indonesia-Malaysia). More than 80% of the trade that passes through is extra-regional and of great strategic importance given the heavy traffic in petroleum and petroleum products. Amongst the indigenous navies of the region possessing major surface and sub-suface equipment, India is the largest. Major interests in the region from non-littoral powers include the USA and, increasingly, China.

Indian Peace Keeping Force (IPKF)

Following the 1987 **Indo-Lanka Accord** an Indian Peace Keeping Force (IPKF) was dispatched on the invitation of Sri Lankan President **Jayawardene** to establish order in the northern and eastern provinces of Sri Lanka. Militant groups were expected to surrender their arms to the IPKF, but the **Liberation Tigers of Tamil Eelam (LTTE)** refused to disarm. Instead of acting as mediator, the IPKF found itself engaged in bloody police action against the LTTE, provoking the ire of India's Tamils. With the government of Sri Lanka failing to prevent either Sinhalese or Tamil extremist action, the Indian forces found themselves losing support from both sides. Recognizing the debacle, India finally withdrew all its forces in early 1990 at the request of newly elected Sri Lankan President **Premadasa**. During the three-year involvement some 1,500 Indian troops were killed and many were wounded in a jungle war in which they had received little intelligence support or co-ordination from political leaders at home and on the ground.

Indian Police Service (IPS)

The Indian Police Service (IPS) is the premier and apex police service in India and deals with issues of public safety and security, including crime prevention and detection, traffic control, accident prevention and management of law and order. For greater efficiency, the IPS is designed to share responsibility with the **Indian Administrative Service** and is present in several departments, such as the Crime Branch, the Criminal Investigation Department (CID), the Home Guards, and the Traffic Bureau. Members of this service are selected through competitive examinations conducted by an independent body, the Union Public Service Commission (UPSC), which is appointed by the President of India.

Indian Space Research Organisation (ISRO)

The Indian Space Research Organisation (ISRO), established in 1969, is the national space agency which operates currently under the Department of Space, government of India. The main objectives of the organization are executing space programmes and developing space technology and its application to various national tasks. The primary aim of space programmes includes the development of satellites, launching of vehicles, sounding rockets and associated ground systems. Besides developing capacities in nuclear technology, the Indian space programme is recognized in many sections of Indian society as the main achievement of post-colonial India.

Indo-Ceylon Agreements (Sri Lanka)

Three Indo-Ceylon Agreements have dealt with the stateless Tamils of Indian origin in Sri Lanka. The first agreement, also known as the Nehru-Kotelawala Pact after the countries' Prime Ministers, was signed on 18 January 1954 and permitted registration for citizenship either in Sri Lanka or India. The pact, however, was not implemented and two more treaties ensued, in October 1964 (Sirima-Shastri Pact) and in 1974 (Sirima-Indira Pact) in which India agreed to repatriate thousands of Tamils to the south Indian state of **Tamil Nadu.** As of October 2003 it was estimated that there were 300,000 stateless people of Indian origin in Sri Lanka.

Indo-Lanka Accord

Signed on 29 July 1987 by the Prime Minister of India, Rajiv Gandhi, and President **Jayawardene** of Sri Lanka, the Indo-Lanka Peace Accord provided for a number of concessions on the part of the Sri Lanka government to Tamil demands regarding the devolution of power to the provinces, a merger of the northern and eastern provinces, subject to a referendum in the east, and official status for the **Tamil language**. India in turn offered to send peace-keeping troops if requested (the **Indian Peace Keeping Force**) to maintain peace in the north east and to convince militant groups to surrender their arms.

Indus Waters Treaty

The waters of the Indus basin begin in the Himalayan mountains of Kashmir. They flow into the Pakistani states of **Punjab** and **Sind**, converging in Pakistan and emptying into the Arabian Sea. The **Partition** of the Indian subcontinent created a conflict over the valuable water resources of the Indus basin, over how to share and manage the intricate system of canals and rivers. As the upper riparian state, India represented a threat to Pakistan and by 1951 negotiations over the allocation of waters had reached a deadlock. Involving the World Bank's good offices in searching for a peaceful solution to the dispute, the stalemate continued until 1960 when the Indus Waters Treaty was finally signed by India and Pakistan, heavily funded by the World Bank. Pakistan obtained exclusive rights for three western rivers, the Indus, Chenab and Jhelum, while India retained rights to the three eastern rivers of Sutlej, Beas and Ravi. A commission was also set up to adjudicate future disputes, providing the machinery for consultation and conflict resolution that has helped the agreement survive two wars (in 1965 and 1971) and facilitated its continued implementation.

Industrial Development Bank of India (IDBI)

The Industrial Development Bank of India (IDBI), established in 1964 under an Act of Parliament, is one of India's premier financial institutions. Its activities include the provision of finance and financial services to aid the establishment and modernization of industry in India. Originally the IDBI was founded wholly as a subsidiary owned by the **Reserve Bank of India (RBI)**.

Industrial Development Bank of Pakistan (IDBP)

The Industrial Development Bank of Pakistan (IDBP), besides being one of the oldest development-financing institutions, is also a scheduled bank owned by the government of Pakistan. The bank finances not only new industrial projects but also supports expansion, modernization and replacement of old projects. IDBP-financed projects have an annual export value of US $133m., and the annual value addition of the completed projects is estimated at around $250m.

Infosys Technologies Ltd

Providing global information technology (IT) services, Infosys is one of India's major IT companies. Established in 1981 in Pune, **Maharashtra**, it later moved to **Bangalore**, where it now has its headquarters. Narayan Murthy, one of the initial founders, is the company's 'Chief Mentor' and its most famous face. Infosys employs approximately 46,000 software professionals in about 30 offices world-wide and in 1999 was the first Indian company to be listed on the Nasdaq. In 2004 Infosys generated revenue in excess of US $1,000m. As a knowledge-intensive company, Infosys has recognized the need to attract, retain and develop its human resouces. As a result, it prioritizes working conditions and has created one of the largest software services campuses in the world, Infosys City near Bangalore.

Institute for Defence Studies and Analyses (IDSA)

Established in 1965, the Institute for Defence Studies and Analyses (IDSA) is considered to be India's top security and strategic studies think-tank. Funded by the Ministries of Defence and External Affairs, the institute conducts research and offers training to government officers from the **Indian Administrative Service (IAS)**, the Indian Foreign Service, the Armed Forces and the Paramilitary Forces.

Integrated Rural Development Programme (IRDP)

A major poverty alleviation programme in India that aimed to generate self-employment. The Integrated Rural Development Programme (IRDP) was launched in 1978–79 and targeted small and marginal farmers, agricultural workers, landless labourers, rural craftsmen and artisans and virtually all families of about five persons with an annual income below the poverty line (which varies across the states). The main aim of IRDP is to help families cross the poverty line on a long-lasting basis by giving them income-generating assets and access to credit. It is required that 50% of beneficiaries belong to **Scheduled Castes** or **Scheduled Tribes**, and that 40% are women.

International Monetary Fund (IMF)

All seven South Asian countries are members of the International Monetary Fund (IMF). India, which had already, before independence, joined the IMF as one of the founding members in December 1945, has contributed 1.95% to the total assets of the Fund, and has a 1.93%-share of the votes in the Board of Governors. It has taken up three major loans from the Fund, one in 1981 (returned in 1984), and two during the financial crisis in 1991 (returned in 1991 and 1993).

Among the other South Asian members, Pakistan has been a member since 1950 and holds US $1,685m. of outstanding debt; Bangladesh, a member since 1972, holds $148m. of debt; and Nepal, a member since 1961, holds $14m. of debt.

Investment Corporation of Bangladesh (ICB)

The Investment Corporation of Bangladesh (ICB) was established in 1976 to encourage and broaden the base of industrial investment. Initially its activities were limited to underwriting the issue of securities, the bridging of financing programmes, and opening/maintaining investors' accounts. Subsequently, the ICB expanded its activities to include providing closed-end and open-end mutual funds, and closed-end unit funds to ensure supply of securities as well as to generate demand for securities. The ICB also operates the **Dhaka Stock Exchange** and Chittagong Stock Exchange as dealers.

Islam, Syed Nazrul

Syed Nazrul Islam (1925–75) was Vice-President of the Provisional Government of Bangladesh, formed at Mujibnagar on 10 April 1971. Starting his political career as an activist of the **Awami League (AL)**, after obtaining an LL B in 1953 from Dhaka University, he was the party's acting president from 1966 until 1969, in the absence of the arrested Sheikh Mujibur **Rahman**. He was elected to the Pakistan National Assembly in 1970 and was deputy leader of the AL parliamentary party. Associated with Sheikh Mujibur Rahman in numerous movements, including the **Six-Point Programme**, anti-Ayub movement and liberation movement, he was a member of Mujibur Rahman's Cabinet after independence and Vice-President in the one-party presidential government in 1975. Following Rahman's assassination and in the aftermath of the 3 November coup of 1975, he was killed along with three others national leaders, all of whom were prominent in the AL and had refused to co-operate with the leaders of the August 1975 coup.

Islami Jamiat i Tulaba (IJT)

Islami Jamiat i Tulaba (IJT) is the student wing of Jamaat-i Islami (JI) of Pakistan. One-third of the JI leadership is recruited from the IJT. The IJT has over the years become increasingly militant and has been involved in violent clashes with other Pakistani student groups. The IJT seeks a state governed by Islamic Law and is opposed to practices such as bank interest, birth control and Western political ideas.

Islami Jatiya Oikya Front (IJOF)

The Islami Jatiya Oikya Front (IJOF—Islamic National United Front) is an alliance of five parties in Bangladesh, led by the **Jatiya Party** (Ershad). Among the four other constituents is the Islamic Shashontontro Andolan. In the 2001 parliamentary elections the front won 14 seats, having received 7.5% of the votes in total.

Islamic Democratic Alliance (IDA/IJI)

The Islamic Democratic Alliance (IDA/IJI) was a coalition of parties founded in 1988, of which the major components were the **Pakistan Muslim League**, the **Muttahida Qaumi Movement** and the IJI. Two years later, in 1990, the IDA/IJI, under the leadership of Nawaz **Sharif**, won the polls and held political power until 1993. The alliance implemented a programme of privatization and economic deregulation.

Islamic Democratic Party (IDP)

The Islamic Democratic Party (IDP) is the fourth officially confirmed political party in the Maldives, registered on 12 December 2005. The moderate Islamic party was founded by Umar Naseer, a businessman and former police officer. It has expressed its solidarity with the government, its main goal being to co-operate with the **Dhivehi Raiyyithunge Party (DRP)** and to support the implementation of President **Gayoom**'s political reform agenda.

Islamic Oikya Jote (IOJ)

The Islamic Oikya Jote (IOJ) is an Islamic political party in Bangladesh and is part of the current ruling coalition led by the **Bangladesh Nationalist Party** since 2001. It is a small party which draws support from traditional religious groups due its attempts to implement Islamic doctrines, and it is working towards a strict enforcement of *Shari'a* law in government policies. It holds two seats in the current parliament but was not allocated any cabinet posts.

J

Jabmi

A term used in Bhutan that literally means 'backer' and which can be understood functionally as a trained advocate, legal council or substitute for a lawyer, who provides representation in civil and criminal cases. The *jabmi* became an integral part of the Bhutanese legal system in August 2003 when the national assembly incorporated guide-lines for legal councils into national law through the Jabmi Act. The main objective was to introduce formal training and licensing for the *jabmi* to improve knowledge of law and professionalism, following criticisms by political observers, especially human rights organizations, about the traditional and under-developed *jabmi* system.

Jaffna

The capital city of Sri Lanka's Northern Province (also referred to as Jaffna Peninsula), Jaffna has great symbolic and strategic importance for the Tamil militants. From about the 11th century Tamil leaders ruled periodically over the northern peninsula from Jaffna before the British took over in 1815. In 1981 the Sinhalese police burned down the Jaffna public library, which housed rare Tamil texts, sparking animosity between the two communities. In 1990, upon the departure of the **India Peace Keeping Force (IPKF)**, the **Liberation Tigers of Tamil Eelam (LTTE)** became the *de facto* administration in Jaffna, but after years of battle Sri Lankan government forces recaptured Jaffna in 1996 and imposed military rule. Jaffna's population has been considerably reduced by the conflict. Many Tamil residents, and also Muslims and Sinhalese, have moved away for fear of what have been described as threats of ethnic cleansing by the LTTE.

Jajmani System

The *jajmani* system describes a system of social relations in terms of the reciprocal bonds of obligations through which social groups owning land are tied to other social groups on the basis of status, occupations and power. Politically, the social bonds of *jajmani* lead to a 'pyramid' of dominance. Politically, the small group of social élites accumulate power, status and wealth, which makes it possible for them to dominate the many others devoid of these resources. Since the bond that thus binds the élite and the non-élite is deeply ingrained, the social pyramid looks like a natural rather than a political construction. Empowered by the principle of universal adult franchise after independence, the relatively powerless bottom of the pyramid quickly learnt how to pool their collective strength and use it as a political resource, leading to a decline in the power of upper social groups.

Jamaat-e-Islami (Bangladesh)

Jamaat-e-Islami (Bangladesh) traces its origin to Jamaat-e-Islami Hind, established in India in 1941 and reorganized as Jamaat-e-Islami Pakistan after independence. From its inception, the founder, Syed Abul Ala Maududi, was opposed to all national movements, including the creation of Pakistan, because he believed in a single party government, the party of God based on the Holy Koran. After Bangladesh's independence, the party was banned because of its strong anti-Bangladesh role during the liberation war. During this period, the party had organized 'peace committees' to root out Bengali freedom fighters and had organized its workers and supporters under auxiliary paramilitary forces called *razakars*, *al-Badras* and *al-Shams* to help the Pakistan army in the battle. The party was indirectly rehabilitated in 1976, when limited party activities were allowed under the Political Parties Regulation (PPR) and many of them joined the Islamic Democratic League (IDL) led by Mawlana Abdur Rahim. The party has organizational units at the central, district, *upazilla/thana* (sub-districts) and union/municipal levels. The central organization consists of *rukn* (members), an *ameer-e-jamaat* (chief) who is elected every three years by direct secret ballot in the *rukn* conference, a *majlis-e-sura* (central advisory committee) and central working committee. The party secured 10 seats and 18 seats in the Jatiya Sangsad (JS) elections of 1986 and 1991 respectively. Although in the 1996 elections the party secured only three seats, in 2001 it emerged as the third largest party, securing 17 seats as a partner of the **Bangladesh Nationalist Party**-led **Four-Party Alliance** that formed the government under Begum Khaleda **Zia**. Two of its members were included in the Cabinet. Critics claim that the Jamaat-e-Islami is partly responsible for the increasing Islamization of politics and the public sphere in Bangladesh.

Jamiat-i-Ulema-i-Islam (JUI)

The Jamiat-i-Ulema-i-Islam (JUI) is a fundamentalist Sunni party in Pakistan, founded in 1945, which adheres to a multi-party democratic system. The party has an extremist militant faction called Anjuman Sipah-i-Sahaba (ASS), which conducted several anti-Shi'a activities. The ASS has been strongly involved in the escalation of the violence between Sunnis and Shi'as since 1997. (*See* **Shi'a–Sunni Conflict in Pakistan**.)

Jamiat-i-Ulema-i-Pakistan (JUP)

Pakistan's Jamiat-i-Ulema-i-Pakistan (JUP) was founded in 1968 and advocates Sunni Islamic principles including enforcement of the *Shari'a*. The organization is considered a moderate, progressive Sunni party, and has a strong presence in urban centres. Its leaders include Shah Ahmed Noorani, Maulana Nasrullah Khan and Maulana Abdus Sattar Khan Niazi.

Jamiat-ul-Ulema-i-Islam (JUI)

Jamiat-ul-Ulema-i-Islam (JUI) is the major representative in Pakistan of *deobandi* (a strand of Islam with its centre of religious learning in **Uttar Pradesh**, India) interests, an Islamic sect which aimed at purifying Indian Islam from 'un-Islamic' practices. The party gathers most of its support in the **North West Frontier Province (NWFP)** and **Balochistan**. The political influence of the JUI is rather weak compared to that of the Jamaat-i Islami.

Jammu and Kashmir

The Himalayan Indian state of Jammu and Kashmir shares disputed borders with Pakistan and China (*see* **Line of Control (LoC)** and **Aksai Chin**). In 2001 the population (in the Indian-administered territories) was 10,143,700, making Jammu and Kashmir one of the least populous states in the country. It is the only Muslim-majority state (67.0% in 2001) in India, although Jammu is Hindu-dominated and Ladakh is largely Buddhist. Most of the population are Kashmiri speakers concentrated in the Valley of Kashmir, the next most common language being Punjabi. In summer the capital is Srinagar, the largest city in the state, and in the winter Jammu. The conflict over Kashmir has retarded economic development in the state where tourism, an important sector of the economy, has been damaged by instability and insecurity. Jammu and Kashmir has a bicameral legislature with a state assembly of 89 seats and returns six members to the **Lok Sabha**.

The dispute over the status of Jammu and Kashmir dates back to the days leading up to the 1947 **Partition** (*see* **Kashmir Dispute**). To mark Kashmir's autonomy, the state was granted special status under Article 370, given its own constitution and special rights for its residents. However, as India sought to integrate the state into the larger polity, these privileges were curtailed, prompting the formation of secessionist groups such as the **Jammu and Kashmir Liberation Front (JKLF)**.

Elections in 1977 returned Sheikh Abdullah's **Jammu and Kashmir National Conference (JKNC)**, but stringent security measures and the stifling of civil liberties alienated the population. The rise of Islamic radicalism and Indira **Gandhi**'s attempts to centralize power, for example her dismissal of the JKNC government in 1984 and elections in 1987 that were widely seen as fraudulent, combined with deteriorating economic and security conditions, transformed what had initially been a peaceful campaign for greater autonomy into a violent, secessionist movement by 1989. The government's crackdown on the insurgency produced a state of siege in the Valley.

Elections since have focused on winning back the trust of the Kashmiri people. General elections held in 1996 were overshadowed in Kashmir by reports of widespread intimidation, particularly in the Valley where the Indian army reportedly coerced the public to vote. Assembly elections in the same year, however, were regarded as a positive development, returning Farooq Abdullah's JKNC to power. In 2002 highly publicized state elections were held which, although not recognized by Pakistan, won international praise and support. Despite threats of violence and boycotts by various groups, including the **All-Party Hurriyat Conference (APHC)**, the polls were declared to have been free and fair, yielding a new winner, the **Jammu and Kashmir People's Democratic Party (PDP)**, which emerged to form a coalition government with the **Congress**. For the 2004 Lok Sabha elections, a highly competitive four-way contest emerged, with Congress, the **Bharatiya Janata Party (BJP)**, the JKNC and the PDP all fighting to emerge as the real representative of Kashmiri interests. Each party polled a significant percentage of votes, but the Congress victory by a margin of two seats marked a comeback for the party which had drawn a blank in the 1999 Lok Sabha elections. The result is attributed to the success of the Congress-PDP alliance at the state level and a renewed faith in the peace process initiated by the state. Voter turn-out for the 2004 elections was 35.20%, an increase of 3% compared with 1999. (*See* **Kashmir Dispute**.)

Jammu and Kashmir Liberation Front (JKLF)

The Jammu and Kashmir Liberation Front (JKLF) was officially founded in Britain in May 1977 by Mohammad Maqbool Bhat, and began the armed movement for Kashmiri 'self-determination' in the late 1980s. Its origins lie in the Plebiscite Front of the 1950s, formed by supporters of the imprisoned leader of the **Jammu and Kashmir National Conference**, Sheikh Abdullah. After Sheikh Abdullah came to an agreement with Prime Minister Indira **Gandhi** and contested elections in 1977, militant, pro-independence members within the Plebiscite Front walked out to continue the struggle for secession. It is reported that the JKLF received Pakistani support and training, but its professed secular ideology and commitment to independence for the state led to its eclipse by other hardline, pro-Pakistan organizations such as **Harkat ul-Ansar** and **Lashkar-e-Toiba**. The JKLF split into two factions in 1995 when Yassin Malik, head of the group in Indian-administered Kashmir, renounced the use of violence, becoming a constituent of the **All Party Hurriyat Conference** and leading a delegation on a visit to Pakistan in June 2005. Amanullah Khan formed his own faction based in Pakistan-administered Kashmir. Discussions to reunite the factions have been initiated.

Jammu and Kashmir National Conference (JKNC)

The Jammu and Kashmir National Conference (JKNC), or National Conference, is a regional political party in India, present mainly in the state of **Jammu and Kashmir**. The JKNC was formed in 1939 and has its roots in Kashmir's first political party, the All Jammu and Kashmir Muslim Conference, which was founded in 1932 under the leadership of Sheikh Mohammed Abdullah. The Delhi Agreement negotiated with Prime Minister Jawaharlal **Nehru** ratified Kashmir's autonomy as ensrhined in Article 370 of the Constitution. However, when Abdullah revived the notion of an independent Kashmir he was was arrested in 1953 and incarcerated until 1964. Winning the elections in 1977, the JKNC won an overwhelming victory in the Valley. Following his death in 1982, Abdullah's son Farooq Abdullah took over leadership of the party and state, winning the 1983 elections on an anti-**Delhi**, pro-Kashmiri autonomy platform, competing directly with the **Indian National Congress (INC)**. By 1984 Farooq's government had been removed and a new government, supported by the Congress, formed. Reaching a *rapprochement* with the centre, the JKNC combined with the INC to contest and win the 1987 elections which were widely dismissed as fraudulent. The partnership with Congress, seen as self-serving, damaged the JKNC's image and popularity, and Farooq's government was ultimately dismissed in 1990 in the face of a mass uprising. Nevertheless, in the 1996 assembly elections the JKNC returned to power, winning significantly even in the regions of Jammu and Ladakh, although turn-out was limited.

Leadership of the party passed to Abdullah's grandson, Omar, in 2002, at the time Minister of State for External Affairs in the **National Democratic Alliance (NDA)** government. In 2002 the National Conference experienced a reversal of fortune when they lost state elections to the Congress and **Jammu and Kashmir People's Democratic Party** alliance.

Jammu and Kashmir People's Democratic Party (JKPDP)

The Jammu and Kashmir People's Democratic Party (JKPDP) is a regional party in the Indian state of **Jammu and Kashmir**. It was formed and led by Mufti Mohammad Sayeed in 1999 as an alternative to the **Jammu and Kashmir National Conference**. In the 2002 assembly elections, the JKPDP won 16 of the 46 seats from the Muslim-majority constituencies in the Kashmir valley, on a campaign promising corruption-free government and unconditional dialogue with the militants. As a result, the JKPDP formed a coalition government together with the **Indian National Congress (INC)**. The JKPDP won its first **Lok Sabha** seat in the 2004 parliamentary elections and became a member of the ruling **United Progressive Alliance (UPA)** at the centre.

Jana Andolan

Led jointly by the **Nepali Congress (NC)** and the **United Left Front (ULF)**, Nepal's Jana Andolan, or People's Movement, was launched on 18 February 1990, the country's **Democracy Day** that commemorates the return of King **Tribhuvan** to Nepal after his self-imposed exile in India, and the end of **Rana Family** rule. Pro-democracy demonstrations in 1990, occasionally violent though mostly peaceful, took place in all major urban areas. Initially attempting to suppress the movement, King **Birendra** ultimately lifted the ban on political parties in April 1990, inviting an all-party interim government to oversee the drafting of a new constitution.

Janajati

A term referring to one of Nepal's disadvantaged and marginalized social groups, janajati is sometimes translated as 'indigenous nationalities'.

Janata Dal—Secular (JD—S)

The Janata Dal—Secular (JD—S) is a regional political party in India. It was founded in 1979 by Raj Narain as an offshoot of the Janata Party, initially deriving its support from opposition to the Hindu nationalist Bharitya Jan Sangh (*see* **Bharatiya Janata Party**), a supporter of the broad coalition (Janata Party) that opposed Indira **Gandhi** during the last phase of the emergency. The party won three seats in the 14th **Lok Sabha** election and is led by the former Prime Minister and party president, H. D. Deve Gowda. The JD—S is not a part of the current ruling **United Progressive Alliance (UPA)** but extends 'outside support' to the **Congress**-led government in the 14th Lok Sabha.

Janata Dal—United (JD—U)

The Janata Dal—United (JD—U) is a regional political party in India. It has its main support base in the state of **Bihar** and is led by the former union cabinet Minister of Defence Georges Fernandes. The party won eight seats in the 14th **Lok Sabha** elections in 2004 and is a constituent of the **National Democratic Alliance (NDA)**, the main opposition in the national parliament. In November 2005 the JD—U, together with its alliance partner, the **Bharatiya Janata Party (BJP)**, defeated the **Rashtriya Janata Dal (RJD)**, its main political opponent, to head the government in Bihar.

Janatha Vimukhti Peramuna (JVP—People's Liberation Front)

Founded in 1965 by Rochana Wijeweera, the Janatha Vimukhti Peramuna (JVP—People's Liberation Front) has been the most successful of Sri Lanka's leftist parties, appealing mostly to students and Sinhalese youth from deprived areas, particularly in the south. In the past the JVP launched two insurgencies against the state, causing thousands of deaths. It was recognized as a legal political party in 1977 and Wijeweera contested the 1982 presidential elections, but the JVP was banned following the 1983 anti-Tamil riots. It has been linked with political killings, but re-emerged under new leadership in 2001 to participate in legislative elections.

The JVP contested the 2004 elections as a member of the **United People's Freedom Alliance (UPFA)**. It has 39 seats under its direct control. In mid-2005 the JVP left the alliance, opposing President **Kumaratunga**'s move to establish a joint mechanism with the **Liberation Tigers of Tamil Eelam (LTTE)** to distribute post-tsunami foreign aid. (*See* **Patriotic National Movement**.)

Jathika Hela Urumaya (JHU—National Heritage Party)

The Jathika Hela Urumaya (JHU—National Heritage Party) is a political party in Sri Lanka led by and composed of Buddhist monks. Launched in early 2004, the JHU contested its first parliamentary elections in April 2004 and won nine out of 225 parliamentary seats. It is seen as a conservative and nationalist party with a manifesto that aims at restoring a 'Kingdom of Dhamma', or the 'correct' way of life and politics as drawn from Buddhist philosophy. (*See* **Buddhist Movement**.)

Jatis

The term *jatis*, signifying local castes which literally means 'born', has its origins in *Sanskrit* and implies that one's existence is determined by birth. *Jatis* operate as a subunit of the Hindu social structure (**caste system**) and are the basic social building block that still governs marriages, social networks, food taboos and rituals in India. There are more than 2,000 *jatis* in India, centred around the performance of traditional occupations and co-existing in an interdependent relationship with other *jatis*. This situation has been changing rapidly because of modernization, urbanization, and government policy, which, through a **reservation policy**, has been opening up top jobs that used to be the prerogative of the upper castes.

Jatiya Party (JP)

The Jatiya Party (JP) of Bangladesh was founded by the former chief-of-staff Gen. H. M. **Ershad** to give a civilian character to his government. Although the party came into being formally in January 1986, it had been operational since 27 November 1983 as 'Jonodol', formed by several prominent leaders of the country, drawn from various political parties. Under the leadership of Ershad, the JP won a majority of seats in the third and fourth parliamentary elections. The results of both elections were contested on account of alleged electoral fraud. The JP advocates Bangladeshi nationalism and claims to operate in favour of the principles of Islam and, at the same time, to promote respect for all religions. Following the political turmoil, Ershad was forced to announce his resignation on 4 December 1990 and many leaders and workers of the party, including Ershad, were imprisoned on charges of corruption. Against the odds, the party secured 35 and 18 seats, respectively, in the elections of 1991 and 2001, thus emerging as a third force in the political arena, by pitting the **Bangladesh Nationalist Party (BNP)** against the **Awami League (AL)** and benefiting from rivalries between their political leaders. However, the party had to manage various splits, including one in 1993 when Shamsul Huda Chowdhury and a breakaway group formed the Jatiya Party (Nationalist). Further splits occurred in April 1999, under Anwar Hossain Manju, who formed the Jatiya Party (Manju), and in 2001, as the **Manjur Faction**, or Jatiya Party (Naziur or Naziur Firoz) separated from the party and joined the **Four-Party Alliance**, the current ruling coalition (since October 2001). Today the party operates under the name Jatiya Party (Ershad), leads the **Islami Jatiya Oikya Front (IJOF)**, and is the fourth largest political force in the parliament, occupying 14 of the 300 seats).

Jatiya Samajtantrik Dal (JSD)

As a breakaway group from the **Bangladesh Awami League (AL)**, the Jatiya Samajtantrik Dal (JSD) was established in October 1972 by Serajul Alam Khan and various partisans, the Seraj faction being a younger group of nationalists who were fighting for independence within the AL and, later, during the **Bangladesh Liberation War**, as the Bangladesh Liberation Front, Mujib Bahini. It was organized as a cadre-based party, identified principally with Marxism and was committed to a scientific, socialist revolution, a classless society and the economic empowerment of the masses. Between 1972 and 1991 the party split into as many as six factions over questions of participation in national and local level elections, alliances with other parties and the movement against Gen. **Ershad**'s military autocracy.

Jatiya Sangsad – *see* Bangladesh, Political Development—Legislature

Jatiyo Rakkhi Bahini – *see* Rakkhi Bahini

Jayawardene, Junius Richard

Leader of Sri Lanka's **United National Party (UNP)** in 1970, Junius Richard Jayawardene (1906–96) prioritized party organization, winning the 1977 elections. In 1978 he was sworn in as President following the introduction of a new Constitution. Economic liberalization and foreign direct investment were encouraged, and administrative decentralization initiated. However, Jayawardene's second term (1982–89) was tarnished by ethnic riots in 1983.

Je Khenpo

Spiritual leader of Bhutan. The *Je Khenpo*, or 'chief abbot', is the administrative head of the influential *Drukpa* monk body and the chairman of the **Council for**

Ecclesiastical Affairs (***Dratshang Lhentshog***). Equal in status (but not in power) to the King, the *Je Khenpo* has historically played a significant role in identifying incarnations, legitimizing accession to the throne, administering the oath of office to the sovereign, and performing other important state rituals. Following the establishment of the monarchy in 1907, the office was retained for the purpose of legitimizing dynastic succession. The *Je Khenpo* is elected by the monks of Bhutan on the basis of his knowledge of Buddhist religion and philosophy, for a period of three to five years. He is responsible for appointing three members of the monk body to the *Tshogdu Chenmo* (National Assembly) and one to the *Lodoi Tsokde* (Royal Advisory Council). Together with approximately 3,300 (ordained) monks, the *Je Khenpo* plays an important role in public and political life.

Jharkhand

Located in northern India, the state of Jharkhand was created in November 2000 out of the southern regions of **Bihar**. Ranchi is the state capital. The population of Jharkhand in 2001 was recorded at 26,945,829, of which 26% were classified as **Scheduled Tribes (STs)**. The state has one of the highest concentrations of tribal peoples, who, in some districts account for more than half of the population. The dominant group is the Santhal, the third largest tribe in India. Hindi is the main language and Hinduism is the majority religion. Despite being rich in natural resources, the state is amongst the poorest in India. Agriculture, forest and extractive industries are the most important contributors to the economy and the state includes the country's biggest coal mines, Dharbad and Jharia region, as well as iron ore deposits and the mines of Jamshedpur and Bokan. The Jharkhand legislative assembly consists of 81 seats and returns 14 members to the **Lok Sabha**. The movement for statehood has its roots in pre-independence India when tribal unrest expressed local resentment against outsider control and encroachment. During the 1970s and 1980s the movement gained momentum and political clout, the **Jharkhand Mukti Morcha (JMM)** emerging as one of the most prominent political forces. Following student agitation, economic blockades and political bargaining between the main national parties, the state of Jharkhand was formed in 2000. Initially under **Bharatiya Janata Party (BJP)** control, in the 2004 Lok Sabha elections an opposition electoral alliance between **Congress**, the JMM, the **Rashtriya Janata Dal (RJD)** and the left resulted in the BJP retaining only one of the 11 parliamentary seats it held. The electoral coalition covered Adivasi voters as well as the **Dalits** and **Other Backward Classes**. High unemployment is also thought to have caused the swing from the BJP.

Jharkhand Mukti Morcha (JMM)

The Jharkhand Mukti Morcha (JMM) is a regional political party in India, based in the state of **Jharkhand**. It is led by the party president Shibu Soren, whose main support base is among the tribal people of the area. The party played a significant role in the struggle for the creation (in 2000) of the state of Jharkhand. In the 14th **Lok Sabha** election the JMM won four seats. It is an ally of the **Indian National Congress** and, as such, part of the currently ruling **United Progressive Alliance (UPA)**.

Jihad/Jehad

Jihad, a complex and diversely interpreted Islamic doctrine, literally means to strive and struggle. To most Muslims *jihad* is a personal struggle for righteousness, but to radical Muslims *jihad* is a compulsory and communal effort to defend and expand the land of Islam.

Jinnah, Muhammad Ali (*Quaid-i-Azam*)

Born on 25 December 1876 in Karachi, Muhammad Ali Jinnah came from a Muslim family belonging to the *Ismaili* community that followed the Aga Khan. Educated first in Karachi, Jinnah went to England in 1892 for further studies, qualifying for the bar in 1896. He returned to India to pursue a career in law and, later, politics. In 1906 Jinnah joined the **Indian National Congress (INC)** and in 1913, while still a member of the INC, the **Muslim League**, gaining an important position in both and earning himself a reputation as the 'ambassador of Hindu-Muslim unity'. Disagreeing with *Mahatma* **Gandhi** on his methods of non-co-operation, Jinnah left the INC in 1919 to focus his attention on Muslim interests, formulating in 1929 an alternative Muslim agenda, the famous 'Fourteen Points', in response to the **Nehru** report which proposed dominion status for India. However, frustrated by the disunity within the All-India Muslim League, he left for England, setting up a practice in London. Persuaded by other Muslim leaders to return in 1934, Jinnah began to reorganize the Muslim League and was elected as its permanent president, gradually moving towards the idea of an independent nation for Muslims first voiced by the Muslim poet-philosopher and Muslim League leader, Muhammad Iqbal.

By 1937 Jinnah was openly accusing the Congress of pursuing a policy that was exclusively Hindu and in 1940 the option of **Partition** was formally raised in the shape of the Lahore Declaration. Thus, under the stewardship of Jinnah, the Muslim League emerged as the third party in negotiations for independence that had previously been conducted between the British and the Congress party. Jinnah launched a 'Direct Action Day' on 16 August 1946 to voice the demand for Pakistan. Meant to be a peaceful act of civil disobediance, it led to wide-scale violence and thousands of deaths, culminating in the Partition of 14 August 1947 and the creation of an independent Pakistan and India.

As Pakistan's first Governor-General, Jinnah was also president of its legislative assembly and deeply involved in establishing the country's government and educational as well as military institutions, which he professed ought to be secular. Although he only lived for 13 months after independence he had to face the refugee problem caused by Partition and the conflict with India over Kashmir. (*See* **Kashmir Dispute**.)

Honoured as the *Quaid-i-Azam* (Great Leader) during his lifetime, Jinnah is revered as the Father of the Nation. Jinnah's death from tuberculosis and lung cancer on 11 September 1948 deprived the young nation of a strong leader at a crucial point in Pakistan's political development.

Jirga

Jirga, a Pashto word meaning council or meeting, refers to a conflict resolution mechanism used mostly among the Pashtun tribes of Afghanistan and Pakistan. Used as an alternative judicial apparatus, a *jirga* consists of tribal notables, religious leaders, or mediation experts who, after listening to contending arguments, announce their decisions which are final and binding on both parties.

K

Kagyupa School

The Kagyupa school was founded in the 11th century and is a major school of Mahayana Buddhism, which is not only one of the most significant schools in Buddhism but also the official state religion of Bhutan. The majority of Buddhists, and especially the ruling *Drukpa* élite in the country, follow this school. The Kagyupa school is headed by the ***Je Khenpo***, who plays an eminent role in the public sphere. In addition, the royal government recognizes this religion as a main constituent of the cultural foundation and integrity of the nation, supporting it through various kinds of subsidies. The preferential treatment of the Kagyupa school is perceived by other religious communities as discriminatory and is a source of political controversy in the country. (*See* **Driglam Namzha**.)

Kahuta Research Laboratories (KRL)

Established in July 1976 by Dr Abdul Qadeer Khan, a Pakistani engineer. Over the past decades Kahuta Research Laboratories (KRL) has evolved into the main centre for nuclear technology and material science in Pakistan. In 2001 Khan was promoted to the inner circle of the country's military leadership as special science and technology adviser to President **Musharraf**. Khan was dismissed in January 2004 when KRL came under investigation following media reports about its alleged involvement in nuclear proliferation.

Kalabagh Dam

The Kalabagh Dam has been the focus of heated debate in Pakistan for the past two decades. The project, if completed, would be the largest public works in Pakistan's history and one of the largest multi-purpose dams in the world. The dam would be built on the Indus River at the confluence point of other rivers in order to tap a catchment area spread over some 285,000 sq km and would serve such purposes as power generation, irrigation supply as well as flood control. Controversy has erupted over the potential environmental effects of the dam and there is disagreement over how to share the benefits of the project among the three provinces through which the Indus River flows. The two smaller provinces of **Sind** and **North**

West Frontier Province (NWFP) claim that reservoirs would benefit only the more prosperous and populous province of **Punjab** while depriving them of water resources.

Kalam, Abdul

Dr Avul Pakir Jainulandeen Abdul Kalam was born on 15 October 1931 in the South Indian state of **Tamil Nadu** and became the 11th President of India on 25 July 2002. Kalam is the third Muslim and the first scientist to hold the post. Having studied for a degree in aeronautical engineering in Tamil Nadu, he joined the **Indian Space Research Organisation** and played a major role in helping to develop India's first indigenous satellite-launch vehicle. Later, Kalam was closely involved in the development and operationalization of the country's missile-delivery systems. Kalam holds India's three highest civilian honours, the *Padma Bhushan* (awarded in 1981), the *Padma Vibhuashan* (1990) and the ***Bharat Ratna*** (1997); and numerous honorary doctorates from universities across the country. His book *India 2020* envisions a developed nation with a core competence in agriculture, energy, education, health care, information technology as well as the strategic sectors of defence and nuclear science.

Karachi Accord (Pakistan People's Party-Muttahida Qaumi Movement Accord)

In November 1988, just before Pakistan's general elections, the **Pakistan People's Party (PPP)** signed a political accord (the Karachi Accord) with the **Muttahida Qaumi Movement (MQM)** to contest the elections jointly. With the support of the MQM, **Benazir Bhutto** was elected as Prime Minister. After the elections the MQM joined the coalition government at the federal level and in the province of **Sind**.

Kargil Conflict

The Kargil conflict, which took place in 1999 between India and Pakistan shortly after a summit between the countries' then Prime Ministers, resulted in more than 1,000 casualties on the Indian side. This was the first conventional war since India and Pakistan became nuclear powers. The effort to seize territory on the Indian side of the **Line of Control (LoC)** around Kargil in the state of **Jammu and Kashmir** was the brainchild of Pakistan's Chief of Army Staff, Gen. Pervez **Musharraf**. It is speculated that while Prime Minister Nawaz **Sharif** was informed, he may not have known details about the operation. The mediating role played by US President Clinton enhanced the influence of the USA in South Asia.

Karnataka

Formerly the state of Mysore, to which India's Kannada-speaking districts of Bombay state were added, Karnataka was named as such in 1973. Located in the south, the state's capital city, **Bangalore**, is an information and technology hub. The overwhelming majority of the population is Hindu but there are substantial minorities, with Muslims accounting for about 12.2% and Christians 1.9% of the population. The state assembly has 224 seats and returns 28 members to the **Lok Sabha**. Karnataka is largely agricultural, its traditional economy characterized by small farmer proprietors. Vokkaligas and Lingayats, the two dominant caste groups in south and north Karnataka respectively, led an anti-Brahmin movement in the early 20th century and have played an active role in state politics. One of the first states to introduce a reservation policy, Karnataka has amongst the highest quotas for **Other Backward Classes**, **Scheduled Castes (SCs)** and **Scheduled Tribes (STs)** in civil service jobs. The **Janata Dal—Secular**, the end product of a long phase of atomization of the Janata movement, is today the major regional political force in the state. H. D. Dewe Gowda (former Chief Minister of Karnataka and Prime Minister of India) is the leader of the party and after the 2004 assembly elections chose to form a minority coalition government with the **Congress** party, thus excluding the **Bharatiya Janata Party** which had won more seats than the other parties.

Kashmir Dispute

Often described as 'the unfinished business of **Partition**', Kashmir has become the focal point of India-Pakistan relations. The conflict has specific territorial reasons and has come to represent competing visions of state and nationhood: for India, a Muslim-majority state of **Jammu and Kashmir** symbolizing the secular nation state, and for Pakistan an Indian-occupied Kashmir representing the incompleteness of Pakistan. The dispute over territory has its roots in the immediate aftermath of independence when the Hindu Maharajah of Kashmir failed to decide whether to join India or Pakistan, a choice which each of the more than 560 former princely states were allowed to make but which in the case of Kashmir was problematic because of the population's religious make-up (largely Muslim) and contiguity with Pakistan. Faced with an armed uprising of local tribesman who had Pakistani backing, the Maharajah appealed for Indian assistance. This was granted on the condition that the Instrument of Accession to the Republic of India was signed. Thus, the Kashmir dispute was born, with the first war between India and Pakistan occurring in 1947–48 as Pakistani forces tried to gain control over Kashmir. Ending with the establishment of a 740-km cease-fire line patrolled then by the **UN Military Observer Group in India and Pakistan**, this has been the *de facto* border ever since. Leaving about 65% of the former princely state under Indian administration (Ladakh, Valley of Kashmir, Jammu) and about 35% under Pakistani administration (**Northern Areas**, **Azad Kashmir**), armed Indian and Pakistani forces are separated by just a few meters. A UN resolution in 1948 directed the two countries to withdraw their troops, first Pakistan then India, after which a plebiscite was to be held to determine public opinion. The plebiscite was never held (partly because troops were never withdrawn), with India negotiating instead special conditions of autonomy with the state's prominent leader, Sheikh Abdullah (*see* **Jammu and Kashmir National Conference**).

Despite a second war in 1965, during which Pakistan tried and failed to instigate mass uprisings in Kashmir, the cease-fire line was maintained. In 1971, the third Indo-Pakistan war, though not fought over Kashmir, produced the **Simla Agreement** of 1972 in which the cease-fire line was turned into the **Line of Control (LoC)**, in the hope of moving towards a mutually acceptable international border. The border, however, remains contested, with regular fighting and skirmishes, a new front opening on the heights of the **Siachen Glacier** in 1984. The emergence of an ethno-nationalist uprising within Kashmir in the 1990s and India's use of force to suppress it (*see* **Jammu and Kashmir**) added a new dimension to the issue, with Pakistan seeking to internationalize the Kashmir issue by pushing for a UN resolution at the Human Rights Commission on India's human rights abuses in Kashmir. India countered by alleging that Pakistan provides aid and sanctuary to militants operating in the area and fans religious extremism through groups such as the **Lashkar-e-Toiba** and **Hizbul Mujahideen**. In 1999 the two countries, by then both nuclear powers, battled at the Kargil sector of the LoC, giving rise to fears of a nuclear conflict.

While armed conflict has changed little about the border, bilateral talks between the countries' leaders have also produced a stalemate (*see* **India, Political Development**—India-Pakistan Relations). Talks with other parties, such as the **All-Party Hurriyat Conference**, an indigenous Kashmiri organization, have also been attempted, but India firmly maintains Kashmir is an internal issue. Since the 11 September 2001 attacks in the USA and the subsequent war on terror, India's complaints about 'cross-border terrorism' in Kashmir have received more attention and in 2004 then Prime Minister **Vajpayee** launched a new peace initiative. Following the earthquake that largely struck Pakistan-administered Kashmir in October 2005, various points along the border were opened to enable families to meet and aid to reach isolated areas. Despite the thousands of civilian casulties as a result of violence in Kashmir, the more than 100,000 Hindus who have migrated from the Muslim-dominated Valley and divided families across the LoC, Kashmir remains an unresolved dispute.

Kerala

An amalgamation of the princely states of Travancore and Cochin on the south-western coast of India, with Malabar districts of the former Madras state, Kerala was formally established in 1956 with Malayalam as the official language and Thiruvananthapuram (formerly known as Trivandrum) as its capital. Kerala has a majority Hindu comunitiy of 56.2% according to the 2001 census, and large minorities of Muslims (24.7%) and Christians (19.0%). There is also a tiny population of Sephardic Jews. The state has an impressive literacy rate of more than 90% and one of the highest rates of popular participation in elections. Despite these positive indicators, Kerala lags behind other Indian states in terms of per capita income and production. Agriculture is the most important economic activity. The state assembly has 140 seats and elects 20 members to the **Lok Sabha**. In 1957 Kerala gained the world-wide distinction of having democratically elected a communist government (dismissed by the ruling **Indian National Congress (INC)** in 1959 under Article 352). Kerala has maintained a preference for left-wing parties, with two rival fronts that have alternately been in power: the INC-led United Democratic Front (UDF) and the **Communist Party of India—Marxist**-led **Left Democratic Front (LDF)**. In the 2004 general elections the Congress was swept out completely, the LDF securing a landslide victory. A **National Democratic Alliance** ally won one seat, returning the first member from the state who is neither a UDF nor an LDF candidate.

Kerala Congress—Joseph (KC—Joseph)

The Kerala Congress—Joseph (KC—Joseph) is a regional political party in the Indian state of **Kerala** led by the former education minister P. J. Joseph. The party has its roots in the Kerala Congress Party (originally named Kerala Pradesh Congress Samudharana Samiti*)*, an offshoot in 1964 from the **Indian National Congress (INC)**. Today the KC—Joseph is one of various fractions of the Kerala Congress Party. It is part of the **Left Democratic Front (LDF)**, a regional, leftist multi-party alliance. Currently, the KC—Joseph possesses one seat in the 14th **Lok Sabha**.

Khalistan

Meaning Land of the Pure, the term Khalistan was used to connote the autonomous state of the Sikhs. Deteriorating centre-**Punjab** relations prompted the **Akali Dal** to mobilize the Sikh peasantry in a major campaign for Punjab's autonomy in 1980. Four core demands presented to the government of India included recasting the Constitution to increase states' autonomy, the return of **Chandigarh** to Punjab, returning the control over river waters to the state and an all-India *gurudwara* act to bring all Sikh shrines and temple under the control of one organization. Threatened by demands for the constitutional recognition of Sikhs as a separate 'nation' and the declaration of Amritsar as a 'holy city', the central government responded with a campaign aimed at breaking up the Akali Dal. One of the ways was to support dissenting voices within the Sikh community, leading **Congress** to support Sant Jarnail Singh **Bhindranwale** as a counterweight. The Khalistan movement lasted throughout the 1980s, propelled by the anti-Sikh violence that followed the assassination of Prime Minister Indira **Gandhi** in 1984 and the imposition of draconian judicial and anti-terrorist measures in the state. By the early 1990s, although a core of militants remained committed to Khalistan, the ideological coherence and moral purpose of the movement had faded with the escalation in violence, mounting civilian casulties and economic destruction that a decade of instability had caused. Much of the support for Khalistan came from an expatriate Sikh community in the form of lobbying international organizations and raising awareness and funds for the campaign.

Khan, Ayub

Ayub Khan, born on 14 May 1907 and educated at Aligarh Muslim University, Aligarh and the British Royal Military College, Sandhurst, was the first native commander of Pakistan's armed forces, chief marshal law administrator and military President (1958–69). The salient features of the Ayub era included the promulgation of the 1962 Constitution, joining US-led anti-Soviet military alliances, the **Indus Waters Treaty** with India, the Indo-Pakistan war of 1965, closer association with communist China, and the introduction of educational and land reforms. Ayub, who was forced to hand over power to Yahya Khan, the commander-in-chief of the Pakistani army in 1969, is best remembered for introducing the **Basic Democracies**.

Khan, Liaquat Ali

The death of **Jinnah** in 1948 brought Liaquat Ali Khan, the first Prime Minister of Pakistan, to the helm of affairs in the nascent state. He had to deal with the refugee crisis caused by **Partition**, formulation of the first Constitution, normalization of relations with India, as well as preparing the ground for sound relations with the West, mainly the USA. He was shot dead by a religious fanatic during a public rally in 1951.

Kidu System

A term used in Bhutan to refer to a royal land grant for poor households (***gung***), which may apply directly to the King for agricultural land. Originating from sources of traditional law, the Kidu system is not manifested as a legal claim but as an entitlement based on binding customs which have legal force. A Kidu is justified if the applicant is landless or does not have enough land to subsist on. This traditional support system is losing significance due to the limited availability of productive land.

Koirala, Bisweswor Prasad

Born in 1914, B. P. Koirala studied in India where he became involved in the Indian nationalist movement, joining the **Indian National Congress (INC)** in 1934. In India he founded the socialist Nepali National Congress in 1947, which in 1950 became the **Nepali Congress (NC)**. Under Koirala's leadership an armed revolution ended the **Rana family**'s century-long rule over Nepal. While the NC was still fighting, the 'Delhi compromise', negotiated between the Ranas and King Tribhuvan, through the mediation of Prime Minister **Nehru** of India, ushered in a fragile interim government. In the 1959 general elections the NC won a landslide victory and B. P. Koirala became the country's first elected Prime Minister. He remained in power for 18 months, during which time he attempted to initiate land reforms and reforms of the bureaucracy, disfavouring him among the conservative feudal circles around the monarchy. In 1960 King **Mahendra** organized a coup and jailed Koirala, holding him without trial until 1968, when he was forced into exile in India. Arrested on various occasions while trying to return to his country, Koirala was also actively engaged in the pro-democracy movement of the early 1980s. However, he did not live to see the restoration of multi-party democracy in Nepal, his funeral in 1982 drawing more than half a million mourners.

Koirala, Girija Prasad

Born in 1922, G. P. Koirala, a leader in the **Nepali Congress (NC)**, is the third and youngest of the Koirala brothers to have become Prime Minister. He has been Prime Minister five times: in 1991, between April 1998 and May 1999, when he headed three governments with different party coalitions, and in 2000, a period during which there were 10 governments in Nepal. After the 1990 introduction of democracy he became one of the most powerful politicians in Nepal. In 2005, despite being aged 83, he was reluctant to give up party leadership and was causing friction within the party (most famously with Krishna Prasad **Bhattarai**) as well as splits.

Kuensel

Kuensel is the national newspaper of Bhutan. Established as an internal government bulletin in 1967, it was enhanced to newspaper format in 1986. It is published in **Dzongkha**, English and Nepali and is also available online. As the first medium of mass communication in the country, its primary role was and is to provide news about Bhutan to the Bhutanese. *Kuensel*'s predominant readership is the urban and educated élite. In 1992 it was transformed into an autonomous corporation, although it continues to receive governmental subsidies. There are no other newspapers or magazines published in Bhutan.

Kumaratunga, Chandrika

On 29 June 1945 Chandrika **Bandaranaike**-Kumaratunga was born into one of Sri Lanka's most important political families. Having studied in France, Chandrika married the actor and politician Vijawa Kumaratunga in 1978. Elected as Prime Minister of a **People's Alliance (PA)** government in 1994, she became President in the same year, ending 17 years of **United National Party (UNP)** rule, and went on to win a second term in 1999. Kumaratunga stepped down in November 2005. Despite campaigning for a negotiated political solution with Tamil rebels and launching new devolution proposals in parliament, ethnic hostilities under Kumaratunga's presidency continued unabated.

L

Lakshadweep

The smallest **Union Territory** of India, Lakshadweep lies in the Arabian Sea off southern India's west coast and comprises three principal islands. In 2001 the population was enumerated at 60,650, of which 93.2% were classified as **Scheduled Tribes (STs)**, the majority speaking a Malayalam dialect, an influence from **Kerala**. In 2001 95% of the population was Muslim and only 4% Hindu. Women play a prominent role in society because of a matrilineal inheritance system that is practised. Lakshadweep became a Union Territory in 1956, with the territorial capital at Kavaratti. The economy is largely based on subsistence agriculture, fishing and tourism, the last limited by the government to preserve the islands' delicate eco-system.

Lashkar-e-Toiba (LET)

The Lashkar-e-Toiba (LET—Army of the Pure) was formed in 1980 by Hafiz Muhammad Saeed as the military wing of the Markaz Dawa-ul-Irshad (MDI). It was originally established as an organization to train fighters for Afghanistan in the struggle against Soviet forces. The LET then identified India as its primary target and has been operating since 1993 in Kashmir, fighting for its accession to Pakistan and the establishment of Islamic rule based on the *Shari'a*. (*See* **Kashmir Dispute**.)

Left Democratic Front (LDF)

The Left Democratic Front (LDF) is a state-wide coalition of leftist parties in **Kerala**, India, and is dominated by the **Communist Party of India—Marxist (CPI—M)**. Its existence is a result of the splits and collaborations between the two dominant communist parties of India, the **Communist Party of India (CPI)** and the CPI—M. In the state elections of 2001 the LDF won 43.7% of the votes, slightly less than in the previous election.

Left Front (India)

The Left Front, the ruling coalition of **West Bengal** for the past two decades, is an alliance of the **Communist Party of India (CPI)**, the **Revolutionary Socialist Party (RSP)**, the All-India Forward Bloc (AIFB) and the **Communist Party of India—Marxist (CPI—M)**, the major communist party in India. It came into existence after relations between the rival CPI and CPI—M, which split in 1964, had improved. Many analysts regard the Left Front to have been a stabilizing factor that reined in the anarchy induced by the Maoist violence and agrarian conflict of the late 1960s. Following the 2004 **Lok Sabha** elections, in which the Left Front further consolidated its position in West Bengal, combined with the **Left Democratic Front**'s **(LDF)** sweeping victory in **Kerala**, the Left Front became an important player in national politics, agreeing eventually to provide outside support to the **United Progressive Alliance** government at the centre. Analysts attribute the Left's success to its wide electoral social base that cuts across caste and economic class lines.

Lhengye Nyamdrel Tshogchung

The term used in Bhutan to refer to the co-ordination committee of the Council of Ministers. It is headed by the chairman of the Council of Ministers and comprises six elected ministers. Today it is one of the most influential bodies in the government.

Lhotshampa

The Lhotshampa are one of three major ethnic communities in Bhutan. The name Lhotshampa, literally 'those living in the south', refers to the Nepalese-speaking people, 60% of whom are of Indo-Aryan origin, settled in Bhutan's border areas, particularly in the south west and south east. Although the Lhotshampa do not constitute a homogeneous social category, they try to retain their Nepalese culture, language (Nepali), religion and traditions. As a result, tensions have arisen between their own group and the ruling **Drukpa** élites who belong to the second major ethnic group, the **Ngalong**, and who identify their own culture as the base for a national identity, advocating it as the cultural heritage of Bhutan. In this context, the Lhotshampa are recognized by some factions of the ruling élite as a threat to the integrity of the country. (*See* **Driglam Namzha**.)

Liberation Tigers of Tamil Eelam (LTTE)

The Liberation Tigers of Tamil Eelam (LTTE) is a guerrilla group, also known as the Tamil Tigers, led by V. **Prabhakaran** and fighting for an independent Tamil state. It has launched attacks against the government, targeting **Tamil United Liberation Front (TULF)** electoral candidates as well as **United National Party (UNP)** candidates, and is held responsible for the assassination of Indian Prime Minister

Rajiv Gandhi in 1991. In 2000, during a presidential campaign, a suspected Tamil Tiger suicide bomber almost killed Chandrika **Kumaratunga**. The LTTE has also been accused of assassinating many Tamil politicians from other Tamil parties who have challenged its claim to be the sole representative of Tamil-speaking people.

Cease-fires between the Sri Lankan government and the LTTE have been announced, broken or simply expired. Since 2002 the LTTE has participated in the Oslo Peace Process, but despite piecemeal progress, a no-war, no-peace situation has persisted. The LTTE continues to have absolute authority over many areas in the north east where it has even installed its own judicial system. A development arm, the Tamil Rehabilitation Organization, is engaged in relief and rehabilitation work and was particularly active following the Asian tsunami of December 2004. The LTTE has over the years established a powerful network of operatives and financiers abroad, although the international debate on banning terrorist groups since the 11 September 2001 attacks on the USA has put pressure on the LTTE to enter into negotiations with the government.

Licence Permit Raj

The Licence Permit Raj (Regime) or Licence Raj is a term used in India to describe the system of distributing industrial and commercial permits to expand or initiate enterprises under state regulations. This created a conglomerate of direct state ownership of 'key' or 'strategic' industries, and legal powers to control and regulate these sectors ceded to private production ventures. In this context, the Licence Raj was one of the main features of the so called mixed economy, which formed the basis of the economic system in post-colonial India. It was introduced by Jawaharlal **Nehru** who was inspired by British Fabian socialism. Critics of the Licence Raj claimed that this system was responsible for the slow rate of India's growth in the past and that it has immense potential for creating shortages and corruption. After 1991 the country altered its economic policy and introduced a process of dismantling the heavily interventionist and regulatory state through the deregulation and opening of many sectors.

Life Insurance Corporation of India (LIC)

The Life Insurance Corporation of India (LIC) was established on 1 September 1956 under the Life Insurance Corporation Act as an autonomous body providing insurance cover against various risks. One of its primary aims has been to channel funds for the benefit of the community at large. Prior to the liberalization of the economy in the 1990s LIC held the monopoly in this field and became synonymous with life insurance. It operates through a network of seven zonal offices, 100 divisional offices and more than 2,000 branch offices across the country.

Line of Actual Control (LAC)

The Line of Actual Control (LAC) refers to the contested border between India and the People's Republic of China, running in the west through sections India claims in **Aksai Chin**, a less controversial 'middle sector' along India's states of **Himachal Pradesh** and **Uttaranchal** and, in the east, through a disputed section in Arunachal Pradesh. (*See* **McMahon Line**; **North East India**.)

Line of Control (LoC)

The 776-km Line of Control (LoC) runs between the Indian state of **Jammu and Kashmir** and the part of Kashmir under Pakistani control. The LoC corresponds roughly to the cease-fire line drawn up after the India–Pakistan war of 1948, later amended under the **Simla Agreement** of 1972, and has been a source of conflict for almost the entire period of both states' existence. Conversion of the LoC into an international border is seen by some as the most feasible solution to the long-running dispute. In 1999 Pakistan's incursions into Kargil led to a brief but fierce battle between India and Pakistan. Under international criticism and American pressure, Pakistani Prime Minister Nawaz **Sharif** issued a joint statement with US President Bill Clinton expressing respect for the LoC, leading to the end of hostilities. An international border, however, could be a soft border with security implications and does not appeal to hardliners in Pakistan and India, nor to those amongst the Kashmiri people who favour independence from both India and Pakistan as the ideal solution. (*See* **Kashmir Dispute**.)

Linguistic Regionalism

Following India's independence in 1947 and the emergence of language movements, the States Reorganisation Commission was formed in 1953 to study the problems involved in redrawing state boundaries. According to the Commission, homogeneity existed when linguistic homogeneity was greater than 70%. Responding to mass popular agitation, almost all of the provinces were reconstituted along linguistic lines and given the power to adopt state languages. Reorganization has been an ongoing process since 1953, beginning with the creation of **Andhra Pradesh** (majority Telegu-speaking). **Mumbai** was reorganized to create **Maharashtra** (majority Marathi) and **Gujarat** (majority Gujarati) in 1960. **Punjab** split in 1966 to create a smaller Punjab (majority Punjabi) and **Haryana** (Hindi) and the new states of the **North East India** in the 1960s and 1970s. In 2000 three new states were formed: **Chhattisgarh**, **Jharkand** and **Uttaranchal**, carved out of **Madhya Pradesh**, **Bihar** and **Uttar Pradesh** respectively, and justified in terms of economic factors and demography in addition to cultural and linguistic reasons.

Lok Jan Shakti Party (LJSP)

The Lok Jan Shakti Party (LJSP) is a regional political party in the Indian state of **Bihar**. The LJSP was founded in 2000 as an offshoot of the **Janata Dal—United** and is headed by Ram Vilas Paswan. The party claims to represent the interest of the minorities, the **Dalits** and other weaker sections of society. As an ally of the **Indian National Congress (INC)**, the LJSP is part of the **United Progressive Alliance (UPA)**, having won four seats in the 14th **Lok Sabha** elections of 2004.

Lok Sabha

The Lok Sabha ('House of the People') is the lower house in the Indian parliament. A maximum of 543 members are directly elected by the general electorate through majority vote in single-member constituencies and two are nominated by the President. Along with the **Raja Sabha**, the upper house, it constitutes the legislative wing of the state. Although both houses are formally equal in power, the Lok Sabha has the decisive voice in the area of budgetary policy.

Luso

A term used in Bhutan to describe a local custom constituting a system of customary law. This system of *luso* is, since the passing of the **Thrimshung Chenmo** (a kind of supreme law), in conflict with the national law given that little of local customary law was incorporated into the national, supreme legal code. However, the fact that the Thrimshung Chenmo is imposed by state regulations and increasingly enforced by the government has not made *luso* irrelevant. Local customs continue to be a determining force in day-to-day judicial and administrative decision-making processes at the grassroots level.

M

Madhesis

The term used for people of Indian plains origin who live in the **Tarai** region of Nepal. It is estimated that 3m.–4m. Madhesis have been denied citizenship papers, necessary to secure property rights, employment and school admissions. The **Nepal Sadbhavana Party (NSP)** has emerged as the main political spokesman for the rights of the Madhesi community. The controversy surrounding the issue highlights the hill-plains divide in Nepal. About two-thirds of Nepal comprises hills inhabited by ethnic hill tribes and the ruling Brahmin-**Chhettri**-Newar castes. The rest comprises southern plains bordering with India, settled over generations by people of Indian origin.

Madhya Pradesh

The state of Madhya Pradesh, formed in 1956, lies at the heart of India with Bhopal as its capital. Relatively poor, with agriculture as the main economic activity of its population, Madhya Pradesh lost some of its valuable resources, namely mineral and forests reserves, in 2000 when **Chhattisgarh** was formed out of its eastern regions. Almost one-fifth of the post-2000 state's population were counted as **Scheduled Tribes (STs)** and a further 15% as **Scheduled Castes (SCs)**. Most of the population practises Hinduism and there is a small minority of Muslims. The legislative assembly of Madhya Pradesh consists of 230 seats and the state returns 29 members to the **Lok Sahba**. The **Bahajan Samaj Party**'s **(BSP)** emergence in the mid-1990s as a player in the state's northern districts, combined with the **Bharatiya Janata Party**'s decision to field as its state leader Uma Bharti, a member of the **Other Backward Classes** category, introduced serious competition.

Despite aligning with the BSP for the 2003 legislative elections, the **Congress** suffered one of its worst defeats in the state. The BJP, campaigning on a slogan of '*bijli, sadak aur pani*', referring to the dismal quality of electricity, roads and water facilities, swept a three-quarters majority of assembly seats. In the 2004 national elections the BJP maintained their electoral advantage in Madhya Pradesh, winning 25 of the Lok Sabha seats and halving the Congress' representation. Although the

BJP successfully courted votes from tribal and backward caste constituencies, players like the BSP and the **Samajwadi Party** have the potential to fracture the political arena.

Madrasas

The term *madrasa* derives from the Arabic language, in which it means 'school', either religious or secular. *Madrasas* have played an important role in countries where the government is unable to provide adequate or, indeed, any educational facilities and have traditionally imparted Islamic teachings at a general, secondary or even elementary level. In South Asia they have played a crucial role. In Pakistan, for example, more than 10,000 are registered, filling gaps in governmental facilities, particularly in regions such as **Balochistan** and the **North West Frontier Province**. Following the 11 September 2001 terrorist attacks in the USA *madrasas* gained international attention and notoriety as places of ideological indoctrination and cadre training, promoting fanaticism and radical Islam. It has been further alleged that, in addition to teaching religious studies, *madrasas* have a history of active engagement with radical Islam. In Pakistan, under President **Zia** ul-Haq, they were used as instruments of Islamization, and during the Soviet occupation of Afghanistan they played a vital role in the resistance, by legitimizing an armed struggle through religion.

Mahajan

Mahajan, in Bangladesh, is a merchant, dealer, banker, money-changer, or money-lender. Until the creation of large-scale institutional credit facilities, *mahajans* were the prime creditors, controlling the agricultural market. Farmers or even entrepreneurs borrowed money from the *mahajans* by mortgaging land, gold and other valuable items. Since the mid-1980s, when NGOs introduced microcredit programmes, the traditional *mahajani* institution has virtually disappeared.

Maharashtra

Located on the country's west coast, Maharashtra is India's third largest state in terms of area and the most populous after **Uttar Pradesh**. In 1960 the erstwhile Bombay state was split into Maharashtra and **Gujarat**, with Marathi and Gujarati as state languages. Maharashtra is home to a variety of indigenous tribes as well as a number of ethnic and religious groups, including the biggest concentration of Parsis in India. Maharashtra's economy is the largest in the country and its capital, **Mumbai**, a major port, is also India's financial and film-industry centre. Maharashtra is one of the few states to have a bicameral assembly. The legislative assembly has 288 seats and there are 48 **Lok Sabha** members. After India's independence in 1947, the areas of the Bombay state which were to become Maharashtra subsequently became a bastion of the **Congress** party, producing influential figures such as Y. B. Chavan (a former defence minister of India). The party enjoyed dominance in state politics until 1995, when the **Shiv Sena** and **Bharatiya Janata Party (BJP)** formed a coalition government. In 1999 the **Nationalist Congress Party (NCP)** fought elections against the Congress but formed a joint government to keep out the Shiv Sena. These two blocks appeared to have solidified as the main players in Maharashtra politics and in the 2004 state elections secured an almost equal share of votes and seats, the NCP-Congress alliance obtaining just enough to form a government. The crucial battleground between the Shiv Sena and the NCP is over the votes of the dominant peasant community, the Maratha-Kunbis, the **Dalits** and the Muslims (10.6% of the population, according to the 2001 census).

Mahatma Gandhi – *see* Gandhi, Mohandas Karamchand

Mahaweli Project

The Mahaweli is Sri Lanka's longest river, running through the central Kandy Mountains down to the north-eastern shores. In 1968 a long-term hydroelectric project was formulated to divert water into the northern dry zone for irrigation and, through a resettlement programme, to reduce population pressure in the wet zones. The project is one of the largest of its kind in the world, covering almost one-third of the country, comprising dozens of different projects, ranging from the building of massive dams to the provision of small health clinics. Five dams have been constructed as regulatory reservoirs, with power-generation capacity of 540 MW. The cost of the Mahaweli Development Project has been estimated at more than US $2,000m., approximately 60% of which has come in the form of overseas development assistance. Criticism of the project has focused on the forced resettlement of people, the spiralling costs of the project and its impact on the environment because of the huge area of jungle that has had to be cleared.

Mahendra, King

The son and successor of King **Tribhuvan**, Mahendra Bir Bikram Shah Dev became King of Nepal in 1955. Despite allowing the country's first general elections in 1959, King Mahendra staged a coup on 15 December 1960, dissolved parliament and installed his chosen Council of Ministers. In January 1961 political parties were banned by royal decree. It has been suggested that a clash of personalities between B. P. **Koirala** (who was imprisoned after the coup) and the young King played a role in these events. Distrustful of party politics and politicians, King Mahendra sought to create a party-less *Panchayat* (village council) democracy. Known as the ***Panchayat* system**, a new Constitution in 1962 established a structure that was to long outlive King Mahendra, who died in 1972 and was succeeded by his son **Birendra** Bir Bokram Shah Dev.

Majeed, Sultan Abdul

Sultan Abdul Majeed (1945–52), a Maldivian monarch, is recognized as a socio-economic reformer and, due to the long-term impact of his measures, as 'the father of modern Maldives'. After his death in Colombo, Ceylon (Sri Lanka), in 1952, the sultanate was formally suspended, the first republic was promulgated and Majeed was succeeded by Muhammad Amin **Didi** as the President of the state.

Majlis

A term used to refer to a council or assembly. There are currently three different types of Majlis in the political system of the Maldives: the **People's Majlis** (parliament), the **People's Special Majlis** (formerly the Citizens' Special Majlis, or constitutional assembly) and the Ministers' Majlis (Cabinet).

Maldives, Republic of

Divehi Rajje ge Jumhuriyya

The Republic of Maldives (formerly Maldive Islands) is an island republic located in the northern Indian Ocean, south-west of the southern tip of India. It comprises a chain of 1,190 small coral islands, none with a land area greater than 13 sq km. The islands are grouped into 26 natural Atolls (rings of coral islands), and divided for administrative purposes into 21 units (20 Atolls and **Malé** as a distinctive first-order administrative division). Area: 298 sq km; capital: Malé; population: 289,480 (2004); official language: Maldivian Dhivehi (a dialect of Sinhala); religion: Sunni Muslim.

History: The first settlers in the archipelago, a race of sun-worshipping people, are generally believed to have originated in Sri Lanka and India (**Kerala** and **Gujarat**), acculturated by Buddhists from Sri Lanka and Hindus from India some time during 500 AD. In this pre-Muslim era, a highly centralized monarchy, frequent exile of political opponents, and a methodical administration of island affairs characterized the political system. The legacy of these features, related to the challenges of the islands' unique geography, has persisted throughout the history of Maldivian governance. The islands, strategically positioned along sea routes between Europe and the Far East, were exposed to Islam by Arab sea traders. In 1153 AD, Islam became the official religion, a significant turning point in the country's history. With the royal conversion to Islam, the former Buddhist King became the first Sultan, beginning a series of Islamic dynasties that ruled until 1968. The conversion is considered to have been an economically pragmatic decision taken by the island-leadership in an attempt to align the Maldives with dominant foreign traders in the **Indian Ocean**. Like other peripheral South Asian states, such as Bhutan or Nepal, no western colonial power ruled the Maldives directly, except the Portuguese who governed for a period of 15 years, capturing Malé in 1558. In the 17th century, the Maldives came under Dutch, and later

British, hegemony although neither power established a colonial administration. Threatened by external attempts to monopolize foreign trade, however, the sultanate formally accepted an alliance with the British and the island state subsequently acquired the status of a British protectorate, in 1887. Consequently, the British government assumed control of Maldivian foreign affairs and defence, while the sultanate retained absolute command over domestic affairs. The sultanate was made elective in 1932 and the islands retained the status of crown protectorate until January 1953, when the first republic was introduced. A new constitution in 1954 restored the sultanate and in 1965 the Maldives gained formal independence. The sultanate was again dissolved when the second republic was formed in November 1968 as the Republic of Maldives Islands, renamed Republic of Maldives in April 1969. The first President, Ibrahim **Nasir** promulgated a new constitution, declaring the Republic of Maldives an Islamic state and endowing the President with immense executive powers, including the right to appoint and dismiss the Prime Minister and Cabinet of Ministers. The Maldives have been a republic continuously since 1968, with a unicameral parliament (**People's Majlis**) as the only legislative body besides the **People's Special Majlis**, whose task has been to amend the Constitution. Both bodies of the Maldivian legislature are only able to enact laws with presidential approval. The head of state and head of government since 1978 has been President Maumoon Abdul **Gayoom**, who is currently serving his sixth term (2003–08), having won the most recent presidential elections with a popular vote of 90%.

Recent Developments: As President, Gayoom has been credited with bringing economic and social progress to the Maldives. Contributions from the fishing industry, tourism, and foreign aid have facilitated rapid economic growth, modernization, and social betterment at many levels. Major progress has been made in the fields of education, health, and poverty reduction. The country has achieved almost universal literacy, and gender inequality is negligible compared to other developing states.

In the mid-1990s international aid donors advocated greater democratization. In response to both external and growing internal demands, various measures to strengthen and democratize the political system were proposed. In 1998 a revised constitution was promulgated with a stronger focus on civil liberties, decentralization, government transparency and greater accountability. Current challenges include conflicting demands from broad sections of society for political liberalization on the one hand, and efforts by the establishment to maintain the *status quo*, as well as enforce a more traditional Muslim way of life, on the other. The stability of the political system has been shaken on various occasions since 2003 as increased political awareness and sophistication has given rise to a reform movement, civil unrest and, following the intervention of security forces, violent riots. The government has gradually introduced elements of a multi-party democracy, a first step being the Political Party Regulations 2005 which permitted political groups to register as political parties. Another dilemma involves the need to preserve the islands' ecosystem whilst developing fishing and tourist industries. One of the gravest issues facing the Republic of Maldives in the 21st century, however, is the threat of inundation if sea levels rise due to global warming.

Maldives, Political Development

The Maldives achieved full independence only in 1965, following periods of Portuguese, Dutch and British hegemony. Since then three major amendments to the Constitution, in 1932, 1968 and 1998, have guided political development towards improved democratic practices and increased respect for human rights. The first Constitution in 1932 was a progressive step towards modern political structures, turning the absolute sultanate into a constitutional and elective monarchy. In 1953, following the inauguration of the first republic, the sultanate was abolished and the modern, Western-orientated Muhammad Amin **Didi** became its first President. Just seven months later, however, Didi was overthrown. Despite his expulsion and subsequent death, he is regarded today as the father of Maldivian nationalism. The sultanate was reinstated under a new constitution in 1954 and Muhammad Farid **Didi** was elected as the sultan of the Maldives. In 1956 the establishment of a British Royal Airforce Base on the island of **Gan** (in the **Atoll** of Addu) was agreed by the British and Maldivian governments. On 26 July 1965 the Maldives became fully independent, regaining its control over external relations and defence and becoming a member of the United Nations. The (second) Republic of Maldives was approved in a national referendum in March 1968, thus dismissing for a second time the sultan, who now effectively ruled in title only. Ibrahim **Nasir**, Prime Minister since 1957, was elected as President, taking over from the last of the sultans, Farid Didi. Following rumours of a coup conspiracy, President Nasir invoked emergency powers in March 1975, dismissed the Prime Minister and dissolved the office of the Prime Minister. Nasir remained in office until 1978, when Maumoon Abdul **Gayoom** was elected and confirmed as President in a national referendum of the same year. Gayoom has remained in power ever since, winning six consecutive elections (the most recent in 2003). Gayoom has had to face three coup attempts, in 1980, when Nasir was implicated in the alleged plot, in 1983, and again on 3 November 1988. Whereas the 1980 and 1983 coup attempts were not perceived as threatening, the third was a serious challenge to Gayoom's political survival, alerting the international community to the security of small states. It has been reported that the coup attempt was organized by Sri Lankan mercenaries linked with a Tamil opposition group, the **People's Liberation Organization of Tamil Eelam (PLOTE)** and hired by Maldivian business interests under the leadership of Abdullah Luthufi. Around 80 sea-borne armed forces landed in **Malé** and attempted to gain control over various key government installations, supported by some 80 others who had infiltrated the country disguised as tourists. Responding to the President's appeal for foreign military assistance, Indian paratroopers, dispatched by Prime Minister Rajiv Gandhi, overwhelmed the coup members within 24 hours and restored law and order in Malé. The political situation since has remained stable, particularly as Gayoom's tenure has produced an environment conducive to economic development. In November 1997 the former Citizens' Special **Majlis** (*see* **People's Special Majlis**) ratified a new constitution, seemingly a step towards greater political pluralism. In mid-February 2005 President Gayoom promulgated a 31-point reform programme to amend the Constitution, moving it towards multi-party democracy, with direct, multi-candidate presidential elections (on the basis of public suffrage rather than the choice of the **People's Majlis**), the reinstalment of the Prime Minister's Office, as well as the separation of the powers of the President as the head of state and the Prime Minister as head of the government. In addition, political parties were legally allowed to function in 2005, as long they were officially registered, having received permission to operate. So far, four political organizations have successfully completed the registration procedure. These moves towards greater democratization have been marked by demonstrations organized by the opposition, demanding a faster pace of political reform and the release of political prisoners. A further concern is the threat of Islamic fundamentalism.

Constitution: The Maldives' first Constitution was introduced in 1932 and was predominantly based upon the British-initiated Constitution of Sri Lanka (*see* **Donoughmore Commission**). It introduced an elected 47-member People's Majlis (assembly) and a Legislative Council of 28 members, partly nominated by the sultan and partly elected by the People's Assembly. This Constitution was replaced in 1937 by a second, which, in turn, was substituted by a third constitution in 1954 (after a constitutional interregnum from 31 January 1940 until 23 April 1942). This formed the constitutional basis for the first republic that lasted a mere seven months, giving way to a reinstalled sultanate in February 1954. Having introduced the system of an elected sultanate already in 1932, the process of recasting the Maldivian feudal political structure culminated in the second republic, formed on 11 November 1968, which brought about the final dissolution of the sultanate. The 1968 Constitution was amended successively in 1970, 1972 and 1975, and again replaced by a new constitution when President Gayoom ratified a 156-article document that came into force on 1 January 1998 and promised to introduce fundamental changes. Until 1998 constitutional reforms had not appeared to have any sustainable impact either on the pace or the pattern of the socio-political system presided over by an Islamic aristocratic oligarchy as the ruling power élite.

The 1998 Constitution describes the Republic of Maldives as a sovereign, independent, democratic and unitary state based on the principles of Islam, affording its citizens equality before the law. Critics view the insufficient recognition of the separation of powers as the main structural failure. Under current regulations, the power to revise and amend the Constitution is held by the People's Special Majlis, with presidential assent.

Executive: Executive powers in the Maldives are vested in the President and in the Cabinet of Ministers (Ministers' Majlis), whose members serve at the

President's pleasure and do not need to be members of the parliament (People's Majlis). The President, who is the head of state, head of government and commander-in-chief of the armed forces and the police, is nominated by parliament for a renewable five-year term of office and elected formally through a public (national) referendum. The Prime Minister's Office existed in the early years of the Republic, but was abolished in 1975 by President Ibrahim Nasir in response to abuses of office. According to the Constitution, the powers vested in the President also include the appointment and removal of the Vice-President, Chief Justice, Speaker and Deputy Speaker of the People's Majlis, ministers, the Attorney General, Atoll Chiefs, judges, the Auditor-General and Commissioner of Elections, as well as the appointment and dissolution of the Cabinet of Ministers. A member of the Cabinet is compelled to resign from office should he be subject to a vote of no-confidence by the People's Majlis. Furthermore, the President is the supreme authority for the administration of justice. No legal proceedings in any court or tribunal may be instigated against the President, whether pertaining to official or private affairs. A motion to remove the President from office requires a proposal from one-third of the members of the People's Majlis, and a resolution from two-thirds of the Majlis to consider the proposal. The Cabinet of Ministers is presided over by the President and consists of the Vice-President (should one have been selected by the President), ministers holding responsibility for the various ministries, and the Attorney General. Their functions include assisting the President in the formulation of government policy, and advising him on matters of social and economic development, the state budget, and international treaties and agreements requiring state ratification. The President holds extraordinary powers as the highest institutional supervisor and protector of Islam, the state religion.

Legislature: Legislative powers are held by the People's Majlis (Rayyithunge Majlis, or parliament), a council comprising 50 members, who serve a five-year term from the date of the first post-election meeting. Of these, eight are appointed by the President for state representation, and 42 are directly elected by the people, two from each of the 20 Atolls and two from Malé, the capital. Three regular sessions are held each year in which the People's Majlis enacts, revises and amends legislation in all areas apart from the Constitution, which can only be amended by the People's Special Majlis. Other powers vested in the People's Majlis include approving the state budget prior to the start of each financial year, and initiating no-confidence motions against members of the Ministers' Majlis (Cabinet of Ministers). Should such a motion be passed, the member must resign from office. Apart from special instances cited in the Constitution (Article 74) that require a two-thirds' majority (34 votes), all proposed matters normally require a simple majority (26 votes) to achieve passage in the People's Majlis. A successfully passed bill comes into force once the President has given his assent. The speaker of the parliament (who is not a member) as well as the deputy speaker (who must be a member) is appointed and removed from office by the President.

Elections/Electoral System: Since the first national referendum of 1968 introduced principles of equal, direct and secret suffrage, the electoral system has essentially remained unchanged. Franchise extends to all Muslim citizens over the age of 21 years who are sound of mind and not serving a prison term. Voting is not compulsory, non-resident Maldivian citizens may not participate in elections and women are entitled to vote. The elected national institutions are the President of the Republic and the legislative institutions, the unicameral parliament, People's Majlis, and the People's Special Majlis. The current electoral provisions derive from the Constitution of the Republic of the Maldives, which came into effect on 1 January 1998, and are operationalized in the laws and regulations on presidential elections as well as general elections (People's Majlis). General elections have been held at regular intervals since the first Constitution was introduced. Since the second Republic was established in 1968 both presidential and parliamentary elections have been held every five years, although not simultaneously. Vacancies arising between general elections are filled through by-elections. The presidential candidate is first elected by parliament (through secret ballot by a selection of screened, qualified persons prepared by the commissioner of elections) and then confirmed in a popular referendum by 51% of the valid votes. In the event of no absolute majority, a re-election between the two strongest candidates is held. If only one candidate stands for the presidency, an absolute majority must still be obtained, otherwise the candidacy process begins anew. Every candidate has to be a Maldivian citizen born of Maldivian parents, male, and at least 35 years of age. Additionally, he must be a Sunni Muslim and must not have committed an offence punishable under the Muslim *Shari'a* law, known in Dhivehi as *sariatu*. There are no legal limits for the re-election of the same presidential candidate. Recent reform proposals include the introduction of a multi-candidate presidential election through a popular referendum.

For the People's Majlis, voters cast their ballots to elect two representatives from each of the 21 administrative units (20 Atolls plus the capital, Malé). Candidates must be Muslim, Maldivian citizens, at least 25 years of age, able to read and write the Arabic and Dhivehi script and of sound mind. Owing to a small population and sparsely inhabited islands, candidates are often unchallenged but must none the less be confirmed by a majority vote. Critics point out that there is a fundamental underweighting of votes by the citizens of Malé, for although the capital comprises around 30% of the country's population it is represented by only two seats, less than 5% of the total number of elected seats in the People's Majlis. Political parties have been allowed since July 2005 and, as indicated in the by-elections for the People's Special Majlis held in December 2005 for two administrative Atolls and Malé, an increasing number of candidates are linked with one of the two major political parties, the **Dhivehi Raiyyithunge Party (DRP)** and the **Maldivian Democratic Party (MDP)**.

Political Organizations: According to the Constitution, the founding of political organizations, particularly political parties, is not explicitly banned. However, despite vaguely formulated conditions about their functions, political parties existed but were not legally recognized by the government until 2005. One assumed reason for this strategy was the potential threat of religious extremist groups and the danger that political parties might use Islam as a tool to challenge the official tolerant version of Sunni Islam as state religion through fundamentalist interpretations. Following the 9 June 2004 constitutional reform agenda, announced by President Gayoom, the current regulatory framework for the creation and operation of political parties was promulgated in June 2005. Alongside a proposed constitutional amendment to provide the right to form and carry out the activities of political parties, such organizations were called upon to register and were invited by the Maldives Law Commission to play an active role in carrying forward the democratic process, including the development of a multi-party system. On 26 June 2005 the Maldivian Democratic Party (MDP) became the first formally registered political party. The Dhivehi Raiyyithunge Party (DRP—Maldivian People's Party), the Maldives Labour Party, the **Adhaalath Party (Justice Party)** and the **Islamic Democratic Party** also submitted applications for registration.

Political Party Regulations 2005: After a fast-tracked presidential decree by Gayoom on 20 May 2005 and a Maldivian parliamentary resolution passed on 2 June 2005, political parties have been allowed to officially register for the first time since 1953. According to subsequently promulgated rules for registration, applications with more than 50 signatures must be submitted in order to receive permission from the Ministry of Home Affairs to begin the process of enlisting a minimum 3,000 signatures of members (Maldivian citizens aged 21 years and above) within a 60-day period (efforts are under way to extend this to nine months) and finalize a party constitution before full registration is granted by the government. However, the incumbents of various governmental posts, such as the Commissioner of Elections, the Auditor-General, judges and magistrates, cannot join a registered political party. This legislation brings the party-less era of independent Maldives to an end.

Social Movements: Due to economic and political inequalities, Maldivian society has experienced the rise of social movements. Fundamental tensions within the country are rooted along two major cleavages, a north-south divide among the Atolls and a confrontation between the centre and the periphery. The first cleavage was visible in the context of the Gan issue already during the process of gaining independence, when some southern Atolls sought to separate to form the autonomous United Suvadives Republic headed by Abdulla Afif Didi. More recently, the second cleavage between the capital Malé and the Atolls appeared because of perceived inequality of access to public resources and the frustrations of citizens from the more remote islands with their inability to influence the decision-making process of the government. The perception of socio-economic deprivation among broad sections of society linked with a more autocratic style of governance, as critics claim, has led to a pro-democratic and reform-orientated movement, backed by the Maldivian Democratic Party (MDP). Further problems are an emerging generation gap between the traditional establishment and a younger generation who have received higher education abroad and have grown up with a greater degree of exposure to foreign cultural influences. This generation is faced with a cultural division and a struggle for adequate employment opportunities. Linked with this are the increasing activities of Islamic groups and their dissatisfaction with socio-political tendencies. A prime concern is whether such groups will use the opening up of the political system to create parties that incite religious divisions and seek to impose a narrow version of Islam imported from abroad. (*See* Nationalism; Political Development.)

Foreign Policy: Key to the foreign policy of the Republic of Maldives are close relations with its vast neighbour, India, which provided military assistance during a 1988 coup attempt, and with which it signed an agreement demarcating the maritime boundary between the two countries in 1976. The Maldivian government has traditionally endeavoured to remain outside of great power politics, seeking to maintain cordial relations with all nations. In this context, the country adheres to the principles of non-alignment. The Maldives participates in several international organizations, having joined the UN in 1965, **South Asian Association for Regional Co-operation (SAARC)** in 1985, the **International Monetary Fund** in 1978 and the Colombo Plan in 1963. The Maldives is also a member of the Asian Development Bank and the Non-Aligned Movement. After 60 years as a British Crown Protectorate, the Maldivian government has retained close relations with Britain, which maintained a military base on the island of Gan until 1976, a critical issue in the relationship between the two countries. As a Muslim nation, the Republic has been a member of the Organization of the Islamic Conference (OIC) since 1976. A further focal point of foreign policy is the Maldives' role in the **Alliance of Small Island States (AOSIS)**, to formulate its concerns about environmental and development issues on a broader international platform.

Judiciary: Justice is administered mainly in accordance with statute law and Islamic law (*Shari'a*) and is supervised by the government under the Ministry of Justice. Elements taken from Islamic law include flogging and the use of banishment to a remote island as a sentence. The supreme law of the land is the Maldivian Constitution. The courts are structured in a hierarchical order, with the High Court of Maldives, established in 1980, as the country's highest court, based in Malé. It comprises the Chief Justice as well as four judges and proceedings are usually heard by a panel of two judges. Its main function is to hear appeals from decisions of the Malé courts and island magistrates courts. In some cases it has the authority to operate as a court of first instance. At the intermediate level, after restructuring the court system in September 1997, there are four courts in Malé: the civil court (*Madani*), criminal court (*Jinaaee*), family court and the juvenile court (combined as *Aaelee*). These trial courts act as courts of first instance and are presided over by a single judge, who is empowered to hear all types of cases. In addition to the Malé courts, there is a court on each inhabited island (currently 200), presided over by a magistrate. These basic judicial units do not have jurisdiction to hear cases involving serious criminal offences and civil cases where the amount in dispute or the subject matter in dispute exceeds a certain amount of money (currently 100,000 Rufiyaa). All members of the judiciary, including the Chief Justice, are appointed by the President and are not subject to confirmation by parliament. Under the current Constitution there are no provisions for a totally independent judiciary and the President possesses the authority to review High Court decisions. In November 1994 a Law Commission was established to carry out reforms of the judicial system, and in February 1995, an Advisory Council on Judicial Affairs, a five-member body functioning under the President's Office, was established by the President. The role of the council is to offer, on request, advice to the President on a range of judicial matters, including appeals following adjudications by the High Court.

Defence (Security): Until the coup attempt of 1988 by foreign mercenaries from Sri Lanka, the Republic of Maldives had not faced any serious external military threat or internal instability. Pursuing a foreign policy of non-alignment (India) and not being party to an international dispute, the Maldives perceived no need to establish military capacities. In the aftermath of the events of 1988 and the emergency call for foreign help, Gayoom strengthened the **National Security Service (NSS)** and built up closer security ties with the USA, the United Kingdom and India. Major security concerns for the Maldives today are primarily environmental as opposed to being defence-related. Sharing a concern for security of the **Indian Ocean** area, the Maldives became a founding member of the South Asian Association for Regional Co-operation (SAARC) and a driving force behind the AOSIS. (*See* **Gan**.)

Military: Given its size and capacities, the Maldives does not possess its own branches of air, naval and ground forces. To provide for external as well as internal security, the country maintains the National Security Service (NSS)—a combined paramilitary force including a security branch (ground forces), air elements, and coast guards to protect the 644 km of coastline—of which the President is the commander-in-chief. To improve its military capacities, the Maldives initiated co-operation between the NSS and the US military in joint exercises that impart training to Maldivian forces by US officers as well as military equipment (small arms). In addition, the Maldives receives large-scale support from India. Female members of the NSS were first recruited in February 1989. In 2004 the military (NSS) expenditure accounted for 5.5% (US $41.1m.) of gross domestic product.

Police: Until September 2004 the Maldives Police Services (MPS) were administered by the Ministry of Defence and National Security. As a paramilitary unit, it formed, together with the NSS, the country's armed forces. Since separating from the NSS it has operated as a civilian body under the Ministry of Home Affairs. Trained by India, their main functions are to investigate crimes, collect intelligence, make arrests and enforce house arrest. In the context of further reforms, major challenges include overlapping responsibilities with the NSS over the maintenance of internal security, the strict limited warrant of the police forces outside Malé in the Atolls and the formulation of legislation to empower and control the MPS. (*See* Security (Defence); Bureaucracy.)

Riots: The emergence of social movements has raised political awareness in Maldivian society. This found its first visible expression in early 2003 when human rights activists publicly demanded the release of arrested journalists. In September of the same year, after the death of a detainee in Maafushi jail, prison riots as well as anti-government protests in Malé broke out. Public unrest turned violent and several government buildings were vandalized or burned. Public expressions of discontent have become more common and in August 2004 the country experienced the first wide-scale political demonstrations in its history when thousands of Maldivians gathered in Malé. Although no statistical data about this civil unrest exists, several observers reported violence by both security personnel as well as demonstrators. In the wake of the civil unrest Gayoom imposed a state of emergency, drawing on security forces to restore law and order in Malé.

Terrorism: The perceived threat of politically or religiously motivated terrorism remains very low in the Maldives largely due to its geographical isolation from direct foreign domination and the liberal outlook of its Islamic society as well as leading religious institutions. Although there are an increasing number of Maldivian students studying Islam abroad in religious schools, so-called ***madrasas***, there is no evidence that fundamentalist, radical pan-Islamic ideas are being disseminated. Despite this, official anti-terror legislation, critics say, has been used against the political opposition rather than against international terror groups. Given its strategically important location in the Indian Ocean, its vast spread of island territory that is difficult to control, there is a concern that the Maldives could become the base for *Jihadi* terrorist groups.

Atoll Chief: The 21 administrative units of the Maldives include 20 Atolls (and the first-order administrative division, Malé), each directed by an Atoll Chief (*Atholhu Veriyaa*). The Atoll Chief is appointed by the President to act like a district officer. The Atoll Chiefs are the immediate superiors of the Island Chiefs (*Katheeb*), who are appointed by the Ministry of Atolls.

Bureaucracy: As in many other aspects of public life in Maldives, the Atoll is the constituent unit in the pyramidal structure of bureaucracy. In this administrative framework, the inhabited islands form the lowest administrative unit, Atolls acting as the intermediate unit leading to the central government, which, at the apex, comprises a number of departments and various ministries, all of which are responsible to or under the direct control of the President, head of the government and the whole bureaucracy. The Atolls are administered by the Ministry of Atoll Administration through its Northern and Southern Regional Offices, Atoll Offices and Island Offices, and are collectively answerable to the President. Each of them has an Atoll Chief (*Atholhu Veriyaa*) who delegates and handles administrative exercises, but who also works on behalf of the central government. Furthermore, an island chief, directly responsible to the Atoll Chief, administrates each inhabited island. The most significant development within the bureaucracy in recent years has been the restructuring of the NSS following the attempted coup in 1988, leading to the establishment of the Maldivian Police Services as an autonomous body.

Citizenship: According to the Constitution, every person was made a citizen of the Maldives at the commencement of the Constitution; every child born to a citizen of the Maldives. However, the current Constitution designates Islam as an official state religion and as a result the government has interpreted citizenship as confined to Muslims while others are given permanent resident permits to live and work.

Corruption: Although there are no official data or indices about corruption, media and individual observers report that corruption is an increasing concern in the Maldives. In 2002 the parliament passed a Bill on Prevention and Punishment of Corruption, broadening the mandate of the Anti-Corruption Board, formed in 1991, to investigate allegations of corruption, bribery, fraud, misappropriation of government funds and property, as well as misuse of government office. According to critics, governmental accountability is limited by the fact that the executive exercises almost complete control over both the legislature and the judiciary, encouraging nepotism and corruption. In the context of the evolving political party system, reports warn that there is the need for strict controls to avoid the practice of 'vote buying' and the misuse of state resources during election time. When international aid poured in after the tsunami, Gayoom's government undertook extra measures to prevent corruption in the public as well as the private sphere and to ensure that funds reached the affected victims.

Decentralization: Until the mid-20th century the Atolls of the Maldives had a relatively high degree of autonomy and decentralized administration. This came to an end with the creation of the strong Atolls Division, a predecessor of the current Ministry of Atolls, in the 1960s. However, the new Constitution of 1998 has made considerable efforts to decentralize the political administration as well as the public sector. In recent years more schools, hospitals or health centres have been placed outside the capital Malé to support regional development through improved infrastructure. Administrative reforms are also planned. According to the current Minister for Planning and Development, Ibrahim Hussein Zaki, the 21 administrative units (20 Atolls and the first-order administrative division Malé) shall be divided into five regions with so-called 'growth centres'. Critics point to the fact that decision-making remains highly centralized.

Federalism: The Constitution of the Republic of Maldives does not provide for a federalist system. The only legislative institution, the unicameral parliament, the People's Majlis, is partly elected by popular vote (42 members) and partly appointed by the President (eight members). Various tensions exist among the Atolls, and between the outer Atolls and the capital, Malé, because of a perceived mismatch in the system of electoral representation. Regardless of population size, all Atolls, including the capital Malé, are represented by two seats in the legislative institutions. Furthermore, it is argued that the current arrangement fails to adequately represent the Malé population where a greater concentration of opposition forces are concentrated. The Maldives has a three-tier hierarchical-federal structure, with Malé at the top and the inhabited islands as the smallest units, holding a certain degree of autonomy and grouped as they are into 20 Atolls. These form the basic framework of the political and administrative system of the Maldives. The introduction of elected Island Development Committees and Atoll Committees in 1994 was meant to legitimize and strengthen the administrative as well as the political structure of the Maldives.

Human Rights: Human rights issues in the Maldives are centred upon the strong constitutional position of the President and the tendency towards a concentration of power. Opponents to the current political situation complain that individual rights are restricted in the areas of freedom of speech, the freedom of the press and freedom of assembly and association. Some human rights organizations identify the use of house arrest, banishment to remote islands and imprisonment as forms of arbitrary punishment practised in the Maldives. Designating Islam as the state religion and the strict interpretation that citizens must be Muslims, combined with the prohibition on publicly practising any other religion seen to be harmful to Islam, are regarded by critics as mechanisms to restrict the freedom of religion. A Human Rights Commission was established in 2003 by the President and in 2005 the Maldives had ratified six of the major international human rights conventions.

Inequality: In the Maldives four main forms of inequality can be identified, namely geographical disparities, disproportionate political representation of the people in the legislative institutions of Malé and the Atolls, economic inequality, and gender-based inequalities. Malé, while comprising around 30% of the country's population, has, like the other political-administrative units (20 Atolls), only two seats in the legislature, creating an imbalance and lack of legitimacy in the political system. Differences in development conditions and infrastructure reflect the geographical disparity between the capital Malé and the Atolls. The Maldives Vulnerability and Poverty Assessment of 1998 observed a higher poverty rate among the Atolls compared to Malé. Furthermore, the modern sectors of the Maldivian economy as well as the members of the social élite are almost all concentrated in the capital.

Nationalism: Nationalism in the Maldives has to take into account the geographical fragmentation of the state as well as its ranking as one of the smallest and least developed countries in the world. Accordingly, the national élite, concentrated in Malé, has claimed that the country is not only an island nation, but also a nation of islands, emphasizing the necessity of belonging as well as the existence of a shared basis of religious and cultural values, expressed in a common history. This is characterized by the self-assertion of an autonomous state that was never conquered by a foreign force, apart from 15 years of Portuguese rule. The fact that the Maldives were a protectorate during the British rule in South Asia until the 1960s is seen as evidence for the determination of an independent Maldives rather than a kind of subordination. This idea of nationalism among the vast number of islands experienced its greatest challenge when a pro-British separatist movement, on the eve of independence and under the leadership of Abdulla Afif Didi in 1959, declared an autonomous state called the United Suvadive Republic, consisting of the southern Addu and Huvadud Atolls. However, by the end of 1963 the administrative control by the centre over the south had been established. Today, the use of nationalism combines the task of promoting Islam as the source of national identity and the limiting of religious fundamentalism.

Participation/Public Action: Maldives has an increasingly active civil society characterized by a rise in political consciousness and sensitivity, particularly with regard to the social and economic disparities in the country. With the introduction, by law, of elected Island Development Committees (IDCs), Atoll Committees and Women's Development Committees, the government has tried to increase participation of the population. These institutions operate as an important link between the centre and peripheral island communities in the development process of the Atolls. However, more significant in this context is a new form of political gathering taking place since 2003 in the country, which has become a focus of national and international attention. Rallies, primarily organized by a self-styled pro-democratic movement, which at the beginning were spearheaded by the then suppressed Maldivian Democratic Party (MDP), have, since the approval of political parties in 2005, been organized by various new political groups. These demonstrations have politicized much of the public sphere, especially on the capital island, which has brought about not only a transformation of political culture and attitudes, but has also created a new 'reformist' élite.

Supreme Council of Islamic Affairs: Established in November 1987 by Gayoom (as President, the supreme authority to propagate the tenets of Islam in the country), the Supreme Council of Islamic Affairs falls under direct presidential control. It operates as an advisory council on matters relating to the state religion of Islam (Sunni).

Maldives, Economic Development

Gross domestic product (GDP) at purchasing power parity (PPP): US $1,250m. (2002 estimate); GDP per capita at PPP: $3,900 (2002 estimate); *agriculture*: 20%; *industry*: 18%; services: 62% (2000 estimates); currency: rufiyaa (MVR).

In the first decade of independence, the Maldivian GDP failed to keep up with the pace of population growth. Nevertheless, a stable political environment and a supportive international community enabled the country to achieve significant social progress and economic growth in the following years. The Maldivian economy experienced a significant rebound in the 1980s, with annual average growth rates of about 9.5%. In addition to foreign aid, the main boost for the country's economy was the introduction of tourism, with the opening of the first resort (Kurumba Island, Malé **Atoll**) in the Maldives in 1972. Until then fisheries had been the dominant industry, exploiting an Exclusive Economic Zone (EEZ) of about 90,000 sq km and based on traditional fishing techniques. Mechanization of the fisheries as well as development of the tourism sector were milestones in the country's economic development. Geographical constraints, such as the lack of arable and cultivatable land, have hindered economic diversification and, together with the boom in tourism, agriculture and manufacturing continue to play a lesser role. In spite of positive trends, the Maldives faces several key development challenges. As a state composed of islands, lacking land-based natural and mineral resources, and with a narrowly-based economy and a dispersed population, the country's development progress is not only unique but also extremely vulnerable to international changes, such as the rise in oil prices, dramatic declines in prices for tuna, environmental catastrophes like the 2004 tsunami and shocks to global tourism. Today, marine biodiversity provides the Maldives with its most significant and vital resource base for future development. Its preservation is a top priority and informs not only environmental protection strategies but also the formulation of economic policy.

Economic Policy/Reforms: The current development philosophy of the government centres on increasing Maldives' self-sufficiency and improving the living standard of inhabitants on the outer islands which suffer from limited resources and geographic isolation. To reduce the considerable gap between the generally prosperous capital **Malé** and the outer islands, primary attention is being given to the regional, Atoll development. Vision 2020, a development strategy, aims to transform the country into a middle-income developing nation with a diversified economy, high-quality education and health services, social and gender equality and democratic governance. A stable political environment and the initiation of economic reforms in 1989, initially through the lifting of import quotas and the opening of parts of the private sector to the export industry, enabled the country to make substantial socio-economic progress in the country's periphery. Because of a liberal trade environment and relaxed regulations allowing more foreign funds, the Maldives were able to attract investors as well as donors to develop key sectors such as fisheries, tourism, services and transport. However, the tsunami in 2004 set the country back in terms of socio-economic development, causing damages equivalent to more than 60% of gross domestic product. The dramatic fall in the number of tourists as a result of the tsunami combined with higher oil prices created a severe budget problem, both a drop in revenue as well as increased costs of transport, so essential for an island state. As a result, the government has sought to stabilize the economy by pursuing policies of fiscal stringency and promoting a more transparent economic environment to maintain as well as attract more attention from international donors.

Private Sector: As a result of the government's regulative economic policy, the Maldivian private sector has remained weak for many years. After various reform efforts in the late 1980s and early 1990s, some export sectors were opened up to the private sector for the first time, enabling significant expansion and diversification, particularly in the fisheries sector. While the governmental sector has focused on providing basic socio-economic services, the private sector plays an increasing role in the development of tourism, resorts, trade, telecommunications, transport and fisheries as well as strengthening domestic food production. According to observers, limited access to long-term finance is one of the main hindrances to the further and sustainable growth of the private sector. (*See* **Maldives Stock Exchange**.)

Public Sector: The public sector in the Maldives consists largely of the services provided by the government and state-owned enterprises, which control access to health care facilities, employment opportunities as well as educational resources and a significant percentage of licences. In particular, the government continues to dominate the emerging sectors of tourism, air and sea transport and commercial fishing. At present the only investment opportunity available to private agents in these sectors is a limited number of shares and debentures on the Maldives Stock Exchange. According to the Companies Act all public enterprises are obliged to have at least 10 shareholders.

Population: The population in 2004 was estimated at around 289,480, with 82,000 in Malé, the capital. The main feature of the Maldivian population is its youth. In 2005 the proportion of the population under 15 years of age was estimated at 43.9%, with 53% of the population falling between the ages of 15–64, and 3.1% aged over 65. The population growth rate is 2.82% and the male/female sex ratio (for the total population) is 1.05. Average life expectancy is 65.42 years (males: 62.76; females: 65.42), with the estimated birth rate recorded at 36.71 births per 1,000 and the death rate at 7.65 deaths per 1,000. The total fertility rate stands at 5.02 children born per woman, with an infant mortality rate of 56.52 deaths per 1,000 live births. The prevalence of HIV/AIDS in adults was estimated in 2001 at 0.1%, with fewer than 100 people estimated as living with HIV/AIDS. Many islands and Atolls are densely populated, raising serious concerns regarding the population growth rate. As a result, a twofold policy remains the main focus, with the dual need to improve health facilities as well as to introduce methods to control population growth.

Family-Planning Policy: Following several improvements in the access to health services, especially for mothers and young children, in the 1960s, the annual population growth rate in the Maldives increased at about 3%, causing the Maldivian population to double in the last four decades. Despite this, changes in the official family-planning policy began relatively late and only after the UN had taken the initiative through the implementation of several family-planning programmes. These programmes included education campaigns and the distribution of various contraceptives. In 2000 the annual population growth rate had declined to about 1.9%.

Migration: Although the Maldivian population is an ethnic mixture of various migrated peoples, such as the Dravidians from **Kerala**, Dhivehi-speakers from Sri Lanka, Arabs and others from Africa, a relatively homogeneous idea of Maldivian citizenship was developed over the last centuries. Today, external migration is not a critical issue and the lack of domestic labour means that expatriates and foreign workforces are welcomed. A more serious concern is internal migration from outer Atolls to Malé due to marked discrepancies in the availability of physical and social infrastructure, such as schools, health care facilities, job opportunities, etc. This increases pressure on the already strained infrastructure and the restricted capacities for housing and limited employment opportunities. Otherwise, inter-Atoll migration is very rare because of the long distances that must be travelled using limited communications facilities. A more pressing issue is the almost 11,500 internally displaced persons, victims of the December 2004 tsunami.

Urbanization: The nearly 300,000 Maldivians living on some 200 of the 1,200 islands that make up the country make it one of the most densely populated areas in the world (970 inhabitants per sq km). The capital, Malé, has about 82,000 inhabitants. Urbanization is relatively low, almost 40% of the total population living in villages of 500 inhabitants or less on the Atolls. This inevitably leads to striking disparities between Malé and the Atolls, particularly in the health sector and in terms of economic and social development. However, due to the rising pressure of internal migration towards Malé, the capital is experiencing a range of developing urban problems, such as air and noise pollution, the lack of a comprehensive system for the collection and disposal of solid waste, a shortage of housing, weakening of infrastructure and increasing congestion.

Minority Groups/Communities: The population of the Maldives is a cultural mixture of various ethnic communities, including Sinhalese, Dravidian, Arab, African and Indian people. Today, officials and observers identify a comparatively high degree of homogeneity within Maldivian society and refer to the country's religious foundation, the Sunni branch of Islam, as a central pillar that pervades in an omnipresent manner the social and cultural life of the whole state. There is only a small ethnic and religious minority group—composed of a few hundred former Indians belonging to a trading community—belonging to the Shi'a branch of Islam. This homogeneity is likely to be affected by the increasing number of foreign workers in the Maldives.

Tribes: Due to the absence of written records, little is known of the tribal origins of the Maldives. Today tribes are not recognized as ethnic communities and aborigines of various descents are subsumed under the major ethnic groups of Sinhalese, Dravidian, Arab and African.

Agriculture/Fishing: The fisheries sector, the second most important sector of the Maldivian economy, contributed approximately 6% of GDP in 2004, compared with 10% in 2002, including fish manufacturing, and employs about 11% of the labour force. The majority of the catch is exported, with raw and fresh fish making up the bulk of fish exports. The highly dispersed islands, with poor soil and scarce arable land, the limited scope for extending production and a shortage of domestic labour have meant that agriculture is restricted to a few subsistence crops, such as coconuts, corn, and sweet potatoes. As a result, the Maldives depends on a significant amount of imported agricultural produce, which has been a major cause of national deficit. The islands are broadly divided into a northern zone, where some monsoon crops are cultivated, an intermediary zone in which there is little agricultural production, and a southern zone in which a number of islands are predominantly agricultural.

Land Reform (Ownership): There are no land ownership laws in the Maldives. On account of geographical conditions and the dominance of fisheries in the country's economy and peoples' livelihoods, conflict over land ownership is rare. With all territory of the Maldives being coastal land, accessibility to the sea is the main source of conflict. A pattern of customary ownership exists, with communities, villages and clans acting as landowners. This community ownership concept includes the right of commercial use of the individual island and its surrounding lagoon and reefs.

Food and Famine/Prevention: Since independence the Maldives has not experienced a serious famine due to its considerable success in achieving food security, including the provision of drinking water. A narrow base of natural resources and poor soil quality has limited the extent of agricultural activities in the country, causing considerable nutritional problems in the past. Domestic production of coconuts, sweet potatoes, fish and corn is insufficent to protect the vulnerable against uncertainties in food availability. In the late 1990s, in order to reduce the high dependence on imported foodstuffs, a local hydroponics project was initiated to address the problems of malnutrition in the country. However, malnutrition among women and children is still a central challenge of Maldives' national development plans.

Industry: The industrial sector in the Maldives accounted only for about 9% of GDP in 2002. Traditional industry consists of boat-building and handicrafts, whereas modern industry is limited to fish processing, coral and sand mining, garment production, coconut processing, a bottling plant, PVC piping, soap, furniture, and food products. Following the decline of the shipping industry in the 1980s, tourism has rapidly grown to become the largest industry in the Maldives, accounting for approximately 20% of GDP, and more than 60% of the Maldives' foreign exchange receipts. More than 480,000 tourists visited the islands in 2002.

Foreign Trade (Import/Export): As a result of its geographical position at the crossroads of maritime trading routes between the Middle and Far East, trade has always been crucial for the Maldives. Today the Maldives have a comparatively liberal trade policy. Since the economic boom following the introduction of tourism in 1972, the need for consumer goods has risen considerably. Today consumers account for about 40% of all imports, consumer goods having become the most important import commodity. The major trade partner of the Maldives for imported goods is Singapore, which provides about 25% of all imports. Europe, Asia (especially India and Sri Lanka) and the Middle East are also important trading partners for imports. The USA is the most important export partner of the Maldives, accounting for about 40% of all exports (mostly clothing), followed by Sri Lanka and Thailand. The major export goods of the Maldives are fish and related marine products (about 57% of total exports). Clothing, mostly driven by foreign investment, is the second most significant export.

Banking System: The Maldives Monetary Authority (MMA), established in 1981, is the central bank of the Maldives with headquarters in Malé. It is the country's bank of issue, manages the foreign exchange policy of the Maldives, and advises the government on banking and money matters. The **Bank of Maldives PLC (BML)**, founded in 1982, is the country's commercial bank. The Maldives' very first bank, established in 1974, was a branch of the **State Bank of India** which remains today one of four foreign banks maintaining branches in the Maldives, together with the Bank of Ceylon (Sri Lanka), Habib Bank Limited (Pakistan), and the Hong Kong Shanghai Banking Corporation. All four are primarily involved in commercial financing and provide short-term loans over 3–4 years only. The BML provides longer-term loans. The Allied Insurance Company of the Maldives was founded in 1985 and provides all classes of insurance, except life insurance. The company is operated by the State Trading Organization (STO), a state-controlled commercial organization.

Foreign Direct Investment (FDI):The major legal framework for foreign direct investment (FDI) in the Maldives is the Law on Foreign Investment, requiring an agreement between the investor and the government. The Maldivian government has taken considerable steps since the late 1980s to ease its regulatory framework for FDI by allowing joint venture companies as well as 100% foreign-owned enterprises and allowing FDI shares and profits thus earned to be freely transferred abroad. Absolute FDI inflows increased from US $5m. in 1985–95 (annual average) to $12m. in 2001. However, as a percentage of gross fixed capital formation, the development of FDI remained static, at about 7%. The government welcomed investments, particularly in the areas of tourism, transport, fisheries, finance, infrastructure development and other services sectors. Recent investments were made in commercial seaweed farming, pearl cultivation and horticulture.

Foreign Investment Services Bureau (FISB): The Foreign Investment Services Bureau (FISB) was established in 1987 as a governmental agency by the Ministry of Trade and Industry and operates as a service centre for promoting and facilitating foreign investment in the Maldives. It provides the institutional framework necessary for effective management of foreign investment and gives assistance at various stages of the investment process.

Foreign Aid: Until the 1980s the largest part of the limited foreign aid to the Maldives came from Arab states such as Kuwait, Saudi Arabia and the United Arab Emirates rather than from the World Bank and the specialized agencies of the UN. Over the past 25 years international efforts have come to support economic development with foreign assistance in the form of grants and loans. With an annual contribution of about US $10m., Japan is one of the biggest donors of foreign aid, besides UN agencies, the World Bank and the ADB. In addition to humanitarian projects, external loans and grants are primarily used for the development of infrastructure and environmental protection and one of the top priorities in the government's economic policy is to maintain donor interest.

Labour: The Maldivian economy suffers from a shortage of skilled labour. Expatriate labour (38,000), around 44.19% of the total employed workforce (86,000) in 2004, plays a significant role in the economic progress of the country. The domestic workforce lacks labour laws to set up trade unions, or minimum legislation to negotiate wage agreements (disputes are resolved by the government) and launch collective action. In practice, no labour movement exists although some workers, linked with the newly registered political parties, have founded informal cells and groups that address labour issues. The **Maldivian Democratic Party (MDP)** has formed various basic units to organize the labour sector. The growing tourism industry, which contributed around 33% to the gross domestic product of the Maldives in 2004, employs around 19.9% of the population and provides, together with fisheries (20%) and the government (38%), the bulk of employment for Maldivians. An unemployment rate of 2.0% was recorded in 2000, a significant increase compared with 1995 when there was close to full employment. There are no records on bonded or forced labour as well as trafficking of persons in the country.

Informal Economy: Together with corruption, the informal sector, or the shadow economy of the Maldives, has increased in recent years. According to one estimate, the shadow economy grew from about 30.3% in 1999 to 31.4% in 2001 and 32% in 2002, as a percentage of the gross domestic product. Illegal fishing, drugs smuggling and arms trafficking have caught the attention of enforcement authorities. Although there is no concrete evidence, observers fear that due to its geographical location the Maldives may have the potential to become a major transshipment point for smuggling in South Asia, especially as part of the Kerala (India)-Sri Lanka–Maldives triangle. The success of anti-smuggling operations shows that the Indo-Maldivian corridor has been used by contrabanders to satisfy the demand for illegal goods since the Maldivian government began strictly to implement its anti-drugs and alcohol laws.

Child Labour: Officially, children's rights are incorporated into Maldivian law, which protects children under the age of 14 from 'places of waged work and from work that is not suitable for that child's age, health, or physical ability'. There is no official data about child labour in the Maldives, but the fact that almost 98% of school-aged children, equal for both male and female, to grade 7 are enrolled in school suggests that the protection of children in the Maldives is effectively implemented. However, it is reported that children work in family-based activities in fisheries, agriculture and commercial enterprises.

Environmental Protection: The Maldives comprises many islands, widely scattered over 859,300 sq km of ocean. Only 33 islands have a land area in excess of 1 sq km, while just three islands have an area larger than 3 sq km. In addition to being very small, all of the islands' surfaces are flat, with elevated areas of no more than 3 m above sea level. The fact that 80% of the total land mass has a mean elevation of only 1 m makes the Maldives one of the most vulnerable countries in the world to rising sea levels. Even slight changes can have devastating consequences for the country. As a result, the Maldives have become a pioneer in the field of global climate protection and, as part of the **Alliance of Small Island States (AOSIS)**, the Maldives have signed and ratified international agreements. Other environmental concerns include land loss due to beach erosion, high population density, deforestation, the depletion of freshwater aquifers, coral reef bleaching and the management of waste and rubbish produced by the tourist industry.

Floods and Natural Disasters: In the past two decades the Maldives has been the victim of three extensive floods. The absence of a land mass, against which waves could build up, reduces their destructive impact and prevents waves from reaching much more than 1.2–1.5 m in height. However, the Maldives is one of the lowest lying countries on earth, and the fact that there are neither dunes nor rocks or hills higher than 3 m above sea level, meant that nearly all of the country was swamped. The first two floods, in 1987 and 1991, caused an inundation of Malé and contaminated drinking water reserves. These experiences triggered extensive projects of environmental protection in the Maldives. Floods following the Asian tsunami of 26 December 2004 affected one-third of the Maldivian islands, resulting in the death of about 82 Maldivians, widespread destruction of housing, tourism and fishing infrastructure on 20 of the 199 inhabited islands, with that of many others severely damaged, 1,113 injured and more than 11,500 people displaced.

Health System/Policy: To implement the governmental goal of health for all, services in the public health care sector are organized into a five-tier referral system, comprising the central health services, including the referral hospital, the regional hospitals, Atoll hospitals, Atoll health centres and island health posts. In addition, health care facilities in the private sector have recently begun to emerge. One of the major constraints to the provision of equal access to health care has been the geographic disparities between Malé and the inhabited islands. Whereas in the capital Malé the ratio of doctors to the population was 2,673:1 in 1989, in the Atolls it was 35,498:1. In the 1990s the Ministry of Health, which is responsible for the allocation of medical and health services, achieved several improvements in the health sector. Due to its policy of preventative health, the infant mortality rate declined from 120 per 1,000 live births in 1978 to 14 in 2003 and life expectancy at birth has increased by around 20 years over the same period. However, maternal mortality as well as fertility has remained high. Universal child immunization has vastly improved the health of children and malaria has been effectively eradicated from the Maldives. Nevertheless, some of the inhabited islands still do not have a permanent doctor or even access to medical care.

Education/Education Policy: The Maldivian education system is not compulsory and consists of government and private schools as well as community/ward schools. Three distinct types of schools exist, including Koranic schools, Dhivehi-language primary schools, and English-language primary and secondary schools. Until the late 1970s, institutes of education in the Maldives were limited to the capital island, Malé. The first primary school outside of Malé opened in 1978, and in 1992 the first secondary school was constructed on another Atoll in accordance with a policy of extending the educational system through launching Atoll Education Centres (AECs) and Atoll Schools (AS) administered in four zones (Northern, Central, Southern and Malé). Primary education begins at six years of age and lasts for five years. Public primary education is free. Secondary education continues from 11 years of age and lasts for up to seven years. Opportunities for higher education are offered through the limited capacities of various institutions, such as the Maldives' college of higher education, which is to be elevated to a university on 1 January 2007. A significant feature of the education system is the co-existence of modern and traditional types of schools. The latter, an institution called *edhuruge*, is today still prevalent in the form of *makthabs* and *madhrasaa*, and which partly deserve credit for the high literacy rate of 97.0% (males: 97.1%, females: 96.9%) in the Maldives.

Social Security/Policy: Traditional Maldivian society, in the form of individual island communities, has in the past developed and provided a natural safety net for people of low social status who are vulnerable to hunger and famine. However, the pressures of modernization and globalization have gradually dismantled these networks, increasing the demands on the public sector. There is no public social security system that provides people with a statutory minimum income. Furthermore, critics point out that access to the limited benefits is dependent on the good will of those in governmental posts, creating an entrenched patronage structure, particularly with regard to educational and employment opportunities. However, current development plans are focused on equalizing access to basic social services, particularly in the public health care sector.

Poverty: Although the country's GDP has improved greatly over the last two decades, economic inequality and poverty are still striking problems in Malé. According to the Maldives Vulnerability and Poverty Assessment (1998), more than 42% of all Maldivians live on less than Rufiyaa 15 per day (US $1.25). One out of four males earns less than US $1 per day. In terms of malnutrition, progress has been achieved and extreme poverty significantly reduced, but the Maldives still rank very low in global terms. Economic development, with its rapidly growing modern sector on the one hand and the disappearance of traditional economic activities on the other, has yet to find a way of integrating most of the population into its processes.

Welfare: Significant to the Maldivian welfare system has been the long-held consideration of health as a basic and human right of each citizen, which has led to a superior health care approach. Public initiatives have been launched to improve the quality and prevalence of educational, health and social services, seeking to ensure that benefits offered in the welfare sector are shared equitably among the population. More recently, private campaigns that tackle welfare issues have gained attention.

Gender Relations/Empowerment: Government efforts to improve access to health services and education, together with the creation of employment opportunities in the public sector to empower women, have enhanced the social and economic status of women in the Maldives. Women enjoy a 98% literacy rate, compared with 96% for men in 2004, and the school enrolment rates for girls and boys are almost equal at a very high level. Official sources claim that Maldivian women are the most emancipated in South Asia and the Islamic world. However, observers stress that discrimination against women persists in economic life and in politics, as well as in the private sphere. Moreover, women constitute only 10% of the representatives in the **Majlis**, or the parliament, and since the first Republic only two women have become cabinet ministers. Furthermore, women are not allowed to contest the presidency. In the civil sector, women are still under-privileged and are not present in significant economic institutions such as the Maldives Association of Tourism Industries or the National Chamber of Commerce and Industry. Furthermore, the interpretation of *Shari'a* law, when applied, tends to disfavour the female population.

Maldives Stock Exchange

The Maldives Stock Exchange is operated by the Securities Trading Floor (STF). The STF was formed on 14 April 2002 and operates within the Capital Market Division (CMD) of the Maldives Monetary Authority (MAA) to implement and enforce the development of a capital market. Currently three companies are listed at the STF: State Trading Organization PLC, **Bank of Maldives PLC** and Maldives Transport and Contracting Company PLC. Control of these shares is not widely held.

Maldivian Democratic Party (MDP)

The Maldivian Democratic Party (MDP) became the first officially registered political party in the Maldives on 26 June 2005. It was formed by a group of 42 activists and, after making an unsuccessful application for permission to register on 28 February 2001, it began operating in exile from Colombo, Sri Lanka, initiating and co-ordinating an initially peaceful movement against the **Gayoom** government which became increasingly violent after 2003. Today the MDP is officially recognized as a political party and pursues activities to promote human rights and democracy in the Maldives. An MDP manifesto emphasizes that the Maldivian nation should be a secular democratic society, based on non-racial, non-sexist principles, but claims that this is not possible under the current Constitution. The current governmental structure is regarded by the MDP as undemocratic and authoritarian and the party has demanded that power be transferred to a national reconciliation government or to a caretaker government. To highlight this demand, the MDP has formed a shadow Cabinet.

Malé

Malé is the capital of the Maldives and is located on Malé Island. Also known as the capital island, it is part of the Kaafu **Atoll**, which is currently administered under the name Malé Atoll (K). Despite its territory belonging to the Kaafu Atoll (or Malé Atoll), it is considered to be an independent, first-order administrative division. As the seat of the central government and the most significant institution in the private as well as the public sector, it is the political, economic and cultural centre of the whole Maldives. Maintaining a commercial harbour and Malé International Airport on an adjacent island, the capital is the centre for trade and tourism and most prosperous business divisions. Rising concerns, besides environmental protection, include the strained socio-economic infrastructure, high population growth (the current population is approximately 82,000) and migration from the Atolls towards Malé. To diminish the pressure and to close the development gap between the capital island and the more remote Atolls, various measures have been initiated, such as the Atoll Development for Livelihoods (ADSL) programme.

Mandal Commission

In 1978 a second commission was appointed by the government to study **affirmative action** for India's backward classes, also known as **Other Backward Classes (OBCs)**. Combined with field survey data and information from the 1961 census, the Mandal Commission's study produced an all-India OBC list of 3,743 castes, together with an even more underprivileged 'depressed backward classes' list of 2,108 castes. With an extensive list of variables and 11 indicators covering educational, social and economic factors, the Commission hoped to find a consensus on a definition of backwardness that would also extend to non-Hindu oppressed groups.

Calculated in total, it was estimated that OBCs constituted about 52% of the total population. However, a **reservation policy** set a quota of 27% for central government positions and university admission was recommended because the Supreme Court had already ruled that the total proportion of reservations under Articles 15 (4) and 16 (4) of the Constitution should be below 50% (**Scheduled Castes (SCs)** and **Scheduled Tribes (STs)** already accounted for 22.5%).

In August 1990 Prime Minister V. P. Singh of the National Front coalition, announced the implementation of the Mandal Commission's recommendations, provoking violent reactions, especially in northern India among upper castes and students. On 16 November the Supreme Court upheld the 27% quota as well as ruling that 'caste' could be used to identify 'backward classes' as long as the caste was socially backward as a whole. In 1993 Prime Minister Narasimha **Rao** announced that he was ready to implement the provisions.

Manjur Faction

The Manjur faction or Jatiya Party (Naziur or Naziur Firoz) split from the **Jatiya Party (JP)**/Jatiya Party (Ershad) and is headed by Naziur Rahman Manur. It is currently part of a **Four-Party Alliance** in power in Bangladesh and is led by the **Bangladesh Nationalist Party (BNP)**. The party won four seats in the parliamentary elections held in 2001. Another breakaway element from the JP is the Jatiya Party (Manju).

Maoist Insurgency – *see* People's War

Marumalarchi Dravida Munnetra Kazhagam (MDMK)

The Marumalarchi Dravida Munnetra Kazhagam (MDMK) is a regional political party in the south Indian state of **Tamil Nadu**. The party was formed by V. Gopalswamy, popularly known as Vaiko, in 1994 as an offshoot of the **Dravida Munnetra Kazhagam (DMK)**. The party is known for its sympathy for the Sri Lankan Tamils and its contacts with the **Liberation Tigers of Tamil Eelam (LTTE)**. On 30 December 2002 Vaiko and his supporters were arrested for comments they had allegedly made in support of the LTTE, under the provisions of India's Prevention of Terrorism Act. Before the party joined the **Democratic Progressive Alliance** it was part of the **National Democratic Alliance (NDA)**. It won four seats in the 14th **Lok Sabha** elections of 2004.

Mastan/Mastani Culture

Mastan, a Bengali word originally used to refer to a person who is in a state of intoxication, is today used to refer to armed individuals who collect 'rent' from businessmen, industrialists, construction contractors, independent professionals or even squatters on government land. So-called *mastani* culture is a common feature of public life in Bangladesh. The government acknowledged in late 2002 that *mastans* were an irritant as well as a threat to the population at large, sending the army into the streets in 'Operation Clean Heart'. The government's solution resulted in its own abuses, however, including at least 40 deaths in custody, after which the government created an élite force, the **Rapid Action Battalion (RAB)**, for anti-*mastan* operations. However, *mastans* have increasingly been incorporated into mainstream politics through their use by ruling as well as oppositional parties to mobilize support and capture votes.

Matubbars

Matubbars are informal village leaders in Bangladesh, generally the oldest people in traditional élite families. In Bangladesh's rural areas they have been historically powerful, controlling and dictating almost every activity of their locality. They participate in the settlement of all types of disputes, control local institutions, organize festivals and even provide support to follow villagers during natural disasters and epidemics. The spread of education, urban influence, and the intervention of governmental and non-governmental organizations in village areas has slowly contributed to their declining grip on rural communities.

McMahon Line

The McMahon Line is located in the eastern Himalayas and constitutes a border between India and China, extending from east Bhutan to Burma (Myanmar). Historically, the Line is based on a British colonial claim, drawn as the frontier between British India and Tibet at the Shimla Conference in 1914. In 1949, however, the newly formed People's Republic of China renounced all agreements concluded between previous Chinese governments and foreign powers, thus nullifying the McMahon Line. India, on the other hand, regarded it as a permanent international border, an issue which became a major cause of tension with China in the 1950s and one of the reasons for the Sino–Indian war of 1962. Heavy fighting occurred along the McMahon Line at **Tawang**, as well as at another disputed section of the border in **Aksai Chin**. The border remains a temporary one, with armies on both sides of what is known as the **Line of Actual Control**.

Microcredit

Bangladesh has one of the largest microcredit programmes in the world. The main focus of this project is credit for the poor. It offers small loans, mainly to poor women and their families to invest in generating self-employment activities at easy repayment rates. In 1976 **Grameen Bank** pioneered the idea to help women gain control over material resources and to advance their socio-economic rights. In recent years more and more NGOs have begun to offer microcredit schemes and international development organizations have also started to support such initiatives as an effective means of pursuing long-term poverty reduction, gender equality and regional development. More than 10m. poor borrowers are reached through microcredit in Bangladesh. Some US $1,000m. is currently disbursed each year. Grameen Bank alone disbursed $319m. in 2003.

Mizo National Front (MNF)

A secessionist political movement in the state of Mizoram (see **North East India**), the Mizo National Front (MNF) was formed in 1959 and for more than 20 years waged a guerrilla war for independence from India. In 1989 a peace agreement was reached with the government of India. Mizoram became a state and Pu Laldenga, founder of the guerrilla movement, became the Chief Minister. In the 1998 state assembly elections the MNF entered office. Following re-election in 2003 Pu Zoramthanga, also a former guerrilla leader, became Chief Minister.

Monopolies And Restrictive Trade Act (MRTP)

Under the 'command and control' model of economic development that India was pursuing, the Indian government introduced the Monopolies and Restrictive Trade (MRTP) Act of 1969 to prevent and regulate the concentration of economic power. The regulatory provisions of the MRTP Act applied to almost every area of business, from production to mergers. The MRTP Act 1969 was amended in 1991 as a part of the new economic reforms. In 2002 a new Competition Act was passed to gradually replace the MRTP Act, directing attention more to consumer freedom and freedom of economic activities rather than the control and elimination of monopolies. A Competition Commission of India, consisting of people from various fields, was formed not as a regulatory body but in order to enforce appellate laws by which firms' monopolistic behaviour could be identified and corrected.

Mujib Bahini

A pro-**Mujibur Rahman** guerrilla organization which was formed during the **Bangladesh Liberation War** and recruited its personnel primarily from the **Awami League (AL)**. Trained and equipped by India, the *c.* 5,000 fighters of Mujib Bahini played an essential part in achieving independence, not only through arms, but also by playing a significant role in organizing uprisings in 1969. In addition, it actively supported the mass movement sparked off by the 11-point programme. Many members later joined the **Rakkhi Bahini**, a post-independence formation.

Mukti Bahini

The Mukti Bahini, or freedom force, trained and equipped by India, succeeded the Mukti Fauj which fought for the liberation of Bangladesh (East Pakistan) from West Pakistani forces. This force was composed of two major components, Bengali personnel serving in the regular units of the Pakistan armed forces, such as the East Bengal Regiment or the East Pakistan Police (also called Niomita Bahini, regular forces), and civilians, especially students, workers, and peasants (known as Gono Bahini, irregular forces). Together with the **Mujib Bahini** and the Shramik League, it was the major force waging the armed independence struggle. As such, its members have been critical of the post-independence formation of paramilitary forces attached to political parties, which have resulted in the fragmentation of the military. However, despite the fact that many of them were incorporated into the regular military, some members chose to join the **Rakkhi Bahini.**

Muluki Ain

Introduced in 1854 as a legal code, the *Muluki Ain* classified the population of Nepal into a five-tier caste hierarchy. Amended several times, it was completely revised in 1963, eliminating differentiated punishment according to caste and lifting the ban on inter-caste marriage. A uniform family law, applicable to all religious communities, was integrated into the *Muluki Ain*. Where the code is lacking, the custom of the particular community applies. Nevertheless, Article 4 (1) of the Constitution, while conceding Nepal to be a multi-ethnic, multi-lingual state, in the same sentence defines the country as a Hindu kingdom.

Mumbai

Formerly known as Bombay, Mumbai is India's largest city, with a population of more than 13m. Located on the west coast in the state of **Maharashtra**, Mumbai is the state's capital and the country's financial centre, home to the **Bombay Stock Exchange** and the **Reserve Bank of India**.

The growth of Mumbai draws upon the legacy of its commercial past. The city's deep harbour brought the Dutch and the East India Company in the 16th and 17th centuries and under British colonial rule it developed into one of the largest Arabian Sea ports, serving the world cotton trade. Local Parsi and Gujarati business families propelled the city's and the country's industrial development in the 19th century through textile mills and steel manufacturing.

Today Mumbai is the headquarters for some of India's leading companies, including Reliance (*see* **Ambani**, Dhirubhai) and **Tata Group**. Mumbai contributes more than 40% of India's foreign trade and has thriving banking, manufacturing and services sectors as well as being the base for an international Hindi film industry known as 'Bollywood'. Built on seven different islands, Mumbai suffers from housing shortages, chronic overcrowding and hugely inflated real estate prices. A vast majority of the city's population lives in slums, many being employed in the domestic and informal sector and contributing 25%–40% of Mumbai's total output.

Musharraf, Gen. Pervez

Born on 11 August 1943 in **Delhi**, Musharraf began his military career in 1964. He fought in the 1965 war against India, receiving an award for gallantry as well as participating in the 1971 war against India as company commander in a commando battalion. He was promoted to the rank of major-general on 15 January 1991, becoming lieutenant-general on 21 October 1995. On 7 October 1998 Pervez Musharraf was appointed as general and chief of army staff, leading Pakistan's armed forces through the **Kargil Conflict** between India and Pakistan in May–July 1999.

Gen. Musharraf became the Chief Executive of Pakistan after a bloodless *coup d'état* on 12 October 1999 when he took over executive powers from the then Prime Minister, Nawaz **Sharif**, who was subsequently exiled to Saudi Arabia. Musharraf was sworn in as the President of Pakistan on 20 June 2001 and his position as head of state was endorsed by a referendum on 30 April 2002. After general elections in October 2002, the National Assembly was paralysed by the opposition, which refused to support Musharraf's constitutional amendments, including the Legal Framework Order giving the general the power to sack the Prime Minister, dissolve parliament and recognizing him as both head of the army and head of state.

A deal in December 2003 with the religious **Muttahida Majlis-e-Amal (MMA)** party, in which Musharraf agreed to leave the army by January 2005, enabled pro-Musharraf legislators to pass the Seventeenth Amendment which, most importantly, retroactively legalized Musharraf's 1999 coup. In January 2004 Musharraf won a vote of confidence and was 'deemed to be elected' to the office of President until October 2007, in addition to his position as head of the army.

Muslim League – *see* Pakistan Muslim League (PML)

Muslim Women (Protection of Rights on Divorce) Bill (India)

Under Prime Minister Rajiv Gandhi, the Indian parliament passed the Muslim Women (Protection of Rights on Divorce) Bill in May 1986. This legislation removed divorced Muslim women from the purview of Section 125 of the Indian Criminal Code, placing them under the exclusive jurisdiction of Muslim Personal Law (*Shari'a* Law). The adoption of the law was accompanied by sharp protests, in particular from women's organizations.

Muttahida Majlis-e-Amal (MMA)

The Muttahida Majlis-e-Amal (MMA) is an alliance of four powerful religious parties in Pakistan: Jamaat-i Islami (JI), **Jamiat i Ulema-i-Islam (F)**, **Jamiat-i-Ulema-i-Islam (S)** and **Jamiat-i-Ulema-i-Pakistan (N)**, which achieved an unexpected electoral victory in the general elections of 2002. The leader of the opposition in the Lower House is a member, and the MMA controls the provincial government in the **North West Frontier Province**. It also forms part of a coalition government in **Balochistan** province. The MMA has 67 seats in the 342-seat National Assembly, of which one-third are held by the JI. The MMA is headed by Maulana Shah Ahmed Noorani, the leader of Jamiat-i-Ulema-i-Pakistan. The party is the political representative of the Barelvi school of Sunni Muslims. The main objective of the MMA is to enforce the implementation of *Shari'a* law. It is strongly opposed to the US campaign against international terrorism in neighbouring Afghanistan and the alliance includes both factions of the pro-Taliban Jamiat Ulema-e-Islam, representing the Deobandi school, Prof. Sajid Mir's Jamiat-e-Ahle Hadith and Allama Sajid Naqvi's outlawed Shi'a group, Tehrik-e-Jafria, which in its present incarnation is known as Pakistan Islami Tehrik.

Muttahida Qaumi Movement (MQM)

Known as the Muhajir Qaumi Movement until 1997, Muttahida Qaumi Movement (MQM) is a political party in Pakistan that originally represented the urban, Urdu-speaking Muhajir population in the province of **Sind**. Initially a student movement, the MQM sought to protest at perceived discrimination against the Muhajir community, particularly following the introduction of a quota system that introduced reservations for university admissions and government posts, favouring Sindi speakers. The MQM successfully contested the general elections of 1988 but factionalism, suppression of the MQM and its choice of violent methods eclipsed the party in the 1990s. It re-emerged in the 2002 national elections, forming the largest bloc in the 167-seat local assembly and becoming an ally of President **Musharraf** in the federal government. Today the party claims to fight against all forms of religious extremism and discrimination. Its leader, Altaf Husain, is known for his strong speeches against Muslim fundamentalism.

N

Naga National Council (NNC)

The Naga National Council (NNC), a political organization, was formed in 1946 with the aim of uniting the Naga people under one administrative unit. In June 1947 the NNC, under the leadership of A. Z. Phizo, announced that the Naga Hills would cease to be part of India with the departure of the British, declaring independence on the eve of India's independence in August 1947. In 1951 the Nagas voted for independence in a plebiscite, boycotting general elections of the same year, with the NNC gradually shifting towards an armed confrontation with the military forces that had been deployed. On 22 March 1956 the NNC announced its own government, the federal government of Nagaland. Finally, in 1975, the government of India and the NNC signed the Shillong Accord which effected a cease-fire. Those who rejected the accord to resume armed activism broke away to form the **National Socialist Council of Nagaland**. (*See* **North East India**.)

Nagaland People's Front (NPF)

The Nagaland People's Front (NPF) is a regional political party in India with a stronghold in the north-east Indian state of Nagaland (*see* **North East India**). One of the party's main objectives is the peaceful resolution of the Indo-Naga political issue and to maintain the unity and integrity of the Naga people. As an ally of the **Bharatiya Janata Party (BJP)** it was part of the **National Democratic Alliance (NDA)** and, together with the BJP, currently leads the state government. In the 2004 **Lok Sabha** election it won one seat. In 2004 it merged with the Nagaland Democratic Party.

Namgyal, Ngawang

Ngawang Namgyal (1594–1651) is considered to be the founder of the modern state of Bhutan. As a Tibetan native, he came to the country in 1616, unifying it under a single authority for the first time. In addition, he strengthened the **Drukpa** *school* and established a dual system of governance, called the *Chhoesi*. He appointed himself as Shabdrung, the spiritual and temporal head of the state, and ruled Bhutan for 35 years. His political system lasted until 1907, when a monarchical system was introduced.

Narayan, Jayaprakash/J. P. Movement

A prominent socialist leader in the Indian movement against British rule and in post-independence politics, J. P. Narayan, popularly known as J. P., was born in the United Provinces (now **Uttar Pradesh**) in 1902. Educated in the USA, J. P. founded the Congress Socialist Party in 1934. Declining to join **Nehru**'s Cabinet in 1952, J. P. refrained from active party politics to dedicate his life to Vinobha Bhave's Sarvodaya and Bhoodan Movements to redistribute land to the landless in India's villages, emphasizing Gandhian principles of personal service, non-violence, and village-centred economic decentralization. J. P. re-entered the limelight in 1973 when he opposed Indira **Gandhi** and her increasingly authoritarian style of politics. Narayan launched the 'J. P. Movement' under his own leadership in 1974, as a protest against increasing inflation, corruption and unemployment. The movement gained national prominence. The People's Union for Civil Liberties and Democratic Rights, formed on his initiative, sought to unite people from various political parties for the defence of human rights. During the emergency regime from 1975 until 1977, the movement became an anti-emergency campaign and J. P. was arrested. In 1977, released from prison, he successfully united the opposition parties and formed the Janata Party coalition, which, in the 1977 elections, for the first time in Indian history defeated the **Congress** party, restoring democratic rule. Once again J. P. declined to lead the new government or to accept an official post, proposing instead Morarji Desai who became India's first non-Congress Prime Minister. But the Janata Party soon lost momentum in factionalism and divisive power politics. Disillusioned, Narayan died in 1979 at the age of 77.

Narmada Dam

India's most controversial dam project, first envisaged in the 1940s by Prime Minister Jawaharlal **Nehru**, but initiated only in 1979 when numerous dams were planned to control the immense Naramada river system running through the states of **Madhya Pradesh**, **Maharashtra** and **Gujarat**. The Narmada Bachao Andolan (Save the Narmada Movement), initiated in the mid-1980s, drew attention to the displacement of more than 200,000 people and the environmental damage that the project would cause, ultimately leading to the withdrawal of World Bank support in 1993. The movement petitioned the Supreme Court, gaining media attention and political importance, particularly through the efforts of renowned activists such as Medha Patkar, who almost died during a 22-day hunger strike in 1991. In 2000 the Supreme Court allowed resumption of construction, imposing some restrictions on the height of the dam.

Nasir, Ibrahim Amir

Ibrahim Nasir, born in 1926, was a leading Maldivian politician, who guided the country as Prime Minister (from 1954) under the last Sultan, Muhammad Fareed **Didi**, to independence, and who dominated the political landscape as President of the second republic after he abolished the sultanate. In 1975, amid rumours of an imminent coup, Nasir invoked emergency rule, dismissed the Prime Minister and disposed of the office of Prime Minister altogether. In the wake of growing political instability, Nasir resigned and, having been charged with government mismanagement, fled to Singapore. He was succeeded by Maumoon Abdul **Gayoom**, who has served as President since 1978. Nasir's presidency is criticized by some observers for its authoritarian style, political repression and misuse of office. In July 1990, despite being accused of involvement in the 1988 *coup d'état* against Gayoom, he was granted a presidential pardon in recognition of his role in the struggle for Maldivian independence.

National Awami Party (NAP)/National Awami Party—Bhasani (NAP—B)

Founded in July 1957 under the leadership of Maulana Abdul Hamid Khan **Bhasani**, president of the (Pakistan) **Awami League (AL)**, the NAP was a leftist faction which split from the AL owing to differences with H. S. Suhawardy, then Prime Minister of Pakistan. The main issue of contention was foreign policy, which Bhasani believed needed to be pursued without being allied to a superpower bloc. However, soon after entering the political arena, increasing tension among the NAP leaders led to a spilt into a pro-Chinese (Maulana Bhasani) and a pro-Moscow (Khan Abdul Wali Khan and Prof. Muzaffar Ahmad) faction in the mid-1960s. After independence, the two factions continued to exist as two separate parties, known as NAP—B (Bhasani) and NAP (Muzaffar). NAP—B contested the first general elections of Bangladesh in 1973 but was unable to secure a seat. It led numerous movements, including one against the India-Bangladesh Friendship Treaty signed on 16 May 1974. After Bhasani resigned in 1974, the party split into several competing factions and splinter groups.

National Bhikku Front (NBF)

The National Bhikku Front (NBF) is a Sinhala nationalist organization of monks with organizational structures in all of the Sinhala majority districts of Sri Lanka. Among other things, the NBF advocates banning NGOs that engage in 'anti-Buddhist activities' and an anti-conversion act. In 2005 the NBF gained international exposure because of its opposition to the Post-Tsunami Operational Management Structure (P-TOMS), which aimed at creating a structure to jointly manage aid, between the Sri Lankan government and the **Liberation Tigers of Tamil Eelam**. (*See* **Buddhist Movement**.)

National Democratic Alliance (NDA)

The National Democratic Alliance (NDA), the ruling coalition in India in 1999–2004, became the official opposition in the parliament after its defeat in the general elections of May 2004. It is a loose and inclusive coalition led by Atal Behari **Vajpayee (Bharatiya Janata Party—BJP)** and includes regional parties such as the **Shiv Sena**, Indian National Lok Dal (INLD), Arunachal Congress (AC), Jantrantrik Bahujan Samaj Party, Samata Party, **Biju Janata Dal (BJD)**, **Akali Dal** and Loktrantik Congress. The political prospects of this coalition have been limited by differences among the partners. During the last years of its tenure in power some parties withdrew from the NDA, for example, on 20 December 2003, the **Dravida Munnetra Kazhagam (DMK)** and, on 12 January 2004, the **Pattali Makkal Katchi (PMK)**, both of which subsequently allied themselves with the **Congress**. Altogether the BJP lost seven allies in the run-up to the election. Confident that it would win, the government had called early elections and launched an 'India Shining' campaign that showcased economic achievements. However, the campaign backfired, enabling opposition parties to appeal to those left out of India's boom and to portray the BJP as the party of the urban middle class. While the BJP did not perform as well as expected, its remaining allies fared even worse.

National Democratic Front of Bodoland (NDFB)

The National Democratic Front of Bodoland (NDFB) was formed in 1988 with the aim of securing an independent Bodoland in the areas north of the river Brahmaputra, in the state of Assam (*see* **North East India**). The Indian government's military operations against the movement forced the NDFB, together with the **United Liberation Front of Assam (ULFA)** with which it has collaborated, to set up camps in neighbouring Bhutan. In December 2003 Bhutan finally agreed to joint military action with the Indian army to flush out insurgents from its territory. In May 2005 the NDFB signed a cease-fire with the Indian government, the first in almost two decades of insurgency.

National Liberation Front of Tripura (NLFT)

The National Liberation Front of Tripura (NLFT) is an active militant group, operating in **North East India**. Founded in 1989 with the objective of forming an independent state of Tripura, the group was banned in April 1997 under the Unlawful Activities (Prevention) Act 1967 and the Prevention of Terrorism Act 2002, following its engagement in terrorist and subversive activities. The NLFT shifted its headquarters to Bangladesh, as well as setting up camps in Myanmar and Bhutan.

National Loktantrik Party (NLP, National Democratic Party)

The National Loktantrik Party (NLP) is a regional political party in India. Its main support base is among the Muslim community in **Uttar Pradesh**, on which the party has a growing influence. The party was founded by Dr Masood Ahmed, a former education minister in the state, to launch a new political forum representing Muslim interests which, in his view, were no longer guaranteed by his former political party, the **Bahajan Samaj Party (BSP)**. The main political aim of the NLP is to oppose politics which it perceives as anti-Muslim, such as the Religious Places Bill introduced by the **Bharatiya Janata Party (BJP)**. The NLP won one seat in the 2004 **Lok Sabha** elections.

National Security Services (NSS)

Until recently, the National Security Services (NSS) of the Maldives operated as the police and army services. Founded in 1892 by Ibrahim **Nasir**, the National Security Guard was upgraded as well as renamed in 1978 by **Gayoom**, the current commander-in-chief. Nevertheless, its organizational outlook remains unchanged as that of a paramilitary force divided into sections rather than one of an army with regular military formations. Following the attempted *coup d'état* of 1988, which was supported by external forces, the government took measures to strengthen and expand the NSS, which currently has around 3,500 personnel (compared with approximately 1,000 in the 1980s). Today, after an organizational spin-off through the Maldivian Police Services (MPS) functioning as military forces of the country, its main duty is to guarantee the country's external security. Equipped with some light armoured vehicles and naval capabilities, it performs army and maritime duties as well as intelligence-gathering. However, the NSS retains a crucial role in maintaining internal law and order and has been involved, on various occasions, in domestic conflicts, during which it has sometimes been accused of human rights violations.

National Socialist Council of Nagaland (NSCN)

The National Socialist Council of Nagaland (NSCN) was established on 31 January 1980 and operates as an active militant group in **North East India**. Its main objective is to establish a Peoples's Republic of Nagaland (Nagalim or Greater Nagaland) based on Mao Zedong's ideology and advocating armed struggle. Internal differences with regard to commencing a dialogue with the Indian government caused the council to split into two factions in 1988. Cross-border links have reportedly been established in neighbouring countries.

National Stock Exchange (NSE)

The National Stock Exchange (NSE) is one of India's two stock exchanges—the other is the **Bombay Stock Exchange (BSE)**. Located in **Mumbai**, the NSE was incorporated in 1992. Recognition as a stock market followed in 1993. Today the NSE is one of the largest and most advanced in India, its network covering more than 40 cities across the country. The NSE was set up to ensure equal access to the capital market to investors from all over the country. NSE is supported by leading financial institutions at the behest of the government of India. The main index of the NSE is the S&P CNX Nifty, a diversified blue-chip index comprising 50 stocks that represent 25 sectors of the economy. To be included in the index a company should have a market capitalization of at least US $113m.

National Unity Alliance (NUA)

Launched in 1986 by H. M. Ashraff, who also founded the **Sri Lanka Muslim Congress (SLMC)**, the National Unity Alliance (NUA) was not meant to be a political rival to the SLMC. However, since Ashraff's death in 2000, the NUA has become more independent. As the two major Muslim parties in Sri Lankan politics, the SLMC and NUA have supported opposite camps, with the SLMC in the opposition and the NUA in the ruling **United People's Freedom Alliance** coalition.

National Women Association of Bhutan (NWAB)

The National Women's Association of Bhutan (NWAB) was established in April 1981 by the government to encourage women's participation in the implementation of development programmes and to improve their socio-economic status, particularly in rural areas. First created as an NGO, it operated from 1985 until 1991 as a non-ministerial department, but has reverted in recent years to the status of NGO.

Nationalist Congress Party (NCP)

India's Nationalist Congress Party (NCP) is a national political party and an important player in the state of **Maharashtra**. The NCP was founded in 1999, when Sharad Pawar, P. A. Sangma and Tariq Anwar were expelled from the **Indian National Congress (INC)** after challenging Sonia **Gandhi**'s leadership on the grounds of her foreign origin. Disagreement within the NCP's leadership over whether to align with the Congress party in 2004 led to a split and under Sharad Pawar the NCP contested the 2004 **Lok Sabha** elections as part of the **United Progressive Alliance (UPA)**, winning nine seats.

Naxalite Movement

The term 'Naxalites' or 'Naxals' refers to different Indian groups using or advocating violent methods of protest on behalf of landless labourers and tribal people against landlords and others in the name of creating a classless society. Based on Mao Zedong's ideology of revolution, Naxalite activities started in 1967 when a peasant uprising in the Naxalbari district of the Himalayan foothills was suppressed by the central government and the **Communist Party of India—Marxist**-led government of **West Bengal**. This later led to the foundation of the political arm of the Naxalites, the Communist Party of India—Marxist-Leninist. The movement later split into several groups as it spread to various parts of India and has created a belt stretching from Nepal to **Kerala**.

Nehru-Gandhi Family

The Nehru-Gandhi family has dominated the Indian political arena since independence in 1947. Motilal Nehru (1861–1931), a prominent lawyer, nationalist leader and freedom fighter during British colonial rule, twice served as president of the **Congress** party. Motilal's daughter, Vijayalaxmi Pandit, was India's ambassador to the United Nations in the 1950s. His son, Jawaharlal **Nehru**, became India's first Prime Minister and occupied this position until his death in 1964. However, the Nehru 'dynasty' continued to dominate Indian politics through his daughter, **Indira Gandhi** (no family ties to Mohandas Karamchand **Gandhi**), who became Prime Minister in 1966. One of her sons, Sanjay Gandhi (his wife Maneka Gandhi and son Varun Gandhi are both members of the **Bharatiya Janata Party**), died in a plane crash in 1980 and Indira Gandhi was assassinated in 1984. Her elder son, Rajiv Gandhi, succeeded her as leader of the Congress party and was India's Prime Minister in 1984–89. His wife, Sonia **Gandhi**, is president of the Congress and was leader of the opposition in 1999–2004. Her children, Priyanka and Rahul Gandhi, are also engaged in politics.

Nehru, Jawaharlal

First Prime Minister of independent India (1947–64). Together with *Mahatma* **Gandhi**, Jawaharlal Nehru is regarded as a founding father of the nation. He is credited with having provided the political stability necessary for a transition from colonial rule to democracy. His vision for a modern India rested upon three main pillars: secular democracy, economic policies that were socialist in leaning and a foreign policy based upon non-alignment. Jawaharlal Nehru's background was a privileged one. Born in 1889 to Motilal Nehru, a successful and prominent lawyer, Nehru was sent to England for his studies. During his university days he came into contact with radical European thinking as well as Indian nationalism. Qualified as a lawyer, Nehru returned to India in 1912 and quickly immersed himself in the freedom struggle. Over the next 30 years Nehru rose within **Congress**, assuming the presidency for the first time in 1929 and ultimately taking over the mantle of Mahatma Gandhi as the leader of the Indian nation upon Gandhi's assassination. Imprisoned on several occasions, Nehru spent this time turning his ideas into books and writing his autobiography. He was personally involved in the negotiations with

Britain after the Second World War and obstinacy on the part of Nehru and the Muslim League's Muhammad Ali **Jinnah** is regarded as one of the factors that made **Partition** inevitable. Nehru's preference for economic planning and large-scale projects contrasted with Gandhi's emphasis on the village community and industry. Under his leadership, three five-year plans were launched and a centralized political structure encouraged. The Hindu Marriage Act 1955 and Hindu Succession Act 1956 were regarded as important steps towards a modern India and Nehru laboured hard against the various divisive forces of regionalism, linguistic, caste and communal demands. Often referred to as the architect of Indian foreign policy, Nehru was a co-founder of the Non-Aligned Movement (NAM) and an active campaigner for arms control and peace. Indian troops were committed to UN operations and Nehru offered his personal offices for mediation during the crises in Korea and Indo-China in the early 1950s. During the Cold War non-alignment was meant to provide India with greater choices and flexibility in foreign policy and economic development but the invasion by China in 1962 raised heavy criticism of Nehru's policies. Two key foreign policy decisions taken by Nehru have had particular long-lasting relevance. The first war with Pakistan, in 1947–48, led to Nehru's appeal to the UN. This internationalization of the Kashmir question and Nehru's agreement to a plebiscite laid the foundations for an ongoing problem. The second decision was to keep India within the Commonwealth on the legal proviso that the republic of India would hold only symbolic allegiance to the British crown. This arrangement enabled numerous others to join. When Nehru died in 1964 Lal Bahadur Shastri suceeded him and after his death in 1966 Nehru's daughter, Indira **Gandhi**, became Prime Minister.

Nepal, Kingdom of

The land-locked Himalayan kingdom of Nepal is bounded by the Tibetan region of China to the north and India to the east, west and south. For administrative purposes Nepal is divided into 14 zones (*anchal*). Area: 140,800 sq km; capital: Kathmandu; population: 2.77m. (2005 estimate), comprising (broadly) ethnic Indo-Nepalese, Tibeto-Nepalese, indigenous Nepalese; national language: Nepali; religion: Hindu (80.6%), Buddhist (10.7%), Muslim (4.2%), Kirat (an indigenous religion, 3.6%), Christian (0.5%), other (0.4%) (2001 census).

Nepal is a constitutional monarchy, with executive powers vested in the King and a 60-member Council of Ministers, responsible for the day-to-day administration of the country. The 1990 Constitution established a bicameral legislature, comprising a 205-seat house of representatives (*Pratinidhi Sabha*) and a 60-seat National Assembly (*Rashtriya Sabha*). The former is directly elected by popular vote and serves a five-year term, the latter by members of the house of representatives for a six-year term. According to the Constitution, the leader of the majority party in parliament is appointed by the King as Prime Minister. As the result of popular protests, democratic politics emerged in Nepal with the general elections of May

1991, although its factionalized character has resulted in frequent changes of government. In the wake of the murder of King **Birendra**, his wife and seven other members of the royal family in June 2001, the King's brother **Gyanendra** ascended to the throne. King Gyanendra has since been confronted with the challenge of the long-standing Maoist rebellion against the government. Following his declaration of emergency in 2001 and subsequent assumption of executive power in 2002, the country is currently governed by the King and his appointed Cabinet, until elections can be held at some unspecified future date.

History: The first known settlers in Nepal's recorded history were the Kiratis, whose rule began around 700 BC. Around the 6th century BC, the founder of Buddhism, Gautama Siddharta, was born in southern Nepal, yet by 200 AD Buddhism had dwindled and Hinduism was introduced by the Licchavis, invaders from northern India, who overthrew the last Kirati King. The ensuing political system, established in the Kathmandu Valley, did not extend its control over all the hill regions of Nepal, despite its otherwise coherent nature. This pattern of rule of high-caste Hindu Kings, unable to cast their influence over the largely tribal communities in the sub-Himalayan region, continued, and by 800 AD Nepal was composed of numerous ethnic communities, many of which had migrated from Tibet, China, South-East Asia and north-east India. As the Licchavi era came to an end, the indigenous Newar community in the Kathmandu Valley achieved prominence and established a trade route passing via Nepal from India to Tibet. This opened up the valley to influence from south and central Asia and was a key factor in its development into an intellectual and commercial centre.

Until the 14th century the Valley of Nepal was repeatedly invaded from India. The concurrent Muslim invasions of India resulted in the flight of many high-caste Hindu families to western hill stations of Nepal and, by extension, a significant restructuring of the political system. Most of the western hill areas came under the social and political influence of this Hindu élite, although traditional tribal practices continued. The advent of the Malla dynasty, founded by Jaya Sthithi Malla, a southern Indian, signified the extension of rule beyond the Valley. In 1488 the kingdom was divided between his four heirs into the independent city states of Kathmandu, Bhatgaon, Patan and Banepa, and remained unchanged until the Gurkha conquest of the 18th century.

The Shah dynasty emerged as rulers in Gurkha, the most easterly principality of Nepal, in the mid-18th century. Prithvinarayan Shah (1730–75), considered the founder of modern Nepal, conquered the Kathmandu Valley and with it the India-Kathmandu-Tibet trade route, refusing British traders entry into Kathmandu. The areas under his control by 1767 provided the territorial identity of the country as it is recognized today.

After the Second World War the Ranas, heriditary Prime Ministers to the nominal rulers of the Shah Dynasty, under pressure from newly independent India, agreed to renegotiate power in 1951. With support from India and the **Nepali Congress (NC)**, the monarch, King **Tribhuvan**, was reinstated and an interim government established. The Cabinet comprised both members of the **Rana family** and popular representatives. The end of Rana domination was thus coupled with the first steps towards democracy.

King Tribhuvan's heir, **Mahendra** Bir Bikran Shah Dev, came to power in 1955. Despite his aversion to parliamentary democracy, a constitution was promulgated under his rule in 1959, providing for a bicameral government. The first general elections, following a week later, were won by the NC, and Bisweswor Prasad **Koirala** was appointed as Prime Minister. Sovereignty remained, however, with the King, who effectively had power of veto over all legislative and constitutional amendments.

On 15 December 1960, amid growing tensions between himself and Koirala, King Mahendra staged a coup, imprisoning the Prime Minister and many senior leaders of the NC. He suspended constitutional rights, dissolved parliament and, in 1961, banned political parties. A party-less ***Panchayat* system**, comprising a four-tier administrative structure that spanned from the village to the national level, was introduced in 1961, followed by a new constitution in 1962. Although decentralized in theory, the *Panchayat* system proved centralized and authoritarian. The Prime Minister and Cabinet, as well as a large proportion of the National Assembly, were appointed by the King.

King Mahendra's successor and son, Birendra Bir Bikram, was formally crowned in 1975. Renewed demand for political change led to a national referendum in May 1980 on the question of retaining the *Panchayat* system. The system won the support of 54.8% of voters, yet in the late 1980s, various campaigns were mounted by banned political parties with the aim of restoring a multi-party parliamentary system. In the face of economic difficulties, deteriorating Indo-Nepalese relations, and internal weaknesses in the *Panchayat* system, political instability in Nepal had by 1989 reached a crescendo. A popular uprising, the pro-democracy **Jana Andolan**, under a co-ordination committee consisting of the NC and the **United Left Front (ULF)**, brought the regime to a collapse. In April 1990 the movement had attracted mass support, and following country-wide demonstrations and riots the King conceded to end the 30-year ban on political parties, dissolve the *Panchayat* system, and to appoint an interim government.

The 1990 Constitution that ensued was, in general, democratic. Sovereignty was invested in the people and the King's role reduced to that of a constitutional monarch with, however, some emergency powers. Provision was made in the Constitution for a bicameral legislature, comprising a 205-seat house of representatives and a 60-seat National Assembly. The first general election for three decades, held on 12 May 1991, resulted in a comfortable majority for the NC, with the **Communist Party of Nepal (CPN**, otherwise known as Unified Marxist-Leninist—UML) winning the second largest majority. G. P. **Koirala** became Prime Minister, but resigned in July 1994. The subsequent dissolution of parliament by the King was followed by new elections which resulted in a majority for the CPN—UML. The communist government was dissolved by parliament in 1996, and Sher

Bahadur Deuba of the NC was subsequently appointed by the King as Prime Minister. In the same year the Nepal Communist Party—Maoist (NCP—M), a radical left-wing party, launched a **People's War** aimed at overthrowing the government, abolishing the monarchy and establishing a people's republic. Although initially limited to remote mountain regions, by the late 1990s violence resulting from the Maoist insurgency had spread to more than half of the country. Political stability remained out of reach, with factionalized politics and numerous party splits resulting in a succession of prime ministerial resignations and appointments, and, by extension, frequent changes of government. Instability was further exacerbated by a struggling economy, large-scale unemployment and illiteracy, and a rapidly expanding, ethnically and religiously fragmented population.

In June 2001 King Birendra and most of his family, including his wife, Queen Aiswarya, were fatally shot by eldest son and heir, Prince Dipendra, in an apparent murder-suicide. Official reports claimed that Dipendra had killed his family members in a drunken rage. Comatose following the injuries he himself sustained during the shooting, he was declared King on 2 June, but died soon after. King Birendra's brother, Prince Gyanendra Bir Bikram Shah, subsequently ascended the throne, on 4 June 2001. Civil unrest erupted again in Kathmandu, coupled with an intensification of the Maoist insurgency. Prime Minister G. P. Koirala, who intermittently served in office for much of the 1990s, was widely criticized for incompetence in dealing with the Maoist rebels, for failure to afford protection to the royal family, and for involvement in a bribery scandal involving the national airline. He resigned in July 2001. Sher Bahadur Deuba, a former Prime Minister, was selected by the ruling NCP to head Nepal's 11th government in 11 years.

The uncertainty of Nepal's political situation intensified when King Gyanendra declared a state of emergency in November 2001. He later dismissed the Prime Minister and his Cabinet in October 2002 when, in the face of the continuing Maoist insurgency, their decision to dissolve parliament led to an inability to hold elections. Thereafter King Gyanendra appointed his own Cabinet, subsequently dissolved it, and reappointed a new Cabinet in 2003. Since taking over executive power in 2002, King Gyanendra has sidelined all political parties, ignored their criticism, and attempted to consolidate royal power.

Recent developments: The collapse of the most recent cease-fire with the Maoist insurgents in August 2003 sparked renewed fighting and bomb blasts in Kathmandu. A week-long blockade of Kathmandu in August 2004 by the Maoist rebels, preventing supplies from reaching the city, was repeated again in December, increasing political instability. Frequent changes in government have continued, and on 1 February 2005 King Gyanendra again dismissed the Prime Minister and his government, declared a state of emergency, and reassumed executive power. The emergency was lifted on 30 April, shortly before the three-month due-date of expiry prescribed by the Constitution, a move welcomed by the Indian government, which, in addition to the USA and Britain, had suspended arms supplies to Nepal. The triangle of tensions between Maoist insurgents, the major political parties, and the monarchy—struggling for the cited goals of a communist state, the re-establishment of democratic elections, and an end to the Maoist insurgency respectively—appear no nearer to a resolution.

Nepal, Political Development

Although Nepal has twice attempted to introduce a democratic political system, it has been repeatedly interrupted in favour of absolute monarchical rule. Since 1951, when the century-old family rule under the Ranas came to an end, Nepal has experienced four monarchs, each of whom has assertively tried to determine the country's political development. As a result, institutions have failed to take root and core issues remain unaddressed. In 1959 general elections were held, but 18 months later King **Mahendra** dismissed the government, dissolved the parliament and banned political parties. A party-less ***Panchayat* system** followed for the next 30 years, during which the state attempted to homogenize the population by centralizing authority and power, declaring Nepali the national language and Nepal a Hindu state. The restoration of multi-party democracy in 1990 was the result of a popular movement (**Jana Andolan**). Between 1990 and 2002 three parliamentary elections were held, governments falling due to inter-party feuds, increasing Maoist violence and, finally, the intervention of the King, who, after declaring emergency rule, indefinitely postponed elections in 2002. Nevertheless, during this period the government has tried to tackle issues of inclusion, providing reservations for women in local government bodies. The Constitution recognizes Nepal to be a multi-ethnic state and attempts have been made to decentralize power.

Constitution: None of Nepal's three constitutions have been the product of an elected constituent assembly. The so-called Delhi compromise of January 1951 had agreed that general elections for a constituent assembly had to take place within two years. This promise was soon dismissed by King **Tribhuvan** and by the time a constitution was introduced in 1959 it had lost much of the original democratic aspect that had been envisioned. All powers remained in the hands of the King, who was the originator of the 1959 Constitution. The following King, Mahendra, used the democratic institutions of the Constitution at his own discretion until he introduced a new constitution in 1962 that established the *Panchayat* system.

The 1990 Constitution established a bicameral legislature and multi-party democracy based on the Westminster parliamentary system. The King is a symbolic head of state and is meant to function as a constitutional monarch, with no real governing power, although he retained the title of supreme commander-in-chief of the army as well as broad emergency powers and control over palace-related issues, including succession. Under Article 4 Nepal is defined as a Hindu kingdom, although no definition of a state religion is given. Nepali, the mother tongue of 48% of the population according to the 2001 census, is also the official language, creating problems for other mother-tongue speakers in the education system, administration and law courts.

Monarchy (Constitutional): Nepal is the world's only officially Hindu kingdom, where a large number of the population considers the King to be an incarnation of Lord Vishnu, one of Hinduism's three supreme gods. Following the end of Rana rule in 1951 the country's first constitution of 1959 ushered in a system where sovereignty was in the hands of the King and the people were his 'subjects'. The King retained enormous executive, legislative and judicial powers which he could exercise at his discretion and various passages in the Constitution allowed him to evade the recommendations of parliament or the Prime Minister. However, in December 1960 King Mahendra invoked emergency powers to dissolve the **Nepali Congress** government and by 1962 introduced a new Constitution under which the King had absolute power. The restoration of democracy in 1990 established the King as the supreme commander of the armed forces but not as the sole source of authority. In a major break with the past the 1990 Constitution vested sovereignty in the people of Nepal not in the King. The King, however, retains formidable emergency powers, although unlike under the 1959 Constitution he was bound to follow the recommendations of the Prime Minister. Article 115 grants the King the unilateral right to proclaim a state of emergency in the event of a 'grave crisis' which must be submitted to the lower house of parliament within three months for approval by a two-thirds' majority. Since 2002 King **Gyanendra** has gradually wrested power, provoking demands not only from Maoist insurgents but also from political parties for an end to the system of monarchy. On 22 November 2005 the seven-party-alliance and the **Communist Party of Nepal—Maoist** formally joined hands and started a common campaign for the abolition of the monarchy and the introduction of a new constitution through an elected constituent assembly.

Executive: The executive powers of the Kingdom of Nepal are vested in the King and the Council of Ministers. The Council of Ministers is composed of a Prime Minister and other ministers. Constitutionally, all official duties undertaken by the King may only be executed on the advice of or with the consent of the Council of Ministers, as announced by the Prime Minister. The Council of Ministers is responsible for directing, controlling and regulating the general administration of the country. The King appoints the leader of the majority party in the house of representatives as Prime Minister, who then appoints the Council of Ministers to serve under his chairmanship. The number of ministers serving varies according to need and it is not unusual for the Prime Minister to assume personal responsibilities for several ministries. Each minister is individually responsible for his respective ministry, and the Council of Ministers is collectively answerable to the house of representatives. Following King Gyanendra's dissolution of the government in 2002, the Council has consisted of members selected by the King rather than according to the Constitution. The current Prime Minister was appointed as the King's own nominee in June 2004. His Majesty King Gyanendra Bir Bikram Shah Dev has been head of state since 4 June 2001. The council of ministers is headed by King Gyanendra himself and mainly consists of leading figures from the former *Panchayat* system who did not join political parties after 1990.

Legislature: According to the 1990 Constitution, the bicameral legislature comprises the King and the two houses of parliament, the Rashtriya Sabha (National Assembly) and the Pratinidhi Sabha (house of representatives). The Rashtriya Sabha has 60 members who serve a six-year term of office and of whom 10 are nominated by the King, 35 (including at least three women) are elected by the Pratinidhi Sabha, and a further 15 are elected by an electoral college consisting of voters (all citizens aged 18 years and above) and the chairman and deputy chairman of village, town and district committees of Nepal's five development regions (three of each region). The Rashtriya Sabha is a permanent body and every two years one-third of its members must retire. The Pratinidhi Sabha has 205 directly elected members, serving a five-year term. Constitutionally, the King has the power to dissolve both houses at any time upon the recommendation of the Prime Minister, but new elections must take place within six months. Bills may be introduced in either house, except for finance bills which may only be introduced in the Pratinidhi Sabha. All bills must pass through both houses before receiving royal assent.

Elections/Electoral System: Nepal's first general elections occurred in 1959 under King Mahendra. The 1959 Constitution provided for a bicameral legislature, within which the 109 members of the house of representatives were to be directly elected according to a plurality system in single-member constituencies. However, on 15 December 1960 King Mahendra abolished the multi-party system and inaugurated the party-less *Panchayat* system. From 1962 until 1980 only indirect parliamentary elections were held. Under King Birendra a referendum was held in 1980 to choose between a return to the multi-party system or the continuation of the *Panchayat* system. The *Panchayat* system was confirmed but a third constitutional amendment allowed for direct elections to the national parliament and in May 1981 the first general elections since 1959 were held. Both parliaments of the 1980s had 140 members, 112 of whom were directly elected in single-member constituencies on the basis of adult suffrage, and 28 nominated by the King. The *Panchayat* system was abrogated before the 1991 elections, which were held on the basis of the 1990 Constitution that reintroduced multi-party democracy. Elections in 1994 and 1999 were held according to the 1990 electoral provisions. The *Pratinidhi Sabha*'s 205 members were directly elected, on the basis of universal adult suffrage for a term of five years. The *Rashtriya Sabha* (National Assembly) has 60 members whose tenure lasts for six years, with one-third of members' terms expiring every two years. Thirty-five, including at least three women, are elected by the *Pratinidhi Sabha* (house of representatives) by single-transferable vote and 15 (three from each of the five development regions) are elected by an electoral college. Ten other members are nominated by the King.

Poorly institutionalized parties and party infighting led to a hung parliament in 1994 and a minority government of the **Communist Party of Nepal—Unified Marxist-Leninist)**, followed by four short-termed coalition governments within three years. An anti-defection law in October 1997 attempted to counter the instability caused by frequent party defection. Winning little more than one-third of the votes, the National Congress gained an absolute majority of seats under the plurality system in the 1999 elections. Governmental instability continued, aggravated by the **People's War** launched by the Communist Party of Nepal—Maoist in 1996. Elections were scheduled for 13 November 2002, but in May King Gyanendra dissolved parliament on the grounds that it was incapable of dealing with the Maoist rebels. In 2004 King Gyanendra announced that parliamentary elections would be held within one year. These have yet to be held.

Political Organizations: Political parties were banned in Nepal in January 1961, and although widely tolerated from 1979 onwards, it was not until the democratic reforms of 1990 that they were allowed to operate and contest elections. Under the 1990 Constitution parties are required to register with the Election Commission. To attain official recognition, 5% of the party's candidates must be female, the party should not be oriented along ethnic or religious lines and a minimum of 3% of all votes cast must be obtained for election to the house of representatives. This in turn entitles the party to a single nation-wide symbol for the following elections.

Nepal's largest political parties have been the **Nepali Congress Party** and the Communist Party of Nepal—Unified Marxist Leninist. The internal organization of most political parties is characterized by a lack of democratic structures, the dominance of **Bahuns** in almost all parties, the defining importance of party leaders above party ideology and extremely powerful individuals often causing parties to split.

In February 2005 King Gyanendra suspended all parties, claiming they were not effectively addressing the civil conflict. However, the suspension's constitutionality is debated.

Social Movements: Nepal has experienced more political than strictly social movements. In 1950/51 and 1990 agitation led to a systemic change, in the former year bringing about the end of Rana rule. In 1990 the introduction of multi-party democracy after the Jana Andolan was the result. There are, of course, great differences between the two movements. The anti-Rana movement of 1950/51 was led by an élite of mainly high-caste Nepalis exiled in India, who used a partisan army, the Mukti Sena, against the Ranas. The 1990 democracy movement was co-ordinated by the Nepali Congress Party, a **United Left Front** and two human rights organizations, Forum for Protection of Human Rights and Human Rights Organization of Nepal, and had broad popular support in many urban centres as well as rural areas of the country. Unlike the 1950/51 movement, the 1990 campaign was peaceful.

However, the agitation in 1990 did not really usher in significant social change, partly due to the continuing dominance of the monarchy in Nepal's politics. Social movements have been attempted on the part of ethnic organizations, or on issues affecting the **Madhesis**, **Dalits** and women but have had limited success. As a result, the Maoists have been able to fill a vacuum by claiming to address social grievances such as caste inequality and rural impoverishment.

Foreign Policy: A small, land-locked country positioned between two vast neighbours, China and India, Nepal's foreign policy has centred on the not always reconcilable task of maintaining friendly relations with both and safeguarding its national security and independence. The long, permeable border with India has necessitated a close yet sometimes acrimonious relationship between the two countries, with Nepal's economy functioning as an appendage to India's. Formal relations with China were established in 1956 and China has provided significant support to Nepal's development. In return, Nepal has been non-critical of China's Tibet policy, with Nepalese authorities constantly repatriating refugees fleeing from Tibet. The intensification of the **Maoist insurgency** since the late 1990s led to hopes of strategic co-operation with major powers. India, the USA and the United Kingdom have provided substantial levels of arms, training and other military assistance to Nepal over the past decade, although this has changed with the emergence of China as the major player in Nepal's foreign relations under King Gyanendra. Since the royal takeover on 1 February 2005, China has provided the Royal Nepal Army with arms and ammunition, India, the United Kingdom and the USA having suspended their dealings with Nepal. It is speculated that in return for China's support of the royal takeover, Nepal lobbied successfully for China to be granted observer status in the **South Asian Association for Regional Co-operation (SAARC)**. Nepal is a member of several international bodies, including the UN (1955), the **International Monetary Fund** and the World Bank (1961), the Asian Development Bank (1966) and the WTO (2004). The country played an active role in establishing the SAARC and is the home to its secretariat.

Nepal-China Relations: To reduce its dependence on India, Nepal has sought to cultivate relations with China. In 1956 Nepal recognized China's sovereignty over Tibet, agreeing to surrender all of its earlier trading privileges, followed by a Treaty of Peace and Friendship in 1960 and the Sino-Nepal Boundary Treaty in 1961. Sharing a 1,414-km frontier between Nepal and Tibet, ties between Nepal and China grew through the 1960s and 1970s, when China steadily provided economic and technical assistance to Nepal. An all-weather highway linking Kathmandu with Tibet was built in 1967, although use of the road was and is heavily controlled by the Chinese, being of great strategic value to them. Relations between the two countries were complicated by India's growing security concerns over Nepal's purchase of weapons from China in the late 1980s, prompting punitive action by India against Nepal and the **Trade and Transit dispute**. Trade between Nepal and China has been increasing and in the 2000s several high-level state visits gave international visibility to ties between the two. Closer ties between the two countries are seen in a number of developments, such as the closure of the Dalai Lama's contact offices in Kathmandu only two days before the King's coup in 2005, Chinese weapons deliveries and increased development support, particularly after other countries, such as the USA, the United Kingdom and India, considered suspending aid in response to the political situation, and King Gyanendra's support for China's candidacy for observer status in the **SAARC**.

Nepal-India Relations: Sharing a 1,751-km border, relations between India and Nepal have been influenced by cultural and historical links, characterized by co-operation and common interests as well as suspicion and resentment. India's role as the midwife of Nepal's democracy was formally acknowledged in the 1950 'Peace and Friendship' treaty signed by the Ranas, which is commonly regarded as an attempt by the Ranas to save their position of power. The treaty agreed on co-operation in security issues, and the granting of reciprocal economic privileges. However, in the late 1950s and 1960s under King Mahendra Nepal's foreign relations were extended to include China, in an attempt to reduce dependence on India (*see* Nepal-China relations). Following the royal coup of 1960 and the official ban on political parties, India supported the National Congress in exile which launched an insurrection from the border areas. This changed after the 1962 India-China border war and India switched to improving relations with the King's government. Trade and transit rights were established and India secured, through a secret agreement, a monopoly on arms sales to Nepal. In the 1970s and 1980s there was economic co-operation between the countries as well as friction over India's support for the Nepalese opposition and Nepal's persistent feeling of vulnerability with India as regional hegemon. King Birendra secret conclusion, in June 1988, of an arms treaty with China and the ensuing Trade and Transit dispute marked a low point in relations.

However, relations improved significantly after a democratically elected government came to power in May 1991, although India's security-related concerns remained. Political instability in Nepal has added to fears of possible anti-India activities (backed by Pakistan's Inter-Services Intelligence) being launched from Nepal. Furthermore, both countries are wary of spill-over effects facilitated by the open border between the two, India being concerned about support cells for India's north east insurgencies generated by the Maoist movement and Nepal by suspicions of co-operation between Indian and Nepali Maoists.

Judiciary: Nepalese law was codified in the **Muluki Ain** (National Code) in 1854 and, together with additional specific legislation, continues to be the central basis of national law. In accordance with the 1990 Constitution, the judicial system has a three-tier structure, consisting of the Supreme Court, 18 appellate courts and 75 district courts. The King appoints the chief justice on the recommendation of the constitutional council and judges on the recommendation of the judicial council. According to Article 31 of the Constitution no questions can be raised in court about any acts of the King.

The house of representatives has the power to impeach Supreme Court justices in cases where incapacity, misbehaviour, or *mala fide* acts are deemed to have been committed in office. An independent judicial service commission, appointed by the King and with the chief justice of the Supreme Court acting as chairman, is responsible for the appointment, transfer, promotion and discipline of civil service officers. A Commission for the Investigation of Abuse of Authority (CIAA), with members who have no specific party affiliation and are appointed by the King on the recommendation of the Constitution Council, is authorized to investigate charges of corruption and abuse of office by public officials. Judicial activism has been practiced over the years in some public interest litigations in areas such as women's rights and environmental protection. The judiciary, however, has come under criticism for increasing corruption and delayed processes. Following the 2002 royal takeover, the Supreme Court has been considering a case about the dissolution's constitutionality.

Defence (Security): Land-locked by China and India, Nepal has, despite its vulnerable position, never faced territorial threats from either. It has had to engage in long-term diplomacy, balancing the needs of its powerful neighbours to advance its own national interests. International disputes have included disagreements over sections of boundary with India, the issue of the 100,000 Bhutanese refugees living in Nepal and, most significantly, the Maoist insurgency. Over the past decade, India, the USA and the United Kingdom have provided substantial levels of arms, training and other military aid to assist the government in the conflict. The Nepalese defence establishment derives its organizational structure from indigenous military traditions, a long association with the British military, and reforms proposed by Indian military advisers in the 1950s and 1960s. In 2005 it was reported that Nepal's armed forces had reached a strength of 94,000 through an ongoing programme of recruitment.

The country's regular armed force is the Royal Nepal Army, though an armed police force was formed in 2001 to combat the Maoist insurgency and numbered 7,000 in 2002. Nepal has no navy and no air force but does fly several non-combat aircraft as part of the army. The country's military expenditure as a percentage of gross domestic product was estimated at 1.5% in 2004, amounting to US $99.2m., a proportion that is projected to rise.

Military: The security forces comprise the Royal Nepalese Army (RNA), including the Royal Nepalese Army Air Service, and the Nepalese Police Force. In August 2002 they together employed 51,000 personnel, and military expenditures amounted to US $295m., or 1.6% of gross domestic product, in 2003. The King of Nepal assumed the role of the Supreme Commander-in-Chief of the RNA in 1951, proceeding to restructure the forces along British, Indian, and Nepalese lines in 1953. Specific to the RNA is its distinct rank-nomenclature, which deviates from that of the colonial successor armies of India, Pakistan, and Bangladesh. Military service is voluntary, esteemed and attractive because of the pay, high by Nepalese standards, the benefits offered, such as a pension scheme, as well as job security and promotion prospects. The history of the RNA is inseparable from that of the Rana Dynasty and its Shah predecessors: the army supported King Mahendra Bir Bikram Shah Dev and his heir, King Birendra Bir Bikram Shah Dev. The royal putsch launched by King Gyanendra in 2002 was possible because of the absolute loyalty of the army leadership to the monarchy.

Military training assistance is provided by the USA, the United Kingdom, India, Pakistan and Bangladesh. The RNA has contributed more than 36,000 peace-keepers to numerous UN-sponsored peace-keeping missions. In response to the Maoist insurgency, an Armed Police Force was established in 2001, which by August 2002 numbered 7,000.

Police: The modern Nepalese Police Force dates back to the 1955 Nepal Police Act which restructured the existing forces along Indian lines. A Central Police Training Centre was established in 1963 in Kathmandu and in 1992 this was upgraded and renamed the National Police Academy. Following the return to democracy in 1990, a Police Reform Commission was created in 1992 to adapt the police organization to the emerging multi-party system of politics. The Police headquarters in Kathmandu operates under the Inspector-General of Police and is the apex body. Occasionally assisted by the military, the Nepalese police are responsible for law and order as well as for monitoring political demonstrations. In 2003–04 the forces comprised more than 46,000 personnel.

Riots: Outbreaks of riots in Nepal have occurred intermittently and often for political reasons. In June 2001 curfews had to be imposed to curtail mounting violence by an angry public demanding the truth behind the royal killings which left King Birendra, the Queen and six other members of the royal family dead and Crown Prince Dipendra fatally wounded. The announcement that Dipendra's uncle, Gyanendra, would accede to the throne provoked further protests by locals who refused to believe that the prince, allegedly because of a family feud, could have committed such a crime.

In September 2005 riot police were dispatched to manage demonstrations against King Gyanendra's assumption of direct power in February. In fact, protests have occurred regularly in Nepal since King Gyanendra suspended parliament and began selecting his own Cabinets in May 2002. Students from Kathmandu's leading Tribhuvan university and opposition parties have been at the forefront of pro-democracy rallies attended by thousands of people.

Terrorism: Since the beginning of the People's War in the mid-1990s, the government of Nepal has treated the Maoist insurgency, despite its valid political motivations, as a terrorist movement. Several countries have offered military assistance and development aid to combat the insurgency, including the USA, India and China. Maoist groups have attacked public facilities, government vehicles and the offices of NGOs, as well as terrorizing the population into observing ***bandhs*** to bring the country's economy to a standstill. In August 2004 Maoist rebels bombed a luxury hotel in Kathmandu, aimed at scaring foreign investors and tourists away, and launched a week-long complete blockade of the capital. Of Nepal's 75 districts, all but one have suffered violence and/or armed conflict relating to the Maoist insurgency. In October 2003 the US Department of State designated the Communist Party of Nepal—Maoist as a terrorist organization, blocking Maoists' assets in the USA and barring most transactions with the Maoists. However, since the events of

1 February 2005 when King Gyanendra assumed executive powers, US support has been less certain.

Bureaucracy: The Nepal Civil Service, established in 1952, was formalized with the passing of the Civil Service Act in 1975 and the introduction of the Civil Service Rules in the same year. Both components were revised and reintroduced in 1993.

Nepal's civil service has an estimated 105,000 approved posts. In recent years the government has attempted to reduce, through institutional reforms, the number of regular civil servants while continuing to permit the entry of better qualified staff, such as advisers and consultants. In the 2001 fiscal year expenditure on government personnel accounted for about 20% of the total government budget.

Since the early 1990s several studies have described the civil service as politicized, inefficient and ineffective. A 1992 Administrative Reform Commission report recommended that its sphere of operation be significantly reduced and some of its power devolved to local bodies.

In November 2001 the ADB approved a US $30m. loan to Nepal with the purpose of improving governance in the country. Objectives of the governance reform programme include the improved performance of key ministries, increased efficiency and responsiveness in the civil service and public-sector organizations, and the development of highly competent and motivated civil servants. Other aims included the efficient allocation of budget resources and the redress of gender inequality in the bureaucracy by way of affirmative action amendments to the Civil Service Act. (*See* ***Aphno Manchhe***; **Bahun**; ***Chakari***; **Chhetris**.)

Citizenship: Nepalese citizenship is based on the 1990 Constitution and the Nepal Citizenship Act of 1964. Laws for acquiring citizenship are stringent, particularly towards those of Indian origin who have long been discriminated against. For instance, in the **Tarai region** amongst the Indian language-speaking (especially Maithili and Bhojpuri) **Madhesi** community it is estimated that there are about 3m. stateless people. According to Article 9.4a of the Constitution foreigners can acquire Nepali citizenship only if they know *Khas Nepali* written in *Devnagari* script and must have resided in Nepal for at least 15 years. The law is also biased against women because children get natural Nepali citizenship only if their father is a Nepali citizen. With regard to citizenship as birthright, landless and nomadic indigenous peoples are particularly vulnerable as few have birth certificates.

Corruption: Corruption in Nepal has primarily taken the form of nepotism and clientelism, practices known locally as *aphno manche* and *chakari*. One manifestation of power abuse has been the politicization of administrative branches, such as the bureaucracy and the police. Ruling parties filled administrative posts with loyalists, party cadres, relatives and caste members, using them later for partisan purposes. Thirty years under the *Panchayat* system contributed to this situation, by establishing patronage as the only way for leaders to widen their support base. Widespread corruption is held as one of the reasons for the downfall of the *Panchayat* system and for Nepal's persistent under-development despite extensive foreign aid. Another consequence of centralized rule has been weak horizontal accountability in Nepal. Key agencies such as the Election Commission, the Commission for the Investigation of Abuse of Authority (CIAA) and the Special Police Department were made dependent upon the Cabinet, which can influence the nomination of commissioners as well as funding and staffing. Furthermore, no institution or mechanism is in place to monitor and hold the above bodies accountable. The CIAA, established in 1990, is meant to play the role of ombudsman and in 2002 was given full legal authority to launch investigations against any public official. Critics say that the CIAA could be used to target political opponents. Following the royal putsch of 2002 the CIAA has been further hindered in its work. In February 2005 King Gyanendra nominated a parallel commission, the Royal Commission for the Control of Corruption. A case in the Supreme Court was introduced regarding the constitutionality of this commission.

Decentralization: Nepal has a tradition of local governance, with forms of voluntary association, resource management and social and economic regulation followed by a number of the country's ethnic groups. State-led efforts at decentralization have had mixed results. In the 1950s two acts established local government units, the Municipality Act of 1953 and the Village Act of 1956, later renamed *Panchayats* in 1962. Facing mounting protests, the King passed the Decentralization Act of 1982 promoting the 'deconcentration' of functional responsibilities to the districts. Following the return to democracy in 1990, the country's new Constitution enshrined decentralization as a fundamental element of democracy. Three acts produced three levels of local administration, the District Development Committee Act of 1991, the Village Development Committee Act of 1991, and the Municipality Act of 1991. In 1999 the Local Self-Governance Act (LSGA) was promulgated. Considered landmark legislation, the LSGA was the first attempt towards devolving administrative, fiscal and judicial powers to the local bodies. However, since 2002, when King Gyanendra dismissed the Prime Minister and the ensuing political instability as well as deteriorating security conditions, local elections have not been held (local elections were last held in 1997). (*See* Bureaucracy; Federalism.)

Federalism: All three of Nepal's Constitutions held Nepal to be a unitary state. Although the 1990 Constitution declares Nepal to be a multi-ethnic, multi-lingual, democratic state, it bans political parties that are formed along religious, community, caste, tribe or regional lines. The Election Commission has been inconstant in its procedures, allowing parties like the Nepal Sadbhavana to represent the Tarai population of Indian origin in elections, while excluding others, such as those representing Tibeto-Mongolian groups. Past attempts at unifying and homogenizing Nepal have included propagation of Nepali as the official language and medium of education, centralized decision-making, administrative units that disregarded ethnic composition, or were aimed at preventing ethnic majorities within districts, and a nationalism that identified the country with its King. However, since the introduction of democracy in 1990 ethnic communities have lobbied for greater regional autonomy and participation in a system long dominated by an élite minority. Such demands have come from organizations of indigenous people (***janajati***) as well as leaders of the Indian-origin Madhesi community and, increasingly, **Dalit** groups.

Human Rights: In fighting the Maoist insurgency the Nepalese government has justified the use of unwarranted force, arbitrary detention, abuse and torture. International reports indicate widespread use of torture and ill-treatment by state security forces. Under the Terrorist and Destructive Activities Act of 2001, the government was permitted to detain suspects without charge. The ongoing insurgency has also been used as a reason to indefinitely postpone elections following the dismissal of the elected government in 2002. Since then the King has appointed three interim governments, but parliament has not been re-established. Furthermore, under Article 53 (4) of the Constitution, the dissolution of the house of representatives becomes invalid if elections are not held within the following six months.

Maoist rebels for their part have been accused of conscripting children, the use of intimidation and abduction. Although improvements were reported in the human rights situation following the government-Maoist cease-fire of 2003, abuses on both sides played a role in the break-down of negotiations. For example, one of the final breaking-points was the killing of 19 Maoists by army members after they had been arrested. In 2000 the National Human Rights Commission was founded in Nepal to act as a watchdog, but in 2005, after its initial term of five years ended, the new members were all nominated by King Gyanendra. So far Nepal has signed most of the major international human rights conventions, but numerous violations of the Constitution occur with hardly any of the citizen's fundamental rights being respected.

Inequality: In 1999 two groups, the Brahmin-Chhetri castes and the Newars, held more than 81.7% of leadership positions in governmental institutions as well as political parties, the media and civil society, while making up 30% and 5.6% of the total population respectively. Indigenous groups, known as the Janajati, tend to be under-represented and economically marginalized, although there is much variation amongst different sections. For example, the Gurung and Magar peoples live in mid-western Nepal, one of the poorest and most underdeveloped regions of the country and the area where the Maoists began their insurgency. The Thakali and Manangpa or Manangi, on the other hand, in northern parts of Nepal, have been traditional traders who have profited greatly from the Nepali state. Capitalizing on caste and gender discrimination, the Maoists have recruited heavily from lower-caste communities. However, it is reported that the Maoist leadership itself continues to be dominated by upper-castes.

A marked spatial variation exists in income distribution, with per capita income in the hill areas 1.6 times higher than in the mountains, 2.5 times higher in urban areas compared to rural regions and nearly four times higher in Kathmandu. Human development indicators, including literacy levels, access to education and health standards, show that 17 of the 25 least developed districts are in the far and mid-western hills and mountains. Income distribution remains skewed, with the bottom 20% of the population accounting for only 6% of total consumption compared with the top 20% accounting for 54%. Economic growth in the late 1990s and early 2000s, which should have reduced poverty, has, as a result of increasing inequality, only been moderately pro-poor.

Nationalism: National identity formation in modern Nepal has centred on the monarchy. During the 1950s and 1960s a policy dubbed 'Nepalism' was spear-headed by King Mahendra to assert Nepal's distinctiveness and independence *vis-à-vis* neighbouring India. Under the 1962 Constitution Nepal was officially made a Hindu state, reviving claims made in the 18th century under Shah rule of Nepal to being the true **Hindustan** (India). In the 1990s there was a burgeoning of ethnic activism. Janajati or 'indigenous peoples' movements emerged to redress the more than century-old domination of the Hindu élite and Kathmandu Valley-centrism. Formed in 1990, the Nepal Janajati Mahasangh, an umbrella grouping of about 48 ethnic organizations, successfully petitioned against the imposition of Sanskrit as a compulsory subject in schools, boosted by the fact that in the 1990s, for the first time, the Constitution recognized other national languages in addition to the official language of Nepali. The fact that many ethnic groups contain a diversity of cross-cutting subgroups has hindered the framing of a common identity and often spawned attempts at Nepali nationalism, such as the policies of King Mahendra in the late 1950s and 1960s.

Participation/Public Action: Political power in Nepal is largely held by a traditional, political élite. About 60% of the members of the house of representatives belong to three caste/ethnic groups, Brahmins, Chhetris and Thakuris, all upper castes which together constitute only 30% of Nepal's total population. Electoral participation of other ethnic groups, such as the hill groups, has actually fallen partly due to lack of representation in leadership positions and state institutions and because the participation of ethnically-based parties in elections is by law forbidden. Female participation in Nepal's political sphere is also limited. Women never make up more than 8% of the 205 members in the lower house, although female candidates are required by the Constitution to make up at least 5% of the candidates in parliamentary elections. From 1991 until 1999 the number of voters increased from 11.2m. to 13.5m., and turn-out remained at nearly 65%. Unlike India, Nepal does not have a policy of reserved posts and quotas in political bodies, civil sector jobs and institutions of higher learning. As a result, though comprising more than 20% of the population, lower castes are dramatically under-represented in the government. The 14 Dalits who have become members of the National Assembly since 1958 have been nominated while only one has been elected to the house of representatives. Participation of the Dalits is similarly low in the administrative and judicial system as well as in the Nepal Royal Army.

Nepal, Economic Development

GDP at purchasing power parity (PPP): US $42,170m. (2005 estimate); GDP per capita at PPP: $1,500 (2005 estimate.); *agriculture*: 40%; *industry*: 20%;

services: 40% (2002 figures); exports: $626m. f.o.b. (2004 estimate); imports: $1,696m. f.o.b. (2004 estimate); currency: Nepalese rupee (NPR).

When Rana rule came to an end in 1950–51 Nepal had an isolated, subsistence economy. Less than 1% of the population was engaged in modern industry and more than 90% of employment and income came from agriculture. Physical infrastructure was minimal, making movement of goods and people nearly impossible. The country's first five-year plan was initiated in 1956 and in 1962 the ***Panchayat* system** was introduced. Under the direct leadership of King **Mahendra** major projects were initiated, including land reform, infrastructure development and the resettlement of population to increase arable land. Through the 1960s and 1970s Nepal received massive foreign aid, but a burgeoning bureaucracy and the government's monopoly over resources encouraged corruption as well as misallocation of funds. In the 1980s Nepal managed to attain a stable growth rate through limited economic reforms and a growing tourism industry. Private-sector and local government involvement were encouraged and spending on agriculture, industry and the social sector was increased. During 1985–90 average economic growth was 4.6%, climbing to about 5% in the 1990s. However, the 1989 **Trade and Transit dispute** with India brought the economy to a near standstill. The ongoing **Maoist insurgency** since 1996 placed new obstacles to economic development and poverty alleviation in Nepal.

Economic Policy/Reforms: Facing a huge budgetary deficit in the early 1980s, Nepal was forced to implement stabilization and structural reforms supported by the **International Monetary Fund**. Changing from a completely state-regulated to a market-oriented economic regime in the mid-1980s, Nepal was in fact one of the pioneers in South Asia in initiating economic reform. Focused initially on fiscal reforms, after the restoration of democracy in 1990 Nepal turned towards liberalization and privatization, acknowledging the need of a small country to integrate with the world economy. Various measures to facilitate trade, encourage exporters within Nepal and stimulate foreign direct investment were taken. On the domestic front financial sector reforms were initiated, as well as a process of privatization. Subsidies, including those on fertilizers, irrigation and food transportation, were also withdrawn. However, despite extensive reform measures during the 1990s the overall impact has been limited. The growth performance of the agricultural sector has been particularly bad, hardly surpassing the population growth rate. Both industrial and the tourism sectors registered negative growth rates and over-dependence on a few exportable products has made the Nepalese economy vulnerable to global events. Most importantly, reforms suffered a setback during the 1990s as political instability took centre stage.

Private Sector: Since the 1990s a concerted effort has been made by the government of Nepal to boost the performance of the private sector. Progress has been made in allowing private operations in sectors that were previously government monopolies, such as telecommunications, banking, insurance and civil aviation, but a number of obstacles have hindered development. Private airlines, for example, proliferated in the early 1990s. However, a decline in the tourism industry due to instability in the country drove at least five domestic airlines into bankruptcy. Under the 1992 Privatization Act 14 state-owned corporations were privatized, of which only two have been taken over by foreign investors, seven corporations were liquidated, and two were closed down. The last privatization completed by the government was in January 2003. In a joint initiative of the private sector and the Ministry of Industry, Commerce and Supplies, a new 'Competition Law' is being drafted to clarify the legal framework. Protection of intellectual property rights is still in its initial stages. Patent registration according to the 1965 Patent Design and Trademark Act is valid for just seven years and can be extended twice. The private sector has access to a variety of credit and investment instruments, including public stock and direct loans from finance companies and joint venture commercial banks.

Public Sector: Most public enterprises (PEs) in Nepal were established during the 1960s and early 1970s when the government played the roles of producer and service provider. Expanding into all sectors, the total contribution to gross domestic product (GDP) of PEs was never much more than about 2%. This was partly due to the dominance of agriculture in Nepal's economy, which was mostly in the form of small-scale, unorganized private farms. Nevertheless, gross domestic investment in PEs remains high, at about 43% of GDP, and PEs are an important source of employment. The expansionary drive in the public sector came to a halt in the sixth five-year plan period (1980–85) when studies revealed the low performance of public enterprises and the difficulties in managing, supervising and controlling them. By the time of the government's eighth five-year plan (1992–97) privatization was being strongly advocated, particularly by the **Nepali Congress (NC)** government of 1992. Under the 1994 Privatization Act 18 PEs were privatized, particularly in the telecommunications sector. However, criticism was raised about the sale of assets to foreigners and the lack of transparency in privatization deals. The early elections of 1994 and the subsequent formation of a series of coalition governments put a brake on the privatization process, as well as the nine-month period of **Communist Party of Nepal—Unified Marxist-Leninist)** government in 1994/95

Between 1997 and 2002 only three of the 30 targeted enterprises were privatized, due to political instability, labour unrest, deteriorating security conditions caused by the Maoist insurgency, a lengthy and cumbersome licensing process and shrinking investor interest. Utilities represent the largest share of public enterprises and they remain Nepal's largest employer of organized labour.

Population: Nepal is a crowded country, with more than 26m. living in an area of about 147,181 sq km. Demographic data show that the total population doubled between 1961 and 1991. Average growth rates between 1991 and 2001 included a high 2.25%, in 2001–05, 2.39% and the sex ratio reported at 99.8 males per 100 females. Nepal has a very young population, with 39.7% under 15 years of age, 56.7% falling within the 15–64 age bracket and 3.6% aged over 65. Nepal is divided ecologically into three regions, mountain, hill and **Tarai**. According to the latest 2001 census, population density has increased in each. Population distribution, however, is skewed towards the Tarai where better resources and infrastructure have resulted in nearly 48% of the population settling there.

The population is extremely diverse, with numerous castes, ethnic and linguistic groups. The 2001 census recorded 106 languages and dialects from Indo-Aryan and Tibeto-Burman families, although other sources report a much greater number. Kathmandu, the country's only metropolitan city, had a population of 671,846 in 2001.

Family-Planning Policy: Over the last 20 years there has been an impressive increase in the use of family-planning methods in Nepal, with the contraceptive prevalence rate rising from 15% in 1986 to 39.2% by 2001. In 1993 the National Health Education, Information and Communication Centre (NHEICC) was established under the Department of Health to support important health programmes such as safe motherhood and family planning. The government's objective to reduce the country's total fertility rate from 4.8 in the late 1990s to 4.2 by the end of the Ninth Plan in 2002 achieved overall success, with a national average of 4.1 reached by 2001. Large differences do, however, exist between fertility levels in urban and rural areas, and Nepal grapples with striking a balance between population growth and economic development. Structural and political impediments, constraints on human resources and capacity, a lack of effective co-ordination and insufficient information and education campaigns continue to impede progress in family planning.

Migration: Internal migration in Nepal, specifically from the mountain and hill region to the Tarai (or plain) areas, has been primarily poverty-driven, the plain areas offering better opportunities, more fertile arable land and infrastructure. The government also encouraged migratory movements with resettlement programmes in the late 1960s. Since the Maoist-led insurgency, the **People's War**, began in 1996 it is estimated that approximately 300,000 people have migrated to the Kathmandu valley and to India. Emigration is largely to neighbouring India as well as to new destinations, such as Saudi Arabia and in South-East Asia. Overseas remittances of Nepalese emigrants are an essential contributor to the economy and an ever-increasing proportion of gross domestic product. In 2002/03 they were estimated at US $855m., more than the value of the nation's merchandise exports. The number of Nepalese workers abroad was estimated at 106,660 in 2003/04.

Urbanization: Nepal is one of the least urbanized of the developing countries. The Municipality Act of 1992 categorized three kinds of municipalities: *Mahanagarpalika* (metropolis), where the population numbers 300,000 or more and there is a minimal annual revenue of Rs.70m. and relevant infrastructure; *Upa-mahanagarpalika* (sub-metropolis), where there is a minimum population of 100,000; and *Nagarpalika* (municipality), where the population numbers 20,000 and more. The capital city, Kathmandu, is the only metropolis and there are four sub-metropolises and 53 municipalities. Within a period of 40 years Nepal's urban population increased from 3.6% of the total population to 14.2%, a growth rate that is much higher than that of the rural population, reflecting rural to urban migration as well as the physical expansion of urban areas to absorb their surroundings.

Minority Groups/Communities: Nepal's population is so varied that no single caste or ethnic group forms a majority. The largest caste, the Brahmin-**Chhetri** groups (the **Bahuns**, 12.7%, the Thakuris, 1.7% and the Chhetris, 15.8%) constitutes around 30% of Nepal's total population and the Newar people of Kathmandu Valley only 5.6%, an ethnic group divided not into clans but according to a **caste system**. In 2002 the government officially recognized 59 **Janajati**, those ethnic groups with their own territorial areas, mother tongue, religions and culture and not falling within the Nepali five-tiered caste hierarchy (according to the 1854 **Muluki Ain**). Amongst the Janajati a majority belong to the Tibeto-Mongolian racial group, speaking Tibeto-Burman languages. To a large extent Buddhism has been the dominant influence but animism or shamanism have also been important elements and the adoption of Hindu practices and customs have made distinctions less clear-cut.

While Hinduism is the state religion, a significant number are Buddhist (10.7%) and Muslim (4.2%). Nepali is the official language but only 48% of the population speaks Nepali as a mother tongue. The 2001 census listed 92 other languages, some of which are designated 'national languages'. (*See* **Tarai (Terai) Region**.)

Agriculture: Nepal is essentially an agrarian-based economy, with more than 80% of economically active citizens involved in agriculture although cultivable land is limited. Principal crops include rice, sugar cane, vegetables and melons, wheat and maize, in addition to livestock products. The predominance of subsistence farming has meant that agricultural production has only just kept up with population growth. Limited investment in agriculture and technological innovation, poor infrastructure, inefficient harnessing of water resources and traditional land tenure arrangements are amongst the reasons for low productivity. In 2002 agriculture contributed only 40% of Nepal's gross domestic product. To boost agriculture the government has initiated market reforms as well as encouraged crop diversification. (*See* **Agricultural Development Bank Nepal (ADBN)**.)

Land Reform (Ownership): In 1964 the Lands Act was introduced, breaking down Nepal's very diverse and complicated traditional land tenure system, initially in 16 of the 75 development districts and thereafter gradually increased to cover the whole kingdom by 1966. However, large absentee landowners, usually senior government officials and members of the Rana nobility and upper castes, continue to own large portions of valuable agricultural land, particularly in the Tarai area. More than 50% of Nepalese households own less than 0.5 ha of land and another 16% owns 1–1.5 ha. Lack of land ownership and secure land titles are among the causes for Nepal's economic and agricultural under-development and also one of the reasons for the Maoist insurgency.

Food and Famine Prevention: Although agriculture is the largest sector of Nepal's economy, it is characterized by low-productivity subsistence production, creating food deficit in a number of districts, especially those in the mountains. Groups that are particularly vulnerable to food insecurity include marginal farm households, rural service castes and agricultural labourers in the mountains and porters and the urban poor of Kathmandu valley, who together make up at least 40% of the country's population. The level of malnutrition is higher in the western districts which tend to have less productive soils, a shorter growing season and erratic rainfall.

Industry: The industrial sector contributed about 20% of Nepal's total gross domestic product in 2002 and employed around 3% of the workforce. Construction accounts for approximately half of Nepal's total industrial activity and is constrained by limited supplies of raw materials. Other industrial activities include processing of agricultural produce, including jute, sugar cane, tobacco, oilseeds and grain, and manufacturing, particularly of garments, carpets and other textiles. Nepal's industry is constrained by small-scale production, lack of capital and the competitiveness of markets in other South Asian countries. Tourism has been a key source of foreign exchange but is sensitive to security concerns raised by the Maoist insurgency.

Foreign Trade: India has long been Nepal's principal trading partner, although its dominance has declined since the 1970s when it accounted for 80% of Nepal's total trade. Despite possessing one of the world's most liberal trade regimes, Nepal has remained largely unsuccessful in promoting export-oriented growth due to high freight costs, falling global demand for Nepalese goods and a lack of foreign investment. According to official statistics, Nepal has had a trade deficit every year since 1965. Exports reached US $626m. f.o.b. in 2004 (excluding unrecorded border trade with India), comprising primarily carpets, clothing and ghee (purified butter) as well as leather, jute goods and toothpaste. In 2004 48.8% of exports went to India, 22.3% to the USA and 8.5% to Germany. Imports amounted to approximately $1,696,000m. f.o.b. in 2004, consisting mainly of gold, machinery, vehicles and spare parts, petroleum products and textiles. Of imported commodities in 2004, 43% came from India, 10% from the United Arab Emirates, 10% from China, 4.4% from Saudi Arabia and 4% from Singapore. One area of significant economic activity has been overseas remittances by the estimated 5% of Nepal's workforce living and working abroad (mid-2003 estimate), which in 2003 reportedly accounted for 14.8% of the country's gross domestic product and continues to rise.

Banking System: Two large banks dominate Nepal's banking sector: Nepal Bank Ltd, of which about 49% is state-controlled, and Rastriya Banijya Bank, in which the government also has a major shareholding. Together the two account for more than 50% of total banking assets, thus creating a near state monopoly on credit although there are a large number of non-performing loans that have been the target of reforms. During the 1980s Nepal opened up the commercial banking sector to foreign participation, attracting a number of joint venture banks. In 1994 the government expanded the role of the Nepal Stock Exchange by allowing private brokers to operate. The Nepal Industrial Development Corporation, established in 1959 with US support, offers financial and technical assistance to private industry, while the Agricultural Development Bank Nepal is the main source of financing for the agricultural sector. The **Nepal Rastra Bank** is Nepal's central bank and the bank of issue. In 2005 Nepal had 17 commercial banks with 382 branches, 18 insurance companies and 25 development banks, with 11 offering microcredit services. In 2001 foreign banks were permitted to have majority ownership in joint ventures but foreign direct investment has been low because of security and other concerns.

Foreign Direct Investment: Foreign Direct Investment (FDI) in Nepal has fluctuated greatly. Commencing in the 1980s, it increased from US $7m. in 1996 to $28.4m. in 1997, then declined to $3.4m. by 2000 before rising again, to $35m., in 2004. In 2004 the greatest proportion of FDI came from India, with 37% of total fixed capital investment, followed by the USA, with 16% of total investment. While the government is keen to increase FDI, particularly in energy and telecommunications, and the country has a relatively liberal trade and investment regime, corruption, a large and inefficient bureaucracy, civil conflict with the ongoing Maoist insurgency, political instability and frequent ***bandhs*** have undermined investment appeal. The Foreign Investment and One Window Policy of 1992 lists acceptable forms of investment, allows foreign shares of up to 100% in designated businesses and outlines general guide-lines. Under the Finance Ordinance of 2004 the process of gradual liberalization and reform was reaffirmed, although following the royal putsch of 2002 there have been no legitimate budgets. The bulk of FDI in Nepal has traditionally derived from small Indian manufacturing enterprises rather than multinational companies. The manufacturing industry accounts for more than 50% of approved FDI and includes food and beverages, tobacco, textiles and garments.

Foreign Aid: Since the mid-20th century foreign aid has played a vital role in Nepal's economy, with more than 65% of Nepal's total government development expenditure derived from foreign aid contributions during the Eighth Plan (1992–97). Bilateral donors (including Japan, China, Denmark, Germany, India, the United Kingdom and the USA) account for 60% of aid while multilateral organizations, such as the World Bank, the ADB and various UN agencies, have provided 40%. Inflow of foreign aid into Nepal increased following the shift to multi-party democracy in 1990 and, in return for his support of the US-led global war on terror, the King of Nepal has been eligible for American military aid to combat the Maoist insurgency, amounting to US $37m. in 2003. However, following the dismissal of the government on 1 February 2005 by King Gyanendra, India, the United Kingdom and the USA have been sending mixed signals about linking future aid to the restoration of multi-party democracy.

Despite the large amounts of aid received, structural hindrances to economic development persist. Contributing to the inability to absorb foreign aid efficiently are administrative inefficiency, widespread corruption and the conflict between the government and Maoists which continues to undermine development efforts and adds to donor fatigue. Aid programmes, run for example by the ADB, typically targeted economic issues but since the early 2000s have begun to address the obstacles to good governance.

Nepal-India Trade Agreements: In 1950 a trade treaty provided Nepal with the unrestricted right of commercial transit of goods through Indian territory and ports.

This treaty was renewed and modified in 1961 and 1971, incorporating provisions for Nepal's trade with a third country. In 1978, at a time when the **Indian National Congress** was out of power, separate agreements (instead of one treaty) on trade, transit and unauthorized trade were concluded. Under Rajiv Gandhi in the late 1980s an attempt was made to return to a single treaty which allowed India to better control Nepal's trade with third countries. While the treaties remained separate, by maintaining the need for periodic renewal, India used the treaties as a bargaining device and an instrument through which to take advantage of Nepal's dependency, as demonstrated in the 1989 Trade and Transit Dispute. A renewed trade agreement in 1996 and transit treaty of 1999 simplified conditions, with India granting automatic renewal for five- and seven-year periods respectively.

Labour: In 2001 58.2% of Nepal's population aged 10 years and older was economically active. Officially, 2% of the population was unemployed. According to government statistics, the structure of employment reveals that 79% of Nepal's population is self-employed, 71% of whom are concentrated in agriculture. Only about 3% are in the organized sector. Annual growth of the labour force during the 1990s was estimated at about 3.5%, creating a huge pool of unemployed with low levels of skills and productivity. A major problem has been the inability of the industrial sector to absorb surplus agricultural labour.

Following grassroots agitation the government officially banned a prominent form of bonded labour in 2000. Limitations on labour unions have been reduced and union publications indicate some improvement in labour practices and worker treatment. One achievement, for example, was the government's decision in 2003 to raise the minimum monthly wage for unskilled labour to US $25, as well as the amended Labour Act allowing for union formation in the unorganized sector. The three largest trade unions are affiliated with legal political parties and the Maoists also have an active affiliated trade union.

Informal Economy: Nepal's informal market is considered to be substantial, especially in consumer goods, labour, construction, currency and the smuggling of weapons. In 1999 it was estimated that more than 73% of the population was employed in the informal sector. Informal workers are unprotected and deprived of legal facilities and social security provisions. Attempts have been made by the government to broaden the scope of trade unions by allowing agricultural labourers and self-employed workers to form a national union. (*See* ***Aphno Manchhe***; ***Chakari***.)

Child Labour: Child labour is a major economic and social issue in Nepal. In 1997 an ILO-supported national child labour survey estimated that 45.2% of 6,225,000 children between the ages of five and 14 years were economically active, the highest percentage amongst South Asian countries. A majority (95%) of child labour in Nepal occurs in the agricultural sector. Under the 1990 Constitution children aged between 14 and 16 years cannot work more than 36 hours per week and minors may not be employed in factories, mines, or similar hazardous locations. The Child Labour Act of 1992 and the Child Labour (Prohibition and Regulation)

Act of 1999 established a minimum age for the employment of minors (16 years for industry and 14 years for agriculture) and prescribed the acceptable working conditions for children. The ILO's Worst Forms of Child Labour Convention was endorsed in 1999, and in recent years government-led public awareness programmes have been conducted.

Environmental Protection: Nepal's extremely rich biodiversity includes Himalayan slopes and Gangetic Plains. More than 80% of the total area is covered by rugged hills and mountains, including Mount Everest and another seven of the world's highest peaks from which originate three major river systems (Karnali, Gandaki and Koshi). Water and forests are Nepal's largest natural resources and, in addition to attracting tourists, represent invaluable raw materials for the country's economic development. Conservation awareness has its roots in Nepalese society, which traditionally worshipped forests as sacred and preserved large expanses of them. In 1957 under the Forest Nationalization Act private forest land was abolished and traditional systems of conservation were replaced by state legislation. However, during the last four decades the forest area has decreased considerably. Compared to 6.4m. ha of forest in 1964, Nepal had 4.27m. ha in 1999. This is attributed mainly to the country's rapid population growth and the burgeoning need for arable land and firewood. To combat problems of soil degradation, deforestation and pollution the government has launched a number of projects aimed at encouraging local participation in conservation through empowerment of bodies at the village and district level. The King Mahendra Trust for Nature Conservation, a non-profit and non-governmental organization established in 1982, has been highly active in conservation work.

Floods and Natural Disaster: Nepal is a disaster-prone country due to geological as well as poverty-related reasons. Common disasters include floods, earthquakes, droughts and epidemics. Flooding and landslides in 2004 affected 800,000 people and partly due to extensive deforestation the country is badly affected by every rainy season. According to the government, more than 18,000 people were killed by various natural disasters between 1983 and 1998. The Natural Disaster Relief Act 1982 is the main piece of legislation regarding natural disasters and the Ministry of Home Affairs acts as the apex body co-ordinating disaster management.

Health System/Policy: In general, the health status of Nepal's population is poor. Lack of potable water and sanitation, contaminated food supplies, and deficient medical facilities are major factors contributing to poor health. Nepal also has high rates of child malnutrition (72% in 2001) and under-five mortality (91.2 deaths per 1,000 live births in 2001). According to UN data for 2003, approximately 60,000 persons between the ages of 15 and 49 had HIV and the HIV prevalence rate was 0.5%. Nevertheless, Nepal's Human Development Index has improved and the government has launched various initiatives, such as the 1991 National Health Policy (NHP), an all-inclusive policy to address service delivery and the administrative structure of the health system. The 9th (1997–2002) and 10th (2002–07)

Health Plan and the Second Long Term Health Plan (SLTHP) (1997–2017) were formulated in resonance with these policy objectives.

Main constraints have included frequent changes of government, the ongoing Maoist conflict, limited national resources, ineffective administration, management and supervision, difficult geographic conditions, slow economic development and a lack of human resources. For example, in 2001/02 it was estimated that there were only 0.54 physicians per 10,000 people. Government allocations for health were around 5.2% of the budget for fiscal year 2004 and foreign aid accounted for about 30%. Increasingly, development of the health sector has involved the private sector. A sexually-transmitted diseases and AIDS programme was launched in the fiscal year 1988/89 and since the early 1990s notable progress has been made in improving primary health care. Nevertheless, Nepal continues to have one of the highest maternal mortality rates in Asia. Gender inequality and a traditional society in which early marriage, short birth intervals, poor maternal nutrition and lack of health care facilities have contributed to the limited success of Nepal's reproductive health programmes.

Education /Education Policy: Almost immediately after his accession to the throne in 1955, King Mahendra introduced a new Nepali nationalism based on the Hindu religion (all Nepalis are or should be Hindus), the Nepali language (an elimination of other ethnic languages and cultures) and an attempt to assert Nepal's distinctiveness and independence from Indian influence. These goals were reflected in the reforms introduced to the education system from 1956 onwards when Nepali became the only medium of instruction in schools, even in the **Tarai** area where many people speak other languages.

In 1959 Nepal's population was largely illiterate. A formal education policy was initiated as part of the effort to stimulate economic development. Primary schooling was made compulsory, beginning at the age of six and lasting for five years, and in 1975 was made free. Secondary education continues from the age of 11 years for another five years. In 2003 there were 789 higher secondary schools, one polytechnic school, four state universities and one private university. The adult literacy rate increased from 20.6% in 1981 to 48.6% in 2003 (males: 62.7%; females: 34.9%). Gender disparities also fell, with the percentage of female students at primary school level (grades one to 10) increasing from nearly 30% to 45.9% between 1990 and 2004. Public spending (as a percentage of gross domestic product) increased from 2.0 in 1990 to 2.9 in 2003.

Social Security/Policy: Social protection in Nepal is very limited, with the formal social security system (provident funds and citizen investment fund) covering mainly civil servants, the army, police and teachers. There are various informal, partly traditional community-based insurance arrangements. Under the Labour Act, some basic protection exists for the workforce (severance pay, protection against lay-offs), but in spite of its minimal nature this has encouraged non-formal employment. The Ministry of Women, Children and Social Welfare is responsible for the needs of the elderly, disabled, widows, children and peoples internally displaced by the Maoist insurgency. Provisions for social welfare are almost non-existent apart from some in the public sector.

Poverty: With a per capita income of US $240 per year, Nepal remains one of the poorest countries in the world. Life expectancy at birth has increased, but, at 60 years, is still lower than neighbouring South Asian countries, while infant and maternal mortality rates are among the highest in the region. In 2003/04 approximately 31% of Nepal's population were living below the poverty line. The incidence of poverty in rural areas is 2.5 times higher than in urban areas. With 88% of the population living in rural areas, poverty is an overwhelmingly rural phenomenon. Within rural areas poverty is greatest in the underdeveloped mountain region due to limited access to resources and services. In general, the **Dalit** communities, scattered across the country, are the poorest due to economic, political and social marginalization. A failure of governance is the cause of Nepal's dismal human development indicators as well as the discriminating social and political system in place, bad land ownership policies and the limited nature of modernization, social and political reforms under Nepal's monarchy.

Public services and expenditure have tended to be urban-biased and have ignored rural areas. Political instability at the centre has hindered effective policy implementation as well as the Maoist insurgency, which has drained resources in addition to making parts of the country inaccessible. Remittance payments from abroad have been one of the few factors helping to raise standards of living. In 2004 total remittances were estimated at $1,000m., making them Nepal's largest source of foreign revenue.

Welfare: Nepal has no official welfare regime and people have had to rely on traditional social networks based on familial structures. While the government has made progress in providing basic amenities through road construction, communications, literacy rates and health services, the quality and efficiency of public services, such as water supply and sanitation, primary and secondary education, remain poor. Furthermore, many of the improvements have occurred in urban areas while rural regions continue to be neglected. NGOs and foreign aid providers are crucial sources of funds and, particularly in the 1990s, encouraged by the emerging multi-party democratic political system, local registered NGOs rapidly increased, growing in number from 222 in 1990 to 5,040 in 1997. Initially suspicious of NGO activity, the state has increasingly co-opted NGOs in areas of health management, assisting children, youth, the elderly, the disabled and women, raising environmental awareness and HIV/AIDS education. For example, the Social Welfare Act of 1992 established the Social Welfare Council (SWC) to promote, co-ordinate, facilitate and mobilize NGO activity. NGOs may mobilize funds from international sources, but must register with the SWC. In the experiment with devolution of power to local administrative units, the government has promoted co-operation between local NGOs and the district and village-level committees. In 2005 an amendment gave new powers to the Ministry of Women, Children and Social Welfare to control and regulate programmes run by the SWC and partner NGOs, leading to fears that NGO activities might be curtailed.

Gender Relations/Empowerment: Women in Nepal suffer from economic, political and social inequality. Despite the constitutional provision for women's participation in politics, the proportion of representation is limited. In 1999 the government introduced the Local Self-Governance Act (LSGA) which provided reserved seats for women in each district municipality and village development committee as well as compelling all political parties to support female candidates, although local elections on the basis of the LSGA have yet to be held. Female representation in Nepal's influential civil service remains at little more than 7% and following the elections in 1999 they made up only about 6% and 15% of the lower and upper houses respectively. Women's access to income and resources is constrained by tradition as well as institutionalized discrimination. For example, women agricultural workers earn 20% less than men and women tend to be active primarily in under-unionized sectors, thus receiving little legal protection. To counter this, one of the most successful government-run programmes has been Production Credit for Rural Women which provides micro-credit for women. Furthermore, the 11th amendment to the **Muluki Ain** in 2001 introduced legal changes in favour of women, granting daughters and widows inheritance rights as well as greater ownership rights within the family. Despite recent improvements, the adult literacy rate for women in 2000 was just over half that of men and Nepal continues to have one of the highest maternal mortality rates in South Asia.

Nepal Rastra Bank

Nepal's central bank, the Rastra Bank, was established in 1956 to guide the country's monetary policy. The bank oversaw foreign exchange rates and reserves, an important role given the free flow of Indian rupees into Nepal and the difficulty of controlling and monitoring exchange rates. A 1960 Act sought to regulate foreign exchange transactions and to encourage use of the Nepalese rupee within the country. Moreover, it was only after the 1960 Trade and Transit Treaty with India that Nepal's foreign exchange earnings no longer passed through the Central Bank of India.

Nepal Sadbhavana Party (NSP)

The Nepal Sadbhavana Party (NSP—Nepal Goodwill Party) was founded in the early 1980s to improve rural conditions and to combat alleged discrimination against the **Madhesis**, as people of Indian plains origin are termed. In the 1991 elections it won six seats and was part of various coalition governments in the 1990s. A core demand has been full citizenship for all Madhesis in Nepal. In 1999 the NSP secured five seats in the house of representatives.

Nepalese Issue/Conflict

The 'Nepalese Issue', also known as the 'Southern Problem', is a major challenge facing the Bhutanese state. It is primarily an ethnic conflict between the **Lhotshampa**, people of Nepalese origin living in southern Bhutan, and the **Ngalong** (of Tibetan stock) who dominate the ruling élite and state institutions. The attempted coup of 1964 by dissidents and the annexation of neighbouring Sikkim in 1975 by India, in which Nepalese allegedly played a significant role, fuelled suspicions and existing prejudices against further immigration of ethnic Nepalese. The numbers of immigrants across open and porous borders increased in the early 1960s at a time when the Bhutanese government was attempting to initiate a process of economic modernization. Gradually portrayed as a threat to national stability and sovereignty, the Bhutanese government, supported by the monastic authorities and the conservative **Drukpa** middle class, implemented a restrictive migration policy in the 1980s and an integration policy to draw the Lhotshampa into the national mainstream. The Lhotshampa, in turn, feeling marginalized and discriminated against, began to perceive this integration as harmful to their own identity and felt the need to resist this process of assimilation into a dominating and exclusive Drukpa culture. Major steps towards a 'Bhutanization' of the Nepali population include the promulgation of **Dzongkha** as the national language and the only official language at schools, the Green Belt proposal, the Bhutan Marriage Act, and the implementation of **Driglam Namzha**. Following various Citizenship Acts, ethnic Nepalese who had migrated to Bhutan after 1958 were labelled illegal or non-national, raising tensions particularly as large numbers were expelled and forced to live as refugees in camps across the borders in Nepal and India. The crisis reached its flashpoint when the Bhutanese census of 1988 identified a significant number of illegal immigrants and landholdings, portrayed by the government as a planned and systematic infiltration of southern Bhutanese districts by the Nepalese. Using the Bhutanese Armed Forces, these people were forced to leave the country, many refugees reporting violations of human rights and the eviction of people who possessed correct citizenship certificates. While it is impossible to identify how many left the country voluntarily or under pressure, it is estimated that more than 100,000 Nepalese live in refugee camps in Eastern Nepal, a major and ongoing cause for tension between both countries.

Nepali Congress (NC)

Nepal's largest political party, the Nepali Congress (NC), has its origins in the Indian independence movement as the Nepali National Congress which officially aimed at peacefully ending the Rana system of rule and the establishment of democratic socialism in Nepal. In 1950, renamed as the NC after merging with the Nepali Democratic Congress which had the financial means to build up a liberation army (*mukti sena*) on Indian soil, an armed struggle against the Rana regime was launched. In 1951, under the 'Delhi compromise' to which the NC was not a party, an interim governing coalition was formed with a Rana Prime Minister, seven other Rana ministers and seven NC ministers under the leadership of B. P. **Koirala**. The breakdown of this government in November 1951 allowed rifts within the NC to surface, especially between B. P. and M. P. **Koirala**, causing the party to split in 1953 and to become sidelined in national politics. Nevertheless, the NC won a landslide victory in the country's first parliamentary elections in 1959, taking 74 out of 109 seats, and B. P. Koirala became Prime Minister. From the start the NC's attempts at reform were opposed by the Gorkha Parishad (19 seats) and the **Communist Party of Nepal** (**CPN**, four seats). King **Mahendra**'s decision to dismiss the government, assume emergency power in 1960 and put many NC leaders into prison without trial forced the NC underground.

Over the next 30 years under the ***Panchayat* system** the NC continued to advocate its programme of eliminating the feudal economy and a return to democracy. After boycotting the general elections of 1981 and 1986, the NC participated in the 1987 local elections. Following an economic crisis in 1989, due to strained Indo-Nepalese relations, and mounting political dissatisfaction, the NC finally opted for direct confrontation, joining the *ad hoc* coalition of communist groups, the **United Left Front (ULF)**, to launch the Movement for the Restoration of Multi-Party Democracy, **Jana Andolan**, in February 1990. On 19 April an 11-member coalition Council of Ministers was appointed, including four representatives of the CPN and three of the ULF, forming an interim government until elections in May 1991.

The NC obtained an absolute majority of seats in the parliamentary elections of 1991 but communist factions formed a united and significant opposition and the government, under G. P. **Koirala**, collapsed in 1994 due to political infighting. Despite winning another parliamentary majority in 1999, the party was unable to form a stable government. Long-standing internal rifts include divisions over policies towards India, economic programmes and, most importantly, support for the constitutional monarchy. The party has tried to portray itself as the sole reliable guarantor of a democratic polity and as the best bulwark against the communists. On economic issues, while initially inclined towards socialism, the NC has supported reform and privatization.

In protest against King **Gyanendra**'s tilt towards assuming direct rule since 2002, the NC officially announced in September 2005 that it was dropping its 60-year-old, written allegiance to the monarchy.

Nepali Congress Party (NC)

Nepal's oldest, continually functioning political party, known today as the **Nepali Congress (NC)**. Founded in 1947 by dissident exiles in India as the Nepali Rastriya Congress (Nepali National Congress), the party subsequently split from and then rejoined the Nepal Democratic Congress, to become the NC in 1950.

Ngalong

The Ngalong are one of three major ethnic communities in Bhutan. The term literally means 'those risen earliest or converted first'. Of Tibetan origin, they are concentrated in the western and northern districts of the country, follow the **Drupka** school and speak **Dzongkha**. Today the Ngalong provide and implement their own culture as the core value of the Bhutanese nation and also dominate the socio-economic and political élite and decision-making institutions of the country. The King's family belongs to this ethnic group. The Ngalong have come into conflict with the second major ethnic group, the **Lhotshampa**, and also, to some extent, with the **Sharchop**. (*See* **Nepalese Issue/Conflict**.)

North East Frontiers Agency (NEFA)

During the time of the British Empire the North East Frontiers Agency (NEFA) was kept deliberately isolated from the rest of India, with the objective of creating a buffer zone between China, Central Asia, Russia and British India. Following independence in 1947, NEFA was administered by the Ministry of External Affairs with the Governor of Assam acting as agent to the President of India. In 1972, under Prime Minister Indira **Gandhi**, NEFA became a **Union Territory** with the name of Arunachal Pradesh and in 1987 statehood was conferred. The state shares a total of 1,630 km of boundary with China, Bhutan and Myanmar. The **McMahon Line** defines the international frontier between India and China and **Tawang** was one of the battlesites during the 1962 Sino–Indian war. It is a border that China still does not officially recognize.

North East India

The 'seven sister' states of Nagaland, Arunachal Pradesh, Mizoram, Manipur, Meghalaya, Tripura and Assam, together with Sikkim, make up the North East region of India. Strategically, this is a highly vulnerable area given that the states border Myanmar, China, Bangladesh, Nepal and Bhutan, all of which have been suspected of deliberately aiding or of turning a blind eye to activities conducted by the many separatist movements in the region. Furthermore, the states are connected to India through a narrow stretch of land only 24 km in width, known as the 'Chicken's Neck' or the Siliguri Corridor. As a result, the Indian army, along with the Assam Rifles, the Border Security Force and the **West Bengal** police, maintain a heavy presence. The region is characterized by extreme ethnic, cultural, religious and linguistic diversity. Mehgalaya, Nagaland and Mizoram are the only Indian states with a Christian majority; there is a sizeable Muslim population in Assam and a variety of tribes that have posed an administrative challenge, requiring a delicate balance of legislation that both protects and conserves cultures yet also provides for economic betterment. Under independent India's Constitution, the

Sixth Schedule provided tribal communities in Assam with autonomy in conducting their administrative, legislative and financial matters. **Partition** in 1947 added further problems, severing inland communication networks, removing crucial economic links, such as the Chittagong port, and bringing in waves of migrants and refugees from east Pakistan that disturbed the demographic balance. The relative geographical isolation of the region combined with indirect rule and underdevelopment during the British colonial period, as well as the numerous indigenous fault lines drawn along tribal differences, tribals versus non-tribals, both groups opposing the state, spawned a number of agitations in the region. Some, like the **All-Assam Students Union (AASU)**, claimed official language status for Assamese in 1960–61, while other groups demanded outright independence, as in the case of the **Bodoland Movement**. Each of the states by the 1980s had experience of violent insurgency movements, aided by foreign arms and external support. In response, the central government of India began to bestow statehood, a first wave occurring in the 1960s and 1970s when Nagaland and Meghalaya were carved out of Assam (in 1963 and 1972, respectively), Manipur and Tripura, which were recognized in 1972, and a second phase under Prime Minister Rajiv Gandhi, when the **Union Territories** of Mizoram and Arunachal Pradesh (formerly, under the British, the **North East Frontiers Agency**) became states in 1986 and 1987 respectively. Politically, however, the North East has been sidelined, partly because, under the system of allotting **Lok Sabha** seats according to population, the states collectively hold only 25 seats (which **Rajasthan** alone has) and thus the major political parties have shown relatively little interest in local politics and issues. In the 1990s there was a proliferation of militant organizations throughout the region and a culture of violence was propagated, in particular by the **United Liberation Front of Assam** and the Bodo outfits. Combining military action (Operation Bajrang in the case of Assam) and support for the electoral process, the government of India has managed to improve conditions to the extent that both the **Bharatiya Janata Party (BJP)** and the **Indian National Congress (INC)** have been competing for local allies. In the 2004 legislative elections, the **National Democratic Alliance (NDA)** joined with the Trinamool Congress in Meghalaya, the **Mizo National Front (MNF)** in Mizoram, the **Nagaland People's Front** in Nagaland and the **Sikkim Democratic Front (SDF)** in Sikkim, making successful inroads into state politics. Security problems continue to trouble the region. For example, in 2004 the imposition of President's rule on Manipur was considered as protests erupted, demanding that the Armed Forces Special Powers Act (AFSPA) be repealed. In place since 1980, the AFSPA grants extraordinary coercive powers to the army. Nevertheless, regular assembly elections have been held in all the North Eastern states and are characterized by a high voter turn-out. Worn out by decades of internal instability and violence, state governments are increasingly looking to opportunities for tourism and the potential of the region's valuable natural resources to generate new employment and stimulate economic development.

North West Frontier Province (NWFP)

North West Frontier Province (NWFP) is the smallest and one of the most backward of Pakistan's provinces, accounting for 12.8% of Pakistan's territory. It is bounded to the north and west by Afghanistan and has been of great historical and strategic importance due to its passes leading into India. The region was separated by the British in 1901 from the **Punjab** of India and in 1947 voted to join newly independent Pakistan. In 1970 the region was granted provincial status and the capital, Peshawar, became the military and political centre of the Afghan anti-Soviet campaign in the1980s. More than 3m. Afghan refugees are still in the NWFP and **Balochistan**. A relatively land-scarce province, the agricultural economy of the NWFP is limited and human development indices of literacy and mortality are worse than those of other provinces. Since the 2002 general elections the religious alliance, **Muttahida Majlis-e-Amal (MMA)**, has been in power in the province.

Northern Areas – *see* Federally Administered Northern Areas (FANA)

Nuclear Non-Proliferation Treaty (NPT)

The Nuclear Non-Proliferation Treaty (NPT) is an international treaty to prevent the spread of nuclear weapons and weapons technology, to promote co-operation in the peaceful use of nuclear energy and to achieve nuclear as well as full disarmament. Opened for signature in 1968, the Treaty came into force in 1970. So far 187 countries have joined the Treaty but both India and Pakistan, for reasons contained in their nuclear policy, continue to withhold signatures to the Treaty. (*See* **Nuclearization**.)

Nuclearization

On 11 and 13 May 1998 India set off five nuclear devices at its test site in Pokhran, in the north-western state of **Rajasthan**. Pakistan followed suit with six tests of its own on 28 and 30 May. Both countries had long possessed the capacity to develop nuclear weapons, and the 1998 tests marked an important threshold arising from a combination of domestic and international pressures. India's programme is traceable back to 1945, when the Tata Institute of Fundamental Research was created on the initiative of nuclear physicist Homi J. Bhabha who later ran the Atomic Energy Commission. Similarly, in 1955 the Pakistan Atomic Energy Commission was set up to promote peaceful uses of atomic energy. India's first test in 1974, under Prime Minister Indira **Gandhi**, combined with the dismemberment of Pakistan in 1971 and the creation of Bangladesh, prompted Prime Minister Zulfikar Ali **Bhutto** to initiate Pakistan's nuclear weapons programme with **Kahuta Research Laboratories** emerging as its main centre.

Pakistan and India remain non-signatories of the **Nuclear Non-Proliferation Treaty** and the **Comprehensive Test Ban Treaty (CTBT)**. Since they became nuclear powers the two countries have twice come to the brink of war: in 1999, when the Kargil crisis resulted in armed conflict between them; and in 2002, when India deployed troops in forward positions along the border following an attack on the Indian parliament in December 2001. Whether conflict between the neighbouring countries will remain more limited and localized as a result of nuclearization remains unclear.

In 2005, according to international estimates, India had a stockpile of approximately 40–50 assembled nuclear weapons. Numbers are more uncertain in the case of Pakistan, but it is reported that the country has between 24 and 48 nuclear weapons. India has several types of aircraft that could be used to deliver a nuclear weapon and has developed *Agni II* intermediate-range ballistic missiles with a tested range of 2,000 km. US-manufactured F-16s are most likely to be used by the Pakistani air force to deliver nuclear weapons and the *Ghauri* missile has a tested range of 1,100 km.

Pakistan does not abide by a no-first use doctrine, which means that in the event of an attack by India, which has superior conventional forces, Pakistan might use its nuclear weapons. India maintains a 'credible minimum nuclear deterrence' under which it will not be the first to use nuclear weapons in a conflict but will respond with punitive retaliation should deterrence fail. In January 2003 India made its nuclear doctrine public and announced the setting up of a Nuclear Command Authority to manage its nuclear arsenal. However, a civil body, the Cabinet Committee on Security, is the final decision-making authority. In the case of Paksitan, an official doctrine has yet to be issued. A centralized command and control structure was established in 2000, comprising President **Musharraf**, cabinet ministers and the chairman of the Joint Chiefs of Staff Committee.

In January 2006, India and Pakistan exchanged lists of their nuclear facilities and installations as stipulated under an accord in place since 1988. The agreement came into force in 1991 and the first such exchange of information took place on 1 January 1992. Both countries have since continued with the practice, even at the height of tensions in 2002.

O

Operation Blue Star

In early 1984 the radical Sikh leader Sant Jarnail Singh **Bhindranwale** conducted his violent campaign out of the *Akal Takht*, the main building within the Golden Temple of Amritsar in **Punjab**, which was transformed into his heavily fortified headquarters. On 5 June the Indian Army entered the Golden Temple in an attack codenamed 'Operation Blue Star'. As the extremists were far better armed and prepared than intelligence reports had estimated, the action turned into a bloody, three-day siege. Total casualties amounted to 92 killed and 287 wounded among the soldiers, and 554 killed and 121 wounded among militants and civilian pilgrims. Bhindranwale and Shabeg Singh, a retired high-ranking officer of the Indian Army who was the military leader of the militants, were among the dead. Parallel to the action in the Golden Temple, a huge security counteroffensive across Punjab was launched, forcing militants underground and leading to the arrest of virtually all mainstream **Akali Dal** politicians, including the former Chief Ministers Badal and Longowal. In a follow-up to the heavy crackdown and the partial destruction of the Golden Temple, Prime Minister Indira **Gandhi** was assassinated by two Sikh members of her security guard on 31 October 1984. (*See* **Khalistan**.)

Operation Enduring Freedom

Operation Enduring Freedom, the military phase of the US-led war on terror, began on 7 October 2001, following the 11 September attacks on the USA. The special engagement of the USA in South Asia is motivated by various security concerns that affect vital US interests, including nuclear proliferation, anti-terrorist operations, regional peace and the reduction of India–Pakistan tensions. As a front line state, Pakistan was a crucial American ally during the campaign to eliminate the Taliban in Afghanistan and has provided assistance in the war on terror by capturing al-Qa'ida members in the border region. The USA, in return, has provided debt relief as well as military and economic assistance to Pakistan.

Orissa

Situated in the east with a coastline along the Bay of Bengal, the Indian state of Orissa was formed soon after independence in 1947, with its capital in Bhubaneshwar. It remained unaffected by the linguistic reorganization that followed as it was already constituted as a state for Oriya-speakers (82.8% of the population in 1991) following a long and intensive agitation by the Oriya-speakers of the earlier province of Bihar and Orissa that led to a separate province of Orissa in 1936.

In 2001 the total population of Orissa was 36,804,660, of which 94.4% claimed Hinduism as their religion, with Christians forming a minority of 2.4% and Muslims 2.1%. **Scheduled Tribes (STs)** constitute a large proportion (22.1%) of the population and a reported 62 different tribal groups live in the state as well as a large number of **Scheduled Castes (SCs)**, accounting for 16.5% of the population. Orissa is a relatively poor state despite its rich natural resources. The vast majority of its population is rural and dependent on agricultural employment. The state's legislative assembly comprises 147 seats and Orissa returns 21 members to the **Lok Sabha**. The **Congress** and Janata Party have traditionally competed for control in this state. However, since 1998 the **Bharatiya Janata Party (BJP)** has been a significant force, managing to capitalize on the backwardness and sense of regional discrimination prevalent in the western part of the state. In 2000 the BJP's rise was further boosted by the formation of the **Biju Janata Dal (BJD)**, which split from the Janata Party and entered into an alliance with the BJP to win an overwhelming victory in the 2000 assembly elections. The BJP-BJD partnership has functioned well, the two parties' support bases complementing one another, with the BJP drawing upper caste votes and the BJD picking up support from **Other Backward Classes** (OBCs) deriving from its Janata Party roots. In 2004 Orissa was one of the few states where the BJP maintained its positions both in state assembly and Lok Sabha elections. The alliance has sustained itself since 2000, partly because the parties have strengths in different areas of the state, with the BJD performing well in the coastal region and the BJP experiencing its growth in the west and tribal areas.

Other Backward Classes (OBCs)

Besides the **Scheduled Castes** and the **Scheduled Tribes**, the Other Backward Casses (OBCs) are the third social group entitled to positive discimination under Article 340 of the Indian Constitution. Much debate has gone into deciding what should be the criteria for 'backwardness'. After the Kalelkar Commission of 1953 failed to produce a consensus, a second commission, known as the **Mandal Commission**, was set up in 1979. Its report in 1980 calculated that the population of OBCs, both Hindu and non-Hindu, constituted around 52% of the country's population. Despite constituting more than half of the total Indian population, the OBCs are entitled to no more than 27% of job reservations in public services. (*See* **Reservation Policy**.)

P

Pakistan, Islamic Republic of

An Islamic republic, bordering the Arabian Sea, flanked by India to the east, Iran and Afghanistan to the west and China in the north, Pakistan is composed of four provinces, **Balochistan**, **North West Frontier Province (NWFP)**, **Punjab** and **Sind**. In addition there are the **Federally Administered Tribal Area** where the federal government has limited control over internal politics, the **Federally Administered Northern Areas**, **Azad Kashmir** and the Islamabad Capital Territory.

Area: 803,940 sq km; capital: Islamabad; population: 153m. (UN 2003), comprising ethnic Punjabis (*c.* 66%), Sindhis (*c.* 13%), Pashtun (*c.* 10.9%), Balochi (*c.* 2.5%) and Muhajir (immigrants from India at the time of **Partition** and their descendants, *c.* 7.6%); official language: Urdu; religion: Muslim *c.* 97% (Sunni 77%, Shi'a 20%), Christian, Hindu and others *c.* 3%. The bicameral parliament (Majlis-e-Shoora) consists of the 100-seat Senate, to which members are elected by provincial assemblies, and the National Assembly, whose 342 members are chosen by popular vote. Both carry a four-year term. The National Assembly selects the Prime Minister to serve for four years, and the President is normally elected by parliament for a five-year term.

History: Pakistan's territory includes the sites of the prehistoric Indus Valley civilization (*c.* 2500–1700 BC). Islam, the dominant religion today, arrived in 711 AD. After a long period of invasions, the Islamic, *Mughal* empire was established in the mid-16th century, ruling over much of present-day Pakistan and large parts of India, to be followed by the British in the mid-18th century. In 1947 Pakistan was carved out of the British Empire as a home for South Asia's Muslims. The **Muslim League (ML)** was formed in 1906, responding to Muslim grievances against a perceived Hindu domination, but the idea of a Muslim nation distinct from Hindu India was introduced only in 1930 by the poet, Muhammad Iqbal. Later, the idea was given political form when the Muslim League, led by Muhammad Ali **Jinnah**, demanded the establishment of Pakistan in areas where Muslims were a majority, giving rise to the Two Nation Theory, formulated in the 1940 Lahore Resolution. Partition of the subcontinent presented Pakistan with a number of institutional as well as geographical challenges. Divided into two sections, East and West Pakistan were separated by about 1,600 km of Indian territory. Demographics combined with ethnic rivalries and provincial particularisms posed an especial problem for the functioning of federalism. Unresolved disputes over the India-Pakistan boundary, most particularly over the control of the state of **Jammu and Kashmir**, ensured bitter relations between the two. Furthermore Pakistan inherited no capital city and no administrative core.

The 1949 Objectives Resolution, formulated by the country's constitution-making body, specified that Pakistan would be Islamic, democratic and federal. However, within 13 months of independence, Jinnah, the country's *Quaid-i-Azam* (Great Leader) was dead and in 1951, the first Prime Minister, Liaquat Ali Khan, assassinated, creating a vacuum right at the start of Pakistan's state- and nation-building process. In the absence of a federally based political party, an essentially migrant political leadership at the centre faced the urgent need to assert central authority over the provinces succumbing quickly to what has been described as a 'bureaucratic authoritarianism', already inherent in the colonial state structure. A succession of unelected civil bureaucrats assumed elective office.

In 1953 Governor-General Mohammad dismissed the Prime Minister, and in 1954 he dissolved the constituent assembly, setting a dangerous precedent for executive intervention. The Constitution of 1956 marked a first attempt at implementing federal principles and a parliamentary form of government whilst at the same time integrating special provisions for Islam. The experiment came to a sudden end in 1958, when Governor-General Iskander Mirza abrogated the Constitution, banned political parties and imposed martial law. Shortly after, he was removed by Commander-in-Chief, Gen. Ayub **Khan**, initiating Pakistan's long descent into military rule. Much vaunted land reforms in 1959 avoided any major overhaul of Pakistan's agrarian structure. Instead, a new class of middling landlords was created, dependent on the state apparatus and further entrenching centralized bureaucratic control.

There was war with India over Kashmir in 1965 and discontent over Pakistan's alignment with the USA grew. In 1969, in the midst of massive anti-government demonstrations, Ayub resigned. Elections were held in 1970 for the first time since independence bringing to the forefront the festering rift between East and West Pakistan. An overwhelming victory of the **Awami League (AL)** in East Pakistan led to demands for independence, to which the central government responded with military occupation. Internal turmoil, followed by India's invasion, resulted in the secession of East Pakistan as Bangladesh in December 1971. Discredited by the military defeat, President Yahya Khan handed over power to the founder and chairman of the **Pakistan People's Party (PPP)**, Zulfikar Ali **Bhutto**. Under Bhutto a formal parliamentary system was set up, restoring the position of Prime Minister to the most powerful. Inaugurating a new constitution in 1973, President Bhutto became Prime Minister of Pakistan. A deadlock produced by the 1977 general elections, in which nine opposition parties united in the Pakistan National Alliance (PNA) to run against Bhutto's PPP, provided the occasion for the military to stage a coup and restore martial law. For the next eight years under Gen. Muhammad **Zia** ul-Haq,

Chief of Army Staff, militarism and Islam became the twin pillars of the regime. Zulfikar Ali Bhutto was hanged, political activity was curtailed and an extensive Islamization programme launched.

Following the Soviet intervention in Afghanistan in 1979 closer ties with the USA were secured with a five-year economic and military aid package worth US $3,200m. for Pakistan. Zia's death in a mysterious plane crash led to elections in 1988, resulting in the victory of the PPP under the leadership of Benazir **Bhutto**. The first woman to head an Islamic state, she was dismissed in 1990 on grounds of corruption and ineptitude by the President. Invested with the power to do so under Zia's 1983 Constitution, the President, acting at the behest of the military, ensured the removal of three elected governments (those of Bhutto in 1990, Sharif in 1993, and Bhutto in 1996). Tense civil-military relations following Prime Minister Nawaz **Sharif**'s attempts to dismiss Gen. Pervez **Musharraf** as Chief of Army Staff and the debacle during the Kargil war with India in 1999 triggered the country's fourth military coup since 1947. Led by Pervez Musharraf in 1999, the military claimed to be acting in the national interest, intervening temporarily to establish a 'real' democracy, to restore the economy and to purge the country of corruption.

In November 1999 a National Accountability Bureau was created to fight corruption and by 2001 both Nawaz Sharif and Benazir Bhutto had been charged and convicted, the former officially in exile and a warrant issued for Bhutto's arrest, effectively removing two of Musharraf's major opponents. The opposition, mobilizing itself under the banner 'Alliance for Restoration of Democracy', closely resembled the Movement for Restoration of Democracy formed during Zia's rule. In a move to strengthen his position, Musharraf assumed the presidency in June 2001. Under growing pressure both from within and outside Pakistan, Musharraf announced elections for October 2002, promising that political parties would be allowed to participate.

Pakistan's new strategic significance following the terrorist attacks of September 2001 presented Musharraf both with an opportunity and a threat to his power, on the one hand securing political recognition and aid from the USA (the lifting of sanctions imposed following nuclear tests in 1998), while on the other his collaboration in 'the war against terrorism' incurred the anger of religious extremists within Pakistan. A national referendum in April 2002 extended Musharraf's presidency by five years. In August Musharraf promulgated the Legal Framework Order that introduced 35 amendments to the 1973 Constitution granting him sweeping powers to dissolve the National Assembly. The National Security Council was created, through which the military acquired a formal role in governing the country.

Latest Elections: Both the PPP and the **Pakistan Muslim League (PML)** under new leaderships were permitted to take part in the October 2002 elections. The PML(Q), the main party supporting Musharraf, did not win an outright majority (77 seats) but was closely followed by the PPP (63 seats) and the **Muttahida Majlis-e-Amal (MMA)**, an alliance of six Islamist parties (45 seats). The PML fared badly, winning only 14 seats. A clear victory for the MMA in the NWFP state elections reinforced the position of the alliance in the National Assembly, which was convened in November. Zafarullah Khan Jamali, the PML (Q) leader, was narrowly elected as Pakistan's Prime Minister and a fragile coalition government established.

Recent Developments: In December 2003 there were two attempts on Musharraf's life, believed to be the work of Islamic militants following the rise in anti-American sentiments as a result of Pakistan's collaboration with the USA in the war against terrorism. Until the 2002 elections the religious parties had never obtained more than 5% of the total vote in the country. In 2002 this rose to nearly 11%. In June 2003 the NWFP voted to introduce *Shari'a* law. In January 2004 President Musharraf secured a vote of confidence in all of the national and provincial assemblies.

Pakistan, Political Development

Pakistan has had a short and turbulent political history, oscillating between military dictatorship and elected political authoritarianism. Despite 98% of the population sharing the common religion of Islam, ethno-linguistic differences (there are more than 20 languages and 300 dialects) and regional diversity have seriously impeded the development of a national identity and stable political system. Intolerance of diversity and an inability to accommodate have been core problems within Pakistan's political tradition. Political élites are drawn mostly from the landed feudal class, businessmen, and religious leaders. Disagreement on the role of religion and the sharing of power between provinces and the centre led to long deliberations over nine years before the country's first constitution could be finalized. A subsequent weakening of the ruling party, continuous regional rifts, ethnic dissension and religious debate paved the way towards dissolution of the first constituent assembly in 1954 and enforcement of martial law in 1958. Under the martial law regime of Gen. Ayub **Khan** the **Basic Democracies** and indirect elections were introduced, giving way to the second constitution of the country in 1962 (abrogated with Ayub's downfall in 1969 after a popular uprising against his rule). In the election of 1970, **Bhutto**'s **Pakistan People's Party (PPP)**, promoting secular ideology, and Mujibur **Rahman**'s **Awami League (AL)**, advocating more autonomy for the east wing, won overwhelming majorities in West and East Pakistan respectively. The politicians' unwillingness to share power, apathy within the civil-military bureaucracy, exacerbated by an already fragile political balance, culminated in the dismemberment of Pakistan and the creation of Bangladesh in 1971.

Though Bhutto's government introduced civil service reforms, land reforms, the quota system and a new constitution in 1973, his economic policies were whimsical and inadequate. Combined with his authoritarian and repressive handling of dissenting elements, they paved the way for the third and longest period of military rule under Gen. **Zia** from 1977. Zia repressed political activities, attempting to legitimize his rule through a programme of Islamization. Elections in 1985 were held on a non-party basis and a new constituent assembly amended the 1973 Constitution, incorporating the 8th amendment which gave the President discretionary powers to dismiss a popularly elected government at his will.

The decade of 1988–98 represented the longest phase of civilian rule in Pakistan, but was marked by unprecedented corruption, law and order problems, economic instability, political victimization and individual authoritarianism, laying the grounds for yet another military *coup d'état* in 1999. Gen. **Musharraf** legalized his presidency through a referendum in April 2002, initiated a series of structural reforms, and has been trying to institutionalize the role of the army in Pakistani politics. Elections held in October 2002 established the pro-Musharraf PML (Q) (*see* **Pakistan Muslim League**) in power and, though not without resistance from opposition religious parties, the parliament passed the 17th amendment to the Constitution, *ex post facto* legalizing the 1999 coup and many of Musharraf's subsequent ordinances.

Constitution: The first attempt to draft a constitution for Pakistan ended in the dissolution of the Constituent Assembly in 1954. A new assembly formed in 1955 promulgated the country's first Constitution in 1956, establishing a federal republic comprising two provinces (East and West Paksitan), with equal representation in a single legislature and devolution of powers to the provincial governments. Soon after, in 1958, martial law was imposed until a new constitution in 1962 provided the basis for an executive system of government under the control of the President. Following the dismemberment of Pakistan and the formation of Bangladesh in 1971 and the emergence of Zulfikar Ali Bhutto, a new constitution was framed with the aim of resolving three core tensions: the role of Islam, the sharing of power between the centre and provinces and the division of responsibility between the President and Prime Minister. The latter was greatly strengthened and a bicameral legislature with a Senate, providing equal provincial representation, and a National Assembly, allocating seats according to size of population, were introduced. The new Constitution failed to bring stability to Pakistan's political development which continued to witness the challenge of balancing executive power between the Prime Minister and President. In 1985, under Gen. Zia ul-Haq, the Eighth Amendment shifted power in favour of the President and in 1997, under Prime Minister Nawaz **Sharif**, the Thirteenth Amendment sought to restore the Prime Minister's powers. On 12 October the Sharif government was overthrown in a bloodless military coup and on 15 October Gen. Musharraf appointed himself Chief Executive, declared a state of emergency and suspended the Constitution. A Legal Framework Order of August 2002 introduced 29 amendments, granting Musharraf the power to dissolve the elected National Assembly, extend his term of office and appoint Supreme Court judges. Following the October 2002 elections, Musharraf officially announced the revival of the 1973 Constitution as part of his promised transition to democracy. Although Musharraf declared the process of restoring the Constitution to be complete in March 2003, controversy persists over his amendments.

Eighth Amendment: In an attempt to strengthen his rule, Gen. Zia pushed the eighth amendment through parliament in November 1985, affecting almost 19 clauses of the Constitution of 1973, and shifting the balance of power greatly in favour of the President. Under this amendment, the President was given the right to nominate the Prime Minister, Governors of the provinces, and High and Supreme Court judges, including the Chief Justice. Article 58 (2) b, the most controversial clause of this amendment, gave the President powers to dissolve the National Assembly at his discretion, altering the entire spirit of the Constitution and almost transforming the system from a parliamentary to a presidential one.

Executive: Since its formation in 1947, Pakistan has faced the challenge of balancing executive power between the two offices of the Prime Minister and President. Powerful individuals and the role of the military have tended to overshadow and undermine the resilience of political institutions. As a result the country has experienced three different Constitutions and four phases of martial law.

At independence, Muhammad Ali **Jinnah** chose to become the country's first Governor-General, and as such ought to have been a figurehead, but in fact, as *Quaid-i-Azam* ('Father of the Nation'), wielded enormous power. Three Governor-Generals followed until 1956, when Pakistan's first Constitution abolished the office and replaced it with that of President within a parliamentary form of government. In 1958, due to increasing instability and factionalism within the government, Iskander Mirza, then President, declared martial law, appointing the Commander-in-Chief of the Armed Forces, Ayub Khan as martial law administrator. Soon after, Ayub Khan, in a bloodless coup, declared himself President, setting a precedent for continuous military involvement in Pakistani politics. Under Ayub Khan's 1962 Constitution, a presidential system augmented the traditional powers of the Chief Executive through control of the legislature, the power to issue ordinances, the right of appeal to referendum, protection from impeachment, control over the budget, and special emergency powers which included the ability to suspend civil rights.

In the next major reversal in Pakistani politics, Zulfikar Ali Bhutto, President and Chief Martial Law Administrator (1971), passed a new constitution in 1973 reintroducing a parliamentary system with himself as Prime Minister (1973). To maintain his own power, it became Bhutto's interest to reduce the presidency to a cipher. Consequently, provisions were included that made it impossible for the National Assembly to remove the Prime Minister. In addition, despite the constitutional provisions for a federal structure with residual powers reserved for the provinces, Bhutto's dismissal of provincial governments that were not ruled by his PPP highlighted his preference for centralized rule. It is argued that the 1973 Constitution went to such an extreme to reinstate the Prime Minister's powers that it virtually invited autocratic rule.

In 1977 Gen. Zia ul-Haq staged a coup and enforced martial law. A referendum in 1984 confirmed his position as President and under him the balance of power tilted dramatically towards the President's office. Through the controversial Eighth Amendment, political authority was given to the President enabling him to appoint and dismiss the Prime Minister and to dissolve both the National and Provincial Assemblies. This provision, which lasted until 1997, was used by President Zia in 1988 to dismiss Prime Minister Muhammad Khan Junejo, by President Ghulam Ishaq Khan to remove Prime Minister Benazir **Bhutto** in 1990 and Prime Minister Nawaz Sharif in 1993, and by President Farooq Leghari to remove Prime Minister Bhutto again in 1996.

In 1997, Prime Minister Nawaz Sharif successfully repealed the Eighth Amendment and introduced a number of measures to bolster the Prime Minister's Office. Among these was the Fourteenth Amendment, which gave party leaders unchecked powers to regulate and dismiss legislators. Since Sharif's party, the Pakistan Muslim League—Nawaz (PML—N), held the majority in parliament, it effectively gave the Prime Minister immunity from being dismissed by a vote of no confidence. Another example was the Ehtesab Act of 1997 which transferred the powers of investigating charges of corruption to a body directly under the Prime Minister's wing.

When, in 1999, Gen. Pervez Musharraf staged a coup to remove Nawaz Sharif from office, he promised a return to democracy under a system with strong checks and balances. Suspending the Constitution, Musharraf has gradually gone about restoring the 1973 version of the basic law, a process that was declared complete in March 2003. Under the 1973 Constitution the President is elected for a five-year term by an electoral college consisting of members from the Senate and the National Assembly as well as members from the Provisional Assemblies. The President may be re-elected, but must not serve more than two consecutive terms. The President may resign, be impeached, or removed from office if there is a two-thirds' vote among members of the parliament. The Prime Minister is appointed by the President from among the members of the National Assembly and is assisted by the Federal Cabinet and a Council of Ministers.

Since appointing himself President in June 2001, Musharraf has made some attempts to strengthen the President's position. The Seventeenth Amendment of 2002 partly restored the President's reserve powers (the ability to dissolve elected councils) but made the exercise of those powers subject to Supreme Court approval or veto within 30 days. Also in 2002, a National Security Council (NSC) was established as a consultative body. Musharraf described the NSC as an insurance against future military coups, and as a mechanism of institutionalizing the role of the military in the government. In January 2004 President Musharraf secured a vote of confidence from the Electoral College, effectively legitimizing his presidency and the right to serve a five-year term ending in 2007. Furthermore, towards the end of 2004 a bill was passed allowing him to retain both the presidency and his military position, representing yet again a distortion of the Constitution. As a result, Musharraf continues to be the active executive of Pakistan's government.

Legislature: Over the past 58 years, since independence, Pakistan has experienced both unicameral and bicameral legislatures, presidential and parliamentary forms of government, as well as one unit and federal state structures. The constituent assemblies in existence on the eve of **Partition** were given the status of dominion legislatures through the Independence Act of 1947. Pakistan's first legislature met on 10 August 1947 in Karachi to elect Muhammad Ali Jinnah as the president of the Constituent Assembly. Entrusted with the responsibility of framing a constitution for the new-born state, the first legislature could only pass the basic norms, called the Objective Resolution of Pakistan, in 1949. Prior to submitting a draft constitution, the legislative assembly was dissolved in October 1954 and a second legislature (constituent assembly) was elected in May 1955 through an electoral college composed from the provincial assemblies. With a total strength of 80, this assembly passed the first Constitution of Pakistan in 1956, declaring Pakistan an Islamic republic, with a unicameral parliament of 310 National Assembly members vested with legislative powers and headed by a President. This Constitution was abrogated by the country's first martial law regime in October 1958. The third federal legislature (National Assembly) came into being under the second Constitution of March 1962, which envisaged a federal system with a presidential form of government and an indirect electoral system consisting of the basic democracies as an electoral college. Total membership of this legislature, which had a three-year term, was 156. Despite a second phase of martial law, imposed in March 1969, Pakistan experienced its first ever general elections based on adult franchise in December 1970. The federal legislature this time consisted of 313 members: 144 from West Pakistan and 169 from East Pakistan. A worsening political crisis culminated in the secession of Bangladesh in December 1971 and the remaining legislature of West Pakistan passed yet another constitution of 1973, which adopted, for the first time, a bicameral legislature: a 210-seat National Assembly and a 63-seat senate, each with five-year terms, and a parliamentary system headed by a Prime Minister vested with executive powers. In the aftermath of a third phase of martial law in 1977, the federal legislature was constituted as a federal council selected by the President (also the martial law administrator) and named the *Majlis-e-Shoora* in December 1981.

In 1985 a quasi-parliamentary system was restored and a newly elected legislature (elected on a non-party basis) adopted the eighth constitutional amendment containing Article 58 (2) (b), which conferred upon the President discretionary powers to dissolve elected governments. Over the next decade this article was invoked on four successive occasions by different Presidents to dissolve elected legislative assemblies and was only repealed from the Constitution through the 13th amendment in 1997. The federal legislature was suspended in October 1999 and subsequently, in June 2001, dissolved after the military take-over by Gen. Musharraf. Formed after the October 2002 elections, Pakistan's 12th legislature passed the 17th amendment to the Constitution, restoring the President's powers to dissolve the federal legislature, but this time subject to approval by the Supreme Court. At present the federal legislature consists of a 342-seat National Assembly (272 general seats, 10 reserved for non-Muslims and 60 for women) and a 100-seat senate (66 general seats, 17 reserved for women and 17 for technocrats). All four provinces have their own independent legislative assemblies with a cumulative strength of 728 members.

Elections/Electoral System: Under Pakistan's first Constitution of 1956 there was to be a parliamentary democracy and direct elections on the basis of adult franchise. By 1962 a new constitution had installed a presidential form of government, with absolute power vested in the President. Ever since, Pakistan has been trying to find its equilibrium somewhere between the two tendencies, despite numerous ruptures to its political system. In 1971 the country was dismembered and Bangladesh was created. Martial law has been declared four times, on each occasion the military leadership declaring that intervention was necessary for the sake of law and order and promising a gradual return to democracy.

In 1970 Pakistan's first general elections under adult franchise were held under an interim formula known as the Legal Framework Order. West Pakistan was divided into four provinces and seats were allocated according to population. The 1973 Constitution restyled the country as the Islamic Republic of Pakistan and set up a bicameral legislature with a National Assembly of 200 seats, whose occupants were elected directly for a five-year term. The Senate was to consist of 63 members, each of the four provinces.

The country's second general elections (and first after the formation of Bangladesh) were held in 1977, but, amidst allegations of widespread rigging by the ruling party, Bhutto's PPP and mounting disruption of public order, martial law was imposed by Gen. Zia ul-Haq in July 1977. In 1979 the Constitution was suspended once again and political parties declared defunct. To legitimize his presidency, Zia staged and won a referendum endorsing his rule in 1984. Elections were finally held in 1985 on a non-party basis. Contrary to expectations a large voter turn-out (53.68% for National Assembly elections and 57.37% for provincial assemblies) ushered in a new political leadership. The constitutional Eighth Amendment of November 1985, however, affecting almost 19 clauses of the Constitution, empowered the President to dissolve the National Assembly, and to nominate the Prime Minister, Governors of the provinces, and judges of the High Court and Supreme Court. Proponents of the amendment argued that such powers would help resolve deadlocks without having to revert to martial law.

Despite the turmoil caused by Gen. Zia's death in an air crash in 1988, elections were held as planned in November. Under a Supreme Court ruling, political parties were allowed to contest the elections and Benazir Bhutto of the PPP was sworn in as Prime Minister. The longest period of civilian rule in Pakistan's history ensued, regimes alternating between the PPP led by Bhutto and the Pakistan Muslim League (PML), led by Mohammad Nawaz Sharif. However, during this period of more than a decade, elections were called in 1990, 1993 and 1997, each time following a presidential decision, under the Eighth Amendment, to dissolve the Assembly. During Nawaz Sharif's rule a number of constitutional amendments were introduced in an attempt to tip the balance in favour of the Prime Minister.

A military coup in 1999 ousted Nawaz Sharif's Government and the Supreme Court ruled in 2000 that the intervention of the armed forces had been necessary to remove a corrupt government, directing Gen. Pervez Musharraf, the Chief

Executive, to hold general elections within three years. A new system of local government was installed in August 2001, under which direct elections on a non-party basis were held in five phases at the level of *zila* (district), *teshil* (town) and union councils. To attract voters, the minimum age for voters was lowered from 21 to 18 years and one-third of seats were reserved for women. How this system will function along with the provincial assemblies remains to be seen.

In October 2002 Pakistan held its eighth national parliamentary elections, which were contested by more than 70 parties, including regional parties with strongholds in their provinces. However, various requirements for candidates were introduced, effectively barring leaders of the two biggest opposition parties, Benazir Bhutto of the PPP and Nawaz Sharif of the PML. Delimitation of constituencies was adjusted to reflect population changes reported in the 1998 census, and as a result the number of National Assembly seats was increased to 272. National and provincial elections were held on the same day, a total of 2,098 candidates contesting the 272 National Assembly seats (from a total of 343, of which 60 were reserved for women and 10 for non-Muslim minorities) and the 728 seats of the Provincial Assemblies. In the 371-seat **Punjab** Assembly, eight were reserved for minorities; in the 168-seat **Sind** Assembly nine; in the 124-seat **North West Frontier Province** Assembly three; and in the 65-seat **Balochistan** Assembly three. For the first time since 1977 the minority communities were allowed to contest and vote for all general seats in the National and Provincial Assemblies, thus ending the separate electorate system.

Under the Legal Framework Order of August 2002, the President is once again empowered to dismiss the Prime Minister and dissolve parliament. Instability has continued to plague Pakistani politics, and following a referendum in May 2002 President Musharraf secured a so-called mandate to fulfil his five year term as President. In November 2004 a law was ratified by parliament allowing Musharraf to occupy the office of both President and head of the army.

Social Movements: A large number of social movements addressing a variety of issues, such as fair trade, economic and educational development, human rights, environmental problems, labour and minority issues, are in operation in Pakistan. Particularly during the 1950s and 1960s, student organizations and trade unions were widely involved in non-party political activism. Though different martial law regimes often interfered with the activities of these organizations, many managed to survive through donations from international circles and Pakistani citizens living abroad who see such movements as potentially contributing towards civil society.

Various social movements in Pakistan perform an important role in monitoring political processes. The People's Rights Movement (PRM), a confederation of social movements across the country, is a prominent actor in Pakistani civil society. Other major organizations include the Anjuman-e-Mazarain Punjab, the Dir Kohistan Forestry Royalties Movement, the Chashma Affectees Movement, and the teachers'/students'/doctors' movement against corporatization. On 12 January 2004 the Pakistan Social Forum was held in Lahore to prepare for the World Social

Forum in that year. The meeting was attended by more than 5,000 members from non-governmental organizations, left-wing parties, trade unions and peasant associations.

Foreign Policy: Pakistan's foreign policy has been determined by a complex balancing process which is the result of its history, religious heritage, and geography. The main concern of that policy has been to preserve the nation's territorial integrity and security, which have been constantly threatened since the state was created in 1947. The military as an institution is well entrenched and in firm control of the state machinery and decisions related to Pakistan's security.

India and Pakistan became adversaries at independence and have remained so. The two countries fought each other shortly after Partition, in 1965, and in 1971 when the dismemberment of Pakistan gave rise to the creation of Bangladesh. Instead of decreasing, India–Pakistan tensions increased after the Cold War. During the Cold War period Pakistan sought security through various alliances, establishing a strategic relationship with the USA to become one of its closest allies in the Muslim world. Following the Soviet intervention in Afghanistan in 1979, Pakistan became a front-line state for the USA. China has also been a major partner in Pakistan's security framework, the two countries having developed strong economic and political ties. The country's relationship with the USA improved in the wake of Pakistan's unconditional accession to the coalition against terrorism after 11 September 2001. The lifting by the USA of sanctions that had been imposed as a result of the nuclear tests carried out in 1998, combined with increased financial assistance, helped draw Pakistan out of its relative isolation following the military coup of October 1999.

The Indian nuclear tests in early May 1998 posed one of the gravest security challenges to Pakistan since independence in 1947. The tests drastically altered the strategic balance in the South Asian region, and in response to the Indian measures Pakistan itself conducted nuclear tests on 28 and 30 May 1998 in the name of security interests and self-defence. Following its tests, Pakistan declared a unilateral moratorium on testing, recognizing the need to prevent a nuclear arms race in South Asia. During foreign secretary-level talks in October 1998, under the agenda item for Peace and Security, Pakistan proposed a Strategic Restraint Regime with India. Based on the precept of preventing a nuclear arms race, the proposal included provision for maintaining nuclear deterrence at minimum levels and the commitment to refrain from introducing new and more destabilizing systems in the region. None the less, the nuclear neighbours clashed at Kargil in May 1999 and in December 2001 seemed to be on the verge of another war. In the recent past Pakistan has shown a strong interest in improving relations with Iran as well as with other Muslim countries. The Gulf States, especially Saudi Arabia, are very important allies of Pakistan, both in terms of financial support and because of the large expatriate Pakistani workforce in the Middle East.

Pakistan-China Relations: Faced with the need for reliable allies as a result of the apparent threat of India, Pakistan, in 1950, became the first Islamic country to recognize the People's Republic of China in 1950. This marked the start of cordial relations, which considerably increased after the Sino–India War of 1962. Both Pakistan and China resolved their border disputes amicably, signing a border agreement in 1963, to the dismay of the Indian government which accuses Pakistan of illegally ceding 5,180 sq km of Indian territory in **Azad Kashmir** to China. The countries collaborated to build the 1,200 km-long Karakorum Highway, the highest international road, of enormous commercial value, connecting Kashgar in China to Abbotabad in Pakistan.

China has consistently provided diplomatic, economic, military and technical assistance to Pakistan and co-operation between the two neighbours ranges from joint constructions of *JF-17* fighter aircraft and naval frigates to trade and investment in the industrial and agricultural sectors. The value of bilateral trade rose to US $2,400m. during 2004, of which Chinese exports represented $1,800m. China's huge contribution, both in financial and technical terms, to the $1,160m.-Gawader port project in Balochistan is a joint project of immense commercial and strategic importance for both neighbours.

Pakistan-US Relations: Pakistan-US relations have been characterized by both close alliance and estrangement. During the Cold War Pakistan played a critical role in US containment of the communist Soviet Union, the opening of China in the 1970s and the campaign against the Soviet presence in Afghanistan. Since the end of the Cold War Pakistan has collaborated with the USA in uprooting the Taliban from Afghanistan and as a front-line partner in the American war on terror. As a strategic ally in American containment policy Pakistan signed a mutual defence agreement with the USA in 1954 and subsequently joined SEATO and CENTO. Economic assistance was provided as well as military aid, although this was suspended during the India–Pakistan War of 1965 and remained so for the next 10 years.

During the 1970s, as the largest single donor (US $712m.) to the Indus Basin Development project, the USA played a major role in the construction of the Tarbela and Mungla dams in Pakistan. However, Pakistan's pursuit of nuclear weapons meant that economic assistance from the USA was cut off in April 1979 under the Symington Amendment. Only after the Soviet invasion of Afghanistan in December 1979 was the old alliance between the two countries revived. In return for its vital role in the campaign against the Soviets in Afghanistan, the USA provided Pakistan with $3,200m. in 1981 and $4,000m. in 1986 in economic and military assistance. However, following the Soviet withdrawal from Afghanistan in 1989, the USA quickly terminated assistance to Pakistan through the Pressler Amendment in 1990. Over the next decade bilateral relations deteriorated, culminating in sanctions under the Glenn Amendment in response to Pakistan's nuclear tests in May 1998. International political dynamics shifted considerably following the terrorist attacks of 11 September 2001, placing Pakistan back in the limelight as America's front-line ally in the 'war against terror'. In return for military bases in Pakistan, the USA provided large amounts of military and development aid and in June 2004 designated Pakistan a major non-NATO ally of the USA, enabling it to acquire defence equipment previously denied.

Judiciary: The Supreme Court is the highest body in the judicial system of Pakistan. It is headed by the Chief Justice of Pakistan and a certain number of judges, laid down by the Constitution. The Chief Justice is directly appointed by the President in consultation with the other judges. The Supreme Court exercises original, appellate and advisory jurisdiction. The apex of the judicial system, the Supreme Court, has the power to pronounce declaratory judgements in dissension between the Federal Government and Provincial Governments or between Provincial Governments. Each province has a High Court. Similar in structure to the Supreme Court, each High Court consists of the Chief Justice and several additional judges. The Supreme Court and the High Courts have been established under the Constitution, while the other Courts have been set up by parliamentary acts or acts passed in the Provincial Assemblies. Each High Court supervises and controls all courts subordinate to it. Any decision of a High Court can override that of the courts subordinate to it. The Federal Shariat Court comprises eight Muslim Judges, including the Chief Justice appointed by the President. Four of the judges have to be qualified as High Court Judges, while three belong to the *ulema* (scholars well versed in Islamic Law). The Court is assigned to examine the accordance of any law with the principles of the Koran.

Federal Shariat Court: The Federal Shariat Court was established on 2 May 1980 to replace the former system in which *Shariat* Benches were set up in Pakistan's four High Courts. This Court consists of a Chief Justice and seven judges, including three *ulemas* (religious scholars).The Shariat Court works separately from the normal legal system and has the power to overturn decisions involving Islamic law, such as in cases of rape, adultery and some cases of murder.

Hadood/Hudood Ordinances (1979): The Hadood Ordinances, promulgated by Gen. **Zia** ul-Haq during his programme of Islamization, include most controversially the criminalization of *zina*, defined as extra-marital sex, including adultery and fornication. The Ordinances have operated in a one-sided manner against women, who are invariably seen as the guilty party even if they have been the victims of rape. The number of female prisoners in Pakistan's jails increased abruptly in the years following the introduction of the Ordinances and more than one-half of them had been convicted on *zina* charges.

State propaganda has nevertheless continued to portray the Hadood Ordinances as an integral part of religious jurisprudence. To review the Ordinances President Musharraf set up a National Commission on the Status of Women in 2000. The Commission reported in 2003 that the ordinances were un-Islamic, having denied women their rights under the Holy Koran, and concluded that they ought to be repealed. The Commission's recommendations have yet to be implemented.

Mohtasib: The office of Mohtasib (Ombudsman), a special feature of the judicial system of Pakistan, is provided for in the Constitution. The Mohtasib is appointed by the President for a period of four years that can neither be extended nor renewed.

The Mohtasib aims at enforcing administrative accountability, through investigating and rectifying any injustice done to a person through maladministration by a federal agency or a federal government official. The Mohtasib has the capacity to award compensation to those who have suffered loss or damage as a result of maladministration. Excluded from jurisdiction are personal grievances or service matters of a public servant and matters relating to foreign affairs, national defence, and the armed services. The institution seeks to bridge the gap between administrator and citizen, to improve administrative processes and procedures, and to curb the misuse of discretionary powers.

Defence/Security: With India seen as the primary threat to security, Pakistan has always devoted a considerable proportion of its resources to defence. Faced with a potential enemy of much greater military strength, uncertain sources of supply and little strategic depth, Pakistan has relied upon a strategy of 'offensive defence', providing for quick pre-emptive strikes to disrupt enemy advances and inflict high costs. Furthermore, close relations have been cultivated with the USA and China to improve Pakistan's defences through direct aid, technology transfer, training and military equipment. The Ministry of Defence comprises the army, airforce, navy and aviation wings, including administrative and financial departments. In 1991 a Ministry of Defence Production was created and made responsible for promoting and co-ordinating indigenous military production. Pakistan's nuclear programme started in earnest after the loss of East Pakistan in the 1971 war with India and on 28 May 1998 Pakistan tested five separate nuclear devices in the desert area of Balochistan.

In 2004 the total military expenditure or Pakistan was US $3,848m., or 4.9% of the country's total GDP.

Intelligence Bureau (IB): Together with the Inter-Services Intelligence (ISI) and the Military Intelligence (MI), the Intelligence Bureau (IB) is one of the three principal intelligence agencies in Pakistan. The IB observes political operatives from countries considered hostile to Pakistan's national interests. It is, however, often accused of being responsible for harassing domestic opposition parties and political leaders.

Inter-Services Intelligence (ISI): The Directorate for Inter-Services Intelligence (ISI) was established in 1948 by a British army officer, Maj.-Gen. R. Cawthome, then Deputy Chief of Staff in the Army of Pakistan. ISI headquarters are located in Islamabad. The ISI and the Intelligence Bureau (IB) are the two main intelligence agencies in Pakistan. While the IB is controlled by the Ministry of the Interior, the ISI is part of the Ministry of Defence. ISI responsibilities include the collection of foreign and domestic intelligence and co-ordinating the intelligence functions of the three military services. Since its creation, a further objective of the ISI has been to gather intelligence in India. It is commonly believed that the ISI plays a key role in politics and decision-making within Pakistan and that all major decisions of domestic importance as well as foreign policy are taken in consultation with the agency.

Military Intelligence (MI): The MI is one of Pakistan's three main intelligence agencies together with the Inter-Services Intelligence (ISI) and Intelligence Bureau (IB). Prior to the imposition of martial law in 1958 it was answerable to the Commander-in-Chief of the Army, but later reported directly to the President, then the Chief Martial Law Administrator of Pakistan. Presently MI reports to the President via the Chief of General Staff. Its sphere of responsibilities includes both the internal and external dimensions of security and intelligence-gathering.

Military: Pakistan's military and bureaucracy were the only two organized institutions at the inception of the country in 1947. In response to the Indian threat, the military was given the highest priority and gradually developed into the country's most powerful institution. Today, the military has a total strength of about 620,000 armed force personnel with a reserve force of 500,000. The military is divided into five different branches, the Army, Navy, Air Force, Civil Armed Forces and National Guard. Military expenditure in 2004 was US $3,848,000m., or 4.9% of the GDP. Given the scale of this expenditure, it is generally felt that the military has been developed at the expense of other civil and political institutions.

Politics in Pakistan have been dominated by the military since the coup of Gen. Ayub Khan in 1958 when martial law was declared. Since independence in 1947 the country has been under direct military rule for more than 28 years. In October 1999 Gen. Pervez Musharraf led a bloodless coup and is the country's President to date, while retaining his army post.

Given the various military regimes and the inability to establish sustainable, representative institutions, the army considers itself to be the one stable institution in Pakistan and the 'guardian of faith', the protector of Pakistan's ideological values. In this way it has justified its repeated involvement in the nation-building process of the state. Due to Pakistan's geostrategic location it has gained substantial US military and financial support, initially as part of the containment policy against the Soviet Union during the Cold War, and more recently as the front-line partner in the 'war against terrorism' since 2001.

Police: Pakistan's police have primary internal security responsibilities but paramilitary forces such as the Rangers and the Frontier Constabulary also provide support in the event of acute law and order problems. The provincial governments control police forces. Generally the police forces in Pakistan are considered to be abusive, corrupt, inefficient and highly politicized. While the government frequently investigates police officials for alleged extrajudicial killings, prosecution is rare. Arduous working conditions, inadequate training and grossly insufficient remuneration are cited as the main causes of poor performance. Since its inception, Pakistan's police have been working under the colonial Police Act of 1861, primarily designed with the imperial intention of keeping subjects under control and not aimed at making the police a politically neutral outfit. Under President Musharraf, the military government promulgated the Police Ordinance (2002) with the objective of improving professionalism in the police services, making them operationally neutral, functionally cohesive and organizationally responsible.

Riots: At the time of **Partition** in 1947 the subcontinent witnessed serious religious and communal violence between Muslims, Hindus and Sikhs. Large religious riots followed independence as more than 14m. people moved across the newly created borders. In 1974 riots and protest marches broke out against the **Ahmadiyya** community in Pakistan. The persecution of Ahmadis ended when the parliament of Pakistan passed an amendment to the Constitution on 7 September 1974, declaring the adherents of Ahmadiyya Muslim Jamaat to be non-Muslims. The controversial blasphemy laws introduced in 1986, which state that 'anyone who directly or indirectly, by word, gesture, innuendo, or otherwise defiles the name of the holy prophet Muhammad will be punished with death or life imprisonment', raised further tensions between religious communities in Pakistan. In many cases, religious minorities have been victims of sectarian and communal violence. Under the blasphemy laws many Christians and Ahmadiyyas have been jailed and some have even been condemned to death. The **Shi'a–Sunni Conflict** divide often produces serious riots in Pakistan in which as many as 4,000 people have died since the early 1980s.

Terrorism: Since 9/11 and the resurgence of al-Qa'ida on the international scene, Pakistan has been considered as one of the states most susceptible to terrorism. Pakistan's perception and definition of terrorism could be described as ambivalent in nature and its link with terrorism is highly sensitive, complex and multi-dimensional. First, the Afghanistan-based al-Qa'ida and Taliban terrorism, despite official condemnation, has had in the past significant support from different Pakistani tribes, some of the religious political parties as well as links with Pakistan's intelligence agencies. Second, so-called terrorist groups in Pakistan are entwined with the ongoing struggle in Kashmir and Pakistan's direct and indirect support to that cause. As a result, several Pakistan-based *jihadi* groups resent the government's pro-US and anti-Taliban policies. Sectarianism is the third dimension of terrorism in Pakistan. Links with terrorism may be supported by different political parties or segments of the intelligence agencies in Pakistan to promote their own ends at home.

Terrorism in Pakistan is a major object of American attention. The government of Pakistan, in collaboration with the US government, is taking both short- as well as long-term measures to control this menace. These include banning various sectarian organizations, the closing down of various ***madrasas*** and the restructuring of their syllabuses, the establishment of an anti-terrorist force and attempts to promote moderate Islamic views, literacy and employment. In the last four years Pakistan has arrested and handed over some 600 alleged al-Qa'ida terrorists to the USA.

Bureaucracy: Since independence a tiny élite in Pakistan, comprising mainly Punjabi feudal leaders, and ranging from the bureaucracy to the military and to politicians, has exercised control over the state's resources. Soon after independence in 1947 the state was instrumentalized by a small political élite, anxious to exclude any competing counter-élites from the decision-making process. The higher bureaucracy has been responsible over a long period, along with the military, for dominating and subverting the political process. Most of the bureaucratic cadres were originally raised out of the colonial Indian Civil Service, whose members were well educated and well trained in Western norms of administration. These standards appear to have declined. Today the bureaucracy is mired in unethical or corrupt practices. Under the rule of Ayub Khan, the army and civil service, together with the small but influential industrial class as well as segments of the landed élite, became part of the political mainstream as the parliamentary government was replaced by a system of basic democracies in 1959. The system, by depriving parties and politicians with provincial bases of any role in the political system, reinforced the importance of bureaucratic patronage.

Citizenship: Under the 1951 Citizenship Act, as originally promulgated, any person born in Pakistan after commencement was declared a citizen of Pakistan. Also included in the category of those entitled to citizenship were parents of Pakistani nationals residing in India, and Commonwealth citizens able to transfer Rs5m. in foreign currency. Citizenship rights are also available (under the Naturalization Act of 1926) to nationals of countries other than those belonging to the Commonwealth once they have resided in Pakistan for a period of five years. Foreign women married to Pakistani nationals and minors (i.e. those below 21 years of age) and Pakistani women married to foreigners are also entitled to a Pakistani passport. Children born after 18 April 2000 to a Pakistani mother and a father who is a foreign national are to be treated automatically as citizens of Pakistan. Any Pakistani citizen residing outside Pakistan who is not a minor and who acquires the citizenship of another country must renounce citizenship of Pakistan.

Civil Service of Pakistan (CSP): The CSP has its origins in the pre-Partition Indian Civil Service. After Partition in 1947 vacancies were filled with quick promotions in the CSP. During the 1950s and 1960s the CSP became a powerful cadre force, wielding great influence in the country's policy-making process. Under Zulfikar Ali Bhutto's civil service reforms of 1973 (see below), the CSP was disbanded and the various administrative services amalgamated under one administrative system.

Civil Service Reforms (1973): Introduced by the government of Zulfikar Ali Bhutto in 1973, the main objective of these reforms was to control and curtail the power and privileges of the Civil Service of Pakistan (CSP). Under these reforms, constitutional protection of civil servants was withdrawn, a system of lateral entry was introduced and the power to arbitrarily dismiss senior officers was given to the chief executive.

Corruption: Corruption in Pakistan has grown exponentially during the various stages of the country's economic development, namely industrialization, nationalization, denationalization, and privatization. In 1996 Transparency International ranked Pakistan as the world's second most corrupt country, out of a total of 54, with a CPI score of 1 (where 10 is corruption-free). While there was an improvement in late 1998, when the score climbed to 2.7, the CPI was reported at 2.1 in the latest index of 2004. The last four elected governments have all been dismissed on charges of corruption. Weak political institutions, a strong and influential bureaucracy, lack of accountability, low meritocracy, highly concentrated sources of power, socio-cultural influences and economic deprivation are a few of the major causes of the corruption that has plagued the country since independence in 1947.

Corruption is institutional, deeply entrenched and all-pervasive in Pakistani society, but the worst cases have been observed among politicians, law enforcement agencies and the judiciary. According to the Transparency International-Pakistan country-wide survey of 2002, the police, power supplies and revenue collection are the three most corrupt institutions in Pakistan. The worst casualty of this widespread corruption is the development sector, which, despite being the recipient of substantial foreign aid, has failed to yield the expected dividends. Estimates of development projects indicate a loss of US $1,000m. (30% of the total value of such projects) due to corruption in 2003.

Since Pakistan's inception five pieces of major anti-corruption legislation have been promulgated and an equal number of anti-corruption agencies established. During the last six years there has been a substantial effort by the government to combat corruption, including the signing of the UN Convention Against Corruption in 2004. Several reforms have been initiated, most importantly the launching of a National Anti-Corruption Strategy, a new Police Order, Access to Justice Programme, Accountability Courts, a Public Procurement Regulatory Authority, and a significantly autonomous National Accountability Bureau (NAB), an unparalleled initiative in the history of the country. At the end of 2004 NAB had filed 740 references in the Accountability Courts and recovered $92m. The State Bank of Pakistan, in collaboration with NAB, has managed to recoup $2,300m. and reschedule $994m. on account of bad loans over the last five years.

National Anti-Corruption Strategy (NACS): The dismissal of Pakistan's last four elected governments on charges of corruption compelled the present military government to tackle the issue. Apart from signing the UN Convention against Corruption in 2004, several reforms aimed at combating corruption have been initiated. These include the launching of a National Anti-Corruption Strategy (NACS) in 2002 with the objective of inculcating high public standards, introducing systematic improvements, and finally eliminating corruption by engaging all stakeholders in an all-inclusive, progressive programme.

National Accountability Bureau (NAB): The National Accountability Bureau (NAB) was created under Pakistan's National Accountability Ordinance (1999), and is the apex anti-corruption agency at the federal level, with regional offices in all four provinces. The NAB implements a three-pronged strategy—prevention, awareness and enforcement—in order to fight corruption. Despite sporadic charges of selective accountability, arm-twisting and political victimization, the Bureau has infused sufficient deterrence against corruption amongst public servants. The recoveries by the NAB are unparalleled in the country's anti-corruption history. At the end of 2004, 740 references had been filed in the accountability courts and US $92m. had been recovered from various corrupt personnel. The State Bank of

Pakistan, in collaboration with the NAB, has managed to recover a total of $2,300m. on account of bad loans over the last five years.

Council of Islamic Ideology: Introduced under Article 228 of the Constitution as an advisory Council of Islamic Ideology in 1962, the Council of Islamic Ideology in Pakistan advises the Majlis e-Shoora, the Provincial Assemblies, the President or a Governor on the issue of whether a law is contrary to Islam. The Council has the responsibility to identify and implement the injunctions of Islam that can be given legislative effect. In case the Council defines a law as incompatible with Islamic doctrines, the President, a Governor, the Majlis e-Shoora or any Provincial Assembly is asked to review the law with retrospective effect. Though such advice is not binding on the government, it is not easy for a government to ignore or overrule the Council's suggestions or opinion. The Council is composed of a minimum of eight and a maximum of 20 members, including a chairman. The members represent various shades of opinion and are expected to possess a knowledge of the principles as well as the philosophy of Islam. Additionally, they are supposed to be experts in economic, political, legal or administrative questions related to the nation. All members and the chairman are appointed by the President of Pakistan.

Decentralization: To transfer administrative and financial power to local governments, Pakistan, in August 2000, adopted a Devolution of Power plan under which local governments were to be elected on a non-party basis. The reform failed to tackle the problem of corruption and did not strengthen accountability of politicians at the local level. Critics of the reform claim that the main reason for the devolution scheme as it was finally introduced was and remains regime legitimacy and survival. The non-partisan nature of the local elections has exacerbated ethnic, caste and tribal divisions and weakened the organizational coherence of political parties. Thought to promote the development of democracy in the provinces, the reforms have rather invigorated the military.

Since elections at the district and sub-district levels, between December 2000 and July 2001, elected governments have been in place in 101 districts and four cities. They are headed by a *nazim* and *naib nazim* (mayor and deputy mayor). The devolution scheme ignores the principal concepts of decentralization, for the delegation of power directly to local bodies has bypassed the provinces. As a result of the reform, the old system subordinating local officials to bureaucrats has been dismantled and elected local officials are now responsible for district administration, management and development.

Federal Public Services Commission (FPSC): The Federal Public Services Commission (FPSC), established in 1947, works autonomously under Article 242 of Pakistan's Constitution, Rules of Business (1973) and FPSC Regulations (1978). The commission consists of a chairman, appointed by the President of Pakistan, and 11 members appointed by the President on the advice of the Prime Minister. The commission's prime function is to devise the syllabus and conduct tests, examinations and interviews for the recruitment and promotion of officers of the civil service of the Federation of Pakistan. The FPSC is one of the few unpoliticized government organizations and has one of the lowest reported incidences of corruption.

Federalism: Article 1 in Pakistan's Constitution states that Pakistan will be a Federal Republic. In the 1973 Constitution, revived by President Musharraf, the Federal Legislative List and Concurrent Legislative List determine the distribution of powers between the Federal and the Provincial Governments. Federal legislation has primacy and the Concurrent Legislative List has often been portrayed as an instrument for limiting provincial autonomy. On 20 June 2001 President Musharraf was officially named Chief of State, although when he took political power in October 1999, following a military coup against the former Prime Minister, Nawaz Sharif, he had adopted the title of Chief Executive. In December 2003 the National and Provincial Assemblies passed the 17th Amendment to the Constitution, transferring a number of powers from the Prime Minister to the President, affirming Musharraf's presidency until 2007. An exemption allowing Musharraf to hold both the presidency and the position of Chief of Army Staff was extended until 2007. The bicameral parliament is composed of the National Assembly (upper house) and a 100-member Senate. While the seats for the National Assembly are allocated to each province and other units of the Federation on the basis of population, in the Senate 22 members are elected by the four provincial assemblies and eight are tribal representatives. Punjab, Sind, North West Frontier Province (NWFP) and Balochistan are each headed by a governor and a provincial cabinet, appointed by the chief executive. The **Federally Administered Northern Areas (FANA)** and **Federally Administered Tribal Areas (FATA)** are governed by the federal government but enjoy substantial autonomy. For instance, Pakistan's law courts have no jurisdiction there; instead, tribal élites maintain their power through ***jirgas*** (extra-judicial tribunals). However, Pakistan has a highly centralized fiscal system in which the Federal Government collects more than 90% of the combined Federal Government and Provincial revenues, and incurs 70% of the combined national expenditure, keeping the provinces tightly dependent upon the centre. Elections for Pakistan's four provinces were held in October 2002. The **Muttahida Majlis-e-Amal**, (**MMA**, the coalition of Islamic parties) performed strongly in the provincial elections, making it possible for it to form the government in the NWFP and to secure a prominent role in the coalition government of Balochistan.

Feudalism: Deep-rooted feudalism and an entrenched feudal mentality are considered among the major problems of Pakistan. Beginning with the Muslim League in 1947, traditional élites have dominated the politico-economic scene of Pakistan. Even among parliamentarians in recent times, about two-thirds can be traced to feudal social origins. This social class is organized in large joint families (*biraderi* system) owning thousands of acres of land that is cultivated by peasants living barely at the subsistence level. Despite a decline in the contribution of agriculture to the GDP from 40% to almost 25%, the feudal class continues to wield immense power as before and is exempted from the majority of taxes. Sensing the economic shift from agriculture to industrialization, it has used its social and economic leverage to multiply its influence by joining the civil service, business, financial and industrial sectors. Authoritarianism being a natural corollary of feudalism, the influence of this class has arrested the growth of liberal democratic institutions and social justice.

Fundamental Property Rights: Articles 8 to 28 of the 1973 Constitution of Pakistan deal with citizens' fundamental rights, stipulating them to be the inalienable right of all citizens who have, under its provisions, the right to enjoy protection of life, liberty, body, reputation, and property and to be treated in accordance with the law. Articles 23 and 24 specify that every citizen is allowed to own and sell his/her property in any part of the country and that no person can be forcibly deprived of his/her property. Any property or land needed in the public interest can be appropriated only after payment of reasonable compensation to the owner has been made.

Human Rights: Pakistan's record of ratifying principal international human rights treaties remains poor. To date, the country is signatory to only five conventions (three on children's rights, one on racial and one on female discrimination) and has signed neither the International Covenant on Civil and Political Rights nor the International Covenant on Economic, Social and Cultural Rights. According to human rights observers, freedom of speech and dissemination of information have been consistently undermined through the arrest and intimidation of journalists. The basic rights of women are limited in the context of the Hadood Ordinances, with the prevention of honour killings a major challenge for the government.

Religious freedom in Pakistan, especially with regard to the minorities, is another source of concern. Discrimination on the grounds of religion persists and all citizens are subject to certain provisions of *Shari'a*, such as the blasphemy laws. Both the President and the Prime Minister must be Muslims and members of the government (including non-Muslims) must take an oath to 'strive to preserve the Islamic ideology, which is the basis for the creation of Pakistan'. The Ahmadi community (*see* **Ahmadiyya/Ahmadis**) continues to be the target of religious extremists and sectarian violence between Sunnis and Shi'as has been on the increase.

Inequality: The Constitution of Pakistan gives equal rights to men and women. However, given the social hierarchy, in which men are usually ranked above women, women rarely appear in positions of power. According to the Human Development Report (1999) of the UNDP, the Gender Empowerment Measure ranks Pakistan 100th among 185 registered UN countries based on measure of control over income and participation in political and economic decision-making.

Rural inequality in Pakistan is usually determined by access to agricultural land and it is important to distinguish between cultivators, who have access to land as small landowners or tenants, and non-cultivators who are landless as unskilled workers. Non-cultivators belong to the poorest section among the rural poor. The UN Human Development Index in 1998–99 put the share of income or consumption of society's poorest 10% at around only 3.7%. For the poorest 20% the estimated share was around 8.8%. In comparison, the share of the richest 10% was 28.3%, and that of the richest 20%, 42.3%.

Punjabis, being the numerical majority, are the most influential ethnic group in Pakistan both politically as well as economically, causing dissatisfaction among other ethnic groups such as the Sindhis, Muhajirs, and Balochis. The Muhajir–Sindhi rivalry in the province of Sind also has its roots in the inequality of means and resources as perceived by the Muhajirs.

Islamization: Under Gen. Zia ul-Haq's leadership a number of Islamic laws were introduced in Pakistan to bring the politics of the state into line with Islamic principles and the *Shari'a*. Gen. Zia introduced the *zakat*, *ushr* (the obligatory charge on farm produce), Islamic Hadood and Penal Code in the country. The *Zakat* and *Ushr* Ordinances to Islamize the economic system were promulgated on 20 June 1980.

Muhajir Dominance: The Muhajirs are Urdu-speaking immigrants from India who came to Pakistan during and after Partition. Predominant in the **Muslim League**, they also subsequently gained a dominant position in state institutions and politics during the initial years after independence. Muhajir ethnic conciousness found its expression in the mid-1980s, first in the form of student activism, later consoldiated into a political party, the **Muttahida Qaumi Movement (MQM)**. The Muhajirs are mainly concentrated in Karachi and other cities of Sind and Punjab.

National Reconstruction Bureau (NRB): In a bid to promote devolution and decentralization, Pakistan's military government created the National Reconstruction Bureau (NRB) in 1999. However, the NRB's major initiative, the Local Government Ordinance (2001), promoting community participation, has not yielded the desired results due to ambiguous procedural rules and a strained relationship between elected representatives and executive officials at the local level.

Nationalism: The creation of Pakistan in 1947 was based on the ideology of Muslim nationalism which held that all Muslims on the subcontinent, regardless of their cultural and social habits, constitute a separate nation. The new state at the beginning of its existence saw itself as a religiously homogeneous state that was ethnically dispersed and geographically divided. However, as the creation of Bangladesh in 1971 proved, religious homogeneity was more a part of state ideology rather than political reality. To protect its religious identity, Pakistan continues to be governed by a civilian-military élite which promotes a combination of religious and militarist nationalism.

During the first years of Pakistan the state was transformed from a relatively decentralized into an ethnically exclusive, centralized polity mostly dominated by the so-called Muhajir élite. Though Bengalis constituted more than half the population, no Bengali in 1956 was above the rank of joint secretary within the All Pakistani Civil Service. In 1970 when the Awami League in East Pakistan secured a clear majority in the general elections, it was prevented from gaining power by the West Pakistani military-civilian élites. In consequence, the Awami League, in co-operation with the **Mukti Bahini**, a local mass movement in East

Pakistan, announced independence from Pakistan as the state of Bangladesh, initiating a separatist movement. A bloody confrontation between the Pakistan army and the people of East Pakistan (subsequently Bangladesh) forced millions of refugees into Indian territory, providing India with a reason to intervene militarily in favour of Bangladesh. The decisive victory of Indian forces in 1971 resulted in the dismemberment of Pakistan and the birth of Bangladesh.

Sub-national movements within Pakistan continue in the form of intra-provincial differences between Baluchis and Pashtuns in Balochistan, between Punjabis and Saraiki in Punjab, between Pashtuns and Hindko speakers in the North West Frontier Province, between Sunnis and Shi'as, and between Sindhis and Muhajirs in Sind. As a result a number of nationalist movements exist in Pakistan that regularly pose a challenge to national integration and stability.

Participation/Public Action: Political instability, periodic miltiary coups, irregular elections, short-lived governments, allegations of corruption and institutionalized clientelism have resulted in a declining voter turn-out whenever elections have been held in Pakistan. Whereas National Assembly elections in 1977 produced a 55% voter turn-out, this fell to 41.8% in the October 2002 general elections. Two types of institutional weaknesses are recognized as possible hindrances to greater participation: structural, operational deficiencies in public-sector institutions and obstacles stemming from social bias or custom. Examples of the first include the need for modern technology to improve the speed, accuracy and transparency of elections as well as the challenge of redrawing present constituency boundaries to make them more representative. The second weakness is most evident in the limited participation of women. Increased membership of women in political parties has not yet led to a significant number of women appointees in important positions within the parties. Quotas established to increase political representation of women require that at least 20% of the 345-member National Assembly and 17% of members in the four provincial assemblies are women.

In the aftermath of the October 2005 earthquake, it was reported that the immediate and extensive response co-ordinated by Pakistan's civil society organizations revealed a sense of national unity and popular engagement not seen since the 1965 war.

Quota System: Article 27 of Pakistan's 1973 Constitution provides safegaurds against discimination in state institutions. Under Zulfikar Ali Bhutto this clause was introduced as the quota system through which 1.4% of the posts in central administration were to be allocated to rural Sindhis, the aim being to correct the preponderance of Muhajirs in the civil service of Sind. Subsequently, in 1974, the National Assembly passed a bill fixing quotas for different provinces. In 1999 the National Assembly passed the 16th Constitutional Amendment, extending the provincial quota system for another 20 years. The Muhajir party, the MQM, opposed the amendment, arguing that the quota system disadvantages the Muhajir community and ought to be revised to take into account population changes.

Pakistan, Economic Development

GDP at purchasing power parity—PPP: US $385,200m.; GDP per capita at PPP: $2,400; *agriculture:* 21.6%; *industry:* 25.1%; *services*: 53.3% (all 2005 estimates); *currency*: Pakistani Rupee (PKR)

Since gaining independence in 1947, Pakistan, an underdeveloped and low-income country, has suffered from internal political rifts, a high population growth rate, increasing poverty and a large military budget. Nevertheless, Pakistan's economy has been resilient in the face of such challenges, achieving an economic growth rate that was better than the world's average during the last century. In fact, during the 1960s Pakistan was regarded as a model state for the growing economies of the developing world. Internal and external conflicts and two full-scale wars (in 1965 and 1971), combined with inconsistent economic and fiscal policies, halted this upward surge of Pakistan's economy. A revival in the 1980s saw economic growth of an average, annual 6%, partly due to generous foreign military and economic aid in the context of the Soviet intervention in Afghanistan in 1979. Again, in the 1990s, reckless policies and rampant corruption jolted the economy, bringing the country to the verge of bankruptcy. Since the start of the 21st century wide-ranging macroeconomic reforms introduced by the government under the aegis of the **International Monetary Fund (IMF)**, coupled with generous foreign assistance and renewed access to global markets, have ameliorated economic conditions and spurred economic growth once again. For the financial year 2005 a high GDP growth rate of 8.4% was recorded.

Initially an agrarian economy, the share of agriculture in Pakistan's economy has gradually declined from 53% of GDP in 1947 to about 22% in 2005. However, the agricultural sector continues to employ almost 42% of the country's labour force. Although per capita agriculture growth has increased almost consistently, it has been overshadowed by the rapid growth in industries such as textiles, apparel, cement and services like telecommunications, transportation and finance. Presently, services account for 53.3% of GDP, while industry has a share of 25% and recorded growth of 10.7% during the 2005 financial year. The removal in 2003 of US economic and military sanctions imposed after President **Musharraf**'s 1999 coup, substantial foreign assistance, growing foreign remittances and better economic management have enabled a record improvement in the foreign exchange reserves of the country, which rose from less then US $2,000m. in 1999 to US $11,636m. at the end of 2005. Current issues on the government's economic agenda include widening the tax base, privatization, good governance, deregulation and improvement of the trade balance.

Substantial growth in the recent past has, however, failed to trickle down and poverty is widespread and constantly on the increase. High inflation (9% during 2005) is a constant threat to economic growth and poorer sections of society in particular are affected. Analysts believe that the longer-term prospects of Pakistan's economy are still uncertain, but in the medium term the opportunities for poverty reduction and job creation are the best they have been in more than a decade. While Pakistan has succeeded in receiving positive endorsements from international financial institutions and a better credit ranking from risk evaluation agencies, there is a dearth of foreign direct investment and pervasive corruption continues to be a major hindrance to the country's economic development. Despite assistance from the international community and financial institutions to rebuild areas affected by the October 2005 earthquake, the economic impact caused by the enormous devastation has yet to be assessed.

Economic Policy/Reforms: To protect its national industries against international imports, Pakistan opted for a protectionist economic policy in the 1950s. Only in the 1980s did the government begin to change former policies of outright bans and quota restrictions, gradually removing licences for certain imports. The government entered into a Structural Adjustment Agreement with the International Monetary Fund (IMF) in late 1988 and three years later liberalization was formally introduced through the Economic Reforms Order of 1991. The most important element of the reform package was to liberalize the financial sector. As a result of this policy, interest rates on domestic credit were liberalized and targeted subsidies on credit for a number of sectors were either removed or severely curtailed.

When Pakistan entered the World Trade Organization (WTO) in 1995, the state committed itself to implementing policies of economic liberalization to simplify matters of international trade. However, because of limited monetary discipline and external factors such as unexpected droughts, most of the programmes failed to achieve their stated purpose. Structural difficulties caused a notable decline in economic performance. Real growth in GDP fell to 1.2% in 1995, compared with 6% in 1994. There have, however, also been significant and positive changes. In the early 2000s tax revenues have grown considerably as the mechanism of tax collection has become more efficient. Together with a reduced fiscal deficit, a surplus on the current account of the balance of payments, the lowering of inflation and the beginning of a decline in the debt/GDP ratio, Pakistan has achieved more macroeconomic stability. Public savings, which were a negative 3%–4% of GDP during the early 1990s, have turned positive and are no longer dependent on foreign grants. These achievements are at least partly due to initiatives taken to provide greater macroeconomic stability, such as Pakistan's Comprehensive Economic Revival Programme that commenced in 1999. The programme worked at restoring Pakistan's relationship with international financial institutions, the implementation of structural reforms, and improvement of economic governance and the revival of major national institutions.

A Stand-By Arrangement with the IMF and assistance from the Fund under its Poverty Reduction and Growth Facility also helped the economic reform process. Reports from the WTO and IMF suggest that Pakistan's long-term economic growth is largely dependent on the consecutive implementation of its Revival Programme, especially with regard to decreasing direct state intervention, as well as improvements in the tax base. Structural reforms were to be directed towards reducing the fiscal deficit by broadening the tax base, reducing the contemporary account deficit through promotion of exports and the introduction of a market-based exchange rate system, maintaining the inflation rate at a low level by alleviating government borrowing from the banking sector and deregulation of the private sector in connection with a two-phased privatization programme.

Nevertheless, the state continues to be an important player in Pakistan's economy and is often considered to be responsible for the slow rate of deregulation. After 35 years, the old price support system was abolished in 2001. Several other economic reforms have been implemented under international pressure. Thus, non-tariff barriers payable on certain items were dismantled in order to open the economy. In adherence with the WTO Agreement on Trade-Related Intellectual Property Rights (TRIPS), Pakistan amended its patent legislation in 1997 to implement TRIPS obligations, passing new legislation on patents, trademarks, and copyrights in 2000.

National Economic Council (NEC): The main responsibility of the National Economic Council (NEC) is to review the economic condition of the country. It formulates plans with respect to financial, commercial and economic policies and the economic development of Pakistan. The Council is guided by the Principles of Policy set out in Chapter 2, Part II, of the Constitution.

Planning Commission: Established in 1958, and presently headed by the Prime Minister, Shaukat Aziz, the Planning Commission is Pakistan's apex planning and development body, functioning under the aegis of the National Economic Council. The commission prepares national plans for the country's socio-economic development, assesses available human and material resources and prioritizes allocation of these resources. The 1960s image of the commission as a dynamic organization committed to the country's development helped Pakistan earn the title of a model developing country. This perception has, however, been tainted with the passage of time, mainly due to political circumstances.

Islamic Economy: The aspiration to establish an Islamic economy in Pakistan is almost as old as the country itself, but the guide-lines to create such a system remain controversial. Pragmatism has usually prevailed over piety, as one can see from the efforts to Islamize the banking system instead of simply removing conventional financial institutions. Even Gen. **Zia** ul-Haq, who attempted to govern Pakistan in accordance with Islamic precepts, opted for 'prudential, incremental' reforms that did not seriously challenge the operations or the corporate interests of domestic banks or Pakistan-based affiliates of multinational banks. This was in spite of his public pledge, in 1979, to eliminate *riba* (the interest system) in Pakistan within a three-year period.

The approach to establish an Islamic economic system is seen as a mixture of financial, theological or legal norms and practices. Some think of the system as a balancing instrument between market, family, society and the state. The issue is directly linked to the challenge of defining Islamic principles as guide-lines for a modern nation state and competing interests as well as contending interpretations have made a consensus on the role of Islam within the constitutional framework of Pakistan far from clear.

Private Sector: Despite an improvement in economic indicators, in the recent past slow growth in private-sector investment has emerged as a prime challenge to Pakistan's economic development. This slow growth is attributed to multiple factors, such as institutional weaknesses, bureaucratic and legal constraints, illegal trade and smuggling, the law and order situation, lack of skilled labour and infrastructure, and a capital market unable to support long-term financing. Private-sector businesses in Pakistan are mostly family-owned, concentrated in a few traditional fields and insufficiently integrated into the larger structure of the political economy.

International organizations, including the World Bank and the Asian Development Bank (ADB), have supported and encouraged Pakistan to improve private-sector performance for the sake of sustainable growth. The ADB alone has provided more than US $400m. in financial assistance to Pakistan's private sector. The present government, for its part, has attempted to create an environment conducive to increased investment in the private sector. Its efforts have included reforms of the financial sector, trade and commerce, small-to-medium enterprises and, above all, the judicial and taxation systems. Besides these, improvement of law and order, eradication of corruption and good governance are high priority areas on the government's agenda. Consequently, sectors such as banking, finance, telecommunications (**Pakistan Telecommunication Corporation Ltd**), pharmaceuticals, automobiles, the textile industry and power generation have attracted considerable private investment.

Public Sector: At independence in 1947 the newly formed government of Pakistan lacked the personnel and resources to play a large role in developing the economy. While exclusive public ownership was reserved for armaments production, generation of hydroelectric power (under the Water and Power Development Authority), railroads, telephone and telegraph communications, the rest of the economy was open to private-sector involvement. In 1972, under the leadership of Zulfikar Ali **Bhutto**, the government nationalized 32 large manufacturing plants in eight major industries, including iron, steel, heavy engineering, motor vehicles, tractor assembly and manufacturing, chemicals, petrochemicals, cement, life insurance, banks, shipping companies and public utilities. The result was a decline of almost 50% in private investment in large-scale manufacturing between 1970 and 1973. After the change of government in 1977, a policy of greater reliance on private enterprise was initiated and continued by successive governments through the 1980s and 1990s. However, the government maintained its role, with public-sector enterprises accounting for about 40% of national industrial output in 1991. From the mid-1990s onwards policies of deregulation, liberalization and privatization have continued apace. Nevertheless, public-sector employment continues to account for more than one-half of waged employment due to the better conditions and greater security associated with public-sector jobs. Furthermore, Pakistan's private sector has yet to prove itself to be more efficient and less susceptible to corruption than the public sector, which has showcased highly successful public enterprises such as the Pakistan Telecommunication Corporation Ltd (PTCL), Pakistan State Oil, the **State Bank of Pakistan** and, in recent years, Pakistan International Airlines.

Population: The majority of Pakistan's population is settled along the Indus River valley, close to the cities of Faisalabad, Rawalpindi, Islamabad, Peshawar and Lahore. The national language is Urdu although it is the mother tongue of only 9% of the population, while 65% speak Punjabi, 11% Sindhi and 24% speak other languages, including Pushtu, Saraiki, Baloch and Brahui (a language which, unlike the others, is of **Dravidian**, not Indo-Aryan, origin). English is commonly used by the government and among officers of the national military and within official institutional circles. The population growth rate is estimated at about 2%, with a birth rate of about 31.2/1000 and an official infant mortality rate of 74.4/1000. Life expectancy is around 62.6 years. At its current rate of growth, Pakistan's population is estimated to double by 2035.

Family-Planning Policy: Despite being one of the few countries which initiated their family-planning programmes in the 1950s, Pakistan's total fertility rate remained as high as 4.14 children born/woman. Although the population growth rate has been brought down from 3.66% in 1972 to 2.04% in 2005, Pakistan still has one of the highest rates in the world. Low literacy rates, particularly among women, a male-dominated socio-cultural milieu and inadequate health facilities are some of the main reasons for the high rate. Although in the 1990s there were improvements in the delivery of family-planning services, with social marketing of contraceptives and an extensive media campaign, the coverage and quality of services remained poor. A much-desired community-based approach has failed to materialize due to the socio-religious environment in the country. A recent trend in family planning is a shift in emphasis from fertility to a comprehensive approach, integrating family planning with reproductive health and also addressing issues such as economic status, education and gender equity and equality. These policies aim at increasing the contraceptive prevalence rate to more than 40%, reducing the growth rate to less than 2% and increasing coverage of the programme to more than 60%.

Migration: To a large extent Pakistan was constituted on migration movements, when millions of Muslims came to Pakistan after they left India in 1947. The next wave of migration in Pakistan was internal. Between 1951 and 1981 people from rural areas came to the urban centres and the urban population quadrupled. The annual urban growth rate during the 1950s and 1960s was more than 5%. The number fell slightly in the 1970s, to 4.4%. During 1980 and in early 1994, it averaged about 4.6%.

The second large movement of people occurred during the 1970s when workers from the urban centres went overseas for employment, mostly to the Middle East. The migration to Persian (Arabian) Gulf countries was accelerated by a severe balance of payments deficit under the regime of Zulfikar Ali Bhutto. To handle the deficit and also to strengthen ties with other Islamic states the government encouraged skilled and unskilled labourers to work in these countries. The Government established a programme in co-operation with the Ministry of Labour, Manpower, and Overseas Pakistanis to implement guide-lines regulating this migration.

Urbanization: Pakistan ranks amongst the most populous countries in the world. Internal migration, mainly from rural to urban areas, has created significant urban agglomerations and, combined with an annual growth rate of 3.44% (2000–05), one of the highest proportions of urbanization in South Asia. The main cities include Karachi, Quetta, Islamabad, Rawalpindi and Faisalabad, whose populations also increased due to the Afghan refugee influx. In 2005 Karachi, with a population of more than 11m., ranked 11th among the world's 30 largest urban agglomerations.

It is estimated that Pakistan's urban population has grown sevenfold, from 6m. in 1951 to about 43m. in 1998, accounting for 32.5% of the total population, and in 2005 it was estimated at 34%. With more than two-thirds of the GDP originating in the urban areas of Pakistan, this prosperity is not equally shared among urban residents and urban centres present acute contrasts of wealth and poverty, with about one-third of urban populations classified as poor. The provision of basic amenities has not kept up with the growing population and problems of housing, sanitation and infrastructure are serious challenges for the government. Urban renewal programmes have been launched by the government and are implemented by the city district governments and *tehsil* municipal administrations, which act as co-ordinating bodies between federal and provincial agencies.

Minority Groups: According to the census of 1998, an estimated 96% of Pakistan's population is Muslim, 2.02% is Hindu, 1.69% is Christian and 0.35% fall into 'other' categories (including Ahmadis). An estimated 10% of the Muslim population is Shi'a, including some 550,000–600,000 Ismailis, mostly followers of the Aga Khan. In the provinces, Christians are mainly concentrated in Punjab. Hindus constitute approximately 8% of the population of Sind where a tiny but influential Parsi community is found in Karachi. The Constitution provides for freedom of religion, yet, in practice, the Government imposes limits. Islam is the state religion and the Constitution requires that laws be consistent with Islam, imposing some elements of Koranic law also on religious minorities. Specific policies that discriminate against religious minorities include the Hudood laws and blasphemy laws. Relations between the different religious groups are often tense, particularly between the majority Sunni and minority Shi'a communities. At the 2002 parliamentary elections, the separate electorate system for minorities was abandoned and minorities were allowed to vote for and contest any seat in the National and Provincial Assemblies. Following the elections there were 10 minorities (all reserved seats) in the 342-seat legislature. Non-representation of minorities in the Senate (upper house of parliament) remains a point of contention.

Tribes: A number of tribes inhabit each of Pakistan's four provinces, but the best known are the hardy, nomadic and semi-nomadic tribes of the **North West Frontier Province (NWFP)**, bordering Afghanistan, and the tribes of **Balochistan**, bordering Iran. Tribes living in the **Federally Administered Tribal Area (FATA)** have their own legal apparatus, known as the *jirga*. Low literacy rates, a war-like attitude, lack of economic activity and idiosyncratic customs among tribal populations have made it difficult for governmental institutions to function, particularly in FATA and Balochistan.

Agriculture: Agriculture is the largest employer in Pakistan, engaging 42% of the total workforce in 2004. However, providing 22.6%, it is not the largest contributor to GDP: industry contributes 24.1% and services 53.5%. Wheat and rice are the most important crops for domestic consumption, providing the staple for a majority of the population. Important agricultural exports include cotton yarn, cotton cloth and rice. Direct rainfall contributes less than 15% of the water needed for crops and other sources of water in Pakistan, including ground water, are scarce and droughts a common occurrence. As a result agricultural activity is concentrated in the fertile Indus River plain in **Punjab** and **Sind**. A number of irrigation projects have been launched by the government, such as the **Kalabagh Dam**, but corruption, the misappropriation of canal water and the maintenance of canals are key challenges as is the growing problem of waterlogging and soil degradation.

Inequality in the ownership of agricultural assets, notably land, is another cause of low yields and low cropping intensities in Pakistan. Large landowners often engage in wasteful rent-seeking behaviour, using influence to manipulate water distribution. The problem of absentee landlords furthermore results in under-utilization of resources while the poor cannot obtain enough land.

Land Reform (Ownership): The debate on land reform in Pakistan has covered a range of perspectives drawn from different political directions. Socialist groups have favoured the elimination of large land holdings. Economists claim that land reforms would enhance productivity since the poor would utilize their land resources more effectively. A strong urban intelligentsia and the business community, however, have argued in favour of granting more political strength to the rural landed groups. International organizations regularly advocate the redistribution of land to enable the rural landless to improve their livelihood and powerful landowners are firmly opposed to any reform that threatens their privileges.

Three land reforms have been instituted in Pakistan since independence in 1947. The first, introduced in 1959, was Martial Law Regulation (MLR) 64 which limited individual land holdings to about 200 ha of irrigated land, or 36,000 produce index units (PIUs). Land resumed was provided to tenants only. The next reform, in 1972, again an MLR, brought the ceiling of land holdings down to 12,000 PIUs, or about 60 ha of irrigated land. The excess land was resumed without compensation, and its allotment to sitting tenants free of charge was protected under MLR 115 of 1972, which in turn was protected under Article 268 (2) (sixth schedule) of the Constitution. The latest land reform was passed in 1977 through the Land Reforms Act of that year which reduced the land ceiling to 8,000 PIUs or about 40 ha of irrigated land, or 80 ha of of unirrigated land, or the aggregate of both. The administrative structure responsible for land reforms includes a Federal Land Commission and four Provincial Land Commissions.

Food and Famine Prevention: Although agriculture accounts for 25% of Pakistan's GDP and the country has almost achieved self-sufficiency in food production, 42m. people still lack adequate resources to purchase food. Because of the long latitudinal extent of the country, Pakistan has a diverse climate and famine occurs due to droughts in Sind and Balochistan once in every 10–15 years, the latest case being in 1998–2002.

During the last 50 years the population has increased fourfold while production of wheat, a major food crop, has not quite trebled. On average, domestic wheat production meets 85% of the requirement and some 2–3m. metric tons of wheat are imported annually. Chronic balance of payment and foreign exchange problems prevent a stable supply of food to the entire population. In consequence, shortages of basic food supplies at some time of the year is a common phenomenon. To meet food and famine problems successfully, the government's long-term plans have focused on economic growth, increased savings and investments, developing physical infrastructures and facilitating human resource development with an emphasis on poverty alleviation.

Industry: At independence only about 5% of the large-scale industrial facilities in British India were located in what became Pakistan. On its formation the country thus had virtually no industrial base. Today the country's industrial sector accounts for about 24% of the GDP. Cotton textile production and clothing manufacturing are the largest industries, accounting for about 64% of exports. Further major industries are cement, fertilizers, edible oil, sugar, steel, tobacco, chemicals, machinery, and food processing. Real GDP growth was around 6.4% during 2003–04, compared to a rate of 5.1% in the previous year. Sectoral shares of GDP in 2001–02 were 24% for agriculture, 18% for manufacturing, 51% for services and 7% for industry. Real growth in manufacturing was 13.4% in 2003–04, compared with 7.7% in 2002–03. The large-scale manufacturing rate was around 18% in 2003. Pakistan still has a large merchandise trade deficit and the budget deficit in 2003–04 was estimated to be equivalent to around 4% of GDP.

Foreign Trade: Pakistan's major exports include raw cotton and cotton products, rice, fruits, leather goods, sports and surgical instruments, while imports, *inter alia*, comprise petroleum and its products, transport equipment, iron and steel, chemical fertilizers, edible oil and agricultural machinery. An agrarian economy dependent upon cotton as the major crop, exports are mostly textile-oriented. There has been a conscious effort in Pakistan to diversify this limited export base. In 2004–05 the total value of exports amounted to US $14,410m., of which $8,600m. was textile-based and, for the first time, a non-textile sector export generated more than $5,000m. ($5,842m.). An increasing trade deficit, mostly caused by heavy imports of petroleum and petroleum products, is an issue of serious concern for the country's policy-makers. By March 2005 the trade deficit had risen to a record high of $4,262,000m.

The USA is the most important market for Pakistani exports, accounting for about 25% of the total in 2005. Other important destinations include the United Kingdom (7%), Germany (5%) and Hong Kong (4%). Middle Eastern markets have either remained stable or have slightly declined, with only Saudi Arabia (2.6%) and Dubai (United Arab Emirates, 2.4%) importing a significant proportion of Pakistani goods. Pakistan's main source of imports is Saudi Arabia, which provides about 12% of the total. Other imporant suppliers include the USA (8%), Japan (7%), the United Kingdom (4%) and Germany (2%).

Banking System: The State Bank of Pakistan (SBP) is the central bank of the country, with responsibility for effective monitoring of the national banking system. Provisions vesting the SBP with power to conduct inspections of banks are laid down in the Banking Companies Ordinance (1962), the State Bank of Pakistan Act (1956) and the Bank's Nationalization Act (1974). The Financial Institutions (Recovery of Finances) Ordinance (2001), Companies Ordinance (1984) and Statutory Regulatory Orders (SROs) represent further important legislation covering activities in the banking system. The financial sector consists of commercial banks, development finance Institutions (DFIs), microfinance banks (MFBs), non-banking finance companies (NBFCs, including leasing companies, investment banks, discount houses and housing finance companies). The SBP has supervisory responsibilities in respect of banks, DFIs and MFBs. These institutions fall within the legal ambit of the SBP. The other financial institutions are supervised by authorities such as the Securities and Exchange Commission and the Controller of Insurance. Religious forces seek the conversion of Pakistan's financial sector into an Islamic banking system.

Foreign Direct Investment: The total amount of FDI released by the Board of Investment, Government of Pakistan, in 2003–04 was US $949.4m. According to the same source, the total amount of FDI in 1989–2004 was estimated at $7,963.2m. The largest investors include the USA, the United Kingdom, Japan, the United Arab Emirates, Germany, South Korea, Saudi Arabia, France and the Netherlands. Sector-wise, from June 2003 to July 2004 most of the capital was invested in power, textile industries, financial business, chemicals, pharmaceuticals and fertilizer production, construction industries, mining and oil exploration, petroleum and chemical refining and food, beverage and tobacco industries. Other sectors of investment include the IT branch and electronics. The legislative framework for foreign direct investment is provided by the 1976 Investment Act and the Economic Act of 1992. The Federal Government may make rules for carrying out the purposes of the two Acts. The Federal Government may, consistent with the national interest, authorize investment in any industrial undertaking for the promotion of foreign private investment. The grounds for such authorization include measures that could contribute to Pakistan's resources; the discovery, mobilization or better utilization of national resources; the strengthening of Pakistan's balance of payments or economic development of the country in any other manner.

Foreign Aid: Pakistan inherited an almost non-existent economy, weak infrastructure, a dearth of skilled human resources, and millions of homeless migrants, inevitably making it heavily dependent on foreign assistance. The Aid-to-Pakistan Consortium, organized by the World Bank in 1960 and consisting of the USA, the United Kingdom, Canada, Japan, Germany, France, the World Bank and the Asian Development Bank, was the main provider of foreign assistance, as Pakistan owed 92% of its total foreign debt to this consortium until 1991. At present the US Agency for International Development (USAID) accounts for around US $7,000m. to Pakistan. In addition, Saudi Arabia and other Middle Eastern countries have been generous donors to Pakistan. Most foreign aid was in the form of loans. However, due to the Afghan war, the proportion of grants increased from 12% in the late 1970s to 25% in the 1980s. At the end of the 2005 financial year Pakistan had a total foreign debt of $34,037,000m. and had paid $2,716,000m. in external debt-servicing.

Board of Investment (BOI): Pakistan's slow economic growth rate is mostly due to the country's inability to attract foreign investment. Consequently, the BOI was created as the central investment promotion and facilitation agency. It works as the focal point between domestic and foreign investors and all related government agencies. Foreign direct investment by June–July 2005 was reported to total US $1,524m., 60% higher than investment in the corresponding period of 2004.

Central Board of Revenue (CBR): The CBR was established as a statutory body by the CBR Act on 1 April 1924. Since Pakistan's independence in 1947 it has undergone various administrative changes and is today responsible for the formulation and administration of fiscal policies, the levy and collection of federal taxes as well as performing a quasi-judicial function of hearing appeals. The CBR currently supports the reform processes of the country through a transformation of the taxation system from an autocratic organism to a service-oriented one.

National Finance Commission (NFC): Pakistan's 1973 Constitution provides for periodically setting up a National Finance Commission (NFC) to advise on the distribution of resources between the centre and provinces. There have been more than seven NFCs, but disputes continue over the criterion for distribution. Some advocate population (which favours Punjab) as the basis for sharing while others promote backwardness (favouring Balochistan and North West Frontier Province) or the amount of revenue collected at the origin (favouring Sind).

Labour: The Industrial Relations Ordinance of 1969 guarantees the right of association, allowing industrial workers to form trade unions, and the right to freely elect representatives, to act as collective bargaining agents, is established by law. However, many restrictions on the formation of unions exclude large sections of the labour force from collective bargaining, e.g. agricultural workers who are not guaranteed the right to strike, bargain collectively, or make any demands on employers. Forced or compulsory labour is prohibited and the minimum age for employment of children is also restricted by law. However, child labour is very common owing to severe poverty and inadequate law enforcement. Acceptable conditions of work are pinpointed under the Pakistan Labour Law (1998), which provides for a monthly minimum wage of about US $42 (1,650 rupees) and for a maximum working week of 54 hours. According to the Economic Survey of Pakistan 2004, around 3.72m. of the labour force were unemployed, representing an unemployment rate of 8.27%.

Informal Economy: Smuggling, over a period of time, has grown exponentially and has assumed the role of a parallel economy in Pakistan, depriving the national exchequer of enormous excise and customs duty, together with income and wealth tax losses. According to estimates, the value of illegal goods smuggled into Pakistan from Afghanistan is US $2,000m.–$3,000m., depriving the Pakistani exchequer of about $1,500m.–$2,000m. per year through excise and custom duty evasion. Markets in areas bordering with Afghanistan as well as in the major cities are flooded with foreign smuggled items ranging from crockery, cosmetics, electronic goods and garments to spare auto parts and even smuggled vehicles. Smuggled goods are not only easily available but are also preferred by the general consumer, undermining local industry, legal imports and the trade in indigenous products. Since the 1950s, the Afghan transit trade, according to which Afghanistan was allowed to import goods through Pakistan without paying duty, has been a major source of illegal trade as most of these goods were smuggled back to Pakistan. Restrictions were imposed on this free trade in 1990 but have had limited success in curtailing illegal activities. Due to geographical proximity, Pakistan is also part of the so-called golden route of drugs-trafficking between Afghanistan, Pakistan and Iran. Efforts by various governments to eradicate this menace have mostly been thwarted by powerful lobbies.

Child Labour: In a society, like Pakistan's, marked by poverty, unequal distribution of wealth and poor educational facilities, child labour is a common phenomenon. Out of a population of 150m. people, of whom 42% are below 14 years of age, it is reported that 23m. children have never attended school. Officially 3.5m., and unofficially as many as 10m. children, labour, mostly in the brick kiln factories, the carpet weaving industry, agriculture, construction, mining, small industries and domestic services. In 2004 the government of Pakistan and the International Labour Organization agreed to a five-year extension of the International Programme for Elimination of Child Labour.

National Pay and Pension Committee (NPPC): The National Pay and Pension Committee (NPPC) consists of financial experts who advise the Pakistani government on how to improve the financial remuneration of public-sector employees. Some recommendations of the committee were incorporated into the 2005 budget when the government announced revised pay scales for public servants.

Pakistan Atomic Energy Commission (PAEC): The Pakistan Atomic Energy Commission (PAEC), the largest science and technology organization of the country, was created in 1956 as the Atomic Energy Research Council. Following subsequent reorganizations it was made a statutory body in 1973. PAEC's research ranges from nuclear power, medicine, agriculture, industry, informatics, biotechnology to defence-related nuclear research. Almost 30 different constituent institutes operate under PAEC.

Environmental Protection: Over the years ineffective natural resource management and high population growth have severely damaged Pakistan's environment. Inadequate environmental protection has resulted in deforestation, water-logging and salinity in rural areas, and in polluted water and air in urban and industrial centres. Air pollution in the two largest cities, Karachi and Lahore, is estimated at 20 times higher than WHO standards. The exponential growth of unmonitored industrial units and vehicles in the last decade are the main source of pollution. Despite a public anti-deforestation campaign, the deforestation rate was as high as 2.1% annually in 2000–05. Mismanagement of industrial and domestic waste and poor sanitation systems cause serious water pollution and water-borne diseases are prevalent. Like many developing countries, Pakistan's preoccupation with economic growth has been at the expense of the environment, with less than 1% of the total public-sector development budget allocated for environmental concerns. Scarce funding, insufficient laws, ineffective application, lack of monitoring and the absence of reliable data are major obstacles to effective environmental protection. In 1992 the government published a National Conservation Strategy Report, the implementation of which stalled due to differences in opinion among political groups, lack of funding and corruption. Recently the WTO's insistence on adequate environmental safeguards for exporting industries has focused national attention on environmental issues.

Floods and Natural Disasters: Pakistan suffers from a plethora of natural disasters including floods, earthquakes, landslides, cyclones, and droughts. Accelerated urbanization, poverty, lack of resources and habitation in geographically unstable locations exposes large numbers of the population to such disasters. Floods alone have affected almost 5m. people and taken the lives of around 4,000 individuals. Droughts in Balochistan and Sind severely affected more than 2.2m. people in 1998–2002. On 8 October 2005 an earthquake of magnitude 7.6 on the Richter scale struck Pakistan, its epicentre in the Pakistan-administered region of **Azad Kashmir**. The official death toll was 87,000 in what was the worst natural disaster in Pakistan's history. It was reported that more than 3m. people were left homeless, exposed to the approaching winter and cut off from sources of aid and communication due to their isolated locations. Wide-scale devastation across the region, particularly in the **Northern Areas** and North West Frontier Province, as well as Islamabad, put estimates of the cost of the damage caused at billions of US dollars.

Health System: The health system in Pakistan is divided into private and public sectors. The private sector provides health coverage to about 70% of the population and the public sector covers the remaining 30%. The Constitution of Pakistan regards health care as a provincial issue and, generally, the respective health departments of the provinces are instructed to implement health policies. The Federal Government is authorized to decide health policies, to formulate plans and to identify health care priorities.

According to the United Nations Population Fund, more than 75% of total annual births occur at home, and the country's maternal mortality rate is around 500 per 100,000 live births. The infant mortality rate was estimated in 2005 at 75.9 deaths per 1,000 live births (the highest amongst **SAARC** countries). In 2005 3.2% of gross domestic product (GDP) was spent on health, Pakistan thus ranking 135th out of 177 countries in terms of health expenditure per capita in the UNDP Human Development Index. The mechanisms to monitor performance of governmental health facilities are generally weak and people have little faith in the public health system.

Education/Education Policy: Pakistan's education system is composed of state primary schools and higher education institutions, a private education sector and a growing number of ***madrasas***. About 2% of Pakistan's GNP is spent on the education sector. Literacy rates remain among the lowest in the world. The Education Policy Plan for 1998–2010 aimed to raise the literacy rate from about 39% to 55% during its first five years, and to 70% by 2010. Currently, approximately 75% of school-age children attend primary school, though only 25% are able to obtain a school-leaving certificate. Regarding the nation's literacy rate, Pakistan (according to UNESCO figures) ranks 142 among 167 states in the world. Salient features of national education policy (in 1998–2010) include the aim to improve the conditions of non-formal education, elementary education, secondary education, higher education, teacher education, and the application of information technology. Education strategy is supervised by the Ministry of Education, which develops and co-ordinates national policies, plans and programmes in education.

Social Security: Social security for Pakistan's employees is regulated under the Workmen's Compensation Act and the Social Insurance Law which provide certain coverage. For the unemployed, homeless and handicapped social security is practically non-existent. Commercial and industrial companies with 50 or more employees must provide group insurance for temporary and permanent disabilities as well as death benefits for employees who earn less than 3,000 rupees per month. Survivor pension is 100% of an insured minimum pension, which must be divided equally if there is more than one widow. The minimum pension in 1991 was 425 rupees. Sickness and maternity coverage is paid to employees in selected industries or establishments earning 3,000 rupees per month or less, including domestic servants. Those excluded from such schemes are employees working in family businesses, the self-employed and persons earning more than 3,000 rupees per month. Once covered, a person remains eligible for benefits. Special systems for public employees, the armed forces, police, local authorities, and railway employees have been established too.

Poverty: While general standards of living have improved over the decades, 33% of Pakistan's population, around 42m. people, were living below the poverty line in 2004 and the gap between rich and poor has widened. The official poverty line adopted by the government was based on a minimum nutritional threshold of 2,350 calories per day for adults. During the 1990s, low rates of economic growth were unable to offset population expansion, while the government failed to provide the basic essentials. Insufficient coverage of public services, child malnutrition, gender biases in education and employment and low literacy levels are key contributing factors to the high incidence of poverty. Poverty levels are considerably greater in rural areas and particularly affect the landless, more than one-half of the rural population. Furthermore, poverty rates also vary across the provinces, with 2001 estimates indicating that North West Frontier Province (NWFP) had the highest rural (44%) as well as urban (31.2%) rates. The relative isolation and inaccessibility of provinces like NWFP and Balochistan are partly responsible for limited economic growth in these areas. To tackle poverty the government emphasizes tax reform to increase state revenues, encouraging investment by targeting corruption, a devolution programme to stimulate development in the provinces (*see* Decentralization) and improvement of public-service delivery (*see* Welfare). Federal budget allocations for education and health programmes have been nearly doubled and efforts are being made to stimulate the rural economy through liberalizing agricultural trade and to improve rural infrastructure.

Welfare: Pakistan's Ministry of Health initiated a Population Welfare Programme early in 1960 and subsequent five-year development plans have made allocations for welfare provisions, with particular emphasis given to family planning and reproductive health. Stabilizing the population growth rate is regarded as a primary developmental challenge and as the key to reducing poverty levels and improving living conditions. Despite governmental efforts, in collaboration with NGOs and private-sector initiatives, Pakistan's population growth rate of 2.1% in 2005 is still relatively high when compared to the average of 1.7% for less developed countries. A parallel problem, partly due to a growing population, has been that Pakistan's per capita income has increased only five times over five decades. The federal government blames the lack of progress on the hindrances of religious, socio-cultural norms of society and low literacy rates amongst women. The impact of family-planning programmes has been generally more visible on urban and educated populations, where fertility rates fell from 6.4% in 1974 to 4.8% in 2000. To expand the coverage of family-planning and health services to rural populations, closer co-operation with community workers at the grassroots level is being encouraged.

Zakat: Originally, *zakat* referred to the concept of transferring a certain amount of surplus wealth to poorer sections of society. The introduction of *zakat* as a public tax in 1980 resulted in a controversial public debate, with Shi'a Muslims declaring the practice un-Islamic according to their interpretation of the Koran.

Gender Relations/Empowerment: Gender disparities in Pakistan appear in different ways and forms. Generally the structure of the country's society is characterized as patriarchal, allocating an inferior status to women. Usually Pakistani women are married within ***biraderis*** (lineages). The institution of *biraderi* provides a certain framework within which women's lives are ordered. Their presence in the public sphere is often limited under the guise of cultural and religious values, restricting their access to education and employment opportunities. Under the Zia regime, the government passed a number of laws that directly (and adversely) affected the socio-legal status of the female population. The Hudood Ordinances of 1979, for example, failed to make a distinction between adultery (*zina*) and rape (*zina-bil-jabr*). Under Musharraf's Government, attempts have been made to improve the status of women, by, for example, reserving 60 seats in the national legislature and 17% of seats in the provincial legislatures for women. In the general elections of October 2002, 13 women were elected to non-reserved seats in the 342-seat National Assembly.

Pakistan Democratic Alliance (PDA)

During the 1990 election campaign Benazir **Bhutto** of the **Pakistan People's Party (PPP)** formed, together with the All-Parties Conference, a joint opposition, the Pakistan Democratic Alliance (PDA), to defeat the Government of Nawaz **Sharif**. This was the first time the PPP had entered into an electoral alliance, which, following Sharif's victory, gradually disintegrated over internal differences.

Pakistan Democratic Movement (PDM)

The Pakistan Democratic Movement (PDM) was formed in 1965 as a joint opposition to free and fair elections, which ultimately followed in 1970 after the end of Ayub **Khan**'s rule.

Pakistan Federal Union of Journalists (PFUJ)

The Pakistan Federal Union of Journalists (PFUJ) is a trade union of working journalists of Pakistan. Founded on 2 August 1950, the PFUJ has a long history in the struggle for press freedom. The Federation consists of nine district unions—UJs. The number of members was estimated at about 5,000 in 2003.

Pakistan Federation of Chambers of Commerce and Industry (PFCCI)

The Pakistan Federation of Chambers of Commerce and Industry (PFCCI) is Pakistan's apex body of trade and industry. It plays an important role in the economic development of the country. Its primary aim is to promote, encourage and safeguard the private sector's interests and to serve as a bridge between the business community and the government of Pakistan.

Pakistan-India Trade Agreement 1951

Following independence in 1947, Pakistan and India had agreed to allow free movement of goods, persons, and capital for one year, India importing raw jute, raw cotton and food grains while Pakistan bought coal, textiles, sugar, matches, jute goods, iron and steel. This agreement broke down and both engaged in a trade war, levying duties on each other's exports. Reaching a crisis in September 1949, when Britain devalued the pound sterling, to which both the Pakistani and Indian Rupee was pegged, an attempt was made to mend relations with the 1951 trade agreement of 26 February. The agreement consisted of three schedules: goods traffic from India to Pakistan and from Pakistan to India, the trade to and from India and Pakistan and, finally, the trade from East and West Pakistan to India. Although trade was resumed, its volume and value steadily declined as both countries developed their international trade links instead. The agreement, negotiated to end on 30 June 1952, was not renewed.

Pakistan Industrial Credit and Investment Corporation (PICIC)

Established in 1957 as a public limited company to promote industrial development, the Pakistan Industrial Credit and Investment Corporation (PICIC) is the pioneer development finance institution of Pakistan in the private sector. It provides finance in both local and foreign currencies to the private sector. Since its inception, PICIC has provided direct assistance to more than 1,300 industrial projects amounting to more than US $641m.

Pakistan Industrial Development Corporation (PIDC)

The Pakistan Industrial Development Corporation (PIDC) was established in 1952 to boost industrial development. It has established more than 50 industrial undertakings in the country. After their successful operation and management, these units were transferred from the public to the private sector.

Pakistan Muslim League (PML)

The Pakistan Muslim League (PML) was founded in 1906 in India as the All-India Muslim League by the Aga Khan III. It won a majority of the Muslim vote in the 1946 elections. After **Partition** of the Indian subcontinent the Muslim League became the major political party in the newly formed Pakistan. The Pakistan Muslim League was established in 1962.

Subsequently, the PML split into several smaller parties. The Pakistan Muslim League—Quaid-e-Azam (PML—Q) was formed in 2001, when the PML split due to internal differences. The PML—Q is now by far the largest faction among these parties and a strong supporter of President Pervez **Musharraf**. The Pakistan Muslim League (N) created in 1993, led by Nawaz **Sharif**, is the second largest faction of the former PML.

Pakistan National Alliance (PNA)

The Pakistan National Alliance (PNA), a coalition of nine opposition parties, with Nizam e Mustafa (Islamic rule) as their joint manifesto, contested the 1977 general election against the ruling **Pakistan People's Party (PPP)**. The PNA fully exploited the alleged misdeeds and secular outlook of **Bhutto**'s Government, thus winning considerable public support. Ironically, the PNA managed to win only 36 of the 200 National Assembly seats and only eight out of 116 seats in **Punjab**, its stronghold, in these elections (popularly believed to have been rigged). Consequently, the PNA boycotted the provincial assembly elections, launching a public protest against Bhutto's government that precipitated the longest period of martial law in Pakistan's history in July 1977.

Pakistan People's Party (PPP)

The Pakistan People's Party (PPP) was founded in 1967 by Zulfikar Ali **Bhutto**, whose immediate aim was to challenge the rule of Ayub **Khan** through a populist movement, blending Islam with socialism. However, although the party espoused policies of land reform, it was largely the product of the wealthy, landed élite and thus unlikely to carry through its radical promises. The PPP came to power in December 1971 when Bhutto was sworn in as President and chief martial law administrator. A large-scale programme of nationalization was launched and in 1977 mounting discontent came to a head when the PPP was accused of electoral fraud. Under Gen. **Zia** ul-Haq's martial law the PPP was banned. Since 1986 the party has re-emerged as a strong political force under the leadership of Benazir **Bhutto**, forming a coalition government in 1988 and again in 1993. Chairmanship of the PPP continues within the Bhutto family, although family feuds have split loyalties within the party. Although Benazir has been in exile since 1999, she is the PPP's life chairperson.

Pakistan Telecommunication Corporation Ltd (PTCL)

Founded as the 'Posts & Telegraph Department' in 1947 and then reorganized under the name 'Pakistan Telephone & Telegraph Department' in 1962, the Pakistan Telecommunication Corporation Act effected the establishment of the Pakistan Telecommunication Corporation (PTC) in 1990. PTCL is the country's largest telephone service provider, a governmental entity and a highly profitable organization in Pakistan. In June 2005 the government approved the sale of a 26% stake in PTCL as part of its bid to strengthen the private sector.

Panchasheela/Panch Shila

A term which has its origin in Buddhism, *panchasheela* was utilized by the **Nehru** administration to describe a concept of five principles of peaceful coexistence, which came to be known as the *panchasheela* doctrine and which was to be the foundation for the relationship between China and India. A 1954 treaty signed between the two countries encapsulated the five principles as: (1) mutual respect for each others' sovereignty and territorial integrity; (2) mutual non-aggression;

(3) mutual non-interference in each other's internal affairs; (4) equality of standing and equal benefits; and (4) peaceful co-existence.

Panchayat System

On 15 December 1960 King **Mahendra** of Nepal staged a putsch, banned all political parties and trade unions and established a party-less *Panchayat* system under the 1962 Constitution. The system originally involved four tiers of government: the zonal, the local, district and national. The zonal *Panchayat* was abolished with the first amendment of the Constitution in 1967, although the zonal assembly remained the electoral body for the National *Panchayat*, of about 90 members, until the third amendment in 1980 which introduced direct elections to the National *Panchayat*. At the local level, two directly elected leaders of each village/town *Panchayat* were automatically members of the District *Panchayat* who then chose remaining members for the district assembly. Additionally, class organizations at each of the levels, for peasants, youth, women, elders, labourers and ex-soldiers, elected their own representatives to the assemblies. The system was officially billed as creating an equal society, free of exploitation and class differentiation and a form of 'guided democracy'. In fact it served the monarchy's interests of self-preservation and legitimization and campaigns like the 'Back-to-the-Village National Campaign' of 1975 were devised by the King to entrench the system by making it as difficult as possible for active party members to gain seats in the *Panchayat* elections.

In December 1980 King **Birendra** introduced the 3rd amendment to the 1962 Constitution on the basis of which direct (though non-party) elections to the national legislature were held on 9 May 1981 for the first time. Over the next nine years the system was gradually eroded and in April 1990 the ban on political parties was removed and, in a proclamation to the nation, various *Panchayat* organizations were dissolved, leading to the November 1990 Constitution.

Panchayati Raj

Panchayat (the rule of five) is a traditional political institution in India that was rejuvenated and recast as the basic foundation stone of democracy at the local level. Based on the findings of the Balwantrai Mehta Committee, it was first developed in western India and then promoted in different parts of the country, with particularly great success in the communist-ruled state of **West Bengal**. This experiment in local self-government was a system of directly elected village, sub-district, and district councils, by the institution of highly localized territorial constituencies. The 73rd Amendment of the Constitution, enacted in 1992, endowed *panchayati raj* institutions with greater degrees of autonomy and independent financial and legislative powers. The legislation makes it obligatory for *panchayats* to have at least a third of the seats occupied by women.

Partition

The territorial division caused by Partition gave rise to the independent states of Pakistan and India on 14 and 15 August 1947 respectively. In February 1947 the Labour Government in London had announced that Britain would quit India by June 1948. Three months later, amidst mounting communal violence, the new Viceroy, Lord Mountbatten, decided to bring the date forward to August 1947. By this point a Partition plan had been formulated and in July the British Parliament passed the Indian Independence Act. The Act, in effect, laid the legal foundations for the transfer of power to two separate authorities, the **Indian National Congress**, representing India, and the **Muslim League**, Pakistan. Furthermore it stipulated that all the Indian princely states were free, in theory, to accede to either state. However, to demarcate boundaries in the former British provinces of Bengal, in **North East India** and **Punjab**, in the north west, two commissions were created, both chaired by Sir Cyril Radcliffe. Each commission was to include four South Asian judges, two selected by Congress and two by the League and was mandated to delimit the new frontiers based on religious affinity, using 1941 census data. Though ambiguously defined, 'other reasons' were also to be taken into account, such as economic or defence considerations.

Under a very tight timetable the Radliffe Award was publicly announced on 17 August, *after* formal independence of the two states. Leaders on both sides protested against the commissions' decisions. In addition to controversy surrounding territory, Partition posed immense infrastructural problems. The irrigation systems of Punjab and Bengal had been built under a single administration and had to be divided. Partition disrupted the economy of the region, dividing cotton production (in Pakistan) from the cotton and jute mills (in India). The two wings of Pakistan, separated by about 1,600 km of Indian territory, represented not only a logistical challenge but also had no prior basis for economic exchange.

Apart from the antagonism and confusion over the sharing of financial assets and the dismantling of common administrative structures such as the Indian Civil Service (*see* **Indian Administrative Services**) and the Indian Police Service, Partition was the cause of extreme violence and of one of the largest exchanges of population in history. In 1951 it was estimated that the inhabitants of close to half of Pakistan's major cities were immigrants or *muhajirs* (refugees from India and their descendants). Partition deaths throughout Pakistan and India numbered between 500,000 and 1m., with some 10–12m. migrants moving across the new borders in Punjab or Bengal. Due to the delayed announcement of the Radcliffe Award, citizens in Punjab and Bengal did not know which country they were in when independence came. While divided families, border tensions and long-lasting conflict over Kashmir are the enduring and visible consequences of Partition, institutional memories of distrust and resentment are also a critical legacy of the events that marked the birth of independent Pakistan and India. (*See* **Kashmir Dispute**.)

Patriotic National Movement (PNM)

The Patriotic National Movement (PNM) in Sri Lanka claims to be an independent conglomerate of Sinhalese nationalists. It has been observed that it has close ties with the **Janatha Vimukhti Peramuna (JVP)**, suggesting that the PNM is a front organization of the JVP. The PNM operates as a body to mobilize the masses and acts as a platform to spread a radical JVP ideology. As a result, the JVP is able to participate in moderate coalitions at the centre, while appealing to Sinhalese nationalist sentiments through the PNM.

Pattali Makkal Katchi (PMK)

The Pattali Makkal Katchi (PMK) is a regional political party in India. The PMK was founded by Dr S. Ramdoss in the mid-1990s. Dominated by the Vanniyars, one of the '**Other Backward Classes**', the PMK has its social base mainly in the state of **Tamil Nadu**. As a former constituent of the **National Democratic Alliance (NDA)** the PMK was, with five seats, a part of the ruling alliance in the 13th **Lok Sabha** (1999–2003). For the 2004 Lok Sabha elections it switched to the **United Progressive Alliance**, winning five seats in the Lok Sabha.

Peljor Gongphel

A term used in Bhutan to refer to a philosophy of economic development whose objective is to improve the material (non-spiritual) constituents of life. It is complementary to the spiritual (non-material) concept of ***gakid*** that strives to attain happiness and peace.

People's Alliance (PA)

The **Sri Lanka Freedom Party**-led People's Alliance (PA) won the 1994 parliamentary elections, ending 17 years of **United National Party** rule (1977–94). The PA comprised disparate parties, such as the Sinhala hardline Mahajana Eksath Peramuna, the Tamil Ceylon Workers' Congress and the leftist Lanka Sama Samaja Party. In 2001 the PA was re-elected, supported by the **Eelam People's Democratic Party** and the **National Unity Alliance**.

People's Democratic Party (PDP) – *see* Jammu and Kashmir People's Democratic Party (JKPDP)

People's Liberation Organization of Tamil Eelam (PLOTE, also PLOT)

During the 1980s in Sri Lanka a number of Tamil militant groups were active and some, like PLOTE, emerged as rivals to the **Liberation Tigers of Tamil Eelam**

(LTTE). Representing the most genuinely Marxist-Leninist of the militant groups, PLOTE was formed in 1980 when its founder split with LTTE leader **Prabhakaran**. After the **Indo-Lanka Accord**, PLOTE entered into electoral politics as the Democratic People's Liberation Front.

People's Majlis

The People's Majlis (Rayyithunge Majlis, or parliament) is the primary legislative body besides the **People's Special Majlis** in the Maldives. The first formal legislative assembly was provided for by the first Constitution of the Maldives in 1932 and designated as the People's Assembly. Later renamed and restructured as the Citizen's Majlis, it has operated since 1998 as the People's Majlis, which has granted greater rights for its members, such as parliamentary immunity, the approval of parliamentary questions and the introduction of a commissioner of election. Consisting of 50 members, eight of whom are appointed by the President and 42 elected, two from each of the 20 Atolls and **Malé**, elections to the People's Majlis have been held at regular five-year intervals since 1932. The most recent parliamentary elections were held in January 2005. (*See* **People's Special Majlis**.)

People's Special Majlis

The People's Special Majlis, established in 1980, has the power to draw up and amend the Constitution of the Maldives. This 108-member **Majlis** consists of eight members appointed by the President, members of the Cabinet of Ministers, members of the **People's Majlis**, and members elected from **Malé** and the Atolls in accordance with the law. Members elected from each constituency should be equal in number to members elected to the People's Majlis from each constituency. The most recent elections to the People's Special Majlis were by-elections held in December 2005 in two Atolls and Malé. To implement amendments of any constitutional article or provision, a majority of votes in the People's Special Majlis and the assent of the President is required. Seventeen years after it was formed for the express purpose of amending the Constitution, the People's Special Majlis passed a new Constitution in November 1997. The revised Constitution was ratified by the President and came into effect on 1 January 1998. Due to the number of presidential appointees and the inclusion of cabinet members (also appointed by the President), critics regard the Majlis as an appendage of the government.

People's War

Launched by the **Communist Party of Nepal—Maoist (CPN—M)** on 13 February 1996, the movement emerged out of disillusionment with Nepal's political system and anger at the plight of the rural poor. One of the main reasons for the movement was that the 1990 Constitution did not really bring about changes in the traditional system of participation and rights. New party élites failed to introduce necessary constitutional, legal, political, social and economic changes, enabling the Maoists to fill a vacuum and launch what can be seen as both a political and social movement.

Aimed at toppling the monarchy, the movement was initially a low-intensity, mainly rural campaign, claiming adherence to a Maoist ideology of peasant-led revolution. Since then the insurgency has grown into one of South Asia's most potent rebel groups and has cost the country more than 12,000 lives, of which a majority were Maoists or 'suspected' Maoists killed by government forces as well as a large number of innocent civilians. Economic costs have also been high, with diminished investor confidence and tourism, damage to infrastructure and lost economic activity due to Maoist-declared ***bandhs***. Life in the rural areas has been severely impacted through continuous killings by both sides and forced recruitment and kidnappings by the Maoists, resulting in large-scale migration from the western parts to the east of the country. There have been many human rights violations on both sides of the conflict, by both the Maoists and the security forces.

People's War Group (PWG)

The People's War Group (PWG) or the Communist Party of India—Marxist-Leninist (People's War) is an extremist, semi-political organization in India and is part of the militant **Naxalite Movement**. Formed in 1980 in the south Indian state of **Andhra Pradesh** by Kondapalli Seetharamaiah, the PWG has two different outfits: a political wing and a military one. The armed forces of the organization operate, since 2000, as the People's Guerrilla Army (PGA). On the political side, the PWG merged in September 2004 with the Maoist Communist Centre (India) to establish the Communist Party of India (Maoist). Today the organization is based primarily in the Indian state of **Bihar**.

Phuntsholing

Phuntsholing is the second largest urban centre in Bhutan, with approximately 30,000 inhabitants. Located in southern Bhutan, it is a border town with India and a hub of commercial activity. All goods imported as well as exported pass through this town. Like **Thimpu**, it has had to face the challenges of rapid urbanization and a lack of social and economic infrastructure to deal with increased population and a growing economy.

Pir

Pir traditionally referred to teachers who gave spiritual guidance. *Pirism* was first introduced to Bengal during the sultanate and forms an integral part of Muslim society. It is popularly believed in Bangladeshi Muslim society that *pirs* have spiritual powers. Often, the graves of *pirs* are turned into *mazars* (literally tombs or shrines) and *murid* (followers of the *pir*) visit the *mazar* on the anniversary of the *pir*'s death. In recent years *pirs* have gained importance in politics, with some taking an active interest in politics, either by running for public office or by supporting candidates or even political parties. For example, Pir Hafizi Huzur contested the presidency in 1986.

Pondicherry

In 1963 the Indian **Union Territory** of Pondicherry was formed out of four enclaves formerly under French rule. Two lie on the Bay of Bengal and the other two are on the opposite coastline of India, along the Arabian Sea. The total population of the enclaves in 2001 was reported at 974,345. The majority of residents are Hindu (86.8% in 2001) though there are significant Christian minorities (6.9%) and Muslim communities (6.1%). The main language is Tamil. Agriculture is an important activity in the territory and each enclave has rich natural resources making it a prosperous part of the country. Each of the enclaves has its headquarters and in 1991 Pondicherry, was granted an elected legislative assembly (30 seats) and a Chief Minister. Pondicherry returns one member to the **Lok Sabha**. A number of parties compete for electoral representation in Pondicherry, including the **Congress**, the **Dravida Munnetra Kazhagam (DMK)** and the **All-India Anna Dravida Munnetra Kazhagam (AIADMK)**, also active in neighbouring **Tamil Nadu** where alliance-making between the two national and two regional parties has an impact on Pondicherry politics.

Ponnambalam, G. G.

Born in **Jaffna** in 1901, G. G. Ponnambalam was the founder president of the **All-Ceylon Tamil Congress (ACTC)** and a popular leader of Tamils in the 1950s. In and out of parliament he was the spokesman for Sri Lankan Tamils, including Indian Tamils. Anticipating the challenges for Tamil-speaking minorities, he appealed to the Soulbury Commissioners in 1945 for a balanced representation. (*See* **Tamil Language**.)

Prabhakaran, Veluppilai

Enigmatic, powerful leader of the **Liberation Tigers of Tamil Eelam (LTTE)**, Prabhakaran was born on 26 November 1954 in **Jaffna**, Sri Lanka, entering Tamil politics at the age of 18. Under his leadership the LTTE has fought the Sri Lankan army despite being vastly outnumbered. To his followers he is a freedom fighter. Others have branded him as a terrorist. The Oslo peace initiative made an effort to induct him and the LTTE into a negotiated resolution of the ethnic conflict. The results so far have been inconclusive.

Prasar Bharati

The Prasar Bharati (Broadcasting Company of India), is a statutory autonomous board, formed under the Prasar Bharati Act in September 1990 of the Indian

Parliament, set up in the late 1990s. The Prasar Bharati is the public service broadcaster and operates **All-India Radio** and **Doordarshan**.

Premadasa, Ranasinghe

Although not a member of Sri Lanka's dynastic élites, Premadasa (1924–93) became President after a controversial election in 1988. Launched into a political career by President **Jayawardene**, Premadasa had projected himself as a friend of the common working man. To force the **Indian Peace Keeping Force (IPKF)** to withdraw and to obliterate the **Janatha Vimukhti Peramuna**, Premadasa initiated talks with the **Liberation Tigers of Tamil Eelam (LTTE)**. In 1993 Premadasa was assassinated in Colombo in a bomb explosion that was officially linked to the LTTE, although they strenuously denied any involvement.

Punjab (India)

Punjab, literally 'Land of Five Rivers', in the north-west of India was partitioned in 1947 between India and Pakistan. In 1956 a state of Punjab was formed combining Punjabi- and Hindi-speaking areas. Under this arrangement Sikhs were only 35% of the population until 1966, when the state was reorganized to create **Haryana** with a 90% Hindu population, a Punjab, with Punjabi as the official language and 63% Sikh, which made it a Sikh majority state, while parts were added to **Himachal Pradesh**. **Chandigarh** continues to serve as a state capital both to Punjab and Haryana. Punjab is known as the grain basket of India and has historically been one of the richest regions. Punjab's Legislative Assembly consists of 117 seats and the state sends 13 members to the **Lok Sabha**.

In 1966 the Centre yielded to demands for a separate state but disputes continued over water sharing with Haryana and **Rajasthan**, over the recognition of Amritsar as a 'holy city' for Sikhs. Demands for greater political autonomy, while initially led by moderate members of the **Akali Dal**, were taken over by extremists and transformed into a militant movement for an independent **Khalistan**, led by Jarnail Singh **Bhindranwale**. Codenamed **Operation Blue Star**, the Indian army was ordered to storm the sacred Sikh Golden Temple of Amritsar in June 1984, to flush out militants, under the leadership of Bhindranwale, who had taken refuge in the shrine. A few months later Prime Minister Indira **Gandhi** was murdered by two of her Sikh bodyguards in revenge, provoking bloody anti-Sikh riots and a crackdown in the state of Punjab. Since then the state has settled into the rhythm of alternating **Indian National Congress** and regional party-rule. Factionalism within the Akali Dal has enabled Congress and, increasingly, the **Bharatiya Janata Party (BJP)** to play a role in state politics, playing one section off against the other. In the 2004 general elections, an alliance between the BJP and Siromani Akali Dal (Badal) merged the BJP's social base of caste Hindus with the Akali's rural Jat-community base, to win 11 of the Lok Sabha seats in a complete reversal of the 1999 parliamentary and 2002 assembly elections.

Punjab (Pakistan)

In the **Partition** of India in 1947 almost 70% of the Punjab became part of Pakistan and it is now the second largest (205,344 sq km) and most populous (72,585,000 inhabitants, according to the 1998 census) of the country's four provinces. Punjab—literally the land of five rivers (Jehlum, Chenab, Ravi, Sutlej and Beas)—is known as the breadbasket, cultural heartland and politically most powerful province of Pakistan. With the world's largest canal system and some 21m. ha of cultivated land, Punjab is the source of about 68% of the country's total grain production, and is the backbone of Pakistan's agrarian economy. Apart from around 39,000 small and cottage-based industrial units, the province also has a vast number of industries producing textiles, sports goods, surgical instruments and electrical appliances. Lahore, Punjab's capital, is the second biggest city and the cultural and academic centre of the country. The location of more than one-half of Pakistan's population, people from the Punjab have dominated the civil-military bureaucracy, the politico-economic arena, socio-cultural circles and sports fields of the country, not without provoking a sense of neglect and deprivation in smaller provinces, especially **Sind** and **Balochistan**.

R

Rahman, Sheikh Mujibur

Referred to as 'Bangabandhu' (the Friend of Bengal), Sheikh Mujibur Rahman was born on 17 March 1920. He rose to prominence before Bangladesh's independence by formulating demands for cultural and political rights and for a just share of economic gains for East Bengal which he expressed in the **Six-Point Programme** in Lahore in 1966. The **Awami League**, which was co-founded by him in 1949, won the majority of seats in the December 1970 general elections. However, President Yahya Khan contrived not to ask Mujib Rahman to form a government and become Prime Minister of Pakistan. Zulfikar Ali **Bhutto**, whose **Pakistan People's Party (PPP)** had become the dominant party in West Pakistan, was opposed to this prospect, compelling Mujib Rahman to insist on his demands for autonomy. After launching a large-scale non-co-operation movement and achieving control over the civil authorities, which made him the 'quasi head of government' of East Pakistan, Mujib Rahman was arrested in East Pakistan and imprisoned in West Pakistan.

After the **Bangladesh Liberation War** in 1971, he was released in 1972 and became the first Prime Minister of independent Bangladesh. He incorporated four pillars, democracy, secularism, socialism and nationalism, into the Constitution. In December 1974 a state of emergency was declared in response to disastrous floods and mounting famine. Four weeks later a presidential system replaced the existing parliamentary system and Mujib became President, with absolute powers. He created the **Bangladesh Krishak Sramik Awami League (BAKSAL)**, which excluded all other parties from the government. On 15 August 1975 army officers staged a military coup and assassinated Mujib along with most of his family. His daughter, Sheikh **Hasina** Wazed, who was living abroad at the time, escaped the massacre and went on to become the leader of the Awami League and to serve the country as Prime Minister between 1996 and 2001. (*See* **Bangla Movement**.)

Rahman, Ziaur

Born in 1936, Maj.-Gen. Ziaur Rahman was a freedom fighter during the **Bangladesh Liberation War** of 1971. He declared independence on the night of 26/27 March 1971 from Chittagong and proclaimed himself provisional President.

In consequence, Ziaur Rahman is recognized as one of the heroes of the struggle for independence. His political career started only after Mujibur Rahman's assassination on 15 August 1975. Ziaur Rahman became chief martial law administrator in 1976 and assumed the presidency in 1977. With his newly founded **Bangladesh Nationalist Party (BNP)** he won the election in 1978 and was thus confirmed in his post. His political achievements include his role as one of the founders of the **South Asian Association for Regional Co-operation (SAARC)**, rural development through the introduction of (*Swanirvar*) ***Gram Sarkar***, and other campaigns based on his Nineteen Points programme. Later, he was responsible for the shift towards Islam in the Constitution and in politics. He was assassinated on 30 May 1981 by an army group. His party is led now by his widow, Begum Khaleda **Zia**.

Raj

The term Raj is derived from Hindi signifying rule, government, realm or sovereignty. Historically, it has been used to refer to the British colonial rule (British Raj). 'Ram Raj' was used by *Mahatma* **Gandhi** during the independence movement to refer to the rule of righteousness, associated with the mythical King Rama of the Ramayana epic.

Rajapakse, Mahinda

A former Prime Minister of Sri Lanka, Mahinda Rajapakse was elected as President of the country in November 2005, representing the **Sri Lanka Freedom Party** in the governing coalition, the **United People's Freedom Alliance**. Rajapakse comes from a political family and was previously labour minister and opposition leader. Winning the November elections by a narrow margin, Rajapakse benefited from a low Tamil turn-out, due to a boycott by the **Liberation Tigers of Tamil Eelam (LTTE)** of the elections in the areas under the control or influence of the LTTE. In pre-poll deals with the Marxist **Janata Vimukthi Peramuna** and the Buddhist **Jathika Hela Urumaya** Rajapakse pledged a hardline stance on the issue of Tamil autonomy.

Rajasthan

Since the creation of **Chhattisgarh** out of **Madhya Pradesh** in 2000 Rajasthan has been India's largest state in terms of area. The modern state of Rajasthan was created in 1948–56, combining 19 princely states and three chieftainships. A largely arid state, the desert of Thar stretches along the 1,070 km border that Rajasthan shares with Pakistan to the north west. Agriculture is the main economic sector, but the harsh climate has meant that the people's livelihood depends on erratic weather conditions. The population is largely Hindu (88.2% in 2001) and the agricultural Jat caste has been a powerful lobby in state politics. In 2001 **Scheduled Castes (SCs)** constituted 17.2% of the population and **Scheduled Tribes (STs)** 12.6%. Minority communities include Muslims (8.5%), Sikhs (1.4%) and Jains (1.3%). Rajasthan's legislative assembly consists of 200 seats and the state returns 25 members to the **Lok Sabha**. The **Congress** party dominated state politics until the 1989 assembly elections which brought the **Bharatiya Janata Party (BJP)** to power. In the 2004 parliamentary elections Rajasthan was one of the few states where the BJP performed well, adding five seats to its tally.

Rajya Sabha

The Rajya Sabha ('House of States') is the upper house in the Indian parliament. Together with the **Lok Sabha** it constitutes the legislative wing of the state. Of its 250 members, 238 are regional representatives, elected by the elected members of the state assemblies and 12 members are nominated by the President. The Rajya Sabha has a term of six years, with one-third of its members retiring every two years.

Rakkhi Bahini

A paramilitary force, also known as Jatiya Rakkhi Bahini, established by Sheikh Mujibur **Rahman** in 1972 and primarily composed of **Awami League** loyalists. As a law enforcing agency, its objective was to maintain internal security. However, its creation and the build-up of a second armed force in the country did not find much support among traditional military organizations like the **Mukti Bahini**, a tendency which was enforced by its increasing role as the personal security force of the government and as a political task force of the Awami League. Following the assassination of Rahman, the Rakkhi Bahini was incorporated into the chain-of-command of the regular Bangladesh armed forces. (*See* **Mujib Bahini**.)

Rana Family

Between 1846 and 1950 members of the Rana family controlled Nepal. Although the King maintained symbolic power, the Ranas ruled the country, institutionalizing the position of Prime Minister as their hereditary prerogative. The Ranas married into the royal family and maintained power by collaborating with the British imposition of colonial rule over India, in the process securing Nepal's own sovereign status. Following Indian independence in 1947 and the pro-democracy movement launched by the **Nepali Congress**, the Rana family gradually lost its guaranteed position of predominance. Nevertheless, through wealth and power acquired over more than a century, the Ranas continue to be influential figures in Nepal's economy and other sectors.

Ranbaxy Laboratories Ltd

As India's largest pharmaceuticals company, Ranbaxy was a pioneer among Indian entreprises in its global strategy. Under its former chairman, Parvinder Singh,

Ranbaxy became a research-based international company and by 2000 was generating almost 50% of its sales outside India, having penetrated markets in China, the EU and the USA. In 2004 Ranbaxy achieved global sales of more than US $1,000m. and ranked among the top 10 generic companies world-wide. Emerging in 1961 as an incorporated company that focused primarily on bulk pharmaceuticals, Ranbaxy has, since the 1990s, increasingly invested in developing new drugs through basic research.

Rao, Pamulaparti Venkata Narasimha

Pamulaparti Venkata Narasimha Rao (1921–2004) served as India's ninth Prime Minister in 1991–96. As a member of the Congress party he served as Chief Minister in **Andhra Pradesh** (1971–73), later holding several cabinet posts under Indira **Gandhi** and Rajiv Gandhi. After Rajiv Gandhi's assassination Rao was chosen to lead the **Indian National Congress**, winning the general elections of 1991 to become India's first Prime Minister outside of the **Nehru-Gandhi family** to serve a full term of five years. As Prime Minister, Rao was at the helm during a period of tremendous transformation in the international system following the end of the Cold War. A landmark accord for maintaining peace and tranquillity and respecting the **Line of Actual Control** was signed in Beijing, China, in 1993 and bilateral official dialogue was pursued with Pakistan. A number of crises erupted during his time in office, including the militancy in **Jammu and Kashmir**, the 1992 destruction of Babri Masjid in Ayodhya and a balance of payments crisis in 1990–91 which brought the country close to bankruptcy. While Rao is criticized for sending the army into Kashmir to quash terrorism, and for not effectively dealing with the violence unleashed by the Babri Masjid crisis, he is invariably remembered as the father of India's economic reforms. Together with his finance minister, Manmohan **Singh**, he initiated a liberalization policy initiating the process of dismantlement of the '**Licence Permit Raj**' and the opening up of the economy. Rao also revived the nuclear and ballistic missiles programme, ultimately leading to the 1998 nuclear tests.

Rapid Action Battalion (RAB)

Bangladesh's **Rapid Action Battalion (RAB)**, formally established on 26 March 2004, is an élite force, which combines troops from six existing forces, the army, the navy, the BDR, the police, the **Ansars and Village Defence Party** and the air force. The RAB commenced full-scale operations on 21 June 2005. At present it consists of seven battalions and has a strength of more than 5,500, involved in anti-crime and anti-terrorist operations across the country. The RAB is alleged to have committed gross human rights violations and extra-judicial killings.

Rashtra

The term *rashtra* is derived from Hindi and means realm, kingdom, country, state or nation depending on the context.

Rashtriya Janata Dal (RJD)

The Rashtriya Janata Dal (RJD) is a regional political party in India, founded as an offshoot of the **Janata Dal** in 1997 by Laloo Prasad Yadav, currently national Minister of Railways, who was Chief Minister of **Bihar** until 1996, when he stepped down on account of corruption charges levelled by the Central Bureau of Investigation. The party's traditional mass base has been the Muslims and the Yadavs (a Hindu caste included among the '**Other Backward Classes**' in some states but not in Bihar). The RJD won 24 seats in the 2004 **Lok Sabha** and is part of the ruling **United Progressive Alliance**. After state elections in 2005 the state of Bihar came under President's rule and, following new elections, the RJD was removed from power after 15 years of rule in the state.

Rashtriya Lok Dal (RLD)

The Rashtriya Lok Dal (RLD) is a regional political party in the Indian state of **Uttar Pradesh**. The party is led by its founder, Ajit Singh (son of former Prime Minister Charan Singh). A former agriculture minister, Ajit Singh claimed to promote the interests of farmers and villagers. The party is an ally of the **Samajwadi Party** and won three seats in the 2004 **Lok Sabha** elections.

Rashtriya Panchayat

Nepal's national legislative body during the ***Panchayat* system** of 1961 and 1990, the Rashtriya Panchayat members were indirectly elected by the local *Panchayats* and representatives from class or professional groups. In the 1981 and 1986 elections members were elected directly by popular vote on a non-party basis and with adult franchise. A certain number were always nominated by the King—after 1980 this was 25% of total members.

Rashtriya Prajatantra Party (RPP)

The birth of the Rashtriya Prajatantra Party (RPP—National Democratic Party) in 1990 was marked by a split when two strong personalities and former ***Panchayat*** premiers, Surya Bahadur **Thapa** and Lokendra Bahadur **Chand**, could not reconcile their differences over leadership. In the 1991 elections RPP (Thapa) and RPP (Chand) contested separately, the former winning one seat and the latter three. Merging together in February 1992, the RPP became a key player after the 1994 elections when it won 20 seats in the *Pratinidhi Sabha*, thereby becoming a balancing power. On 12 September 1995 the RPP entered into a coalition government with the **Nepali Congress (NC)** and the **Nepal Sadbhavana Party**, when the ruling **Communist Party of Nepal—Unified Marxist-Leninist (CPN—UML)** was defeated in a vote of confidence. Like other political parties in Nepal, the RPP fell prey to internal factionalism and the instability of coalition politics, its Chapa wing entering into an alliance with the CPN—UML in 1996 while the Thapa wing remained close to the NC. Contesting the 1999 elections separately, the RPP (Thapa) obtained 11 seats and the RPP (Chand) none. The party is influenced more by the personalities of the two leaders rather than by ideology. It is generally perceived to be a conservative party, supporting constitutional monarchy.

Rashtriya Swayamsevak Sangh (RSS)

The Rashtriya Swayamsevak Sangh (RSS—National Volunteers' Corps) was founded in 1925 by Keshav Baliram Hedgewar in India. Over the years, it has created a wide network of affiliated organizations, commonly referred to in Indian politics as the **Sangh Parivar** (Parivar meaning extended family) which undertakes a large variety of activities in all areas of public life, such as education, social welfare, trade union and intellectual activities. The constitution of the RSS claims that the *Sangh*, as such, has no political affiliation and is devoted to purely cultural work, defining its primary function as 'character building', and the promotion of Indian nationalism on the basis of Hindu values and traditions. The core ideology of the organization is a modified version of ***Hindutva*** as the basis of the Indian nation and it aims to project itself as a model for the regeneration of Hindu society. The structure of the RSS is strictly hierarchical and based on the idea of obedience to the supreme leader (*Sarsanghchalak*). The RSS structure is divided into a network of local branches (the *Shakha* technique) and a system of *pracharakas* (voluntary, full-time workers). A loyal, dedicated and highly disciplined cadre of *pracharakas* forms the organizational and ideological backbone of the *Sangh Parivar*. The electoral success of Hindu nationalism has inevitably led to ideological compromises, creating some tensions between the RSS and its political affiliate, the **Bharatiya Janata Party**, on issues of doctrine, recent reform measures and modernizing processes, such as economic liberalization. The RSS is often portrayed by its critics as a Hindu fundamentalist organization.

Rasta Roko/Railway Roko

Terms used in India to describe particular forms of collective protest. Rasta Rocko means, literally, 'block the road' and railway roko refers to blocking the railway system.

Reliance Group – *see* Ambani, Dhirubhai

Republican Party of India (A) (RPI—A)

The Republican Party of India (A) (RPI—A) is a regional political party in the Indian states of **Maharashtra**, **Andhra Pradesh** and **Karnataka**. The stronghold of the party is Maharashtra where the party holds 20 seats in the state assembly. It is led by Ramdas Athavale and claims to represent the interest of the **Dalits**. As an ally of the **Indian National Congress (INC)**, it is part of the **United Progressive Alliance (UPA)** and won one seat in the 2004 **Lok Sabha** elections.

Reservation Policy/Anti-reservation Movement

After India's independence in 1947, Dr B. R. **Ambedkar**, spokesman for India's '**untouchables**' and an architect of India's Constitution, campaigned to officially abolish 'untouchability' and to introduce political and economic provisions for **Scheduled Castes (SCs)** and **Scheduled Tribes (STs)**. Accordingly Article 15 (4) declared that the state could make 'special provision' for the advancement of STs and SCs. Articles 330 and 331 reserved seats in the **Lok Sabha** and the state assemblies in proportion to SC and ST numbers living in the represented territory. Article 335 reserved state and central government jobs for STs and SCs on condition that such provisions be reviewed after 10 years. Since then parliament has periodically amended the Constitution to extend reservations. According to all-India lists STs and SCs together constitute about 22.5% of the total population. Efforts to develop a similar version of **affirmative action** for India's former 'untouchables' and **Other Backward Classes (OBCs)** were finally implemented in 1993 following delays and protests against the **Mandal Commission** report issued in 1980. OBCs are entitled to 27% of job reservations in public services.

Anti-reservation reactions have included violent protests, particularly in reaction to the Mandal Commission's recommendations, as well as ongoing discussions about the success of such policies in uplifting and empowering disadvantaged groups. More recently the proposal under the **United Progressive Alliance** government to extend reservations to private businesses has reignited the debate.

Reserve Bank of India (RBI)

The Reserve Bank of India (RBI) was established in 1935 and nationalized on 1 January 1949. Founded as India's central bank, it formulates, implements and monitors the monetary policy of the government and is responsible for monetary price stability, management of the currency and supervision of the financial as well as the payments system.

Revolutionary Socialist Party (RSP)

The Revolutionary Socialist Party (RSP) is a regional political party in India, organized as a left-centrist party in **West Bengal**, **Kerala** and **Uttar Pradesh**. It is part of the **Left Front** governments in West Bengal and Tripura and, in Kerala, of the **Left Democratic Front** government. The party defines itself as part of the Marxist-Leninist tradition, advocating socialist rule and the rights of the working class. In 2001 the party branch in Kerala split, leading to the emergence of the Revolutionary Socialist Party (Bolshevik). The RSP won three seats in the 2004 **Lok Sabha** elections.

Rohingya Issue

Rohingya refers to one of the five distinct Muslim communities which migrated and settled in Arakan, Myanmar (former Burma). However, Arakan, with a substantial Muslim community, was attached to Buddhist Burma after the British left the region. Since 1942 severe tension has developed between the Arakanese Buddhist Maghs and the Muslim Rohingyas, resulting in violent riots and the exodus of approximately 1.5m. Rohingyas to the southern Chittagong district in Bangladesh, especially in 1991 and 1992 when there were 250,000 arrivals. The Rohingyas became an international refugee concern and a sensitive issue between Myanmar and Bangladesh. According to an agreement between the two countries, most of the Rohingya refugees were repatriated between October and December 1979. None the less, 15,000–20,000 Rohingya refugees remain in Bangladesh.

S

SAARC – *see* South Asian Association for Regional Co-operation

Samajwadi Janata Party—Rashtriya (SJP—R)

The Samajwadi Janata Party—Rashtriya (SJP—R), or Socialist People's Party—National is a regional political party in India. The party is an offshoot of the Samajwadi Janata Party and is led by former Prime Minister Chandra Shekhar. The party's main objective in the 2004 **Lok Sabha** elections was to challenge the **National Democratic Alliance (NDA)** under the leadership of the **Bharatiya Janata Party (BJP)**. The party has one seat in the 14th Lok Sabha.

Samajwadi Party (SP)

The Samajwadi Party (SP—Socialist Party) is a regional political party in India, founded by the current party president, Mulayam Singh Yadav, on 4 October 1992 in the northern state of **Uttar Pradesh**. The party stands for democratic socialism on the basis of equality and prosperity. Its political agenda consists of supporting the agricultural sector and medium-scale industries, which it presents as the key sectors of the Indian economy, reservations in jobs and education for the backward classes, and a controlled market entry for MNC's. The SP did not join the **United Progressive Alliance (UPA)** but has agreed to extend outside support to the **Congress**-led government in the 14th **Lok Sabha**.

Sangh Parivar

Sangh Parivar refers to a variety of organizations broadly constituting the Hindu nationalist movement, namely, political parties, cultural and religious organizations and other affiliates that adhere to the philosophy of ***Hindutva***. The *Sangh Parivar* (or family) operates with a kind of division of labour among its several affiliates. Among these, the main ones are the **Bharatiya Janata Party (BJP)**, which acts as the electoral wing, the organizational and ideological backbone, the **Rashtriya Swayamsevak Sangh (RSS)**, and the **Vishwa Hindu Parishad (VHP)**, which provides a youth wing for men and women, with the Bajrang Dal and Durga Vahini (the female wing) covering religious issues.

Sarvodaya

Literally meaning 'universal uplift' or 'progress of all' in Hindi and Sanskrit, the term *sarvodaya* is used widely across South Asia. It was coined by Vinoba Bhave and refers to the principles of Mohandhas Karamchand **Gandhi** and the independence movement. *Sarvodaya* emphasizes and combines the ideas of service, and non-violence and has been applied by post-independence Gandhians in socio-economic movements across South Asia. In India, J. P. **Narayan** was a prominent advocate of *sarvodaya*.

Satyagraha

A philosophy of non-violent resistance, employed most famously by Mohandas Karamchand **Gandhi** against British colonial rule in India and racial discrimination in South Africa. The term *Satyagraha* ('holding on to truth') was used by Gandhi to replace 'passive resistance' and to refer to 'civil disobedience'. It includes three core principles: (1) *Sat* (truth, honesty and fairness); (2) ***Ahimsa*** (non-violence, refusal to inflict injury upon others); and (3) *Tapasya* (willingness and effort for self-sacrifice). In April 1930 thousands of followers joined *Mahatma* Gandhi on his Salt *Satyagraha*, a 390-km march to the coastal town of Dandi in **Gujarat**, where, on 6 April, Gandhi broke the British salt tax which declared the private production or collection of salt illegal. In its current usage, *Satyagraha* is often indistinguishable from other forms of direct political action, with those engaged in it not always following the lofty ideals that Gandhi considered indispensable.

Savarkar, Vinayak Damodar

Savarkar (1883–1966), a controversial figure in Indian politics, has become the object of attention by academics as well as the larger public because of his militant activism and nationalism during the struggle for independence. Some have seen in his writings the portent of an exclusive brand of Hindu nationalism, while, for his admirers, his ideas indicate an effort, howsoever rudimentary, to bring the multiple faiths of India under the roof of a strong, cohesive Indian nation. He coined the term ***Hindutva*** in his book of the same name, in which he attempted to define who is a Hindu.

Implicated in the murder of a British official, Savarkar was sentenced to 50 years' imprisonment at the infamous Cellular jail in the **Andaman and Nicobar** islands. After his release from prison (he was incarcerated in 1911–24) his movement was restricted to the district of Ratnagiri and he was prohibited from participating in politics. The ban was lifted in 1937 and Savarkar joined the Hindu Mahasabha, occupying its presidency from 1937 until 1943. Despite, or perhaps because of, his extreme social and political views, he was never able to build up a broad support base, either for his social work (which included upliftment of the lower castes) or his political campaigns (for example the wider use of Hindi) during his lifetime. His alleged but as yet unproven involvement in the assassination of *Mahatma* **Gandhi** adds to the controversy surrounding his life and ideology.

Scheduled Castes (SCs)

The category of Scheduled Castes (SCs) includes communities consisting of formerly 'untouchable' Hindu castes. They were traditionally excluded from the *chaturvana* system of Hinduism as they were considered polluted in view of their traditional occupations, such as scavenging and the removal of dead bodies and other polluting substances. Following independence, the practice of '**untouchability**' was legally forbidden (under Article 17 of the Indian Constitution). Article 341 of the Constitution allows the government to compile a schedule (hence the term Scheduled Castes) of castes, races and tribes that are economically and socially disadvantaged, entitling them to reservations and protection under the Constitution. This comprises the reservation of jobs in public services and college places for SCs in proportion to their numbers in Indian society. The 2001 census recorded 166m. SC members across the country, about 16.20% of the total population. The largest numbers were in **Uttar Pradesh**, **West Bengal**, **Bihar**, **Andhra Pradesh** and **Tamil Nadu**. SCs are not listed by name in the Constitution. (*See* **Dalits**; ***Harijan***; **Other Backward Classes**; **Scheduled Tribes**.)

Scheduled Tribes (STs)

Article 342 of the Indian Constitution allows the government, after consulting with the state government concerned, to designate groups as Scheduled Tribes (STs) in relation to a particular state or **Union Territory**. The criteria for attaining ST status are not spelt out in the Constitution but are generally accepted to include indications of primitive traits, distinctive culture, geographical isolation and backwardness. In the 2001 census the ST population, at about 84m. people, constituted 8.1% of the total population. Large concentrations are found in **North East India**. Illiteracy rates and poverty are particularly high amongst these groups which tend to live in forest and hilly areas.

Special provisions, such as reservations in the **Lok Sabha** and state assemblies in accordance with the proportion of the ST population (Articles 330 and 332) and claims to services and posts (Article 335), are operationalized through the tribal sub-plan of the planning commission and administered by the tribal development ministries of each state. The fifth and sixth schedules of the Constitution deal with the administration of scheduled and tribal areas. Nine states have scheduled areas, including **Himachal Pradesh**, **Gujarat**, **Maharashtra**, **Rajasthan**, **Madhya Pradesh**, **Chhattisgarh**, **Jharkhand**, **Orissa** and **Andhra Pradesh**. Each scheduled area has a tribes advisory council that advises the governor of the state on the welfare and advancement of STs.

Senanayake, Don Stephen

Born in 1884, Don Stephen Senanayake was at the forefront of Sri Lanka's struggle for independence from Britain and is popularly known as 'the father of Sri Lanka'. Together with other prominent nationalist leaders, such as S. W. R. D. **Bandar-anaike**, he founded the **United National Party (UNP)** in 1946 and became the country's first Prime Minister in 1948. An anglophile and a nationalist, Senanayake strongly believed in the Commonwealth's importance and the need to establish a secular nation state. Engaged deeply in combating Sri Lanka's agricultural problems, he devoted considerable attention to improving rural conditions, encouraging crop diversification and boosting food production. After Senanayake's death in a riding accident in 1952, his son Dudley S. Senanayake succeeded him as Prime Minister, creating what was to become one of the most important political families in Sri Lanka. In September 1953 Sir John Kotelawala, Dudley Senanayake's cousin, assumed the leadership of the UNP government and remained in power until April 1956. In 1970 leadership of the party passed to a distant relative, Junius Richard **Jayawardene**.

Shah Bano Case

Shah Bano, a Muslim woman and mother of five children, was divorced by her husband in 1978. She having approached the courts for maintenance, a verdict was reached by the Supreme Court in 1985 which ruled in her favour, entitling her to maintenance under Section 125 of the Criminal Procedure Code 1973, with an upper limit of Rs. 500 a month. The ruling provoked strong opposition from orthodox Muslims, who perceived this to be an encroachment by the state on Muslim family law (under the purview of personal law in India). The All-India Muslim Personal Law Board was formed and agitation and protests were mounted, prompting the then Prime Minister, Rajiv Gandhi, ultimately to concede defeat in the name of secularism. In 1986 the **Congress** party, which had an absolute majority in parliament, passed an act nullifying the Supreme Court's judgement. Also in 1986 the **Muslim Women (Protection of Rights on Divorce) Bill (India)** was enacted, granting the right to maintenance, but, in accordance with Muslim law, restricting it to the period of *iddat* (about three months) after the divorce, shifting the onus of maintenance to the woman's relatives or the Wakf Board. The Shah Bano case is considered to be a landmark case as it revived the debate on the uniform civil code in India and the need to reform orthodox personal laws that disadvantage women.

Shah Dynasty

The Shah dynasty, originating in the tiny hill state of Gorkha (**Gurkha**), was the unifying force in Nepal following the 1768/69 conquest of the Kathmandu valley by Prithvinarayan Shah. Land and property in the conquered territories was seized and distributed to supporters, installing the system of rural suppression and exploitation and the promotion of so-called higher castes. Their period of expansion ended with the Anglo–Nepali war of 1814–16. After Prithvinarayan's death in 1775 a string of Shah kings ascended the throne as minors, enabling powerful regents or Prime Ministers from aristocratic families (especially the Thapa and Pande) to dominate Nepali politics. The Shah dynasty gradually gave way to the Rana system in 1846, during which the King, divested of any real power, was maintained as a symbol of unity and continuity. In 1951, when Nepal initiated its first experiment with democracy, King **Tribhuvan**, together with an interim government, took back the reins of power. Although attempts have been made since to establish a constitutional monarchy, Nepal's Shah dynasty has re-emerged as the country's central power-broker.

Shaheed

A term used in South Asian political discourse, *shaheed* refers to the traditional concept of martyr, which is deeply embedded in various religions and values within as well as outside the region. Today it is primarily used by people who advocate ***jihad*** as a term to indicate 'suicide bombers'.

Shalish

Shalish is a traditional method of dispute resolution widely practised in Bangladesh, especially in rural areas, for the informal adjudication of petty disputes, both civil and criminal. The third party, which acts as a mediator between two contending parties, is referred to as a *shalishkar* (adjudicator). These are usually the leaders of the community. *Shalish* has been traditionally organized by the *gram* (village) *panchayats*, led by local notables who are commonly called *matbars* (leaders). At the same time, union *parishad*, the lowest tier of local government, are also authorized to resolve disputes through village courts. In rural areas *shalish* has three implications: it is a means to establish social solidarity; it provides for the legal needs of the community; and it is a means of reinforcing the power of rural élites. In recent years a number of NGOs, including the Madaripur Legal Aid Association, and Ain-o-Shalish-Kendro, have emerged as substitutes for the traditional *shalish* system.

Shanti Bahini

The Shanti Bahini (peace force) in Bangladesh, mostly drawn from the Chakma tribes, was founded in 1972 as the armed wing of Parbattya Chattagram Jana Samhati Samiti (the Chittagong Hill Tracts People's Solidarity Association) and has fought since the mid-1970s for political independence for the Chittagong Hill Tracts. On 2 December 1997 the political wing of the Shanti Bahini signed a Peace Accord with the government and two months later formally surrendered their arms. The realization of the high level of autonomy demanded for the three districts of the Hill Tracts and envisaged in the CHT peace agreement has yet to be achieved.

Sharchop

The Sharchop claim to be the oldest of the three major ethnic communities in Bhutan, with various sources identifying them as among its earliest inhabitants. The term Sharchop refers to the people living in the east. They are of Indo-Mongoloid (Burmese) stock and speak Tsangla. Despite the fact that many of them have been assimilated into the **Drukpa** culture of the **Ngalong**, sections of the Sharchop still retain their close cultural and socio-economic ties with **North East India** and Myanmar (Burma). In addition, the Sharchop usually follow the Nyingmapa school of Mahayana Buddhism and not the **Kagyupa school**, which is recognized by the government as the core constituent of the nation's cultural foundation. Interactions between the Sharchop and neighbouring India and Myanmar are regarded with suspicion by the ruling Drukpa élite, which feels similarly threatened by links between the **Lhotshampa** and bordering Nepal and India. (*See* **Driglam Namzha**.)

Sharif, Mian Nawaz

Sharif (1948–) first entered Pakistani politics in 1981 as finance and sports minister in the **Punjab** provincial cabinet. With the support of Gen. **Zia** he became chief minister of the province in 1985. In 1990 he was elected as Prime Minister until 1993, and he returned to power in 1997. He was overthrown by Gen. **Musharraf** in a coup in 1999 and forced into exile to Saudi Arabia where he has remained since. His party, the Pakistan Muslim League (N) continues in Pakistan although Sharif was barred from participating in the 2002 general elections.

Shi'a–Sunni Conflict in Pakistan

Shi'as constitute 15% of the world's Muslim population and more than 20% of Pakistan's population. Sectarian violence, or mainly the Shi'a–Sunni rift, is a serious challenge facing the government of Pakistan. Differences between these two sects of Islam can be traced back to the succession issue after the death of the Prophet Muhammad in 632 AD. In Pakistan this cleavage mainly surfaced in the early 1980s when mostly Sunni Islamic radical groups received funding from the USA and Saudi Arabia to fight the Soviet invasion of Afghanistan. Concurrently, the Shi'a Islamic revolution of 1979 in Iran promoted Shi'a radicalism in the region, resulting in the foundation of Tahreek-e-Nifaze Fiqa-e-Jafria (TNFJ) in Pakistan to safeguard Shi'a interests against the Sunni majority and the Islamization process initiated by Gen. **Zia**. Iranian support for Shi'a elements in Pakistan, and the mostly

Sunni Afghan ***jihad***, encouraged Sunni extremism, supported by an anti-Iranian block in the Muslim world.

International proponents of this proxy war provided political, financial, and ideological support to their respective factions, this phenomenon coinciding with Gen. Zia's religious revivalism. Consequently, Sipah-e-Sahaba (a Sunni sectarian party) was founded in 1985. Sipah-e-Sahaba and TNFJ had Lashker-e Jhangvi and Sipah-e-Muhammad as their respective hardline armed factions, to conduct subversive activities such as targeted killings, mosque bombings and suicide attacks against the rival community. Since 1980 more then 4,000 people have been killed in sectarian violence in Pakistan. Attempts by the government to counter sectarianism have mostly proven ineffective, partly because sectarian groups have themselves been used for political purposes and also because socio-economic factors such as low literacy rates, high unemployment and the unequal distribution of wealth continue to contribute to frustration and intolerance within society.

Shiv Sena

The Shiv Sena is a regional political party in India, founded in **Mumbai** on 19 June 1966 by party president Bal Thackeray. Formed as a 'sons of the soil' movement, the Shiv Sena originally saw itself as guarding the interests and rights of native Maharashtrians, who, the founder believed, were threatened by an influx of ethnic migrants, including South Indians and Muslims. **Maharashtra** is the Shiv Sena's stronghold, the party having taken power there in the 1995 assembly elections in coalition with the **Bharatiya Janata Party**, although it lost the 2004 state elections. In 1998 the Srikrishna Commission indicted the Shiv Sena for its involvement in riots in Mumbai, particularly those that occurred in 1992–93.

Siachen Glacier

A glacier located in the disputed Kashmir region and claimed by both India and Pakistan, Siachen, at an elevation of more than 5,000 m, is the world's highest battle ground. Both countries maintain permanent military personnel on the glacier and have intermittently fought for control of it since 1984. The roots of the conflict lie in the fact that the glacier was left undemarcated under the cease-fire line of 1948 and the subsequent **Line of Control** following the 1972 **Simla Agreement**. Pakistan's attempts to project the line north east towards the Karakoram Pass have met with stiff resistance from India, which seeks to prevent the creation of a China-Pakistan link via the Karakoram Pass. Both India and Pakistan have troops on the glacier, with the Indian Army controlling the heights and two of the three passes and the Pakistani army controlling lower access to the glacier. Talks have been under way to demilitarize this area where more soldiers die from harsh weather conditions than actual fighting. (*See* **Kashmir Dispute**.)

Sikder, Siraj

Siraj Sikder (1944–75) was the chief leader of a revolutionary Marxist and a pro-Beijing party, Purba Bangla Sarbahara Party in Bangladesh. He took part in the **Bangladesh Liberation War** with his party cadres and the party's armed wing. Opposed to the involvement of India, his group operated independently of other liberation forces, which had Indian support. After independence in 1971 Sikder continued his armed struggle against the government to establish supremacy of the *sarbahara* (proletariat), continuing to issue anti-Indian propaganda and receiving substantial support from the tribes in the Chittagong Hill Tracts. He was arrested during the emergency rule in 1974 and killed in early January 1975 by the police.

Sikh Conflict – *see* Khalistan; Operation Blue Star

Sikkim Democratic Front (SDF)

The Sikkim Democratic Front (SDF) is a regional political party in the north Indian state of Sikkim. The party was established on 4 March 1993 and is led by Pawan Kumar Chamling. It won one seat in the 2004 **Lok Sabha** elections. It is the most significant regional party in Sikkim where it has been in power since 1994.

Siliguri Corridor

Also known as the 'chicken's neck', the Siliguri Corridor describes the narrow, strategically important strip of land located between Bhutan and Bangladesh that connects India's mainland with the north-eastern states.

Simla Agreement

Following the 1971 war and the creation of Bangladesh, the Simla Agreement, signed on 3 July 1972, sought to normalize relations between India and Pakistan. Sub clause 4 (ii) stated that the **Line of Control (LoC)** in **Jammu and Kashmir** resulting from the cease-fire of 17 December 1971 shall be respected. Furthermore, a commitment to resolving all conflicts between the two countries through bilateral negotiations was undertaken. A private understanding between Indira **Gandhi** and Zulfikar Ali **Bhutto** supposedly provided for the LOC to gradually become an international border. No written record exists as Bhutto argued that an official statement would threaten both his political survival and the chance of working towards gradual acceptance. (*See* **Kashmir Dispute**.)

Sind

Named after the Sindhu (Indus) River and home to the 4,000-year-old Indus Valley civilization, Sind is the south-eastern province of Pakistan, adjacent to **Punjab**,

Balochistan, India and the Arabian Sea. With Karachi as its capital, the country's commercial and industrial hub and the biggest contributor to federal revenue, Sind has an area of 140,914 sq km and a population of around 40m. Cotton, rice, wheat, and sugar cane are the major crops of Sind. The province is linguistically divided into two distinct segments, the urban, Urdu-speaking Muhajirs and the Sindhi-speaking natives of rural background. Sind is the only province which has an internal quota system distinguishing between urban and rural areas, causing a sharp division among the populace. It experienced some of Pakistan's worst ethnic, sectarian and political clashes in the provincial capital during the 1980s and early 1990s.

Singh, Ganesh Man/Ganesh Man Singh Shrestha

Born in 1915, Ganesh Man Singh was one of Nepal's most prominent leaders of the pro-democracy People's Movement, the **Jana Andolan**, forcing King **Birendra** in 1990 to introduce multi-party democracy. One of Bisweswor Prasad **Koirala**'s closest associates from the formation of the **Nepali Congress (NC)**, in 1951 he became a minister in the Rana-NC interim government and, again, in the 1959 NC Cabinet. Like most ministers, he was imprisoned by King **Mahendra** on 15 December 1960 and released in 1968. In the late 1980s he was given the title of Supreme Leader of the NC although he rejected the office of interim Prime Minister offered to him by King Birendra in 1990. Ganesh Man left the NC in 1994 after a serious rift with Prime Minister G. P. **Koirala**. Man Singh's death in 1997 ended his almost 50-year struggle against Nepal's monarchy.

Singh, Manmohan

The 14th Prime Minister of India, Manmohan Singh, a member of the **Indian National Congress**, was sworn in on 22 May 2004. Born on 26 September 1932 in West Punjab (now Pakistan), Singh is the first Sikh to hold the office of Prime Minister. Beginning his career in the administrative services in 1971, Singh was economic adviser in the Ministry of Commerce, then chief economic adviser in the Ministry of Finance, as well as serving as deputy chairman of the Planning Commission, governor of the Reserve Bank and adviser to the Prime Minister. Brought in as finance minister in 1991 under Narasimha **Rao**, Singh is regarded as the architect of India's economic reforms. His decision to devalue the Indian currency by a tremendous 18% against the US dollar and, later, his dismantling of the infamous **Licence Permit Raj**, are examples of his crucial role in the liberalization process. Singh is widely seen to be the least corrupt politician in India, but doubts have been voiced about his ability to lead a coalition government, especially one that is dependent on the left parties (which in the past disapproved of his economic policies) for survival. He has never won a popular election and sits, with the support of the INC, in the upper house of parliament, the **Rajya Sabha**, whose members are elected indirectly by the elected members of state assemblies. A trusted confidant of Sonia **Gandhi**, Singh was nominated by her for the office of Prime Minister after the 2004 elections, to head a coalition government. In June 2005 Singh became India's first leader to visit front-line troops on Kashmir's **Siachen Glacier**, in order to boost their morale.

Singh, Moni

Moni Singh (1901–94) began his political career as a member of an armed revolutionary group while he was a student in secondary school. Subsequently, he joined the **Communist Party of India** and successfully led various anti-British campaigns, such as a peasants' movement against traditional systems of revenue-extraction, which brought him to the forefront of politics as a revolutionary as well as a nationalist leader across undivided, pre-**Partition** Bengal. After the end of colonial rule in 1947, he organized the Communist Party in Pakistan and was one of the driving forces behind the founding of the new Communist Party of East Pakistan, later the **Communist Party of Bangladesh (CPB)**, in 1968. He played a role in the **Bangladesh Liberation War** as a member of the advisory council of the *Mujibnagar* government, founded on 10 April 1971 as the first government of the People's Republic of Bangladesh. After the independence of Bangladesh, he led the CPB as its elected president, co-operating with the regime of Mujibur **Rahman** and advocating a pro-Moscow foreign policy.

Singh, G. Zail

India's seventh President (1982–87), Zail Singh (1916–1994) was the first Sikh to hold the post. Post-independence, as Minister for Revenue and Agriculture, Singh played a key role in India's agrarian reforms. Elected to be Chief Minster of **Punjab** in 1972, Singh accelerated industrialization and the **Green Revolution** in his state. Becoming home minister in 1980 under Indira **Gandhi**, and later President, Singh was formally India's Commander-in-Chief of the Armed forces during the storming of the Amritsar Golden Temple in 1984. Against all normal political conventions, Zail Singh was instrumental in installing Rajiv Gandhi immediately after Indira Gandhi's death.

Sinhala Only Policy

During the elections of 1956 the **Sri Lanka Freedom Party**, under the leadership of S. W. R. D. **Bandaranaike**, campaigned using a 'Sinhala Only' slogan, promising to replace English with Sinhala as the only official national language. Having produced a landslide victory, the campaign unleashed two powerful forces: Tamil resentment and Buddhist/Sinhala sentiments of supremacy. Previously Bandaranaike had been in favour of having two official languages, but under the pressure of his electoral victory, the bill was introduced into the house of representatives and became the Official Language Act No. 33 on 15 June 1956, with the support of the

United National Party. Riding upon Tamil fears of being assimilated into the Sinhala mainstream, the Ilankai Tamil Arasu Kadchi (ITAK), also known as the **Federal Party**, organised ***hartals*** in the north and eastern provinces. Communal tension and violence increased from 1956 onwards and finally in August 1958, as a gesture towards accommodation, Bandaranaike enacted the **Tamil Language** (Special Provisions) Act, authorizing the Prime Minister to frame regulations to give effect to the use of Tamil in the north and eastern provinces. In 1987, following the **Indo-Lanka Accord**, the 13th Amendment to the Constitution introduced Tamil as an official language and English as the link language.

Six-Point Programme

The Six-Point Programme, presented by Sheikh Mujibur **Rahman** in Lahore, Pakistan, at the conference of opposition parties on 6 February 1966, while Gen. Ayub **Khan** was in power, became a core programme of East Pakistan and of the **Awami League** in particular, in the effort to remove the disparity between the two wings of Pakistan. The Six-Point Programme included a parliamentary form of government with the supremacy of a legislature directly elected on the basis of universal adult suffrage; apart from defence and foreign affairs all other residuary subjects were to be vested in the federating states; two separate currencies for the two wings; the right of the federating unit to levy taxes and duties and to establish trade links with foreign countries; separate accounts for the foreign exchange earnings of the two wings; and a separate militia or paramilitary force for the East Wing (now Bangladesh). The government rejected the six points, which it saw as a device to dismember Pakistan, and arrested Mujib Rahman by initiating the **Agartala Conspiracy Case** against him. While Mujib was in jail widespread agitation broke out in East Pakistan, forcing the government to release him unconditionally on 22 February 1969.

Small Farmers Development Project (SFDP)

The Small Farmers Development Project (SFDP), a major poverty alleviation programme in Nepal, was born out of a development support workshop jointly organized in 1975 by the then Ministry of Food, Agriculture and Irrigation, the Ministry of Land Reforms, the FAO/Asian Survey on Agrarian Reform and Rural Development and the Asian Development Bank of Nepal, which now serves as its executive agency. Its main objective is to help improve the socio-economic status of the rural poor through a collective approach, and in 1998 it was providing services to more than 180,000 small farmers. Institutional development is one of the major activities under the SFDP, in addition to economic activities, social and community development, community irrigation, environmental conservation, women's development, and collaboration with NGOs.

Sonali Bank

Sonali Bank is the largest commercial bank of Bangladesh, with 1,304 branches, including one overseas branch. Started in 1972 under Presidential Order No. 26, Sonali Bank took over the assets and liabilities of the erstwhile National Bank of Pakistan, Bank of Bhowalour and Premier Bank, functioning in then East Pakistan.

Soulbury Commission

Headed by Lord Soulbury, the Soulbury Commission, a second royal commission from Britain following the **Donoughmore Commission**, arrived in 1944 to consult with local leaders on the drafting of a new constitution for Sri Lanka. The Soulbury Constitution became the basic document for the independent country's Constitution, establishing a parliamentary system modelled on Britain's.

South Asian Association for Regional Co-operation (SAARC)

The South Asian Association for Regional Co-operation (SAARC) is an association of seven South Asian countries, namely Bangladesh, Bhutan, India, Maldives, Nepal, Pakistan, and Sri Lanka. It was established on the basis of an initiative of Bangladesh's President Ziaur **Rahman**, under the SAARC Charter during the first SAARC Summit held in Dhaka, Bangladesh, on 7–8 December 1985. Its growth as a regional organization has been stymied because of Indo-Pakistani hostilities and suspicion among India's neighbours of India's hegemonic intentions. The Association's primary objective is the strengthening and acceleration of regional co-operation, particularly in the area of economic development. Further aims, as stipulated by the SAARC Charter, include the promotion of mutual trust and collective self-reliance among South Asian countries; collaboration and mutual assistance in economic, social, cultural, technical and scientific fields; and the strengthening of co-operation with other developing countries and international and regional organizations. The Association operates according to the principles of sovereign equality, territorial integrity, political independence, non-interference in the internal affairs of other states and mutual benefit. Agreed areas of co-operation are intended as a complement to bilateral or multilateral co-operation rather than a substitute and must remain consistent with bilateral and multilateral obligations of member states.

The highest authority of the Association rests with the heads of state or government, who meet at an annual summit. A council of ministers, comprising the foreign ministers of member states, is mainly responsible for formulating policies, reviewing progress and deciding on new areas of co-operation. The council meets twice a year and may also hold extraordinary sessions on the agreement of member states. A standing committee, comprising the foreign secretaries of member states, is involved in monitoring, co-ordinating, approving and financing programmes;

mobilizing regional and external resources; and identifying new areas of co-operation. The SAARC Secretariat was established in Kathmandu on 16 January 1987, taking on the role of co-ordinating and monitoring the implementation of SAARC activities, facilitating Association meetings and acting as a communication channel between SAARC and other international organizations.

In 1993 the SAARC countries signed the **SAARC Preferential Trading Agreement (SAPTA)**, which came into effect in 1995. At the 12th SAARC summit, held in Islamabad in 2004, member states signed the **South Asia Free Trade Agreement (SAFTA)**.

South Asia Free Trade Agreement (SAFTA)

The South Asia Free Trade Agreement was reached at the 12th summit of the **South Asian Association for Regional Co-operation (SAARC)** by its seven South Asian member states in Islamabad, Pakistan, on 6 January 2004. Conceived as a step forward from the earlier **South Asia Preferential Trade Agreement (SAPTA)**, which it superseded, SAFTA came into effect in January 2006, reducing tariffs for intra-regional trade among the seven SAARC members down to zero customs duty on the trade of nearly all products in the region by the end of 2012. India, Pakistan and Sri Lanka are required to reduce customs duties to 20% within a two-year period, and to zero, through annual cuts, by 2012. The 'least developed countries' in the region, namely Nepal, Bhutan, Bangladesh (designated as such by the United Nations) and Maldives are afforded an additional three years to achieve zero duty.

The Agreement makes provision for the SAFTA Ministerial Council (SMC), the highest decision-making body of SAFTA, which is responsible for the administration and implementation of decisions and arrangements made under the Agreement, and consists of the Ministers of Commerce/Trade of member states, who should meet at least once every year. The SMC is supported by a Committee of Experts (COE), comprising one nominee from each member state, which should meet at least once every six months to monitor, review and facilitate implementation of the Agreement and, when necessary, to act as a dispute settlement body. The SMC and COE are each chaired by an individual country on an annual rotation basis and both enjoy the support of the SAARC Secretariat in the discharge of their functions.

SAARC Preferential Trading Agreement (SAPTA)

The SAARC Preferential Trading Agreement (SAPTA), signed by **SAARC** members in Dhaka, Bangladesh, on 11 April 1993, provided for the adoption of various instruments of trade liberalization on a preferential basis. The primary aim of SAPTA was to expand regional trade through the exchange of concessions as a means of stimulating national economies and strengthening intra-regional economic co-operation. Based on principles of reciprocity and mutual advantage, SAPTA took into account member states' respective levels of economic and industrial development and patterns of external trade as well as trade and tariff policies. The

Agreement recognized special needs of the region's 'least developed states' (designated as such by the United Nations), affording them preferential treatment. A Committee of Participants was established under SAPTA, consisting of representatives from each member state who meet at least once a year to review the progress made in the implementation of the Agreement and to ensure that trade expansion benefits all SAARC states equitably. SAPTA transformed into the **South Asia Free Trade Agreement (SAFTA)** at the start of 2006.

Sramik Karmachari Oikyo Parishad (SKOP)

Sramik Karmachari Oikyo Parishad (SKOP) is a united front of workers and employees in Bangladesh, constituted in 1984. Numerous individual and company unions are joined together under the banner of SKOP, forming a non-partisan group for labour unions. As a collective bargaining agency, SKOP has the right to deal with the government and management or employers on issues of minimum wages, improved working conditions and health and safety conditions. SKOP has been prominent in major issues, such as the reopening of Adamjee Jute Mills and other closed industries and the slowing down of the privatization of state-owned enterprises in the public sector.

Sri Lanka, Democratic Socialist Republic of

The Democratic Socialist Republic of Sri Lanka comprises one large island and several islets, lying east of the southern tip of India. It is divided into nine provinces and 25 administrative districts. Since 1988 the northern and eastern provinces have technically been jointly administered. Area: 65,610 sq km; capital: Colombo (Sri Jayewardenepura Kotte is the legislative capital); population: 19m. (UN estimate, 2003), comprising ethnic Sinhalese (74%), Tamils (18%), Moor (7%), Burghers, Malays, and Veddas (1%); official language: Sinhala (official and national language); religion: Buddhist 70%, Hindu 15%, Christian 8%, Muslim 7% (1999). Executive power is invested in the President who is elected by popular vote for a six-year term. The unicameral parliament consists of 225 members elected for a six-year term. One hundred and ninety-six are elected through a system of proportional representation and the remaining 29 are chosen using a formula based on the aggregate votes received by each party.

History: Sri Lanka's history chronicles an embittered relationship between two peoples—the Sinhalese who arrived from northern India around 500 BC and eventually set up Buddhist kingdoms on the north-central plains, and the Tamils who followed a few centuries later from southern India. The ancient linkage of northern Sri Lanka with the Tamil kingdoms of southern India has not been forgotten by today's Sinhalese who see in the proximity of India's southern **Tamil Nadu** a source of psychological and political support for Tamil separatists on the island. Following the Portuguese and Dutch, it was the British who in the late 18th century succeeded in uniting the island. A national movement emerged in the late

19th century, taking institutional form as the Ceylon National Congress in 1919. In 1931 universal suffrage was granted, Ceylon being the first of Britain's Asian colonies to secure this right. Following independence in February 1948, the **United National Party (UNP)** won the country's first general elections. Under the leadership of D. S. **Senanayake**, the UNP attempted to establish an anti-communist, intercommunal parliamentary form of government. In July 1951, however, the party experienced its first shock when the left-of-centre bloc seceded to form the **Sri Lanka Freedom Party (SLFP)** under the leadership of S. W. R. D. **Bandaranaike**. Together the two parties have since dominated Sri Lankan politics. The 1956 election marked the first instance of serious communal disharmony. Bandaranaike of the SLFP ran on a '**Sinhala Only Policy**' platform, promising that Sinhalese would be the only official language and emphasizing the country's Buddhist origins. It has been argued that the emotive nature of the 1956 elections politicized, for the first time, the two communities, pitting the one, Sinhalese and Buddhist, against the other, Tamil and Hindu. In May 1958 an anti-Tamil rumour sparked nation-wide communal riots, instigating a state of emergency and the forcible relocation of more than 25,000 Tamil refugees from Sinhalese areas to Tamil areas in the north. Following her husband's assassination in 1959, Mrs S. R. D. Bandaranaike contested the 1960 general election, winning an absolute majority in parliament to become Sri Lanka's seventh, and the world's first woman, Prime Minister. While in office, she vigorously enforced legislation, such as the Official Language Act, openly placing Sinhalese interests over Tamil. Returning to power in 1970, Mrs Bandaranaike led the United Front coalition, which included the SLFP and two other parties. A new threat to stability emerged when the Maoist **Janatha Vimukhti Peramuna (JVP—People's Liberation Front)** attempted to overthrow the government. The insurrection was suppressed but later in the 1980s an invigorated JVP was to arise, garnering strength from the anti-Indian sentiment that followed the arrival of Indian troops in 1987. A new constitution in 1972 declared Sri Lanka a republic, and the protection of Buddhism a constitutional principle. The Tamil community, including the **Federal Party** which had from the start advocated a more federal system, reacted collectively against the new Constitution and in May 1972 founded the Tamil United Front (in 1976 the **Tamil United Liberation Front—TULF**). At about the same time the **Liberation Tigers of Tamil Eelam (LTTE)** emerged, building upon the political disillusionment of Tamil youth which had intensified during the Bandaranaike years. By this time the separatist call for a *Tamil* ***Eelam***, or homeland for Tamils, was increasingly accompanied by attacks on government targets. The 1977 elections returned the UNP to power under the leadership of J. R. **Jayawardene**. Declaring that his government would inaugurate an era of *dharmishta*, or righteous society, Jayawardene crafted a new constitution the following year, changing the previous Westminster-style parliamentary government to a new presidential system modelled on France. The 1978 Constitution, unlike its predecessor, made substantial concessions to Tamil sensitivities. Also marking a break with the post-independence period was the shift in economic policy away from a socialist orientation. However, in July 1983 the ambush and killing of 13 Sinhalese soldiers by the Tamil Tigers unleashed a Sinhalese backlash. An unprecedented wave of violence engulfed the country, initiating an intermittent civil war. A ban on the advocacy of separatism imposed in August caused all TULF members of parliament to resign. In 1985, with the active participation of Indian Prime Minister Rajiv Gandhi, a dialogue with the TULF was reopened. Tamil demands focused on the issue of devolving central legislative, administrative, and judicial authority, but progress was soon halted as the moderate TULF had little credibility among the militants fighting for a *Tamil Eelam*. To dislodge this opposition a military campaign was launched by the government that succeeded in wresting part of the **Jaffna** Peninsula stronghold from the Tamil Tigers but which also drew strong criticism from the Indian government. Good relations with India had been of great importance to Sri Lanka since independence but the ethnic crisis between the Sinhalese and the Tamils, culminating in the mid-1980s, caused the relationship to turn acrimonious. India alleged that the Sri Lankan security forces were committing atrocities against the Sri Lankan Tamils and Sri Lanka accused India of encouraging Tamil separatism and of providing Tamil guerrillas with sanctuary and training facilities in the southern Indian state of Tamil Nadu. Overcoming much bitterness, the **Indo-Lanka Accord** was finally signed by Prime Minister Rajiv Gandhi and President Jayawardene in July 1987. A key concession negotiated was a temporary merger of the Northern and Eastern provinces to ensure that an elected provincial council in the Tamil majority areas enjoyed substantial power to administer Tamil affairs. Indian military assistance was also officially accepted, with the **Indian Peace Keeping Force (IPKF)** arriving in the north to monitor a cease-fire. By early September violence had broken out in the Eastern Province where Sinhalese and Muslims perceived the merger of the provinces and the resultant Tamil majority as a threat. Bandaranaike's SLFP capitalized on this discontent, launching an election campaign based on the government's 'betrayal' of the non-Tamil population in the Eastern province. In the mean time Sinhalese extremists of the JVP took advantage of the quagmire in the Northern Province to launch armed raids on military camps in the south. With increasing attacks from both subversive JVP and extremist Tamil Tiger members the 1988 presidential elections turned into a veritable battle of ballot versus bullet. Against the odds, UNP candidate **Premadasa** won by a large margin over the SLFP's Bandaranaike. Under Premadasa's presidency the five-and-a-half-year state of emergency declared by his predecessor was lifted, the remaining 45,000 Indian soldiers were recalled, and parliamentary elections were held for the first time in 11 years. However, soon after the withdrawal of Indian troops, fighting between the LTTE and government forces resumed, culminating in the assassination of Prime Minister Premadasa in 1993. The SLFP, the main party in the **People's Alliance (PA)** coalition, returned to power in 1994 for the first time in 17 years, with Chandrika **Kumaratunga** as Prime Minister. Kumaratunga later won the November 1994 presidential elections, pledging to abolish the executive presidency, a promise she has yet to fulfil. A new dual strategy was formulated, focusing on the military defeat of the Tamil Tigers but coupled with the new element of a constitutional settlement granting more autonomy to Tamil majority areas. A devolution initiative gathered momentum during the mid-1990s but continuous violence and the lack of a political consensus in parliamentary discussions stalled the process. Following an election in 1999, widely condemned as fraudulent, and an assassination attempt on President Kumaratunga, the PA was returned to power. In the elections of December 2001, the UNP entered the coalition government, promising a strong commitment to economic and social sector reforms, deregulation, and private-sector development. Thus, two historically opposed parties governed Sri Lanka in a delicate and highly strained cohabitation. In February 2002 Mr Wickremasinghe's government and the LTTE signed a permanent cease-fire agreement and in December the government agreed to peace talks in Norway. Mrs Kumaratunga, accusing the Wickremasinghe government of leniency, declared a state of emergency on 4 November 2003 while Prime Minister Wickremasinghe was visiting the USA, taking control of three ministries, including defence. In January 2004 a joint document issued by Kumaratunga's PA and former leftist revolutionaries, the JVP, claimed the peace process put Sri Lanka's territorial integrity at risk. The alliance was transformed into the United People's Freedom Alliance to contest the April elections, called almost four years ahead of schedule by Kumaratunga.

Latest Elections: Snap elections were held in April 2004. Kumaratunga's coalition, the United People's Freedom Alliance, won 105 seats, thus failing to achieve a majority, implying that it needed the support of minority factions. The rival UNP, the party of ousted Prime Minister Wickremasinghe, suffered a loss of seats. The **Tamil National Alliance** achieved an unprecedented victory, winning four electoral districts to emerge as the third largest party in the new parliament with 22 seats. In what was viewed as a concession to the powerful Buddhist clergy, Mr Mahinda Rajapakse, a devout Buddhist and senior leader of the SLFP, was sworn in as Prime Minister.

Recent Developments: Following the elections, the JVP holds 39 of the alliance's seats and is insisting on more power than Mrs Kumaratunga has offered. Peace talks were resumed through Norwegian intermediaries following factional infighting within the Tamil Tigers that led to the emergence of a breakaway group in early April 2004. In November 2005 Rajapakse won presidential elections, with Kumaratunga stepping down after 11 years as President.

Sri Lanka, Political Development

Although Sri Lanka became formally independent of British colonial rule in 1948, universal adult suffrage was already in force under the Donoughmore Constitution from 1937. During the 50 years following independence two political families have dominated Sri Lankan politics: the Senanayake-**Jayawardene** clan and the **Bandaranaike family**. Both prominent nationalist leaders, D. S. **Senanayake** and

S. W. R. D. Bandaranaike, together with others, formed the **United National Party (UNP)** in 1946. However, Bandaranaike, who later broke with Senanayake, went on to found the rival **Sri Lanka Freedom Party (SLFP)** in September 1951. The UNP ruled first from 1948 to 1956 under three Prime Ministers: D. S. Senanayake, his son Dudley, and Sir John Kotelawala. The SLFP swept the UNP out of office in 1956 on a wave of Sinhala nationalism, with S. W. R. D. Bandaranaike becoming Prime Minister, and then, after his assassination in 1959, his widow, Sirimavo. Under Dudley Senanayake the UNP returned to power in 1965. In 1970 Mrs Bandaranaike resumed the premiership, governing in coalition with the leftist Lanka Sama Samaja Party (LSSP) and the Communist Party of Sri Lanka. A year later an armed uprising against the government led by the Maoist **Janatha Vimukthi Peramuna (JVP)** was suppressed through emergency rule that lasted six years. In 1972 a new republican constitution allowed the ruling coalition an additional two years in power. Under J. R. **Jayawardene** the UNP returned to power in the 1977 general elections, winning 140 of the 168 National Assembly seats. The **Tamil United Liberation Front (TULF)** emerged as the main opposition party and, for the first time, a Tamil, Appapillai Amrithalingam, became leader of opposition. A new constitution in 1978 established a strong executive presidency, with Jayawardene as President. A national referendum prolonged the life of parliament by a further six years and the UNP extended its control through by-elections and local elections. In July 1983 the country's worst ethnic violence resulted in a state of emergency. The sixth amendment officially banned separatism, compelling all TULF parliamentary members to resign. Increasing violence in the north and east caused Indian intervention in the conflict and in 1987 the **Indo-Lanka Accord** committed Indian peace-keeping troops. Under Mrs Bandaranaike's leadership a new opposition front, the United Socialist Alliance, was formed, with the Communist Party, the LSSP and a Tamil party, the **Eelam People's Revolutionary Liberation Front**. The UNP's Ranasinghe **Premadasa** narrowly defeated Mrs Bandaranaike in the 1988 presidential elections but managed to recover its position by winning an absolute majority in parliament in 1989. However, in 1993 Premadasa was assassinated by the **Liberation Tigers of Tamil Eelam (LTTE)**. Following the 1994 parliamentary elections the SLFP returned to power for the first time in 17 years. First appointed Prime Minister, Chandrika Bandaranaike **Kumaratunga**, later won the presidential elections, designating her mother, former Prime Minister Sirimavo Bandaranaike, to replace her. In the north east the war had intensified, with the government engaged in a protracted military campaign against the LTTE. These had been the first elections fought on a platform promising peace. In January 1995 the first formal truce was negotiated with the LTTE, but by April fighting had resumed. Turning towards devolution proposals as an alternative strategy, Kumaratunga kept up the military offensive which, finally in December, regained control over **Jaffna** province. Prior to the 1999 elections voter apathy seemed to threaten both presidential candidates, but an assassination attempt on Kumaratunga just before polling ensured victory for the **People's Alliance (PA)**.

With a very narrow majority in parliament, however, Kumaratunga's devolution plans stagnated. In April 2000 the government was badly humiliated and forced to seek help abroad when the LTTE captured the strategic Elephant Pass. Parliamentary elections in 2001 brought the UNP into the government, with Ramil Wickremasinghe, earlier Kumaratunga's presidential rival, as Prime Minister. An uneasy cohabitation government came to an abrupt end when, in November 2003, President Kumaratunga took control of three key ministries while Wickremasinghe was abroad. Early elections were called and in January 2004 the SLFP and the JVP formed the **United People's Freedom Alliance (UPFA)**. In the April parliamentary elections the UPFA received 45% of the vote, while the UNP obtained 37%.

Constitution: Constitutional reform has become a political battleground in Sri Lanka. In 1978 then Prime Minister J. R. Jayawardene of the United National Party (UNP) amended the Republican Constitution of 1972 to institute an executive presidency in Sri Lanka, concentrating all power in the elected head of state and government and introducing elections based on proportional representation for the first time. It was argued then that stability and accelerated development required a strong executive, freed from the whims of the legislature. However, the introduction of measures such as the Fourth Amendment (December 1982), extending the life of parliament to six years, or the Sixth Amendment (August 1983), obliging members of parliament to renounce support for separatism, came to be seen as the UNP's strategy of entrenching its power. In her 1994 campaign Chandrika Kumaratunga of the People's Alliance promised to abolish the presidential form of government and to reinstate parliamentary government. Amendment of the Constitution requires a two-thirds' vote of parliament. Moreover, measures that affect 'the independent, unitary, and democratic nature of the state', the Buddhist religion, fundamental rights, the President's term of office or parliament must be approved by a popular referendum. Over the last decade, however, abolishing the presidential form of government along with other constitutional reforms, such as the granting of autonomy to the Tamil-dominated north and east, have been deadlocked.

Executive: Sri Lanka shifted from a prime ministerial to a presidential system in 1978 when, under J. R. Jayawardene of the United National Party (UNP), a new Constitution granted extensive executive powers to the President. Under the 1978 Constitution the President is popularly elected for a term of six years and may serve no more than two consecutive terms. With parliament's approval, the President appoints the Prime Minister and together they select the members of the Cabinet. It is the chief executive, rather than the Prime Minister, who presides over the Cabinet's deliberations, and who may assume any ministerial portfolio. The 1978 Constitution envisaged both President and Prime Minister to be from the same party. This has not been the case since the December 2001 parliamentary elections when Ranil Wickremsinghe of the UNP became Prime Minister. Ever since then there have been serious cohabitation strains. The Kumaratunga-led alliance of parties has on the whole favoured a tougher stance on the Tamil question and has had more socialist leanings. The UNP, on the other hand, has been pressing for a negotiated settlement with the Liberation Tigers of Tamil Eelam (LTTE), including concessions for the Tamils and other minorities. In November 2003, citing national security concerns and taking advantage of Wickremsinghe's absence, Kumaratunga used her executive powers to suspend parliament and sack three key ministers. A state of emergency was declared allowing detention for up to one year without charge as well as widening the powers of the military, a provision that was widely used by previous governments to crack down on the Tamil rebellion. Through her actions Kumaratunga paved the way for the dissolution of parliament in February 2004, calling for early elections, thus ousting the UNP from the government. Ironically, Kumaratunga contested the April 2004 elections with the same promise that she made in 1994 of scrapping the presidency to restore full parliamentary democracy. Under the 1978 Constitution the President is a fixed executive, unremovable while in office except for specific reasons. A resolution calling for impeachment of the President that is not supported by two-thirds of parliament is referred by the speaker to the Supreme Court. Once the process of impeachment has been initiated the President cannot prorogue or dissolve parliament. In 2001 the opposition moved a resolution to impeach not only the President on charges of corruption and abuse of power, but also the chief justice on the grounds of partiality.

Legislature: Sri Lanka's unicameral legislature, the National Assembly, has 225 members, elected for a six-year term, of whom 196 are elected from 22 multi-seat constituencies and 29 by proportional representation. Proportional representation was introduced in 1978 when the second republican constitution established the executive presidency and a parliamentary legislature. The legislature reserves the power to make all laws and the nation's President has the power to summon, suspend or end a legislative session and to dissolve parliament. Except in the 1989 polls, when the United National Party won 51% of the vote and obtained 125 seats, no party has been able to achieve a majority on its own. The support of the minority parties has been a crucial component in tipping the scales in favour of either of the major parties. In 1994, for instance, when President Kumaratunga swept the polls to form the first People's Alliance government, her party had received an all-time high of 48.9% of the vote but still could not secure a majority in its own right, with 105 seats. Most recently the President dissolved parliament in February 2004, after a two-year term. Elections were held in early April, contested by a record 2,337 independent candidates. Kumaratunga's Sri Lanka Freedom Party, allied with the Janatha Vimukthi Peramuna, secured the most seats by a single party but failed to achieve a majority. As a result the very first vote in parliament was lost: that of appointing the speaker.

Elections/Electoral System: Sri Lanka was the first colony to have universal suffrage (1931) and to hold parliamentary elections, in 1947, a year *before* independence. The two major parties, the United National Party (UNP) and the Sri Lanka Freedom Party (SLFP), have generally alternated rule. There are five different elections in Sri Lanka, namely the presidential, parliamentary general, provincial councils and local authorities elections, and the referendum. An elector must be a citizen of Sri Lanka of at least 18 years of age. Registration takes place annually, irrespective of whether elections are due to take place. Problems have arisen over the great number of persons displaced by the ethnic conflict in the north and east who have slipped through the legal provisions for registration. Soon after the 1977 general elections a new constitution introduced a strong executive presidency and J. R. Jayawardene was sworn in as the country's first President. Following this Constitution the President is today directly elected by the people for a six-year term. For the election of members of parliament the 1978 Constitution introduced a modified form of proportional representation on the grounds that the earlier first-past-the-post system did not suit Sri Lanka's multi-ethnic composition. The Third Amendment to the Constitution, approved in 1982, allows the President to hold a presidential election at any time following his fourth year in office. In 1980 parliament approved legislation to divide Sri Lanka's eight provinces into 24 district development councils, which were meant to abolish village councils in order to encourage common development projects. The 13th Amendment to the Constitution (1987) introduced provincial councils as the key institution presiding over all local bodies. Provincial and local government elections also adopted the PR system. The party winning the most votes in each district received a proportional number of seats in parliament plus one bonus seat, awarded automatically. Meant to be a step towards the decentralization of power, the first 1981 local elections in the north were marred by violence, including the assassination of the UNP's leading candidate, and scandal due to alleged voting irregularities. Soon after, in 1982, a controversial referendum to extend the life of parliament further eroded the credibility and legitimacy of the electoral process. Since then local and provincial elections have intermittently been postponed by the government, which has often used emergency regulations, as in 1998, to put off provincial council elections. In particular, the government has prevented local elections in the northern and eastern parts on the grounds that the area is occupied by rebels. However, general and presidential elections have been held, for example in 1994 when Jaffna was not under the control of government forces. Over the last decade the existing PR system has been increasingly criticized by both the government and the opposition. Partly, this has been an attempt to blame the electoral process for problems of violence and intimidation in recent elections. During the 1994 elections both parties pledged to change the system to one modelled on the German electoral system. Since then proposals have been tabled but electoral reform remains an ongoing debate. Minority parties, however, which have gained immense bargaining power as the king-makers in coalition politics, are not in favour of changing the current electoral system. It is also feared in some quarters that the TULF may actually benefit from a first-past-the-post system, as it did in 1977 when, as a result of the demographic profile of the island, the TULF emerged as the main parliamentary opposition party.

Social Movements: One of Sri Lanka's best known and largest social movements is the Sarvodaya Shramadana Movement, founded by A. T. Ariyaratne during the

1950s. Drawing its inspiration from *Mahatma* **Gandhi** and Vinoba Bhave, the movement also infused Buddhist values into its grassroots activities. Striving for a rural 'reawakening', the movement began by Buddhist monks addressing village needs and offering an alternative to the top-down development programme of local government. The movement rejected both the capitalist model of development that encourages competition, consumerism and individualism, and also the communist model of revolution and forced redistribution. Instead, the movement preached spiritual awakening and a programme of community services to encourage both self-reliance and the maximum participation of villagers. In 1972 the movement was legally recognized by a special act of parliament, its work attracting donor funds from Western organizations. Today the movement has spread throughout the country and is also promoting its vision and philosophy abroad. This movement has, however, been linked with a Buddhist revivalism and an exclusivist Sinhala nationalism that is based upon a belief in Sri Lanka being the protector of Buddhism. This phenomenon is sometimes blamed for the early ethnic tensions that emerged in the 1950s and 1960s. (*See* **Buddhist Movement**.)

Provincial Councils/System: Following conditions agreed to in the **Indo-Lanka Accord** of 1987 and the subsequent 13th amendment to the Constitution, the government of Sri Lanka introduced the provincial council system. Thus, devolution of power was introduced for the first time into the post-colonial Sri Lankan Constitution, allowing provinces to directly elect councils for a six-year term. The creation of provincial councils proved to be highly controversial, denounced on the one hand by the Buddhist nationalist opposition, the Sri Lanka Freedom Party and the radical Janatha Vimukthi Peramuna for giving in to Indian demands and, on the other hand, boycotted by the Tamil United Liberation Front and the Liberation Tigers of Tamil Eelam who criticized the arrangement as superficial and minimal. Elections to all eight provincial councils were held for the first time in 1988. An elected north-east provincial council was constituted, but, due to mounting violence, was dissolved in June 1990. Elections have yet to be held either under a single or divided administrative unit. (*See* **Buddhist Movement**.)

Foreign Policy: Sri Lanka's overriding concern has been how to manage relations with its giant neighbour, India. Through the Non-aligned movement (NAM), and as a founding member, Sri Lanka tried to establish an independent policy, to pursue what S. W. R. D. Bandaranaike called a 'dynamic neutralism'. One of the high points of the NAM was in fact reached in 1976 at the Colombo Summit, where an impressive array of leaders congregated. Relations with India reached a low point during the 1980s when the **Indian Peace Keeping Force (IPKF)** was sent to monitor a cease-fire in Sri Lanka. As a member of the **South Asian Association for Regional Co-operation (SAARC)**, Sri Lanka has also attempted to build relations across the region, lobbying for and signing in 1998 a free-trade agreement with India, one of the first such agreements in the region. A triumph for Sri Lankan diplomacy occurred in 1997 when the USA classified the Liberation Tigers of Tamil Eelam as a 'terrorist' organization, a designation that was renewed in 2003. Another important, recent milestone was the decision in 2000 to formally resume diplomatic ties with Israel after more than two decades. This was widely seen as a move to win more military assistance for the civil war. (*See* **Indo-Lanka Accord**.)

Sri Lanka-India Relations: With India just 20 km away, relations between the two countries have gone through highs and lows. In the early decades after independence Sri Lanka sought to pursue an independent line of foreign policy, inclining towards the Western powers, occasionally to the chagrin of India. A challenge that both faced early on was the fate of more than 900,000 Tamils of Indian origins living in Sri Lanka who, under the 1948 Ceylon Citizenship Act, had been rendered stateless. The issue of their citizenship was subsequently addressed in two major bilateral agreements, the Srimavo-Shastri Pact of 1964 and the Srimavo-Indira Gandhi Pact of 1974 and several consequent legislative acts.

Drawn into Sri Lanka's ethnic conflict because of its own Tamil population in the south, India's attempts at mediation resulted in the Indo-Lanka Accord of 1987 and the dispatch to Sri Lanka of the IPKF. Producing mixed reactions in Sri Lanka, Indian involvement came to an end when newly elected Sri Lankan president Ranasinghe **Premadasa** demanded the withdrawal of the IPKF. Ever since, India has chosen to focus on economic issues as a basis for improved relations and co-operation. In 1998 Sri Lanka and India signed a Free Trade Agreement, the first of its kind in the region and a promising model for India's relations with other neighbouring countries. Since 1998 trade between the two has increased threefold and discussions are under way for a Comprehensive Economic Partnership Agreement envisioning integrated markets and increased investment. India is the largest source of imports for Sri Lanka and the fourth largest direct investor. Building on growing economic interdependence, better security relations have followed, with India becoming a major player in Sri Lanka's energy interests, defence co-operation and improved communication on sensitive matters such as fishing rights.

Following the 2004 **Indian Ocean** tsunami, the Indian navy was deployed immediately to provide emergency relief and aid in search and rescue operations. A three-year moratorium on the repayment of Sri Lankan debt was part of India's tsunami assistance.

Judiciary: Sri Lanka's highest court is the Supreme Court, headed by a chief justice and 6–10 associate justices. Supreme and High Court justices are appointed by the President. Superior court justices can be removed on grounds of incompetence or misdemeanour by a majority of parliament, whereas High Court justices can be removed only by a judicial service commission consisting of Supreme Court justices. The Supreme Court has the power of judicial review; it can determine whether an act of parliament is consistent with the principles of the Constitution and whether a referendum ought to be taken on a proposal, such as the 1982 proposition to extend parliament's term by six years. It is also the final court of appeal for all criminal or civil cases. Concerns about the judiciary's independence have led to allegations that the system encourages a subservient judiciary. Partly for political motivations, the opposition has been trying since 2001 to push through a motion to impeach the chief justice. International watchdogs have criticized the policing and prosecution system and have drawn attention to the use of emergency regulations. The government is engaged in an ongoing project for legal and judicial reform, aimed at improving efficiency and transparency. (*See* **Donoughmore Commission**; **Soulbury Commission**.)

Defence (Security): Internal security has been the overwhelming concern for the Sri Lankan government. Since the early 1980s the insurgency led by the Liberation Tigers of Tamil Eelam (LTTE) has claimed more than 60,000 lives. As the crisis intensified in 1989 the government was forced to accept an Indian Peace Keeping Force on Sri Lankan soil and has had to cope with attacks on civilian and military targets. For example, in 2000, after heavy fighting, the Tamil Tigers captured the strategic Elephant Pass which links Jaffna to the rest of Sri Lanka and in 2001 launched a suicide attack on Sri Lanka's international airport. As part of their military strategy, the Sri Lankan armed forces were stationed on a permanent basis in the north east. These camps grew in size and number and by the early 1990s there were more than 200 of what came to be known as high security zones (HSZ). Today, during the peace talks, the LTTE has been insisting that the government reduce the HSZs in the north to allow the internally displaced to return to their lands. Meanwhile, the government argues that first the LTTE must disarm. More recently the defence ministry became a political battleground when President Kumaratunga took over the ministry in late 2003. Constitutionally the defence and external affairs portfolio should be held by the Prime Minister, whom Kumaratunga accused of compromising national security during the peace process.

Military: By 1949 Sri Lanka's army, navy, and air force had been established. In the mid-1950s the army's officer corps was dominated by Tamils, but in just over 10 years this balance was reversed. Due to a mutual security agreement with Britain the military budget could be kept relatively small during the 1950s. With the sudden growth of the Tamil separatist movement in the early 1980s, the activities of the armed forces evolved from civil patrol to anti-terrorism, counter-insurgency and guerrilla warfare. The army and the special task force of the police played the central role in these operations, whilst the navy patrolled the coasts to interdict arms shipments. In 1986 the insurgency was strong enough to seize control of Jaffna Peninsula, leading finally, in May 1987, to 'Operation Liberation', a co-ordinated land, sea, and air attack involving 3,000 troops, the single largest force ever deployed by the Sri Lankan government. Bogged down in an ongoing civil war, the armed forces have been accused of gross human rights violations. However, despite the regular use of the armed forces in the 1980s there has not been an attempt by the military to undermine .civilian power. Military expenditure in 2004 was 2.60% of gross domestic procuct.

Police: The 60,000-member police force responsible for internal security in most areas of the Sri Lanka has also been used in military operations against the Liberation Tigers of Tamil Eelam, particularly the paramilitary police Special Task

Force (STF). More recently, the STF has also been used for VIP security, undergoing training from British as well as Indian security forces. In addition there is the home guard, an armed force that is allegedly mainly Sinhalese, responsible to the police and meant to provide security for Muslim and Sinhalese village communities in or near the north and east. These militia groups have been unpopular, often exceeding their original mandate for self-defence, avenging terrorist attacks by the indiscriminate killing of Tamil civilians.

Riots: Anti-Tamil riots throughout the 1970s culminated in July 1983 when communal riots erupted in Sri Lanka in apparent retaliation for the ambush of an army patrol in the north that left 13 Sinhalese soldiers dead. The mob violence that followed, mostly in Colombo, was reported as deliberate and highly organized. The unprecedented breakdown in law enforcement led some to accuse the government of connivance. 'Black July', as it is known, is often portrayed as a watershed in Sri Lanka's ethnic struggle that hardened the militancy of the Tamil movement. The 1983 violence also had an anti-Indian element and members of the Indian mission in Colombo were targets of attack. The riots also initiated the flight of Sri Lankan Tamil refugees to India. At least 150,000 Tamils fled the island. An official inquiry into the anti-Tamil riots of 1983 suggested estimates ranging from 500–10,000, it remains unclear how many died. Sri Lanka's second largest minority after the Tamils, the Muslims, have also been drawn into communal clashes, especially following their demands that the east be treated as a separate entity in the government's peace talks with the rebels. The potential for communal violence in the north and east remains real and tension between the Tamil Tigers and the military continues to trigger sporadic riots. The Liberation Tigers of Tamil Eelam have been accused of deliberately attacking civilians in the north to force non-Tamils to flee Jaffna Peninsula. (*See* **Buddhist Movement**.)

Terrorism: Over more than two decades of civil war, terrorism has become ingrained in Sri Lanka's political system, besides undermining its economy. The Liberation Tigers of Tamil Eelam (LTTE), though it has not always been conclusively proven, is held responsible for some 200 suicide bombings, blasts and targeted killings, including the May 1991 assassination of former Indian Prime Minister Rajiv Gandhi, the May 1993 assassination of Sri Lankan President Ranasinghe Premadasa, and the two December 1999 suicide bombings in Colombo that wounded Sri Lankan President Chandrika Kumaratunga. The LTTE is designated a foreign terrorist organization by the USA. State security forces have also employed methods of terror and intimidation in the fight against Tamil rebels. The 1979 Prevention of Terrorism Act, originally a temporary measure, remains in force today and allows the authorities the freedom to arrest suspects almost at will, and for prolonged custody without trial.

Bureaucracy: Under colonial rule, Sri Lanka developed a strong and centralized administrative structure. Since independence Sri Lanka's bureaucracy has suffered under the legacy of colonial rigidity, growing inter-departmental rivalry and a swollen public sector. Adding to inefficiency is the tendency for parties in power to use administrative positions as patronage, thus politicizing the system. Since the 1970s attempts have been made to reform the system, particularly through decentralization. Following the 1971 Janatha Vimukthi Peramuna (JVP)-led insurrection, the government promoted political leadership at the local level, setting in motion various efforts to create institutions at the district level. The 1987 introduction of a Provincial Council System tried to create more responsive methods of public service delivery but lack of co-ordination between different levels of government, bureaucratic resistance and poor management have hindered attempts at decentralization. New public management initiatives have turned attention to increasing transparency and accountability within the system, improved recruitment practices and regular performance assessments.

Citizenship: Citizenship laws are based on the Citizenship Act of Sri Lanka 1972, amended in 1987. Late in 2003 the Sri Lankan parliament passed an amendment to the Citizenship Act to grant citizenship to more than 170,000 Tamils of Indian origin. First brought to Sri Lanka by the British in the 1820s as labourers for the plantations, the Tamils of Indian origin found themselves without civil rights after the 1948 Ceylon Citizenship Act denied them nationality. In 1964 the Sirimavo-Shastri Pact negotiated repatriation to India for some and Sri Lankan citizenship for others, but a significant number fell through the process, with critics arguing that India deliberately delayed and obstructed the process of granting Indian citizenship. After more than 40 years of lobbying the latest bill grants citizenship to any person of Indian origin who has been a permanent resident of Sri Lanka since 30 October 1964, or who is a descendant of such a person. Politically the interests of the Tamils of Indian origin have been largely represented by the Ceylon Workers Congress under the leadership of Tondaman, the estate workers' main trade union organization.

Corruption: Corruption in Sri Lanka is considered a serious problem, with all sectors of the economy affected and officials from both ruling parties accused of corrupt practices. A lack of resources, limited legal and administrative safeguards against corruption as well as an extensive public sector and an opaque regulatory system have provided the scope for considerable bureaucratic discretion. The lack of a freedom of information law has hindered the ability of the media to act as a public watchdog, with the publicly funded media serving as the government's mouthpiece. The link being made by international donors between good governance and aid has caused the government to pay more attention to corruption and how donor funds are disbursed. This is an important step towards countering the domestic as well as international perception that politicians appropriate a significant portion of the aid given to Sri Lanka. In March 2004 Sri Lanka became the second country in the world to ratify the United Nations Convention against corruption. This should entail new domestic legislation to deal with corruption in both the private and the public sector. However, in the mean time yet another special committee has been appointed by President Kumaratunga to deal with bribery and corruption.

Decentralization: Sri Lanka comprises nine provinces and 25 administrative districts, each with an appointed governor and an elected development council. In

November 1987 an amendment to the Constitution was adopted providing for the creation of eight provincial councils (the northern and eastern provinces temporarily counted as one administrative unit). Responsibilities were divided into central, provincial and 'shared' subjects. In practice this formula tilts towards the centre, especially since the provinces have virtually no independent financial authority. On sensitive issues such as law and order, policing and land distribution, power has gravitated to the centre. Elections were held to all eight provincial councils for the first time in 1988. The north-east province council was dissolved in June 1990 and elections have not been held there since. At the district and local level there is a network of 68 *pradeshiya sabhas* (district councils), introduced in early 1988, as well as municipal and urban councils. The debate on power sharing at the national, regional and district levels has been an ongoing discussion in Sri Lankan politics. Since the 1980s and 1990s it has become a core issue in the attempts to resolve the ethnic conflict.

Federalism: Article 2 of Sri Lanka's Constitution asserts that Sri Lanka is a unitary state. Local government institutions have played a limited role in the political process and administrative divisions have been in the form of districts. In November 1987 the 13th Amendment introduced devolution of power for the first time into the Sri Lankan Constitution. Although it was to be applied nation-wide, it was seen primarily as a possible solution to the ongoing ethnic conflict. However, devolution was also then perceived to be the result of Indian pressure, particularly as the Sri Lankan government had to agree to a temporary merger of the northern and eastern provinces in the Indo-Lanka Accord of July 1987, a highly unpopular move with the Sinhalese who feared the emergence of an autonomous Tamil state. What has come to be known as the 'devolution package' includes proposals to remove constitutional barriers such as Article 2 and to create eight regionally organized administrative entities. However, devolution remains a highly contentious issue since any move towards a federal structure can be portrayed as giving in to separatist forces. More recently an attempt has been made to deflect attention from the core issue of Sinhala versus Tamil nationalism by promoting devolution as a form of necessary administrative reorganization and regionalization. (*See* **Sinhala Only Policy**; **Tamil Language**.)

Human Rights: Sri Lanka has ratified 13 international human rights conventions, including the Convention against Torture and the Optional Protocol to the International Covenant on Civil and Political Rights. A National Human Rights Commission was established in 1997. More recently, efforts have been made by the government to improve the human rights situation, especially with regard to the treatment of detainees. Previously detainees could be held without charge for one year if they were suspected of being supporters of the Liberation Tigers of Tamil Eelam (LTTE). The LTTE itself has had a negative human rights record. In 2001 violations both inside and outside LTTE-controlled areas were reported. Attacks against civilians have also continued and the recruitment of child soldiers has been an issue of international concern for many years. Demobilization and child protection programmes have been initiated. Accusations of human rights abuse on either side have helped fuel Sri Lanka's civil conflict. Restrictions on the freedom of the press have been eased, but controlled access to areas under the LTTE remains a serious impediment to accurate reporting on the human rights situation in conflict areas. Violence and discrimination against women and institutionalized ethnic discrimination against Tamils continue to be problems.

Inequality: Despite an entrenched welfare system, the distribution of income in Sri Lanka is only marginally more equitable than that of its South Asian neighbours. In 1996/97 the Gini index (a measurement of the extent to which the distribution of income among individuals or households deviates from an equal distribution) was estimated at 0.43: the lowest quintile received 5.5% of all income, and the highest 50.2%. In addition, access to services and opportunity varies across the country, affecting income levels. While the North and East suffer from conflict-related poverty, the South suffers from structural poverty due to differences in resource endowments. Perceptions of inequality and marginalization have been a key cause of the ongoing conflict in Sri Lanka. Recently, an ADB loan to improve secondary education in Sri Lanka emphasized supporting Tamil-speaking teachers in the north-east region as a means to reduce perceptions of exclusion. However, in terms of income and employment, rather than ethnicity being a determining factor, a significant gender disparity is found to exist. On the whole, gender seems to be the prime cause of inequality as represented in figures on health, school attendance and political participation.

Nationalism: Cultural nationalism, stemming, respectively, from Sinhala and Tamil identity, has long been an important component of Sri Lankan politics. Already in the 1930s political rhetoric spoke in terms of religious and linguistic identities as well as directly targeting different minorities. The distribution of population and the system of representation created two political zones: the north, where Tamil parties dominated and tended to adopt a position of opposition, and a southern zone where mostly Sinhala politicians competed for government power. In 1956 this division was crystallized when the Sri Lanka Freedom Party was elected to power on a wave of Sinhala Buddhist populism. Decisions to establish Sinhala as the official language helped spark the country's first communal riots. By the late 1970s Tamil politics had moved from non-violent protest and calls for federalism to guerrilla warfare and demands for a separate Tamil state. The Liberation Tigers of Tamil Eelam (LTTE) emerged as the militant group in the north and east whilst in the south the government faced the radical Sinhala Janatha Vimukthi Peramuna (JVP), which also took to violence in the 1980s. Since then attempts by the government to negotiate concessions for the Tamils have often met with a political or violent backlash, especially over proposals to merge the northern and eastern parts into a Tamil-dominated province. (*See* **Buddhist Movement**; **Tamil Language**.)

Participation/Public Action: Rather than taking specific affirmative action Sri Lanka has focused on decentralization as a means by which to encourage participation in government decision-making and development programmes. For example, at the local level *pradeshiya sabhas* were set up in 1987 with the express objective of enhancing community participation in decision-making and development at a local level.

Despite the fact that Sri Lankan women achieved the right to vote in 1931 and have a high literacy rate, female representation in Sri Lanka's governing bodies is surprisingly low even by South Asian standards. Even at the local level socio-cultural and economic constraints seem to prevail and female membership of local government councils fluctuates between 2%–3%. Proposals for a quota or reservation system for women have been considered but not yet implemented.

In dealing with participation of the minorities, the government has toyed with federalism but has noted that under a federal system most of the Sri Lankan Tamils would be outside the Tamil federal unit, if the eastern province were to remain separate. Instead, district councils have been advocated as the best regional unit to accommodate ethnic, cultural and social variations, supplemented by safeguards to protect the minorities within.

Sri Lanka, Economic Development

Gross national income (GNI): US $16,100m. (2002); GNI per capita: $850.0 (2002); GDP at PPP: $73,700m. (2002); GDP per capita at PPP: $3,700 (2002); exports: $4,600m. f.o.b. (2002); imports: $5,400m. f.o.b. (2002); currency: Sri Lankan Rupee (LKR)

At independence high levels of literacy and a smoothly functioning, commodity-based export economy implied a promising economic future for Sri Lanka. A decade later a growing balance-of-payments deficit forced a reorientation towards more protectionist, import-substitution strategies. Government participation in the economy increased, especially under the second coalition government (1970–77) headed by the **Sri Lanka Freedom Party (SLFP)**. During this period the state came to dominate the plantation, financial, and industrial manufacturing sectors and major trade unions outside the plantation sector. In 1977 the **United National Party (UNP)** returned to power and, in response to the poor economic outlook, launched a programme of economic liberalization, including trade policy reform and a process of privatization. Foreign direct investment in export-oriented manufacturing was the primary boost to GDP growth until the mid-1980s when service sectors also flourished as a result of the public-sector investment boom. The change of government in 1994, when the SLFP-led alliance came to power, was significant in the sense that it did not lead to major changes in economic policy. Since then market-oriented reforms have endured and been broadened despite the intermittent civil war. Following the economy's contraction in 2001, the government has focused on the mounting external debt.

In 2002 the combined services sector (including transport, communications, financial services and tourism) accounted for 62% of GDP, manufacturing for

16% and agriculture for 20%. Wholesale and retail trade is the single largest sector, generating 21% of GDP. Of the 7.3m.-strong workforce in 2002 at least one-quarter was employed in agriculture. Three cash crops (tea, rubber and coconuts) have traditionally dominated Sri Lanka's exports, but in 2002 they jointly accounted for only 2.9% of GDP. Instead, garments, textiles and other manufactured exports accounted for 77% of total export earnings in 2001/02. Principal imports include mineral products, foodstuffs and machinery. The largest market for Sri Lankan exports in 2002 was the USA and the principal supplier of imports was India. Sri Lanka's electricity requirements are met from fossil fuel (51.7%) and hydroelectric power (48.3%).

The fiscal imbalances in Sri Lanka continue to be a pressing problem. During 1996–2003 the budget deficit averaged 9% of GDP, reaching its highest level, 10.8%, in 2001. Also in 2001 the country experienced negative economic growth, of -1.5%, for the first time since independence, contracting from the 6% growth in GDP attained in 2000. As a result of fiscal mismanagement, combined with a severe drought and a global slowdown, investment as a proportion of GDP declined from 28% in 2000 to 22% in 2001, affecting private as well as state-run business. A high inflation rate of 11% aggravated the economic recession. Following its entry into the government the UNP's first state budget in March 2002 pledged to cut the budget deficit. Greater fiscal discipline, tax reforms, a booming stock market and a negotiated cease-fire with the **Liberation Tigers of Tamil Eelam (LTTE)** helped to bring the budget deficit down to 8.9% in 2002 and assisted a recovery in GDP growth. In 2003 the government committed to the Fiscal Management Act, promising to reduce the deficit to 5% of GDP and the public debt to 85% of GDP by 2006.

The services sector is a major foreign exchange earner for Sri Lanka. Since the 2002 peace initiative, tourism has gathered momentum and the government has been moving towards greater private as well as foreign participation. Port services also recovered strongly in 2002, buoyed by the removal of the war-risk surcharge. The floating of the Sri Lanka rupee in January 2001 allowed monetary authorities to accumulate foreign reserves and, more recently, to relax restrictions on foreign exchange transactions, thus easing financial services. Furthermore, in early 2003 the privatization programme was boosted with the floating of Sri Lanka Telecom on the stock exchange.

Economic Policy/Reforms: One of the first developing economies to implement economic reforms, Sri Lanka moved in the late 1970s from an inward-looking strategy of import-substitution to a more export-oriented, open economy. The reforms were initially aimed at promoting exports in manufacturing, especially textiles and clothing, but have since been extended to other areas of the economy. Until 2001, and despite a long civil war, the country's GDP had never declined year on year. The main challenge facing the government is how to achieve economic growth while at the same time fighting a secessionist civil war that has been a drain on Sri Lanka's resources. In 1982, just before the conflict intensified, the government spent US $54m. (3.1% of the budget) on the security forces. In 1990 the amount was $364m. (12.5%) and in 2000 it rose to $1,018m. (17%), causing fiscal difficulties and detracting from investment in the private sector. However, it has been pointed out that, unlike other countries suffering from protracted conflict, there has been no destruction of the formal economy in Sri Lanka. In fact, during the 1990s, which was a period of intense conflict, average annual economic growth of 5% was recorded. One argument suggested is that the high security and state of emergency allowed the government to carry out World Bank-proposed structural reforms and liberalization plans without meeting the kind of political resistance that such reforms have sparked elsewhere. For example, in the early 1990s some of the largest national companies—including the national airline, gas and telecommunications companies and major tea plantations—were privatized.

Despite the shift towards privatization in the 1990s the government is still involved in a number of loss-making commercial activities. The main objective of privatization has been to raise revenues rather than to improve the economic efficiency of the enterprises and sectors involved. Thus, privatization largely took place in the manufacturing sector whilst state-owned enterprises, in electricity, petroleum and public transport in particular, continue to be highly indebted. The electricity sector went through a severe crisis in 2001 when there were prolonged power cuts which damaged the country's output and productivity. The Electricity Reforms Act passed in 2002 stipulated the separation of generation, transmission and distribution at the Ceylon Electricity Board, a state-owned monopoly, and called for greater private-sector participation. However, with 1m. public servants, the Sri Lankan government is, in per capita terms, one of the biggest in the world. The executive comprises 57 ministries, leading to overlapping jurisdictions, which hinders effective policy formulation and implementation.

Following the 2002 cease-fire the government launched an initiative—'Regaining Sri Lanka'—aimed at co-ordinating the reconstruction and development process. The strategy envisioned accelerating privatization, reform of the legal and regulatory system and increased efficiency of critical government functions. The assessment also took into account rehabilitation of the north and east, including the need for local administration. However, the **United People's Freedom Alliance (UPFA)** contested and won the April 2004 elections on the basis of a 'pro-poor' campaign, capitalizing on a sense of dissatisfaction with the impact of previous reforms. In government, the UPFA released an economic policy document, entitled 'Creating our Future, Building our Nation'. Highlighting the former UNP government's failure to improve poor and rural areas, the need to continue with reforms was affirmed but steps towards increasing government involvement were envisioned.

Private Sector: At independence Sri Lanka's economy was dominated by the production of primary commodities, tea, rubber and coconuts accounting for 90% of the country's exports. When the prices of these crops collapsed in the 1950s the need to reorient production became urgent. Under the Sri Lanka Freedom Party (SLFP) government a number of state-owned enterprises were initiated or existing enterprises nationalized to encourage domestic production. By the mid-1970s a shift towards liberalization and deregulation was under way and under United National Party (UNP) rule in 1977 the economy was opened up to foreign capital, technology and competition. The second wave of liberalization, initiated in 1989, included a privatization programme. Around 40 state-owned commercial enterprises were partially or fully privatized. Despite a change of government in 1994 to the traditionally more left-wing SLFP-led **People's Alliance**, and trade union discontent, the privatization programme was extended to utility and service sector enterprises.

Returning to power in 2001 the UNP promised an acceleration of the reform process and privatization in the remaining state-owned sectors of electricity, petroleum, water services, bus and railway operations and state banks. While the government still retains control over a great deal of infrastructure, it has moved towards privatization in key areas such as telecommunications, banking and insurance. The United People's Freedom Alliance coalition government elected in April 2004 has emphasized the need to focus on small and medium enterprises in manufacturing and cash crop sectors which contribute more than 50% of gross domestic product.

Public Sector: Sri Lanka's economy is burdened with a bloated public sector whose performance has deteriorated over time. Nearly 19% of the workforce is employed in government and quasi-governmental agencies. The privatization programme has helped to reduce semi-governmental employees and public sector rationalization features high on the government's reform agenda. The government suspended recruitment in the state sector from June 2002. Since 1977 there has been deregulation, privatization and an opening up of the Sri Lankan economy to international competition. State-owned companies have been sold, including a large number of plantation management companies. The state nevertheless continues to determine the price of basic goods, such as bread, flour, petroleum, bus and rail fares, telecom rates, water and electricity (though this is likely to change), and maintains control over infrastructure. Key state corporations, such as the Ceylon Electricity Board and the two state banks that previously dominated the financial system, are not to be privatized, but restructured with a more autonomous corporate structure under the supervision of the Strategic Enterprise Management Agency. In March 2002 Sri Lanka opened the services sector for 100% foreign investment, a step towards greater private sector participation and competition. Import controls on rice and other food items have also been removed. Recently Sri Lanka Telecom, a state-owned enterprise, was privatized and other sectors have been earmarked to follow.

Population: Sri Lanka's population was estimated at 19.4m. in 2003, with a net population growth of 1.3%. The first systematic and scientific population census was undertaken in 1871. The 13th census was conducted in 2001 after a time lag of 20 years and, although able to cover important towns in the north and east, such as **Jaffna** and Ampara, had to exclude major areas due to the security situation. Studies reveal that until the mid-1940s both the birth and the death rate were high, hence the natural population increase remained at moderate levels. Rapidly falling death rates and almost stable birth rates during the 1940s to early 1960s caused a high level of natural increase. A steady decline in the birth rate since has been largely responsible for the reduced gap between birth and death rates, lowering the natural increase of population. Declining fertility together with family planning has narrowed the pyramid base, whilst declining mortality levels have expanded the top. As a result, Sri Lanka is facing the prospect of an 'ageing' population. Sinhalese make up 74% of the population and are concentrated in the densely populated south west. Ceylon Tamils, whose South Indian ancestors have lived on the island for centuries, total about 12% and live predominantly in the north and east.

Family-Planning Policy: In 1965 the Sri Lankan government, by a cabinet decision, accepted family planning as a national policy, initiating the 'Small is Beautiful' programme that distributed condoms and gave incentives to people willing to undergo sterilization. The United Nations Population Fund holds Sri Lanka as a prime example of a successful family-planning campaign. From 1950 until 1990 the population growth of countries in the South Asian region averaged more than 2% growth annually, with Sri Lanka having the least rapid growth rate, 2.02%. Having achieved its demographic goal of a low growth rate, Sri Lanka faces the task of shifting the focus of the country's health system from family planning to a reproductive health approach. This includes coping with the threat of HIV/AIDS, the high rate of abortion, adolescent health, the challenge of an ageing population and the need to spread health services to peripheral parts of the country, particularly in the northern and eastern areas. With an estimated 63,000 people having been killed during the course of the long-running civil war, the implications for population growth rates in the north east are not fully known.

Migration: Given its size Sri Lanka has one of the biggest internal refugee populations in the world. An estimated 1m. people have been forcibly displaced as a result of two decades of conflict. The majority were Tamils forced to flee the war-torn north-east province, although substantial numbers of Sinhalese and Muslims have also been affected. An estimated 200,000 people fled overseas, while the large majority remain internally displaced on the island. When travel restrictions were lifted and military activities ended in early 2002, many of the displaced returned. By the end of 2003 more than 345,000 were reported by the international media to have returned, with more than half having moved to the Jaffna district. Major obstacles hinder their resettlement, including the lack of infrastructure, the unresolved restitution of property, security concerns, especially with regard to landmines, and the continued existence of high-security zones, areas declared by the government to be off-limit. In December 2001 the Sri Lankan government established the Ministry of Rehabilitation, Resettlement and Refugees and during 2002 launched a national framework for relief, rehabilitation and reconciliation.

Apart from war refugees Sri Lanka also has a very large number of labour migrants. In 2000 it was estimated that of about 858,000 migrant workers, more than one-half were women, the majority of whom were unskilled labour, mostly working as housemaids, with the Middle East as the most favoured destination. Remittances from abroad are important for the economy and have also had an impact on family structures by motivating more women to gain employment.

Urbanization: In the last three decades Sri Lanka's housing situation has improved in terms of the size and structural quality of buildings. Nevertheless in Colombo, with a population of 2.2m., more than 50% of the houses are still classified as 'under served' dwellings lacking access to adequate water, sanitation and waste disposal facilities. Population growth, internal migration and industrialization have all contributed to the growing pressure on land, both in terms of rural and urban settlements. Currently about 28% of Sri Lanka's population live in urban areas where the population is growing twice as fast as the rest of the population. Government agencies, such as the Urban Development Authority, have tried to tackle growing infrastructural problems through urban planning programmes. A recent example is the Sustainable Townships Programme, which aims to provide slum dwellers with free housing paid for by releasing the newly acquired land to the market. Another innovative idea has been to encourage private property developers' investment in housing for middle- and lower-income groups. The official definition of urban settlements extends only to those areas under the direct administration of the municipal and urban councils. As a result, rapidly changing villages, emerging towns and urban settlements near towns tend to be neglected.

Minority Groups/Communities: Due to historical settlement patterns, Sri Lanka's ethnic groups are concentrated in certain areas. The Indian Tamils are primarily in the highland, plantation areas where they constitute almost one-half of the population, whilst the Sri Lankan Tamils make up more than 95% of the population in the Jaffna peninsula and constitute substantial minorities in the north and east. While the Sinhalese can be separated into up-country Kandyan Sinhalese, who tend to look down on the low-country, coastal Sinhalese, the Tamils are divided into an older community of island Tamils and the Indian Tamils (brought in as plantation labour in the 19th century).

Muslims are not in the majority anywhere but make up large minorities in areas in the north-west and east coast districts. Although the Sinhalese are by far the majority, they feel threatened by the Tamil community for historical reasons and because of the geographical proximity to India's Tamils. The Sinhalese community is largely Buddhist. Tamils tend to be Hindu, although there are also many Christian Tamils, and most of the Muslims practice Sunni Islam. According to the most recent census, in 2001, Buddhists make up 69.1% of the population, Muslims 7.6%, Hindus 7.1% and Christians 6.2%, while the religion of the remaining 10% is unspecified. Other minority groups include Burghers, Eurasians, Malay and Veddha.

The Sinhala-Tamil confrontation is well known, but more recently the Muslim community has entered into the political fray, in particular since 1990 when the Liberation Tigers of Tamil Eelam launched a brutal campaign of ethnic cleansing against the Muslims in the north. In 1986 the Sri Lanka Muslim Congress (SLMC) was declared a national political party. In June 2001 their withdrawal from the People's Alliance created a crisis for the government and forced President **Kumaratunga** to invite the opposition leader to become Prime Minister. The SLMC has demanded that the Muslims be treated as a separate entity in peace talks with Tamil Tiger rebels.

Agriculture: Historically, the dominant sector of the Sri Lankan economy has been wet rice cultivation and the country has an ancient irrigation system of major and minor reservoirs. Under the British, agriculture was commercialized through the introduction of plantations. Today about 44% of cultivated land is used for three principal export crops: tea, rubber and coconuts. Irrigation in Sri Lanka has been a complicated task of modernizing existing traditional systems and balancing the interests of ethnic communities threatened by resettlement policies (*See* **Mahaweli Project**).

In recent times, agriculture has lost its relative economic importance. In 2002 agriculture accounted for 20.1% of GDP, compared with about 28% in the early 1980s. As a proportion of GDP, the contribution of Sri Lanka's agricultural sector is one of the lowest in South Asia. Rapid growth in industry and services is changing the structure of the economy as well as attracting rural labour, drawing people from the countryside to the cities. By 2002 the share of employment provided by agriculture was 33%, compared to 47% in 1990. At the same time, labour productivity has stagnated over the last decade. As a result the government is turning its attention to rural development as a means of promoting economic growth. About 80% of Sri Lanka's population lives in rural areas where poverty is a major concern and low-value, low-productivity activities, such as traditional paddy production, dominate. Obstacles to agricultural diversification include lack of credit, insufficient technical advice, continued government intervention in commodity and factor markets and the multiplicity of government agencies involved in agricultural policy-making at the centre.

Land Reform (Ownership): Under the 1935 Land Development Ordinance the government had the authority to distribute land under various schemes for cultivation and housing. Since Sri Lanka's independence various measures of land tenure have been passed, particularly in the paddy sector. Management of land has passed from public to private hands but the state maintains strong control, owning today approximately 80% of land in Sri Lanka. Two land reform acts, passed in 1972 and 1975, invested a total of some 400,000 ha of private and plantation lands with the state, some of which was distributed in smallholdings to the landless. Various restrictions on leasing, sales, inheritance, land use and transfer have resulted in ill-defined property rights, limited investment and have failed to create the necessary incentives to maximize production. The majority of the rural poor cultivate land to which they do not hold official title. Following a poverty reductions strategy proposal, submitted to the **International Monetary Fund** in 2002, the government has committed itself to transferring full ownership of land to farmers. This will improve farmers' access to credit by making land more attractive as collateral for banks. Land law reform is of particular concern because of its potential to cause mass rural to urban migration, as well as inter-ethnic conflict, especially in the Eastern Province.

Food and Famine Prevention: Despite government efforts to increase domestic rice production and attain self-sufficiency Sri Lanka is classified as a food-deficit country. Irrigation remains largely dependent on rainfall to replenish tanks and reservoirs. Consecutive droughts cause significant reductions in paddy production. The intermittent civil war has been a major cause of food insecurity, with the Northern and Eastern provinces suffering the most. A recent World Food Programme survey found that at least a quarter of children entering school in the north east suffered from acute malnutrition. Food has been used as an instrument of leverage if not openly as a weapon of war. During the civil war the central government sealed off the northern jungles to prevent food and medicine supplies falling into rebel hands, in the process victimizing civilians and particularly children. Despite the fragile peace this part of the island continues to suffer from severe food deprivation. In the mid-1990s rice imports were liberalized and prices of paddy largely determined on the open market. The government, no longer involved in paddy marketing or storage, encourages the private sector to import rice to meet national shortfalls in production.

Industry: At independence Sri Lanka had little industrial infrastructure, the colonial economy having been focused on agriculture and plantations. In 1948 tea, rubber and coconuts provided the bulk of export earnings. Heavy industries in manufacturing, mining and oil refining were established in the late 1960s, mostly in the state sector. In 1978, following economic reforms, the advent of export processing zones and the initiation of privatization, manufacturing received a vital boost and became the driving force of Sri Lanka's economic growth in the 1990s. In 2002 manufacturing accounted for 16% of GDP. Garments and textiles were the leading sector, contributing 77% of total visible export earnings during 2001/02. Total output of factory industries grew by 4.6% in 2003, compared with 2.8% in 2002. In 2005 the Multi-Fibre Agreement, which for the previous 25 years had established quotas in the textile and clothing industry limiting exports to countries whose domestic industries were still developing, expired. The sector now faces intense global competition, spurring the government to search for ways to diversify the industrial base towards higher-value, skill-intensive areas. This has included efforts to deregulate the industry and to improve the business environment through, for example, the exchange control legislation announced in the 2003 budget.

Foreign Trade (Import/Export): *Exports*: US $5,306,000m. f.o.b. *Export commodities*: textiles and apparel; tea and spices; diamonds, emeralds, rubies; coconut products; rubber manufactures; fish. *Major markets*: USA (32.4%), United Kingdom (13.5%), India (6.8%), Germany (4.8%). *Imports*: $7,265,000m. f.o.b. *Import commodities*: textile fabrics; mineral products; petroleum; foodstuffs; machinery and transportation equipment. *Major suppliers*: India (18%), Singapore (8.7%),

Hong Kong (7.7%), China (5.7%), Iran (5.2%), Japan (5.1%), Malaysia (4.1%) (all figures 2004 estimates).

Following independence Sri Lanka's tree crop exports suffered from a deterioration in terms of trade. After the 1977 economic reforms the economy shifted towards manufacturing and international trade was seen as an important component of economic growth. Unilateral tariff reductions and reduced non-tariff barriers made Sri Lanka one of the most open economies in South Asia. In the last decade Sri Lanka has concluded a number of bilateral economic agreements, gradually shifting its market orientation from the United Kingdom to the Middle East and North America. Also, in recent years Sri Lanka has been expanding its trade links within South Asia, concluding free-trade agreements with both India and Pakistan in 2002. Trade policy continues to be formulated and implemented mainly by the Ministry of Commerce and Consumer Affairs. An original member of the World Trade Organization, Sri Lanka, together with other developing countries, has been seeking greater market access for non-agricultural goods in the developed world.

Export Processing Zones (EPZ): Sri Lanka opened its first Export Processing Zones (EPZs) in 1978 as part of the country's strategy of investment promotion, under the Greater Colombo Economic Commission (renamed Board of Investment—BOI—in 1991). The newly elected United National Party (UNP) government of 1977 established a garment factory in every parliamentary constituency with concessions to foreign investors and collaborators. Today, any export enterprise can apply to be under the business-friendly BOI regulations, even if it is located outside the demarcated zones. Ninety per cent of all EPZ workers are women, which has prompted concerns over the status and treatment of female labourers especially in the EPZs where trade union activity is curbed. EPZs continue to contribute a significant share of Sri Lanka's industrial export earnings. In 2000 this was reported at 30.5%, with EPZs employing 110,000 workers, or 10% of the national workforce. Over time investment has shifted from being purely concentrated in garment manufacturing to electronics and electrical goods.

Banking System: Commercial banking today accounts for 64% of the total assets in the Sri Lankan financial system. Post-independence, the banks were marshalled to promote and foster economic development through practices such as interest rate control and priority sector lending. The Banking Act of 1995 provides the legal framework for the banking industry and gave the Central Bank of Sri Lanka, the country's sole bank of issue, wide supervisory powers. The bank has had an increasingly important role in developing credit facilities for special groups, such as peasant farmers, small businesses and the self-employed. In 2001 there were 11 domestic commercial banks operating. At the end of 2002 foreign banks had a total of 35 bank offices and domestic banks had extended their networks to 1,128 offices. Two state-owned banks dominate: the **Bank of Ceylon** and the People's Bank which together account for more than 60% of total bank deposits. Over the past two decades private banks have been increasingly involved in the financial system.

Private finance companies that fund consumer durables and transportation equipment have a significant presence in the market. Innovative steps by the government have included the establishment of offshore banking facilities, merchant banking, leasing companies and venture capital suppliers.

Foreign Direct Investment (FDI): During 2002 total inflows of FDI were recorded at about US $246m. Although a sharp increase from 2001, this is far below levels reached by comparable countries and the government is currently focusing on measures to attract FDI, including reforms of the tax and regulatory framework and promoting Sri Lanka's comparative advantages abroad. Since 1977 government policy has aimed at improving investment conditions. In 1978 the Greater Colombo Economic Commission was set up, reconstituted in 1992 as the Board of Investment (BOI), to oversee the export processing zones (EPZs). Created to attract export-oriented foreign firms, there are currently eight in operation which contribute significantly to Sri Lanka's export earnings. In 1990 a new investment policy abolished various restrictions in the ownership structures of joint-venture projects outside the EPZs which, combined with the privatization programme, created opportunities for FDI to expand beyond manufacturing into sectors such as telecommunications. In 1997–2000 Singapore was, cumulatively, the largest investor, followed by the United Kingdom. After the success of the Indo-Lanka Free Trade Agreement, India became Sri Lanka's largest investor in 2002. A prime attraction for India has been the ability to re-export to India whilst taking advantage of the lower tariffs on raw materials in Sri Lanka.

Foreign Aid: Foreign Aid has been essential in preventing acute foreign exchange shortages in Sri Lanka. Between 1978 and 1986 it accounted for around 9% of GDP and took the form of grants or concessionary loans. The World Bank and most aid donors strongly supported liberalization of the economy during the decade after 1977, at times linking aid to the government's commitment to free-market policies. More recently international aid has focused on the challenges of post-conflict reconstruction and has been contingent upon the state of the peace process. In 2002 US $74m. was received as grants and the government borrowed a further $408m. Japan has been the single largest donor to Sri Lanka over the past two decades and since 2002 has also been engaged in peace negotiations. In June 2003 a donor conference in Tokyo pledged $4,000m. aimed at rebuilding the tea and rubber industries, reviving the rural economy and repairing infrastructure. A key problem has been underutilization of donor funds due to a lack of counterpart funds, limited capacity for implementing projects, the ongoing civil war and local political struggles. In a bid to improve management the World Bank was invited to administer Sri Lanka's international funds for reconstruction.

Labour: More than 20% of the 6.1m.-strong labour force of Sri Lanka, excluding the north and east, is unionized. Trade union membership, however, is on the decline. The Ceylon Workers Congress (CWC) and the Lanka Jathika Estate Workers Union are the two largest unions representing workers in the heavily unionized plantation sector. Many unions have political affiliations. For example, the CWC's agenda includes political issues, such as citizenship status for stateless Indian Tamils.

The unemployment rate has declined over the years and fluctuates around 10%. The rate of unemployment among high school and college graduates, however, remains proportionally higher than the rate for less-educated workers. Labour law reforms are under way and the government has been working on ways to facilitate dispute resolution as well as to reform the social security schemes. Much of Sri Lanka's labour law is contained in a worker's charter enacted in 1995. Sri Lanka does not have a national minimum wage, but the law provides for and enforces the decisions of wage boards for the specific sectors and industries.

It is interesting to note that women comprise the majority of Sri Lanka's workforce in the two key foreign exchange-earning sectors of the economy, the garment industry and overseas remittances.

Informal Economy: According to a 2004 World Bank study, Sri Lanka has one of the largest informal economies in Asia, measuring 44.6% of official gross national income (GNI). The average size of the informal economy in Asia was 35.7% of official GNI. Home-based production of garments for sale is a popular occupation of women in Sri Lanka's informal sector, usually involving cut piece sewing. These home-based workers are either self-employed or subcontracted. Spared the hardships of factory routine and excessive labour control, the subcontracted worker is, however, at the mercy of intermediaries and without union protection. The growing 'informalization'of the economy, however, has caused a rise in the number of women who work. Such self-employed women are increasingly seen as micro-entrepreneurs, engaged in economic activity, whose working conditions and prospects can be improved through micro-financing. Most farming in Sri Lanka also falls under the informal economy, except for the estates and large holdings, which employ wage labour. In addition, rural credit depends on an informal network of intermediaries and money-lenders. The government, together with international organizations, has made efforts to build a rural financial system.

Child Labour: A pressing and much publicized problem in Sri Lanka has been and continues to be the use of child soldiers by the Liberation Tigers of Tamil Eelam (LTTE) in the civil conflict. But other children, not directly involved in the conflict, have also been affected by the war in multiple ways. Due to hardship and lack of options, child labour is on the rise, especially in households headed by women. Child labour in Sri Lanka primarily takes the form of agricultural work. To combat this, the government made education and attendance at school compulsory for every child aged between 5 and 14 years. Whilst this has brought literacy levels up, it has not prevented a high drop-out rate from school. Since 1994 the government has devoted increasing attention to the protection of children, raising the minimum age for employment from 12 to 14 years, setting up a National Child Protection Authority (NCPA) in 1999 and working with international organizations to prevent the trafficking of children as well as to campaign for the demobilization of child soldiers and their reintegration into society. The NCPA operates in four main areas: protection, advocacy, rehabilitation and legal reform.

Environmental Protection: High population density and efforts to improve living standards have put tremendous pressure on Sri Lanka's natural environment. Five key environmental issues have been recognized by the government, including land degradation, inadequate disposal of solid and liquid waste in urban areas, pollution of inland waters, loss of biodiversity and degradation of coastal resources. Increasing pressure of population has led to a rapid decline in the land:man ratio as well as extensive deforestation caused by land clearing for agriculture, cropping by the landless poor, illegal logging and commercial timber extraction. Flooding and soil erosion have further worsened land conditions for the rural poor. In 2001 a new Ministry of Environment and Natural Resources began work on conservation legislation as well as methods to improve the regulatory and institutional framework for natural resource management. Increasingly, attention is being given to land use planning as a way of reducing the pressure on land. In addition to conservation efforts aimed at preserving the natural forests and preventing soil degradation, this will also require reform of the land ownership system to tackle the problem of landlessness. The Asian tsunami of December 2004 damaged a vast area of coastline stretching from Jaffna in the north down the entire eastern and southern coast and up the west coast to north of Colombo.

Floods and Natural Disasters: Drought is the most significant natural hazard in Sri Lanka. In addition, unpredictably, flash floods, landslides and cyclones affect the island. The worst ever natural disaster in Sri Lanka's history was the December 2004 tsunami which left at least 31,000 dead and between 800,000–1m. homeless and damaged 75% of the country's coastline. Inevitably the most vulnerable were the poor living in makeshift housing, and particularly the elderly and children. International organizations, national governments, UN agencies as well as private individuals donated money and help to the Sri Lankan government. The government and the Liberation Tigers of Tamil Eelam vied for control over distribution of aid in the north-eastern areas, delaying the relief and rehabilitation work by their politics.

Health System/Policy: Education and health have been the cornerstones of the Sri Lankan government's strategy for socio-economic development. Health policy has been adapted to challenges, initially tackling life expectancy (in 2003 life expectancy at birth was 71 for the total population, compared to a regional average of only 61 years), maternal and infant mortality and malaria control, and then extending to new concerns, such as the increasing prevalence of non-communicable diseases, HIV/AIDS, drug abuse, the high incidence of suicide, particularly among youth, as well as the emerging problems of an ageing population. In 1989 a major organizational change took place, with the devolution of certain powers and functions from the centre to provincial councils. In the health sector the management of all health care institutions (other than teaching hospitals and special hospitals) and public health services became the responsibility of provincial councils and the respective provincial health ministry. Financial resources for health care stem mainly from the government, which meets the health care needs of the vast majority of the population. The private sector's contribution has been comparatively small in terms of service provision and financing, but has been growing, mainly in urban areas. In 2002 total expenditure on health by the government represented 3.7% of gross domestic product.

Education/Policy: Sri Lanka's human development figures have been amongst the most impressive in South Asia, including high adult literacy (92% in 2001), near-universal school enrolment and gender parity in school-going children. Three institutions shape education policy: the Ministry of Education, the National Education Commission and the National Institute of Education. In 1997 the government made school attendance compulsory for children aged 5–14 years. To attract poor children the government offered free school textbooks and uniforms. Schools were nationalized in 1968 with the objective of abolishing disparities in quality and academic achievement. Over the past 40 years the public schooling system has perhaps kept differences at a minimum but at the expense of overall quality. Faced with fiscal constraints as a result of the rising costs of civil conflict, the government has been forced to turn towards greater public-private partnerships. Especially in secondary and tertiary education, it is hoped that diminished state involvement will allow the system to be more responsive to market requirements, thus reducing the high level of graduate unemployment. Modernization of the education system is currently regarded as one of the main pillars of economic and social development and as a key to reducing inter-community and regional disparities.

Social Security: A number of social security schemes are in operation in Sri Lanka, including pension schemes, provident fund schemes and state-run social assistance schemes. A looming challenge, however, is the support system for an ageing population. Sri Lanka expects its population aged 60 years and over to double in less than 20 years. Life expectancy, currently 73 years for men and 76 for women, is close to that of OECD countries. Combined with a still low female participation rate in the labour force, the dependency ratio for future generations in Sri Lanka threatens to rise considerably. Current formal and informal arrangements of income support for the elderly are unsuited to tackling pensioner poverty. Pension schemes are all state-run, operate with low returns on savings and currently cover just over one-quarter of the working-age population. Deregulation of the sector is under consideration to allow greater opportunity for private-sector providers.

Poverty: Despite having one of South Asia's highest per capita rates of gross domestic product, without the burden of a huge, fast-growing population, Sri Lanka's poverty-reduction efforts have been disappointing. Currently it is estimated that between one-fifth and one-third of the population live below the poverty line. Rural poor account for about 90% of the poor in Sri Lanka. One positive sign has been the apparent decline in urban poverty, although regional and sectoral disparities have widened. Development has been concentrated in the Western Province (Colombo and surroundings), with conflict areas in the north and east being the worst affected. According to reports, up to 70% of the population in these areas live below the poverty line. Amongst the government's poverty alleviation schemes there have been food subsidies, income-transfer initiatives and rural development programmes, as well as the recent attention given to governance issues, social mobilization and community empowerment. Launched in 2002, 'Regaining Sri Lanka' is a poverty-reduction strategy that emphasizes the importance of peace, growth and equitable development. It is argued that annual economic growth of 5% is simply not enough to realize a breakthrough in poverty reduction. Others have emphasized the need for factor market liberalization where structural impediments constrain agricultural growth.

Welfare: Sri Lanka has a long history of social assistance programmes, which in part account for its impressive human development indicators. The effectiveness of social welfare has, however, been questioned and criticisms made that spending on social welfare comes at the expense of other sectors, such as education or physical infrastructure. Universal food subsidies were used in the past but since the 1977 economic reforms the government has preferred to implement targeted income transfers. The largest welfare programme in operation currently is *samurdhi*. Launched in 1995, the programme has three components: a welfare grant to purchase essential household commodities; savings, credit, insurance and social security schemes that improve access to finance and a community infrastructure development initiative. *Samurdhi* claims about one-half of the total welfare budget (excluding education and health), or almost 1% of GDP, and is a growing strain on the country's budget. There has also been criticism that the distribution of *samurdhi* welfare is not need-based but is instead used as an instrument to satisfy the supporters of the leading political party. A welfare benefit law is under consideration to spell out entry and exit criteria for all welfare schemes, and to protect them from becoming politicized. In addition, the government has begun to encourage the development of social security schemes on a commercial and competitive basis.

Gender Relations: The economic and social status of Sri Lankan women is relatively better than in other South Asian countries, with adult female literacy at 88.6% in 1999. Nevertheless, achieving gender equality and empowerment is an ongoing process. Two decades of armed conflict have resulted in a disproportionate number of widows, especially in the north and east. It has been estimated that there are 30,000 war widows. Women have thus been thrown into positions of heads of households, responsible for their families' upkeep. The problem is compounded by the fact that women tend to be concentrated in low-paying, semi-skilled and labour-intensive work, such as the tea and garment sectors, and are subject to long hours, job insecurity and subordinate positions with few promotion opportunities. Legislation and systematic data collection remain in need of a gender perspective. Unemployment rates for women, while falling faster than those for men, remain higher. Marriage law in Sri Lanka has been revised to enforce a minimum marriage age of 18, but Muslim personal law co-exists and has no such minimum age.

Although women have led the government and held positions on Supreme Court benches, their representation in politics and public life remains very low.

Sri Lanka Freedom Party (SLFP)

Founded in 1951 by S. W. R. D. **Bandaranaike**, the Sri Lanka Freedom Party (SLFP) promoted a **Sinhala Only Policy**. In 1960 the party came to power in coalition with Marxist parties. Since then the SLFP has been in and out of power and in 2004 formed the government with President **Kumaratunga** as part of the **United People's Freedom Alliance**.

Sri Lanka Muslim Congress (SLMC)

A prominent Muslim party in Sri Lankan politics, the Sri Lanka Muslim Congress (SLMC) was founded in 1981 by H. M. Ashraff, who later also founded the **National Unity Alliance** that was to become a rival Muslim party. In 2001 the SLMC, a constituent party in the **People's Alliance (PA)** coalition government, prompted a crisis when its members resigned from all government positions, ending the PA's majority in parliament and crossing over to the opposition **United National Party**. The SLMC holds five seats in the national legislature.

State Bank of India (SBI)

The flagship of Indian banking in terms of profits, assets, deposits, branches and employees. With more than 9,000 branches across the nation and an international network with several branches in 34 other countries, the State Bank of India is the country's largest commercial bank. The bank has its corporate office in **Mumbai**.

State Bank of Pakistan

The State Bank of Pakistan, located in Karachi, was created in 1948 and is Pakistan's central bank. The main functions of the bank include regulation of the financial system, to act as the lender of last resort, and to conduct monetary policy. It is responsible for the management of public debt and foreign exchange and advising the government on financial policy.

Stranded Pakistanis (Biharis)

Stranded Pakistanis in Bangladesh are referred to as Biharis, Urdu-speaking, non-Bengali Muslims who originally migrated from various parts of India, mostly from the state of **Bihar** to Bangladesh (then East Pakistan) during the **Partition** of British India in 1947. Some of them sided with West Pakistan during the **Bangladesh Liberation War** in 1971 and found themselves abandoned and unwelcome after the surrender of the Pakistani army. However, most of them rejected Bangladeshi citizenship but are too poor to move too Pakistan and remained stranded. There are approximately 250,000–300,000 stateless Biharis living in 66 camps in 13 regions across Bangladesh, awaiting repatriation to Pakistan. However, Pakistan has been reluctant to allow them to return due to the costs of resettlement and the threat of creating internal tensions.

Swadeshi

Meaning 'of one's own country, made from its own resources', *swadeshi* is a term that was used to refer to the consumption of only home-made goods. Against this background, *swadeshi* originated as a call to boycott British goods in favour of Indian products, and to encourage self-sufficiency, particularly in cottage-industry items such as hand-loomed cloth. The term was popularized by *Mahatma* **Gandhi** during the freedom struggle.

Swanirvar

A term used in Bangladesh to refer to a concept of local development focused on the self-reliance of villages, with the help of village councils (*gram sarkar*). It is also used in relation to demands for independence from foreign assistance.

Swaraj

The term *Swaraj* is derived from the Hindi language and used widely across South Asia. Literally it means self-rule or self-determination and at the political level refers to a concept developed during the struggle for independence by Mohandas Karamchand **Gandhi** in 1909 and expressed in his well-known pamphlet *Hind Swaraj*. Today the term is applied in different contexts. It is sporadically used in the political rhetoric of sub-national movements in South Asia to formulate claims for a separate homeland or more autonomy for a particular region or ethnic minority; and has been used to support the economic policy of protectionism aimed at creating a self-sufficient Indian market.

T

Taher, Col Abu

Abu Taher was one of 11 sector commanders of the Bangladesh Liberation Force in the 1971 war. He proposed the formation of a people's army, but government and military officers rejected it. Entering politics in 1972, he was elected as vice-president of **Jatiya Samajtantrik Dal (JSD)**, a left-wing off-shoot of the **Bangladesh Awami League**. During coups and counter-coups of 1975 Taher led the 'soldier-people' uprising (coup) on 7 November. In the aftermath Taher was arrested and executed in 1976.

Taluka

The term *taluka* (also *taluk* or *talook*) is used in India to denote an administrative division below a district consisting of an average of 80–100 contiguous villages. In the northern states these areas, which are usually revenue districts, are called *tahsil* or *tehsil.*

Tamil Eelam Liberation Organization (TELO)

Formally founded in 1976, the Tamil Eelam Liberation Organization (TELO) was a dominant Tamil resistance organization until eclipsed by the **Liberation Tigers of Tamil Eelam** in the late 1980s. Today it is one of the groups within the **Tamil National Alliance**. In the 2001 parliamentary elections the TELO won four seats in the north east.

Tamil Language

Tamil is spoken by all Tamils in Sri Lanka, in the north east, central and southern parts of the country, as well as by the Muslims living in the north east. The struggle to gain official recognition for Tamil became a central concern after the government's decision in 1956 to recognize only Sinhala as the national language. Although legislation providing for 'reasonable use of Tamil' was passed in August 1958, the regulations for its implementation were not created until 1966. The status of Tamil changed under the 1978 Constitution and following the **Indo-Lanka**

Accord, in the 13th constitutional amendment of 1987, Tamil was made an official language alongside Sinhala. Despite the efforts of the Official Language Commission, government language policies have often not been implemented and many state institutions still issue official documents in Sinhala or Sinhala and English.

Tamil Nadu

Located at the southern tip of India, the state of Madras (formed in 1956) was renamed Tamil Nadu in 1968. Tamil is the official language in the state and Chennai, formerly Madras, is the state's capital. The state assembly has 234 seats. Tamil Nadu returns 39 members to the **Lok Sabha**. Tamil Nadu is the second most industrialized state of India, with the highest level of urbanization and one of the best systems of infrastructure in place. Textiles are a major industry and the city of Chennai hosts a number of manufacturing multinationals. At the same time, agriculture is a traditional and important source of employment. The **Dravidian** movement began in Tamil Nadu, under the leadership of 'Periyar', as an intellectual and social movement that aimed to uplift the socially repressed classes and challenge the ideology behind the **caste system**. To mobilize support, the movement emphasized its Dravidian identity (**Tamil language** and culture as opposed to the Indo-Aryan sources of North Indian culture), eventually spawning the **Dravida Munnetra Kazhagam (DMK)** in 1949. Under the DMK, Tamil nationalism was brought to the fore, especially over the issue of Hindi as a national language in the 1960s. The **All-India Anna Dravida Munnetra Kazhagam (AIADMK)**, formed in 1972, has been the main competitor to the DMK, although both parties essentially claim to represent Tamil interests. Larger-than-life figures have often dominated Tamil Nadu's politics, e.g. Marudur Gopalamenon Ramachandran (or MGR) and AIADMK leader, Jayalalitha. Inceasingly members of parliament from Tamil Nadu have played an important role in the formation and functioning of coalition governments at the centre. In the 2004 general elections the DMK-led **Democratic Progressive Alliance (DPA)** captured all 39 Lok Sabha seats.

Tamil National Alliance (TNA)

Known as Illankai Tamil Arasu Kachchi, or Sri Lanka Tamil Government Party, the Tamil National Alliance (TNA) is a Tamil separatist alliance. Composed of the **All-Ceylon Tamil Congress (ACTC)**, the **Eelam People's Revolutionary Liberation Front (EPRLF)**, the **Tamil Eelam Liberation Organization (TELO)** and the **Tamil United Liberation Front (TULF)**, it was formed in 2001 just before the general elections. Political goals range from ensuring equal rights for the Tamil minority to the creation of an autonomous Tamil homeland in the north east. In the 2004 elections the TNA secured 22 seats in parliament.

Tamil United Liberation Front (TULF)

In the mid-1970s the Tamil United Liberation Front (TULF) was formed as part of an attempt to unite Tamil forces in Sri Lanka. At the time the TULF was under the growing influence of a disenchanted Tamil youth population. Absorbing among others the **Federal Party (FP)**, which had lobbied for a federal system, the TULF extended its demands to include the creation of an independent state for the Tamils. The subsequent emergence of the **Liberation Tigers of Tamil Eelam (LTTE)** in 1976 and the outbreak of civil war in the early 1980s undermined efforts to form a united Tamil front. Unlike the LTTE, the TULF has persistently pursued the path of electoral politics, and in 1977 emerged as the main parliamentary opposition party. The LTTE has generally viewed the TULF as being too moderate and in 1989 even assassinated its secretary-general, A. Amirthalingam, in Colombo. For the 2001 parliamentary elections four Tamil parties, including the TULF, joined together to form the **Tamil National Alliance (TNA)**. Disagreement, however, emerged over whether the LTTE was the sole representative of the Tamils. TULF contested the 2004 parliamentary elections as part of the TNA, this time alongside the LTTE-backed Illankai Tamil Arasu Kachchi (the Federal Party). The TNA, which won 22 seats in the five north-eastern electoral districts, is an emerging political force.

Tarai (Terai) Region

A once densely populated area of southern Nepal bordering with India, Tarai is traditionally seen as a marginal frontier area. The Tarai region, despite being the national granary, continues to be regarded as the periphery that sustains the core, mid-hill areas. Local communities of the Tarai, among them the **Madhesis** of Indian origin, have also been traditionally sidelined. However, this has been partly offset by the fact that a large number of the 205 parliamentary constituencies are now located in the Nepal Tarai, although a large number continue to be nominated by the **Bahun**-dominated central party élite in Kathmandu.

Tashkent Agreement

Accord signed in Tashkent, USSR, on 10 January 1966 by India's Prime Minister, Lal Bahadur Shastri (who died the next day), and Pakistan's President, Ayub **Khan**, ending the 17-day war between Pakistan and India in August–September 1965. A cease-fire secured by the United Nations Security Council on 22 September 1965 and third-party mediation offered by the Soviet Union led to an understanding between the warring parties to withdraw to pre-conflict positions, not to interfere in internal affairs and to work towards restoring economic and diplomatic relations.

Tata Group

Today comprising 93 operating companies in seven business sectors, including information systems and communications, engineering, materials, services, energy, consumer products and chemicals, the Tata Group was founded by Jamsetji Tata in the mid-19th century. It is now one of India's largest and most respected business conglomerates with revenues in 2004–05 of US $17,800m. The group has operations in more than 40 countries, employing some 220,000 people. Major Tata companies include Tata Steel, Tata Motors, Tata Power, Tata Tea and Indian Hotels. Tata Sons is the premier promoter company. Ratan N. Tata is the present chairman, having taken over from the legendary J. R. D. Tata in 1991.

Tawang

Tawang is one of the unresolved border issues between India and China. The district of Tawang covers about 2,085 sq km and is located in the north west of the Indian state of Arunachal Pradesh (*see* **North East India**). To the north it borders Tibet and to the south west it lies next to Bhutan. For administrative purposes it is sub-divided into Lumla, Jang and Tawang. The district headquarters are located at Tawang.

Telangana Rashtriya Samithi (TRS)

The Telangana Rashtriya Samithi (TRS) is a regional political party in India based in the state of **Andhra Pradesh**. The party is led by union cabinet minister K. Chandrasekhar Rao and participated in elections for the first time in 2004. The party won five seats in the 14th **Lok Sabha** elections, with the issue of demanding a separate state of the Telangana region in Andhra Pradesh. It is an ally of the **Indian National Congress (INC)** and part of the ruling **United Progressive Alliance (UPA)**.

Telugu Desam Party (TDP)

The Telugu Desam Party (TDP—Party for Telugu Nation or Land) is a regional political party in **Andhra Pradesh**, India, with its headquarters in Hyderabad. It was founded by N. T. Rama Rao (known as N. T. R., a former popular Telugu film star) on 29 March 1982, drawing its support from the local, dominant Kamma community. The ideology of the party was originally founded on identity politics, cultural pride, Telugu culture, Telugu people and Telugu land. Under the leadership of Chandrababu Naidu, it embraced economic growth and modernization as its main policy, which cost it the support of small and marginal peasants. The TDP ruled the state of Andhra Pradesh from 1983 until 1989 and returned to power in November 1994. During the 1990s the Telugu Desam became a major player in the **Lok Sabha** and a tactical supporter of the **National Democratic Alliance (NDA)**. TDP became the major opposition party in Andhra Pradesh after losing the 2004 assembly elections to the **Congress** party.

Thapa, Surya Bahadur

Once a close collaborator of King **Mahendra**, under whom he served as premier from 1966 until 1969 during the ***Panchayat* system**, Thapa, a veteran politician and pro-monarchist, was appointed by King **Gyanendra** as Prime Minister of Nepal on 4 June 2003 to replace Lokendra Bahadur **Chand**. This was the fifth time in his political career that he had assumed the office of Prime Minister. Thapa resigned on 7 May 2004 amidst mounting pressure from major political parties, including his own, the **Rashtriya Prajatantra Party (RPP)**, demanding restoration of fully-fledged democracy.

Thimpu

Thimpu, located in the north west of Bhutan, is the largest urban settlement and capital of the country, with an estimated population of 50,000–65,000. It is not only the centre of the royal government, but also the country's religious and economic headquarters. Established in 1952 to replace the ancient capital of Punakha, Thimpu's economy is characterized by a dominating bureaucratic sector, strong industrial production (39% of the country's total industrial activities) and various transport activities. The geographical terrain of Thimpu, enclosed as it is in an extremely narrow valley, makes large-scale expansion impossible. The major challenge, as in other Bhutanese urban centres, is how to cope with the pressures of a rapidly growing population and rural-urban migration. (*See* **Phuntsholing**.)

Thram

A term used in Bhutan to refer to a land deed number and certificate issued by the Land Record as proof of ownership of registered land. In this context, Thram is a form of cadastre and comprises information on family and property as well as documents, which are organized and collected on a family, block and district basis. Since the early 1980s the Thram has become an immensely politicized issue as the government has made it mandatory for all people in Bhutan to register and to obtain identity cards on the basis of house number and Thram number, issued by the government. (*See* **Nepalese Issue/Conflict**).

Thrimkhang Gongma

The term Thrimkang Gongma refers to the High Court in Bhutan. located in the capital, **Thimpu**. It was introduced to the political system by the King in 1968 in order to separate the judiciary from the executive and the legislature. The court comprises seven judges, all of whom are appointed by the King, who also has the right to dismiss them. The chief justice is the *primus inter pares*, i.e. the most senior. Although the Thrimkong Gongma is considered the highest court in the country, the

King reserves the powers of the highest court of appeal and has both appellate and original jurisdiction. Critics object that there are no lawyers or juries and that the judge acts as investigator.

Thrimshung Chenmo

The term *Thrimshung Chenmo* refers to the legal code of jurisdiction in Bhutan, first laid down by Shabdrung *Ngawang Namgyal*. Since its enactment by the National Assembly in 1957, the *Thrimshung Chenmo* has been commonly perceived and described as a 'general law of the country'. Today Bhutan's legal base is in the process of being modernized through measures such as the Civil and Criminal Procedure Code (2001) and the Bhutan Penal Code (2004). The *kasho* and *kadyon* play a significant role in Bhutan's judiciary, executive and legislature.

Trade and Transit Dispute

Nepal-India relations deteriorated dramatically in 1989 when India refused to renew trade and transit agreements in retaliation for a major arms deal between Nepal and China. Annual economic growth in Nepal, which had averaged 4% in the 1980s, declined to 1.5% in 1989/90 as India imposed a virtual economic blockade. The arms deal was regarded in India as a threat to its own security environment as well as directly contravening the established structure of friendly India-Nepal relations. Economic discontent as a result of the embargo, combined with mounting political instability during the **Jana Andolan** movement, pressured Nepal's King to reach an agreement with India. In June 1990 a joint Kathmandu-New Delhi communiqué granted commercial privileges to India, reopened transit routes for Nepal's exports to India and restored co-operation on security matters.

Tribes – *see* Scheduled Tribes (STs)

Tribhuvan, King

On 18 February Nepal celebrates **Democracy Day**, commemorating the return in 1951 of King Tribhuvan from exile in India which signified the end of Rana rule. Under King Tribhuvan assembly elections were continuously postponed and a succession of short-lived governments, partly due to the King's interference, prevented the emergence of a constitution during his lifetime. Following Tribhuvan's death in 1955, his son **Mahendra** succeeded him.

Tsa-Wa-Sum

In Bhutan the term *Tsa-Wa-Sum* literally means the King, Country and the Government and refers to the law codex of **Thrimshung Chenmo** that declares any act against one of the three elements as, possibly, an anti-national offence punishable by life imprisonment or death. In March 1990 the National Assembly (*Tshogdu Chenmo*) confirmed and approved the death sentence for offences against *Tsa-Wa-Sum*. The law has been criticized for imposing limitations on freedom of opinion, while the royal government emphasizes the law's importance for national security and the integrity of the country.

U

Union Territory

In addition to India's 28 states, there are six Union Territories (as of 2004). **Delhi** was a Union Territory until 1991, when it was made into a national capital territory with a special status. Union Territories are administered by the central government through an appointed Lt-Governor or Chief Commissioner, on the President's recommendation in consultation with the Prime Minister. The territories have councils of ministers and legislative assemblies but although they can make laws in state matters, as enumerated in the seventh schedule of the Constitution, the **Lok Sabha** may overrule their decisions.

United Left Front (ULF)

The United Left Front (ULF) coalition, comprising seven communist factions, was formed in late 1989 as part of Nepal's pro-democracy movement. It joined forces with the **Nepali Congress (NC)** to launch strikes and demonstrations, the **Jana Andolan** movement, in Nepal's major cities. The interim government (April 1990–May 1991) comprised four representatives of the NC, three from the ULF and two nominees of the King. By December 1990 the ULF had split in anticipation of the 1991 elections.

United Liberation Front of Assam (ULFA)

Established in 1979, the United Liberation Front of Assam (ULFA) projected itself as leading a national liberation struggle against occupation by India. ULFA's methods have included kidnappings, targeted assassinations, ambushes on security forces as well as attacks on the local population. In 1990 the government of India banned the ULFA, classifying it as a terrorist organization, and launched military operation 'Bajrang' against it. (*See* **North East India**.)

United National Liberation Front (UNLF)

The United National Liberation Front (UNLF), founded on 24 November 1964, is the oldest insurgent group in the north-eastern Indian state of Manipur. Its objective was to achieve an independent and socialist state. In 1990 the UNLF launched an armed struggle to 'liberate' Manipur, establishing its own armed wing, the Manipur People's Army. The UNLF reportedly has reported contacts with Bangladesh, China and Myanmar, and has collaborated with the many other insurgency movements in **North East India**.

United National Party (UNP)

Formed in 1946 by D. S. **Senanayake**, Sri Lanka's United National Party (UNP) played a key role in the transition to independence. Although appearing to be, like the **Indian National Congress**, an umbrella party, the UNP represented a small group of notables from the island's English-speaking élite. Furthermore, while seeking political support from the Sri Lankan Tamils in the north and north east, the UNP took a less accommodating stance towards the large population of Indian Tamils. From the 1950s onwards the UNP's development must be seen alongside the **Sri Lanka Freedom Party (SLFP)**. Created in 1951, when S. W. R. D. **Bandaranaike**'s left-of-centre bloc seceded to form the SLFP, the two Sinhalese parties have since dominated Sri Lankan politics. Between 1946 and the early 1970s the UNP was organized around powerful personalities and politically influential families. In 1970 the new leader, J. R. **Jayawardene**, departing from the personality-dominated system, established a strong party organization. To provide the electorate with a clear-cut alternative to the leftist SLFP and other groups, the UNP has remained a party of the moderate right. The UNP's popular support has been in the Sinhalese majority areas of central, southern and western Sri Lanka, but it has been less closely identified with Sinhalese chauvinism than the SLFP. Membership of the party today is 1.4m.

United Nations Commission for India and Pakistan (UNCIP)

Following the invasion of **Jammu and Kashmir** by armed tribes supported by regular Pakistani troops in 1948, India requested the United Nations to intervene in the dispute. The Security Council adopted Resolution 39 (1948) establishing the UN Commission for India and Pakistan (UNCIP) in January 1948 to investigate and mediate in the **Kashmir Dispute**. In April 1949, Resolution 47 (1948) enlarged the membership of UNCIP and recommended measures to facilitate restoring peace, including the holding of a plebiscite and the use of observers. In July 1949 India and Pakistan signed the Karachi Agreement establishing a cease-fire line to be supervised by UNCIP observers. When UNCIP was terminated in March 1951, through Resolution 51 (1951) the **United Nations Military Observer Group in India and Pakistan** was created to continue its functions.

United Nations Military Observer Group in India and Pakistan (UNMOGIP)

Replacing the **United Nations Commission for India and Pakistan (UNCIP)**, the United Nations Military Observer Group in India and Pakistan (UNMOGIP) was deployed in January 1949 to observe, report and investigate complaints of cease-fire violation in the state of **Jammu and Kashmir**, following fighting between India and Pakistan in 1948. Following the 1971 war and the **Simla Agreement** which further defined the **Line of Control (LoC)** in Kashmir, India argued that the mandate of UNMOGIP had lapsed. Pakistan, however, did not agree. In view of the disagreement, the Secretary-General ruled that the UNMOGIP can be terminated only be a decision of the Security Council. In the absence of such a decision, UNMOGIP contines under the same mandate and with the same functions. In 2005 UNMOGIP consisted of 44 military observers, supported by 21 international civilian personnel and 47 local civilian staff.

United People's Freedom Alliance (UPFA)

Since April 2004 the ruling coalition party in Sri Lanka, the United People's Freedom Alliance (UPFA) was formed in February when **Kumaratunga**'s **Sri Lanka Freedom Party (SLFP)** formed an electoral alliance with the **Janatha Vimukhti Peramuna (JVP)**. The alliance party won 45.6% of the popular vote and 105 of 225 seats in the legislature.

United Progressive Alliance (UPA)

The ruling coalition in India since the 14th **Lok Sabha** elections of 2004, the United Progressive Alliance (UPA) is under the leadership of the **Indian National Congress (INC)**. Its major constituents are **Rashtriya Janata Dal** (**RJD**, 23 seats), **Dravida Munnetra Kazhagam** (**DMK**, 16 seats), the **Nationalist Congress Party** (**NCP**, nine seats), **Pattali Makkal Katchi (PMK**, 16 seats), **Telangana Rashtriya Samithi** (**TRS**, five seats), **Jharkhand Mukti Morcha** (**JMM**, five seats), **Marumalarchi Dravida Munnetra Kazhagam** (**MDMK**, four seats) and **Lok Jan Shakti Party** (**LJSP**, four seats). The UPA government draws support from outside through the **Left Front**, with the UPA-Left Co-ordination Committee acting as the interface between them.

'Untouchables'/'Untouchability'

Hinduism is characterized by its classification of society into four castes, or *varnas*, of which the lowest were considered to be the *Shudras*. Below even the *Shudras* were groups of offspring resulting from the mixing of *varnas*, who were usually condemned to occupations considered abhorrent by other Hindus, such as shoemaking, scavenging and sweeping. In 1871/72 the British produced their first all-India census in which they tried to place each group within the four-*varna* framework. The census revealed that a significant population was disadvantaged, a group that came to be known by the terms depressed or backward castes as well as the English term 'untouchables'. The 1935 Government of India Act entitled 'degraded' groups to special electoral representation and in 1936 the provincial governments prepared lists or 'schedules' of officially designated **Scheduled Castes (SCs)** and **Scheduled Tribes (STs)**.

Following Dr **Ambedkar**'s efforts, Article 17 of the Constitution declared 'untouchability' to have been abolished and any disability arising from untouchability as an offence 'punishable in accordance with law'. Under Ambedkar's leadership the Constitution also initiated a policy of **affirmative action** in the form of a **reservation policy**, and, following his example, when millions of 'untouchables' converted to Buddhism they adopted the name **Dalits**.

Uttar Pradesh

Located in the north of India, Uttar Pradesh is the country's most populous state, with nearly 176m. inhabitants in 2000. Known as the United Provinces under the British administration, this region of India was one of the centres of political activity during the freedom struggle. Following independence in 1947, the state of Uttar Pradesh was established and has since produced eight of India's Prime Ministers. Uttar Pradesh has been a crucial force in modern Indian politics, not least because of the 80 members it returns to the **Lok Sabha** and the 31 it returns to the **Rajya Sabha**. Despite its political importance, Uttar Pradesh is one of the poorest states of the union, partly the result of sheer population pressure as well as a record of bad governance. Agriculture is the main occupation of the population. In 2001 **Scheduled Castes (SCs)** accounted for a high 21.1% of the state's population. According to the 2001 census, 80.6% of the population were Hindus, 18.5% Muslims and 0.4% Sikhs. Uttar Pradesh has a bicameral legislature with a state assembly of 403 seats and an upper house of 108 seats. The **Congress** party dominated state politics until the 1970s when the political emergence of lower-caste groups tilted the balance towards alternatives such as the Janata Party or the **Bahujan Samaj Party (BSP)**. The emergence of the **Bharatiya Janata Party (BJP)** in the 1990s further squeezed Congress out of politics in Uttar Pradesh, with the BJP capitalizing on the Ayodhya issue. Following the 2002 assembly elections, BSP leader, Mayawati, supported by the BJP, became Chief Minister. Corruption allegations led to the eventual dissolution of this partnership, allowing Mulayam Singh Yadav of the **Samajwadi Party (SP)** to return to prominence. In the 2004 general elections the BJP lost 15 of the seats it had held in the **Lok Sabha** (it held 25 after the 1999 polls) while the Congress retained nine, one of which was won by Sonia **Gandhi**'s son, Rahul Gandhi. The BJP's decline was attributed to infighting within the party and rural dissatisfaction, as well as the fractured nature of politics in Uttar Pradesh which favoured most of all the SP. The SP's secularist principles received overwhelming support from the Muslim community, increasing its parliamentary representation to 35 seats, while the BSP, retaining its traditional **Dalit** support base, won 19 seats.

Uttaranchal

In November 2000 Uttaranchal became the 27th state of India, formed out of the mountainous northern region of **Uttar Pradesh**, with Dehradun as its capital, and fulfilling long-voiced demands by the people of the Kumoan and Garhwal hills of north-western Uttar Pradesh for a separate state based on cultural, social (caste), and economic distinctiveness. In the north east the state borders Tibet, and to the south east Nepal. Compared to the other hill states, Uttaranchal has a small tribal population, recorded at 3.0% of the total in 2001. The 2001 census reported religious affiliation as 85% Hindus and 11.9% Muslims. Uttaranchal is rich in mineral resources, yet the population remains very poor. Agriculture is the main economic activity, but tiny landholdings result in inefficient production. The tourism industry is a major economic sector, with nature reserves and several hill stations being among the most frequented destinations in India. Excessive logging, deforestation and economic as well as social discontent caused the hill peoples of Uttar Pradesh, long shunted between different princely domains and neglected, to launch the peaceful **Chipko Movement** in the 1970s.

Uttaranchal's legislative assembly comprises 70 seats and the state returns five members to the **Lok Sabha**. In the 2004 parliamentary elections, the state's first general elections, the **Bharatiya Janata Party** managed to retain three Lok Sabha seats, losing one to the **Samajwadi Party (SP)**. Congress held its Lok Sabha seat.

V

Vajpayee, Atal Behari

Born on 25 December 1924 in the city of Gwalior in **Madhya Pradesh**, Atal Behari Vajpayee served as Prime Minister of India from 16 May 1996 until 1 June 1996, from 19 March 1998 until 27 April 1999 (in acting capacity following the government's fall in April 1998) and from 13 October 1999 until 22 May 2004, leading the **National Democratic Alliance (NDA)** coalition government until its electoral defeat in 2004. Educated in Gwalior and later **Uttar Pradesh** in political science, Vajpayee pursued various literary and artistic avenues, and is a recognized poet with published anthologies of his own poems. India's longest serving Prime Minister outside of the **Indian National Congress** and one of the most senior members of the **Bharatiya Janata Party (BJP)**, Vajpayee retired from active politics in December 2005.

A member of parliament for almost 50 years, Vajpayee's political career began during the independence struggle when he joined the 'Quit India Movement' of 1942–45. Initially sympathetic to the left, in 1951 he became a founder member of the Hindu nationalist Bharatiya Janata Sangh (BJS), the predecessor of the BJP. Opposing the emergency period (1975–77) under Prime Minister Indira **Gandhi**, he was imprisoned in 1975. From 1977 until 1979 he was foreign minister in the Janata coalition government of Prime Minister Morarji Desai, the first non-Congress government since independence. In 1980 Vajpayee was a co-founder of the BJP, serving as its first president, in 1980–86. Often described as the moderate face of the Hindu-nationalist BJP, Vajpayee developed a nation-wide appeal that was instrumental in the BJP's rise to prominence.

As Prime Minister, his governments were marked by defining events like the nuclear tests soon after the NDA came to power in May 1998 and his bus journey to Pakistan in February 1999 followed shortly by the **Kargil Conflict** and the communal violence during the **Gujarat** riots of 2002. Announcing the resumption of formal talks with Pakistan in January 2004, Vajpayee is credited with having injected new momentum into the peace process.

Vishwa Hindu Parishad (VHP)

The Vishwa Hindu Parishad (VHP—World Hindu Council) is an affiliate of the ***Sangh Parivar***. It was formed in 1966 in Allahabad by the **Rashtriya**

Swayamsevak Sangh (RSS), its primary goal being the political unification of Hindus irrespective of linguistic, regional, sectarian and class differences. Three core objectives dominate their programme: (1) to consolidate and strengthen Hindu society; (2) the protection and spread of Hindu values, both ethical and spiritual, and to make them relevant to contemporary India and abroad; and (3) the establishment and invigoration of contacts amongst Hindus overseas. This also includes eliminating the practice of '**untouchability**' and the conversion and readmission of Hindus who have been converted to Christianity or Islam. The VHP runs schools, temples and medical centres. Since the 1980s the VHP has been involved in raising public support and awareness about Ram Janmabhoomi, the attempt to build a Ram temple in Ayodhya in place of the Babri Masjid.

Vote Bank

A term used widely across South Asia to denote a predictable voting bloc, a group of voters whose votes are presumably ensured by catering to special interests related to religion or caste.

W

Wangchuck Dynasty

The hereditary monarchy of Bhutan was established in 1907, emerging from a 250-year-old dual system of administration, comprising the *Druk Desi*, responsible for the temporal administration of the country, and the ***Je Khenpo***, responsible for religious matters. In 1907 the lay and ecclesiastical leadership of Bhutan agreed to establish a hereditary monarchy in the person of Ugyen Wangchuk, the son of the 51st *Druk Desi* and powerful governor of Tongsa. Ugyen Wangchuck signed a coronation agreement with the British and became Bhutan's first King. The country has since been ruled by Jigme Wangchuck (1926–52), Jigme Dorji Wangchuck (1952–72) and Jigme Singye Wangchuck (since 1972), thus remaining under the continous rule of the Wangchuck dynasty. Ugyen Wangchuck was succeeded by his son Jigme Wangchuck, and during the four decades of their rule Bhutan was unified and brought under the direct control of the monarchy. The third monarch, Jigme Dorji Wangchuck, was active in the promotion of education, technological development, and political reform. In 1953 he guided Bhutan towards a constitutional monarchy by establishing a National Assembly over which he initially retained veto power. His 1968 decree, which furnished the National Assembly with institutional sovereignty and the power to remove the King through a vote of no-confidence, came into force from 1969. He was, however, careful to secure the Wangchuck dynasty, by stipulating that a successful vote of no-confidence would result in the next Wangchuck family member in the line of succession automatically acceding to the throne. In 1963 the King altered his title to ***Druk Gyalpo*** (Dragon King), with the aim of asserting a distinct Bhutanese identity. The present monarch, Jigme Singye Wangchuck, has continued his father's modernization policies, yet remains equally committed to upholding a centralized and uniform culture, attaching more value to **Gross National Happiness** than simply to rapid economic development. In 1979 Jigme Singye Wangchuck married four sisters, descendants of the rulers under the ***Chhoesi*** system. Dasho Jigme Gesar Namgyal Wangchuck, the *Druk Gyalpo*'s eldest son, is next in line to the throne.

West Bengal

The state of West Bengal, situated in north-eastern India on the Bay of Bengal, shares international borders to the east with Bangladesh, with Bhutan to the north east and with Nepal to the west. West Bengal also connects the Republic of India with the north-eastern states (*see* **North East India**). Soon after India's independence in 1947, the state of West Bengal was formed, gradually incorporating the surrounding Bengali-speaking areas. The total population in 2001 was recorded at 80,176,197 of which the majority were Bengali-speaking (86% in 1991) followed by Hindi speakers (6.6%) and Urdu speakers (2.1%). In 2001 72.5% of the population were Hindu and there was a substantial Muslim minority of 25.2%. Urban agglomeration is centred on the state capital, Kolkata (previously Calcutta). West Bengal is the most prosperous state in eastern India, its wealth stemming from traditional commerce and trade. However, the vast majority of the population, largely rural, remains very poor. The state's legislative assembly comprises 295 seats and returns 42 members to the **Lok Sabha**. Since the 1960s state politics has been dominated by the rivalry between **Congress** and the communists. West Bengal holds the world record of having the first democratically elected communist government, under the **Communist Party of India—Marxist (CPI—M)**, which was elected in 1977 and has since remained in power, for most of this period under the veteran leader Jyoti **Basu**. Since the late 1990s the Nationalist Trinamool Congress (renamed **All-India Trinamool Congress—AITC**), led by Mamata Banerjee, has been a player in state politics but the **Left Front** remains an indomitable force in West Bengal, having consolidated its position in the state elections of 2003 as well as in the Lok Sabha elections of 2004, when it increased its tally of parliamentary seats from 29 to 35.

Wipro Infotech

Together with Infosys, Wipro is one of India's premier software companies. Chairman Azim Premji, having transformed his father's company Wipro, that largely sold edible oils, into a multinational computer giant, is considered to be one of the world's most successful businessmen and in 2005 was listed the richest Indian. The company was listed on the Nasdaq in 2000 and in 2004 its value crossed the US $1,000m. mark. An Azim Premji Foundation invests in social sector development and in 2004 Wipro threatened to shift operations out of **Bangalore**, where it is headquartered, if the city's infrastructure was not improved.

Women's Action Forum (Pakistan)

The forum was established in 1981 in response to the process of Islamization under the regime of Gen. **Zia** ul-Haq. The organization aimed at, and continues to focus on, strengthening women's position in society and the improvement of their legal status as citizens. The Women's Action Forum has played an important role in exposing controversies in the various interpretations of Islamic law.

Workers' Party of Bangladesh

The Workers' Party of Bangladesh is a Marxist-Leninist-oriented party which was a member of the left-wing alliance headed by the **Bangladesh Awami League** during the regime of Gen. **Ershad**. Later the party joined a five-party alliance in opposition to the military regime, but subsequently the party split. One faction, under the leadership of Nazrul Islam, participated in the 1986 legislative elections and won three seats. After the fall of the military regime, the party won one seat in the 1991 parliamentary elections.

Z

Zaki, Ahmed

Ahmed Zaki (1931–96) was a Maldivian statesman and Prime Minister. After being appointed as Prime Minister by President **Nasir** in December 1968, he was subsequently arrested on the President's orders following a non-violent *coup d'état* in March 1975, after which the office of the Prime Minister was abolished. During his term in office he was elected as a member of the Citizens' Majlis (**People's Majlis**) in 1973. Nasir identified his rising popularity as a threat to his own position. Zaki's banishment to a remote **Atoll** and the simultaneous dissolution of the Prime Minister's office are regarded as landmarks in the political development of the country towards a presidential form of government and the introduction of autocratic elements into the political culture. After 50 days in jail, Zaki was released in September 1974 and served his country in various international functions, including as the High Commissioner of Maldives to the United Kingdom.

Zhiwey Zhung yog

A term used in Bhutan to refer to a basic principle of governance. Derived from Buddhism, it has been internalized by the King and the country's civil servants and describes the endeavour to reach a peaceful solution of current issues and conflicts. (*See* ***Dragpo tewa***.)

Zia, Begum Khaleda

Begum Khaleda Zia (1945–) has served as Bangladesh's Prime Minister first in 1991–96 and again since 2001. Zia began her political carrier as vice-chairman of the **Bangladesh Nationalist Party (BNP)**, which elevated her on 10 May 1984 to the position of chairperson. Her first political activities were marked by the consolidation and strengthening of the party apparatus, which was deeply split after the assassination of her husband, Ziaur **Rahman**, former President of Bangladesh, on 30 May 1981. Additionally, Khaleda Zia launched a campaign, between 1983 and 1990, to dislodge the military government of Gen. **Ershad**, forming a coalition called the seven-party alliance and engaging in joint opposition with her rival, Sheikh **Hasina** Wajed, and the Awami League until 1987. She was detained seven times during the alliance movement. After Gen. Ershad handed over power to a neutral **caretaker government** in 1990, Khaleda Zia was elected as Bangladesh's first female Prime Minister in the 1991 elections and, immediately after taking office, guided the transformation from a presidential to a parliamentary form of government. During the period of the Awami League government, in 1996–2001, she led numerous oppositional movements to unseat the government, forming the **Four-Party Alliance**. Following national elections of 2004 she was once again sworn in as the Prime Minister, having won two-thirds of the seats in parliament.

Zia ul-Haq, Gen. Muhammad

Gen. Zia ul-Haq (1924–88) held power in Pakistan for 11 years as chief martial law administrator (1977–85) as well as President (1979–88). During his rule he launched a programme of Islamization of state institutions and increased the President's power through constitutional measures. Zia ul-Haq died in an air crash on 17 August 1988.

APPENDIX: COUNTRY-BY-COUNTRY LIST OF ENTRIES

SOUTH ASIA

Bay of Bengal Initiative for Multi-Sectoral Technical and Economic Co-operation (BIMSTEC)

Comprehensive Test Ban Treaty (CTBT)

Confidence-building Measures (CBMs)

Dharma

Dharna

Fatwa

Indian Ocean

Indus Waters Treaty

International Monetary Fund (IMF)

Jihad/Jehad

Kargil Conflict

Kashmir Dispute

Nuclear Non-Proliferation Treaty (NPT)

Nuclearization

Operation Enduring Freedom

Partition

Raj

Shaheed

Siachen Glacier

South Asian Association for Regional Co-operation (SAARC)

South Asia Free Trade Agreement (SAFTA)

SAARC Preferential Trading Agreement (SAPTA)

Tashkent Agreement

United Nations Commission for India and Pakistan (UNCIP)

United Nations Military Observer Group in India and Pakistan (UNMOGIP)

BANGLADESH

Agartala Conspiracy Case

Agrani Bank

Ahmed, Tajuddin

Aid to Bangladesh Consortium

Ansars and Village Defence Party (VDP)

Ashraf

Association of Development Agencies in Bangladesh (ADAB)

Bangla Movement

Bangladesh, People's Republic of

History

Latest Elections

Recent Developments

Bangladesh, Political Development

Constitution

Executive

Legislature (Jatiya Sangsad)

Elections/Electoral System

Political Parties Regulation (PPR)

Social Movements

Foreign Policy

Bangladesh-India Relations

Judiciary

Defence (Security)

Military

Police

Riots

Terrorism

Bureaucracy

Citizenship

Corruption

Decentralization

Federalism

Human Rights

Inequality

Nationalism

Participation/Public Action

Bangladesh, Economic Development

Economic Policy/Reforms

Private Sector

Public Sector

Population

Family-Planning Policy

Migration

Urbanization

Minority Groups/Communities

Tribes

Agriculture

Land Reforms (Ownership)

Food and Famine Prevention

Industry

Foreign Trade

Export Processing Zones (EPZ)

Banking System

Foreign Aid

Foreign Direct Investment (FDI)

Foreign Investors' Chamber of Commerce and Industry (FICCI)

Labour

Informal Economy

Child Labour

Trade Unions

Environmental Protection

Floods and Natural Disasters

Health System/Policy

Education/Education Policy

Non-Formal Primary Education (NFPE)

Social Security /Policy

Poverty

Welfare

Gender Relations/Empowerment

Bangladesh Academy for Rural Development (BARD)

Bangladesh Awami League (AL)

Bangladesh Bank (BB)

Bangladesh Chemical Industries Corporation (BCIC)

Bangladesh Institute of Development Studies (BIDS)

Bangladesh Krishak Sramik Awami League (BAKSAL)

Bangladesh Liberation War

Bangladesh Nationalist Party (BNP)

Bangladesh Rifles (BDR)

Bangladesh Rural Advancement Committee (BRAC)

Bangladesh Shilpa Rin Sangstha (BSRS)

Bangladesh Student Politics

BASIC Bank

Bhasani, Maulana Abdul Hamid Khan

Bikalpa Dhara Bangladesh (BDB)

Caretaker Government

Chittagong Hill Tracts (CHT) Conflict

Choudhury, Badruddoza

Communist Party of Bangladesh (CPB)

Dhaka Stock Exchange Ltd (DSE)

Eleven-Party Alliance

Ershad, Gen. Hossain Muhammad

Export Promotion Bureau (EPB)

Farakka Issue

Four-Party Alliance

Fourteen-Party Opposition Movement

Gano Forum (People's Forum)

Gherao

Gono/Gana Adalat

Gram Sarkar (*Gram Parishad*)

Grameen Bank Project

Hasina Wazed, Sheikh

Hossain, Kamal

Imam, Jahanara

Investment Corporation of Bangladesh (ICB)

Islam, Syed Nazrul

Islami Jatiya Oikya Front (IJOF)

Islamic Oikya Jote (IOJ)

Jamaat-e-Islami Bangladesh

Jatiya Party (JP)

Jatiya Samajtantrik Dal (JSD)

Mahajan

Manjur Faction

Mastan/Mastani Culture

Matubbars

Microcredit

Mujib Bahini

Mukti Bahini

National Awami Party (NAP)/National Awami Party—Bhasani (NAP—B)

Pir

Rahman, Sheikh Mujibur

Rahman, Ziaur

Rakkhi Bahini

Rapid Action Battalion (RAB)

Rohingya Issue

Shalish

Shanti Bahini

Sikder, Siraj

Singh, Moni

Six-Point Programme

Sonali Bank

Sramik Karmachari Oikyo Parishad (SKOP)

Stranded Pakistanis (Biharis)

Swanirvar

Taher, Col Abu

Workers' Party of Bangladesh

Zia, Begum Khaleda

BHUTAN

Bhutan Broadcasting Service Corporation (BBS)

Bhutan Chamber of Commerce and Industry (BCCI)

Bhutan People's Party (BPP)

Bhutan Trust Fund for Environmental Conservation (BTF)

Bhutan, Kingdom of Bhutan

History

Recent Developments

Bhutan, Political Development

Constitution

Monarchical System/Monarchy

Bhutan Royal Government

Executive

Council of Ministers (*Lhengye Zhungtshog*)

Royal Advisory Council (Lodoi Tsokde)

Legislature

National Assembly (Tshogdu Chenmo)

Elections/Electoral System

Political Organizations

Social Movements

Foreign Policy

Bhutan-China Relations

Bhutan-India Relations

Bhutan-Nepal Relations

Judiciary

Department of Legal Affairs (DLA)

Defence (Security)

Military

Police

Riots

Terrorism

Block Development Committees

Bureaucracy

Citizenship

Bhutan Citizenship Act 1985

Corruption

Decentralization

District Development Committee

Federalism

Human Rights

Inequality

Nationalism

Participation/Public Action

Royal Civil Service Commission (RCSC)

Royal Pardon

Royal Vote of Confidence

Bhutan, Economic Development

Economic Policy/Reforms

Private Sector

Public Sector

Population

Family-Planning Policy

Migration

Urbanization

Minority Groups/Communities

Tribes

Agriculture

Land Reform (Ownership)

Food and Famine (Prevention)

Industry

Foreign Trade (Import/Export)

Banking System

Foreign Direct Investment (FDI)

Foreign Aid

Labour

Informal Economy
Child Labour
Compulsory Labour
Environmental Protection
Green Belt Policy
Floods and Natural Disasters
Health System/Policy
Education/Education Policy
Social Security/Policy
Poverty
Welfare System
Gender Relations/Empowerment
Marriage Act of 1980
Royal Audit Authority (RAA)

Chhoesi
Chimi
Chipon
Council for Ecclesiastical Affairs (Dratshang Lhentshog)
Dragpo tewa
Dratshang
Driglam Namzha
Druk Gyalpo (Dragon King)
Drukpa
Drukyul
Dzong
Dzongkha
Dzongkhag
Gakid
Gewog
Gross National Happiness (GNH)

Gung

Gup

Indian Military Training Team (IMTRAT)

Jabmi

Je Khenpo

Kagyupa School

Kidu System

Kuensel

Lhengye Nyamdrel Tshogchung

Lhotshampa

Luso

Namgyal, Ngawang

National Women Association of Bhutan (NWAB)

Nepalese Issue/Conflict

Ngalong

Peljor Gongphel

Phuntsholing

Sharchop

Thimpu

Thram

Thrimkhang Gongma

Tsa-Wa-Sum

Wangchuck Dynasty

Zhiwey Zhung yog

INDIA

Aditya Birla Group

Advani, Lal Krishna

Affirmative Action

Ahimsa

Aid-to-India Consortium

Akali Dal

Akhil Bharatiya Vidyarthi Parishad (ABVP)

Aksai Chin

All-Assam Students' Union (AASU)

All-India Anna Dravida Munnetra Kazhagam (AIADMK)

All-India Forward Bloc

All-India Majlis-e-Ittehadul Muslimen (AIMIM)

All-India Radio (AIR)

All-India Railwaymen's Federation (AIRF)

All-India Sikh Student Federation (AISSF)

All-India Trade Union Congress (AITUC)

All-India Trinamool Congress/Nationalist Trinamool Congress (AITC)

All-Party Hurriyat Conference (APHC)

All-Tripura Tiger Force (ATTF)

All-Assam Gana Sangram Parishad (AAGSP)

All-India Hindu Mahasabha (HMS)

Ambani, Dhirubhai

Ambedkar, Dr Bhimrao Ramji

Andaman and Nicobar, Union Territory

Andhra Pradesh

Arthasastra

Asom Gana Parishad (AGP)

Ayodhya Conflict

Bahujan Samaj Party (BSP)

Bajrang Dal (BD)

Bandh

Bangalore

Basu, Jyoti

Bharat

Bharat Ratna

Bharatiya Janata Party (BJP)

Bharatiya Kisan Union (BKU)

Bharatiya Mazdoor Sangh (BMS)

Bhindranwale, Jarnail Singh

Bhopal industrial accident

Bihar

Biju Janata Dal (BJD)

Bodoland Movement

Bofors Scandal

Bombay Stock Exchange (BSE)

Border Security Force (BSF)

Bullock Capitalists

Caste System

Centre of Indian Trade Unions (CITU)

Chandigarh

Chhattisgarh

Chipko Movement

Communist Party of India (CPI)

Communist Party of India—Marxist (CPI—M)

Confederation of Indian Industries (CII)

Congress System

Dadra and Nagar Haveli

Dalit

Daman and Diu

Delhi

Democratic Progressive Alliance (DPA)

Doordarshan

Dr Reddy's Laboratories Ltd

Dravida Munnetra Kazhagam (DMK)

Dravidian

Federation of Indian Chambers of Commerce and Industry (FICCI)

Gandhi, Indira

Gandhi, Mohandas Karamchand

Gandhi, Sonia

Goa

Green Revolution

Gujarat

Harijan

Harkat ul-Ansar/Harkat ul-Mujahideen (HuM)

Hartal

Haryana

Himachal Pradesh

Hindi-Chini bhai bhai

Hindustan

Hindutva

Hizbul Mujahideen (HM)

India, Republic of

- *History*
- *Latest Elections*
- *Recent Developments*

India, Political Development

- *Constitution*
- *Executive*
- *President's Rule*
- *Legislature*
- *Elections/Electoral System*
- *Social Movements*
- *Emergency*
- *Anti-defection Law*

Poverty

Welfare

Gender Relations/Empowerment

National Development Council (NDC)

India Trade Promotion Organization (ITPO)

Indian Administrative Service (IAS)

Indian Federal Democratic Party (IFDP)

Indian National Congress (INC)

Indian National Trade Union Congress (INTUC)

Indian Police Service (IPS)

Indian Space Research Organisation (ISRO)

Indo-Ceylon Agreements

Industrial Development Bank of India (IDBI)

Infosys Technologies Ltd

Institute for Defence Studies and Analyses (IDSA)

Integrated Rural Development Programme (IRDP)

Jajmani System

Jammu and Kashmir

Jammu and Kashmir Liberation Front (JKLF)

Jammu and Kashmir National Conference (JKNC)

Jammu and Kashmir People's Democratic Party (JKPDP)

Janata Dal—United (JD—U)

Janata Dal—Secular (JD—S)

Jatis

Jharkhand

Jharkhand Mukti Morcha (JMM)

Kalam, Abdul

Karnataka

Kerala

Kerala Congress—Joseph (KC—Joseph)

National Stock Exchange (NSE)

National Unity Alliance (NUA)

Nationalist Congress Party (NCP)

Naxalite Movement

Nehru, Jawaharlal

Nehru-Gandhi Family

North East Frontiers Agency (NEFA)

North East India

Operation Blue Star

Orissa

Other Backward Classes (OBCs)

Panchasheela/Panch Shila

Panchayati raj

Pattali Makkal Katchi (PMK)

People's War Group (PWG)

Pondicherry

Prasar Bharati

Punjab

Rajasthan

Rajya Sabha

Ranbaxy Laboratories Ltd

Rao, Pamulaparti Venkata Narasimha

Rashtra

Rashtriya Janata Dal (RJD)

Rashtriya Lok Dal (RLD)

Rashtriya Swayamsevak Sangh (RSS)

Rasta Roko/Railway Roko

Republican Party of India (A) (RPI—A)

Reservation Policy/Anti-reservation Movement

Reserve Bank of India (RBI)

Horse Trading

Foreign Policy

Non-Alignment

India-China Relations

India-Pakistan Relations

India-Russia Relations

India-USA Relations

Judiciary

Uniform Civil Code

Defence (Security)

Military

Police

Central Reserve Police Force (CRPF)

Central Industrial Security Force (CISF)

Central Bureau of Investigation (CBI)

Research and Analysis Wing (RAW)

Riots

Terrorism

Bureaucracy

Cattle Preservation Bill

Citizenship

Corruption

Decentralization

Directive Principles of State Policy (DPSP)

Federalism

Human Rights

Inequality

Nationalism

Participation/Public Action

Third Front

Khalistan

Lakshadweep

Lashkar-e-Toiba (LET)

Left Democratic Front (LDF)

Left Front (India)

Licence Permit Raj

Life Insurance Corporation of India (LIC)

Line of Actual Control (LAC)

Line of Control (LoC)

Linguistic Regionalism

Lok Jan Shakti Party (LJSP)

Lok Sabha

Madhya Pradesh

Maharashtra

Mandal Commission

Marumalarchi Dravida Munnetra Kazhagam (MDMK)

McMahon Line

Mizo National Front (MNF)

Monopolies And Restrictive Trade Act (MRTP)

Mumbai

Muslim Women (Protection of Rights on Divorce) Bill (India)

Naga National Council (NNC)

Nagaland People's Front (NPF)

Narayan, Jayaprakash/J. P. Movement

Narmada Dam

National Democratic Alliance (NDA)

National Democratic Front of Bodoland (NDFB)

National Liberation Front of Tripura (NLFT)

National Loktantrik Party (NLP, National Democratic Party)

National Socialist Council of Nagaland (NSCN)

Revolutionary Socialist Party (RSP)

Samajwadi Janata Party—Rashtriya (SJP—R)

Samajwadi Party (SP)

Sangh Parivar

Satyagraha

Sarvodaya

Savarkar, Vinayak Damodar

Scheduled Castes (SCs)

Scheduled Tribes (STs)

Shah Bano Case

Shiv Sena

Sikkim Democratic Front (SDF)

Siliguri Corridor

Simla Agreement

Singh, G. Zail

Singh, Manmohan

State Bank of India (SBI)

Swadeshi

Swaraj

Taluka

Tamil Nadu

Tata Group

Tawang

Telangana Rashtriya Samithi (TRS)

Telugu Desam Party (TDP)

Union Territory

United Liberation Front of Assam (ULFA)

United National Liberation Front (UNFL)

United Progressive Alliance (UPA)

'Untouchables'/'Untouchability'

Uttar Pradesh

Uttaranchal

Vajpayee, Atal Behari

Vishwa Hindu Parishad

Vote Bank

West Bengal

Wipro Infotech

MALDIVES

Adhaalath Party

Alliance of Small Island States (AOSIS)

Atoll

Bank of Maldives PLC (BML)

Dhivehi Raiyyithunge Party (DRP)

Didi, Abdulla Afif

Didi, Muhammad Amin

Didi, Sultan Muhammad Farid (Fareed)

Gan

Gayoom, Maumoon Abdul

Islamic Democratic Party (IDP)

Majeed, Sultan Abdul

Majlis

Maldives, Republic of

History

Recent Developments

Maldives, Political Development

Constitution

Executive

Legislature

Elections/Electoral System

Political Organizations
Political Party Regulations 2005
Social Movements
Foreign Policy
Judiciary
Defence (Security)
Military
Police
Riots
Terrorism
Atoll Chief
Bureaucracy
Citizenship
Corruption
Decentralization
Federalism
Human Rights
Inequality
Nationalism
Participation/Public Action
Supreme Council of Islamic Affairs

Maldives, Economic Development
Economic Policy/Reforms
Private Sector
Public Sector
Population
Family-Planning Policy
Migration
Urbanization
Minority Groups/Communities

Tribes

Agriculture/Fishing

Land Reform (Ownership)

Food and Famine/Prevention

Industry

Foreign Trade (Import/Export)

Banking System

Foreign Direct Investment (FDI)

Foreign Investment Services Bureau (FISB)

Foreign Aid

Labour

Informal Economy

Child Labour

Environmental Protection

Floods and Natural Disasters

Health System/Policy

Education/Education Policy

Social Security/Policy

Poverty

Welfare

Gender Relations/Empowerment

Maldives Stock Exchange

Maldivian Democratic Party (MDP)

Malé

Nasir, Ibrahim Amir

National Security Services (NSS)

People's Majlis

People's Special Majlis

Zaki, Ahmed

NEPAL

Adhikari, Man Mohan

Agricultural Development Bank Nepal (ADBN)

Aphno Manchhe

Bahun

Bhattarai, Baburam

Bhattarai, Krishna Prasad

Birendra, King of Nepal

Chakari

Chand, Lokendra Bahadur

Chhetris

Communist Party of Nepal (CPN)

Communist Party of Nepal—Maoist (CPN—M)

Communist Party of Nepal—Unified Marxist-Leninist (CPN—UML)

Comrade Prachanda (Pushpa Kamal Dahal)

Democracy Day

Gurkha (Gorkha)

Gyanendra, King

Jana Andolan

Janajati

Koirala, Bisweswor Prasad

Koirala, Girija Prasad

Madhesis

Mahendra, King of Nepal

Muluki Ain

Nepal, Kingdom of

History

Recent Developments

Nepal, Political Development

Constitution

Monarchy (Constitutional)

Executive

Legislature

Elections/Electoral System

Political Organizations

Social Movements

Foreign Policy

Nepal-China Relations

Nepal-India Relations

Judiciary

Defence (Security)

Military

Police

Riots

Terrorism

Bureaucracy

Citizenship

Corruption

Decentralization

Federalism

Human Rights

Inequality

Nationalism

Participation/Public Action

Nepal, Economic Development

Economic Policy/Reforms

Private Sector

Public Sector

Population

Family-Planning Policy

Migration

Urbanization

Minority Groups/Communities

Agriculture

Land Reform (Ownership)

Food and Famine Prevention

Industry

Foreign Trade

Banking System

Foreign Direct Investment (FDI)

Foreign Aid

Nepal-India Trade Agreements

Labour

Informal Economy

Child Labour

Environmental Protection

Floods and Natural Disaster

Health System/Policy

Education /Education Policy

Social Security/Policy

Poverty

Welfare

Gender Relations/Empowerment

Nepal Rastra Bank

Nepal Sadbhavana Party (NSP)

Nepali Congress (NC)

Panchayat System

People's War

Rana Family

Rashtriya Panchayat

Rashtriya Prajatantra Party (RPP)

Shah Dynasty

Singh, Ganesh Man/Ganesh Man Singh Shrestha

Small Farmers Development Project (SFDP)

Tarai (Terai) Region

Thapa, Surya Bahadur

Tribhuvan, King

Trade and Transit Dispute

United Left Front (ULF)

PAKISTAN

Ahmadiyya/Ahmadis

Aid-to-Pakistan Consortium

All-Pakistan Mohajir Students Organization (APMSO)

All-Pakistan Muslim Parties Convention

All-Pakistan Women's Association (APWA)

Al-Zulfikar Organization

Anti-Ahmadiyya Movement

Anti-Blasphemy Law

Associated Press of Pakistan (APP)

Awami National Party (ANP)

Azad Kashmir

Balochistan

Basic Democracies (BD—Pakistan)

Bhutto, Benazir

Bhutto, Zulfikar Ali

Biraderi System

Democratic Action Committee (DAC)

Federally Administered Northern Areas (FANA)

Federally Administered Tribal Area (FATA)

Hundi System (Pakistan)

Industrial Development Bank of Pakistan (IDBP)

Islami Jamiat i Tulaba (IJT)

Islamic Democratic Alliance (IDA/IJI)

Jamiat i Ulema i Islam (JUI)

Jamiat-i-Ulema-i-Pakistan (JUP)

Jamiat-ul-Ulema-i-Islam (JUI)

Jinnah Muhammad Ali (*Quaid-i-Azam*)

Jirga

Kahuta Research Laboratories (KRL)

Kalabagh Dam

Karachi Accord (Pakistan People's Party-Muttahida Qaumi Movement Accord)

Khan, Ayub

Khan, Liaquat Ali

Madrasas

Musharraf, Gen. Pervez

Muttahida Majlis-e-Amal (MMA)

Muttahida Qaumi Movement (MQM)

North West Frontier Province (NWFP)

Pakistan, Islamic Republic of

History

Latest Elections

Recent Developments

Pakistan, Political Development

Constitution

Eighth Amendment

Executive

Legislature

Elections/Electoral System

Social Movements

Foreign Policy

Pakistan-China Relations

Pakistan-US Relations

Judiciary

Federal Shariat Court

Hadood/Hudood Ordinances (1979)

Mohtasib

Defence/Security

Intelligence Bureau (IB)

Inter-Services Intelligence (ISI)

Military Intelligence (MI)

Military

Police

Riots

Terrorism

Bureaucracy

Citizenship

Civil Service of Pakistan (CSP)

Civil Service Reforms (1973)

Corruption

National Anti-Corruption Strategy (NACS)

National Accountability Bureau (NAB)

Council of Islamic Ideology

Decentralization

Federal Public Services Commission (FPSC)

Federalism

Feudalism

Fundamental Property Rights

Human Rights

Inequality

Islamization

Muhajir Dominance

National Reconstruction Bureau (NRB)

Nationalism

Participation/Public Action

Quota System

Pakistan, Economic Development

Economic Policy/Reforms

National Economic Council (NEC)

Planning Commission

Islamic Economy

Private Sector

Public Sector

Population

Family-Planning Policy

Migration

Urbanization

Minority Groups

Tribes

Agriculture

Land Reform (Ownership)

Food and Famine Prevention

Industry

Foreign Trade

Banking System

Foreign Direct Investment

Foreign Aid

Board of Investment (BOI)

Central Board of Revenue (CBR)

National Finance Commission (NFC)

Labour

Informal Economy

Child Labour

National Pay and Pension Committee (NPPC)

Pakistan Atomic Energy Commission (PAEC)

Environmental Protection

Floods and Natural Disasters

Health System

Education/Education Policy

Social Security

Poverty

Welfare

Zakat

Gender Relations/Empowerment

Pakistan Democratic Alliance (PDA)

Pakistan Democratic Movement (PDM)

Pakistan Federal Union of Journalists (PFUJ)

Pakistan Federation of Chambers of Commerce and Industry (PFCCI)

Pakistan-India Trade Agreement 1951

Pakistan Industrial Credit and Investment Corporation (PICIC)

Pakistan Industrial Development Corporation (PIDC)

Pakistan Muslim League (PML)

Pakistan National Alliance (PNA)

Pakistan People's Party (PPP)

Pakistan Telecommunication Corporation Ltd (PTCL)

Punjab

Sharif, Mian Nawaz

Shi'a–Sunni Conflict in Pakistan

Sind

State Bank of Pakistan

Women's Action Forum (Pakistan)

Zia ul-Haq, Muhammad

SRI LANKA

All-Ceylon Buddhist Congress

All-Ceylon Tamil Congress (ACTC)

Bandaranaike Family

Bank of Ceylon (BOC)

Buddhism Movement (Sri Lanka)

Donoughmore Commission

Eelam

Eelam People's Democratic Party (EPDP)

Eelam People's Revolutionary Liberation Front (EPRLF)

Federal Party (FP)

Gramodaya Mandalas

Indian Peace Keeping Force (IPKF)

Indo-Lanka Accord

Jaffna

Janatha Vimukhti Peramuna (JVP)

Jathika Hela Urumaya (JHU)

Jayawardene, Junius Richard

Kumaratunga, Chandrika

Liberation Tigers of Tamil Eelam (LTTE)

Mahaweli Project

National Bhikku Front (NBF)

Patriotic National Movement (PNM)

People's Alliance (PA)

People's Liberation Organization of Tamil Eelam (PLOTE, also PLOT)

Ponnambalam, G. G.

Prabhakaran, Veluppilai

Premadasa, Ranasinghe

Rajapakse, Mahinda

Senanayake, Don Stephen

Sinhala Only Policy

Soulbury Commission

Sri Lanka, Democratic Socialist Republic of

History

Latest Elections

Recent Developments

Sri Lanka, Political Development

Constitution

Executive

Legislature

Elections/Electoral System

Social Movements

Provincial Councils/System

Foreign Policy

Sri Lanka-India Relations

Judiciary

Defence (Security)

Military

Police

Riots

Terrorism

Bureaucracy

Citizenship

Corruption

Decentralization

Federalism

Human Rights

Welfare

Gender Relations

Sri Lanka Freedom Party (SLFP)

Sri Lanka Muslim Congress (SLMC)

Tamil Eelam Liberation Organization (TELO)

Tamil Language

Tamil National Alliance (TNA)

Tamil United Liberation Front (TULF)

United National Party (UNP)

United People's Freedom Alliance (UPFA)